The Decipherment
of Linear A

The Decipherment of Linear A

Crete, Egypt, and the End of the Minoan Empire

Mark Cook

FCA, JIEB, CFE, MPhil, MA, MAncHist

First published in Great Britain in 2025 by
Pen & Sword History
An imprint of Pen & Sword Books Limited
Yorkshire – Philadelphia

Copyright © Mark Cook 2025

ISBN 978 1 03613 463 1

The right of Mark Cook to be identified as
Author of this Work has been asserted by him in accordance
with the Copyright, Designs and Patents Act 1988.

A CIP catalogue record for this book is
available from the British Library.

All rights reserved. No part of this book may be reproduced, transmitted, downloaded, decompiled or reverse engineered in any form or by any means, electronic or mechanical including photocopying, recording or by any information storage and retrieval system, without permission from the Publisher in writing. NO AI TRAINING: Without in any way limiting the Author's and Publisher's exclusive rights under copyright, any use of this publication to "train" generative artificial intelligence (AI) technologies to generate text is expressly prohibited. The Author and Publisher reserve all rights to license uses of this work for generative AI training and development of machine learning language models.

Typeset by Mac Style
Printed in the UK by CPI Group (UK) Ltd, Croydon, CR0 4YY.

The Publisher's authorised representative in the EU for product safety is Authorised Rep Compliance Ltd., Ground Floor, 71 Lower Baggot Street, Dublin D02 P593, Ireland.
www.arccompliance.com

For a complete list of Pen & Sword titles please contact

PEN & SWORD BOOKS LIMITED
47 Church Street, Barnsley, South Yorkshire, S70 2AS, England
E-mail: enquiries@pen-and-sword.co.uk
Website: www.pen-and-sword.co.uk
or
PEN AND SWORD BOOKS
1950 Lawrence Road, Havertown, PA 19083, USA
E-mail: uspen-and-sword@casematepublishers.com
Website: www.penandswordbooks.com

To my parents:

*my father, a better accountant than me,
and my mother, the real historian of the family*

Preface

Linear A has intrigued me ever since I watched the documentary series *The Birth of Europe* on BBC 2 in 1991 with my mother. Episode 2 discussed the Minoans and what the programme proclaimed was Europe's first written language, Linear A, which the Minoans had used in Bronze Age Crete. The quartermaster of the palace of Knossos who first recorded the palace inventories in Linear A, so the programme stated, was probably the first man in Europe to be able to write, but no one knew what he had written.[1] This seemed something of a tragedy. Time has moved on, and so has our understanding (the earliest Linear A finds are from Phaistos, and the first use of Cretan hieroglyphs predates Linear A), but Linear A has nonetheless remained undeciphered. I guess this has always been at the back of my mind for had I not watched that programme then, I would not have written this book now…

---

1. *The Birth of Europe – Episode 2: Colliding Continents & The Age of Bronze*: https://www.youtube.com/watch?v=0Ynju8_f9PQ&t=2290s (see video at 37:17) (accessed 1 January 2021)

Contents

List of Pictures	xiii
List of Diagrams of Tablets, and List of Tables	xiv
List of Graphs, and List of Maps	xv
Middle and Late Bronze Age Chronology of Crete and Egypt, and Rulers of Egypt During the 18th Dynasty	xvi

Chapter 1   The Problem   1

Chapter 2   The Mathematical "proof" and the Emergence of a Theory   7
       Excursus 2.1: Rotation of Symbols in Ancient Texts   21

Chapter 3   The Theory   24
       Excursus 3.1: The interaction of shorthand and Egyptian grammar   33
       Excursus 3.2: Abbreviation to the first, last, or a middle letter of a word in shorthand   40

Chapter 4   The reconstructed history of Egypt's involvement in Middle and Late Bronze Age Crete   47
       Excursus 4.1: Why hieroglyphs?   56
       Excursus 4.2: Why did the Egyptian colonial administration continue to use Linear A (and, by implication, hieroglyphs)?   59
       Excursus 4.3: The end of the Minoan Empire and the coming of the Egyptians (before the Greeks)   72
       Excursus 4.4: The missing Fourth (and Third) Campaign   84
       Excursus 4.5: What was in this for Egypt?   87
       Excursus 4.6: Why Herodotus does not state that Egypt owned Crete   109

Chapter 5   The Translations   122
       Selected tablets, translations, and commentary   129

x   The Decipherment of Linear A

| Part I | Tablets reflecting the Hagia Triada temple acting as agent of the state | 129 |

Tablet HT 123A 129
Analysis 1. Evidence regarding the Egyptian administration on Crete 157
2. Evidence for the size of Hagia Triada's area of administrative responsibility 158
3. The interaction between the Egyptian calendar and the shearing season on Crete 161
4. Evidence of continuity between the Egyptian and Mycenaean regimes and the Dk series of Linear B tablets 163

Tablet HT 102 171
Excursus 5.1: The male = symbol 175

| Part II | Tablets reflecting the Hagia Triada temple acting as principal, as a religious institution | 190 |

1. Records of goods received, to be received, and issued 190
   (a) Goods wholly and partially received exhibiting certain characteristics of the Mc series of Linear B tablets 191

   Tablet HT 14 191
   Excursus 5.2: What was a phyle? 194

   Tablet HT 114A 208
   Excursus 5.3: Linear A symbol L76 to Linear A symbol L2' (+ male = symbol) 214
   Excursus 5.4: Certain aspects of the relationship between Middle Egyptian, Linear A, and Linear B 217

   Tablet HT 121 221
   Analysis 1. The tithe-like tax payable to Egyptian temples on Crete and the Mc series of Linear B tablets 229
   2. Minoan units of measure of weight 234
   3. The use of Linear A on the Mc series of Linear B tablets 235

   (b) Others goods wholly and partially received 243

   Tablet HT 13 243

   Tablet HT 2 257

   Tablet HT 86A 266
   Analysis 1. Evidence of contemporary Egyptian administrative practice at Hagia Triada 278

	Contents	xi

Tablet HT 95A	281
Tablet HT 95B	291
Tablet HT 36	300

(c) Receipts of goods from a certain source, and their subsequent issue during the same period ... 304

Tablet HT 91	304

(d) Issue of goods (animals) to the phyle of priests ... 318

Tablet HT 19 ... 318
Analysis 1. Further evidence that Linear A is Middle Egyptian (written in shorthand) ... 325

Tablet HT 17 ... 326

2. Inventories ... 333
   (a) Inventory (animals and some fodder) belonging to the temple and held "on hand" ... 333

   Tablet HT 7A ... 333
   Excursus 5.5: The many Linear A representations of Hieroglyph N13 ... 342

   (b) Inventory (animals and some fodder) belonging to the temple held by the herdsmen, grazed on the margin of the temple's vineyards, and in the storehouse / barn ... 346

   Tablet HT 120 ... 346

   (c) Inventory (animals and fodder) belonging to the temple but held at nearby Phaistos ... 362

   Tablet HT 21A ... 362
   Tablet HT 21B ... 370

3. End of month accounting ... 371

   Tablet HT 89 ... 371
   Analysis 1. The timing of temple receipts and payments using sheep (ewes) ... 386

   Tablet HT 118 ... 387
   Tablet HT 18 ... 395

4. Forecasts ... 401
   (a) Evidence of annual forecasts being prepared in the temple at Hagia Triada ... 401

   Tablet HT 92 & Tablet HT 133 ... 401

		(b) Forecasts for cattle and livestock use in future periods	405
		Tablet HT 116A	405
		Tablet HT 116B	429

Part III	Tablet from the temple at Khania acting as principle, as a religious institution	433
	Tablet KH 11	433

Chapter 6	The end of the beginning?	457

Appendix 1: Identified Linear A symbols	463
Appendix 2: Identified Linear A number and fraction symbols	470
Appendix 3: The forms of Egyptian words we need to consider	472
Appendix 4: Place names	475
Appendix 5: Goats	481
Appendix 6: Ordinals	486
Appendix 7: Grain	492
Excursus 7A.1: The expected recording of wheat	494
Appendix 8: Dates	496
Select bibliography	508
Index	520

List of Pictures

Chapter 1
Picture 1.1:   Linear A and Linear B ideograms and example of counterpart resemblance, according to Palmer 4
Picture 1.2:   Examples of animal symbols in Linear B 5

Chapter 2
Picture 2.1:   Photograph of Linear A Tablet HT 21B 7
Picture 2.2:   Example of a page marked "this page is intentionally left blank" 8
Picture 2.3:   Transcription of Tablet HT 91A 9
Picture 2.4:   Transcription of Tablet HT 123A 11

Chapter 3
Picture 3.1:   Transcription of Tablet HT 123A 30
Picture 3.2(a) and (b): A comparison of the transcriptions of Tablet HT 95B and Tablet HT 86A 44

Chapter 4
Picture 4.1:   Statue of User found at Knossos 55
Picture 4.2:   Intermediary statue of (Nakht)weser(?) found at the Temple of Amun, Karnak 55
Picture 4.3:   The Aegeans (Cretans) portrayed in the tomb of Senenmut (Theban Tomb 71) 64
Picture 4.4:   The Aegeans (Cretans) portrayed in the tomb of Useramun (Theban Tomb 131) 65
Picture 4.5:   The Aegeans portrayed in the tomb of Rekhmire (Theban Tomb 100) 67
Picture 4.6:   First World War US Army recruitment poster 74
Picture 4.7:   The Golden Bowl of General Djehuty 80
Picture 4.8:   The Temple of Amun at Karnak with the Annals 82
Picture 4.9:   The "Botanical Gardens of Thutmose III" at the rear of the Festival Hall, Karnak 85
Picture 4.10: Recording of Kefti ships in the Peru-nefer naval dockyard 88
Picture 4.11: The Flotilla Fresco 94
Picture 4.12: New South Wales, View of Sydney from the East Side of the Cove No. 2 97
Picture 4.13: Front face of the statue base E_N PWNV at Kom el-Hetan 112
Picture 4.14: Left side of the statue base E_N PWNV at Kom el-Hetan 113
Picture 4.15: Amenhotep III with Queen Tiye receiving gifts on the occasion of his third jubilee 117
Picture 4.16: The royal family receives tribute in Year 12, from the tomb of Meryre II 119

List of Diagrams of Tablets

Chapter 1
Diagrams 1.1(a), (b), and (c): Linear A symbol L42 and L67 on tablets from
    Hagia Triada (HT)   5

Chapter 2
Diagram 2.1: Sketch of Tablet HT 123A   10
Diagram 2.2: Selection of tablet fragments from Khania (KH)   17

Chapter 3
Diagram 3.1: Sketch of Tablet HT 123A   30
Diagram 3.2: Sketch of Tablet HT 14   31
Diagram 3.3: Sketch of Tablet HT 86A   36
Diagram 3.4(a), (b), and (c): Tablet fragments from Khania (KH)   39
Diagram 3.5(a) and (b): A comparison of the sketches of Tablet HT 95B and
    Tablet HT 86A   44

List of Tables

Chapter 2
Table 2.1: Possible solutions to the Row One and Row Four equations, Linear A
    Tablet HT 123A   15

Chapter 4
Table 4.1: Attributed dates of Linear A tablet finds   48
Table 4.2: Finds of Egyptian commercial wares in Crete from the Late Minoan
    Period (by known Sub-Period)   60
Table 4.3: Finds of Syria-Palestinian and Cypriot commercial wares in Crete from
    the Late Minoan Period (by known Sub-Period)   62
Table 4.4: Captions in the tomb of Rekhmire (Theban Tomb 100)   69
Table 4.5: Believed stages in the ordering of place names on statue base E_N PWNV,
    Kom el-Hetan   115

Chapter 5
Table 5.1: Analysis of the Mc series of Linear B tablets' data   231
Table 5.2: Analysis of certain Linear A tablets' data   232

List of Graphs

Chapter 2
Graph 2.1: Solution to the Row One and Row Four equations, Linear A Tablet
HT 123A — 15

Chapter 4
Graph 4.1: Linear A tablets found in Crete by attributed date (Sub-Period mid-point) — 49
Graph 4.2: Finds of Egyptian commercial wares in Crete from the Late Minoan period (by known Sub-Period) — 60
Graph 4.3: India's post-independence trade with Great Britain as a percentage of total trade — 63

List of Maps

Map 1: Bronze Age Crete — xvii

Chapter 4
Map 4.1: Peru-nefer — 92
Map 4.2: Katsambas, Knossos, and Mount Iouktas — 100

Middle and Late Bronze Age chronology of Crete and Egypt

Dominant culture on Crete	Cretan Archaeological Sub Period	Chronology	Egyptian involvement in Crete	Egyptian Dynasties (non-native)	Egyptian Dynasties (native)	Egyptian Peroid
					↓	↓
	Middle Minoan IIA	1850 BC - 1800 BC	?		12th Dynasty (1991 BC - 1803 BC)	
Cretan city states?	Middle Minoan IIB	1800 BC - 1700 BC			13th Dynasty 1803 - 1649 BC	Middle Kingdom (2055 BC - 1650 BC)
	Middle Minoan III	1700 BC - 1600 BC	Trading relationship with Egyptian expatriate presence	15th Dynasty (Hyksos) (1650 BC - 1550 BC)	14th Dynasty (1725 - 1650 BC)	Second Inter-mediate period (1650 BC - 1550 BC)
Minoan	Late Minoan IA	1600 BC - 1500 BC			16th Dynasty (1649 BC - 1582 BC) 17th Dynasty (1582 - 1540 BC)	
	Late Minoan IB	1500 BC - 1450 BC				
Egyptian	Late Minoan II	1450 BC - 1400 BC	Egyptian protectorate Rebellion		18th Dynasty (1539 BC - 1296 BC)	New Kingdom (1550 BC - 1069 BC)
	Late Minoan III A1	1400 - 1375 BC				
Mycenaean	Late Minoan III A2	1375 1300 BC	Treaty based relations			↓

Rulers of Egypt during the 18th Dynasty

Ruler	Reign
Ahmose	1539 BC - 1515 BC
Amenhotep I	1515 BC - 1494 BC
Thutmose I	1494 BC - 1483 BC?
Thutmose II	1482 BC? - 1479 BC
[Queen] Hatshepsut	1479 BC - 1458 BC
Thutmose III	1479 BC - 1426 BC
Amenhotep II	1425 BC - 1400 BC
Thutmose IV	1399 BC? - 1380 BC
Amenhotep III	1379 BC - 1342 BC
Amenhotep IV / Akhenaten	1341 BC - 1325 BC
Nefertiti / Smenkhkkare / [Queen] Ankh[et]kheperure-Neferneferuaten	1330 BC - 1322 BC
Tutankhamun	1322 BC - 1314 BC
Ay	1313 BC - 1309 BC
Horemheb	1309 BC - 1296 BC

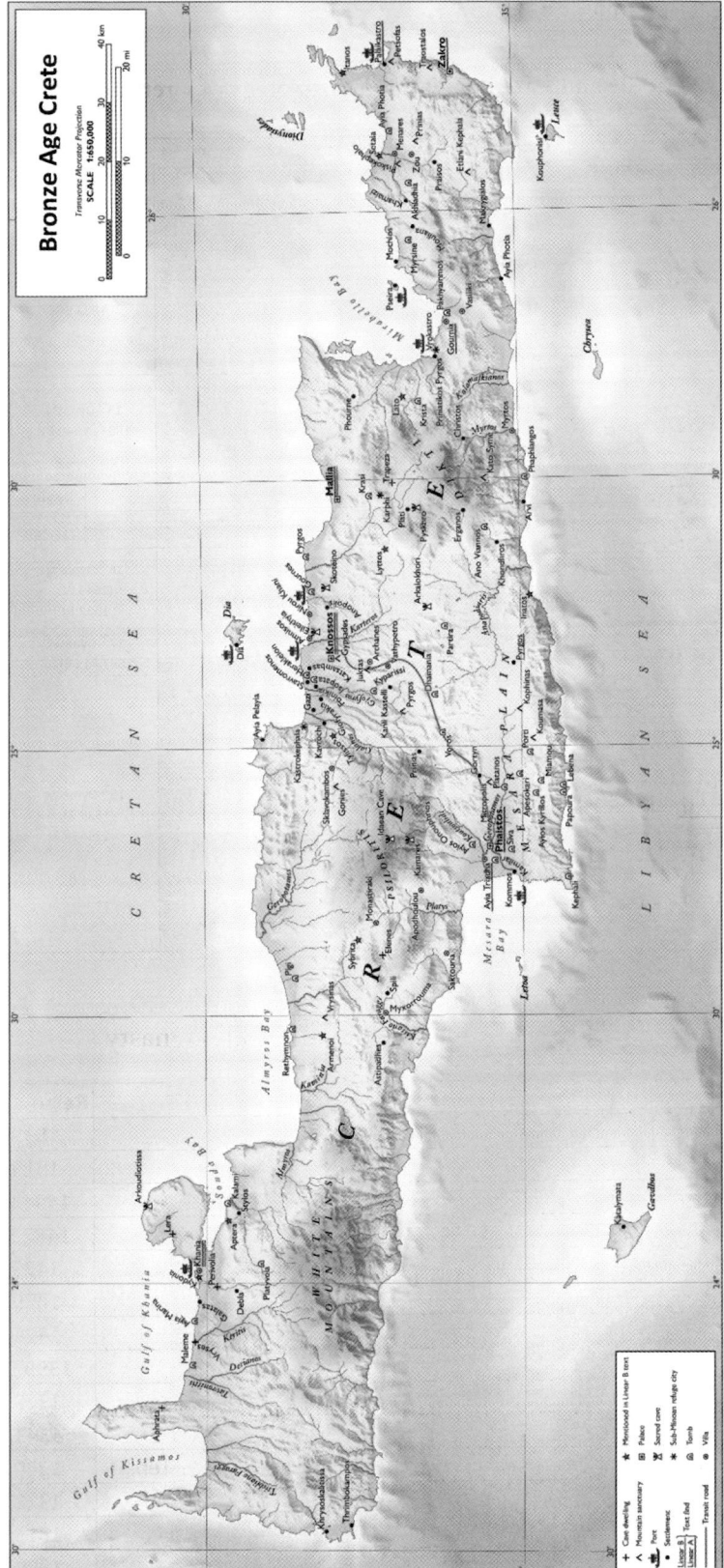

Chapter One

The Problem

"We're not that dumb, and we're not that smart."
(Donald Keough (Coca Cola director regarding the
replacement and reintroduction of Coke), 1985)[1]

In 1952 British architect Michael Ventris, building on the sadly curtailed work of Alice Kober, an American academic who had died just two years before, deciphered Linear B. Both Ventris and Kober were astonishingly smart. I think it wise to point out in paragraph one of page one of this book that I am not that smart. This has, however, perhaps helped me to decipher Linear A.

As the reader is no doubt aware, Linear A is a script that is believed to have been used principally on Crete from c.1800 BC to c.1450 BC. It was primarily used on clay tablets, seals, and nodules. Since the 1950s, as had been the case with Linear B before it was deciphered, there have been continual attempts to decipher Linear A "by reputable scholars, by talented amateurs and by cranks of all kinds from the lunatic fringe…"[2] As to which category I should be considered to fall into, I will leave it to the reader to decide. However, from the very beginning of my work deciphering Linear A it was apparent that there was a lot of "noise" out there.[3] I have tried to tackle the decipherment from a fresh perspective focussing on the primary evidence, not others' perspectives on it. Intentionally, therefore, I did not focus on previous, failed, decipherment attempts. Indeed, there seemed little point; to bring a fresh perspective to decipherment, and achieve success where others had failed, the "noise" had to be ignored.

As to why at the outset I thought I might be able to bring a fresh perspective to decipherment, I should probably tell the reader a little about myself. Beyond an obvious passion for history, I am a Chartered Accountant. My most recent professional roles have been working as a forensic accountant investigating insurance claims for employee theft and fraud. Piecing together disparate pieces of information to determine what actually happened, when that may have been deliberately obscured, is central to that role. I am also a qualified Insolvency Practitioner. When a business fails its records are typically in a poor and incomplete condition. Reviewing these to identify any potentially nefarious

---

1. https://www.snopes.com/fact-check/new-coke-fiasco/ (accessed 27 June 2020)
2. Michael Ventris & John Chadwick, *Documents in Mycenaean Greek* (2nd Ed.)(Cambridge: Cambridge University Press, 1973), p11
3. "Noise" is used in the sense conveyed by Norman F. Dixon, who characterises it as incorrect or deficiently analysed information that delays or prevents a correct analysis being undertaken (in the context of a general directing a battle). See Norman F. Dixon, *On the Psychology of Military Incompetence* (London: Jonathan Cape, 1976), pp28–31

2 The Decipherment of Linear A

transactions that have taken place that, again, might have been deliberately obscured is one of the principal roles of an Insolvency Practitioner, who may then challenge those transactions to recover assets for creditors. The Linear A tablets are partially complete accounting records so an accountant reviewing them makes sense. Oddly, it might even be the case that I am the first qualified accountant to look at them since they were created 3,500 or so years ago. Moreover, it was the logical mind of a professional architect who ultimately deciphered Linear B. Perhaps external professional input would yield fruit yet again?

In fact, my approach seems to follow that of Alice Kober, who made the first significant steps towards the decipherment of Linear B. She wrote:

> *"In attempting to decipher documents written in an unknown language with an unknown script, the first step is to establish the facts that are obvious from an inspection of the available documents. The second step is to find, by careful analysis and logical deduction, what conclusions can be drawn from these fundamental facts."*[4]

It seems to me that attempted (and failed) decipherers have not followed Alice Kober's wise words, and it is for this reason that I focussed on the Linear A tablets only, as they contained the most information and, therefore, were most likely to lead to success.

There are two principal schools of attempted decipherment of Linear A. In adopting different, and conflicting, methods from the outset we can tell with certainty that at least one of them is wrong. In fact, both are.

The first school of attempted decipherment is what might be called the "syllabic comparative school of attempted decipherment". In 1954 Michael Ventris and John Chadwick, a British academic, jointly published their seminal work on Linear B, *Documents in Mycenaean Greek*. In it we are told that "for the convenience of the printer and of those unfamiliar with the Mycenaean script, texts and words have generally been printed in… syllabic transliteration".[5] Mycenaean (Linear B) symbols, and the words formed using them, were transcribed into our Latin alphabet, spelt phonetically. This was not problematic for Linear B as it had already been deciphered.

A large number of Linear B symbols are visually similar to Linear A symbols. Beginning with Ventris and Chadwick,[6] it was assumed that the Linear B symbols, having presumably been derived from the visually similar Linear A symbols, had the same phonetic values in Linear A as they had in Linear B. Accordingly, Linear A was also transcribed into our Latin alphabet applying those believed phonetic values. I disagree with the logic of this approach. As historian Emmett L. Bennett Jr noted in 1953, the Linear A and Linear B scripts are radically different and when the same sign was used in both Linear A and

---

4. Michael Ventris & John Chadwick, *Documents in Mycenaean Greek* (2nd Ed.)(Cambridge: Cambridge University Press, 1973), p15
5. Michael Ventris & John Chadwick, *Documents in Mycenaean Greek* (2nd Ed.)(Cambridge: Cambridge University Press, 1973), pxviii
6. Michael Ventris & John Chadwick, *Documents in Mycenaean Greek* (2nd Ed.)(Cambridge: Cambridge University Press, 1973), p39

Linear B there was no guarantee that the same value should be assigned to it.[7] As we shall see, Bennett was correct to have his doubts.

The resulting "language" revealed by this process, however, has been assumed (by virtue of the tablets being found in Crete), to be Minoan. From the words identified by this approach it had been hoped that the language revealed could be aligned to a language family, thus revealing the origins of the Minoans. No such revelation has taken place, however, and the "language" was incomprehensible. To me, this is unsurprising. The approach is inherently flawed, as the aspiring decipherer is placed one step removed from the source material, using uncertain phonetic transcriptions rather than focusing on the texts themselves, which Alice Kober so wisely stated one must focus on.

The failure of this approach can be seen in three so-called "transactional" words that have purportedly been identified by using it (their meanings inferred from their contexts on the tablets, and their pronunciations based on their symbols' phonetic values in Linear B). Archaeologist Helena Tomas identifies these as:

- "Total" (written ∃＋ and purportedly pronounced "ku-ro");
- "Grand total" (written ɁͰ∃＋ and purportedly pronounced "po-to-ku-ro"); and
- "Deficit" (written ఆ＋ and purportedly pronouced "ki-ro").[8]

However, as we shall see in Chapter Two, these are all unfortunately incorrect, and the words have different meanings (and pronunciations).

The second principal school of attempted decipherment, which might be called the "pictorially comparative school of attempted decipherment", also uses Linear B as its guide. Historian Ruth Palmer summarised the purported decipherment achievements of this approach in 1995 when she wrote that:

> *"The identities of 9 commodities in the Linear A tablets are secured, based on the resemblance of the 9 Linear A signs to their Linear B counterparts in both form and function within the texts."*[9]

Both of these schools cannot be correct, for taking both schools' arguments to their logical conclusion you would have: symbols in Linear A that sound like they do in Linear B; and

---

7. Michael Ventris & John Chadwick, *Documents in Mycenaean Greek* (2nd Ed.)(Cambridge: Cambridge University Press, 1973), p37, citing Emmett L. Bennett Jr, "The Mycenae Tablets", *Proceedings of the American Philosophical Society* 97(4)(1953), p439
8. *Helena Tomas – It's All Linear B to Me*: https://www.youtube.com/watch?v=OBUIMjXkHZU (accessed 11 October 2020) (see video at 18:45 onwards); Ilse Schoep, "Tablets and Territories? Reconstructing Late Minoan IB Political Geography through Undeciphered Documents", *American Journal of Archaeology*, 103(2)(April 1999), p208; and W. C. Brice, *Inscriptions in the Minoan Linear Script of Class A* (Oxford: Oxford University Press, 1961), p5
9. Ruth Palmer, "Linear A commodities: a comparison of resources", in Robert Laffineur & Wolf-Dietrich Niemeier (Eds.), *Politea: Society and State in the Aegean Bronze Age: proceedings of the 5th International Aegean Conference/5e Rencontre égéenne internationale, University of Heidelberg, Archäologisches Institut, 10–13 April, 1994* (Bruxelles & Austin: Université de Liège & University of Texas at Austin, 1994), p144

4   The Decipherment of Linear A

symbols in Linear A that, by virtue of what they look like, represent the same thing as they do in Linear B. Looking the same, sounding the same, and meaning the same, would make Linear A equal Linear B, which clearly it does not.

To continue with the "pictorially comparative school of attempted decipherment" in its own right, as regards the nine commodities, I disagree with Palmer's logic. In the same way we cannot be certain that a symbol sounds the same in one language as it does in another, we cannot be certain that a symbol means the same thing in one language as it does in another based simply on it appearing similar. Indeed, the shortcomings in the findings resulting from this approach can immediately be seen if we consider two examples of Linear A symbols whose meanings have purportedly been determined based on their similarity to Linear B symbols with known meanings. Indeed, even their "secured" meanings are quickly revealed to be incorrect when all facets of the Linear B language are considered.

The Linear B symbol for barley (*120) has been believed to convey the same meaning to the similar Linear A symbol L42 (AB 120); this is one of Palmer's nine symbols with a secured meaning. Similarly, Linear A symbol L67 (A304) is also believed by Palmer (by virtue of, it seems, a process of elimination given the secured meanings that have been identified) to represent a crop.[10]

Picture 1.1: Linear A and Linear B ideograms and example of counterpart resemblance, according to Palmer[11]

Per Palmer:	Linear A symbol	Linear B symbol
Linear A symbol with a Linear B counterpart having a resemblance leading to a "definite identification"	Symbol AB120 or L42	Symbol *120 GRA - barley
Linear A symbol with "no Linear B parallel"	Symbol A304 or L67	

---

10. Ruth Palmer, "Linear A commodities: a comparison of resources", in Robert Laffineur & Wolf-Dietrich Niemeier (Eds.), *Politea: Society and State in the Aegean Bronze Age: proceedings of the 5th International Aegean Conference/5e Rencontre égéenne internationale, University of Heidelberg, Archäologisches Institut, 10–13 April, 1994* (Bruxelles & Austin: Université de Liège & University of Texas at Austin, 1994), p141. L67 has also been assumed not to be an animal by Palmer as it appears in fractions, such as on Tablet HT 21A. This does not, however, take into account either the possibility that the animal may already have been slaughtered and part consumed or may have been part owned with another party (of which, as we shall see, there is some evidence).

11. See Ruth Palmer, "Linear A commodities: a comparison of resources", in Robert Laffineur & Wolf-Dietrich Niemeier (Eds.), *Politea: Society and State in the Aegean Bronze Age: proceedings of the 5th International Aegean Conference/5e Rencontre égéenne internationale, University of Heidelberg, Archäologisches Institut, 10–13 April, 1994* (Bruxelles & Austin: Université de Liège & University of Texas at Austin, 1994), p155 Plate XXI (Palmer's symbol AB120 with the = through the stem is too angular, as can be seen in Diagram 1.1). Throughout this work references to Linear A characters use the system adopted by Carratelli (Michael Ventris & John Chadwick, *Documents in Mycenaean Greek* (2nd Ed.)(Cambridge: Cambridge University Press, 1973), p33 Figure 6), and Brice (W. C. Brice, *Inscriptions in the Minoan Linear Script of Class A* (Oxford: Oxford University Press, 1961), Table 1).

However, as Alice Kober correctly determined, in Linear B the presence of two horizontal bars, akin to an equals sign (i.e. =), crossing the vertical stem of a symbol representing an animal, indicate that symbol represents a male animal.[12]

Picture 1.2: Examples of animal symbols in Linear B[13]

109ª	ox/bull	*21	sheep
109ᵇ	cow	106ª	ram
		106ᵇ	ewe
*22	goat	*85	pig
107ª	he-goat	108ª	boar
107ᵇ	she-goat	108ᵇ	sow

Both Linear A symbol L42 and L67 appear with and without these horizontal bars meaning that they represent male and female animals, respectively:

Diagrams 1.1(a), (b), and (c): Linear A symbols L42 and L67 on tablets from Hagia Triada (HT).[14]

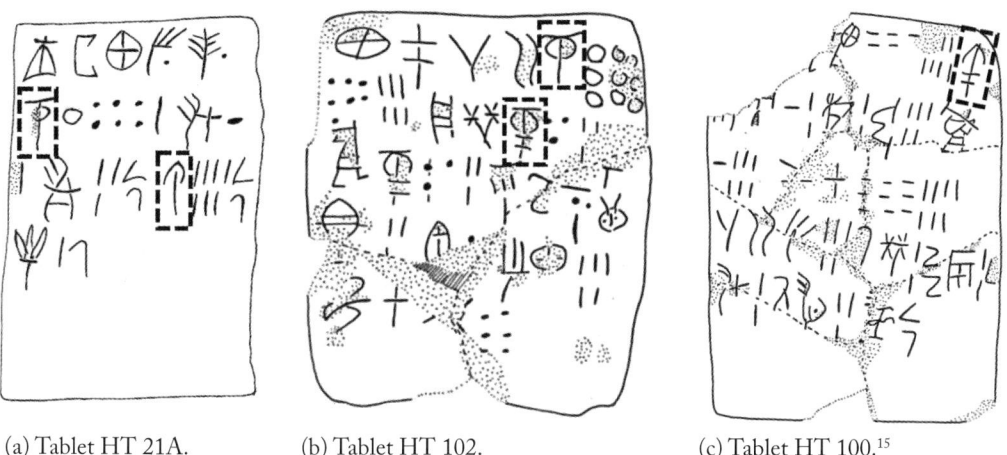

(a) Tablet HT 21A.   (b) Tablet HT 102.   (c) Tablet HT 100.[15]

---

12. John Chadwick, *The Decipherment of Linear B* (2nd Ed.)(Cambridge: Cambridge University Press, 1967), p45; Michael Ventris & John Chadwick, *Documents in Mycenaean Greek* (2nd Ed.)(Cambridge: Cambridge University Press, 1973), pp196, 208
13. See Michael Ventris & John Chadwick, *Documents in Mycenaean Greek* (2nd Ed.)(Cambridge: Cambridge University Press, 1973), p195
14. Louis Godart & Jean-Pierre Olivier, *Recueil des Inscriptions en Linéaire A, Volume 1: Tablettes éditées avant 1970* (Athens: École Française D'Athènes, 1976) (Archaeological Museum of Heraklion, Ministry of Culture – Hellenic Organisation of Cultural Resources (copyright))
15. Linear A symbol L67 with the male = symbol joined to it, as here, is, in fact, Linear A symbol L10.

When the male = symbol is attached to Linear A symbol L42 and Linear A symbol L67, as on Tablet HT 100 and Tablet HT 102, it demonstrates that the symbols to which it is attached record something male and, by inference, when it is not attached to those same symbols, they record something that is female, as shown on Tablet HT 21A and Tablet HT 102. Linear A symbol L42 and Linear A symbol L67 cannot represent crops; they must therefore represent animals (so, cattle or livestock). The "pictorially comparative school of attempted decipherment" has, therefore, only taken account of information from Linear B that supports its, unfortunately premature, conclusions and has not taken account of the information from Linear B which shows those conclusions to be incorrect.

In considering how a decipherment of Linear A should be approached, Ventris and Chadwick quoted T. J. Dunbabin in *Documents in Mycenaean Greek* as expressing a hope for the discovery of a Rosetta Stone to allow a comparison of Linear A to another known language so providing a template for Linear A's decipherment.[16] Sadly there is no such thing. However, by an examination of the original texts themselves, we have the next best thing. This is discussed in Chapter Two.

---

16. Michael Ventris & John Chadwick, *Documents in Mycenaean Greek* (2nd Ed.)(Cambridge: Cambridge University Press, 1973), p23

Chapter Two

The Mathematical "proof" and the Emergence of a Theory

"Follow the money."
(Deep Throat, *All the President's Men* (1976))[1]

Linear A, of course, was used almost a millennia before money was invented. Given my professional background, however, it was perhaps natural that I would first focus on the numbers recorded on the Linear A tablets, and this is where the decipherment story begins.

Two tablets provide us with a mathematical "proof" as to what Linear A really is. They are Tablet HT 21B and Tablet HT 123A. Both are from Hagia Triada (abbreviated to "HT") in southern central Crete where the majority of the surviving Linear A tablets have been found. Let us start with Tablet HT 21B:

Picture 2.1: Photograph of Linear A Tablet HT 21B[2]

This side of this tablet might seem an odd choice for the key to deciphering Linear A. After all, while the other side of the tablet, Tablet HT 21A (which we saw in the last chapter and which is translated in Chapter Five), has symbols and values recorded against those symbols, this side has only a single ‡ symbol, Linear A symbol L2, covering it in its entirety. This only occurs in one other instance in the Linear A corpus, on Tablet HT 1B (however, it has not been recognised as such because Tablet HT 1B is somewhat scuffed and is broken and incomplete). Indeed, while included in W. C. Brice's *Inscriptions in the Minoan Linear Script of Class A* (Oxford: 1961) (referred to as "Brice" throughout this work), this side of the tablet has been seen as so inconsequential that it was omitted from L. Godart and

---

1. https://www.imdb.com/title/tt0074119/characters/nm0000602 (accessed 31 July 2022)
2. W. C. Brice, *Inscriptions in the Minoan Linear Script of Class A* (Oxford: Oxford University Press, 1961), Plate III (© The Society of Antiquities of London)

8 The Decipherment of Linear A

J. P. Olivier's otherwise comprehensive five volume *Recueil des Inscriptions en Linéaire A* (Paris: 1976–1985) (referred to as "Godart & Olivier" throughout this work).

Other than this single symbol, the entire side of Tablet HT 21B is blank but, I believe, this was intentional and reflects what the symbol was meant to convey. It fulfilled the same function as the phrase "this page is intentionally left blank" that is used by modern printers, for example:

Picture 2.2: Example of a page marked "this page is intentionally left blank"[3]

This page is intentionally left blank.

---

3. Boris Jerorović, *A Concise Dictionary of Middle Egyptian* (Oxford: Griffith Institute, Ashmolean Museum, 2002), p44

The Mathematical "proof" and the Emergence of a Theory 9

This is what the ‡ symbol across the whole side of the tablet was meant to convey; that this side of the tablet was intentionally left blank or, indeed, that it was intentionally empty and had no (i.e. zero) content. While superfluous (most tablets do not have this symbol on their reverse side, and I have always been puzzled as to why modern printers feel it necessary to print "this page is intentionally left blank" in today's books), we are lucky that the scribe included it.

If the ‡ symbol was being used to convey the fact that this side of the tablet was empty and had no (i.e. zero) content, then if the symbol were then used in a numerical context, we would expect it to have the numerical value of "zero". This is seemingly confirmed by Tablet HT 91A, Brice's transcription of which is set out below:

Picture 2.3: Transcription of Tablet HT 91A[4]

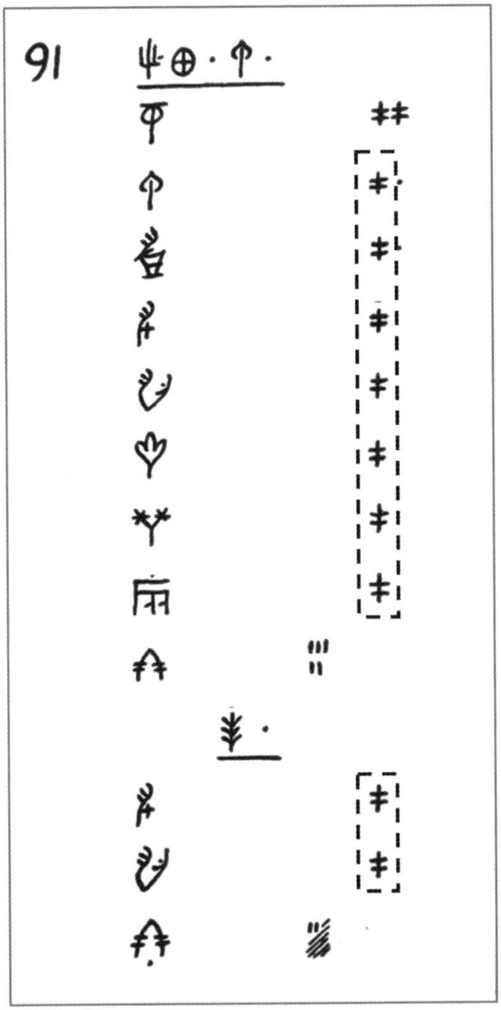

---

4. W. C. Brice, *Inscriptions in the Minoan Linear Script of Class A* (Oxford: Oxford University Press, 1961), Plate VIIIa (© The Society of Antiquities of London)

10   The Decipherment of Linear A

In Linear A, fraction values and certain larger numerical values were conveyed by symbols. On Tablet HT 91A nine different things, be they commodities, cattle, or livestock (and from Chapter One we know that the first highlighted category above, and the unhighlighted one before that,[5] are cattle or livestock), are recorded with an amount conveyed by the ✢ symbol. It has been assumed that the ✢ symbol represents a fraction value when used in a numerical context (Linear A fraction symbol A). However, it would defy logic to imagine, if the ✢ symbol had a specific fraction value, that all those categories of items being recorded at that particular point in time (including at least one type of animal) were present in that same fractional amount. It would also defy logic for the ✢ symbol to uniformly represent a large number for that same reason. Realistically, given its use on Tablet HT 21B, it could only be the case that ✢ represents zero.

With this in mind, let us now look at Tablet HT 123A, which is set out below:

Diagram 2.1: Sketch of Tablet HT 123A[6]

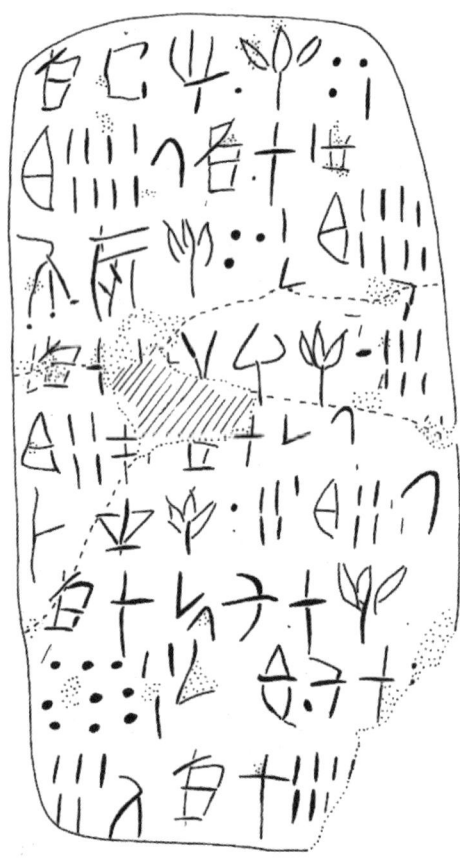

---

5. There are two ✢ symbols next to the first category on the tablet. This is discussed further on page 306.
6. Louis Godart & Jean-Pierre Olivier, *Recueil des Inscriptions en Linéaire A, Volume 1: Tablettes éditées avant 1970* (Athens: École Française D'Athènes, 1976) (Archaeological Museum of Heraklion, Ministry of Culture – Hellenic Organisation of Cultural Resources (copyright))

The Mathematical "proof" and the Emergence of a Theory   11

This format of tablet is somewhat confusing, so Brice's tabulated transcription is used for the purpose of analysis here and is set out below. This shows three columns of "commodities" (identified by numbered circles), split across four rows of category groupings (identified by numbered squares), and then totals for each of the three columns. We see the "zero" symbol in Row Three Column Two:

Picture 2.4: Transcription of Tablet HT 123A[7]

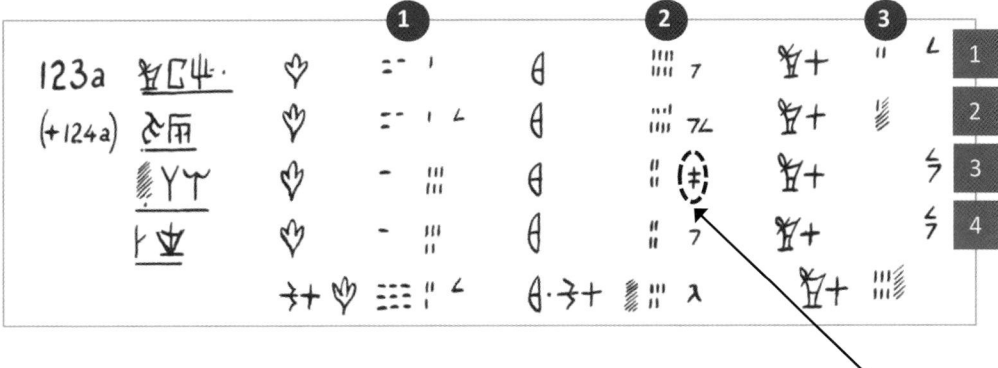

As can be seen above, the highlighted Linear A symbol L2 / fraction symbol A, ✢, is that which was shown on Tablet HT 21B (and Tablet HT 1B) and which, on the basis of that tablet and Tablet HT 91A, we have deduced to equal zero. Taking the ✢ symbol as zero (or, more properly here, a sign denoting a zero value of fractional units), we can see that Row Three of Tablet HT 123A records the "commodities" thus:

Row Three: [transcription box]

In Linear A, a horizontal tally mark has a value of 10 and a vertical tally mark has a value of 1. Thus, there are 16 units of the first commodity and 4 units (or, four single units plus a zero value of fractional units) of the second commodity. As to why Linear A symbol L2 / fraction symbol A was needed, it would seem that for some reason the scribe felt the need to explicitly state that there was no fractional value of the second commodity (perhaps because all the other counts of the Column Two commodity had fractional values).

The ratio of the first two commodities in Row Three is, therefore, 4:1 which is highly significant. On the Dk series Linear B tablets that recorded flocks of sheep and consignments of wool at Knossos, Ventris and Chadwick noted that the ratio of sheep (rams) to wool was 4:1.[8]

---
7. W. C. Brice, *Inscriptions in the Minoan Linear Script of Class A* (Oxford: Oxford University Press, 1961), Plate XXa (© The Society of Antiquities of London). Brice was uncertain but he believed there might originally have been a symbol after the ✢ symbol that is circled. I do not.
8 Michael Ventris & John Chadwick, *Documents in Mycenaean Greek* (2nd Ed.)(Cambridge: Cambridge University Press, 1973), pp119, 204

One of the underlying assumptions I have adopted is that while the transition from Linear A to Linear B evidently represented a political change, there was no change in the underlying economy of Crete and its sources of wealth. Further, while links between the two scripts of Linear A and Linear B are not yet fully understood, that there was a link demonstrates a degree of administrative continuity from one regime to the next. We might expect, therefore, a degree of similarity in the economic transactions that were recorded as well as a degree of similarity in how they were recorded. It seems reasonable to conclude, therefore, that as with the Dk series of Linear B tablets, here on Tablet HT 123A we are likely looking at sheep (rams) and wool. Column Three, as was also recorded in the Dk series of Linear B tablets, therefore, represents a "deficit" i.e. the amount of wool not yet delivered (against the obligation to do so).

It is worth noting at this point that the accounting is slightly different between the Dk series of Linear B tablets and Linear A Tablet HT 123A (the only tablet of this type surviving in the Linear A corpus so, yet again, we are lucky that this particular tablet survived). On the Dk series of Linear B tablets, the wool value represents an amount delivered to date and the deficit is a current deficit (the original total obligation, which is not shown, less deliveries to date). Therefore the 4:1 ratio is observed by comparing the total of sheep (rams) to the combined total of wool (the amount delivered to date) *plus* the deficit (the current obligation outstanding). The Dk series of Linear B tablets shows the position on an individual debtor's account that would in the modern day be recorded in the debtor's ledger. An example is set out below.

Numerical analysis of Linear B tablet Dk 1072

	Sheep (rams) [at start of period]	Wool [amount delivered to date]	Deficit [current obligation outstanding]
Recorded amounts	100	13 ¹⁄₃	11 ²⁄₃
Totals (not on tablet)	100	25	
Ratio:		4:1	

On Linear A Tablet HT 123A, the sheep (rams) and wool units by themselves demonstrate the 4:1 ratio. The wool units are, therefore, a gross, not a net, obligation (i.e. the original total amount owed, without any deduction for subsequent deliveries). As the wool obligation has not changed over time with deliveries made, and the wool value therefore represents the original total obligation calculated as owed, the number of sheep (rams) on which that value is calculated must also be the number at that fixed point in time when the obligation was calculated. Conversely, the deficit in Column Three is still a current deficit, showing the amounts that were outstanding when the tablet was written (taking into account deliveries made since the gross obligation was assessed) but it is a memorandum entry, not part of the ratio calculation. The amounts delivered to date would be found by deducting the current deficit from the original total wool obligation amount.[9] Tablet HT 123A also differs from the Dk series of Linear B tablets in that it evidently shows more than one debtor's account, given that four times it repeats differing numbers of the same three categories of items (sheep (rams), wool (payment obligation), and deficit); as we shall see in Chapter Five, these are, in fact, four groups of debtors.

Numerical analysis of Linear A tablet HT 123A Row 3			
	Sheep (rams) [at start of period]	**Wool** [obligation to deliver at start of period]	**Deficit** [current obligation outstanding]
Recorded amounts	16	4	[fraction value]
Ratio:		4:1	

With the value of ⨯ being zero, and from this being able to show that a 4:1 ratio was present on Row Three (when comparing the Column One value to the Column Two value), and inferring that Columns One, Two, and Three record sheep (rams), wool, and deficit, respectively, we can prove the point further if the same 4:1 ratio is also evident on the other rows of the tablet. From the outset, however, we can see that this ratio is broadly present between the totals for Column One and Column Two at the bottom of HT 123A ([93 + an unknown fraction] vs [25 + an unknown fraction]), suggesting, in turn, that each row on Tablet HT 123A also exhibits a 4:1 ratio.

Algebraically, there is only sufficient evidence to test whether Rows One and Four also exhibit the same 4:1 ratio. To do this, the value of another fraction symbol has to be calculated, namely Linear A fraction symbol E (i.e. 𐄳). To begin, we need to take the commodity values in Column One and Column Two for these two rows:

Row One: ❦   ⋮⁻ ᛁ   ᚦ   ⦙⦙⦙⦙ 𐄳

Row Four: ❦   ⁻ ⦙⦙⦙   ᚦ   ⦙⦙ 𐄳

---

9. The small values of the current deficits in Column Three on Tablet HT 123A, when compared to the original obligations in Column Two, indicate, even before we undertake any further analysis, that the shearing of the sheep in question was complete. Sheep shearing takes place in Crete from mid-May to mid-June (http://www.wondergreece.gr/v1/en/Articles/Architecture/8721-Mitata_in_Crete (accessed 31 July 2022)), so we know, therefore, that the tablet was written after this point in the year.

On the assumption that we will see a 4:1 ratio across all rows on the Linear A tablets, four times the Column Two value will equal the Column One value on both Row One and Row Four, and (importantly) the value of the fraction symbol "7" will be the same on each row. Therefore, taking Row One values and converting this into a simple algebraic equation (where four times the Column Two value equals the Column One value):

Row One equation:

Column 1 commodity amount: 31 = 4 x Column 2 commodity amount: 8 + fraction "7"

To put this algebraically (where x is the faction "7"):

$31 = 4(8 + x)$

$31 = 32 + 4x$

$-1 = 4x$

$X = -0.25$ or, as a fraction, $-¼$

We should then arrive at the same answer using the values on Row Four:

Row Four equation:

Column 1 commodity amount: 15 = 4 x Column 2 commodity amount: 4 + fraction "7"

To put this algebraically (where x is the faction "7"):

$15 = 4(4 + x)$

$15 = 16 + 4x$

$-1 = 4x$

$X = -0.25$ or $-¼$

The two different equations give us the same fractional value for "7" if we assume the ratio of 4:1 between the Column A and Column B values. This is not a coincidence.

Perhaps, however, let us look at this another way, and not assume a 4:1 ratio between the Column One commodity values and the Column Two commodity values, but simply assume that they are in a fixed proportion but that the ratio between them is unknown (so, instead of just 4:1 we will try to determine the unknown value "y" in the ratio y:1). If the fixed ratio between Column One values and Column Two values is the ratio y:1, and the value of fraction symbol 7 (x) is also unknown but is the same in both the "Row One equation" and "Row Four equation", we can determine both the value of x and the value of y.

As we vary either x or y in the "Row One equation" and "Row Four equation", so the value of the other unknown (y or x) will change in order for the equations to balance. This

The Mathematical "proof" and the Emergence of a Theory 15

gives us a number of solutions for each, which can be plotted as lines on a graph known as "solution curves". If the intersection of the solution curves for the "Row One equation" and "Row Four equation" is at a single point, at that single point we can see what the single value of x and y is that solves both equations simultaneously, telling us both the fixed ratio and the value of this fraction symbol. Moreover, not only will this give us the fixed ratio between the Column One values and Column Two values and the value of Linear A fraction symbol E value, if it is 4:1, matching Row Three, it will "prove" our theory.

The analysis is set out below:

Table 2.1: Possible solutions to the Row One and Row Four equations, Linear A Tablet HT 123A

Value of x (i.e. "7") (both equations)	Value of y Row One equation	Value of y Row Four equation
x	y1	y2
(2.00)	5.17	7.50
(1.75)	4.96	6.67
(1.50)	4.77	6.00
(1.25)	4.59	5.45
(1.00)	4.43	5.00
(0.75)	4.28	4.62
(0.50)	4.13	4.29
(0.25)	4.00	4.00
0.00	3.88	3.75
0.25	3.76	3.53
0.50	3.65	3.33
0.75	3.54	3.16
1.00	3.44	3.00
1.25	3.35	2.86
1.50	3.26	2.73
1.75	3.18	2.61
2.00	3.10	2.50

Graph 2.1: Solution to the Row One and Row Four equations, Linear A Tablet HT 123A

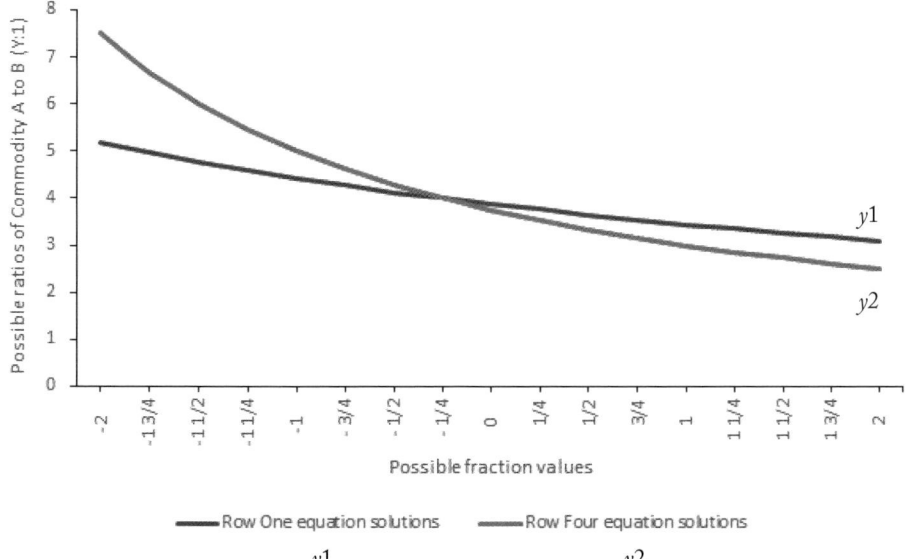

16   The Decipherment of Linear A

As Graph 1 shows, if there is a fixed ratio of the commodity in Column One to the commodity in Column Two that is exhibited by Row One and Four, it can only be 4:1, the ratio that we determined from Row Three, and the value of Linear A fraction symbol E (7) can only be –0.25 or –¼. While we made the assumption that Commodity One and Commodity Two were in proportion on Row One and Row Four, the 4:1 ratio again being evident, and this also being the ratio evident on Row Three, cannot be a coincidence. While memories come flooding back of my Maths A-Level teacher writing on my homework that "EVIDENCE <u>NEVER</u> EQUALS PROOF", there comes a point when the reasonable rational person accepts the evidence before them as sufficient proof (or, we would all be smoking as if it were still the 1950s). The evidence here is more than sufficient to prove, beyond reasonable doubt, that a 4:1 ratio exists between these two items on at least three rows of the tablet (with the final row also exhibiting this ratio, as will be set out in Chapter Five).

That the value of Linear A fraction symbol E (i.e. 7) is a negative fraction, namely –0.25 or –¼, will no doubt come as a surprise to the reader. Indeed, such a notion might be scoffed at by potential detractors. However, as those of us who learned French at school will remember, if one wants to say that the time is 7:45, one might say "il est huit heures moins le quart" (literally "it is 8 hours minus a quarter"). The concept of negative fractions does, therefore, exist; it is just a question of convention as to whether such a concept is used.

On the assumption that the Cretan economy exhibited the same characteristics during the Mycenaean period when Linear B was used as it did in the earlier period when Linear A was used, and that its underlying transactions were similar and, administratively, they were similarly recorded, on the basis of this ratio being present in the Linear B records, the two commodities in question are:

- Column One: "sheep (rams)":
  This is, therefore, the meaning here of Linear A symbol L49, which is written here as:

  As we shall see, however, the scribe of Tablet HT 14 wrote it more accurately as:

- Column Two: "wool":
  This is, therefore, the meaning here of Linear A symbol L90:

The Mathematical "proof" and the Emergence of a Theory

Further, as noted, we can also be equally certain that, following the format of the Dk series of Linear B tablets, in Column Three we have the "deficit"; this (or, as we shall see, "deficiency") is, therefore, the meaning of Linear A symbol L103, namely:

Archaeological support for the mathematical "proof"
Archaeological evidence can be found to support the mathematically driven findings at this point. Ruth Palmer notes that, on the basis of her ascribed meanings for certain Linear A symbols as derived from a comparison to Linear B, it is surprising that there are no instances of sheep being recorded at Khania on the surviving Linear A tablets.[10] Of course, what is and is not shown on the Linear A tablets is always subject to the random nature of archaeological survival and all of the Linear A records recording sheep at Khania may not have survived. However, there are three instances of the Linear A symbol for wool that we have identified on Tablet HT 123A appearing on the surviving Linear A tablets from Khania:

Diagram 2.2: Selection of tablet fragments from Khania (KH)[11]

Tablet KH 12

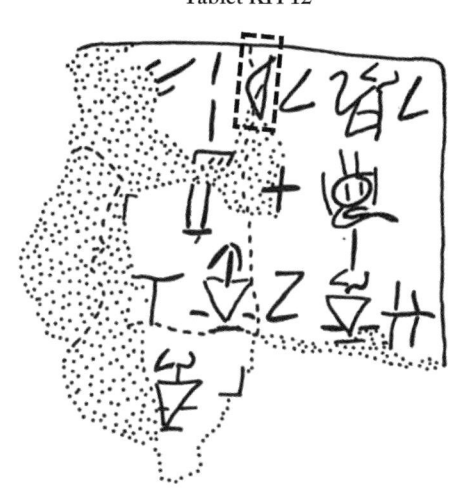

Tablet KH 56

Tablet KH 85

---

10. Ruth Palmer, "Linear A commodities: a comparison of resources", in Robert Laffineur & Wolf-Dietrich Niemeier (Eds.), *Politea: Society and State in the Aegean Bronze Age: proceedings of the 5th International Aegean Conference/5e Rencontre égéenne internationale, University of Heidelberg, Archäologisches Institut, 10–13 April, 1994* (Bruxelles & Austin: Université de Liège & University of Texas at Austin, 1994), p146
11. Louis Godart & Jean-Pierre Olivier, *Recueil des Inscriptions en Linéaire A, Volume 3: Tablettes, Nodules et Rondelles éditées en 1975 et 1976* (Athens: École Française D'Athènes, 1976) (Archaeological Museum of Chania, Ministry of Culture – Hellenic Organisation of Cultural Resources (copyright))

18   The Decipherment of Linear A

If there was wool, there must have been sheep. Therefore, now that the symbol for wool has been identified correctly, Palmer's detailed understanding of the Cretan economy is shown to be correct.

Clues as to the language of Linear A
The words for sheep (rams), wool, and deficits are all written as single Linear A symbols. As we shall see, this gives us a clue as to the nature of Linear A. For now, however, let us consider, again, the symbol for zero which has given rise to the above mathematical analysis and the identification of the meanings of our first Linear A symbols.

Looking at Linear A symbol L2 / fraction symbol A, ‡, and now knowing its meaning, it is clear that it was derived from Egyptian Hieroglyph F35 which, in Middle Egyptian (the form of the Egyptian language spoken when Linear A was used), spelled the word *nfr* meaning "zero"[12]:

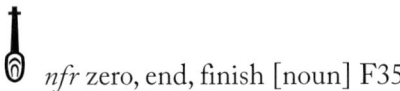
nfr zero, end, finish [noun] F35

From a side-by-side comparison of Linear A symbol L2 / fraction symbol A with Hieroglyph F35, we can see the changes that have occurred (the stem has been simplified to a single line, and the oval and its detail at the base has been simplified to a horizontal line intersecting the stem):

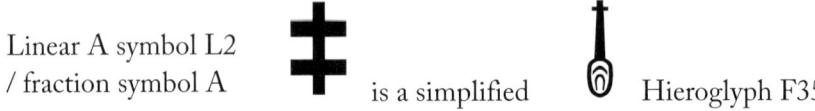
Linear A symbol L2 / fraction symbol A   ‡   is a simplified   Hieroglyph F35

This change is easily understandable if one thinks about the medium in which Linear A was principally used. The Linear A scribe incised the symbols he wrote in clay using a stylus. The hieroglyph-based script he evidently used was designed to be inscribed on monuments, on a large scale that allowed for intricately detailed (indeed ornate) masonry work. To be incised in clay (a medium for which hieroglyphs were not designed), the hieroglyph had to be simplified. It would not be easy incising two lines close to each other in clay for the vertical shaft of the hieroglyph, so it was simplified to a single vertical stroke. It would be difficult to incise the oval and its interior detail at the bottom of the shaft in clay, so this was simplified to a single horizonal line.[13]

---

12. F35 is the hieroglyph's alphanumeric code from Gardiner's sign list which I will use to refer to all hieroglyphs in this work (see A.H. Gardiner, *Egyptian Grammar: Being an Introduction to the Study of Hieroglyphs* (3rd Ed.) (Oxford: Griffith Institute, 1957), pp438–548)
13. It is perhaps interesting to note at this point that, in the later Classical Greek shorthand writing (which, as discussed subsequently, I believe was based on and applied largely the same methodology of the earlier Egyptian form of shorthand writing seen in Linear A), words beginning with the Greek letter Omikron (O) could be abbreviated to single a bar (albeit a slanted bar) (see F. W. G. Foat, "On Old Greek Tachygraphy", *The Journal of Hellenic Studies* 21(1901), p252). Though Classical Greek shorthand was not written on clay tablets, the characteristics of Linear A as well as methodology seem to have persisted.

The Mathematical "proof" and the Emergence of a Theory

Perhaps there will be an element of the story of *The Emperor's New Clothes* here about perceiving and recognising the similarity between this Linear A symbol and the hieroglyph upon which it is so clearly based (and, indeed, the Linear A symbols and the hieroglyphs upon which they are based more generally). Those with a vested interest in not deciphering Linear A (once, deep down, they know what it is) will not want to see this truth before them. However, as we go through the corpus (and the other evidence) that position will become so untenable as ultimately to be a source of amusement rather than a serious academic concern. I shall proceed on the assumption that the reader is not one who will give us cause for such amusement.

The mathematical "proof" shows us that this similarity between Linear A symbol L2 / fraction symbol A and Hieroglyph F35 is no mere coincidence. Once we understand why the hieroglyph has had to be modified, we are faced with the fact that the symbol looks like a hieroglyph because it is a hieroglyph and it has demonstrably kept the same meaning. The maths has proved this beyond reasonable doubt (as, indeed, we shall encounter a number of times throughout the corpus).

That Linear A symbol L2 / fraction symbol A demonstrably means "zero" on Tablet HT 21B and Tablet HT 123A, and that Linear A symbol L2 / fraction symbol A was based upon Hieroglyph F35 which spelled a word also meaning "zero" in Middle Egyptian, gives us a mathematical "proof" that Linear A was a form of Middle Egyptian. While not the Linear A Rosetta Stone that Dunbabin had hoped for, this mathematical "proof" is, I think, the next best thing. Moreover, we have already noted that sheep (rams), wool, and deficit are conveyed by just one symbol, yet the Middle Egyptian words that had those meanings (unlike the word for zero) had many hieroglyphs. The most likely explanation to account for this is, therefore, that we are dealing with a form of shorthand.

That Linear A was Middle Egyptian written using a form of shorthand is evident from the symbols that appear elsewhere on Tablet HT 123A and this can again be demonstrated mathematically. Considering, again, Brice's tabulated transcription of this tablet (that we saw in Picture 2.4 previously):

Two symbols appear next to the totals at the bottom of Column One and Column Two (but not Column Three):

20   The Decipherment of Linear A

These are Linear A symbols L98 and L22, respectively. Brice, in 1961, stated that he believed that these, together, represented the word for "total".[14] This, however, is not quite right.

While evidently all columns are totalled, and it can reasonably be assumed that this is indicated by the one symbol that is next to all three column totals (Linear A symbol L22), the reader will recall that earlier in this chapter it was evident that the Column One and Column Two totals represented totals at a fixed point in time (and that the total deficit in Column Three, being "current", did not represent an amount at that fixed point in time). The first symbol, therefore, represents a date.

A simple visual inspection shows us that Linear A symbol L98 is Egyptian Hieroglyph F14 rotated by 90 degrees anticlockwise:

This hieroglyph does not form a word by itself, but it is the first hieroglyph in both ways of writing the Middle Egyptian word *wpt rnpt* which means "New Year's Day":

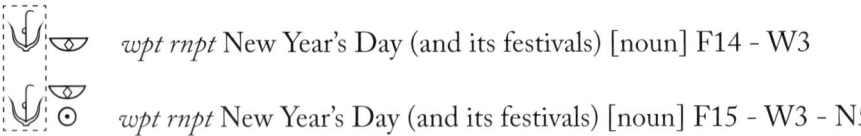

New Year's Day is, of course, the start of the New Year, and this would seem the most likely meaning conveyed here (when the number of sheep (rams) were likely counted and the wool payment obligations arising thereon were likely calculated). That an obligation owed was calculated on the first day of the New Year (which we can consider as equivalent to the last day of the old year) is not surprising to us with our concept of payment of taxes annually according to a calculation undertaken after the start of the New Year based on numbers as at the end of the old year. Given that this word is abbreviated to a symbol representing its first hieroglyph, we again appear to be looking at a form of shorthand and, moreover, the rotation of the hieroglyph to become the Linear A symbol is itself indicative of this, as discussed in the following excursus.

---

14. W. C. Brice, *Inscriptions in the Minoan Linear Script of Class A* (Oxford University Press: Oxford, 1961), p5

The Mathematical "proof" and the Emergence of a Theory   21

> **Excursus 2.1: Rotation of symbols in ancient texts**
>
> To my knowledge, there are only two circumstances in the ancient world where symbols in one script were rotated when they appear in another script.[15]
>
> The first circumstance where letters in the alphabet of one language were used to become the alphabet of another written language, such as when the Phoenician alphabet was used to create the Classical Greek alphabet in the 8th Century BC. Then, reversals and rotations were the result of scribal error.[16] If we believed that this was the case with Linear A, we would again be considering Linear A to be a Minoan language written with modified Egyptian hieroglyphs. As noted, however, all approaches to the decipherment of Linear A on the basis that it is Minoan have failed, so this is discounted as a possibility.
>
> The second circumstance where letters were rotated (and / or reversed) is when they are used in the Greek form of shorthand writing.[17] This characteristic clearly fits with our now emerging theory that Linear A is Middle Egyptian written in hieroglyphs using a method of shorthand. Given this common characteristic, in the next chapter we focus on the Greek shorthand method that, in effect, provides us with a cipher by which we can de-code Linear A.

Returning to Tablet HT 123A, however, we know that the second Linear A symbol, L22, means total (or, indeed, coming at the end of the tablet and list of all items, grand total). In Middle Egyptian *dmd sm3* means "grand total". It is written in hieroglyphs as:

 *dmd sm3* grand total [noun] N14 - F36

Again, we are faced with modification of the first hieroglyph to become a Linear A symbol. Hieroglyph N14 is a five pointed star but is modified in Linear A to become a four pointed "star" i.e. a cross:

★ becomes ✚

The reason for this change is because it is simpler to incise in clay a vertical stroke and a horizontal stroke that intersect than it is to create a five pointed star. It is, of course, also quicker to write (one of the desirable characteristics of shorthand), requiring two incissions rather than five.

---

15. Cuneiform pictographic symbols were rotated by 90 degrees anticlockwise during that script's development. The reason for this is not understood (C. B. F. Walker, *Reading the Part: Cuneiform* (London: The Trustees of the British Museum, 1987), pp14–15), but it was not to move from or distinguish between one script and another.
16. L. H. Jeffery, *The local scripts of archaic Greece: a study of the origin of the Greek alphabet and its development from the eighth to the fifth centuries B.C.* (Oxford: Clarendon Press, 1961), pp14–15, 23 (in the case of *Alpha* being written sideways), pp23 (the Attica I version of *Alpha* being a reversed Phoenician *'ālep*), and p30 (the *Lambda* in certain cases being a reversal of the Phoenician *lāmed*).
17. T. W. Allen, "Miscellanea", *The Classical Quarterly* 24(1)(1930), p41 and H. J. M. Milne, *Greek Shorthand Manuals: Syllabary and Commentary* (London: Egypt Exploration Society, 1934), p2

Thus, we have against the Column One and Two totals the symbols ∃+ that, together, tell us "[on] New Year's Day, grand total" for sheep (rams) and wool (obligation), respectively. As anticipated, the amounts in these two columns are at a fixed point in time, namely on New Year's Day, the start of the new year (and the end of the old year) (as we shall see in Chapter Five, this is, in fact, a tax calculation). As also anticipated, "[on] New Year's day" is missing from the third column total because this is a "current" total, i.e. whenever this tablet was written (after the start of the year), this was the (current) deficit then outstanding. Finally, as we had with the symbol for "zero", we have yet more instances of symbols being hieroglyphs (modified as we would expect them to have been because they were being incised in clay), demonstrating the characteristics of ancient shorthand (i.e. being rotated). Moreover, we have those symbols representing words that, if written in full in Middle Egyptian written in hieroglyphs, have meanings that match those determined from the mathematical analysis of the tablet and comparison to Linear B. Linear A is demonstrably Middle Egyptian written in shorthand using hieroglyphs.

What then of "sheep (rams)", "wool" and "deficit" (actually deficiency)? I am going to be circumspect at this stage as to which particular Middle Egyptian words, written in hieroglyphs, are represented on this tablet using shorthand. The reader may infer, however, that not only have the words been identified and, similarly, so have the hieroglyphs on which the Linear A symbols representing those words are based, but when used on the tablet they, again, represent a consistent use of the shorthand methodology seen thus far.

For now, however, with our progressively more and more evidenced theory that Linear A was Middle Egyptian written in shorthand using hieroglyphs we can return briefly to the point made in Chapter One and say with confidence that:

- ∃+ does not mean just "total" (it means "[on] New Year's Day, grand total") and it was not pronouced "ku-ro";
- ⊰𐆑∃+ cannot mean "grand total" and it was not pronounced "po-to-ku-ro"; and
- 𐆇+ does not mean just "deficit" (as we will see, it means "deficiency, grand total") and it was not pronounced "ki-ro".

With the analysis of Tablet HT 123A (and Tablet HT 21B) this allows us to:

- Deduce the meaning of six symbols ("zero", "sheep (rams)", "wool", "deficit" (or, as we will see, deficiency), "New Year's Day", and "grand total"); and
- Determine that the Linear A symbols representing three of these ("zero", "New Year's Day", and "grand total") were representations of the first hieroglyphs only of the spelling of those words in Middle Egyptian written in hieroglyphs;

then, given that certain Linear A symbols, on occasion, also demonstrate characterics of ancient shorthand writing (namely being rotated), the evidence means we must form the opinion that Linear A is a form of Middle Egyptian written in shorthand using (modified) hieroglyphs. Consequently, Linear A cannot be Minoan. The shorthand method used, however, was not simply in the style of modern acronyms with words abbreviated to just their first hieroglyph (or a symbol representing just their first hieroglyph), although that is all we have seen thus far. Chapter Three, therefore, sets out the mechanics of how the particular form of shorthand that was Linear A worked.

Chapter Three

The Theory

"When I see a bird that walks like a duck and swims like a duck and quacks like a duck, I call that bird a duck." (James Whitcomb Riley)

Background

Intuitively, Linear A being a form of shorthand writing makes sense. Clay tablets, on which the majority of the surviving Linear A text was written, were only meant to be preserved for the short term. If not created for an ad hoc purpose, after their contents were written up in a more permanent form (and after a period in temporary storage prior to reuse), the information on the clay tablets would be erased and the tablet would be reused.[1] Linear A being a form of shorthand and, therefore, intended for use only in the short term, matches the short-term nature of the medium in which that information was being temporarily recorded.

On the basis of the initial findings discussed in Chapter Two, and the outline theory that Linear A was a method of writing Middle Egyptian in shorthand using hieroglyphs, the next steps towards decipherment were:

1) To identify the Egyptian hieroglyphs represented by the Linear A symbols. As we will see, Linear A tablets can only be translated with certainty if all of the hieroglyphs represented by the symbols on them are identified.
2) To identify the method of shorthand used. Again, Linear A tablets can only be translated if, once the hieroglyphs represented by the symbols are identified, we know how they were used.
3) In the light of (1) and (2), to test the resulting translations against our historical knowledge of, or our reasonable assumptions concerning, Middle and Late Bronze Age Crete (as, in effect, we did with Tablet HT 123A in the last chapter).

This sounds straightforward, and it is deliberately so, for I wish to spare the reader from the many dead ends that were encountered along the path to decipherment. Michael Ventris found his early efforts at the decipherment of Linear B "puerile",[2] and I feel the same.

---

1. Michael Ventris & John Chadwick, *Documents in Mycenaean Greek* (2nd Ed.)(Cambridge: Cambridge University Press, 1973), p114
2. John Chadwick, *The Decipherment of Linear B* (2nd Ed.)(Cambridge: Cambridge University Press, 1967), p34

As regards (1) the reader can refer to Appendix 1 and then Chapter Five to see the derivation of each individual Linear A symbol from the hieroglyph or hieroglyphs that it represents (in so far as they have been identified, which is the vast majority).

As regards (3), a key difficulty in testing the translations against our historical knowledge is that existing interpretations of the history of Bronze Age Crete prior to its conquest by the Mycenaeans are incorrect (or, maybe more accurately, incomplete). They consequently do not lend themselves to aiding a successful decipherment of Linear A by anyone. A critical reassessment of the existing evidence has, therefore, been necessary. Indeed, it appears to me that it has long been overdue irrespective of the additional evidence provided by Linear A. Fortunately, the outcome of this reassessment is not reliant upon the Linear A evidence; we do not have to contend with a circular argument.

This is not to say that the Linear A evidence should not play a part in a revised history of Middle and Late Bronze Age Crete. Indeed, as the reader will see, detailed conclusions are certainly drawn in this regard after the broader historical reassessment has been undertaken. The successful decipherment of Linear B prompted a major revision in the interpretation of Late Bronze Age Cretan history (although, for that reason, the decipherment of Linear B was not, at least at first, welcomed by all for, as John Chadwick recalled, when Linear B was found to be Mycenaean Greek, "most of the archaeologists were predjudiced against the Greek solution"[3]). Nonetheless, history is "a continuous process of interaction between the historian and his facts, an unending dialogue between the present and the past".[4] When new facts become known, the historian must revise his views.

Chapter Four therefore sets out a revised history of certain aspects of Middle and Late Bronze Age Crete (primarily those concerning Crete's relationship with Egypt and vice versa). For the purposes of understanding this chapter now, however, it must be understood by the reader at this stage that, from the Middle Minoan IIB period onwards (from c.1800 BC) at least, parts of Crete were under the significant influence but not control of Egypt as a result of a relationship that probably arose through trade. Then, beginning in the Late Minoan IB period (currently dated 1500–1450 BC), Crete briefly became part of Egypt's empire immediately prior to the Mycenaean conquest of the island.

For now, this chapter focuses on (2) and the shorthand method that was applied to Middle Egyptian written in hieroglyphs when modified and simplified to be incised in clay. This resulted in a script (not a language) that we now know as Linear A.

The Greek shorthand method

From written accounts and correspondence that survives, as well as from the few surviving examples of its use, shorthand, first evidenced in a 4th Century BC inscription from the Acropolis, was used in both Classical Greece and Rome and on into the Byzantine world

---

3. John Chadwick, *The Decipherment of Linear B* (2nd Ed.)(Cambridge: Cambridge University Press, 1967), p68
4. E. H. Carr, *What is History?* (2nd Ed.)(Camberwell, VIC: Penguin, 2008), p30

up to the 15th Century AD.⁵ It has been argued that in the 4th Century BC Xenophon recorded the works of Socrates in shorthand,⁶ and it is known that the proceedings of the Roman Senate were recorded in shorthand at the instigation of Cicero on 5 December 63 BC.⁷ The historian H. J. M. Milne believed, on the basis of Cicero's 45 BC letter to Atticus and his use of a Greek technical expression to mean shorthand (διὰ σημείων), that the Romans, borrowing as they frequently did from the Greeks, based their system of shorthand on the system used by the Greeks.⁸

Virtually nothing survives of the Graeco-Roman use of shorthand. In 1901 the historian F. W. G. Foat counted a mere 5 examples of Greek shorthand as surviving from what he called the Ptolemaic and Roman periods (but in which he included the 4th Century BC example from the Acropolis).⁹ In 1934 Milne added a further 11 examples from Roman Egypt.¹⁰ The corpus is, therefore, hardly extensive (indeed, it is significantly less extensive than the Linear A corpus).

Whatever has survived from the ancient world is, however, always very fragmentary. All things being equal, less and less survives from further back in history. More than this, however, records written in shorthand were only ever meant to be retained temporarily and, after use (such as the information being transferred to the permanent record), the temporary records would have typically been destroyed by their creators or, if different, their users. Consequently, it is unsurprising that surviving examples of the use of shorthand in Greece and Rome are particularly scarce. It would typically only be through exceptional circumstances that such records would have survived (events such as the Linear A clay tablets being fired during the destruction of the buildings in which they were stored). The 4th Century BC stone inscription from the Acropolis is, therefore, something of an aberration (for temporary shorthand records are not recorded in stone and the later remaining examples that survive are, in terms of medium, more representative, being recorded on wax tablets and papyri).

Despite the lack of surviving texts, shorthand writing was, nonetheless, likely to have been commonplace in the Graeco-Roman world, including, of relevance to this work, Egypt. A surviving papyrus tells us, for example, that in AD 155, during the reign of the Roman Emperor Antoninus Pius, an ex-cosmetes of Oxyrhynchus (in Egypt), Panechotes, contracted to place his slave, Chaerammon, with a shorthand teacher for two years for a fee of 120 silver drachmae.¹¹ Panechotes was highly unlikely to be the only slave owner who needed a slave able to read and write shorthand; Chaerammon was highly unlikely

---

5. H. J. M. Milne, *Greek Shorthand Manuals: Syllabary and Commentary* (London: Egypt Exploration Society, 1934), pp7–9
6. Diogenes Laertius, *Lives of Eminent Philosophers* (2.6)
7. Plutarch, *Parallel Lives: The Life of Cato the Younger* (23.3)
8. Cicero, *Letters to Atticus* (DCIX (A XIII.32)), cited by H. J. M. Milne, *Greek Shorthand Manuals: Syllabary and Commentary* (London: Egypt Exploration Society, 1934), p1
9. F. W. G. Foat, "On Old Greek Tachygraphy", *The Journal of Hellenic Studies* 21(1901), p243
10. H. J. M. Milne, *Greek Shorthand Manuals: Syllabary and Commentary* (London: Egypt Exploration Society, 1934), p7
11. Apprenticeship to a shorthand writer: http://papyri.info/ddbdp/p.oxy;4;724 (accessed 24 June 2020)

to be the only slave who learned to read and write shorthand; and his teacher was highly unlikely to be the only teacher who taught shorthand. There was a demand for the skill of reading and writing in shorthand even in the commercial world and the extent of this demand, while it cannot be fully gauged, was highly likely to have been extensive.

The survival of the 4th Century BC stone inscription from the Acropolis, therefore, when likely more representative examples of more commonplace day-to-day use on more perishable mediums that, despite their likely greater original number, will not have survived, may have skewed our perspective as to the ultimate origins of shorthand. While Foat acknowledged that this inscription was the basis for ascribing shorthand to the Greeks,[12] notwithstanding the language used on the surviving texts, this assertion should be treated with caution when we know that what has survived is not likely to be representative.

While the method of shorthand used by the Greeks is believed to have originated in Greece,[13] what if it did not? The majority of the few surviving shorthand texts originate from Egypt. We might expect more examples to survive from Egypt, given its more arid conditions aiding survival, but what if there was another reason? What if its use was more extensive there and what has survived reflects this? What if its use was more extensive there because that was where it had originated? If we discounted Greece as the origin of the shorthand method, the most likely candidate for where shorthand originated, based on number and location of finds, would be Egypt.

Until this book (if anyone had even considered the matter) the ancient Egyptians were not believed to have had a form of shorthand writing. Yet, with their more enduring civilisation than the Classical Greeks and Romans, abductive reasoning dictates it is likely they would have had a need for one. Indeed, before the advent of modern technology and computers, the need to quickly and/or concisely summarise information for temporary retention prior to the creation of a more permanent record was perhaps a requirement of all administrations in all civilisations. This need certainly gave rise to the Pitman shorthand method in the 19th Century AD.

With the earliest surviving example of shorthand coming from 4th Century BC Greece, if we wanted to assert that shorthand had instead originated in Egypt it would need to be attested there before the 4th Century BC, before its conquest by Alexander the Great and before the Ptolemaic Dynasty that this gave rise to. But, if shorthand had been used in Egypt before the Ptolemaic Dynasty, it would not have been Greek that it was used with.

No use of shorthand is, however, attested in pre-Ptolemaic Egypt, but we would not necessarily restrict our focus to just Egypt, for if shorthand were used in pre-Ptolemaic Egypt (and we assume that evidence of its use has simply not survived), then it would also have been used in pre-Ptolemaic Egypt's overseas interests and possessions. Again, however, no use of shorthand is attested in pre-Ptolemaic Egypt's *known* overseas interests and possessions. Therein, however, lies the crux of the matter. If a territory were not known to have been an Egyptian overseas interest or possession, and a shorthand text was found there written in Egyptian but in a script that was not known in Egypt, it might not be

---

12. F. W. G. Foat, "On Old Greek Tachygraphy", *The Journal of Hellenic Studies* 21(1901), p245
13. F. W. G. Foat, "On Old Greek Tachygraphy", *The Journal of Hellenic Studies* 21(1901), p242

recognised for what it actually was. It might even be mistaken for the local language of the place in question.

The reader will accept then, I hope, that if we assumed that the Linear A texts found in Crete were Egyptian, and, effectively as a cipher being used to decipher encrypted text, we could apply (in reverse) the later Graeco-Roman shorthand method to the Linear A texts found in Crete and obtain meaningful translations, we would demonstrate two things. First, we would demonstrate that it was the Egyptians who created and used the shorthand method subsequently passed to and used by the Greeks (presumably between the end of the Greek Dark Ages, when writing in Greece resumed, and its first attested use in Greece in the 4th Century BC). Second, we would demonstrate that Crete (or parts of it) was at least an overseas interest of Egypt at the time that Linear A was in use, which fact has not previously been known to us. Given that I labour the point, the reader may correctly infer that this is exactly what we can do and this is exactly what we can demonstrate.

The Egyptian shorthand method – principal characteristics

As Milne notes, the Greek (and Roman) shorthand systems were based on the normal alphabet and it was the distinctive part of a letter that was taken to produce the symbol used in shorthand.[14] We first saw that this was the case for Linear A in Chapter Two where Linear A symbol L2 / fraction symbol A represented Hieroglyph F35, Linear A symbol L22 represented Hieroglyph N14, and Linear A symbol L98 represented (a rotated) Hieroglyph F14. However, while we saw in Chapter Two that the words for "grand total" and "New Year's Day" were abbreviated to just their first hieroglyph, we are not dealing with a shorthand system where words are simply abbreviated to their first letter (or, rather, hieroglyph). We are not dealing with a method of shorthand akin to modern acronyms.

H. J. M. Milne identified the characteristics of the Greek system of shorthand writing thus[15]:

1. **The use of the first letter or syllable standing for the whole word.**
   Milne gives the examples of:

   - ὅτι which is abbreviated to ὅ, and
   - ἐστί which is abbreviated to ἐσ.

2. **The use of the final syllable or syllables standing for the whole.**
   Milne gives the examples of:

   - κοινή which is abbreviated to νή, and
   - βασιλεύς which is abbreviated to εύς.

---

14. H. J. M. Milne, *Greek Shorthand Manuals: Syllabary and Commentary* (London: Egypt Exploration Society, 1934), p2
15. H. J. M. Milne, *Greek Shorthand Manuals: Syllabary and Commentary* (London: Egypt Exploration Society, 1934), p6

The Theory 29

3. **The first letter or syllable plus the last letter or syllable representing a whole phrase.**
   Milne gives the examples of:
   - ἐν Σαλαμῖνι ναυμαχία which is abbreviated to ἐα, and
   - θεοῦ σώζοντος which is abbreviated to θος.

4. **Some distinctive letter or syllable (from the body of the word in question, not being the first or the last) + the final syllable standing for the whole.**
   Milne gives the examples of:
   - μακρὸν ἂν εἴη λέγειν which is abbreviated to ρειν, and
   - Κάριον πέλαγος which is abbreviated to ριος.

While, as we shall see, there were some changes to the finer details of the shorthand method in its more than 30 centuries of use across three languages, from the deductions made in Chapter Two, we can already see that elements of this shorthand method were used to write, and can be used (in reverse) to translate, Linear A Tablet HT 123A, namely (1) and a slightly simplified application of (4). With examples of (2) and (3) being drawn from the subsequent body of this work for illustrative purposes at this stage, examples of each of the above are set out below:

Examples of the use of the Egyptian shorthand method

1. **The use of the first letter or syllable standing for the whole word**
   In Chapter Two, we saw on Tablet HT 123A that the word for "New Year's Day" was abbreviated to its first hieroglyph:

   ⋮ wpt rnpt New Year's Day (and its festivals) [noun] F14 - W3
   ⋮ wpt rnpt New Year's Day (and its festivals) [noun] F15 - W3 - N5

   This hieroglyph was rotated by 90 degrees (a characteristic of ancient shorthand writing) and then simplified to be written in clay:

   became (which are highlighted, in dashed ovals, below)

   We also saw on Tablet HT 123A that the word for "grand total" was also abbreviated to its first hieroglyph:

   ⋮ dmd smȝ grand total [noun] N14 - F36

   Again, however, we saw that this hieroglyph had been modified from being a five-pointed star to become a four-pointed star (i.e. a cross).

30   The Deciphermen of Linear A

✶ became ✝ (which are highlighted, in dotted rectangles, below)

Diagram 3.1:
Sketch of Tablet HT 123A

Picture 3.1:
Transcript of Tablet HT 123A

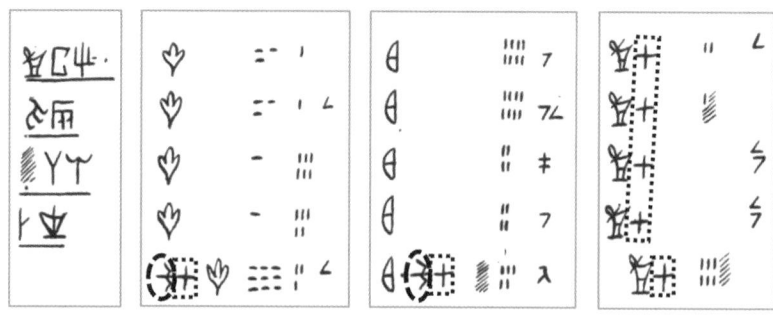

2. **The use of the final syllable or syllables standing for the whole**
   We have not analysed the tablet yet, or translated it (which we do in Chapter Five), but if we look at Tablet HT 14 let us consider the highlighted symbol, Linear A symbol L51 ⊤, below:

Diagram 3.2: Sketch of Tablet HT 14[16]

We already know we are dealing with a tablet that concerns the recording of cattle and/or livestock: in the list of five categories of items that repeats itself, the first and the fourth, as we saw in Chapter One, are ones that appear elsewhere in the corpus with the male = sign (thus they are animals); and the final symbol, as we saw on Tablet HT 123A, was determined to mean "sheep (rams)".

With this then in mind, it is unsurprising that we see an abbreviation for the Middle Egyptian word for "small cattle", represented by its final hieroglyphs:

‛wt small cattle, herds, flocks, goats [noun - ani.] T14 - Z7 - X1 - Z5 - Z2

Taking the final two hieroglyphs, Hieroglyphs Z5 - Z2, we see not only the characteristic of this shorthand method, where the last letter(s) (or, rather, hieroglyph(s)) are used to abbreviate the whole word, but also the characteristic of that letter(s) (or, rather. hieroglyph(s)) are rotated:

\
ı ı ı is rotated by 180 degrees to

ı ı ı
\ and modified (top bar added) to become

---

16. Louis Godart & Jean-Pierre Olivier, *Recueil des Inscriptions en Linéaire A, Volume 1: Tablettes éditées avant 1970* (Athens: École Française D'Athènes, 1976) (Archaeological Museum of Heraklion, Ministry of Culture – Hellenic Organisation of Cultural Resources (copyright))

32 The Decipherment of Linear A

𝌀 which is Linear A symbol L51

The top bar is added so that the four vertical strokes that would otherwise make up the symbol are not confused with four vertical tally marks counting 4.

With a symbol representing Hieroglyphs Z5 - Z2 that in turn represents the Middle Egyptian word 'wt, being its last hieroglyphs, not only does the same theme, that of a record of cattle and/or livestock, continue to emerge, but also we see a word being abbreviated to its final hieroglyph(s), as the Greek shorthand method could abbreviate words to their final letter(s).

This is also evident in the Linear A symbol that Linear A symbol L51 is joined to (and preceded by) on this tablet, which is highlighted below:

Diagram 3.2 (repeated): Sketch of Tablet HT 14

That we have joined symbols means, as we shall see, we are dealing with a phrase. The symbol in question is Linear A symbol L89 ↷. It represents a rotated and reversed Hieroglyph D3:

 is rotated by 90 degrees to

 and reversed

 which is Linear A symbol L89

This, in turn, represents the last hieroglyph in the word:

𓏇𓈖𓆰𓏥 *šnw* grass (cattle fodder) [noun - flora] V7 - N35 - W24 - Z7 - D3

These two joined symbols therefore mean "grass (cattle fodder) [for the] small cattle".

Putting the further consideration of phrases to one side momentarily, at this stage we must consider how these first two characteristics of the shorthand method would have interacted with Middle Egyptian, and the consequent differences between the Egyptian and Greek methods of shorthand.

Excursus 3.1: The interaction of shorthand and Egyptian grammar

While very similar, Linear A does not share all of the characteristics of the later Greek shorthand method (despite the latter evidently being based on the former). Whereas the Greek shorthand method abbreviated grammatically correct Greek or Latin (in respect of Greek, this was seen in the examples previously given), Linear A abbreviated a much simplified and, as a result, grammatically incorrect form of written Middle Egyptian.

There is precedent that we can rely on in asserting this. Nouns change in Middle Egyptian according to their number (i.e. singular, plural, or dual), with (generic) endings added to reflect a noun being plural or dual. However, in Middle Egyptian we know that, when list items were recorded (i.e. nouns followed by a number), nouns were typically written in the singular.[17] That the noun was plural (or dual) was obvious by the number of items recorded after it on the list, i.e. the context in which the noun appeared indicated what the grammatically correct way of writing the noun would have been.

Differing from, and simpler than, the Greek shorthand method of over a thousand years later, this approach was applied to the nouns abbreviated in Linear A. The form of the noun that was abbreviated was always singular. This, of course, make sense, for if, in English, you were to abbreviate a noun to its last letter, and it was written in the plural, it would end with the letter "s", and it would thus be indistinguishable from any other noun written in the plural that was also abbreviated to its last letter. Nouns appear in Middle Egyptian dictionaries as they are attested: in the male or female gender (the two genders in the Egyptian language), and in the singular. Conveniently for us, therefore, this is the form of the noun that was then abbreviated in Linear A.

Similarly, in the case where the noun was the subject of a passive verb, the (generic) prefix particle added to the beginning of the noun was ignored, so that, as a noun abbreviated to its last hieroglyph(s) would not be abbreviated to its generic plural or dual ending, it would not be abbreviated to its generic prefix particle hieroglyph(s) beginning (or, again, it would be indistinguishable from any other such nouns). More generally, the case of a noun, as we would know it, is determined in Middle Egyptian primarily by the

---

17 Boyo G. Ockinga, *A Concise Grammar of Middle Egyptian* (Darmstadt/Mainz: Verlag Philipp von Zabern, 2012), p22

order of the words in a sentence (with the exception of the aforementioned subjects of passive verbs which have an added particle prefix). However, word order poses further problems in deciphering Linear A. The language it represented (Middle Egyptian) was not used in a literary context; it was used in an administrative context recording accounting information and, consequently, we should not expect to see grammatically correct sentences. We shall consider the implications of this shortly.

This logical concept is extended further to the rest of the Middle Egyptian language as it was written and then how it was abbreviated in Linear A, in particular regarding verbs. Verbs appear in Linear A in headings and subheadings as well as some list items. In Middle Egyptian, the abstract grammatical concept of the stem of a verbform is known as the root (this is the form that verbs appear in dictionaries, which is again convenient for us, as we shall see). As a verb conjugates, its root is modified by reduplication of a radical (a root consonant), by the addition of a (generic) causative prefix, and (unwritten) vowels, and by the addition of (generic) grammatical endings and other elements.[18] How, then, would a system of shorthand that could abbreviate words to their first or last hieroglyph(s) be applied to verbs when their spelling changed as they conjugated?

Again differing from, and simpler than, the Greek shorthand method of over a thousand years later, the same approach as was used with nouns was applied to verbs when they were abbreviated in Linear A. When a Middle Egyptian verb was written in shorthand in Linear A it was an abbreviation of the root of that verb. The context in which the verb appeared would (again) indicate how that verb would have been written if it had been conjugated in a grammatically correct way.

Finally, with both nouns and verbs being represented in such a simplified form, perhaps needless to say that, when there were any prepositions that might otherwise have been required to have been written had a phrase been written in a grammatically correct way, these were omitted in their entirety in Linear A. Indeed, only verbs and nouns (and adjectives) were included in Linear A shorthand, in their root or attested form, respectively, leaving us to infer the finer points of grammar. Similarly the grammatically-driven vocabulary that would have surrounded these nouns and verbs, such as prepositions, also has to be inferred.

This makes Linear A simpler than its later Greek counterpart in some respects. However, in other respects it also makes it more difficult for us to decipher. A string of abbreviated grammatically incorrect words that was little more than an aide memoire but which was clear to its author (or, if different, to its user who we can assume would be someone familiar with the typical phraseology used), is less clear to us almost 3,500 years later. As a result, to translate the tablet we have to use as much contextual information as possible, from knowing the history of the institution that produced the Linear A tablets on Crete, to the relationships reflected in the numerical information recorded on them.

---

18 Boyo G. Ockinga, *A Concise Grammar of Middle Egyptian* (Darmstadt/Mainz: Verlag Philipp von Zabern, 2012), p33

The Theory   35

3. **The first letter or syllable plus the last letter or syllable representing a whole phrase**
   We can best see this characteristic if we consider two Linear A tablets: Tablet HT 14, which we considered previously, and Tablet HT 86A.

   As we will see in Chapter Five, the scribe for Tablet HT 14 wrote the second subheading on the tablet as an abbreviation of four individual words that appeared within it:

Diagram 3.2 (repeated): Sketch of Tablet HT 14

This sequence of four Linear A symbols has been arrived at by a combination of shorthand characteristics. For its translation, the reader should consult pages 199 to 202 in Chapter Five, but for our purposes now, this subheading means "sustenance deficiency now, [to be] receive[d]". Most importantly for us now, as will be seen subsequently, the first symbol was arrived at using shorthand characteristic (1) (i.e. the symbol represents the first word's first hieroglyph) and the last symbol was arrived at by shorthand characteristic (2) (i.e. the symbol represents the last word's last hieroglyph). When the second subheading on Tablet HT 86A was written, the scribe has then been able to use shorthand trait (3), when, instead of abbreviating all four words, he simply abbreviated the first and the last words when he wrote "sustenance [to be] receive[d]" the subheading on this tablet:

36   The Decipherment of Linear A

Diagram 3.3: Sketch of Tablet HT 86A

Therefore, on Tablet HT 86A, the whole phrase is abbreviated to just the first letter (or, rather, hieroglyph) of the first word plus the last letter (or, rather, hieroglyph) of the last word representing the whole (four word) phrase "sustenance [deficiency now,] [to be] receive[d]".

As regards the abbreviation of phrases, in addition to this characteristic (3) of Linear A shorthand, which was present in the Greek form of shorthand, as we have seen Linear A also had the characteristic of phrases being abbreviated to the joined symbols that were the shorthand abbreviation of their component words, which was not present in the Greek form of shorthand. It appears that the decision whether or not to join symbols together was, ultimately, one of scribal preference.

4. **Some distinctive letter or syllable (from the body of the word in question, not being the first or the last) + the final syllable standing for the whole.**
As we saw in Chapter Two, the word "wool" was represented by Linear A symbol L90, i.e.:

As we have seen, this symbol appears frequently on Tablet HT 123A, which concerns the calculation of a wool tax obligation:

Diagram 3.1 (repeated):
Sketch of Tablet HT 123A

Picture 3.1 (repeated):
Transcript of Tablet HT 123A

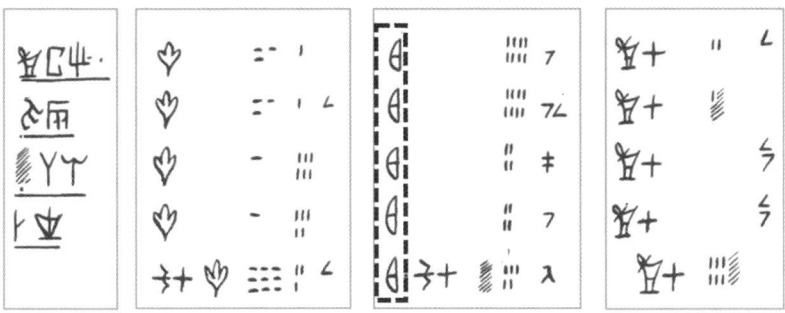

The Middle Egyptian word for wool, written in hieroglyphs (at least the one we must concern ourselves with here (which is discussed further in Appendix 3)), is:

šnw hair, wool [noun - bod.] V49 - X1 - Z4 - D3

Milne believed that distinctiveness was the reason for a letter from the middle of the word, rather than its first or last letter, being chosen to represent it in the Greek form of shorthand. Distinctiveness, however, is quite subjective and while that may be the governing factor in certain cases, on other occasions more practical reasons appear to have determined whether a letter(s) (or, here, hieroglyph(s)) from the middle of the

38   The Decipherment of Linear A

word would be chosen to represent it. This is, for example, the case for the Middle Egyptian word *šnw*:

- As we have seen, and as we will see, Hieroglyph D3 was frequently used in the Linear A corpus to represent the commonly recorded commodity "grass (cattle fodder)". This suggests that a symbol representing Hieroglyph D3 would not have been used to represent the word for "wool" which was also probably commonly recorded in the original (although not surviving) corpus.
- Hieroglyph V49 was visually similar to Hieroglyph M12 (especially when written in clay). When Hieroglyph M12 was used by itself (in hieroglyphs, not Linear A) it represented the number 1,000 (see page 187). If a Linear A symbol visually similar to that representing Hieroglyph M12 had been used to represent the word *šnw*, meaning "wool", it might have appeared that, instead of wool being recorded, there were a thousand items of the item that appeared before it on the list in question. This suggests that a symbol representing Hieroglyph V49 would not have been used as an abbreviation for the word *šnw*.
- Similarly, Hieroglyph M12 was the first hieroglyph in the word *ḥrps*, which means "loaves". A symbol representing that hieroglyph that, in turn, represented that word also briefly appears in the corpus (see page 187). If it was used for what was a commonly occurring commodity in the original (although not surviving) corpus, then this again suggests that a symbol representing the visually similar Hieroglyph V49 would not have been used as an abbreviation for the word *šnw*.
- That left Hieroglyphs X1 - Z4.

Hieroglyphs X1 - Z4 appear in the middle of the word, and they are modified to become a Linear A symbol:

is rotated to become…

but if the hieroglyphs were used to represent wool like this, it would confuse the reader: Hieroglyph Z4, when rotated, could appear as two horizontal tally marks (which might incorrectly infer a count of 20) or the rotated Hieroglyphs X1 - Z4 might be confused with Linear A symbol L47 which had another meaning. For these reasons, as well as also to save space horizontally (a consistent theme throughout the corpus), Hieroglyphs X1 - Z4 (rotated), are modified, with Hieroglyph Z4 being written *inside* Hieroglyph X1 (with one line instead of two),[19] as

which is Linear A symbol L90.

---

19. We see a similar treatment with ordinals (see Appendix 6).

This transcription of Linear A symbol L90, above, is mine. The standard transcription of ◁ is not quite accurate (at least not in how the symbol *should* be written). Taking the three examples that we briefly considered in Chapter Two from Khania, we can see this symbol, with its single line inside a rotated semi-circle:

Diagram 3.4(a), (b), and (c): Tablet fragments from Khania (KH)

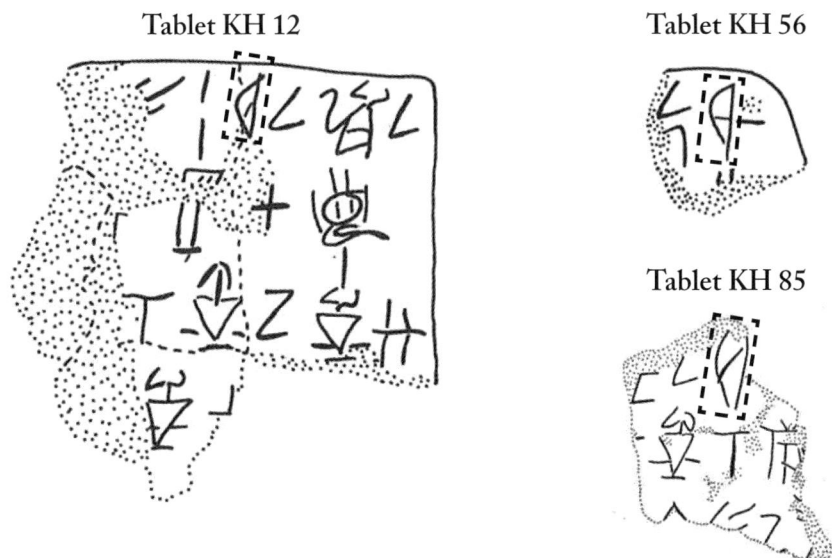

As the scribe should have, in the case of Tablet KH 12 and Tablet KH 85, the line within the semi-circle is slanted upwards (bottom left to top right). In the case of Tablet KH 56, however, as with Tablet HT 123A, the scribe has not bothered and has simply written the line horizontally within the semi-circle. The reason for this upward slant is that it reflects the upward slant that would be visible on the lines of Hieroglyph Z4 after they have been rotated by 90 degrees anticlockwise (and the two lines have been merged into one, and inserted into the semi-circle). In deciphering Linear A in the 21st Century AD, we have to understand how and why the hieroglyphs were modified to become Linear A symbols as well as then also contending with individual scribes' handwriting preferences in the 15th Century BC (and before).

Returning to the shorthand method, however, here we have another departure from the Greek system. In contrast to the later Greek system of shorthand (which it would be reasonable to presume evolved in the 30 or more centuries of use across at least three languages), in the Egyptian method of shorthand (i.e. Linear A) the letter or syllable (or, rather, hieroglyph) from the middle of the word that represented it was not accompanied by the final syllable of the word (or, rather, hieroglyph).

Therefore, as will be seen, Linear A exhibits the following characteristics, with words abbreviated to:

- Their first hieroglyph(s);
- Their last hieroglyph(s); or
- Occasionally, a hieroglyph(s), not being the first or the last hieroglyph(s) of the word, coming from the body of the word (that was, perhaps, distinctive or, perhaps more likely, chosen for some other practical reason).

Phrases could be further abbreviated to:

- The first hieroglyph(s) of the first word and the last hieroglyph(s) of the last word, as in the later Greek shorthand method; or
- They could be abbreviated to the joined symbols that were shorthand for its principal component words.

The version of the words that were abbreviated were also always:

- If a noun, in the singular form in which it was attested; or
- If a verb, in its root form.

At this stage it might help to consider how this shorthand method worked by using a very basic modern-day setting.

> **Excursus 3.2: Abbreviation to the first, last, or a middle letter of a word in shorthand**
>
> In our own language, let us consider what a shopping list of foods to be purchased from a greengrocer would look like where each item was abbreviated to just its first letter. Let us consider the list of items: ten apples, twelve bananas, and thirteen carrots. This would be abbreviated to:
>
> $$A - 10$$
> $$B - 12$$
> $$C - 13$$
>
> Consider, however, if the list were more Australian in character and, in addition to those items just listed we also required eleven avocados. A uniform approach could not now be followed, because, if it was, the list would become:
>
> $$A - 10$$
> $$A - 11$$
> $$B - 12$$
> $$C - 13$$

If we could only use one letter to represent each item, because the "A" already represents "apples", we could instead abbreviate "avocado" to its last letter, the "O" or, rather its last letter in the singular, for abbreviating it to "S" as the last letter in the plural, i.e. avocados, could be mistaken for anything else in the plural. We would thus arrive at the list:

$$A - 10$$
$$O - 11$$
$$B - 12$$
$$C - 13$$

While this is not the way we do things, this is a perfectly logical approach. If, then, it was customary for shopping lists to include apples and avocados, the "A" and "O" abbreviations would become the convention. If, by exception, a list was made that had no apples, but only avocados, bananas, and carrots, we might still expect to abbreviate avocados to "O", even though that would not then be strictly necessary, in order to follow the convention.

If, in 3,500 years' time, all the shopping lists written in this form of shorthand survived and were analysed by future decipherers, they would understand the logic behind this choice. If, however, only the exceptional shopping list survived with avocados and no apples and an attempt was made to decipher it, and if "O" were nonetheless determined to be avocados, there would be some confusion as to why avocados were not abbreviated to "A". The confusion, however, would be a modern problem, arising through the lack of data that would have been derived from the entire body of shopping lists if they had survived (which they have not) or, perhaps, lack of knowledge as to the typical shopping list from surviving historical accounts of consumer activity (which also might no longer exist). Either would indicate the reason for the choice. The choice, nonetheless, was logical at the time.

Alternatively, the author of the exceptional shopping list might have chosen "A" for avocados because, with no apples on his or her list, he or she could then use "A". In that case, the future decipherer might never know that "avocados" was ever abbreviated to "O", or he or she might mistakenly assume that, as apples are more common, this is what the scribe wrote with "A" and he or she would produce an incorrect translation. Ultimately, across two different lists, the same word might be abbreviated to different letters. The same is true of Linear A (as it was in the later Greek shorthand system[20]).

---

20. This is seen in a number of instances in the surviving Greek shorthand corpus where the same word was abbreviated to different symbols, for example: the word ϵντων can be abbreviated to either the Greek shorthand symbol 306 or 349; the word ϵυμενος can be abbreviated to either the Greek shorthand symbol 187 or 376; and the word μεθα can be abbreviated to either the Greek shorthand symbol 331 or 746 (see H. J. M. Milne, *Greek Shorthand Manuals: Syllabary and Commentary* (London: Egypt Exploration Society, 1934), pp73–74).

We have convention and scribal choice giving a number of possible outcomes that may be equally correct and consistent in their translated form and yet at the same time inconsistent in their abbreviated un-translated form.

Continuing with this logic, let us consider the case where the list had ten apples, eleven avocados, twelve bananas, thirteen carrots and fourteen oranges, and oranges were more frequently on the shopping list than avocados so that "O" was already used as an abbreviation for them. An alternative letter would then have to be chosen to represent avocados.

In the shorthand method we are considering, a "distinctive" letter (or, rather, hieroglyph(s)) not being the first or last was sometimes used to represent the word. In our own language, the letter "V" is somewhat distinctive; in Scrabble, for example, a "V" tile is worth 4 points, whereas the "A", "B", "C" and "O" tiles are all worth less (1, 3, 3, and 1 points, respectively). It also comes second in the word and, having discounted the first and the last letters, the next most sensible letter might be the second. We might, therefore, choose to abbreviate avocados to the letter "V", thus giving us the list:

A – 10
V – 11
B – 12
C – 13
O – 14

This makes most sense when the list covers all five items. However, if the list only dealt with, say, avocados ("V", because this is now the convention), bananas ("B"), and carrots ("C"), to someone picking up this list 3,500 years without the knowledge of the method of shorthand used, and absent data from all lists, the use of V would be baffling, for what fruit or vegetable begins with V? The list might never be fully deciphered (and the language it represented might never be recognised). In approaching the decipherment of Linear A from its limited surviving corpus (which had previously been felt to be too small to allow for decipherment at all), we are therefore fortunate that the Greeks used the earlier Egyptian shorthand method (albeit with some amendment) and that the surviving Greek corpus allowed historians to formulate the rules that we can now apply (in reverse) to de-code Linear A, much in the way of using a cipher to decipher encrypted text.

The shorthand method – word order

As we have previously noted, the case of a noun, as we would know it, is determined in Middle Egyptian primarily by the order of the words in a sentence. This is the final aspect to consider in this chapter.

With Linear A, we are not dealing with sentences (the clay tablets are temporary administrative output, not literature). We thus have to adjust our mindset from imagining that what we would ever encounter would be fully formed sentences (they are not). If we are not dealing with fully formed sentences, then we should not expect to deal with Middle Egyptian words that, while nonetheless abbreviated, were written in the correct order (and, again, they are not). With the administrative context in which Linear A was used in mind, we have to think one step further when approaching the translations. The administrator is not a grammarian, especially, and in particular, when he (or she) is writing in shorthand.

We can rely on modern administrative practices to guide us at this stage. If an administrator worked in the storeroom of the shop selling the items noted in Excursus 3.2 above and was recording a shortfall in a delivery from a supplier, the administrator could just as easily write "apples to be received from the supplier", "apples, from the supplier, to be received", "to be received, from the supplier, apples", "to be received, apples, from the supplier", "from the supplier, apples, to be received", or even "from the supplier, to be received, apples". Which was chosen would depend on the administrative preferences of the institution as well as the administrator's stylistic preferences. All of these iterations, conveying the same information, are clearly written in English, yet none of them are written in grammatically correct English, the words being either written in the wrong order or there being words missing. We must expect this (different, and grammatically incorrect, word ordering) to be the case with Linear A.

Perhaps the most immediately obvious example of this that can be seen is identified by a comparison of the next two tablets: on each, four categories of items are written using the same three symbols in the same order, and yet a fifth category of item (written under the same subheading each time it appears) is written each time with the same symbols but written in a different order. This is the result of different administrators' work; this category on each, despite its symbols being written in a different order, and despite word order being so important in Middle Egyptian grammar when used in a literary context, records the exactly same thing.

44   The Deciphermentof Linear A

Diagram 3.5(a) and (b): A comparison of the sketches of Tablet HT 95B and Tablet HT 86A[21]

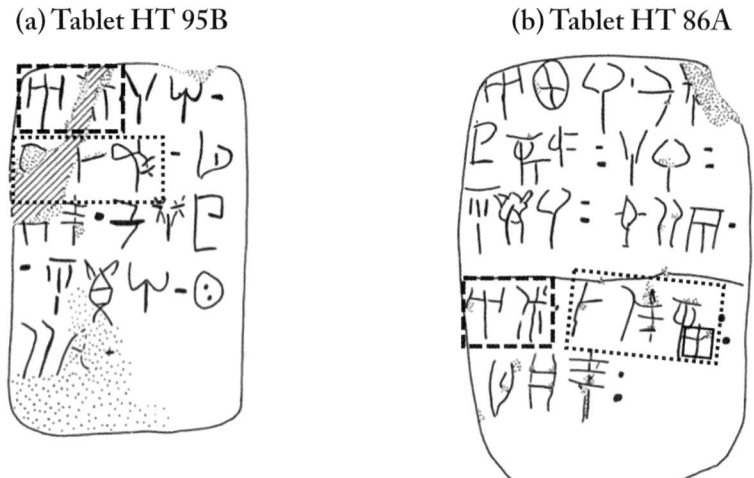

(a) Tablet HT 95B   (b) Tablet HT 86A

Picture 3.2(a) and (b): A comparison of the transcriptions of Tablet HT 95B and Tablet HT 86A[22]

(a) Tablet HT 95B   (b) Tablet HT 86A

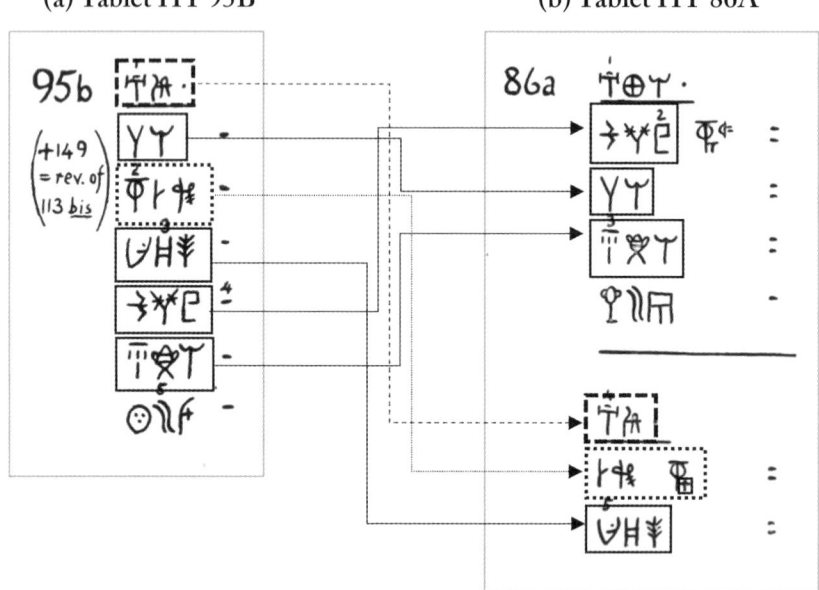

---

21. For sketch diagrams: Louis Godart & Jean-Pierre Olivier, *Recueil des Inscriptions en Linéaire A, Volume 1: Tablettes éditées avant 1970* (Athens: École Française D'Athènes, 1976) (Archaeological Museum of Heraklion, Ministry of Culture – Hellenic Organisation of Cultural Resources (copyright)). For tabular transcriptions: W. C. Brice, *Inscriptions in the Minoan Linear Script of Class A* (Oxford: Oxford University Press, 1961), Plate VIa (© The Society of Antiquities of London)
22. W. C. Brice, *Inscriptions in the Minoan Linear Script of Class A* (Oxford: Oxford University Press, 1961), Plates VIIa & VIIIa (© The Society of Antiquities of London)

Key

☐ = Subheading

☐ = items recorded with symbols in the same order (i.e. the same items)

☐ = items recorded with symbols in a different order (but still the same items)

☐ = subscript descriptor

Another good example will be seen through a comparison of the translations of Subheading Two on Tablet HT 14 (see pages 199 to 202), which (in order of words represented by their Linear A symbols) is "sustenance deficiency now, to [be] receive[d]", and the Subheading on Tablet HT 2 (see pages 262 to 263) which (in order of the words represented by their Linear A symbols) is "deficiency [of] food [in the] storehouse / barn now". Most obviously, at the start of each, the symbols for sustenance and deficiency, and deficiency and food, are reversed, again demonstrating the disapplication of the rules of grammar of Middle Egyptian, in particular, here, word order, when used in a shorthand administrative context.

For this reason, therefore, when we reach the translations in Chapter Five, we should not expect grammatically correct complete sentences to have been written (in shorthand), and we should not expect the incomplete sentences' words to be written in the grammatically correct order.

This will be something of an anathema for (academic) linguists who have attempted and failed to decipher Linear A. To successfully decipher Linear A, and realise that the Middle Egyptian language would have been used differently in a commercial setting (especially when written in shorthand) and that use would have disapplied many of the rules of grammar (as we do with our own language today), one needed to have practical commercial experience (which, generally, academics do not). The wrong people from the wrong background with the wrong skills have tried to decipher Linear A. The task needed someone from outside of this group.[23]

The Egyptian shorthand method – Conclusion

If this method is the correct one, what would we expect to see on the Linear A tablets? We would see tablets covered in Egyptian hieroglyphs (or symbols that clearly represent them) where some are rotated (we shall consider why this occurs for individual symbols during the course of Chapter Five and ultimately in Appendix 1). Nonetheless the symbols would be identifiable as hieroglyphs because, ultimately, they were meant to be identified as such. The sequences of hieroglyphs would not spell words because we are dealing with

---

23. Indeed, I imagine that were Linear A shorthand to have been used in a more literary, and not accounting, context, the typical word order of Middle Egyptian would have been used. This may well be determined to be the case if the Byblos Script proves to be Middle Egyptian written in shorthand using hieroglyphs (i.e. written in grammatically correct Linear A), as what survives of its use is clearly more literary than the clay tablets found on Crete.

shorthand, and the words they represented, if they had been written out in full, they would not spell out complete or grammatically correct sentences with the correct word order, because that is not the nature of the evidence that has survived. This, as we will see in Chapter Five, is exactly what we see.

Having identified the shorthand method used, producing translations nonetheless remains difficult. Linear A is very different to Linear B, and we cannot gain certainty that our decipherment of one symbol in one area of the corpus is correct by simply applying it to all the other instances of that symbol across the corpus as a whole as was ultimately the proof for Linear B (hence the "mathematical proof" set out in Chapter Two was so important to demonstrating what Linear A actually is). Milne faced the same problem when translating Greek shorthand; the only way to mitigate this uncertainty was by assessing the texts in their correct historical context. He wrote:

> *"Everything, of course, depends on the context. The same sign might theoretically admit of various expansions, and to decipher shorthand without a clue to the meaning would baffle the most ingenious."*[24]

And therein lies yet another problem. History as it is currently incorrectly (or, rather, incompletely) written simply does not allow for the notion of administrative records ever having been written in Egyptian by Egyptians in Crete. As well as Linear A, the imbroglio that is the history of Middle and Late Bronze Age Crete also needs to (independently) be solved in order for both the decipherment and history to have meaning.

It is for this reason that Chapter Four now sets out a reconstructed history of Egypt's involvement in Crete before we then embark upon the decipherments of the individual Linear A tablets in Chapter Five. Applying the shorthand method to the Linear A tablets can only produce meaningful translations in the context of the reconstructed history of Egypt's involvement in Middle and Late Bronze Age Crete. Only through approaching matters in this order will the reader be able to understand the Linear A tablets and be assured that the translations presented in this work are correct.

---

24. H. J. M. Milne, *Greek Shorthand Manuals: Syllabary and Commentary* (London: Egypt Exploration Society, 1934), p5

Chapter Four

The Reconstructed History of Egypt's Involvement in Middle and Late Bronze Age Crete[1]

"This is what we call an orgy of evidence."
(Danny Witwer, *Minority Report* (2002))

To reconstruct the history of Egypt's involvement in Middle and Late Bronze Age Crete we must begin with an assessment of the evidence at hand.

The Linear A tablets, being written in Middle Egyptian in shorthand using hieroglyphs and now capable of translation (with those translations set out in Chapter Five), are an evidence source in their own right. Beyond the details they reveal in their content, in their quantity they reflect Egypt's involvement in Crete and the changing extent of that involvement. Analysis of the archaeological finds on Crete has resulted in a consensus opinion amongst historians that the use of Linear A on Crete abruptly ceased at the end of the Late Minoan IB period (c.1450 BC) due to the conquest of Crete by the Mycenaeans (who subsequently used Linear B).[2] There is less consensus as to when Linear A was first used in Crete. While some historians believe that the earliest recorded use of Linear A on Crete occurred in the Middle Minoan IIA period (1850–1800 BC), this is not universally accepted.[3] The earliest uncontested evidence of the use of Linear A

---

1. https://www.imdb.com/title/tt0181689/characters/nm0568180 (accessed 1 January 2022)
2. Helena Tomas, "Saving on Clay: The Linear B Practice of Cutting Tablets", in Kathryn E. Piquette & Ruth D. Whitehouse, *Writing as Material Practice: Substance, Surface and Medium* (London: Ubiquity Press, 2013), p176. As we shall see, this is not strictly true.
3. Massimo Perna and Helena Tomas state that the earliest use of Linear A is attested by a tablet fragment (Tablet KN 49) found in the Southwest House at Knossos which has been dated to the Middle Minoan IIA period (1850 BC–1800 BC). Both Perna and Tomas, however, note that doubts exist on this interpretation (Massimo Perna, "The Birth of Administration and Writing in Minoan Crete", in Dimitri Nakassis, Joann Gulizio, Sarah A. James (Eds.), *KE-RA-ME-JA: Studies Presented to Cynthia W. Shelmerdine* (Philadelphia: INSTAP Academic Press, 2014), p254; Helena Tomas, "Saving on Clay: The Linear B Practice of Cutting Tablets", in Kathryn E. Piquette & Ruth D. Whitehouse, *Writing as Material Practice: Substance, Surface and Medium* (London: Ubiquity Press, 2013), p176). In 2007 Maurizio Del Freo gave credence to various speculative proposals put forward by Jean-Pierre Olivier as to what the tablet might have said (and so he came down on the side of Linear A)(Maurizio Del Freo, "Rapport 2001–2005 sur les textes en Écriture Hiéroglyphique Crétoise, en Linéaire A et en Linéaire B" in A. Sacconi, M. del Freo, L. Godart & M. Negri (Eds.), *Colloquium Romanum: Atti del XII Colloquio Internazionale di Micenologia. Roma, 20–25 febbraio, 2006* (Pisa & Rome: Pasiphae, 2007), pp204–207); Ilse Schoep, however, does not believe that the signs on the tablet in question can be identified and the script in question (Cretan hieroglyphs or Linear A) cannot be established with any certainty (Ilse Schoep, "The Inscribed Document" in C. F. Macdonald & C. Knappett (Eds.), *Knossos: Protopalatial deposits in early magazine A and south-west houses* (British School of Athens Supplementary Volume 41)(London: British School of Archaeology at Athens, 2007))(both cited by Helen Tomas, "Saving on Clay: The Linear B Practice of Cutting Tablets", in Kathryn E. Piquette & Ruth D. Whitehouse, *Writing as Material Practice: Substance, Surface and Medium* (London: Ubiquity Press, 2013), p176).

on Crete is seen in tablets dating from the Middle Minoan IIB period (1800–1700 BC) found in the remains of the First Palace of Phaistos (near Hagia Triada).[4] Of course, the Middle Minoan IIB dating is a *terminus ante quem* for the first use of Linear A, and it could have been in use before this, so perhaps the point is moot.

All things being equal, the number of Linear A tablets found and their attributed dates can reasonably be taken to represent the relative levels of Linear A usage over time (of course the random nature of archaeological survival is such that this is not always the case as, for one, the further back in time we go the lower the rates of survival of evidence, but this is the working assumption that it is most sensible to adopt). The numbers of Linear A tablets found and their attributed dates are set out in Table 4.1 and Graph 4.1 below. For graphing purposes, unless a more specific date has been assigned to the finds, the mid-point of the relevant archaeological Period or Sub-Period to which the tablets have been assigned has been taken as the data point for graphing purposes:

Table 4.1: Attributed dates of Linear A tablet finds[5]

Place	No.	Period / Sub-Period	Date range	Date
Arkhanes	7	LM I	1600 - 1450 BC	1525
Haghia Triadha	147	LM IB	1500 - 1450 BC	1450
Khania	94	LM IB	1500 - 1450 BC	1450
Knossos	6	LM IA	1600 - 1500 BC	1550
Mallia	6	MM III	1700 - 1600 BC	1650
Petras	2	MM III	1700 - 1600 BC	1650
Phaistos	26	MM IIB	1800 - 1700 BC	1750
Palaikastro	1	MM IIIB	1650 - 1600 BC	1625
Myrtos Pyrgos	2	LM IA	1600 - 1500 BC	1550
Tylissos	2	MM IIIB	1650 - 1600 BC	1625
Zakro	31	LM IB	1500 - 1450 BC	1450
	324			

---

4. Helen Tomas, "Saving on Clay: The Linear B Practice of Cutting Tablets", in Kathryn E. Piquette & Ruth D. Whitehouse, *Writing as Material Practice: Substance, Surface and Medium* (London: Ubiquity Press, 2013), p176, citing Giovanni Pugliese Carratelli, "Nuove epigrafi minoiche di Festo", in *Annuario della Scuola Archeologica di Atene e delle Missioni Italiane in Oriente* (Vol. XXXV-XXXVI)(Nuova Serie XIX-XX)(1957–1958)(Roma: Instituto Poligrafico Dello Stato, 1958), p386

5. Arkhanes: Louis Godart & Jean-Pierre Olivier, *Recueil des Inscriptions en Linéaire A: Tablettes, Nodules et Rondelles édités en 1975 et 1976* (Paris: Lirairie Orientaliste Paul Geuthner, 1979), pxvi; Hagia Triada, Khania, and Knossos: Ilse Schoep, "Tablets and Territories? Reconstructing Late Minoan IB Political Geography through Undeciphered Documents", *American Journal of Archaeology* 103(2)(April 1999), p205; Mallia: Michael Ventris & John Chadwick, *Documents in Mycenaean Greek* (2nd Ed.)(Cambridge: Cambridge University Press, 1973), p31; Petras: Jacques Raison, "Du nouveau sur la chronologie du linéaire A", *Bulletin de l'Association Guillaume Budé*, 3 (October 1960), p316; Phaistos: Giovanni Pugliese Carratelli, "Nuove epigrafi minoiche di Festo", in *Annuario della Scuola Archeologica di Atene e delle Missioni Italiane in Oriente* (Vol. XXXV-XXXVI)(Nuova Serie XIX-XX)(1957–1958)(Roma: Instituto Poligrafico Dello Stato, 1958), p386, and Helena Tomas, "Saving on Clay: The Linear B Practice of Cutting Tablets", in Kathryn E. Piquette & Ruth D. Whitehouse, *Writing as Material Practice: Substance, Surface and Medium* (London: Ubiquity Press, 2013), p176; Palaikastro: Michael Ventris &

The Reconstructed History of Egypt's Involvement in Middle and Late Bronze Age Crete   49

Graph 4.1: Linear A tablets found in Crete by attributed date (Sub-Period mid-point)

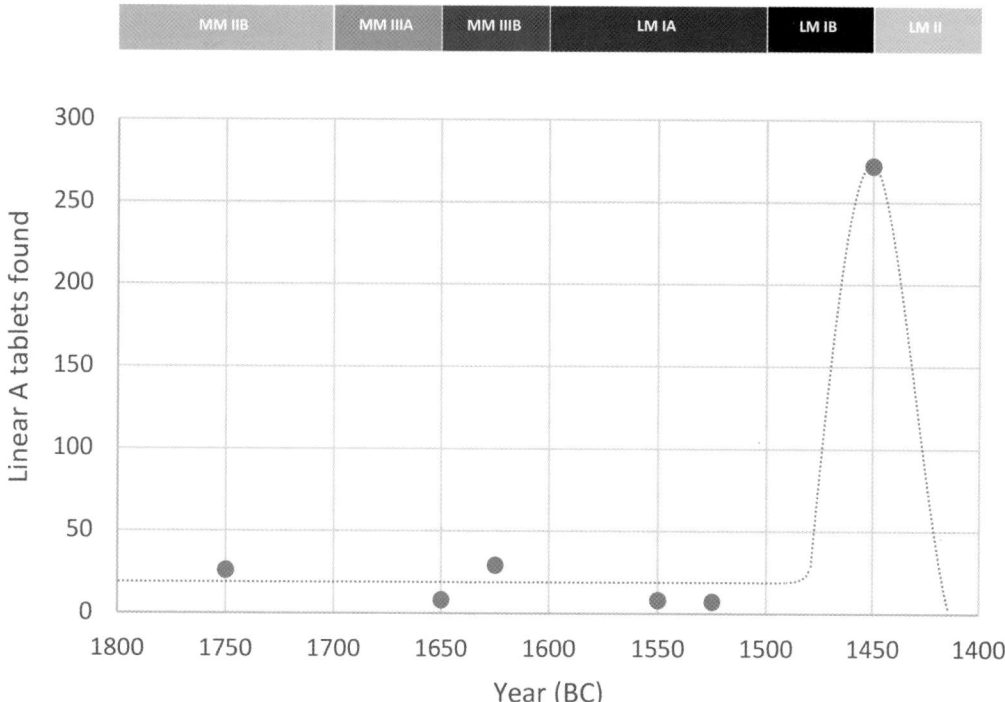

On the basis of the archaeological finds and their attributed dates, Linear A appears to have been used on Crete at a low level from at least the Middle Minoan IIB period for almost three hundred years. Then, in the Late Minoan IB period (1500–1450 BC) there was a significant apparent increase in Linear A usage before its use abruptly ceased. The level of finds suggests that the circumstances prevailing in the Late Minoan IB period were different to the periods that had preceded it. If Linear A reflects the output of Egyptian administrators, as the evidence indicates, then the nature of Egypt's involvement in Crete appears to have changed.

John Chadwick, *Documents in Mycenaean Greek* (2nd Ed.)(Cambridge: Cambridge University Press, 1973), p32; Myrtos Pyrgos: Gerald Cadogan, "Pyrgos, Crete, 1970–1977", *Archaeological Reports* 24(1977–1978), pp77, 79; Tylissos: Michael Ventris & John Chadwick, *Documents in Mycenaean Greek* (2nd Ed.)(Cambridge: Cambridge University Press, 1973), p32; and Zakro: Ilse Schoep, "Tablets and Territories? Reconstructing Late Minoan IB Political Geography through Undeciphered Documents", *American Journal of Archaeology* 103(2)(April 1999), p205. The keen eyed will note, in my subsequent discussion on the need for specificity when considering finds of Egyptian commercial wares in Crete, that I prefer to use archaeological Sub-Period dates for data points and discount data that cannot be assigned accurately to a Sub-Period. My reason for including Mallia, Petras, and Arkhanes in the above table despite this preference, given that they can only be dated to a Period (MM III, MM III, and LM I, respectively) and not a Sub-Period, is that these 15 tablets are sufficiently small in number compared to the whole 324 (<5%) that they will not skew the overall picture had they been dated to either Sub-Period into which they might have fallen (i.e. MM IIIA or MM IIIB, or LM IA or LM IB). The same is not true of the more limited Egyptian commercial ware data.

The profile of Linear A finds which, as we shall see, is reflective of the other archaeological and historical evidence in Crete and Egypt that we shall consider, suggests, in fact, that there were two distinct periods of Egyptian involvement in Middle and Late Bronze Age Crete that had very different characteristics. As this chapter will show, first there was a period when Egypt enjoyed significant influence in, but not control of, Crete. This lasted from the Middle Minoan IIB period (1800–1700 BC) onwards up to the Late Minoan IB period (1500–1450 BC). As this chapter will then go on to show, in the second period, beginning in the Late Minoan IB period, for three decades, maybe slightly longer, perhaps all of Crete became part of the Egyptian empire. With the Mycenaean conquest of Crete, which thus far has been dated to c.1450 BC (though now it can be more securely dated to two and a half decades later), Egypt's involvement in Crete ceased and Crete henceforth became an inseparable part of the Greek world. We shall consider these two phases of Egyptian involvement in Crete, and the further evidence relating to them, in turn.

Part I: The period of significant Egyptian influence but not control (up to the Late Minoan IB period)

The history of this period of Egypto-Cretan relations really derives in the first instance from the contrasting perspective of the succeeding period. The reader will, therefore, have to grant a degree of forbearance at this stage as matters are addressed chronologically. In retrospect, when the reader reconsiders this period again in the light of the subsequent period, all will become clear.

As we shall see, in the succeeding period the majority but not, at least initially, all of Crete (and certain of the Aegean Islands including, in particular, Thera) voluntarily became part of Egypt's empire; in this preceding period we know Crete was not, therefore, part of Egypt's empire. As we shall also see, in the succeeding period Linear A tablet finds peak precisely because of Egypt's ownership of Crete. Moreover, their translations reflect the administration of Egyptian temples operating on the island. In this period, despite Crete not being part of Egypt's empire, there were, nonetheless, also Egyptian temples operating on Crete. For such extraterritorial legal concessions to be given to the Egyptians, who were, by implication, in Crete, it implies that the Egyptians were in a position of significant influence (but not yet control).

It is important not to think of Crete as a single political entity during the Middle Minoan IIB period (1800–1700 BC) onwards up to the Late Minoan IB period. It is most likely that the island was formed of a number of separate city states in the same manner as was Classical Greece a millennia later with its more than one thousand independent *poleis*. This is not to say that Crete was proto-Greek (necessarily), but as with the different Greek *poleis*, the people were from the same culture but they were not all in political union. Absent a surviving written record, this political but not cultural separation on Crete has been difficult to determine from archaeology alone.

There is some historical evidence to support the belief that Crete was formed from a number of separate city states. During the reign of Thutmose III (who ruled Egypt during and beyond the Late Minoan IB period in Crete, from 1479 to 1425 BC), an inscription found in the tomb of his Vizier, Rekhmire, records "the arrival in peace of the chiefs of Keftiu-land [Crete] (and) the islands which are within the Great Sea [the Aegean Islands]…"[6] Note the use of plurals here for "chiefs". In the same tomb there is also a record of "the arrival in peace of the chiefs of Retenu [Syria-Palestine[7]] and all the lands of Further Asia…"[8] We know that, when Thutmose III conquered Syria-Palestine up to the borders of the Mitanni Empire, the area was comprised of a number of separate city states. Those city states' chiefs (plural) are recorded as they represented a (plural) number of separate city states (albeit under varying degrees of Mitanni influence prior to their conquest by Egypt). We can infer, by comparison, that up to this point Crete was, therefore, comprised of a number of separate city states (albeit with varying degrees of importance).

We know, however, of the so-called Minoan Empire. How does this fit with the portrayal in Rekhmire's tomb and, indeed, our other sources? Even the great (perhaps legendary) King Minos is credited with having unified only three cities on Crete in an account written by the 1st Century BC Greek geographer, philosopher, and historian Strabo.[9] This was clearly not the whole island and, moreover, if this achievement was worthy of record it suggests, again, that the previous norm was for the Cretan city states not to be unified.

In fact, my analogy for the political structure of Crete towards the end of this period, far from an ancient one, would be something like Germany in the period 1866–1871. The Minoans (like the Kingdom of Prussia) had conquered a portion of the island to create their own empire (the equivalent of the North German Confederation within

---

6. Norman de Garis Davies, *The Tomb of Rekh-mi-re' at Thebes: Volume 1* (New York: The Metropolitan Museum of Art Egyptian Expedition, 1943), p20
7. Diamantis Panagiotopoulos, "Foreigners in Egypt in the Time of Hatshepsut and Thutmose III", in E. Cline & D. O'Connor (Eds.), *Thutmose III: A New Biography* (Ann Arbor: University of Michigan Press, 2006), pp373–374, 377. The Syria-Palestinian region was divided into three areas, Djahy, Remenen, and Retenu. The exact boundaries of these three areas are uncertain and they appear, at times, to overlap. Djahy roughly corresponds to Palestine, and Remenen, broadly, denoted Lebanon. However, Retenu, in addition to Syrian territory, evidently included parts of Djahy. Panagiotopoulos believes that Retenu was, in fact, the designation for Syria, coastal Lebanon and parts of northern Palestine (from the inscriptions on the sixth and seventh pylons at Karnak, it included Hazor, Aqqo, Megiddo, and Tanaach) and Joppa (Jaffa) (Diamantis Panagiotopoulos, "Foreigners in Egypt in the Time of Hatshepsut and Thutmose III", in E. Cline & D. O'Connor (Eds.), *Thutmose III: A New Biography* (Ann Arbor: University of Michigan Press, 2006), p374). I agree. The important distinction, I believe, is that these are all territories that were conquered by Thutmose III's armies (Jaffa is listed in the topographical lists of conquered regions from the reign of Thutmose III but is not recorded on the Annals (Colleen Manassa, *Imagining the Past: Historical Fiction in New Kingdom Egypt* (Oxford & New York: Oxford University Press, 2013), p74, citing W. Max Müller, *Die Palästinaliste Thutmosis III* (Berlin: W. Peisner, 1907), p21 and pl. 2, no. 62; and Wolfgang Helck & Eberhard Otto, *Lexikon der Ägyptologie: Band III, Horhekenu – Megeb* (Wiesbaden: Otto Harassowitz, 1980), columns 269–270)). Presumably Jaffa was conquered by an Egyptian force separated from the main forces under the command of Thutmose III (that went on to fight the Battle of Megiddo) and, as a result, the account of its capture was not included in the Annals. Djahy and Remenen were, in my opinion, names of geographical regions; Retenu was, in my opinion, the name for the territories that were conquered by Egypt during Thutmose III's reign which could, and did, overlap with those regions described on a purely geographical basis. For convenience, therefore, I shall refer to Retenu as "Syria-Palestine".
8. Norman de Garis Davies, *The Tomb of Rekh-mi-re' at Thebes: Volume 1* (New York: The Metropolitan Museum of Art Egyptian Expedition, 1943), p27
9. Strabo, *Geography* (X.4.14)

Germany or, rather, *Kleindeutschland*). While the chronology of all of their allocations to this period remains "debatable",[10] this I think is the most likely reason for the destruction of certain Cretan settlements in the Late Minoan IA period (1600–1700 BC) in the aftermath of the eruption of Thera (while the Minoans had an Aegean maritime empire before this, I presume the Thera eruption gave rise to such political changes on Crete as to allow the Minoan Empire to expand on the island, from its Knossos capital and its environs, to reach its overall zenith thereafter). The Minoans, no doubt, had their allies on the island, coerced or otherwise (for Prussia, these were the Kingdom of Bavaria, the Kingdom of Württemberg, and the Grand Duchy of Baden). There were also some states that remained outside of this grouping, such as those of the Polichnites and the Praesians (who Herodotus refers to and which we shall discuss later in this chapter[11]), who I imagine were equivalent in status, but probably not in significance, to the Grand Duchy of Luxembourg and the Principality of Liechtenstein, both of which retained their independence and were left out of the 1871 unification of Germany.

I think the scales were not tipped quite so much in the Minoans' favour and they were relatively weaker in Late Minoan Crete than was Prussia in 1866–1871 Germany, with allies less coerced and, perhaps, with proportionately more of the island remaining independent outside the empire and its network of allies. Nonetheless, when the Minoans voluntarily became part of the Egyptian empire, it seems that the majority (but not all) of Crete (though enough for the Egyptians to simply refer to the whole of the island in Rekhmire's tomb) and certain of the Aegean Islands (including, in particular, Thera) came with them. However, within that part of Crete that came with them there were still separate, if not wholly independent, political entities for, as noted, in Rekhmire's tomb it is the chiefs (plural) of Keftiu who brought tribute, not the chief (singular) of Keftiu who brought tribute.[12] This is, therefore, how I see Crete at the end of the Late Minoan IA period; conversely, before the Late Minoan IA period, indeed before the c.1625–1600 BC eruption of Thera, there was probably no single dominant state on the island.

With this broad framework in mind we can also infer something of Egypt's involvement in Crete up to the Late Minoan IB period. With a fragmented political structure on the island, Egyptian influence could more easily be exerted upon individual Cretan city states. While the degree, no doubt, varied from place to place and from time to time as political circumstances changed (Egyptian influence presumably shrank (relatively) at Knossos as the Minoan Empire grew, for example), that there was significant influence at certain times and in certain places is evidenced by the presence of Linear A.

The Linear A tablets demonstrate, being reflective of the administration of Egyptian temples (written in Middle Egyptian in shorthand using hieroglyphs), that: there were

---

10. Jan Driessen & Colin F. MacDonald, *The Troubled Island: Minoan Crete Before and After the Santorini Eruption* (Liège: Université de Liège, 1997), p35
11. Herodotus, *The Histories* (VII.170.1–2)
12. Similarly, to extend the analogy with the North German Confederation and Germany, the Kingdom of Bavaria, the Kingdom of Württemberg, and the Grand Duchy of Baden were separate signatories to the 1871 Treaty of Versailles (despite having just become part of the newly proclaimed German Empire): http://gander.chez.com/traite-de-francfort.htm (accessed 1 January 2022)

Egyptians on Crete (at this stage, most appropriately called expatriates); and there were Egyptian temples on Crete (as Chapter Five will show) that had income and assets that were recorded in a script that would have been unlikely to be understood by the local Cretans.

As to why there would have been Egyptians on Crete, I think it is probably safe to say that the first links between Crete and Egypt arose through trade. With trade comes traders, and I suspect this is the origin of these Egyptian expatriates on the island. After all, Egypt did not own Crete in this period so these cannot have been colonists. Indeed, the second largest grouping of Linear A tablets that have been found comes from Khania (Chania) a harbour town on the island's north coast (while these tablets have been attributed to the Late Minoan IB period, this is only the end date for the activities undertaken at this site which led to their creation).

That these expatriates were granted the extraterritorial legal concession of having their own religious institutions allowing them to worship their own gods, I think, follows this. Indeed, similar concessions were also not unknown for expatriate trading communities in the ancient world (or, at least, its successor regimes).

A Muslim mosque was present in Orthodox Christian Constantinople from at least the 10th Century AD. Under the terms of a treaty with the Fatimid Caliph of Egypt, the Byzantine Emperor, Constantine IX Monomachos, rebuilt the mosque in 1049. It was, however, destroyed by rioters in 1201. Later, as a concession to Saladin, the Sultan of Egypt and Syria,[13] a second mosque was built for the city's Muslim traders by the Emperor Isaac II Angelus during his first reign (1185–1195). It was, however, destroyed by Latin crusaders of the Fourth Crusade in August 1203. A third mosque was built by Emperor Michael VIII Palaiologos after the Byzantines recaptured Constantinople from the Latin Empire in 1261.[14] The relative powers of the Byzantines and the Muslims are significant to note here; the Byzantine Empire was becoming weaker and the Muslims were becoming stronger. The granting of extraterritorial concessions is, therefore, reflective of relative weakness.

What, however, of the finds of Linear A tablets in and around the Cretan palace complexes? To me their location infers a political dimension to the relationship. We can, I think, draw an analogy with the early modern era to infer what was happening.

In the early modern era, following the Reformation, Catholic foreign embassies in Protestant countries were allowed their own Catholic "embassy chapels". These were an extraterritorial legal concession that allowed the Catholic powers' ambassadors and expatriate community members to worship in their own faith, where otherwise doing so would be prohibited within the nation in question (e.g. the Spanish and Portuguese embassy chapels in London close to the Palace of Westminster at the end of the sixteenth and start of the seventeenth century). Here we are dealing with the Egyptian temple equivalent. Embassy chapels are, of course, a modern diplomatic concession that has arisen through the modern ambassadorial system which did not exist in the ancient world. That Egyptian temple

---
13. Jonathan Harris, *Byzantium and the Crusades* (2nd Ed.)(London: Bloomsbury Publishing Plc, 2014), pp140–141
14. R. Janin, *Constantinople Byzantine. Developpement Urbain et Repertoire Topographique* (2nd Ed.)(Paris: Institut Français d'études Byzantines, 1964), pp258–259

equivalents were located in and around the Cretan palace complexes nonetheless suggests the Egyptian traders possessed a degree of political influence (but not the presence of a representative of the Egyptian state).

In the Egyptian temple chapels in and around the Cretan palatial complexes, therefore, Egyptians could worship Egyptian gods with impunity. That there were so many Egyptian embassy temple chapels located within the Cretan palaces reflects both the fragmented political structure of Crete and the widespread Egyptian influence which was probably facilitated by that fragmentation. Nonetheless, presumably driven in the first instance by concerns regarding their principal activity, namely their commercial dealings, and presumably thereafter also adopted by the temple chapels once those concessions were granted, the Egyptians appear to have wanted to keep their affairs beyond the immediate purview of the Cretans, and Linear A appears to have been the solution.[15]

There might even be written evidence to support the notion that there were Egyptian temple chapels within the Cretan palace complexes. Diodorus Siculus, writing in the 1st Century BC, tells us that the Labyrinth on Crete was built for King Minos; Sir Arthur Evans identified this to be at Knossos.[16] Diodorus Siculus states that it was "like" the labyrinth in Egypt,[17] which Karl Lepsius and Flinders Petrie identified to be at Hawara,[18] and which Lloyd determined was a temple.[19] Writing a millennia and a half after the event, Diodorus has, undoubtedly, got some things wrong, but his record of the construction of something "like" an Egyptian temple within the Palace of Knossos is not a coincidence; it was "like" one because it was one. It was an Egyptian temple chapel.

Moreover, as the later Linear A tablets reveal (which are translated in Chapter Five), at least two of these temple institutions on Crete were dedicated to the Egyptian goddess Hathor (at Hagia Triada and Khania). She is exactly the goddess we would expect an overseas Egyptian temple to be dedicated to, as Hathor was believed to escort enterprising Egyptians on voyages abroad and in foreign lands (as, indeed, was also the case in Byblos, which we shall return to later in this work).[20]

If we accept that an Egyptian temple chapel was located within the Minoan Palace of Knossos even before Crete became part of Egypt's empire, the presence of a statue of an

---

15. With Linear A, a monumental (and older) Egyptian script (hieroglyphics) was used, out of context, to keep Egyptian activities beyond the purview of the Cretans. Evidence, however, only remains of its use by religious institutions, not in commercial dealings. A similar example exists from the ancient commercial world, with a Middle Babylonian clay tablet from Mesopotamia (dated to 1400–1200 BC), where the craftsman author used cuneiform signs with their least common values and in truncated form, spelling certain words differently in the course of the text, and even including puns on homonyms of words to conceal the formula for making glaze that he was recording (C. J. Gadd and R. Campbell Thompson, "A Middle-Babylonian Chemical Text", *Iraq* 3(1)(1936), pp87–88). (https://www.britishmuseum.org/collection/object/W_1929-0715-1). The resulting form of cuneiform has been called a cipher (David Kahn, *The Codebreakers: A Comprehensive History of Secret Communication from Ancient Times to the Internet* (New York: Scribner, 1996), p75); if it is, so too is Linear A.
16. Sir Arthur Evans, *The Palace of Minos: A comparative account of the successive stages of the early Cretan civilization as illustrated by the discoveries at Knossos. Volume 1* (London: Macmillan and Co, Ltd, 1921), pp286–290
17. Diodorus Siculus, *Bibliotheca Historica* (I.61.1–3)
18. Alan B. Lloyd, "The Egyptian Labyrinth", *The Journal of Egyptian Archaeology* (56)(1970), p90
19. Alan B. Lloyd, "The Egyptian Labyrinth", *The Journal of Egyptian Archaeology* (56)(1970), p94
20. C. J. Bleeker, *Hathor and Thoth: Two Key Figures of the Ancient Egyptian Religion* (Leiden: E. J. Brill, 1973), pp72–73

Egyptian goldsmith named User that was found in the palace becomes much easier to explain. The presence of this statue has, it is fair to say, baffled historians and prompted some bizarre theories that I am too polite to mention here. In fact, this statue is an intermediary statue (a statue that purported to aid communication between worshippers and the god or goddess of the temple in question). Its presence reflects Egyptian religious practices being carried out in the Egyptian temple chapel inside the Minoan palace complex as well as, more broadly, the presence of an Egyptian commercial expatriate community in Crete and the political influence it enjoyed.

A picture of the statue of User and a similar intermediary statue found in Egypt is set out below. Thereafter we can usefully have an excursus to consider further why hieroglyphs were used in this previously unknown form on Crete by the Egyptians.

Picture 4.1: Statue of User found at Knossos[21]

Picture 4.2: Intermediary statue of (Nakht)weser(?) found at the Temple of Amun, Karnak[22]

---

21. Sir Arthur Evans, *The Palace of Minos at Knossos. Volume I: The Neolithic and Early and Middle Minoan Ages* (London: Macmillan and Co., 1921), p288 Figure 220
22. Statue of (Nakht)weser(?); B.V. Bothmer (CLES), © Brooklyn Museum (CLES)/Egyptian Museum, Cairo JE 36719 /IFAO https://www.ifao.egnet.net/bases/cachette/?descr=Or&os=25#galerie (accessed 27 June 2024). The late 18th to early 19th Dynasty statue of (Nakht)weser(?) portrays the individual seated holding the Hathoric element against his chest. It appears in raised relief, but the handle is held with both hands in his lap, suggesting he has a three-dimensional object in his hands (Eleanor Beth Simmance, *Communication with the Divine in Ancient Egypt: Hearing Deities, Intermediary Statues, and Sistrophores* (PhD: University of Birmingham, 2017) pp458–459). User's statue does not appear to have held such an element (we might presume it would have been Hathoric if it had), but the inclusion of such elements in intermediary statues was not universal e.g. the

> **Excursus 4.1: Why hieroglyphs?**
>
> Hieroglyphs were the first written form of the ancient Egyptian language, but by the time of the New Kingdom hieroglyphs were used for:
>
> - Monumental inscriptions, principally on buildings but also for "monumental" inscriptions on small objects (for example, commemorative scarabs);
> - Religious, legal, and historical texts recorded in official and public locations, especially temples; and
> - Captions to reliefs and paintings (for example, in burial tombs).
>
> Hieratic was the script of day-to-day administration and commerce having become such in c.2700 BC, some considerable time before the period we are considering here.[23]
>
> As has been stated it seems reasonable to assume that the first links between Egypt and Crete arose through trade (after all, until the reign of Thutmose III, Egypt did not have an ocean-going navy[24]). Trade would have been recorded (on the Egyptian side) in hieratic and as a result it would seem likely that the Cretans would have had knowledge of hieratic with some of them possibly able to read it. Conversely there would have been no practical need for a non-Egyptian to learn hieroglyphs, so it seems considerably less likely that the Cretans understood hieroglyphs. The Egyptians, in choosing to record their activities in Crete, relied upon this, I believe.
>
> During this period, the Egyptians in Crete had significant influence but not control. One might imagine therefore that they wanted to keep their commercial affairs outside the immediate purview of the Cretan authorities lest their position become subject to scrutiny and challenge. The use of Linear A shorthand, based on hieroglyphs that were unknown to the Cretans, was a practical response to this situation and it helped keep the Egyptians' dealings in Crete free from Cretan interference. As the scripta franca in use in commerce, it was then also used (by the same individuals) in the operations of the Egyptian temple chapels. Linear A was a simple invention; it used a method of shorthand writing that was likely then in use in Egypt with the hieratic script (although no examples of its use there have survived), and it applied the same methodology to

---

differently-styled 18th Dynasty (Amenhotep III) statue of Amenhotep son of Hapu, also from the Temple of Amun at Karnak (http://wayback.archive-it.org/7877/20160919162339/http://dlib.etc.ucla.edu/projects/Karnak/resource/ObjectCatalog/1853 (accessed 20 January 2022)). User was evidently a member of the commercial classes; similarly intermediary statues in Egypt also portray members of the commercial classes e.g. the (again) differently-styled 19th to 20th Dynasty statue of Bahy from Nag el-Mecheikh who was the Overseer of the Weavers (https://www.pba-auctions.com/lot/16862/3399363?npp=150& (accessed 20 January 2022)).

23. John Baines, "Literacy and Ancient Egyptian Society", *Man* 18(3)(September 1983), p582. The surviving archaeological evidence has not indicated that Egyptian hieroglyphs were used for record keeping in ancient Egypt, although the 2013 discovery of the Diary of Merer, dealing with the transport of limestone from Tura to Giza in the 4th Dynasty, and which was written in both hieroglyphs and hieratic, suggests this picture may not be as absolute as was once thought.
24. Richard A. Gabriel, *Thutmose III: The Military Biography of Egypt's Greatest Warrior King* (Washington, D.C.: Potomac Books, Inc., 2009), p126

> the same language, Middle Egyptian, but written instead in hieroglyphs. The Cretans would not have understood it.
>
> Beyond demonstrating to us that Egyptian institutions existed and operated in Crete, the surviving Linear A tablets, being day-to-day missives produced in the administration of Egyptian temples, are not as revealing to us as would have been the permanent records (of the temples or traders' commercial activities), originally presumably retained on papyrus but which have not survived, and it is the latter, in particular, holding the more sensitive information that the Egyptians probably sought to keep confidential. They too were presumably written in hieroglyphs, given that Linear A was written using hieroglyphs (in shorthand), and that was the scripta franca, rather than hieratic.
>
> Finally, before returning to our narrative, we might usefully consider the following evidence attesting to the suitability of hieroglyphs rather than (solely) hieratic as the basis for a new script.
>
> The later Proto-Sinaitic semitic script, to which we will return in Excursus 5.4, contains elements drawn from both hieroglyphic and hieratic Egyptian scripts.[25] For elements of the former script (hieroglyphics) to be included, for the creators of the Proto-Sinaitic script something, in terms of capability or capacity, must have been missing from the latter script (hieratic). While Linear A, as we shall see, draws upon hieratic for some of its fraction symbols (see Appendix 2), for the reasons set out above (namely the desire to initially keep presumably Egyptian commercial dealings discrete from the Cretans), hieroglyphs are virtually the sole source of Linear A symbols. That Proto-Sinaitic also drew upon hieroglyphs even when there was no similar desire to keep dealings discrete indicates there were occasions when there were valid reasons for choosing hieroglyphs over hieratic and, even if those valid reasons may not be wholly perceived by today's academics, it shows us that hieratic was not all things to all men all of the time – and, when it was not, hieroglyphs could be and, indeed, were used. With the creation of Linear A, therefore, we must also expect that, while the circumstances on Crete also dictated it, the benefits of hieroglyphs over hieratic, whatever they may have been, might also be considered as likely to have been a consideration in determining the final form of that script too.

The use of hieroglyphs in the Egyptian temples' administration in this period, therefore, reflects the Egyptians on Crete having significant influence but not control. This close and enduring economic and, it seems, partly political relationship reflected the existence of two distinct cultures on Crete. This was the necessary precursor to the next stage in Egypto-Cretan relations when the Cretans, specifically the Minoans, faced probably their greatest challenge since the eruption of Thera. When it occurred, they turned to their longstanding partner for help.

---

25. F. Simons, "Proto-Sinaitic – Progenitor of the Alphabet", *Rosetta* 9(2011), p17

Part II: Crete as part of Egypt's empire (from during the Late Minoan IB period)

Towards the end of the Late Minoan IB period (1500–1450 BC) the evidence is clear; for a brief period, probably of just over three decades, Crete became part of Egypt's empire. There is significant evidence for this change:

- First, as we have seen, within Crete there is a jump in Linear A tablet finds attributed to the Late Minoan IB period compared to prior periods suggesting a significantly increased bureaucratic output which would be consistent with Crete becoming part of Egypt's empire.
- Second, archaeological evidence found in Crete, specifically finds of Egyptian commercial wares, also peak in the Late Minoan IB period. This concurrent peak is due, I believe, to imperial preference guiding trade to a greater extent than it had been previously.
- Third, the re-evaluation of a number of tomb inscriptions in Egypt (some of them surprisingly specific and unambiguous) indicates (or, in fact, states) that Crete became part of Egypt's empire.
- Fourth, archaeological evidence found in a burial tomb of Djehuty, a general of Thutmose III's army, explicitly states that he was governor of Crete.
- Fifth, a critical re-evaluation of the Annals, an inscription at Karnak detailing Thutmose III's military campaigns and tribute received, reveals when Crete became part of Egypt's formal empire.
- Sixth, a critical re-evaluation of the "Flotilla Fresco" in ancient Akrotiri on Thera (modern Santorini) reveals that it depicts the moment Crete became part of Egypt's empire.

That there was a significant change in the nature and extent of Egypt's involvement in Crete in the Late Minoan IB period is indicated in the first instance by a jump in the number of Linear A tablets found and dated to this period. As we saw in Table 1 and Graph 1 in this chapter, over 80% of the Linear A tablets that have been found have been dated to the Late Minoan IB period, which lasted a mere 50 years according to archaeologists, compared to less than 20% dated to the archaeological periods covering the almost three hundred years before that. Even taking into account the expected lower rate of survival of evidence from the further back in time we look, such that, all things being equal, we would expect fewer tablets to survive from, say, 1800 BC compared to, say, 1450 BC, it is reasonable to interpret this pattern nonetheless as suggesting that a significant change took place.

If there was a change, and Crete became part of Egypt's empire, that would have led to the Egyptian temples flourishing as they catered for more expatriates (now colonists), and a greater volume of administrative records (broadly, the more active the institution, the more records it produces). In addition, as we shall see in Chapter Five, in common with Egypt proper where, during the New Kingdom period, the Egyptian state increasingly used the larger temples as its agents as well as or in place of the provincial administrators used previously,[26] Linear A was also used in the conduct of the administration of the state.

---

26. Brian P. Muhs, *The Ancient Egyptian Economy: 3000–30 BCE* (Cambridge: Cambridge University Press, 2016), pp115–116

> **Excursus 4.2: Why did the Egyptian colonial administration continue to use Linear A (and, by implication, hieroglyphs)?**
>
> Excursus 4.1 set out why Linear A (and hieroglyphs) were used in the Egyptian temples on Crete during the period that Egypt had significant influence but not control of Crete; its use reflected the political circumstances on Crete and the Egyptians' desire to keep their activities beyond the purview of the Cretans. After Crete became part of Egypt's empire, conditions clearly changed, Egypt then having control and Egyptian institutions on Crete being able to operate freely. Why, therefore, was Linear A still used (rather than hieratic as was the case in Egypt proper)?
>
> The explanation is, I think, institutional lethargy. The same people ran the temples the day before Crete became part of Egypt's empire as the day after Crete became part of Egypt's empire. If the same people were doing the same thing, then despite the political changes around them, why change day-to-day practices?[27] After all, as Bert Lance said, "if it ain't broke, don't fix it."[28] Linear A was the scripta franca of the Egyptians on Crete, and it continued to be used in the temples in relation to temple activities.
>
> In contrast to the other territories conquered by Thutmose III, however, as Crete had an established network of Egyptian temples it made sense for Egypt to administer this new territory through that temple network in the same way that Egypt was. As in Egypt, the Egyptian temples acted as agents of the state.
>
> While the form of Middle Egyptian that is Linear A reflected past conditions on Crete, when the Egyptians had significant influence but not control, this pre-existing practice continued and expanded thereafter, despite Egypt having control after Crete became part of Egypt's empire. Consequently, as we shall see in Chapter Five, in addition to the records produced using Linear A in this period showing the temples acting as principal in their dealings (i.e. as religious institutions conducting religious activities), as they had done previously, they also show them acting as agents of the state, conducting the administration of government.

The peak in Linear A tablet finds in the Late Minoan IB period is matched by a concurrent peak in the second evidence type we shall consider, namely Egyptian commercial wares found in Crete. Two concurrent peaks in two different types of Egyptian archaeological evidence found on Crete is not a coincidence.

Levels of finds in Egyptian commercial wares over time can reasonably be seen to equate to levels of imports of Egyptian goods. However, unlike the abrupt cessation in the use of

---

27. Though I believe that Linear A (and hieroglyphs) was the scripta franca of the Egyptian colonial administration, I also believe that local Cretans likely came to learn it following the commencement of Egyptian rule of the island in 1455 BC. This meant that, when Egypt withdrew in c.1424 BC, there was sufficient knowledge amongst those remaining on Crete for Linear B to be created (although the exact relationship between Mycenaean Greek and Linear B and Middle Egyptian and Linear A is not yet understood).
28. https://www.phrases.org.uk/meanings/if-it-aint-broke-dont-fix-it.html (accessed 1 January 2022)

60 The Decipherment of Linear A

Linear A, of which there are no attested finds after the Late Minoan IB period and the conquest of the island by the Mycenaeans, finds of Egyptian commercial wares in Crete tail off gradually after the Late Minoan IB period. Table 4.2 and Graph 4.2 below show the level of finds of Egyptian commercial wares in Crete when they can be attributed to a known archaeological Sub-Period e.g. Late Minoan IA or Late Minoan IB, rather than simply a broader archaeological Period, e.g. Late Minoan I.[29]

Table 4.2: Finds of Egyptian commercial wares in Crete from the Late Minoan period (by known Sub-Period)[30]

Sub-Period	Date range	Sub-Period mid-point	Number of finds
LM IA	1600 - 1500	1550	2
LM IB	1500 - 1450	1475	25
LM II	1450 - 1400	1425	21
LM IIIA1	1400 - 1375	1388	15
LM IIIA2	1375 - 1300	1338	10
LM IIIB	1300 - 1200	1250	3
LM IIIC	1200 - 1060	1130	0

Graph 4.2: Finds of Egyptian commercial wares in Crete in the Late Minoan period (by known Sub-Period)[31]

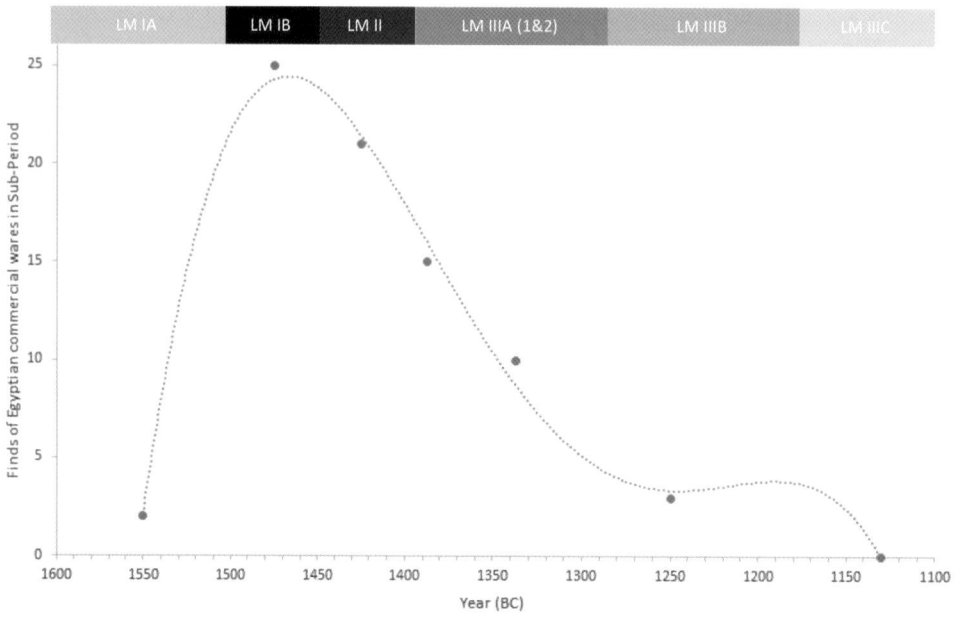

29. The reason for requiring such specificity is that only by using the most accurate archaeological data relating to Sub-Periods (rather than Periods) can we hope to draw the correct conclusions. Less specific data that can only be attributed to longer archaeological Periods (rather than Sub-Periods) cannot be used to infer what was a much shorter period of Egyptian rule that lasted for less than one Sub-Period.
30. Eric H. Cline, "The Nature of the Economic Relations of Crete with Egypt and the Near East during the Late Bronze Age", in Angelos Chaniotis (Ed.), *From Minoan Farmers to Roman Traders: Sidelights of the Economy of Ancient Crete* (Stuttgart: Franz Steiner Verlag, 1999), p117 Table 1 values
31. Eric H. Cline, "The Nature of the Economic Relations of Crete with Egypt and the Near East during the Late Bronze Age", in Angelos Chaniotis (Ed.), *From Minoan Farmers to Roman Traders: Sidelights of the Economy of*

The pattern of finds of Egyptian goods tailing off gradually following the Mycenaean conquest is also consistent with Crete having been and then ceasing to be part of Egypt's empire. Historian Eric Cline, for one, notes the falling off of trade with Egypt after the Late Minoan IB period "might" be linked to the destruction of Knossos in c.1450 BC (and the Mycenaean conquest of the island).[32] It is. In the Late Minoan IB period (and slightly beyond), Crete was part of Egypt's empire and purchases of Egyptian commercial wares by Crete were driven by imperial preference; after the Mycenaean conquest, imperial preference was superseded by more rational economic choice. The tailing off of finds of Egyptian commercial wares, reflecting a gradual reduction in Egyptian imports, might appear surprising, for if the Mycenaeans conquered Crete from the Egyptians (which, as we shall see, was the case) then how could they have continued to purchase Egyptian goods? The answer is the prevailing anti-clockwise sea current in the eastern Mediterranean.[33] This meant that Egyptian commercial wares could still be purchased in Mycenaean Crete, transported there as before via the Levant and Southern Anatolia and, more importantly, via intermediary merchants thus avoiding the need for purchases to be made directly from the Egyptians (with whom the Mycenaeans were, for a time at least, presumably still at war following their conquest of the island).[34] These purchases diminished over time but, at least to begin with, despite the political change, commercial buying patterns did not.

Therefore, it is no coincidence that the Linear A finds (and implied levels of usage) and finds of Egyptian commercial wares (and implied levels of imports) both peak at the same time, when Crete was part of Egypt's empire.

It might, perhaps, be argued that the peak in finds of Egyptian commercial wares (and, therefore, implied levels of imports) could simply be due to economic growth in Crete leading to higher imports but, if so, this would be reflected in the levels of imports from all of Crete's major trading partners. However, there are no concurrent peaks in finds originating from Syria-Palestine and Cyprus, Crete's other apparent principal trading partners (based on the levels of archaeological finds). We are not, therefore, dealing with

---

Ancient Crete (Stuttgart: Franz Steiner Verlag, 1999), p117 Table 1 values. It is worth briefly commenting on the limited number of finds of Egyptian commercial wares in Crete dated to the Late Minoan IA period (2); more might have been expected in the context of Crete forming part of Egypt's informal empire. I think, however, the explanation might be found in the conditions prevailing in Egypt at this time. The Hyksos controlled northern Egypt for much of this time (1650–1550 BC) and, I think, this must have led to: a weakening of the bond between Crete and Egypt (given the fragmentation of the Egyptian state) such that less Egyptian influence led to less purchasing of Egyptian commercial wares; the Hyksos having more of an Asiatic focus given their background perhaps also led to their ignoring Egypt's previous commercial markets; and the impact of war between the Hyksos and the Theban princes for the last 30 years of their time in Egypt (which would have left little time to focus on trade).

32. Eric H. Cline, "The Nature of the Economic Relations of Crete with Egypt and the Near East during the Late Bronze Age", in Angelos Chaniotis (Ed.), *From Minoan Farmers to Roman Traders: Sidelights on the Economy of Ancient Crete* (Franz Steiner Verlag: Stuttgart, 1999), p121
33. Eric Cline, *1177 B.C. The Year Civilization Collapsed* (Princeton: Princeton University Press, 2014), p25
34. There were still Mycenaean imports into Egypt (A. R. David, *The Pyramid Builders of Ancient Egypt: A Modern Investigation of Pharoah's Workforce* (Boston: Routledge and Kegan Paul, 1986), p183), but one might imagine that these did not come from Crete (now an enemy of Egypt) or its mainland Mycenaean allies but, rather, the other city states of mainland Greece.

a Late Minoan IB period economic boom on Crete drawing in goods from all of Crete's major trading partners. In contrast, after the Mycenaean conquest, there are concurrent peaks in finds from Syria-Palestine and Cyprus in the Late Minoan IIIA1 / A2 period (1400–1300 BC) (as well as continued trade with Egypt).

Table 4.3: Finds of Syria-Palestinian and Cypriot commercial wares in Crete from the Late Minoan period (by known Sub-Period)[35]

Sub-Period	Date range	Number of Syria-Palestinian finds	Number of Cypriot finds
LM IA	1600 - 1500	3	2
LM IB	1500 - 1450	3	7
LM II	1450 - 1400	0	3
LM IIIA1	1400 - 1375	21	11
LM IIIA2	1375 - 1300	13	8
LM IIIB	1300 - 1200	1	3
LM IIIC	1200 - 1060	0	0

Simultaneous peaks in finds from two trading partners likely indicating a period of general economic growth.

That there were concurrent peaks in trade with two regions does suggest broad economic growth drawing in a higher level of imports. The earlier peak in Egyptian trade only suggests dominance by that one power at the expense of the others; it reflects imperial preference.

The pattern of Crete's trade with Egypt after the island ceased to be part of Egypt's empire and imperial preference was superseded, reflects similar patterns of trade experienced by the former territories of the British Empire after their independence following the Second World War. After the war, when a territory was granted independence, this typically led to a change in the buying preferences of that territory as rational economic choice prevailed over (former) imperial preference. Following British India's independence in 1947, for example, there was a steady tailing off of trade between India and Britain. The pattern is remarkably similar to post 1450 BC Crete (albeit, in the case of India, it took place over a shorter time period as would be expected in a more dynamic world economy with more competition, better global transport links, and more goods capable of substitution):

---

35. Eric H. Cline, "The Nature of the Economic Relations of Crete with Egypt and the Near East during the Late Bronze Age", in Angelos Chaniotis (Ed.), *From Minoan Farmers to Roman Traders: Sidelights of the Economy of Ancient Crete* (Stuttgart: Franz Steiner Verlag, 1999), p117. Note, the use of the term "Syria-Palestinian" here is not entirely synonymous with the territory of Retenu conquered by Thutmose III (see footnote 7 in this chapter).

The Reconstructed History of Egypt's Involvement in Middle and Late Bronze Age Crete 63

Graph 4.3: India's post-independence trade with Great Britain as a percentage of total trade.[36]

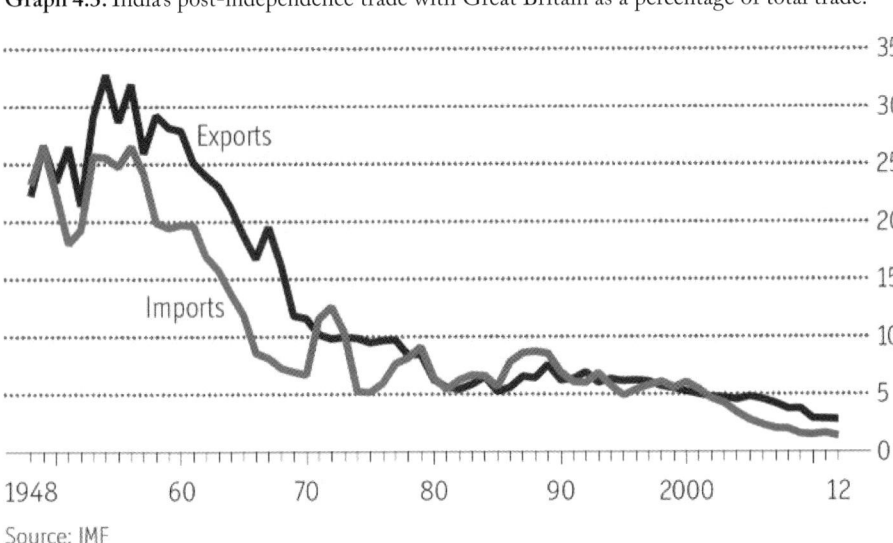

Source: IMF

The peak of finds of Egyptian commercial wares in Crete reflects Crete being part of Egypt's empire during (and, as we shall see, slightly beyond) the Late Minoan IB period. The tailing off of finds thereafter reflects rational economic choice prevailing over (former) imperial preference.

Our third body of archaeological evidence supporting the assertion that Crete was part of Egypt's empire in the Late Minoan IB period (1500–1450 BC) is found in Egypt. It is surprisingly specific and unambiguous in character. Three contemporary portrayals of Cretans are found in Egyptian tomb chapels dating from this period. In believed chronological order, they are found in the tombs of:

- Senenmut, the architect of Queen Hatshepsut[37] (who ruled c.1473/72–1459/58 BC[38]);
- Useramun, who was Vizier from Year 5 of King Thutmose III's reign (1475/74 BC) until some time between Year 28 (c.1453/52 BC) and Year 34 (c.1446/45 BC) of Thutmose III's reign[39]; and

---

36. https://www.economist.com/special-report/2013/11/07/paying-its-way (accessed 23 June 2020) (© The Economist Group Limited, London (7 November 2013))
37. Eric Cline, *1177 B.C. The Year Civilization Collapsed* (Princeton: Princeton University Press, 2014), p23
38. Aiden Dodson, "The Coregency Conundrum", *Kmt: A Modern Journal of Ancient Egypt*, 25(2)(2014), p30
39. J. J. Shirley, "Viceroys, Viziers & The Amun Precinct: The Power of Heredity and Strategic Marriage in the early 18th Dynasty", *Journal of Egyptian History* 3(1)(2010), pp83–84 and footnote 49. Year 5 is provided by Papyrus Turin I. Year 28 of Thutmose III is the last attested date of Useramun as Vizier, provided by a stela in the tomb of his steward, Amunemhat (Theban Tomb 82) (B. Porter and R. Moss, *Topographical Bibliography of Ancient Egyptian Hieroglyphic Texts, Reliefs, and Paintings I: The Theban Necropolis, Part 1: Private Tombs* (2nd ed.) (Oxford: Clarendon Press, 1960), pp163–167). Papyrus Louvre E. 3226 provides the earliest date for Rekhmire as Vizier, in Year 34 of Thutmose III's reign.

64   The Decipherment of Linear A

- Rekhmire, Useramun's nephew and successor as Vizier,[40] who became Vizier some time between Years 28 (c.1453/52 BC) and Year 34 (c.1446/45 BC) and who served until shortly after King Amenhotep II became ruler (1425 BC).[41]

The tomb of Senenmut shows Aegeans (Eric Cline is "unequivocal" that they are Cretans) carrying their wares[42]:

Picture 4.3: The Aegeans (Cretans) portrayed in the tomb of Senenmut (Theban Tomb 71)[43]

This portrayal has been claimed to be the earliest known depiction of Aegeans (Cretans).[44] When attempting to date this portrayal, however, we need to understand that we are dealing with a large number of unknowns. The events portrayed (of which we will learn more shortly) would naturally have taken place before Senenmut's death and the sealing of his tomb. The date of his death is, however, not known. Not knowing the date of Senenmut's death means that it is also impossible to say with certainty when (or, at least, the latest date at which) the events portrayed in his tomb could have taken place. The assertion that these are the earliest portrayals of Aegeans (Cretans) is, therefore, conjecture.

---

40. James Henry Breasted, *Ancient Records of Egypt: Volume 2* (Champaign: University of Illinois Press, 2001), p267
41. R. S. Merrillees, "Aegean Bronze Age Relations with Egypt", *American Journal of Archaeology* 76(3)(1972), p287. Rekhmire is shown presenting a bouquet to King Amenhotep II, who is portrayed and is referred to without reference to Thutmose III. Consequently, Thutmose III would appear to have died and this therefore represents the start of Amenhotep II's sole rule (in 1425 BC) rather than the start of his period of co-rule (in 1427 BC).
42. Eric Cline, *1177 B.C. The Year Civilization Collapsed* (Princeton: Princeton University Press, 2014), p23. This would concur with Evans, who made the point that the bovine head on this bowl echoes that of the Minotaur (he also linked the cult of the bull on Crete to that of the Egyptian Goddess Hathor (J. Alexander MacGillivray, *Minotaur: Sir Arthur Evans and the archaeology of the Minoan Myth* (London: Jonathan Cape, 2000), p243). Evans may well have been correct to do so.
43. Nina de Garis Davies, *Ancient Egyptian Paintings I* (Chicago: Oriental Institute of Press, 1936), Plate XIV (Image copyright © The Metropolitan Museum of Art. Image source: Art Resource, NY)
44. R. S. Merrillees, "Aegean Bronze Age Relations with Egypt", *American Journal of Archaeology* 76(3)(1972), p293

There is no mention of Senenmut in the surviving record after Year 16 of Thutmose III's reign (c.1464/63 BC),[45] and this has influenced some historians' views as to the likely date of Senenmut's death. Historian Barbara Switalski Lesko has, however, speculated that Senenmut may have served on into the period of Thutmose III's sole rule (which began in 1459/58 BC).[46] I agree. After all, we know that burial tombs took many years to prepare,[47] and while construction of Senenmut's tomb has been dated according to an ostracon found in it dating to Year 16 of Thutmose III's reign (so it had begun by at least 1463 BC),[48] of all the people we might expect to build their own tomb significantly before they needed it, would we not expect a royal architect to do so? Consequently, agreeing with Lesko that Senenmut served on into the earlier years of Thutmose III's sole rule, what was ultimately portrayed in the tomb could, as a result, have occurred (and been painted) at a later date than has been thought. In fact, far from being the earliest depiction (of a separate event), I believe they relate to the same events that were recorded in the tomb of Useramun.

In the tomb of Useramun, Thutmose III's Vizier, there is a similar portrayal of Aegeans to that in the tomb of Senenmut:

Picture 4.4: The Aegeans (Cretans) portrayed in the tomb of Useramun (Theban Tomb 131)[49]

---

45. B. Switalski Lesko, "The Senmut Problem", *Journal of the American Research Centre in Egypt*, 6(1967), p113, citing H. E. Winlock "The Egyptian Expedition 1925–1927", *The Metropolitan Museum of Art Bulletin* 23(2)(February 1928), p30
46. B. Switalski Lesko, "The Senmut Problem", *Journal of the American Research Centre in Egypt*, 6(1967), p117
47. R. S. Merrillees, "Aegean Bronze Age Relations with Egypt", *American Journal of Archaeology* 76(3)(1972), p288
48. B. Switalski Lesko, "The Senmut Problem", *Journal of the American Research Centre in Egypt* 6(1967), p113
49. Eberhard Dziobek, Erik Hornung & Yvonne Marzoni Fecia di Cossato, *Die Gräber des Vezirs User-Amun Theben Nr. 61 und 131* (Mainz am Rhein: Verlag Philipp von Zabern, 1994), Plate 20. Note also, in a further similarity to the portrayal in the tomb of Senenmut, that a bull's head (left) and a bull figurine (right) are carried by the Aegeans (Cretans).

The men in the painting, again carrying their wares, wear folded loin cloths of a similar type to those portrayed in the tomb of Senenmut, thus the historians Jean Vercoutter and R. S. Merrillees conclude that they represent the same people.⁵⁰ Again, these are Cline's Cretans. Alongside them Syria-Palestinians are also portrayed, carrying their wares. The portrayals are also accompanied by a caption which reads:

> *"Receiving the tribute which the might of His Majesty brought back from the foreign countries in the north of the confines of Asia [Syria-Palestine] and the Isles in the Midst of the Sea [the Aegean Islands, including Crete], by the prince, Count, Ouseramon [Useramun]."*⁵¹

Of relevance later in this chapter, it is important to note that those bearing the tribute (and, therefore, also those portrayed bearing tribute in the tomb of Senenmut) are not stated to be, and are not, chiefs (or princes). With that oblique statement made, for now let us consider what the text of this caption tells us.

The text tells us that Thutmose III went overseas. He went to Syria-Palestine, and the Isles in the Midst of the Sea (the Aegean, including Crete), and, as a result of being there, through his "might", he was able to send tribute back to Egypt where it was received by Useramun, the Vizier. We know from the Annals (a source which we will consider shortly), that in the course of his campaigns, Thutmose III personally commanded an Egyptian army that conquered Syria-Palestine. We would expect him thereafter to have sent the tribute he received back to Egypt following that territory's subjugation. Crete is placed on a par with Syria-Palestine, a conquered territory. If the caption wording of the tomb indicates that Thutmose III went to Syria-Palestine, as we know he did, and that through his might Syria-Palestine became part of Egypt's empire (paying tribute), as we know it did, then, given that the two are treated on a par, surely the caption wording also means that Thutmose III went to Crete and that Crete too became part of Egypt's empire (paying tribute), and that this occurred at around the same time, given the joint record, though after Syria-Palestine, as Crete is mentioned second? Indeed, as we shall see later, other evidence clearly shows that Thutmose III personally went to Crete to receive its submission (and tribute) shortly after he first subjugated Syria-Palestine.

As regards the portrayal of the receipt of tribute from Syria-Palestine, it is worth considering just how exceptional this event was (and thus worth memorialising). In 1457 BC Thutmose III led the Egyptian army to victory at the Battle of Megiddo and in its subsequent conquest of the three principal ports of the Levant coast, Tyre, Sidon, and Biblos.⁵² Following this, for the first time, an Egyptian king received tribute from this territory that was, no doubt, sent back to Egypt. This exceptional event (and the receipt of the tribute back in Egypt) was worth memorialising. Whatever happened with Crete was therefore also similarly exceptional and worth of memorialising.

---

50. R. S. Merrillees, "Aegean Bronze Age Relations with Egypt", *American Journal of Archaeology* 76(3)(1972), p289
51. R. S. Merrillees, "Aegean Bronze Age Relations with Egypt", *American Journal of Archaeology* 76(3)(1972), p289
52. Richard A. Gabriel, *Thutmose III: The Military Biography of Egypt's Greatest Warrior King* (Washington, D.C.: Potomac Books, Inc., 2009), p120. The ports' capture is omitted from the Annals; perhaps the Egyptian forces that captured them were not led by Thutmose III, hence record of their capture was not felt worthy of inclusion.

If, as the caption implies, Crete became part of Egypt's empire and the Egyptian king received tribute from it (in person) for the first time, and that tribute was then sent back to Egypt, its arrival in Egypt, like that from Syria-Palestine, would have been an exceptional event worth memorialising. Of course, it did not arrive at the same time as the tribute from Syria-Palestine, for the king could not have received tribute from both territories in person and have dispatched the two sets of tribute back to Egypt thereafter such that they arrived in Egypt at the same time, so the combined reference in the caption is a figurative conflation of the two events. The combined treatment of the two territories suggests, however, that both territories enjoyed a similar relationship with Egypt thereafter and knowing the nature of one territory's relationship with Egypt we can infer the nature of the other territory's relationship with Egypt.

If Crete became part of Egypt's empire, therefore, the tomb painting and its caption suggests that this rule began:

(a) After the period of co-rule between Hatshepsut and Thutmose III, which ended in c.1459/58 BC (for it is only "the might of His Majesty" (singular) which led to the tribute being received and brought back);
(b) After the Battle of Megiddo in 1457 BC as, after this, the chiefs of Syria-Palestine became vassals of Thutmose III and paid him tribute for the first time, and the tribute from the chiefs of Crete was listed as received after this in the tomb caption; and
(c) Before the end of Useramuns' tenure as Vizier, which was some time between c.1452/53 BC and c.1446/45 BC.

For now, therefore, we can make the safe working assumption that Egyptian rule of Crete began within the relatively narrow window of 1457 BC–1445 BC.

In the third tomb that we consider in this work, that of Rekhmire, Vizier of Thutmose III and Amenhotep II, we again see a portrayal of Aegean men carrying their wares:

Picture 4.5: The Aegeans portrayed in the tomb of Rekhmire (Theban Tomb 100)[53]

---

53. https://www.flickr.com/photos/manna4u/32544493391/?map=1 (accessed 1 January 2020)

Later in this chapter we shall return to the portrayal but, for now, we will consider its accompanying caption. The caption above the portrayal of the Aegeans in this tomb is the most detailed that has been found accompanying any such portrayal and has therefore been the focus of historians' analysis. For us, the wording of this caption gives us our first details of how Crete became part of Egypt's empire. Based on the implicit assumption that Egypt did not own Crete, however, historians have misinterpreted the portrayal in Rekhmire's tomb (and the tombs of Useramun and Senenmut). In order that we do not do the same we must examine not just the caption relating to the Aegeans but also to the other three peoples represented bearing tribute or, as some historians would have it, bearing diplomatic gifts (which in one case (not the Aegeans) they are). These four captions are set out below:

The Reconstructed History of Egypt's Involvement in Middle and Late Bronze Age Crete 69

Table 4.4: Captions in the tomb of Rekhmire (Theban Tomb 100)[54]

Who?	Caption	Bringing tribute [or gifts]?	Seeking the "breath of life"?	Why do they want the "breath of life"?
People of Punt	"The arrival in peace of the chiefs of Punt, with respectful obeisance, at the place where His Majesty, the King of Both Egypts, Men-kheper-Re' — may he live for ever — was, **bringing their tribute**, diverse acceptable offerings of their land — a land on which no others have set foot — because of the greatness of his might throughout their lands; for every land is subject to His Majesty."	Yes	No	N/A
People of Keftiu (Crete) and the Aegean	"The arrival in peace of the chiefs of Keftiu-land (and) the islands which are within the Great Sea, in respectful obeisance to the might of His Majesty, the King of Both Egypts, Men-kheper-Re' — may eternal life be given him — **of whose victories throughout all lands they have heard with their tribute** on their backs, **in the hope that vital breath would be given them because of loyalty to His Majesty, in order that his might should be allowed to protect them**."	Yes	Yes	1. Because of loyalty to His Majesty 2. In order that his might should be allowed to protect them
People of Nubia	"The arrival in peace of the chiefs of the southern land, (namely) the Iuntiu-sety and Khenty-hen-nufer, with respectful obeisance and prostration, **bearing their tribute** . . . . (to) the King of Both Egypts, Men-kheper-Re' — may he live for ever — **in the hope that there would be given to them the breath of life.**"	Yes	Yes	N/A
People of Retenu (Syria-Palestine)	"The arrival in peace of the chiefs of Ret[e]nu and all the lands of Further Asia in deferential obeisance, their tribute on their backs, **in the hope that there would be given to them the breath of life because of loyalty to His Majesty; for they have seen his very great victories — yea, his terribleness has dominated their hearts.**"	Yes	Yes	1. For they have seen his very great victories, and 2. His terribleness has dominated their hearts

---

54. Norman de Garis Davies, *The Tomb of Rekh-mi-re' at Thebes: Volume 1* (New York: The Metropolitan Museum of Art Egyptian Expedition, 1943), pp20, 25, 27

Four peoples are portrayed in Rekhmire's tomb: the Puntites, the Cretans (and Aegeans), the Nubians, and the Syria-Palestinians (from Retenu). Analysis of the captions relating to them allows us to determine the nature of Egypt's relationship with Crete.

Historian Diamantis Panagiotopoulos, in a work edited by Eric Cline, believes that the Middle Egyptian word for tribute, *inw*, which is used in all four captions alongside the portrayals, should be taken to mean "diplomatic gifts" in the case of the Cretans and, as a result, Crete was not part of Egypt's empire (because the Cretans gave diplomatic gifts).[55] "Diplomatic gifts" is acknowledged as a possible meaning of the word *inw*.[56] The Puntites are universally agreed never to have been the Egyptian king's vassals, for example, so they cannot have brought tribute; their emissaries can only have brought diplomatic gifts.

However, Eric Cline, writing with Steven M. Stannish, believes that to receive "the breath of life" means to receive "diplomatic recognition".[57] Of the four captions alongside portrayals of peoples in Rekhmire's tomb, the Puntites, despite being universally acknowledged never to have been vassals, are the only ones that are not recorded as also seeking "the breath of life". The portrayal of an exceptional Puntite emissary (for it must have been exceptional to have warranted depiction) bringing diplomatic gifts (according to Panagiotopouolus, edited by Cline) from a faraway people who were not then also seeking diplomatic recognition (according to the meaning ascribed by Cline and Stannish) is clearly so contradictory as to demonstrate error. Moreover, the Nubians and the Syria-Palestinians, who were undeniably a subject people of the Egyptian empire, cannot have sought diplomatic recognition, and yet they too are recorded as seeking "the breath of life" in Rekhmire's tomb.

The interpretation of "the breath of life" as "diplomatic recognition" can only be incorrect and, therefore, as the Cretans did not seek diplomatic recognition there is no certainty that Panagiotopoulos, in turn, is correct when he argues that, for Crete, *inw* meant "diplomatic gifts" (as opposed to "tribute"). The word *inw* has more than one potential meaning when translated into our language: it can mean "diplomatic gifts", as it did in the case of the Puntites, or it can mean "tribute", as it did in the case of the Nubians and the Syria-Palestinians. Absent any other information, it could mean either in the case of Crete. In the Egyptian language something paid (tribute) or given (a gift) by a non-Egyptian ruler to the king of Egypt, whether as a vassal (tribute) or an independent diplomatic counterparty (a gift), was viewed without distinction (all other rulers were perceived as equally inferior to the King of Egypt). We therefore cannot infer either way that the word described a gift or tribute without correctly interpreting it from its context. The correct interpretation of the phrase "the breath of life" is, therefore, vital.

The position adopted by Cline and Stannish contradicts historian David Lorton's detailed (indeed, unsurpassed) consideration of the instances where the phrase "the breath of life" was used in the 18th Dynasty in the context of international relations. He believes

---

55. Diamantis Panagiotopoulos, "Foreigners in Egypt in the Time of Hatshepsut and Thutmose III", in E. Cline & D. O'Connor (Eds.), *Thutmose III: A New Biography* (Ann Arbor: University of Michigan Press, 2006), pp397–398
56. Raymond O. Faulkner, *A Concise Dictionary of Middle Egyptian* (Oxford: Griffith Institute Ashmolean Museum, 2017), p27
57. Eric H. Cline and Steven M. Stannish, "Sailing the Great Green Sea? Amenhotep III's "Aegean List: from Kom el-Hetan, Once More", *Journal of Ancient Egyptian Interconnections* 3(2)(2011), p10

that "breath" relates to entering into a treaty relationship, whether as a sovereign or on the basis of equals, and "[of] life" likely means agreed under oath.[58] I agree. This is why the Puntites did not seek "the breath of life". They brought diplomatic gifts; they did not seek a treaty-based relationship bound by oath.

Consequently, when the defeated Syrians became vassals of Thutmose III after the Battle of Megiddo, they did so in a relationship codified by way of a treaty bound by oath. Perhaps making the point even more clearly is their plea to become vassals recorded in the Annals (an account of Thutmose III's military achievements discussed later in this chapter):

"Grant that we survive: we shall make deliveries to your majesty and we shall send trade goods [for your treasury!... There has never been a king who did] what your majesty has done in this land! Then my majesty commanded that the "breath of life" be given to them."[59]

In return for their submission following his exceptional military victory, Thutmose III granted them "the breath of life" i.e. he recognised the defeated princes as his vassals and they were obliged to send trade goods to him thereafter in a relationship codified by a treaty sworn under oath. The trade goods they sent were not diplomatic gifts, they were tribute, and the tribute was payable in return for being given "the breath of life" and the rights and obligations as vassals that entailed.

What, then, of Crete (and certain of the Aegean Islands)? Let us again consider what the caption in Rekhmire's tomb tells us about what "the vital breath" (and, we can safely say was also implied – for all parties to treaties swear to uphold their terms) "of life" was to be granted for, as this will tell us about the nature of the relationship between Crete and Egypt (and indicate the correct meaning, in our language, of *inw* when used in this context).

The caption in Rekhmire's tomb tells us that the chiefs of Crete and the Aegean Islands came to Thutmose III because they had heard of his "victories throughout all lands" (i.e. surely a reference to the military victories won by Thutmose III in Syria-Palestine and, in particular (at least), the Megiddo campaign after which, Useramun's tomb implied, Crete became part of Egypt's empire). They wanted to be loyal to Thutmose III "in order that his might should... protect them". The word "protectorate", more familiar to us from the more recent history of the British Empire, did not then exist but what does this caption say other than that the Cretans and Aegeans sought to become a protectorate of Egypt (thus becoming part of Egypt's empire)? For a period, this is exactly what happened and, under the terms of a treaty (sworn on oath) (a treaty of accession, in modern parlance), Crete became an Egyptian protectorate and, as explicitly stated and portrayed in the tombs of Useramun and Rekhmire, and portrayed in the tomb of Senenmut, they paid tribute for that privilege. Only from the caption in Rekhmire's tomb do we get an indication of why

---

58. David Lorton, *The Juridical Terminology of International Relations in Egyptian Texts through Dynasty XVIII* (The John Hopkins University Press: Baltimore, 1974), pp136–144
59. Kurt Sethe, *Urkunden der 18. Dynastie, Abteilung IV, Band III* (Leipzig: JC Hinrichs'sche Buchandlung, 1907), 759, 8–15, cited in David Lorton, *The Juridical Terminology of International Relations in Egyptian Texts through Dynasty XVIII* (The John Hopkins University Press: Baltimore, 1974), p138. See also James Henry Breasted, *Ancient Records of Egypt: Volume 2* (Champaign: University of Illinois Press, 2001), p190, paragraphs 441–442

they voluntarily submitted to the King of Egypt, and it is the political act of submission by the Chiefs of Crete and (certain of) the Aegean Islands that is portrayed together with their resulting payment of tribute.

After the long period of Crete being under significant Egyptian influence, the choice of Egypt as protector was a natural one if the (what would have to have been exceptional) circumstances demanded it. At this stage it is appropriate to have a brief excursus to set out why the Cretans and Aegeans voluntarily submitted themselves to Egyptian rule.

> ### Excursus 4.3: The end of the Minoan Empire and the coming of the Egyptians (before the Greeks)
>
> Writing in the 5th Century BC (so, 1,000 years after the events we are discussing) Herodotus tells us of a failed Minoan military expedition to the island of Sicily and the destruction of the Minoan fleet:
>
> *"Minos, according to tradition, went to Sicania, or Sicily, as it is now called, in search of Daedalus, and there perished by a violent death. After a while the Cretans, warned by some god or other, made a great expedition into Sicania, all except the Polichnites and the Praesians, and besieged Camicus (which in my time belonged to Agrigentum) by the space of five years. At last, however, failing in their efforts to take the place, and unable to carry on the siege any longer from the pressure of hunger, they departed and went [on] their way. Voyaging homewards they had reached Iapygia, when a furious storm arose and threw them upon the coast. All their vessels were broken in pieces; and so, as they saw no means of returning to Crete, they founded the town of Hyria, where they took up their abode, changing their name from Cretans to Messapian Iapygians, and at the same time becoming inhabitants of the mainland instead of islanders...*"[60]
>
> After a digression, Herodotus returns to the story:
>
> *"...the Praesians say that men of various nations now flocked to Crete, which was stript [sic] of its inhabitants; but none came in such numbers as the Grecians..."*[61]
>
> Herodotus' account appears to be the most reliable,[62] but he is not alone in recording a naval and military catastrophe. Diodorus Siculus, in the 1st Century BC (400 years

---

60. Herodotus, *The Histories* (VII.170.1–2)
61. Herodotus, *The Histories* (VII.171.1)
62. As we shall see subsequently, the Flotilla Fresco in the so-called West House in ancient Akrotiri on Thera (modern Santorini) depicts Thutmose III travelling to Crete to receive the submission of the Cretan and (certain) Aegean Island chiefs. It seems reasonable to expect that the accompanying fresco, the "Assembly on the Hill and the Ship Wreck", portrays the events leading up to the calamitous outcome of the Minoan expedition to Sicily, especially given that, from what little remains, the details appear to agree with the details of Herodotus' account (i.e. the ships are wrecked, not burned): https://web.archive.org/web/20120306172922/http://www.

after Herodotus), less plausibly recorded that Minos was murdered in Sicily whilst bathing and the Cretan fleet was burned whilst ashore.[63]

The common theme in both sources, of which we can therefore have a greater degree of certainty, was that the Minoan fleet was destroyed and its expeditionary force failed to return to Crete.[64] This no doubt also entailed the loss of a substantial portion of the upper echelons of Minoan (male) society and Minoan military manpower who were either dead or unable to return to Crete (hence, perhaps, Herodotus refers to Crete as having been "stripped" of its inhabitants[65]) as well as a large proportion of its matériel. This loss would likely have had major repercussions for the Minoan Empire's relations with its neighbours on Crete as well as further afield. In both respects the situation facing the Minoan Empire was probably a critical one.

Within Crete, as we might infer from Herodotus, there were a number of peoples who did not support the expedition to Sicily (the Polichnites and the Praesians were absent, we are told). We might reasonably speculate that the destruction of the Minoan fleet and the loss of its expeditionary force drastically weakened the Minoans' position as regards its allies and as regards those that were not its allies (such as, perhaps, the Polichnites and the Praesians). Consequently, at home, the Minoans may have felt threatened.

Internationally, the destruction of the Minoan fleet and loss of its expeditionary force can also be expected to have had major repercussions, resulting in a major shift in the balance of power in the Aegean. In the First World War, at the Battle of Jutland in 1916, the Commander in Chief of the Grand Fleet, Admiral Sir John Jellicoe, was described by Winston Churchill as being "the only man on either side who could lose the war in an afternoon".[66] If the German High Seas Fleet destroyed the Grand Fleet, Great Britain would be forced into submission. The fate of the British Empire was, therefore, in Jellicoe's hands. In the 15th Century BC it seems he had a (less successful, at least when it came to tackling the forces of nature) Minoan equivalent.

In a benign geopolitical situation this might not be problematic; in this case, however, I suspect the geopolitical circumstances were not benign. It is never good practice to base history on legend. However, let us consider the mythological story of the Minotaur. As we all know seven noble youths and seven noble maidens were required to be delivered up by Athens to Crete every seven or nine years (depending on the version of the story) and they would then be eaten by the Minotaur in the Labyrinth. When it came to the third batch of victims, Theseus, son of the Athenian

---

therafoundation.org/wallpaintingexhibition/assembly-on-the-hill-and-ship-wreck/wallpainting (accessed 1 January 2021).

63. Diodorus Siculus, *Bibliotheca Historica* (IV.79.1–5)
64. As an aside, Sicily seems a long way for such a force to have travelled, and yet the Athenians did the same thing and sent a force to Sicily during the Peloponnesian War in 415–413 BC (also unsuccessfully).
65. Although, in fact, this might more likely refer to the Cretans that were evacuated to Egypt when the Egyptians withdrew from Crete in c.1424 BC (see pages 105 to 108).
66. Winston S. Churchill, *The World Crisis, Volume 3* (New York: Charles Scriber's Sons, 1927), p106

king, volunteered to go to Crete in order to slay the Minotaur. With the help of King Minos' daughter Ariadne, he succeeded and then escaped. There is obviously figurative embellishment here, but, if the reader believes myths have their origin in fact, what kernels of truth might there be in the story?

The regularity of the requirement to deliver up victims (or, one hopes, hostages – which would be more in line with Plutarch's rationalisation of the story in his *Life of Theseus*[67]) suggests, to me, a formal peace settlement imposed on Athens by the Minoans.[68] If this was a formal peace settlement, a confrontation had preceded it. The requirement for Athens to periodically give hostages to the Minoans would be to ensure that Athens kept the peace with the Minoans (rather than satiate the needs of a mythical monster) and while the periodic requirement remained it would suggest that a true rapprochement had not occurred. For me, therefore, the Minotaur legend is at least symptomatic of the enmity between Athens and the Minoan Empire. We might even consider it Greek propaganda demonising the Minoans. Indeed, as we can see from events closer to our own time, one does not create a bogeyman who comes from a friendly nation.

Picture 4.6: First World War US Army recruitment poster[69]

The loss of naval and military resources entailed by the destruction of the Minoan expedition to Sicily would likely have caused a major shift in the balance of power in Crete and the wider Aegean. The Minoans' neighbours (such as, it seems, Athens) who had hitherto been subjugated, dominated or otherwise prevented from achieving

---

67. Plutarch, *Life of Theseus* (19.4)
68. Bettany Hughes also thinks along the same lines: https://www.youtube.com/watch?v=7VJqnTlbCS0 (accessed 11 October 2020) [see 12:15–30].
69. Harry R. Hopps, *Destroy this mad brute Enlist - U.S. Army* (1918) [Photograph] Retrieved from the Library of Congress, https://www.loc.gov/item/2010652057/ (accessed 2 January 2022)

their own aspirations, would have seen this as their chance to permanently remove the Minoans as a threat. It seems likely that the surviving Minoan hierarchy foresaw this existential threat and they turned to Egypt for protection.[70]

The logical question to ask at this stage, however, is if the Minoans had lost their fleet, why did they not simply build another one? Aside from the loss of manpower they had suffered, meaning they would not have had the trained crews to man it, we can find the answer in the archaeology of Crete.

The archaeology of Knossos reveals what J. D. S. Pendlebury interpreted to be a growing shortage of wood around Knossos, the Minoan capital according to Evans,[71] from the Middle Minoan IIIB period (1650–1600 BC) to the Late Minoan IA period (1600–1500 BC) resulting, in particular, in gypsum replacing wood in building construction.[72]

It has been argued by some historians that a shortage of good oak hampered the operations of the Royal Navy during the Dutch Wars (1652–1654, 1665–1667, 1672–1674, and 1780–1784), the American War of Independence (1775–1783), and the Napoleonic Wars (1803–1815). The "timber problem" affected not only the Royal Navy, but also manifested itself in international law, in naval architecture, and in England's foreign, colonial, commercial, and forest policies.[73] However, while serious, this "timber problem" was never so acute as to have impacted on the choice of materials used in building construction in Great Britain as it appears to have for the Minoans.

There are a large number of imponderables that we are dealing with here. We do not know the size or composition of the Minoan fleet, so we do not know it's construction needs; even if we did know that, we do not know the extent of the shortage of wood near Knossos. What it is perhaps safest to say, however, is that even if there were sufficient wood for the fleet's regular replacement needs, when a shortage of wood was manifesting itself in the choice of materials used in building construction, the construction of an entirely new fleet in one go could easily have exhausted stocks that might have ordinarily been sufficient. On the basis of what information we have, therefore, it seems safe to say that the loss of the Minoan fleet and expeditionary force likely prompted a crisis in matériel as well as manpower, and the Minoan Empire simply did not have the wood to build another fleet.

---

70. It is beyond the scope of this book to consider the point, but I wonder whether Athenian 5th Century BC notions of empire, specifically a naval empire based in the Aegean, were based on the benchmark of the Minoan Empire. King Minos was credited by the Athenians as having been the first person to organise a navy (Thucydides, *History of the Peloponnesian War* (I.4.1)); Athens built its navy under Thermistocles (483 BC). Athens also later embarked upon the nonsensical Sicilian Expedition (415–413 BC). Perhaps, in respect of the latter, Athens hoped to succeed where the Minoans had failed?
71. Sir Arthur Evans, *The Palace of Minos: A comparative account of the successive stages of the early Cretan civilization as illustrated by the discoveries at Knossos. Volume 1* (London: Macmillan and Co, Ltd, 1921), p533 footnote 1
72. J. D. S. Pendlebury, *A Handbook to the Place of Minos: Knossos* (2nd Ed.)(London: Macdonald and Jane's, 1974), pp35, 59, 66
73. Robert G. Albion, *Forests and Sea Power: The Problem of the Royal Navy 1652–1862* (Cambridge: Harvard University Press, 1926), ppvii-ix

Who did have the wood to build the new navy needed to protect Crete? From 1457 BC, Egypt. In 1457 BC, following his victory at the Battle of Megiddo, Thutmose III captured the Levant ports of Tyre, Sidan, and Byblos.[74] These are the victories that the chiefs of Crete and the Aegean Islands had heard of, as recorded in the tomb of Rekhmire and which led to them requesting "the vital breath" (of life) from Thutmose III; these had given Egypt control of the export of cedar from Lebanon which the Minoans now needed to rebuild their fleet. Scarcity of resources in Crete and Egyptian military success in Syria-Palestine forced the Minoans into a deal with the Egyptians. If Crete were to be protected by a new fleet, then that fleet would now have to be Egyptian.

Is the notion of one nation voluntarily surrendering its sovereignty to another realistic? Examples have happened in history, and I cite two here, both of which occurred when an adverse balance of power necessitated it.

The first example occurred in AD 1885 when King Khama III sought Great Britain's protection for Bechuanaland (now mostly Botswana) in order to forestall the encroachment of Boer freebooters from the south and German colonists from the west. The balance of power then prevailing was clearly not in Bechuanaland's favour. British missionaries, such as John Mackenzie who championed Bechuanaland's cause, had "preceded the flag", so there was at least a degree of cultural affinity that facilitated King Khama III's appeal to Great Britain. In response most of Bechuanaland became a protectorate and remained part of the British Empire until 1966.

The second example is Great Britain itself, after World War Two. Although victorious in the war, Great Britain was exhausted. Facing an adverse balance of power in Europe, with the Soviet Block facing down Western Europe, Great Britain was forced to join the (informal) American Empire. This ensured that the British (and Western European) way of life endured and Soviet expansion did not fill the power vacuum left by Britain's wartime exhaustion (and France's military defeat). As Hastings Ismay, the first Secretary General of NATO, said NATO's purpose (and, though he did not say it, British foreign policy) was "to keep the Soviet Union out, the Americans in, and the Germans down".[75] For Great Britain, in becoming part of the American Empire, the very high degree of cultural affinity between the two nations meant that the move was not an overly difficult one.

The Minoans faced this same choice after the destruction of their fleet and the loss of their expeditionary force. They wanted to keep at least certain Greeks out (legend indicates this included the Athenians), the Egyptians in, and, perhaps, the dissenting Cretans down (be they wayward allies or troublesome unallied neighbours). The Minoans (as did Great Britain after World War Two) had to make the best of the bad

---

74. Richard A, Gabriel, *Thutmose III: The Military Biography of Egypt's Greatest Warrior King* (Washington, D.C.: Potomac Books, Inc., 2009), p120. As we have noted, like the capture of Joppa (Jaffa), the capture of these ports is not explicitly recorded in the Annals.
75. https://www.nato.int/cps/en/natohq/declassified_137930.htm (accessed 27 December 2021)

situation in which they found themselves. They probably hoped that by becoming an Egyptian protectorate it would result in relatively little cultural change given that parts of Crete had been subject to significant Egyptian influence for centuries (indeed, given that I have drawn on the example of mosques in Constantinople as exemplifying this relationship, this view is perhaps even mirrored in the extreme sentiment of the last Byzantine *megas doux* (commander in chief of the navy) and *mesazon* (chief minister) Loukas Notaras who, presumably feeling less affinity with the Latin west than with the Muslim Ottomans, the historian Doukas records as saying "I would rather see a Turkish turban in the midst of the City [i.e. Constantinople] than the Latin mitre"[76]). As a result of the degree of cultural affinity that already existed between Crete and Egypt, the move was an easier one.

The Minoans, therefore, simply asked for Egypt's protection (as the caption in Rekhmire's tomb records). While the difference in wording between the captions relating to Crete and Syria-Palestine has been noted by some historians, Panagiotopoulos, for example, rightly drawing the distinction between the Cretans who had "heard" (*nḥtw*) of Thutmose III's victories and the Syria-Palestinians who had "seen" (*m33*) them,[77] they have not, however, concluded as to its significance. This difference in language reflects Crete voluntarily becoming part of the Egyptian empire in contrast to the Syria-Palestinians who were conquered by it. They both became, nonetheless, subject territories of the same empire and their chiefs became vassals of the same king.

Despite all the evidence pointing towards Crete being part of Egypt's empire, and this being explicitly stated in Rekhmire's tomb, historians have concluded otherwise. I imagine this is probably because it is not (or, rather, no longer) explicitly stated to have been the case on the Annals, which we consider later in this chapter, and it perhaps being too difficult to believe that Crete had belonged to another nation before being conquered by the Mycenaeans. As Lady Bracknell might say, to be subjugated by one people may be regarded as a misfortune; to be subjugated by two looks careless!

Historians have had to draw upon extraneous evidence to address the contradiction between Crete's stated vassal and (incorrectly) believed non-vassal status in the caption in Rekhmire's tomb. Panagiotopoulos writes:

"The fact that dignitaries from subjugated cities retained a gift-based political relationship with their overlord is not contradictory to their status, since the giving of compulsory gifts to pharaoh[s] is well attested in the correspondence of the Amarna archive about a century later."[78]

---

76. Doukas, *Historia Turco-Byzantina* (37.10)
77. Diamantis Panagiotopoulos, "Foreigners in Egypt in the time of Hatshepsut and Thutmose III", in E. Cline & D. O'Connor (Eds.), *Thutmose III: a new biography* (Ann Arbour: University of Michigan Press, 2006), pp397–398
78. Diamantis Panagiotopoulos, "Foreigners in Egypt in the time of Hatshepsut and Thutmose III", in E. Cline & D. O'Connor (Eds.), *Thutmose III: a new biography* (Ann Arbour: University of Michigan Press, 2006), pp374–375

This analogy is, however, fallacious and an important distinction needs to be drawn. Diplomatic gifts may well have accompanied correspondence between subjugated local vassal princes and their overlord the King of Egypt (and, similarly, independent kings and the King of Egypt), but that correspondence would have been delivered by an emissary; the chiefs (or princes) did not travel with the gifts that accompanied written correspondence as the correspondence, and emissary, would have then served no purpose with in-person communication being possible instead. The (figurative) portrayal in Rekhmire's tomb of chiefs themselves delivering gifts or tribute is, therefore, clearly representative of something else (not a situation akin to that recorded in the Amarna correspondence).

Moreover, Panagiotopoulos does not state which specific Amarna correspondence he is referring to, and there is certainly correspondence within that body of evidence that indicates we should not apply his point to all vassals in all circumstances. For example, compulsory gifts were demanded by the King of Egypt (either Amenhotep III or Akhenaten) in correspondence when he wrote to his vassal Milkilu, ruler of Gazru (in Palestine). He demanded that Milkilu "send [40] extremely beautiful cupbearers in whom there is no defect", but the request was accompanied by payment from the King of Egypt for the female cupbearers in the form of "silver, gold, linen garments: *ma-al-ba-ši* [the translation for which is not known], carnelian, all sorts of (precious) stones, an ebony chair…"[79] The Amarna correspondence reveals that "gifts" had to be paid for; while, for a vassal, their giving was "compulsory", the relationship between lord and vassal was nonetheless a reciprocal one.

The Amarna correspondence indicates, in fact, that Milkilu had been granted "the breath of life", for when "the breath of life" was granted to a vassal by the King of Egypt the vassal's rights were enshrined in a treaty sworn on oath and, in particular, it would be expected as a result that the King of Egypt would pay for what property he demanded (over and above any tribute payable) as he evidently did in this transaction. This is also exemplified in the later (believed fictional) *Report of Wenamun*, dated to the end of the 20th Dynasty, which relates the story of the Prince of Byblos (in Syria-Palestine) protesting to the king's agent, Wenamun, that payment had to be made for goods, in this case timber, when they were demanded (and they had kept the records that showed this was the case).[80] Payment was required for anything demanded over and above the tribute payable.

The caption in Rekhmire's tomb therefore describes a very different relationship to that described by certain historians. It shows the chiefs of Crete, Nubia, and Syria-Palestine in a (figurative) display of personal loyalty bearing their tribute to the king, not a relationship maintained by correspondence (carried by emissaries) accompanied by gifts. It is incorrect to conflate a gift that accompanied bilateral correspondence (and which was reciprocated) with the portrayal of a vassal chief (or prince) bearing tribute, in person, in an economic demonstration of fealty (which would not be, and was not, reciprocated, materially).

---

79. Amarna Letter EA 369, cited in William L. Moran, *The Amarna Letters* (Baltimore & London: The John Hopkins University Press, 1992), p366
80. James Henry Breasted, "The Report of Wenamon", *The American Journal of Semitic Languages and Literatures* 21(2)(1905), p106.

Another way in which historians have obliquely tried to address their irreconcilable problem of the (subject) Syria-Palestinians and (purportedly non-subject) Cretans both bearing diplomatic gifts was because local taxes were levied in Syria-Palestine (but not in Crete) and these were not visible in the Syria-Palestinians' tomb depictions. As only the diplomatic gifts are shown, Crete and Syria-Palestine can be portrayed on a par, so the implied argument goes.[81] This does not, however, actually address the specific status of Crete, or demonstrate with any evidence that it was any different to Syria-Palestine; in fact, Rekhmire's tomb portrayal and caption wording indicates Crete, unlike Punt, was on a par with Syria-Palestine (both were given "the breath of life") in the same way that both were portrayed on a par in Useramun's tomb. That they held the same status should, therefore, be the default presumption. We have already seen that, in the case of Crete, it brought tribute (as did Syria-Palestine) but, if we play devil's advocate and assume both brought diplomatic gifts, then at the same time as purportedly sending diplomatic gifts, taxes were being paid in one that was part of the empire that are invisible to the portrayals in the tombs (Syria-Palestine, it is argued), but surely taxes can equally have been paid in another part of the empire and similarly not be shown (such as Crete). Historians' implied argument, for Crete, is that absence of evidence is evidence of absence, but the fallacy of this argument is clear if it is applied equally, rather than selectively. Like Panagiotopoulos I believe the subject territories of Syria-Palestine would have paid taxes locally but record of this has not survived. However, as we saw in Chapter Two and as we will see further in Chapter Five, in Crete taxation was paid, and record of this has survived. Based solely on surviving local taxation records there is, therefore, better evidence existing for Crete having been part of Egypt's empire than there is for Syria-Palestine having been part of Egypt's empire though, of course, I am not arguing that Syria-Palestine was not part of Egypt's empire! The position that Crete was not part of Egypt's empire is really untenable.

While historians have previously believed that Rekhmire's tomb portrayed two subject peoples (the Nubians and the Syria-Palestinians) and two non-subject peoples (the Cretans and the Puntites),[82] following Lorton's correct understanding of the phrase "the breath of life", and correctly identifying why the militarily defeated Syria-Palestinians (and Nubians) "hoped" to receive it, why the Cretans "asked" to receive it, and why the Puntites never asked to receive it, we can see that the evidence tells us there were three subject peoples and, further, it shows us that the Cretans became a subject people by their own volition.

Crete forming part of Egypt's empire is further evidenced in archaeological finds from Egypt, in particular, the Golden Bowl of General Djehuty, which is our fourth piece of evidence that Crete was part of Egypt's empire. General Djehuty was an Egyptian general who served in Thutmose III's army, and his golden bowl was found in his burial tomb at Saqqara, the necropolis of Memphis.[83]

---

81. Diamantis Panagiotopoulos, "Foreigners in Egypt in the time of Hatshepsut and Thutmose III", in E. Cline & D. O'Connor (Eds.), *Thutmose III: a new biography* (Ann Arbour: University of Michigan Press, 2006), pp374–375
82. Diamantis Panagiotopoulos, "Foreigners in Egypt in the time of Hatshepsut and Thutmose III", in E. Cline & D. O'Connor (Eds.), *Thutmose III: a new biography* (Ann Arbour: University of Michigan Press, 2006), p390
83. https://www.louvre.fr/en/oeuvre-notices/bowl-general-djehuty (accessed 20 January 2022)

80   The Decipherment of Linear A

Picture 4.7: The Golden Bowl of General Djehuty[84]

The Golden Bowl of General Djehuty is, perhaps, the most ignored piece of historical evidence in the history of history (and the reader can consult historians' published works to see which historians have included it in their narratives and which historians have not; the latter will, I am sure, be the most ardent critiques of this work). The inscription on the bowl states:

"Given through the favour of the king, the King of Upper and Lower Egypt, Menkheperre [Thutmose III], [to the] hereditary noble, nomarch, god's father, beloved of the god, one who fills the heart of the king in every foreign country and in the islands which are in the midst of the sea [the Aegean Islands, here including Crete], one who fills the storehouses with lapis lazuli, silver, and gold…"[85]

As historian James Henry Breasted stated, this tells us that Djehuty was the governor ("one who fills the heart of the king") in, amongst other places it seems, the Aegean islands (including Crete) ("the islands which are in the midst of the sea").[86] This evidence is vital in two respects.

---

84. *Coupe au nom du général Djéhouty* © Musée du Louvre
85. Christine Lilyquist, "The Gold Bowl Naming General Djehuty: A Study of Objects and Early Egyptology", *Metropolitan Museum Journal* 23(1988), p25. Explanatory text in square brackets in the translation is my own, and is consistent with James Henry Breasted's interpretation (see James Henry Breasted, *Ancient Times: A History of the Early World* (Ginn and Company, Boston, 1944), p298). For the avoidance of doubt, I give no credence whatsoever in Claude Vandersleyen's subsequent theory regarding the bowl inscription, namely that the islands "in the midst of the sea" were the islands of the Nile Delta. This wholly incorrect theory, in my opinion, seems to derive from a desire to reconcile the (false) notion that Egypt did not own Crete (and certain of the Aegean islands) with the inscription on the Golden Bowl of General Djehuty which explicitly states (in fact) that it did. Christine Lilyquist rightly has her doubts and highlights a number of issues with Vandersleyen's rationale (Christine Lilyquist, "The Gold Bowl Naming General Djehuty: A Study of Objects and Early Egyptology", *Metropolitan Museum Journal* 23(1988), p25 footnote 156 citing Claude Vandersleyen, "Le sens de Ouadj-our," *International Congress of Egyptologists' Abstracts of Papers* (Munich, 1985), pp246f, and Claude Vandersleyen "Ouadj-our ne signifie pas 'mer': qu'on se le dise!", *Giittinger Miszellen*, 103 (1988), pp75–80). My view is consistent with Breasted and his unsurpassed opinion on the matter.
86. James Henry Breasted, *Ancient Times: A History of the Early World* (Ginn and Company, Boston, 1944), p298

First, the bowl demonstrates that Crete and (certain of) the Aegean Islands became part of Egypt's formal empire during the reign of Thutmose III (as Breasted believed when he wrote in the 1940s,[87] before Linear B was deciphered and presumably made the notion of both the Egyptians and the Mycenaeans as having owned Crete too implausible to consider). Crete and the Aegean islands had an Egyptian governor because Crete and (certain of) the Aegean Islands were part of the Egyptian empire.

Second, the bowl demonstrates the omissions from Thutmose III's Annals. This record of the military achievements of Thutmose III's reign, which we shall consider next, makes no reference to a senior officer of Thutmose III's army being appointed as governor of Crete and (certain of) the Aegean Islands or why he might have received such an appointment (which was surely the result of an exceptional event worthy of record). The Annals, in fact, have been doctored and this is incontrovertible evidence of that fact. Moreover, it clearly indicates the subject area in relation to which they have been doctored, Egypt's ownership of Crete.

The Annals are, therefore, the fifth piece of evidence that helps us confirm that Crete was part of Egypt's empire. As noted above, they are an account of the military campaigns of Thutmose III and the tribute that he received, that was inscribed on the walls of the Temple of Amun at Karnak, near Thebes, covering the years 1457 BC to 1437 BC.

---

87. James Henry Breasted, *Ancient Times: A History of the Early World* (Ginn and Company, Boston, 1944), p298. Historian Michael Rostovtzeff thought the same (see, for example, M. Rostovtzeff, *Caravan Cities* (Oxford: Clarendon Press, 1932), p15).

Picture 4.8: The Temple of Amun at Karnak with the Annals[88]

The Annals tell us that they were inscribed in 1437 BC, after the campaigns they relate.[89] They are a written history and as with all histories the bias of the author (or commissioner) will be present. In particular the Annals are an official history and the bias of the state that commissioned that official history (or, more particularly in the ancient world, the ruler of the state) will be present. We would, therefore, expect the Annals to have exhibited the propaganda wishes of Thutmose III when they were (literally) set in stone. More than this, however, as exemplified by the usurpation of Tutankhamun's legacy by Horemheb a century later,[90] we must also expect the Annals to exhibit the propaganda wishes of Thutmose III's successors who may also, for their own subsequent needs, have doctored the official record.

We have already noted the glaring absence of reference to General Djehuty being appointed governor of the Islands in the Midst of the Sea (Crete and (certain of) the

---

88. https://en.wikipedia.org/wiki/Thutmose_III#/media/File:ThutmosesIII-AnnalsOfThutmosesIII-Karnak.png
89. James Henry Breasted, *Ancient Records of Egypt: Volume 2* (Champaign: University of Illinois Press, 2001), p217
90. Marianne Eaton-Krauss, *The Unknown Tutankhamun* (London and New York: Bloomsbury Academic, 2016), pp35–36, regarding Horemheb's usurpation of Tutankhamun's achievements set out in the Restoration Stelae.

Aegean Islands), and why he received that appointment (surely an exceptional event in the history of Egypt and an achievement for Thutmose III worth memorialising). More generally, there are few references to Crete, prompting Panagiotopoulos, for example, to note that the "Cretans are curiously absent [from the Annals]… yet this may be due to its numerous lacunae"[91]; "may", however, suggests other possibilities, but Panagiotopoulos does not suggest what these might be.

We would clearly not expect Thutmose III to have recorded the submission of Crete and (certain of) the Aegean Islands and them being part of the Egyptian empire if they had already been lost by the time that the Annals were inscribed in 1437 BC as it would detract from his otherwise spectacular record of military success. In that eventuality Crete would probably be entirely omitted from the record. The few remaining references to Crete in the Annals, however, suggest this was not the case. Alternatively, if the details surrounding the submission of Crete and (certain of) the Aegean Islands being part of the Egyptian empire were originally recorded but they were subsequently (irretrievably) lost by Egypt, we would expect reference to them to have been removed from the permanent record (perhaps, however, leaving some of the more innocuous references that might otherwise be explained away). If they did not, and Crete was lost after 1437 BC by Thutmose III or one of his successors, it would publicly highlight that king's failings.

With the latter seemingly more likely, and with our likely date range of 1457 BC to 1445 BC as to when Egypt's rule of Crete commenced, we should consider where the record of Crete becoming part of Egypt's empire might have originally been recorded. The account of the submission of one empire to another would have taken up considerable space, and with that in mind there really is only one place that it could originally have been inscribed.

I, like Panagiotopoulos, find it odd (Panagiotopoulos says "unexpected"), that Thutmose III's Annals focus on flora and fauna of Syria (referred to by historians as the "Botanical Gardens of Thutmose III"), at the rear of the temple in the Festival Hall, in the space for the Third Campaign (the record of the flora and fauna is explicitly dated Year 25 i.e. 1455 BC).[92] Panagiotopoulos notes that such a focus was "exceptional".[93] The inclusion of reliefs representing flora and fauna in a monument that otherwise records successful military campaigns and tribute being received is such an aberration that it is utterly implausible that this was the original inscription. Squarely within our date range of 1457 BC to 1445 BC, in particular after the date that Thutmose III conquered the Levant coast ports and thereby gained control of the supply of Lebanon cedar that the Minoans needed to rebuild their fleet, this is where I believe record of the Minoan Empire's submission to Thutmose III, and Crete and (certain of) the Aegean Islands becoming a protectorate of Egypt, was originally set out (together with details of the Third Campaign, which was presumably undertaken in Crete). We can infer this took place in 1455 BC.

---

91. Diamantis Panagiotopoulos, "Foreigners in Egypt in the time of Hatshepsut and Thutmose III", in E. Cline & D. O'Connor (Eds.), *Thutmose III: a new biography* (Ann Arbour: University of Michigan Press, 2006), p394
92. James Henry Breasted, *Ancient Records of Egypt: Volume 2* (Champaign: University of Illinois Press, 2001), p192
93. Diamantis Panagiotopoulos, "Foreigners in Egypt in the time of Hatshepsut and Thutmose III", in E. Cline & D. O'Connor (Eds.), *Thutmose III: a new biography* (Ann Arbour: University of Michigan Press, 2006), pp404–405

Excursus 4.4: The missing Fourth (and Third) Campaign

The Annals numbered the military campaigns that were led by Thutmose III in person.[94] As we have seen, the account of the Third Campaign is missing from the Annals, replaced by the "Botanical Gardens of Thutmose III". We have deduced that Thutmose III went to Crete in 1455 BC primarily to grant "the vital breath" (of life) to the Minoans and their Cretan allies at the time of their becoming his new vassals. Yet, a military action that constituted the Third Campaign also took place this year. The most logical location for this military action to have taken place, especially given that the account of it was also replaced by the "Botanical Gardens of Thutmose III", was in Crete.

Although it is also missing from the Annals as they survive now, we can infer that the Fourth Campaign, led by Thutmose III in person, must have taken place between Year 26 (1454 BC) and Year 28 (1452 BC) (inclusive), given that the Third Campaign took place in Year 25 (1455 BC) and the Fifth Campaign took place in Year 29 (1451 BC). It would seem most likely that, record of the Fourth Campaign also having been erased, its account appeared, chronologically, following the Third Campaign and, therefore, its account was also most likely replaced by the "Botanical Gardens of Thutmose III". Again, therefore, this suggests that it also took place in Crete (and, given the logistical effort involved in Thutmose III taking his retinue to Crete, it would seem most likely that he did not return to Egypt between campaigns, and that the campaigns took place in successive years).

What was the nature of these campaigns? As the Annals show in later years, what might be labelled as a numbered military campaign led by the King could, in reality, be quite a modest affair. For example, as historian Antony Spalinger points out, in Year 31 (1449 BC) the Seventh Campaign only records the capture of one town, Ullaza, because, Spalinger believes, the King did not conquer much territory that year.[95]

We know at this stage that Egypt did not have an ocean going navy so it could not transport a sizeable military force to Crete to undertake a military campaign. Nonetheless, Thutmose III was presumably supported by a sizeable personal retinue (of which we see evidence of the "Flotilla Fresco" which is considered later in this chapter). With a low benchmark to qualify as a campaign included in the Annals, Thutmose III would not have needed sizeable forces significantly beyond those put into the field by the Minoans and their allies plus his own retinue in order that limited local successes in two consecutive campaigns in two consecutive years could be counted as numbered military campaigns in the Annals. These could be recorded as the Third Campaign and Fourth Campaign in the Annals but they were each little more than a demonstration of power, to show the King's personal presence in, and commitment to, Crete and his new vassals.

---

94. Anthony Spalinger, "A Critical Analysis of the "Annals" of Thutmose III (Stücke V-VI)", *Journal of the American Research Centre in Egypt* 14(1977), p49
95. Anthony Spalinger, "A Critical Analysis of the "Annals" of Thutmose III (Stücke V-VI)", *Journal of the American Research Centre in Egypt* 14(1977), p45

Picture 4.9: The "Botanical Gardens of Thutmose III" at the rear of the Festival Hall, Karnak[96]

Beyond the missing reference to General Djehuty and the circumstances of his appointment, and the out of place flora and fauna being exactly where we would expect the details of the Minoan Empire's submission to be, is there any other evidence of the official record set out in the Annals having been doctored? Yes, there is.

While the reasons for doing so are not fully understood, towards the end of Thutmose III's reign, he ordered the removal of all representations of Hatshepsut in reliefs, texts, cartouches, and wherever else they appeared.[97] Where she was exorcised, her image was replaced with images of her dead husband Thutmose II.[98] Whatever the reason, it seems reasonable to conclude that one result of this action was that what had been Hatshepsut's achievements were no longer attributed to her. This process of exorcising Hatshepsut from the official record is believed to have been carried out in c.1433/32 BC.[99] It did not, however, remove all mention of her and some references survived, and, importantly for our purposes now, burial tombs were one of the locations where the record of her remained intact (because, presumably, they were sealed by the time of her exorcism).[100]

In contrast to the omission of reference to Crete in the Annals, Cretans and Aegeans are portrayed in the tomb of Senenmut, and stated and portrayed in the tombs of Useramun and Rekhmire, to have brought tribute (as we have seen, as vassals). If references to Crete's submission (and payment of tribute) were exorcised from the Annals because it

---

96. https://www.tripadvisor.com.au/Attraction_Review-g294205-d16723984-Reviews-Botanical_Garden_of_Thutmosis_III-Luxor_Nile_River_Valley.html#photos;aggregationId=&albumid=&filter=7&ff=476125306 (accessed 1 January 2022)
97. Richard A. Gabriel, *Thutmose III: The Military Biography of Egypt's Greatest Warrior King* (Dulles, Virginia: Potomac Books, Inc, 2009), p25
98. Announcement by the Ministry of Antiquities (14 April 2016): https://www.facebook.com/permalink.php?story_fbid=482652288606587&id=336764893195328 (accessed 1 January 2022)
99. Ian Shaw, *The Oxford History of Ancient Egypt* (Oxford & New York: Oxford University Press, 2003), p241. The exorcism took place 25 years after her death in 1458 BC.
100. Donald B. Redford, *History and Chronology of the 18th dynasty of Egypt: Seven studies* (Toronto: University of Toronto Press, 1967), p87

was subsequently lost it is no coincidence that record of it nonetheless survives in the same types of places where reference to Hatshepsut survived the exorcism of her name. It was infeasible (and presumably sacrilegious) to reopen all of the tombs of all of the dead to confirm which captions and portrayals needed to be updated (and these tomb captions and portrayals are, therefore, our most unbiased source as to what originally occurred). The process of exorcism in each case was similarly flawed: the flaws evident in the process of exorcising Hatshepsut from the official record are similarly evident in the process of exorcising Crete from the official record, such as the Annals. Ultimately that there were the same type of flaws in the same process (conducted at different dates) demonstrates that the exorcism of Crete and (certain of) the Aegean Islands being part of Egypt's empire took place.

The out of place flora and fauna that took the space of the Third Campaign in 1455 BC (and Fourth Campaign thereafter), therefore, gives us the date of the event portrayed in Senenmut's tomb and the event portrayed and described in Useramun's tomb (in so far as Crete (and the Aegean) is concerned), with tribute being sent back from Crete (and the Aegean) for the first time, and that exceptional event being recorded in the tombs of the officials that witnessed it. The tomb of Rekhmire (who was not yet Vizier at the time but who presumably nonetheless held a relatively senior office while his uncle was Vizier so also recorded the events) additionally relates that this was due to the submission of Cretan (and Aegean) chiefs, asking to become a protectorate of Egypt, and Thutmose III granting them "the vital breath" (of life).

The similarly exceptional receipt of tribute after the Battle of Megiddo from the Syria-Palestinians is recorded and portrayed in Useramun's tomb and Rekhmire's tomb, as well as the Annals (in Year 24 (1456 BC) as we have seen), and the receipt of tribute from the Nubians is also recorded and portrayed in Rekhmire's tomb as well as in the Annals (in Years 31, 33–35, 38, and 40–42 (1449 BC, 1447–1445 BC, 1442 BC, and 1440–1438 BC)). The receipt of diplomatic gifts from the Puntites is also recorded and portrayed in Rekhmire's tomb as well as in the Annals (twice, in Year 33 (1447 BC) and also Year 38 (1442 BC), so presumably there was a second deputation to the king and the two deputations were conflated in Rekhmire's tomb). The omission of the Cretans and the Aegeans, who are recorded and portrayed in Useramun's tomb and Rekhmire's tomb (although in the latter, importantly, they were subsequently painted over), but not in the Annals, is so conspicuous as to only be the result of the deliberate doctoring of the record set out in the Annals, after the event.[101]

This solves Panagiotopoulos' conundrum as to why Crete is largely absent from the Annals, and addresses his observation concerning the unexpected and exceptional nature of the inclusion of the flora and fauna of Syria in the space for the Third Campaign in

---

101. The reason that only the Syria-Palestinians and the Aegeans are depicted in Useramun's tomb is that these were the peoples of the two territories conquered or taken possession of, respectively, by Thutmose III (i.e. they were his achievements, during Useramun's term as Vizier). Conversely, the Nubians had been conquered by Thutmose I (1506–1493 BC), so were not included, and the Puntites had merely sent emissaries bearing diplomatic gifts to Thutmose III, so they were not included either.

The Reconstructed History of Egypt's Involvement in Middle and Late Bronze Age Crete 87

1455 BC (and Fourth Campaign in 1454 BC). It might be argued that the evidence is circumstantial (but for the translations of the Linear A records), but this date for the commencement of Egypt's rule of Crete falls squarely within the 1457 BC to 1445 BC range that can be inferred from the caption in Useramun's tomb, the believed reasons for the Minoan approach to Egypt based on Herodotus' account and the archaeology of Knossos, and the progress of Egypt's military campaign in the Levant. This is not a coincidence.

We shall return to consider when the Annals were doctored to remove reference to Crete being part of the Egyptian empire (which happened after Crete was lost). At this juncture, however, having considered the Annals' record of Thutmose III's campaigns, as ultimately preserved, and what it infers is the likely date of the commencement of Egyptian rule of Crete, let us briefly return to consider why Egypt agreed to Crete becoming its protectorate which, on the face of it, seemed to entail an assumption of potential military obligations at a time when Egypt was already heavily engaged in its campaigns in Syria-Palestine.

> ### Excursus 4.5: What was in this for Egypt?
>
> As noted above, the evidence suggests that Crete most likely became a protectorate of Egypt in 1455 BC, Year 25 of Thutmose III's reign. The years before this had seen Thutmose III conducting his First Campaign and Second Campaigns into Syria-Palestine and the Egyptians' likely experience in these campaigns suggests the principal reason for Egypt agreeing to the Minoans' request for protection.
>
> For both of his first two campaigns Thutmose III's military forces had to travel by land, across the Sinai Peninsula and into Palestine, in order to reach their area of operations. This weakened his army (in terms of fatigue as well as cost in matériel) before his campaign could even begin. It also shortened the period of the campaigning season available to Thutmose III, limiting his ability to achieve his strategic goals. He might achieve victory in a battle but he would have little time thereafter to consolidate his gains. In these circumstances, Egyptian power could never be projected to its full extent. Presumably to address this, Thutmose III constructed Egypt's first seagoing navy.[102] It was undoubtedly a force multiplier, allowing the Egyptian army to be more rapidly deployed to its chosen theatre of operations in better condition for a longer period of time.
>
> How was this change to Egypt's fighting forces actually achieved? The historian Torgny Säve-Söderberg has stated that Thutmose III was the first commander in history to conduct large-scale amphibious operations on the open sea.[103] This, of course, is incorrect for, as we have discussed, the failed Minoan naval and military expedition to Sicily predates the use of Thutmose III's navy. Nonetheless, he was the

---

102. Richard A. Gabriel, *Thutmose III: The Military Biography of Egypt's Greatest Warrior King* (Washington, D.C.: Potomac Books, Inc., 2009), p126
103. Torgny Säve-Söderbergh, *The Navy of the Eighteenth Egyptian Dynasty* (Uppsala, Sweden: Uppsala University Press, 1946), p34, cited by Richard A. Gabriel, *Thutmose III: The Military Biography of Egypt's Greatest Warrior King* (Washington, D.C.: Potomac Books, Inc., 2009), p138

88   The Decipherment of Linear A

first Egyptian able to do so on any scale for, while in the 5th Dynasty King Sahure had a navy sufficient to transport troops to the Syrian coast in 2480 BC, and, later, in the 6th Dynasty, Egypt transported troops to Palestine by sea in 2340 BC,[104] these were small affairs.

Thutmose III was the first Egyptian king in almost a millennium to conduct such operations and the first to conduct them on such a grand scale. The historian Manfred Bietak believes, and it is also my belief, that it was Cretan know-how that helped to construct Egypt's first sea going navy[105]; Thucydides tells us, after all, that the Minoans were the first to build a navy.[106] In support of his theory Bietak cites, in particular, British Museum Papyrus 10056, from the Egyptian naval base at Peru-nefer which lists the materials needed to construct and repair vessels. It also, importantly, refers to Keftiu (i.e. Cretan) ships.[107]

Picture 4.10: Record of Kefti ships in the Peru-nefer naval dockyard[108]

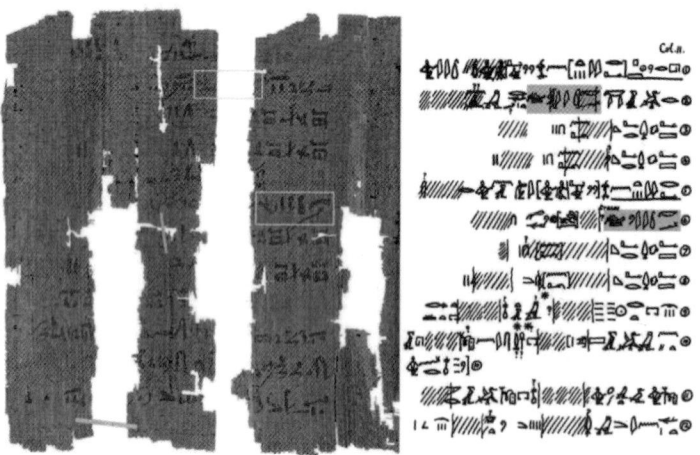

Egypt allowed Crete to join its empire as a protectorate in 1455 BC in order to gain this know-how. In the years after 1455 BC, military historian Richard A. Gabriel believes that between Year 26 and Year 29 of Thutmose III's reign (1454–1451 BC) Egypt was constructing its new seagoing navy at the new naval dockyard at Peru-nefer so that it could be used for the first time to transport the Egyptian army to the coast of Lebanon for Thutmose's Sixth Campaign in Year 30 (1450 BC).[109] It is not a

---

104. Richard A. Gabriel, *Thutmose III: The Military Biography of Egypt's Greatest Warrior King* (Washington, D.C.: Potomac Books, Inc., 2009), p138
105. Manfred Bietak, "Minoan presence in the pharaonic naval base of "Peru-nefer"", *British School at Athens Studies* 18(2010), p21
106. Thucydides, *History of the Peloponnesian War* (I.4.1)
107. Manfred Bietak, "Minoan presence in the pharaonic naval base of "Peru-nefer"", *British School at Athens Studies* 18(2010), pp11, 24
108. BM Papyrus 10056 (© The Trustees of the British Museum)
109. Richard A. Gabriel, *Thutmose III: The Military Biography of Egypt's Greatest Warrior King* (Washington, D.C.: Potomac Books, Inc., 2009), pp126, 136, 139, 140, 148

coincidence that the naval construction programme began immediately after the date we have identified as being when Crete became part of Egypt's empire.

Moreover, this is also why Thutmose III's grand palace at Peru-nefer was decorated by Minoan artists (or maybe Minoan-trained local artists). At the same time as naval construction was underway, Thutmose III's palace was decorated with Minoan-style frescoes, presumably to celebrate Crete becoming part of Thutmose III's empire (in the same way as, in the 19th Century AD, the architecture of the Brighton Pavilion reflected the imperial possessions of the growing British Empire in India.[110])

The new Egyptian navy's role was not, however, solely one of transporting the Egyptian army as it did in the Sixth Campaign in Year 30 (1450 BC). The Annals have numerous lacunae within the text that was originally inscribed, but Year 32 (1448 BC) is missing altogether. After this, however, in Year 34 (1446 BC), the Annals record, for the first time, tribute being delivered by Cyprus, of copper and lead (the former of which, at least, appears to be the most important element of the tribute), and other luxury items. Year 36 is missing from the Annals, but further tribute is given: in Year 38 (including copper but a lacuna follows what was recorded next); in Year 40 (including copper and lead again); and in Year 42 (if the unknown country that delivered copper, amongst other things, was Cyprus). It appears most likely that Cyprus had a biennial tribute obligation to Egypt, primarily of copper and lead. An obligation of such regularity suggests imposed terms. The missing Year 32 appears the most likely candidate for when these terms were imposed two years before the first biennial payment was received. For a year to be missing in its entirety suggests the record has, again, been doctored.

We can infer further details of the campaign that is now missing from this year. The campaign in Year 30 is referred to as "the sixth expedition of his majesty" (so, the King's Sixth Campaign). There is no explicit reference to the events in Year 31

---

110. Given that Crete became part of Egypt's empire in 1455 BC, we would expect the Minoan frescoes to have been painted after this date. The most recent archaeological opinion is that the wall paintings date to the first half of the reign of Thutmose III: https://www.orea.oeaw.ac.at/en/research/tell-el-daba-publications/tell-el-daba-late-minoan-wall-paintings (accessed 1 January 2022). The mid-point of Thutmose III's reign was 1452 BC; archaeologists therefore date the wall paintings to the period 1479 to 1452 BC, the final years of which also coincide with Minoans assisting naval construction. Therefore it seems most likely that the Minoan frescoes were also painted in the final years of this period.

Of course, this obviously cannot have been the case for the other (earlier) palaces that had Minoan-style paintings, namely Tel Kabri in Israel, Alalakh in Turkey, Qatna in Syria, and Dab'a in Egypt, which date to the 17th and 16th Centuries BC. If the Minoan empire collapsed in the 15th Century BC, then it might well have been at its peak in the 17th and 16th centuries BC (and, as noted, I believe the Minoan empire rose after the eruption of Santorini in 1627–1600 BC). In 18th Century AD Europe, royal palaces copied the baroque style of the Palace of Versailles of Europe's most powerful ruler, King Louis XIV: https://www.vam.ac.uk/articles/inside-the-baroque-palace (accessed 1 January 2022).

The style chosen by the most powerful ruler of the day often sets the standard that is emulated by other lesser monarchs, so we should not be surprised that the same thing occurred in the Bronze Age if Minoan styles were emulated by lesser rulers than the Minoan kings. Egypt, after all, was not the most powerful nation in this period, its north being occupied by the Hyksos for more than 100 years before their expulsion by Ahmose I (1550–1525 BC), so its style would not have been emulated at this time.

(1449 BC) constituting a campaign, but reference is made to the King capturing the city of Ullaza in the Levant, so we can assume this was the King's Seventh Campaign. After the missing Year 32, in Year 33 (1447 BC) there is, again, no explicit statement that events constituted a campaign, but we can assume that it was considered such as the King fought a battle in Naharin; that would make this the King's Eighth Campaign. In Year 34, three towns are recorded as surrendering to the King in the land of Zahi, which would be counted as the King's Ninth Campaign. In Year 35, the King is recorded as being in Zahi "on the tenth victorious expedition", so the King's Tenth Campaign.[111] What happened in Year 32 then? By virtue of the numbering of the campaigns in the text of the Annals, Spalinger is correct to conclude that, if there was a campaign in Year 32, as he believes there was, the King did not lead it in person.[112] I believe it was a naval campaign that concerned Cyprus, and the maritime nature of the campaign explains the reason for the King's atypical absence.

If Spalinger is correct, as I believe he is, to suspect that there was a campaign in Year 32 but it was not led by the King, then, as Breasted believed that the Fourth Campaign account had been recorded elsewhere but he did not know where (though we have now solved that conundrum),[113] so too must we conclude that the Year 32 campaign was also recorded elsewhere (as might be appropriate for a solely maritime campaign not involving the king).

There is other evidence for Egypt having imposed terms upon Cyprus. The Poetical Stela of Thutmose III,[114] originally located in the Temple of Amun at Karnak (the location of the Annals), states in its narrative, when the god Amun-Re addresses Thutmose III, that:

> "I [i.e. Amun-Re] have come to let You [i.e. Thutmose III] smite the West, Keftiu [Crete], Isy [Cyprus] are in awe of you."[115]

To put Crete (which we now know to have been an Egyptian protectorate) and Cyprus on a par, both "in awe" of Thutmose III, suggests, given Cyprus' apparent biennial tribute commitment from Year 34 onwards, that Cyprus had at least been coerced by Egypt into a favourable settlement. Perhaps Cyprus had previously been in the orbit of the Mitanni, as had been the Levant coast prior to it being conquered by Egypt in 1457 BC, but, I think, the arrival of the Egyptian fleet forced it to switch allegiance to

---

111. James Henry Breasted, *Ancient Records of Egypt, Volume 2: The Eighteenth Dynasty* (Chicago: University of Chicago Press, 1906), pp197–207
112. Anthony Spalinger, "A Critical Analysis of the "Annals" of Thutmose III (Stücke V-VI)", *Journal of the American Research Centre in Egypt* 14(1977), p49
113. James Henry Breasted, *Ancient Records of Egypt, Volume 2: The Eighteenth Dynasty* (Chicago: University of Chicago Press, 1906), p193
114. Cairo Museum 34010
115. Miriam Lichtheim, *Ancient Egyptian Literature: Volume II* (Berkeley: University of California Press, 1976), p37

The Reconstructed History of Egypt's Involvement in Middle and Late Bronze Age Crete 91

> Egypt, and this relationship persisted for over a century.[116] The navy that the Minoans helped the Egyptians to construct therefore not only gave Egypt a logistical capability it had not previously had, but also an offensive capability in its own right.

We know now that Thutmose III received tribute from Syria-Palestine and Crete and (certain of) the Aegean Islands for the first time in person and that this took place in person in 1455 BC, the year the Minoan Empire became an Egyptian protectorate. Although it has never been recognised as such, we are lucky that there is yet more evidence, the sixth that we shall consider, which is extraordinarily detailed and which confirms that this personal visit by Thutmose III to Crete took place (and further evidences the extent to which the Annals have been doctored).

Let us consider, first, a topographical map of the Egyptian port of Peru-nefer (or, Avaris[117]) where the Egyptian fleet was constructed with the help of the Minoans. The city dated back to the 12th Dynasty and had been the Hyksos capital of northern Egypt before its reconquest by the early 18th Dynasty Egyptian kings. It was located on the eastern Pelusiac branch of the Nile and was ideally located for travel to Syria-Palestine.

---

116. I think this relationship with Cyprus persisted for some considerable time. In Amarna Letter EA 35 (British Museum No. 29788) from the King of Alashiya to the King of Egypt (Amenhotep III or Akhenaten), the former sends a "greeting gift" (šulmānī) of 500 units of copper. The units, however, are not stated (the text says "500 copper"). This has caused some confusion amongst historians. Some translate the units as talents, but this would result in the consignment weighing 28,653 pounds (13 tonnes, to the nearest tonne). In volume, this is equivalent to 3,072 pints or, in the metric system, 1.45m³. Moran notes that it is "somewhat curious" for the King of Alashiya to apologise to the King of Egypt for sending only "500 [talents] of copper" when this is the largest amount mentioned in the entire Amarna correspondence (William L. Moran, *The Amarna Letters* (Baltimore: The John Hopkins University Press, 1992), p107, and p108 note 2). Presumably for this reason, Oppenheim translates the text as "500 [pounds (lb)] of copper" (A. Leo Oppenheim, *Letters from Mesopotamia: Official, Business, and Personal Letters on Clay Tablets from Two Millennia* (Chicago & London: The University of Chicago Press, 1967), p120). This, I think, is more accurate, though perhaps still not entirely correct. The letter is written in Akkadian and it seems incongruous to expect that anything other than an Akkadian measure of weight would have been used in it. The Akkadian Talent (as well as the Attic Talent) was divided into 60 Minas, each weighing 1 pound 1.8 ounces. If the consignment were, say, 500 Minas, they would, in total, weigh 556 pounds 4 ounces. This amount of "greeting gift" (šulmānī) or, in Middle Egyptian, diplomatic gift (inw), or even Oppenheim's believed 500 pounds, is much easier to comprehend and, indeed, would correspond to the "tribute" recorded in the Annals as being received by Thutmose III from Cyprus. In Year 34, after the Ninth Campaign, Thutmose III is recorded as receiving 2,040 deben of copper, which Breasted calculated as approximately 408 pounds (James Henry Breasted, *Ancient Records of Egypt: Volume 2* (Champaign: University of Illinois Press, 2001), p206 footnote e). I believe the two correspond to each other and the 408-pound copper tribute recorded as paid, apparently biennially, in the Annals continued to be paid, with an uplift no doubt to reflect the fluctuating value of copper (either to Oppenheim's 500 pounds or my 556 pounds 4 ounces), into the reign of Amenhotep III or Akhenaten (and perhaps even until the island was conquered by the Hittites under Tudhaliya IV or his son Suppiluliuma II (Eric Cline, *1177 B.C. The Year Civilization Collapsed* (Princeton: Princeton University Press, 2014), p99–100). Perhaps it was only at this stage that the details of the naval campaign of Year 32, wherever they were originally inscribed, were exorcised from the record.
117. Manfred Bietak, "The Tuthmoside stronghold of Perunefer", *Egyptian Archaeology: The Bulletin of the Egyptian Exploration Society*, 26 (2005), p18; Manfred Bietak, "Perunefer: the principal New Kingdom naval base", *Egyptian Archaeology: The Bulletin of the Egyptian Exploration Society* 34(2009), p15

92 The Decipherment of Linear A

Map 4.1: Peru-nefer[118]

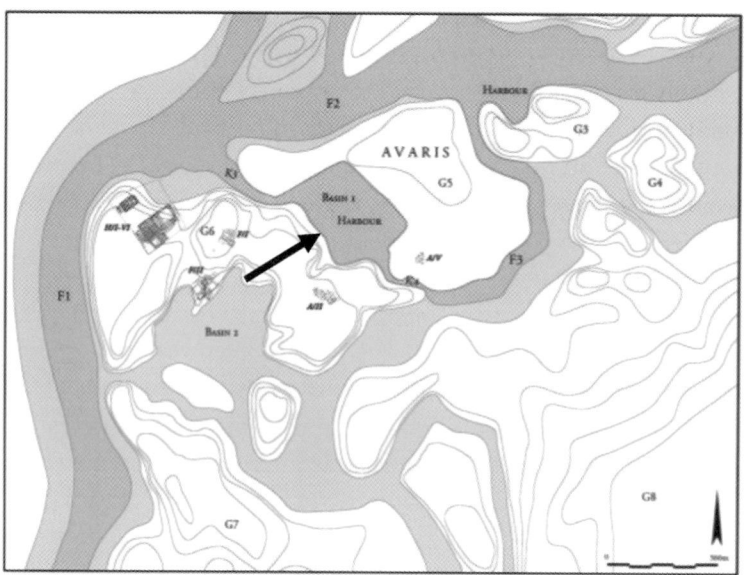

Perhaps unfairly, archaeologists and ancient historians do not enjoy a popular reputation for spatial awareness; in *Indiana Jones and the Last Crusade* (1989) Professor Marcus Brody (played by Denholm Elliott) was even said to have got lost in his own museum![119] However, this is the skill that must be employed now. We must create in our minds a three-dimensional topographical image of Peru-nefer: the harbour, the city, the island, and the Nile beyond, based on the two-dimensional map above.

Imagine, therefore, we were looking at the harbour at Peru-nefer from a raised perspective on the island opposite the harbour, in the direction of the arrow in the above map, so that we could see the horizon beyond the island in front of us. What would we see, working from the foreground towards the horizon? First, we would see the harbour basin (a promontory would extend furthest towards us on the left). Then, we would see the city beyond the harbour on the island. The island would appear to be surrounded by a waterway with land immediately beyond (on the left, the waterway is the easternmost main channel of the Nile). To the right rear of the island as we looked at it we would see two islets that, if portrayed at low tide would be joined to the adjacent headland on the right. Beyond and partially concealed by the islets, we would see the Nile branching away from the waterway surrounding the island, disappearing towards the horizon (whence it would reach the Mediterranean Sea).

Now, let us consider the "Flotilla Fresco" found in the so-called West House at ancient Akrotiri on Thera (modern Santorini), an island that was part of the Minoan Empire.[120]

---

118. Manfred Bietak, "The Tuthmoside stronghold of Perunefer", *Egyptian Archaeology: The Bulletin of the Egyptian Exploration Society*, 26 (2005), p18; Manfred Bietak, "Perunefer: the principal New Kingdom naval base", *Egyptian Archaeology: The Bulletin of the Egyptian Exploration Society* 34(2009), p15
119. https://www.imdb.com/title/tt0097576/characters/nm0001186 (accessed 1 January 2022)
120. https://web.archive.org/web/20120308114124/http://www.therafoundation.org/wallpaintingexhibition/flotilla/wallpainting (accessed 1 January 2022)

The Reconstructed History of Egypt's Involvement in Middle and Late Bronze Age Crete

This has traditionally been dated to the Late Cycladic I period (1600–1500 BC), although archaeologist Thomas F. Strasser includes it in a genre of specific landscapes (or seascapes) that had counterparts at Knossos dated to the Late Minoan I period (1600–1450 BC).[121] This latter date range naturally extends slightly beyond the Late Cycladic I period, and I agree with that latter suggestion, for the painting depicts events in 1455 BC, as will become clear. The fresco shows a flotilla of ships sailing from a port of origin on the left to a destination port on the right. It is shown on the following page.

---

121. Thomas F. Strasser, "Location and Perspective in the Theran Flotilla Fresco", *Journal of Mediterranean Archaeology* 23(1)(2010), pp3, 20

Picture 4.11: The Flotilla Fresco

The Reconstructed History of Egypt's Involvement in Middle and Late Bronze Age Crete   95

Let us compare the port of origin, on the left of the fresco (shown on the top line of the previous page) and place this next to the map of Peru-nefer, marking off seven key points we would expect to see in a depiction of Peru-nefer from the vantage point we have discussed.

Map 4.1 (repeated): Peru-nefer (annotated)

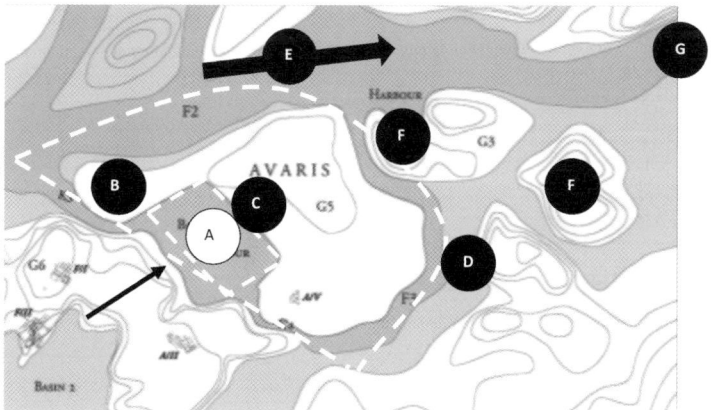

Picture 4.11 (repeated, in extract): The Flotilla Fresco (annotated)

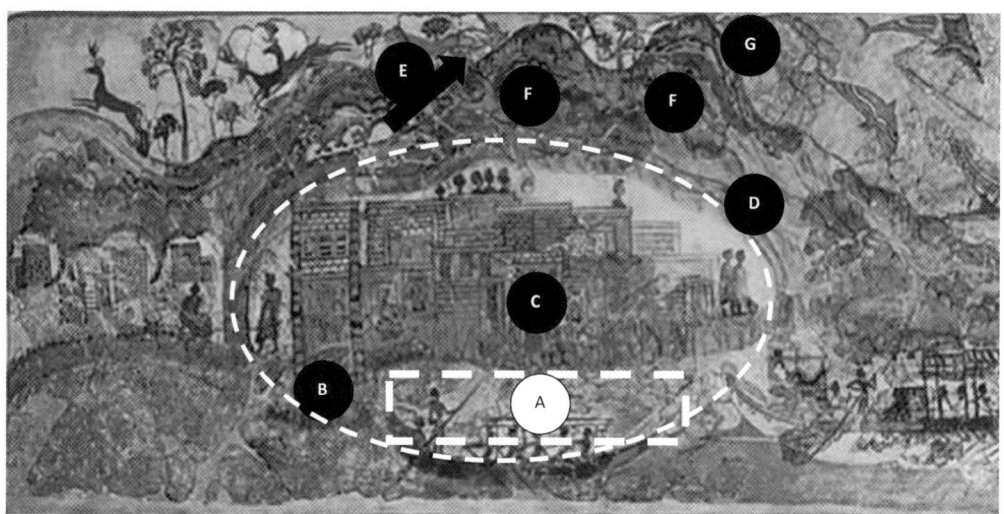

Key: Points labelled on both map and picture are:
A. the harbour;
B. the promontory on the western side of the harbour;
C. the town beyond the harbour;
D. the channel surrounding the harbour;
E. the Nile branching off behind the harbour island, to the north on the map and to the left rear of the island on the mural;
F. to the right rear of the island, beyond the channel that surrounded the island on which Peru-nefer was located, what would be two islets at high tide but at low tide would appear joined to the adjacent headland; and
G. the Nile entering the Mediterranean.

With such a high degree of agreement between the representation of the port in the Flotilla Fresco and the geography of Peru-nefer, the flotilla's port of origin as represented in the fresco can, clearly, only be Peru-nefer, with its harbour (A), the promontory to the left of the harbour (B), the town beyond on the island (C), the harbour island surrounded by a channel (D), with the Nile branching off behind it (E), as well as two hills, which would be islets at high tide, joined to the adjacent headland (F) (indicating this is low tide), and the Nile continuing behind them to where it reaches the Mediterranean (G). Yes, ships that left Peru-nefer's harbour for the open sea in real life would have sailed left round the promontory and follow the branch of the Nile towards the horizon and the sea, and not sail towards the viewer then to the right, but I think that this reflects the use of artistic licence to create the image of the journey from its origin in Egypt, on the left of the fresco, to its destination on the right of the fresco, with both harbours seen from a similar perspective. It can have been shown no other way if this was the artist's objective.

It has been thought that the flotilla's port of origin represented in the fresco was on Thera (the modern island of Santorini). Why? This is where the painting was located, and the animals depicted in the surroundings of the town are believed to have been from the Aegean. Therefore, it has been assumed, the location of the town was also in the Aegean.[122] However, an example from the British Empire shows us why this was not the case.

After the colony of New South Wales was founded in 1788, its early history was recorded in landscape paintings produced as watercolours and prints. These were of two sorts: those where the preparatory sketches were prepared in the nascent colony and the paintings based on those sketches were also executed in the colony; and those where the preparatory sketches were prepared in the colony and the paintings based on those sketches were executed back in Great Britain. Of the latter in particular, Patricia R. McDonald tells us that:

"Such images cannot be interpreted literally, however, but must be juxtaposed with current [i.e. contemporary] philosophical and aesthetic ideas emanating from Great Britain together with the demands of the engraving trade."[123]

---

122. Thomas F. Strasser, "Location and Perspective in the Theran Flotilla Fresco", *Journal of Mediterranean Archaeology* 23(1)(2010) p16
123. Patricia R. McDonald, "By Who and for Whom? British Reactions to the Landscape of New South Wales, 1788–1830", in *The World Upside Down: Australia 1788–1830* (Canberra: National Library of Australia, 2000), pp28–29

Picture 4.12: New South Wales, View of Sydney from the East Side of the Cove No. 2[124]

In the paintings executed in Great Britain, although based on sketches prepared in New South Wales, Australia was portrayed through a British lens. Consequently many of the early paintings are idealised portrayals of the new colony, shaped by the perspectives of those who had never been there. Australia was portrayed as looking like England and its countryside when it did not (and, moreover, I imagine that if those paintings are found in three and a half thousand years by future archaeologists in England, they will think that it was England that was portrayed).

The landscape (and animals) on the "Flotilla Fresco" at Akrotiri were also similarly painted more for the painting's target audience than for realism. That explains why a detailed Egyptian geographical setting has Aegean plants and animals surrounding it. Egypt is being portrayed in Minoan (Aegean) terms.

The fresco was, no doubt, expensive to produce and, no doubt, it was in the house of someone wealthy and powerful. If the house belonged to a non-governmental personage, it demonstrated a personal commitment to the new Egyptian regime. If the house belonged to an official, the fresco would have been propaganda, purposely demonstrating the similarity between Egypt and Crete in the medium of the day. In a later era, with the medium of that day, Powell and Pressburger's film *A Canterbury Tale* (1944) was intended to help strained relations between American servicemen stationed in England

---

124. John Heaviside Clark (c.1770–1863) after John Eyre (b. 1771), *New South Wales, View of Sydney from the East Side of the Cove No. 2* (London: J. Booth, 4 June 1810): https://nla.gov.au/nla.obj-135288358/view

98   The Decipherment of Linear A

and their English hosts during the Second World War.[125] In one scene in particular, US Army Sergeant Johnson (whose rank insignia stripes are (light heartedly) stated by the English characters throughout the film to be upside down, because they are not worn the British way) and the villagers of fictional Chillingbourne in Kent discuss the workings of the timber (or, lumber) industry. The evident similarities between UK and US approaches are clearly meant to show that the Great Britain and USA were cut from the same cloth. Similarly, this is also why Aegean flora and fauna appear on the fresco's portrayal of Peru-nefer. The Egyptians were being shown as cut from the same cloth as the Minoans in the medium of their day.

What, then, was the destination port at the right-hand side of the mural? Well, given that the origin of the flotilla is in Egypt, despite the mural being located on Thera, which was then part of the Minoan Empire, it is reasonable to assume that the destination for such a major event being recorded would involve the heart of that empire, Crete (and, in particular, Knossos). Having shown that the port of origin was faithfully represented geographically, the port of destination will likely be as well, and details in the painting show us the exact location of where this destination port was located. Let us consider the surroundings of the destination port and, in particular, the area to the left of it in the fresco:

Picture 4.11 (repeated, in extract): The Flotilla Fresco (annotated)

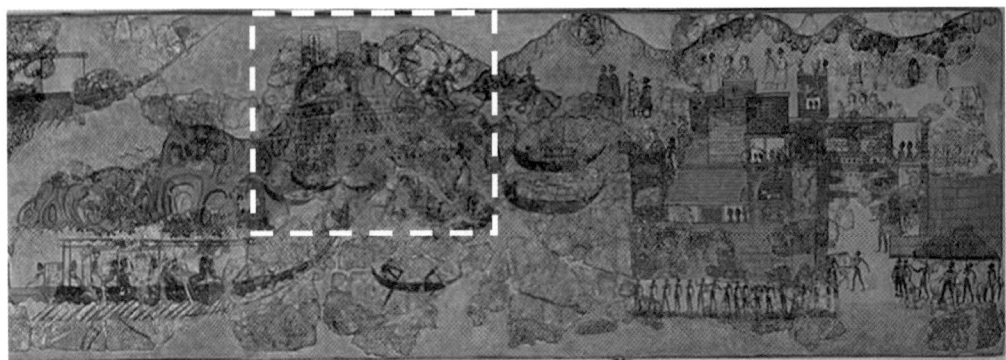

Half way to the horizon, we can see a large building and, directly behind it, a separate structure on the hilltop. Given the assumption that the destination port is in Crete, these are, respectively, a Minoan palace complex and Minoan hilltop sanctuary (with, it appears, a goddess' statue in the doorway).

---

125. https://www.cineaste.com/winter2006/a-canterbury-tall (accessed 12 January 2021)

The Reconstructed History of Egypt's Involvement in Middle and Late Bronze Age Crete 99

Picture 4.11 (repeated, in extract): The Flotilla Fresco (annotated)

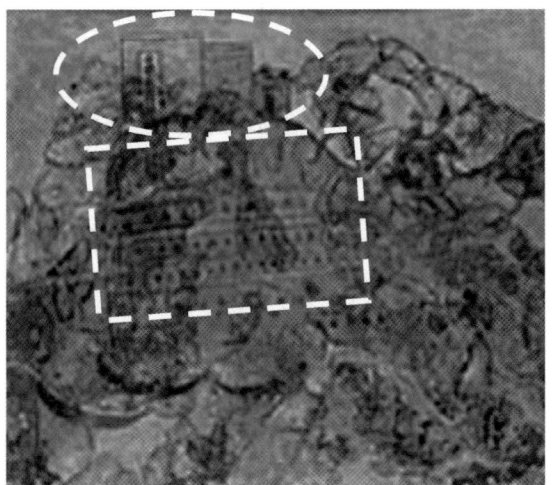

The alignment of the mountain sanctuary and the palace complex directly in front of it allows us to pinpoint the exact location we are viewing the scene from. In fact, there is only one possibility. The mountain top sanctuary is Mount Iouktas and the palace complex directly in front of it is the Minoan palace at Knossos, the capital of the Minoan Empire. Richard Bosanquet, Sir Arthur Evans' co-director of the Cretan Exploration Fund and fellow excavator in Crete, recorded that you could see the sea from his room in the upper storey of Evans' Villa Ariadne that was built next to the Knossos ruins.[126] It follows that if you could see the sea from the top of the Villa Ariadne, you could have seen the sea from the upper parts of the Minoan palace of Knossos; and if you could see the sea from the upper parts of the palace of Knossos, the palace of Knossos could be seen from the sea.

Given this, where was the artist's offshore vantage point? There must be one, because he has painted a panorama of the shoreline on which the destination port stands. If Mount Iouktas and Knossos are in line, let us extend that axis and see where it goes…

---

126. J. Alexander MacGillivray, *Minotaur: Sir Arthur Evans and the Archaeology of the Minoan Myth* (London: Jonathan Cape, 2000), p238, citing E. S. Bosanquet, *Robert Carr Bosanquet: Letters and Light Verse* (Gloucester: John Bellows, 1938), p169.

Map 4.2: Katsambas, Knossos, and Mount Iouktas

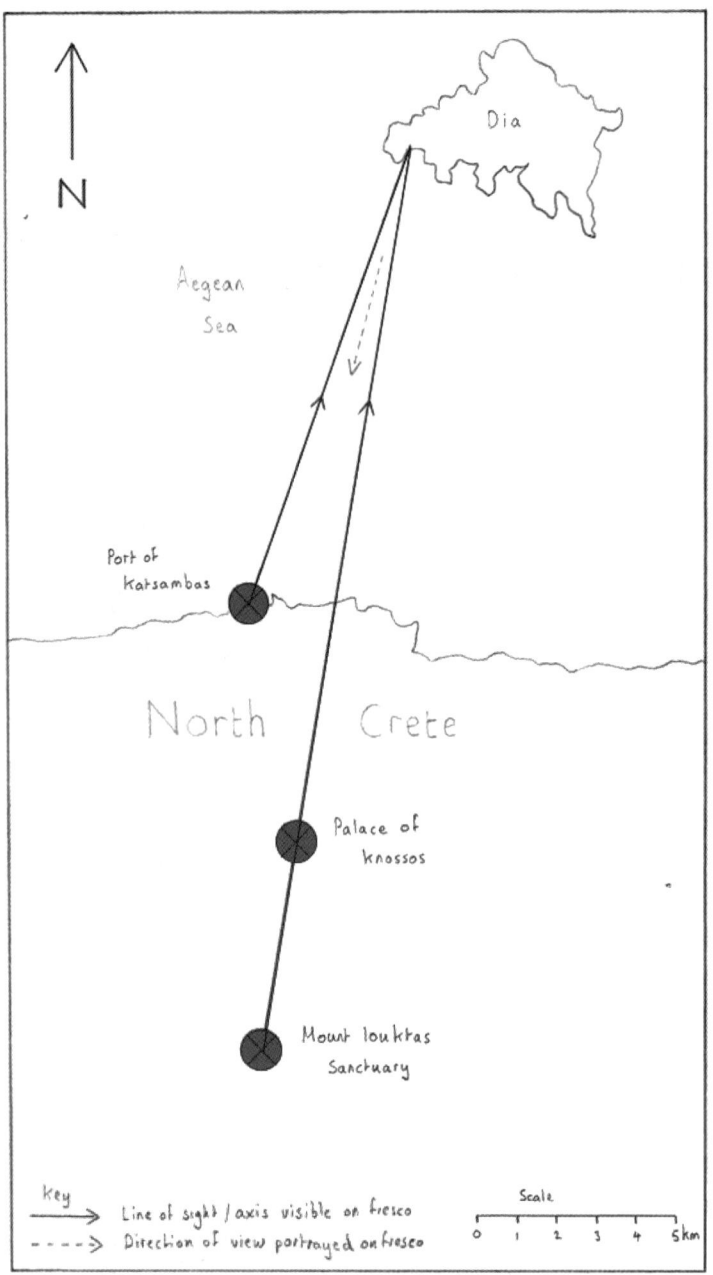

The axis goes to the Island of Dia, so this is where the artist made his preparatory sketches. We can be certain that this is the correct location for there is no other Minoan hilltop sanctuary and Minoan palace complex that align in such a way that that axis leads to an offshore island (especially one which you can then see a port from). The artist's method in Egypt and Crete was the same, with a similar vantage point offshore from the harbour and surroundings that he was to paint.

From this vantage point on the Island of Dia, the artist sat in 1455 BC (or shortly thereafter), facing the Cretan coast, and recording (or reimagining) the scene. To the right of the axis where Mount Iouktas and Knossos are aligned, the artist would see the port of Katsambas, the port of Knossos and the destination of the Egyptian flotilla.

Picture 4.11 (repeated, in extract): The Flotilla Fresco (annotated)

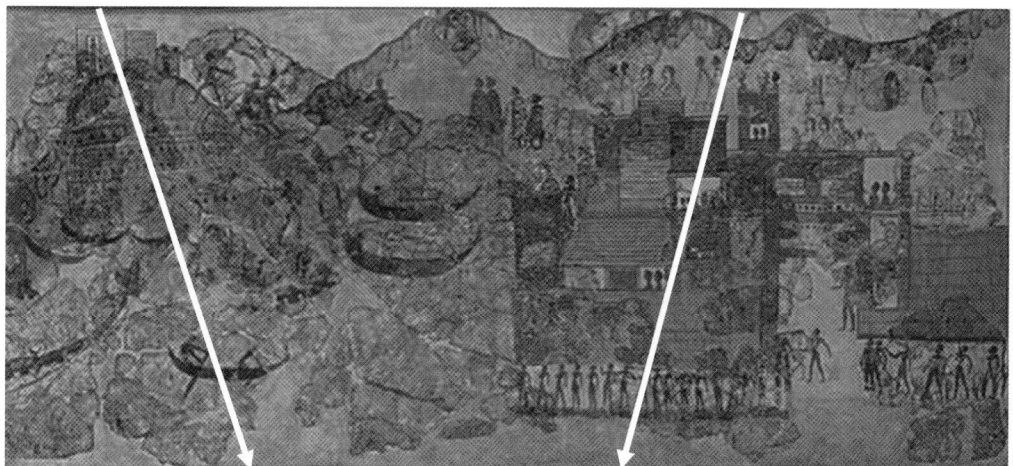

As our analysis of the caption in the tomb of Useramun indicated, Thutmose III had gone to Crete in person. Thutmose III went to receive (and send back) tribute which was subsequently received in Egypt by Useramun, the Vizier. This was implied to have taken place at a date after he had gone to Syria-Palestine to receive tribute there for the first time. The Annals indicate Thutmose III went to Syria-Palestine (Asia) in Year 24 (1456 BC) and received tribute (in person) from that territory for the first time (he had received trade goods from the chiefs immediately after he granted them "the breath of life" in the aftermath of the Battle of Megiddo the previous year, but these were not termed tribute).

From our analysis of the Annals, we can infer that, in the following year, Year 25 (1455 BC), Thutmose III went to Crete to receive the tribute (in person) from the Isles in the Midst of the Sea (Crete and (certain of) the Aegean Islands) for the first time (and that tribute, as Useramun's tomb records, was sent back to Egypt). The caption in Useramun's tomb conflates those two separate events. As regards the latter, the Flotilla Fresco is the Minoan portrayal of the arrival of Thutmose III in Crete prior to him granting "the breath of life" to the Minoan chiefs and their allies in 1455 BC. It celebrates the Minoan Empire becoming an Egyptian protectorate. This event (and the subsequent military campaigns) was what was described in the Annals before it was erased and replaced with the "Botanical Gardens of Thutmose III".

One ship in the flotilla stands out, that which is in the centre of the painting (which is where you would expect the focus of the work to be). It is the only one that has bunting flown from stem to masthead to stern. This ship is obviously carrying the most important person in the fleet.

102　The Decipherment of Linear A

Picture 4.11 (repeated): The Flotilla Fresco (extract)

The ship is also painted yellow. Yellow, as those interested in heraldry will know, is the colour used to portray gold. This, therefore, is Thutmose III's ship, for who else other than the King of Egypt would be portrayed in a golden ship travelling from Egypt to Crete? Indeed, we know that the King of Egypt had a golden river barque, for there survives a description of Ramesses III's river barque, just over 250 years later; it was:

> "…*overlaid with fine gold to the water line…a great cabin was in the midst of it, of fine gold, with inlay of every precious stone, [finials in the same of] rams heads of gold from front to rear, and [fitted] with uraeus-serpents wearing atef-crowns.*"[127]

It would have been risky to sail in such a vessel across the open seas… but, for Thutmose III, it was worth it!

* * *

The Linear A records relating to the period when Crete was part of Egypt's empire reveal most about the character of the Egyptian administration (which, given Egypt's long prior involvement on the island was likely to be distinct from its other imperial possessions). These, and what can be inferred from them, are set out in Chapter Five. Next, therefore, we shall consider how and when Egypt's rule of Crete came to an end.

There are two key pieces of evidence from Egypt which we have already touched upon that give us our best indications of when Egypt's rule of Crete came to an end. The first piece of evidence is, again, the Annals. In Year 42 of Thutmose III's reign (1437 BC, the year that the Annals were inscribed on the walls of the temple at Thebes), the Annals tell us that the Chief of Tinay (or, as archaeologist and philologist Paul Faure elsewhere transcribed the word, Ta-na-jou[128]) gave "a silver vessel the work of Keftiu", together with

---

127. Susan Redford, *The Harem Conspiracy: The Murder of Ramesses III* (DeKalb: North Illinois University Press, 2002), p91, citing James Henry Breasted, *Ancient Records of Egypt, Volume 4: The Twentieth to the Twenty-Sixth Dynasties* (Chicago: University of Chicago Press, 1906), p120 and the Great Harris Papyrus, Plate 7.
128. Paul Faure, "Toponymes Créto-Mycéniens Dans Une Liste D'Aménophis III (environ 1380 avant J. C.)", *Kadmos* 7(1968), p146

other items, to Thutmose III while he was in Syria-Palestine on campaign.[129] Historian Malcom H. Weiner states that the Tanajou are most likely to be the Danaoi.[130] The Danaoi were, as use of the term in Homer's *Iliad* tells us, the Mycenaeans.[131] That the Mycenaeans were bringing Cretan objects to the Egyptians has been taken to suggest that Crete had already been conquered by the Mycenaeans,[132] for how else could they give something from (and, as historians have correctly inferred, representing) Crete?

This interpretation agreed with the Annals as they currently stand, where the details of the Minoans' submission to Egypt in 1455 BC have been erased and replaced with the "Botanical Gardens of Thutmose III". There is no longer reference to Crete being an Egyptian protectorate as it was when the Annals were inscribed in 1437 BC and, therefore, as it was when the Mycenaeans gave tribute to Thutmose III for the island earlier that year; but there was originally, and the Mycenaeans arrived on Crete when it was still an Egyptian protectorate.

This is confirmed by the second piece of evidence we have to support the theory, namely the portrayal of the Aegeans in Rekhmire's tomb. Merrillees and others have observed that the portrayal is, in fact, one that painted over an earlier portrayal. Both the initial and final portrayals represent Aegeans but they wear different clothing:

> "The original painting appears to have had foreigners wearing loin cloths like the figures in the tomb of Sen[en]mut, but the superimposed scene depicts Aegeans dressed in different garments of the kilted type."[133]

Historian Gerald Cadogan believed this change reflected a political change taking place after the portrayal was first painted (i.e. the change from Minoan to Mycenaean control of the island).[134] Despite the logic of this assertion, it is not wholly correct because it was made absent of the knowledge that Crete was (still) an Egyptian protectorate when the Mycenaeans arrived.

The portrayal, as we have seen, originally reflected the political decision of the (Minoan) chiefs of Crete and (certain of) the Aegean Islands to voluntarily join Egypt's empire. Why would that portrayal be changed to show Mycenaeans rather than Minoans paying that tribute?

---

129. James Henry Breasted, *Ancient Records of Egypt, Volume 2: The Eighteenth Dynasty* (Chicago: University of Chicago Press, 1906), p217
130. Malcolm H. Weiner, "The Mycenaean Conquest of Minoan Crete", in Colin F. McDonald, Eleni Hatzaki, and Stelios Andreou (Eds.), *The Great Islands: Studies of Crete and Cyprus presented to Gerald Cadogan* (Kapon Editions: Athens, 2015), p136
131. Malcolm M. Willcock, *A Companion to the Iliad, based on the translation by Richard Lattimore* (Chicago: The University of Chicago Press, 1976), p4, citing Richard Lattimore, *The Iliad of Homer* (Chicago & London: Chicago University Press, 1951), p19
132. Malcolm H. Weiner, "The Mycenaean Conquest of Minoan Crete", in Colin F. McDonald, Eleni Hatzaki, and Stelios Andreou (Eds.), *The Great Islands: Studies of Crete and Cyprus presented to Gerald Cadogan* (Kapon Editions: Athens, 2015), p136
133. R. S. Merrillees, "Aegean Bronze Age Relations with Egypt", *American Journal of Archaeology* 76(3)(1972), p287
134. Gerald Cadogan, *Palaces of Minoan Crete* (London: Barrie & Jenkins Ltd, 1976), p40

That the Mycenaeans came to Crete while it was still an Egyptian protectorate means that they did so with the consent of Thutmose III. That they did so with the consent of Thutmose III means they must have become his vassals, hence they are recorded as paying him tribute in the Annals in Year 42 (1437 BC). The portrayal in Rekhmire's tomb was changed, in the first instance, to reflect this new arrangement (Rekhmire was, after all, the Vizier when this took place; the portrayal was not changed in the tomb of Useramun because he was no longer Vizier, so we know the Greeks settled on the island some time after 1453 BC–1445 BC). The changed portrayal reflects more than just this, however. As we shall see, Herodotus states that the Greeks that settled on Crete did so in significant numbers.[135] The changed portrayal in Rekhmire's tomb therefore also indicates that the Mycenaeans had supplanted the Minoans as Thutmose III's principal vassals on the island, in terms of the wealth and power they contributed to his rule.[136]

Perhaps we can also infer something of Thutmose III's style of rule in Crete at a time when he faced rebellion in Syria-Palestine and his forces, we may assume, were stretched thin; perhaps Thutmose III could not impose his rule on Crete as he might otherwise have wished (and perhaps there was even some unrest amongst some of the Minoans due to their need to support Thutmose III's perpetual campaigns in Syria-Palestine). As regards his rule in Crete, like a weak dictator benefitting from the rivalries of competing agencies and adopting a divide and rule approach,[137] perhaps Thutmose III allowed the Mycenaeans to settle and supersede the Minoans in the imperial hierarchy. That they did so was reflected in the changed portrayal in Rekhmire's tomb.

As regards Egypt's foreign (and imperial) policy, permitting the settlement of the Mycenaeans on Crete also had benefits. Thutmose III and Egypt's main land forces were perpetually engaged in Syria-Palestine, which the Annals suggests was seemingly always on the verge of, if not actually in, rebellion. This was at least part of the cause of military action: in Year 29 the Fifth Campaign suppressed the rebellion in Zahi and sacked the city of Arvad; in Year 30 the Sixth Campaign sacked Kadesh, which Breasted believes was the instigator of the revolt,[138] and sacked Arvad again; in Year 36 the Tenth Campaign suppressed the rebellion of an unnamed foe backed by Naharin (i.e. Mittani); and in Year 42 the Seventeenth Campaign suppressed the rebellion of Tunip and Kadesh. While rebellion is not stated, and perhaps the region had not been completely pacified, in Year 38 the Thirteenth Campaign also involved military action in the district of Nuges, which Thutmose III had already campaigned in during Year 34, in the Ninth Campaign. Thutmose III's empire was clearly very expensive to police and manpower resources would not have been in abundant supply.

---

135. Herodotus, *The Histories* (VII.171.1)
136. As a result of the Cretans being portrayed in his tomb as wearing kilts as they bore tribute (Theban Tomb 86), we can also infer that the official Menkheperraseneb served on as, amongst other things, Overseer of the foreign lands, until late in Thutmose III's reign (see: https://www.metmuseum.org/art/collection/search/544600 (accessed 4 June 2022).
137. David Williamson, "Was Hitler a weak dictator?", *History Review* 42(March 2002), p11
138. James Henry Breasted, *Ancient Records of Egypt: Volume 2* (Champaign: University of Illinois Press, 2001), p197

Perhaps, as the military situation became more acute, the Egyptians adopted the same solution as did the Western Roman Empire in the 4th and 5th Centuries AD. When Rome needed to increase the size of its military (and ameliorate pressure on its frontiers, which may also have been the case here, especially given subsequent Greek migration to the island), the Romans permitted peoples from outside the empire to settle within its borders as *foederati* in return for providing military levies when the circumstances required it. The Mycenaeans appear likely to have a similar obligation. This would explain their presence in Syria-Palestine while the king was on campaign; after all, the Mycenaean chief is specifically stated to have paid tribute to Thutmose III while he was on campaign in Syria-Palestine (not, ceremonially, in Egypt). Why else would the Mycenaeans have been there?

Presumably given past animosities the Mycenaean Greeks that were permitted to settle on Crete by Egypt were not Athenians (given the Minotaur myth), or any other Greeks that the Minoans had sought protection from in the first place. As with Rome, where the loyalty of the *foederati* was not guaranteed, the Mycenaeans ultimately rebelled (although, unlike with Rome, on Crete I believe a section of the Minoan populace aided the rebels[139]).

The archaeological evidence supports this conclusion. We know that at the end of the Late Minoan IB period, all of the palaces on Crete, with the exception of Knossos, were destroyed and not rebuilt. Many settlements were also abandoned or deliberately destroyed by fire. Moreover, administrative centres were particularly targeted, "indicating a desire to destroy the political infrastructure".[140] The extent of the destruction across Crete has perplexed historians, who have been unable to formulate a theory that explains

---

139. The so-called Pylos Combat Agate (https://en.wikipedia.org/wiki/Pylos_Combat_Agate), a Minoan-made engraved sealstone from the Late Helladic II period (1500–1400 BC) that was found in the Griffin Warrior Tomb at Pylos, depicts a Mycenaean warrior, wearing only a breechcloth, plunging his sword into another warrior's neck. This second warrior wears a plumed helmet, similar in style to the headwear depicted on the Chieftain's Cup from Hagia Triada (https://commons.wikimedia.org/wiki/File:Chieftain_cup_from_Hagia_Triada_01.jpg), and the Prince of the Lilies fresco at Knossos (https://en.wikipedia.org/wiki/Prince_of_the_Lilies). Given that the second warrior and his fallen comrade wear kilts of the type depicted as worn by the Cretans in Rekhmire's tomb, I take them to be Mycenaean *foederati* fighting for the Egyptians on Crete (wearing the traditional Cretan plumed helmet). Bethany Hughes believes the first Mycenaean depicted on the sealstone was the warrior buried in the Griffin Warrior Tomb: he is depicted with long hair, and ivory hair combs and a bronze mirror were found in the tomb, and he is depicted with a necklace and a sword, both of the type as found in the tomb (*Treasures Decoded*, Season 7 Episode 4: Mystery of the Golden Warrior: 25:50–26:50: https://www.imdb.com/title/tt15380176/?ref_=tt_cl_eps_sm_1). I agree with Hughes. The sealstone depicts (and commemorates) the defeat in combat of Mycenaean *foederati* fighting for the Egyptians, reflecting the successful Mycenaean rebellion on Crete with at least some Minoan support, which we can infer because the commemorative sealstone was Minoan-made. As to why Mycenaeans wear different clothing (breechcloth and kilts), we know from Herodotus that Greeks from different parts of the Greek world had different fashions (Herodotus, *The Histories* (V.87.3)). There is no reason to think that, a thousand years before he wrote, Greeks from different parts of the Greek world were any different. However, more than this, I think the kilt, whichever part of Greece it came from, was part of a generic representation of a Mycenaean *foederati* in Egyptian service.
140. Helène Whittaker, "Symbolic Aspects of Warfare in Ancient Crete", in Geoff Lee, Helène Whittaker, Graham Wrightson, *Ancient Warfare: Introducing Current Research: Volume 1* (Newcastle upon Tyne: Cambridge Scholars Publishing, 2015), p9, citing Jan Driessen & Colin F. MacDonald, The Troubled Island: Minoan Crete Before and After the Santorini Eruption (Liège: Université de Liège, 1997), pp35–41

the archaeological findings in their entirety. That there were two waves of destruction in some locations within a short timescale has similarly perplexed historians but, as we shall see, understanding this is central to understanding the evidence in its entirety.

Intuitively such widespread destruction was not the collateral damage of conquest, for conquerors (including participants in a rebellion) do not want to have to rebuild everything from scratch; they wish to retain as much as possible of the value generating infrastructure (including, perhaps, the administration) for their own future purposes. After all, as the 6th Century BC Chinese military strategist Sun-Tzu tells us, "in war, better take a state intact than destroy it."[141] In terms of magnitude, I can think of no other event in history where such a level of widespread and simultaneously targeted destruction inferred by Crete's archaeological record would have occurred other than as a result of a scorched earth policy coinciding with a military withdrawal (destroying those palaces and settlements not already lost to the rebels, which themselves had probably also been damaged in the uprising, leaving us with the picture of near total destruction that we have in the archaeological record).

We can infer that the rebellion was not, at first successful across the whole island and, for a time, things hung in the balance. Where there was only one event of destruction, then either the rebellion was permanently successful and the Mycenaeans were left in control, or the rebellion did not touch the location or was defeated without damage and only upon the Egyptian withdrawal was the location destroyed. The former scenario (namely the success of the rebellion) explains why, at Myrtos-Pyrgos, it was only the house of the local ruler (presumably an Egyptian or pro-Egyptian Minoan) that was destroyed by fire (presumably begun by the rebelling Mycenaeans) while the remainder of the site was spared.[142] The latter scenario (namely destruction upon withdrawal) also explains the lack of both high value items and human remains, despite widespread destruction, at Khania, which was presumably evacuated (Maria Andreadaki-Vlazaki writes of the populace's "timely departure").[143] This also explains why there was a lack of human remains at Pseira and Gournia, despite their destruction.[144] These were the sites that, it seems most likely, had been spared from the destruction of the first wave of the rebellion and remained in Egyptian hands until the time of withdrawal.

Where there were two events of destruction then it seems most likely that the initial wave of rebellion in that locale was defeated, but the settlement was damaged nonetheless, and the scorched earth policy destroyed the settlement upon the Egyptians' withdrawal.

---

141. Sun-Tzu, *The Art of War* (Melbourne: Penguin Group (Australia), 2009), p12
142. Sinclair Hood, "Warlike Destruction in Crete c.1450 BC", in Theocharēs Eustratiou Detorakēs (Ed.), *Pepragmena tou 5. Diethnous Krētologikou Synedriou (Hagios Nikolaos, 25 Septemvriou–1 Oktōvriou 1981)* (Héraklion, 1985), p177
143. Maria Andreadaki-Vlazaki, "LM 1B pottery in Khania", in Thomas M. Brogan and Erik Hallager (Eds.), *LM IB Pottery: Relative Chronology and Regional Differences. Acts of a Workshop Held at the Danish Institute at Athens in Collaboration with the INSTAP Study Center for East Crete, 27–29 June 2007 - Monographs of the Danish Institute at Athens, Volume 11,1* (Athens: The Danish Institute at Athens, 2011), p74
144. Sinclair Hood, "Warlike Destruction in Crete c.1450 BC", in Theocharēs Eustratiou Detorakēs (Ed.), *Pepragmena tou 5. Diethnous Krētologikou Synedriou : (Hagios Nikolaos, 25 Septemvriou–1 Oktōvriou 1981)* (Héraklion, 1985), p172

This is why there were two events of destruction evidenced to have struck the settlement and Palace of Zakros within a short timescale.[145]

Similarly, this explains why, in the Late Minoan IB period, evidence suggests preparations against attack, such as the construction of defensive walls at Makyrygialos or the reinforcement of the peribolos wall at Zakros,[146] and the stockpiling of defensive matériel, namely slingstones, at Pseira.[147] This would suggest none of these locations were the initial focus of the rebellion (which I presume, also most successfully, to have been at Knossos, especially given the elements of administrative continuity that we shall see there in Chapter Five). These were sites that, it seems most likely, had been spared from the destruction of the first wave of the rebellion and remained in Egyptian hands and were preparing to defend themselves from the rebels.

Finally, we can then see the implementation of the scorched earth policy adopted by the Egyptians upon withdrawal. At Zakros, for example, the tops of pithoi were sawn off (presumably by the withdrawing Egyptians) so that their contents would burn more easily when they were deliberately set fire to, as part of a "carefully planned and executed arson".[148]

A deliberate and pre-planned, if hurried, withdrawal (by Egypt) also explains how inhabitants had time, despite the destruction, to hide their valuables when they could not carry them away leaving archaeologists to find what have been described as "hoards" (i.e. these items were not found where they simply fell, they have been found where they were deliberately hidden).[149] At Gournia, the hoard included bronze bars (surely a repository of wealth), and bronze tools and weapons (also items of value) that appear to have been hidden.[150] At Mochlos objects made of precious metals appear to have been removed, but for two buried hoards that included two groups of bronze vessels (clearly items of value) that were both, again, apparently hidden.[151] It explains the bronze ingots (surely a

---

145. Lefteris Platon, "Zakros: one or two destructions around the end of the LM IB period", in Thomas M. Brogan and Erik Hallager (Eds.), *LM IB Pottery: Relative Chronology and Regional Differences. Acts of a Workshop Held at the Danish Institute at Athens in Collaboration with the INSTAP Study Center for East Crete, 27–29 June 2007 - Monographs of the Danish Institute at Athens, Volume 11,2* (Athens: The Danish Institute at Athens, 2011), p610
146. L. Vance Watrous, "The Harbor Complex of the Minoan Town at Gournia", *American Journal of Archaeology* 116(3)(2012), p537
147. Philip P. Betancourt and Ioannis Frangakis, "The Slingstones", in Cheryl R. Floyd, Philip P, Betancourt, Costis Davaras, *Pseira III: The Plateia Building* (Philadelphia: University of Pennsylvania Museum, 1998), pp119, 123
148. Tim Cunningham, "Havoc: The destruction of power and the power of destruction in Minoan Crete", in J. Bretschneider, J. Driessen, and K Van. Lerberghe (Eds.), *Power and Architecture: Monumental Public Architecture in the Bronze Age Near East and Aegean* (Leuven, Paris & Dudley: Uitgeverij Peeters, 2007), p39, citing N. Platon, Ανασκαφη Ζακρον, in Πρακτικα της Αρχαιολογικης Εταιρειας, 117(1962), p159
149. Hara Georgiou, *The Late Minoan Destruction of Crete: Metal Groups and Stratigraphic Considerations. Monograph IX* (Los Angeles: Institute of Archaeology, University of California, 1979), p55
150. Sinclair Hood, "Warlike Destruction in Crete c.1450 BC", in Theocharēs Eustratiou Detorakēs (Ed.), *Pepragmena tou 5. Diethnous Krētologikou Synedriou (Hagios Nikolaos, 25 Septemvriou-1 Oktōvriou 1981)* (Héraklion, 1985), p174, and Hara Georgiou, *The Late Minoan Destruction of Crete: Metal Groups and Stratigraphic Considerations. Monograph IX* (Los Angeles: Institute of Archaeology, University of California, 1979), pp11–12, 55
151. Sinclair Hood, "Warlike Destruction in Crete c.1450 BC", in Theocharēs Eustratiou Detorakēs (Ed.), *Pepragmena tou 5. Diethnous Krētologikou Synedriou (Hagios Nikolaos, 25 Septemvriou-1 Oktōvriou 1981)* (Héraklion, 1985), p175, and Hara Georgiou, *The Late Minoan Destruction of Crete: Metal Groups and Stratigraphic Considerations. Monograph IX* (Los Angeles: Institute of Archaeology, University of California, 1979), pp41–42, 55

repository of wealth rather than a votive object) and also tools and weapons made from bronze and precious metals (again, items of value) that were hidden in the Arkhalochori Cave.[152] These all reflect a hurried but orderly Egyptian withdrawal (no doubt taking with them the individuals who buried or hid their wares who, unable to take all their possessions with them, hoped that they would return to the island at some time in the future to retrieve them, forlornly as it turned out).

The success of this policy, if one can call it that, meant that whereas in the Late Minoan IB period there were 32 deliberately occupied settlements on Crete, in the Late Minoan II period (after the Mycenaean conquest) there were only 10.[153]

What of the Cretans who were evacuated? Well, historian Jean Vercoutter believed a considerable number of Cretans settled in the Nile valley in the first half of the 18th Dynasty (i.e. before c.1421 BC).[154] It seems most likely that these were the Cretans who had been supporters of the Egyptian regime and when the defeated Egyptians withdrew, as with the Americans in Saigon in 1975 and Kabul in 2021, they took with them some (but not all) of those who had supported them.[155] Perhaps no military withdrawal is ever entirely orderly.

So, why was the brief reference to the Mycenaeans left in the Annals in Year 42? Well, the Egyptians still thought of their king as the divinely ordained king of all, and if there was a singular reference to a people on a faraway island paying tribute to an Egyptian king (or, rather, what could be interpreted instead as diplomatic gifts now for, as we have seen, the Middle Egyptian word *inw*, as used on the Annals here, was the same), that was a comment that could be taken at face value and no one would question the matter years after the event (as, indeed, they have not). The ambiguity (or, perhaps, multi-faceted character) of the word assisted the Egyptians themselves at times.

When did this rebellion take place? The tomb of Rekhmire ultimately gives us our best indication. The final inscription in his tomb records Rekhmire travelling to Hatsekhem to meet the new king, Thutmose III's son Amenhotep II, after Thutmose III had died in

---

152. Hara Georgiou, *The Late Minoan Destruction of Crete: Metal Groups and Stratigraphic Considerations. Monograph IX* (Los Angeles: Institute of Archaeology, University of California, 1979), p10
153. Jan Driessen & Colin F. MacDonald, *The Troubled Island: Minoan Crete Before and After the Santorini Eruption* (Liège: Université de Liège, 1997), p38
154. R. S. Merrillees, "Aegean Bronze Age Relations with Egypt", *American Journal of Archaeology*, 76 (3) (1972), p285.
155. Presumably those that were left behind included sufficient members of the administration for at least some aspects to be successfully adopted by the Mycenaeans, such as the wool tax regime (as discussed in Chapter Two and which is further discussed in Chapter Five). While not yet fully understood, Linear B also drew from Linear A and Middle Egyptian written in hieroglyphs, also suggesting a degree of continuity from one regime to the next. Indeed, that there were Egyptians left behind on Crete by the withdrawal is perhaps evidenced; Eric Cline cites a Linear B tablet from Knossos that records the name *a3-ku-pi-ti-jo*, meaning "Memphite" or "Egyptian" in Mycenaean Greek, who was in charge of a flock of sheep at the Cretan site of *su-ri-mo*; (Eric Cline, "The Nature of the Economic Relations of Crete with Egypt and the Near East during the Late Bronze Age", in Angelos Chaniotis (Ed.), *From Minoan Farmers to Roman Traders: Sidelights on the Economy of Ancient Crete* (Franz Steiner Verlag: Stuttgart, 1999), pp126–127), citing Linear B Tablet Db 1105). As Cline notes, gentilics (personal names derived from place names) demonstrates a link between Egypt and Crete; in my opinion, there is no more likely explanation than *a3-ku-pi-ti-jo* being a descendant of those left behind by the withdrawal.

1425 BC.¹⁵⁶ Rekhmire was still Vizier but, thereafter, the narrative abruptly ceases. By this time, the Mycenaeans were on Crete (according to the surviving portions of the Annals we can infer that they had been there since at least Year 42 of Thutmose III's reign (1437 BC)) and the portrayal in Rekhmire's tomb had been changed to reflect this.

While we know that tombs took many years to complete, as we saw with the tomb of Senenmut, in the case of Rekhmire, however, I think that a combination of his age (we can be reasonably certain he was over 50 when Amenhotep II assumed the throne) and his wealth (he held the highest office in the land) meant that his tomb would have been kept up to date with all of his latest achievements. Thus, if he was removed from office in disgrace as is hypothesised, we can infer that this disgrace arose shortly (perhaps very shortly) after 1425 BC. Historian Sigrid Hodel-Hoenes believes that Rekhmire may have fallen from royal favour because of Amenhotep II's policy of appointing his favourites to high political positions.¹⁵⁷ This is, however, to mix cause and effect.

Given that Rekhmire was Vizier when the Mycenaeans were allowed to settle on Crete, when that policy failed, and the Mycenaeans rebelled, it seems most likely that it was he who received the political blame for it (after all, Thutmose III was dead and Amenhotep II, as king, could not be seen to be at fault). Amenhotep II, therefore, blamed Rekhmire and, as has been inferred but it has not been known why, he left office in disgrace. Shortly after 1425 BC, therefore, is the best date we can give for the end of Egyptian rule on Crete. Moreover, it was, therefore, most likely Amenhotep II who doctored the Annals when he could not recover the island. Crete having been lost, he did not want to suffer the embarrassment of his inability to recover it. The story of the end of the Minoan Empire was, therefore, lost to history because Amenhotep II could not maintain the empire he inherited from his father and he did not want posterity to know that.

At this juncture we shall make another excursus to consider why Herodotus does not explicitly state that Crete was once owned by Egypt.

> ### Excursus 4.6: Why Herodotus does not state that Egypt owned Crete
>
> Despite Amenhotep II's efforts to erase the episode from history, he was not wholly successful. Herodotus, for example, does make an oblique reference to Crete having been part of Egypt's empire. Let us return to the second part of the Herodotus' quote that we considered earlier (in Excursus 4.3), namely:
>
> *"…the Praesians say that men of various nations now flocked to Crete, which was stript [sic] of its inhabitants; but none came in such numbers as the Grecians…"*¹⁵⁸

---

156. Norman de Garis Davies, *The Tomb of Rekh-mi-re' at Thebes: Volume 1* (New York: The Metropolitan Museum of Art Egyptian Expedition, 1943), p27
157. Sigrid Hodel-Hoenes, *Life and Death in Ancient Egypt: Scenes from Private Tombs in New Kingdom Thebes* (Ithaca and London: Cornell University Press, 2000), p140 citing Wolfgang Helck, *Untersuchungen zu den Beamtentitlen des ägyptischen Alten Reiches* (Glückstadt, Hamburg, New York: J. J. Austin, 1954), pp294–295
158. Herodotus, *The Histories* (VII.171.1)

Herodotus states that the men of "various nations" (plural) flocked to Crete, most numerous of whom were the Grecians. While the most numerous, they were <u>not the only</u> foreigners to visit upon the island as the final comparative statement indicates; the Greeks came to Crete in greater numbers than the other unnamed foreigners. Moreover, the Greeks are also suggested to have been the last to flock to the island as they are mentioned last and, indeed, we know it was the Mycenaeans who ultimately ended up in possession of the island. Therefore, whoever the other foreigners were, we know they came to the island before the Grecians and we know they came to Crete in lesser numbers than (ultimately) did the Grecians.

Whilst they are alluded to, why does Herodotus not expressly state that it was the Egyptians who preceded the Greeks, and that, for a short period, Crete was part of Egypt's empire before the Mycenaean conquest of the island? There are two reasons.

First, Herodotus claims to have travelled to Egypt and relied upon Egyptian sources for portions of his work. His journey to Egypt was, however, roughly a thousand years after the events we are considering in Crete, and his Egyptian sources may have had their deficiencies. Herodotus tells us, for example, that he spoke to the priests in Memphis, Heliopolis, and Thebes (where the Temple of Karnak, and the Annals, was located).[159]

If Herodotus relied on Egyptian priests for his knowledge, and the Egyptian priests relied upon inscriptions for their knowledge, and their inscriptions had been doctored, Herodotus' work was at risk of importing the bias of his sources (or, rather, the bias of his sources' sources). In particular, if his sources' sources included the Annals, we now know this had significant deficiencies due to Amenhotep II exorcising all explicit references to Egypt owning Crete.

This, however, posed a problem for Herodotus as a different oral tradition evidently existed in Crete. What exactly the Praesians recalled is not stated, but people from another nation which, given the evidence already discussed could only be Egypt, also "flocked to Crete". Herodotus' two sources were ultimately, therefore, irreconcilable: an oral tradition in Crete, and Egyptian sources ultimately based on written records. The latter would typically be more reliable than an oral tradition, despite the oral tradition's specificity (we may infer). This is why Herodotus uses the opaque term "various nations". Like many of today's ancient historians, he hedged his bets. Herodotus truly was the Father of History!

Secondly, Herodotus was Greek and, when he wrote, Crete was Greek. He may not have wished to state that the Egyptians had owned Crete before the Greeks (especially if the Praesians recalled that the Egyptians had taken ownership of Crete by invitation rather than by conquest as had the Mycenaeans). To do so would be to acknowledge that the Egyptians had a better claim to the island than the Greeks (hopefully sufficient time has passed that the good people of Greece will not object

---

159. Herodotus, *The Histories* (II.3.1)

The Reconstructed History of Egypt's Involvement in Middle and Late Bronze Age Crete 111

> to me writing this now!). While elsewhere in *The Histories* Herodotus presents both evidentiary arguments when they are in conflict,[160] here he does not for this reason. When historians write they have an agenda and Herodotus' omission here was driven by his Greek pro-Greek sentiment.
>
> Herodotus' account is, therefore, to quote one of the great Presidents of the United States, Bill Clinton, "both true and misleading". Like President Clinton's testimony, it is intentionally so.

Having examined, and re-examined, the evidence the conclusion is plain; from 1455 BC up to c.1424 BC, Crete was part of Egypt's empire.[161] So, what happened next between Crete and Egypt?

Postscript – Creto-Egyptian relations after the Late Minoan IB period (after c.1424 BC)

After Egypt withdrew from Crete it was some time before there was a true rapprochement between the Greeks and the Egyptians. The first evidence we have that this took place dates from the reign of the Egyptian king Amenhotep III (1379–1342 BC) and is found on the base of one of the five (V) statues of Amenhotep III in the northern (N) half of the west (W) portico of the Peristyle Court (P) in his mortuary temple at Kom el-Hetan on the west bank of the Nile across from Karnak (Statue Base List E_N PWNV). Around the head of the base of the statue there is a caption that reads:

> "…all of the difficult lands north of Asia. All of the lands of the Phoenicians and Nubia are at the feet of this great god… the great ones of all of the southern and the northern foreign lands, who did not know to come to Egypt since the god's time, come on their knees united in one place so that the breath of life may be given to them, their tribute on their backs."[162]

The statue base was evidently incomplete with inscriptions beneath this only on the front face and left side of the base (beneath the right foot of the statue). Indeed the five statue bases that survive in the northern half of the East Portico are not inscribed at all and this has been assumed to be because they were also incomplete.[163]

---

160. See, for example, the differing histories of the Carians given to Herodotus by the Cretans and the Carians themselves, both of which he records (Herodotus, *The Histories* (I.171.2,5–6)).
161. If I may be so bold, I would, in fact, suggest that the Late Minoan IB and Late Minoan II period dates are adjusted to reflect this. I would end the Late Minoan IB period in 1455 BC (as opposed to 1450 BC), and I would begin the Late Minoan II period in c.1424 BC (as opposed to 1450 BC). The period in between, from 1455 BC to c.1424 BC would become the Late Minoan IIIC period. Perhaps, indeed, the time has come for us to rename the Late Minoan II period onwards as Mycenaean, since that is what we have known them to be since the 1950s.
162. Eric H. Cline and Steven M. Stanish, "Sailing the Great Green Sea? Amenhotep III's "Aegean List: from Kom el-Hetan, Once More", *Journal of Ancient Egyptian Interconnections* 3(2)(2011), p7
163. Eric H. Cline and Steven M. Stanish, "Sailing the Great Green Sea? Amenhotep III's "Aegean List: from Kom el-Hetan, Once More", *Journal of Ancient Egyptian Interconnections* 3(2)(2011), p7, citing H. Sourouzian,

In the centre of the front face of the statue base, beneath the caption there are two cartouches bearing Amenhotep III's prenomen and nomen. The cartouches rest upon the heads of two squatting and bound prisoners. On either side facing these are further depictions of standing but bound prisoners, two on the right with space for a third and three on the left. On the left hand side of the statue base are a further twelve standing bound prisoners face right towards the front of the statue. All prisoners have superimposed upon them a crenelated oval (a cartouche-like oval with a crenelated edge, as if a city wall). On the front face, to the right of the king's name, these crenelated ovals state the place names *Keftiu* (Crete) (closest to the king's name) and *Tanaja* (Greece) (furthest from the king's name). On the front face, to the left of the king's name, they state, left to right, the place names Kydonia, Phaistos, and Amnisos (all in Crete). On the left face of the statue base, left to right, were: two unknown locations; Siteia (Crete); Lyktos (Crete); Amnisos (Crete); Knossos (Crete); Eleia (Crete) (or Elos (Greece) or Aulis (Greece)); Kythera (Greek island); Naupilion (Greece); Messenia (Greece); Thebes (Greece) or Tegea (Greece); and Mycene (Greece).

Picture 4.13: Front face of statue base E_N PWNV, Kom el-Hetan[164]

R. Stadelmann, N. Hampikian, M. Seco Alvarez, I. Noureddine, M. Elesawy, M. A. López Marcos, and C. Perzlmeier, "Three seasons of work at the temple of Amenhotep III at Kom El Hettan. Part III: Works in the dewatered area of the Peristyle Court and the Hypostyle Hall", *Annales du Service des Antiquités de l'Égypte* 80(2006), p414

164. John Strange, *Caphtor / Keftiu: A new investigation* (Acta theologica Danica Vol. 14, Leiden: Brill, 1980) p22 Fig. 1 Text no. 3, statue-base at Kom el-Hetan, front

The Reconstructed History of Egypt's Involvement in Middle and Late Bronze Age Crete   113

Picture 4.14: Left side of statue base E$_N$ PWNV, Kom el-Hetan[165]

The order of the individual place names (from left side left (Crete) to left side right (Greece) to front face left (Crete again), i.e. Crete – Greece – Crete), has prompted some historians, such as Eric Cline, to believe that this represents a diplomatic voyage.[166] It does not (and, it seems, I am not the only one who thinks so[167]). Indeed, we cannot take the order of place names as significant as the statue base was unfinished.

Confusion has arisen exactly because the place names, their order, and the statue base more broadly, were never completed and evidently went through a number of phases of being inscribed where the place name inscriptions were changed but where the ultimately intended arrangement was never arrived at. It is known, for example, that the three cartouches on the left of the king's name were changed from all being Greek cities to all being Cretan cities. Thus, rather than viewing the final series of cities as being Cretan – Greek – Cretan (which has led to the mistaken belief that this represented the itinerary of a voyage), the replacement of the three Greek cities on the front with Cretan cities shows us that the inscription order was being changed from the initial Cretan – Greek (running from left side left to front face middle) to Greek – Cretan, but only the front side's three cartouches were changed before work halted. This is why Amnisos appears twice; its later (ultimate) position was on the front face, and its former position (where it still also remains because it had not been overwritten when work halted) was in the middle of the left side. This was also the case with Amyklai. It was originally inscribed on the left hand side of the front face of the statue base, then it was moved to appear closest to the king's name (so it now appeared twice because the original had not been removed at

---

165. John Strange, *Caphtor / Keftiu: A new investigation* (Acta theologica Danica Vol. 14, Leiden: Brill, 1980) p23 Fig. 1 Text no. 3, statue-base at Kom el-Hetan, left side nos. 5–12
166. Eric H. Cline and Steven M. Stanish, "Sailing the Great Green Sea? Amenhotep III's 'Aegean List: from Kom el-Hetan, Once More", *Journal of Ancient Egyptian Interconnections* 3(2)(2011), pp9, 11
167. For example, historian Nicholas Reeves appears to have his doubts (see Nicholas Reeves, *Akhenaten: Egypt's False Prophet* (London: Thames & Hudson, 2001), p57).

this stage) before it was removed from the front altogether presumably to be inscribed in another location on the base, in which it never was because the base was never completed.

These were stylistic changes, and no particular significance is demonstrated beyond that. Having the Cretan place names closest to the king's name on the left matched the country names to the right of the king's name, where Crete was also closer than Greece. Reordering the place names would, stylistically, mean that both sides matched; the task, however, was simply never finished (as, indeed, the inscription as a whole was not, with the right and rear faces left blank).

However, we do not even need to go into matters in all this detail to disprove the theory that the list represented a diplomatic voyage for, whatever the reason for the repeated reordering, the repeated reordering demonstrates what the inscription absolutely is not. If, to play devil's advocate, the list of place names did represent the itinerary of a diplomatic voyage, then that voyage must have taken place before the list was inscribed (because you would not memorialise something that had not happened yet). Why, then, was the (past) voyage itinerary, where the itinerary was known, repeatedly changed (and this was not a question of simply reversing the place names, to swap direction of travel)? There is no answer to that question, thus the list cannot be the itinerary of a diplomatic voyage. The notion that it was is demonstrably incorrect.

Perhaps underlying Cline's mistaken belief that this sequence of place names inscribed on the statue base represented the itinerary of a diplomatic voyage is his belief, in turn, that "the breath of life" meant "diplomatic recognition" and that the peoples referred to in the caption means that the peoples referenced (and the Greeks and Cretans depicted) were seeking diplomatic recognition.[168] However, as we have seen from our analysis of Rekhmire's tomb, and as David Lorton had previously convincingly shown, this is not the meaning of that phrase[169]: "the breath" (a treaty relationship) "of life" (sworn on oath) being given by Amenhotep III to the great ones from lands "who did not know to come to Egypt since the god's time" (i.e. for a long time) indicates a new treaty based relationship between Egypt and those place names on the base. This, therefore, represents a rapprochement between Egypt and the Greeks (who were now on Crete as well as the mainland, with both groups being represented). The depictions, therefore, represent a peace treaty.

If completed, presumably also on this statue base (where they are specifically mentioned in the caption), or on another incomplete statue base in the complex (if the caption on this base was to have been repeated on those other bases too), Phoenicia and Nubia (and cities therein) would also have been depicted as bound prisoners with crenelated ovals showing place names. Presumably elsewhere in the complex so too would the Mitanni have been represented as it is to them that "the difficult lands north of Asia" would seem to obliquely refer and it is they who are believed to have had a peace treaty with Amenhotep II and

---

168. Eric H. Cline and Steven M. Stanish, "Sailing the Great Green Sea? Amenhotep III's "Aegean List: from Kom el-Hetan, Once More", *Journal of Ancient Egyptian Interconnections* 3(2)(2011), pp10–11
169. David Lorton, *The Juridical Terminology of International Relations in Egyptian Texts through Dynasty XVIII* (The John Hopkins University Press: Baltimore, 1974), pp136–144

The Reconstructed History of Egypt's Involvement in Middle and Late Bronze Age Crete 115

Table 4.5: Believed stages in the ordering of place names on statue base E_N PWNV, Kom el-Hetan

	First iteration (Amyklai erroneously first on front rather than last)	Second iteration (Crete followed by Greece, left to right from rear of left side)	[Never overwritten before progressing to third iteration]	Final iteration (only complete on front) (Greece followed by Crete)
Left hand side (left to right, back to front)		Unknown (Crete) Unknown (Crete) Siteia (Crete) Lyktos (Crete) Amnisos (Crete) Knossos (Crete) Eleia (Crete) (or Elos (Greece) or Aulis (Greece)) Kythera (Greek island) Nauplion (Greece) Messenia (Greece) Thebes (Greece) or Tegea (Greece) Mycene (Greece)		
Front left (left to right)	Amyklai (Greece) Pisaia (Greece)	[Never overwritten before progressing to third iteration]		Kydonia (Crete) Phaistos (Crete) Amnisos (Crete)
	[Never inscribed before progressing to second iteration]	Pisaia (Greece) Amyklai (Greece)		
Amenhotep III's name	Prenomen	Prenomen		Prenomen
Amenhotep III's name	Nomen	Nomen		Nomen
Front right (left to right)				Keftiu (Crete itself) Tajana (Greece itself)

Thutmose IV.[170] Presumably reference to them here relates to the treaty having been renewed at the start of the reign of Amenhotep III.

The depiction of the Greeks as prisoners, as would have been the Mitanni, and the Phoenicians and the Nubians (both still owned by Egypt at this stage) suggests, in propaganda terms, that the objective was to portray Egyptian dominance. As regards the Greeks (and the Mitanni if they had been portrayed), not only had the king brought peace, he had achieved it on Egyptian terms.

We can draw on other similar depictions (not considered by the advocates of the incorrect itinerary theory) to confirm the meaning of the portrayal of the bound prisoners and crenelated ovals.

If we look at the tomb of Kheruef (Theban Tomb 192), Steward to the Great Royal Wife, Queen Tiye (Amenhotep III's consort), we see a depiction of Amenhotep III and Queen Tiye seated under a baldachin on top of a dais. On the side of the dais that faces us we can see depictions of captives with superimposed crenelated ovals with place and people names written inside them:

---

170. James M. Weinstein, "The World Abroad: Egypt and the Levant in the Reign of Amenhotep III", in David O'Connor and Eric H. Cline (Eds.), *Amenhotep III: Perspectives on His Reign* (Ann Arbor: The University of Michigan Press, 2001), p256

The Reconstructed History of Egypt's Involvement in Middle and Late Bronze Age Crete 117

Picture 4.15: Amenhotep III with Queen Tiye receiving gifts on the occasion of his third jubilee[171]

The captives (and their place and people names) are the "Nine Bows" of Egypt, namely: *Haut-Bebu* and *Shat* (the far north and far south, respectively); *Ta-Shema*; *Sekhet-Yam*; *Ta-Mehu*; and Pedjtiu-Shu (which refer to "Greater Egypt" along the cardinal points comprising Upper Egypt, the Western Oases, Lower Egypt, and the Eastern nomadic

---

171. The Epigraphic Survey in cooperation with the Department of Antiquities of Egypt, *The Tomb of Kheruef: Theban Tomb 192* (Chicago: The Oriental Institute of the University of Chicago, 1980), Plate 49 (courtesy of the Institute for the Study of Ancient Cultures of the University of Chicago). The Nine Bows are highlighted at (1). The title "ruler of the Nine Bows" is highlighted at (2).

groups, respectively); and *Tjehenu* (Libya), *Iwnntiw-Setet* (the tribes of Nubia), and *Mentiw nw Setjet* (the Bedouins of Asia) (three races from outside of Egypt proper).[172] Here at least, the "Nine Bows" were the king's domains and certain peoples within his domains over which he had dominion. The king is depicted as their master by being portrayed larger-than-life on top of representations of them. Indeed one of Amenhotep III's titles was "ruler of the Nine Bows" and this is written in hieroglyphs in the tomb portrayal on the right support of the baldachin (as well as being figuratively displayed in more expansive detail beneath him).

The larger-than-life portrayal of Amenhotep III in the tomb of Kheruef, sitting upon representations of the king's possessions and subjects portrayed as bound prisoners with their place and people names displayed in crenelated ovals, is obviously an assertion of dominance. At Kom el-Hetan the larger-than-life depiction of Amenhotep III (this time in the form of a statue), sitting upon representations of bound prisoners with the names of Greek and Cretan cities in crenelated ovals is, again, obviously an assertion of dominance.

Although Crete was no longer part of the Egyptian empire, and Greece proper never was, we are meant to infer from the caption at Kom el-Hetan that the terms of the peace treaty were onerous upon Crete and Greece (this is the propaganda at least). The Cretans and Greeks depicted were evidently required to bring tribute, as the caption states (and I think was the case), and, therefore, they were subject to a form and degree of economic domination that allowed Egypt, at least, to portray them as prisoners on Amenhotep III's statue base; they could be portrayed as economic captives, but they were not political captives.

This is also how they could appear as requesting "the breath of life" alongside territories that we know were owned by Egypt and were part of its empire at this time: Crete and Greece were portrayed as (economic) prisoners as they wanted relations underpinned by a peace treaty sworn on oath and they were prepared to pay for it; the Mitanni would have been portrayed as (economic) prisoners as they wanted relations underpinned by a peace treaty sworn on oath and they were prepared to pay for it; Phoenicia and Nubia, if they had been depicted, would have been portrayed as (political) prisoners as they wanted their vassal status underpinned by a treaty sworn on oath (and, whatever happened, they were going to be paying for it!). To borrow a phrase that British accountants will be familiar with, and American accountants will not be, the portrayal is one of commercial substance over legal form. Those subject to economic domination were portrayed as prisoners of equal status to those alongside them who were subject to political domination (and, therefore, economic domination as well) who were also portrayed as prisoners.

The peaceful treaty-based relationship between Greece and Crete and Egypt which, in so far as Egyptian propaganda wished to portray it, reduced the Greek and Cretan parties to the treaty to economic vassals, is portrayed again in the reign of Akhenaten, Amenhotep III's successor.

---

172. The Epigraphic Survey in cooperation with the Department of Antiquities of Egypt, *The Tomb of Kheruf: Theban Tomb 192* (The University of Chicago Oriental Institute Publications: Chicago, 1980), p55; and William Cooney, "Egypt's encounter with the West: Race, Culture and Identity", *Durham theses* (Durham University, 2011), pp74–75 (http://etheses.dur.ac.uk/910).

The west wall of the tomb of Huya (Amarna Tomb 1), the Chief Steward of Queen Tiye (by this stage the widow of Amenhotep III), records an event in Year 12 of the reign of Akhenaten, where an inscription tells us that Akhenaten and Nefertiti were:

"...to receive the tribute of Kharu [Syria] and Kush [Nubia], the west and the east. All foreign countries gathered as one, and the islands in the midst of the sea [Crete and the Aegean Islands] are presenting products to the king upon Akhet-Aten's great throne of receiving the dues of every foreign country, while the granting of the breath of life is made to them."[173]

The caption therefore records largely the same countries as Amenhotep III's statue base at Kom el-Hetan had listed before (although not Greece proper and not Mitanni).[174]

This event is also portrayed on the east wall of the tomb of Meryre II (Amarna Tomb 2), royal scribe, steward, overseer of the two treasuries, and overseer of the royal harem of Queen Nefertiti, the wife of Akhenaten (the inscription simply referring to the "chieftains of every foreign land are presenting [products to the king and] begging peace from him, so that [they might be] allowed to breathe the breath [of] life"[175]):

Picture 4.16: The royal family receives tribute in Year 12, from the tomb of Meryre II[176]

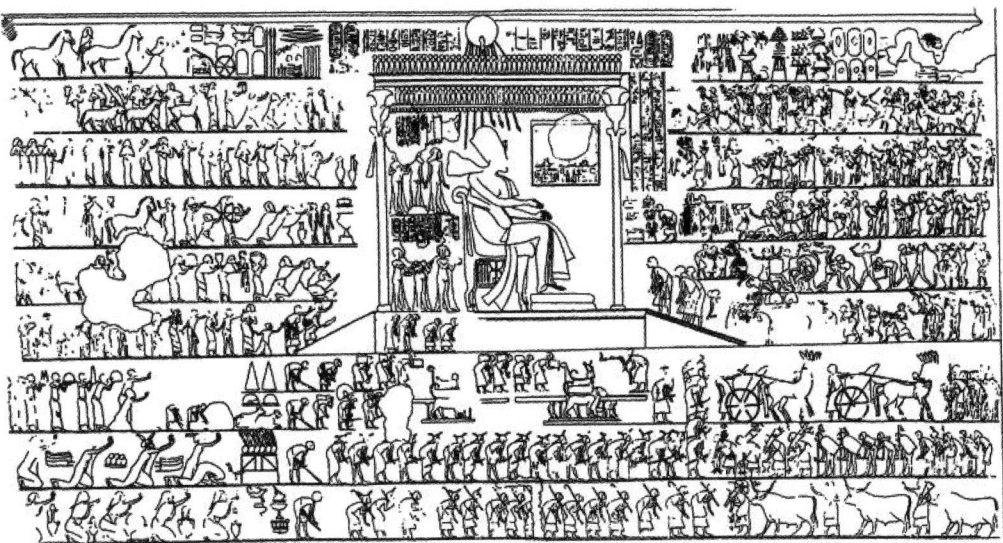

---
173. William J. Murnane, *Texts from the Amarna period in Egypt* (Atlanta: Scholars Press, 1995), p135
174. It is, of course, worth pointing out to those historians who believe that "the breath of life" means diplomatic recognition (who do not consider the inscription in the tomb of Huya), that Crete had already received diplomatic recognition from Egypt during the reign of Amenhotep III according to their line of argument (by virtue of the portrayal and inscription at Kom el-Hetan), so it would not have needed to receive it again from Egypt's next king, Akhenaten. Again, therefore, the evidence indicates this cannot be the meaning of this phrase.
175. William J. Murnane, *Texts from the Amarna period in Egypt* (Atlanta: Scholars Press, 1995), p162
176. William J. Murnane, *Texts from the Amarna period in Egypt* (Atlanta: Scholars Press, 1995), p163, Figure 8

If the Cretans, in particular, are already recorded as having been granted "the breath of life" (peaceful treaty-based relations sworn on oath) in Amenhotep III's reign, why do they seek it again? Lorton states that, under the Egyptian system, treaties appear to have only been valid for the lifetime of the royal signatory and that arrangements had to be made to renew the peace at each succession.[177] We should, therefore, expect reference to such treaty renewals with successive rulers.

If peace treaties were renewed at each succession, and the captions in the tombs of Huya and Meryre II and the depiction in the tomb of Meryre II refer to Akhenaten renewing the peace treaty with the Cretans (and Aegeans) in Year 12 of his reign (and, given the other attendees, presumably concurrently renewing the treaties enshrining the state of his vassals then in Egypt's empire), Lorton presumes that the captions in the tombs of Huya and Meryre II and the depiction in the tomb of Meryre II relate to the start of Akhenaten's period of sole rule after a period of co-regency with his father Amenhotep III.[178] Coming in Year 12 this implies that Akhenaten had a long co-regency with his father, something which has been debated by historians for some considerable time.[179]

Lorton is correct in his view that "the breath of life" would be regranted following the succession of a new monarch. The captions in the tombs of Huya and Meryre II and the depiction in the tomb of Meryre II, relating and depicting as they do this occurring, do relate and depict the ceremony accompanying the regranting of "the breath of life" at the commencement of a new monarch's reign. Lorton has, however, attributed the captions in the tombs of Huya and Meryre II and the depiction in the tomb of Meryre II to the commencement of the wrong new monarch's reign. It was not that a co-regency had ended and sole rule was beginning; it was that a co-regency (with a new monarch) was beginning.

Historian Nicholas Reeves believes, as do I, that the depiction in Meryre II's tomb, in fact, depicts the commencement of Queen Nefertiti's joint rule as Akhenaten's co-regent (as Ankhkheprure).[180] Therefore, as David Lorton correctly believes, with the commencement of a new monarch's reign (even that of a co-regent), peace treaty relationships were renewed and "the breath of life" was re-granted (and tribute was paid). This is why Akhenaten and Nefertiti are virtually superimposed upon one another in the portrayal; while co-regents, their rule was as one.[181]

The conclusion to draw from our analysis for now is that the inscriptions on the base of Amenhotep III's giant statue at Kom el-Hetan and in the tombs of Huya and Meryre II at Amarna record the effects of a peace treaty ("the breath of life") that had been agreed by Amenhotep III and then, having evidently been renewed by Akhenaten in his own right (of which record does not survive), being renewed upon Nefertiti's coronation as

---

177. David Lorton, *The Juridical Terminology of International Relations in Egyptian Texts through Dynasty XVIII* (The John Hopkins University Press: Baltimore, 1974), p143
178. David Lorton, *The Juridical Terminology of International Relations in Egyptian Texts through Dynasty XVIII* (The John Hopkins University Press: Baltimore, 1974), p144
179. See, for example, Aidan Dodson, "The Coregency Conundrum", *Kmt: A Modern Journal of Ancient Egypt* 25(2)(2014), pp28–35
180. Nicholas Reeves, *Akhenaten: Egypt's False Prophet* (London: Thames & Hudson, 2001), pp162, 172
181. Nicholas Reeves, *Akhenaten: Egypt's False Prophet* (London: Thames & Hudson, 2001), pp171–173

The Reconstructed History of Egypt's Involvement in Middle and Late Bronze Age Crete

Akhenaten's co-regent. The Greeks and Cretan parties to the treaty are portrayed on the base of the statue at Kom el-Hetan as bound prisoners; given that the caption records they were paying tribute to Egypt, the peace was implicitly, economically (though not politically), on Egypt's terms. That the Cretans are portrayed alongside Syria and Nubia, the terms of the peace were (from an Egyptian propaganda perspective at least) such that the Cretans could be portrayed as economic vassals (indeed, prisoners) of Egypt, if not actual vassals (indeed, prisoners) of Egypt as were Syria and Nubia, and tribute was evidently payable at least at inception and renewal.

* * *

With the history of Crete, and Egypt's relations with Crete, during the relevant periods now reconstructed, we can move on to the Linear A tablets and their translations, and see what these tell us about Egypt's involvement in Crete prior to the Mycenaean period.

Chapter Five

The Translations

"Look man. I lay it out for y'all to play it out."
(Huggy Bear, *Starsky and Hutch* (2004))[1]

We now have all the components necessary to translate the Linear A tablets: the symbols are sufficiently identified (as can be seen in Appendix 1 as well as throughout this chapter), the shorthand method has been identified (as set out in Chapter Three), and the historical context for Linear A has now been determined (as set out in Chapter Four).

Nonetheless, translating Linear A remains far from easy for even if two people today were to be given something as mundane as the same shopping list written in this method of shorthand, both knowing the context in which it was written (including the intentions of the person that wrote it), they could both still easily read it differently and purchase two different sets of goods. We therefore also need to rely upon some of the additional information that is recorded on, and can be inferred from, the tablets themselves to arrive at sound translations. We saw something of this process in Chapter Two, where analysis of Tablet HT 123A (in conjunction with Tablet HT 21B in particular) revealed the meaning of six symbols on that tablet and helped us to identify the hieroglyphs represented by three Linear A symbols (and, indeed, all the rest will follow in the further analysis and complete translation of that tablet in this chapter).

As to the mechanics of how the tablets have been translated, it is one of translating the symbols in progressive stages of certainty, so as, in turn, to progressively reduce the amount of uncertainty that exists for the fewer and fewer symbols remaining to be deciphered. As to the levels of certainty, the translation process can be divided in two: first, those elements of the translations that are certain beyond reasonable doubt; and, second, those elements of the translation that are certain on the balance of probability. These are considered, in turn, below:

1. <u>Elements of the translations that are certain beyond reasonable doubt</u>

    a) As the Linear A tablets are the temporary product of administrators, as a matter of administrative convention we would typically expect them to:

        i. Begin with:

            - A date, which would be the date that the items listed on the tablet were recorded or the period that transactions recorded on the tablet related to (and we see this); or

---

1. https://www.imdb.com/title/tt0335438/characters/nm0004879 (accessed 1 January 2022)

- A place name, which would be the origin or location of the items in question if, say, the tablet recorded a receipt of goods or inventory, respectively (and we see this); and

ii. If the tablets' contents are totalled, we would expect the total (at the end of the tablet) to be labelled as such (which we have already seen in Chapter Two).

By identifying the hieroglyphs that are represented by the Linear A symbols and, by applying (in reverse) the shorthand method, identifying the words that they in turn represent, that these words have the meanings we would expect them to have based on their contexts on the tablets provides us with greater certainty not only that the translation is correct but also that the shorthand methodology employed is correct. The success of this approach adds towards the proof that the Linear A shorthand method we have determined is the correct one. If what we reasonably expect to see on a tablet is what we can see was recorded using the shorthand method we are applying, it is most likely that we are using the correct method of translation.

b) We are, additionally, assisted by the degree of administrative continuity between the period when Linear A was in use and the period in which Linear B was in use. This is not only evidenced in the creation of Linear B (which, although the relationship between scripts is not fully understood at this stage, evidently drew upon Linear A and Middle Egyptian written in hieroglyphs), it is also evidenced in the degree of continuity of the prevailing taxation regimes and, through identifying the same mathematical relationships between items recorded on the Linear A tablets as existed between similar items recorded on the Linear B tablets, further certainty can be added to both the translations themselves and the methodology we are using.

We see this in two respects:

i. <u>Dk series of Linear B tablets:</u>
As we saw in Chapter Two, the tax calculation based on sheep (rams) numbers and resulting in a wool tax payment obligation was the same on Tablet HT 123A as it was on the Dk series of Linear B tablets. The same mathematical relationship existing between items recorded in Linear A and similar items recorded in Linear B allows us, in so far as translating Linear A is concerned, to:

- Identify the meanings of the symbols representing those items (those meanings being drawn from the deciphered Linear B and the mathematical relationship between the items in question);
- Identify the Middle Egyptian words used to convey those meanings;
- By applying the shorthand method to those words, identify the hieroglyph(s) that would represent those words, and the Linear A symbols that would represent the hieroglyph(s); and
- Confirm these are the symbols on the Linear A tablet in question (thus also confirming the correct method of decipherment is being used).

ii. Mc series of Linear B tablets:
As discussed later in this chapter, the Mc series of Linear B tablets represents a tithe-like tax being paid to the Egyptian temples on Crete. Again, the same mathematical relationship exists between items recorded on certain Linear A tablets (Tablet HT 14, Tablet HT 114A, and Tablet HT 121) and the (partially translated) Mc series of Linear B tablets, which, again, allows us, in so far as Linear A is concerned, to adopted the same approach as before:

- Identifying the meanings of the symbols representing those items (those meanings being drawn from the deciphered Linear B and the mathematical relationship between the items in question);
- Identify the Middle Egyptian words used to convey those meanings;
- By applying the shorthand method to those words, identify the hieroglyph(s) that would represent those words, and the Linear A symbols that would represent the hieroglyph(s); and
- Confirm these are the symbols on the Linear A tablet in question (thus also confirming the correct method of decipherment is being used).

By virtue of the mathematical relationship between items recorded in Linear A being the same as between items recorded in Linear B, and thereby being able to identify the meanings of the symbols, and the Middle Egyptian words that have those meanings, and the hieroglyphs that would represent those words if the shorthand method were applied, and the Linear A symbols that represent those hieroglyphs, and confirm that these are the symbols on the tablet, we can confirm that the tablets record the same things in Linear A as in Linear B and, again, that we are using the correct method of decipherment. In practical terms, therefore, the certainty of this aspect of the decipherment of Linear A relies on the decipherment of Linear B before it.

c) In some cases, once the hieroglyph that is represented by a Linear A symbol is known, it is clear that there is only one possible meaning. For example:

- Linear A symbol L49, representing Hieroglyph F155 (which we saw on, and will see further in the analysis of Tablet HT 123A), can only conceivably represent (and could only represent using the shorthand methodology) the collective noun *wp* meaning "horned cattle" given that the one other word that it appears in would not have been recorded in an accounting record (it can mean "Jupiter") and that other word in which it appears would not have been abbreviated to that hieroglyph in any event; and
- Linear A symbols L43 and L69/96, representing Hieroglyph O10 (which we will see on Tablet HT 17, Tablet HT 19, and Tablet HT 89), can only represent (and could only represent using the shorthand methodology) the name of the goddess Hathor as this the only word that uses that hieroglyph (and Hathor is exactly the goddess we would expect to see worshipped by

Egyptians in an Egyptian overseas interest or possession and recorded as such in the records of the institution where she was worshipped).
- Similarly, although with slightly less certainty, Linear A symbols L48, L48', and L79, representing Hieroglyph N13, can only represent (and could only represent using the shorthand methodology) one of two Middle Egyptian words (a day half way through the month, or the festival of the half month).

2. <u>Elements of the translation that are certain on the balance of probability</u>

   a) In Chapter One we saw that symbols representing certain animals could be identified as such by those symbols being joined to the male = symbol within the corpus. Knowing that Linear A is Middle Egyptian written in shorthand using hieroglyphs, and having identified the hieroglyphs represented by the Linear A symbols in question, we can identify the most likely animals that they, in turn, represent (though in some cases we see the male = symbol used slightly differently, instead of indicating that the symbol to which it was joined represented an animal that was male, the symbol to which it was joined represented a type of man, so this rule is not as absolute as one would hope).
   b) In the Linear A corpus we see the use of similar terminology to that used in the Linear B corpus. Given the degree of administrative continuity, we can, on the balance of probability, be certain that when similar terminology is revealed by translations as being used, those translations are also correct. Most obviously, this is seen in the use of the collective noun for animals of *iw 'w*, meaning "quadrupeds", which is used in both the Linear A corpus and the Linear B corpus.
   c) The layout of certain tablets is similar such that, while a different Middle Egyptian word with a different abbreviation was chosen by the different scribes, we can infer that the same meaning was intended across different tablets. As an example, we see this, most obviously, in two tablets that have similar layouts and which show amounts received in the first half, and amounts to be received in the second half. In the subheading detailing the latter, different words for "deficiency" are represented:

      - On Tablet HT 14 the word *ḥꜣw ḥrt ʿ* (which is represented by Linear A symbol L34 which, in turn, represents Hieroglyph M16); and
      - On Tablet HT 2 the word *gbi* (which is represented by Linear A symbol L103 which, in turn, represents Hieroglyph G1).

      Despite different Middle Egyptian words being represented by different Linear A symbols, we can infer from common scribal practice as regards tablet layout that, on the balance of probability, the words in question have the same overall meaning (and the same meaning in English).

      The layout of other tablets also similarly helps us. Tablet HT 89 (and Tablet HT 27A, which is too damaged to include in this work) is an end of month account of income (before the total) and the different categories of expenditure (after the total). Identifying the latter as such helps us determine not only what the broad categories of expenditure were within the temple organisation but this also helps us when tablets have less straightforward descriptions (such as when amounts received are described by their alternative future intended payee from that originally intended e.g. on Tablet HT 114A).

d) If there are competing potential translations then the archaeological record of Crete can assist us in narrowing the list of possible meanings of symbols representing commodities. For example, on Tablet HT 13 and Tablet HT 36, Linear A symbol L101 clearly represents Hieroglyph M34 which could be the shorthand abbreviation for a word meaning emmer, barley, or grain. As we shall see, emmer has not been recorded by archaeologists as having been grown on Crete in the period. On the balance of probability, therefore, we can remove emmer from the list of possible meanings for the symbol in question.

e) Finally, as will be seen, the tablets are the temporary administrative product of an Egyptian temple. We can, therefore, draw from the Egyptian temple and certain other provincial administrative records that have survived in Egypt proper so as, in effect, to create a lexicon of Middle Egyptian words that were more likely to have been used in the administration of an Egyptian temple in Crete.

If this were the only approach adopted, I would say there would be an extreme risk that the process of translating the tablets would simply be one of self-validation; we would be looking for the answer that we had already assumed to be there, ultimately proving nothing. For this reason, this approach is principally used in a confirmatory manner. Moreover, with the other steps taken to reach this point, both in terms of historical reconstruction and analysis of the tablets themselves (in particular through steps set out in 1(a), 1(b), and 1(c) above proving the shorthand method), this risk is more than sufficiently mitigated and on occasion we can go beyond mere confirmation. As a case in point, in the previous example, in deciding between barley or grain being recorded, due to the terminology used in temple administration in Egypt, we can determine that, on the balance of probability, it is the latter that is more likely to have been recorded.

Additionally it should be noted that, although these texts were written in hieratic, as we know the hieroglyph equivalents of the characters of the hieratic script, in creating a lexicon of the Middle Egyptian words for use now, we know exactly which version of the spelling of these words would have been used if they had been written in hieroglyphs (there are, after all, many instances of many words being spelt many ways in hieroglyphs), and it is this version of the spelling of these Middle Egyptian words that is compared to the Linear A text when identifying its symbols.

Cumulatively, however, the whole is greater than the sum of its parts, and once a theme of a tablet is known with a greater level of certainty, determining the most likely meaning for the remaining symbols becomes progressively easier and more certain as, ultimately, a tablet must be internally consistent.

As we are dealing with shorthand, however, there are limits as to how far even this analysis can be advanced, especially when tablets are broken or damaged and text is missing (or, indeed, if the layout of the tablet lacks a certain level of logic because, for example, it has been overwritten or added to, or because the scribe was simply less structured in his work). There is significantly less certainty as to the meaning of even identified symbols on the tablets when a tablet heading is missing, for example, and the possible meanings of the remaining symbols almost exponentially increase in that scenario (although, that said, the themes evident across the corpus do still mean that inferences might still be capable of being drawn and in the conclusion to this work, Chapter Six, I propose a way to advance further the analysis of the tablets that are not covered in this work). For now, however, the tablets included in this work are only those which, for the reasons set out, I am certain that the translations are accurate.

Given that over 80% of the surviving Linear A tablets have been found at Hagia Triada and these have been dated to the Late Minoan IB period (which, as we have seen, was the period in which Egypt began its approximately three-decade rule of Crete that lasted from 1455 BC to c.1424 BC), it is perhaps unsurprising that within the entire corpus the best-preserved tablets are found within this group of tablets. With one exception, therefore, these are the focus of this chapter. As we shall see, the tablets are the temporary administrative product of the workings of an Egyptian temple, be they ad hoc reports (presumably drawn from the permanent ledgers of the temple), accounting workings (presumably to check the entries made in the permanent ledgers), or a record of the accounting entries themselves (temporarily recorded, to be entered into the permanent ledgers of the temple in the future).

128 The Decipherment of Linear A

> **Notes to the translations set out in this chapter**
> To avoid being too repetitive in this chapter, headings for tablet sketch diagrams and photos of tablets have been dispensed with as, unless otherwise stated:
>
> 1. Sketch diagrams and pictures of Linear A tablets are taken from Godart & Olivier, specifically:
>
>   - For tablets from Hagia Triada (HT): Volume 1.[2]
>   - For the tablet from Khania (KH): Volume 3.[3]
>
> 2. Tabulated transcriptions of Linear A tablets are taken from Brice.[4]
> 3. Middle Egyptian dictionary extracts are taken from Mark Vygus' online dictionary, which is available at: https://www.egyptologyarchive.com/2018/10/book-no2-middle-egyptian-dictionary.html
>
>   This dictionary of Middle Egyptian words, spelt in hieroglyphs, has Gardiner's alphanumeric hieroglyph referencing which can, if exported to an excel spreadsheet, provide a database that is searchable and from which one can find all occurrences of a particular hieroglyph or group of hieroglyphs and where they appear first, last, or within Middle Egyptian words.
>
> All these sources have been vital in deciphering Linear A, and I am grateful to their authors for what must have taken many hours of hard, diligent, work to complete. Linear A could not have been deciphered without them.

---

2. Louis Godart and Jean-Pierre Olivier, *Recueil des Inscriptions en Linéaire A, Volume 1: Tablettes éditées avant 1970* (Athens: École Française D'Athènes, 1976) – for tablets found at Hagia Triada (Archaeological Museum of Heraklion, Ministry of Culture – Hellenic Organisation of Cultural Resources (copyright)) – which applies throughout, including subsequent appendices.
3. Louis Godart and Jean-Pierre Olivier, *Recueil des Inscriptions en Linéaire A, Volume 3: Tablettes, Nodules et Rondelles éditées en 1975 et 1976* (Athens: École Française D'Athènes, 1976) – for tablets found at Khania (Archaeological Museum of Chania, Ministry of Culture – Hellenic Organisation of Cultural Resources (copyright)) and for tablets found at Zakros (Archaeological Museum of Agios Nikolaos, Ministry of Culture – Hellenic Organisation of Cultural Resources (copyright)) – which apply throughout, including subsequent appendices.
4. W. C. Brice, *Inscriptions in the Minoan Linear Script of Class A* (Oxford: Oxford University Press, 1961) (Images copyright: © The Society of Antiquities of London).

The Translations

Selected tablets, translations, and commentary

As we shall see, the Linear A tablets found at Hagia Triada reflect the dual role of an Egyptian temple in the period:

- First, acting as agent of the state (i.e. undertaking certain functions for and on behalf of the state); and
- Second, acting as principal in its dealings (as a religious institution).

These are set out in Parts I and II of this chapter, respectively. Part III of this chapter then briefly considers a tablet from Khania, where an Egyptian temple was also acting as principal in its dealings. We shall begin now with the first of these.

Part I: Tablets reflecting the Hagia Triada temple acting as agent of the state

Tablet HT 123A

It is perhaps appropriate, given that this tablet provided us with the mathematical "proof" as to the nature of Linear A (in Chapter Two), that we should begin the translations set out in this chapter with Tablet HT 123A.

Given the complex nature of the record that this tablet sets out, we shall work from not only Godart & Olivier's sketch diagram of the tablet but also from Brice's columnar tabulation, both of which are set out below. The translation is set out in column order.

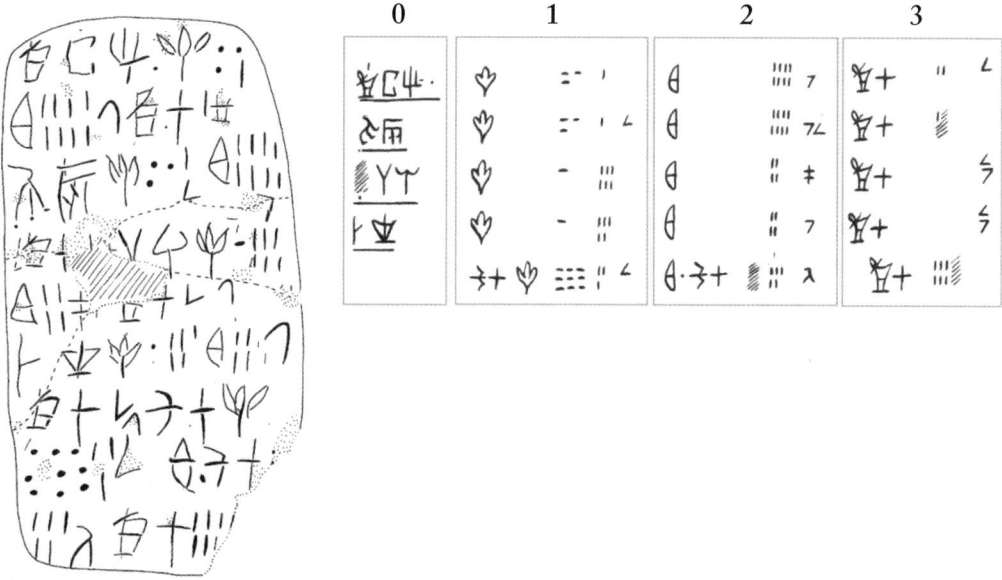

As discussed in Chapter Two, this tablet appears akin to what we today would describe as a summary of the debtors ledger in respect of tax debts. The debtors are on the left of Brice's tabulation (Column Zero), then their assets on New Year's Day (sheep (rams))

130   The Decipherment of Linear A

(Column One), then their tax obligations calculated on New Year's Day that were to be paid in wool (Column Two), and then their current deficits that had not been paid as at the date the tablet was written (Column Three). Individuals' names are, naturally, problematic when deciphering shorthand, for how do you know that a letter represents a name rather than a word? I do not believe, however, that this is what Column Zero records.

If Tablet HT 123A is a summary of debtors in the area in question, that there are only four debtors seems odd. However, we know from the E series of Linear B tablets from Pylos that landholdings could be recorded under the names of "corporate" groups, such as smiths and priestesses, as well as in the name of individuals.[5] Indeed, it is landholding groups that are recorded here (which is further indicated by one of the four groups recorded here also appearing in another tax record, Tablet HT 14, which we will see later in this chapter). We are, therefore, seeing the records of individual debtors aggregated by type.

Heading + Subheading One: Transcription Column Zero, Row One, Symbols One to Three:

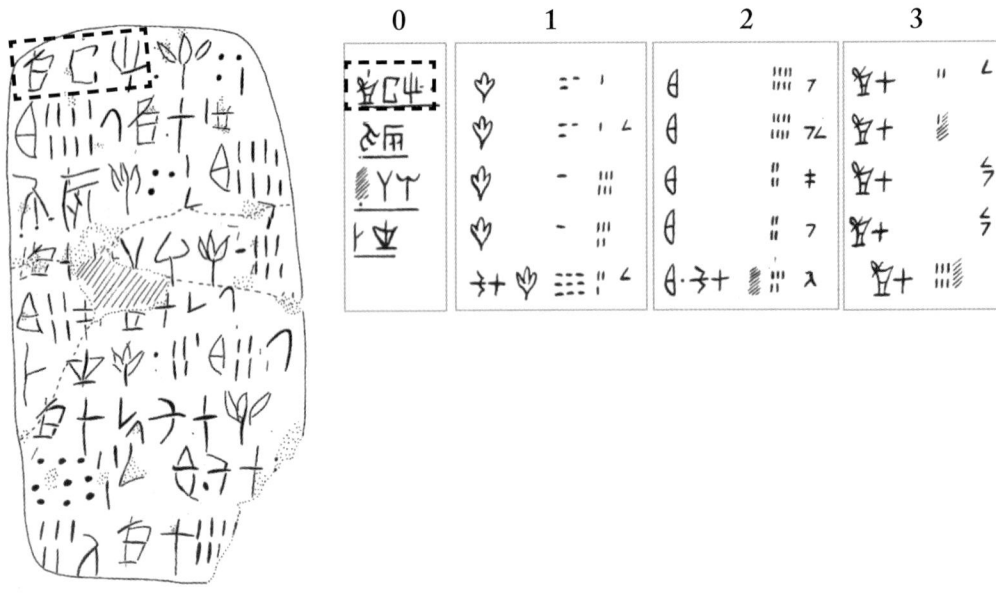

Hieroglyph G1 / simplified / Linear A symbol L103
Here, this Linear A symbol is a simplified representation of Hieroglyph G1, and it represents the word:

---

5. Ruth Palmer, "Bridging the Gap: The Continuity of Greek Agriculture from the Mycenaean to the Historical Period", in David W. Tandy (Ed.), *Prehistory and History: Ethnicity, Class and Political Economy* (London: Black Rose Books, 2001), p56

The Translations 131

◌ 𓅃 𓏭𓏭 ◠ *g3wt* tax, tribute [noun] W11 - G1 - M17 - M17 - X1 - Y1

◌ 𓅃 ◁ 𓌢 ⸗ *g3wt* tax, tribute [noun] W11 - G1 - O37 - M2 - Z3A

That taxation was the subject of this tablet was identified in Chapter Two. As we have already seen, all the parties recorded on the tablet are paying tax at the same rate (25%) on the number of assets held, so there is some justification for this symbol being seen as a heading, rather than just being applicable to the party listed first.

Although most symbols undergo a degree of simplification in their transition from a detailed hieroglyph normally inscribed in stone on a temple wall to a Linear A symbol incised in clay, the derivation of this symbol is less clear than most. Moreover, while a characteristic of shorthand that we saw in Chapter Two, this word being represented by a symbol representing a distinctive hieroglyph that is not its first or last is also less common. In arriving at this translation, the only reason that this word has been identified is because Hieroglyph G1, represented by this symbol, can be demonstrated to represent another word on this tablet when it also appears second in its spelling (again, after Hieroglyph W11). The symbol representing that word, meaning "deficiency", is written in Column Three of this tablet's transcription and it was only identified from the known meaning that it could be inferred to have through a comparison with the Dk series of Linear B tablets.

As this is the ultimate reason for ascribing the symbol its meaning here, the identification of this symbol (and why it was chosen to represent that word) is discussed subsequently when Column Three is translated. For now, however, this symbol is taken here to mean "tax".

Hieroglyph O1 ⌷/ rotated ⌷/ Linear A symbol L74 ⌷
Here, Hieroglyph O1 has been rotated by 90 degrees to become Linear A symbol L74. The rotation of hieroglyphs to become Linear A symbols is a common theme throughout the Linear A corpus. As a result, a symbol that was wide (horizontally long) takes up less room horizontally and, indeed, I think this was the intention (which is discussed further in Appendix 1). As we are dealing with landholder groups, and their landholdings, here this symbol represents the last hieroglyph in the word:

△⌷ *s3 pr* pasture ground, byre [noun - arch.] J17 - O1

|△⌷ *s3 pr* pasture ground, byre [noun - arch.] S29 - J17 - O1

Hieroglyph D46 ⌒/ rotated ⎵/ simplified / Linear A symbol L100 ψ
Here Hieroglyph D46, a lifelike representation of a hand, is rotated by 90 degrees so that it takes up less space (horizontally). It is also simplified to be drawn as a "stick hand".

Again, as we are dealing with landholder groups, here this symbol represents the first hieroglyph in the word:

dmi town, village [noun] D46 - W19 - M17 - M17

dmi town, village [noun] D46 - W19 - M17 - M17 - O49 - Z1

dmi town, village [noun] D46 - W19 - M17 - M17 - X1 - N23 - Z1

dmi town, village [noun] D46 - W19 - M17 - M17 - X1 - N23 - Z1 - O49

dmi town, village [noun] D46 - W19 - M17 - M17 - X1 - N23 - Z1 - Z3A - O49

dmi town, village [noun] D46 - W19 - M17 - N21 - Z1

dmi town, village [noun] D46 - W19 - M17 - O49

dmi town, village [noun] D46 - W19 - M17 - X1 - N23 - Z1 - O49

dmi town, village [noun] D46 - W19 - M17 - Z5 - Z5 - O49

dmi town, village [noun] D46 - W19 - M17 - Z7 - X1 - N23 - Z1 - O49

dmi town, village [noun] D46 - W19 - N23 - Z1 - M17

These three symbols therefore mean "tax [from the] pasture grounds [of the] villages".

    Translations of the E series of Linear B tablets, which revealed to historians details of the patterns of land ownership in the Mycenaean period, indicated that certain land was termed as *ki-ti-me-na* or *ke-ke-me-na* (or, *ktimenai/?kekeimenai*). This term was believed by the Italian historian Giovanni Pugliese-Carratelli to indicate that the land in question (fields or plots) was "cultivated". The term was normally used in the contexts of fields administered by the *dāmos*, or village.[6] When it comes to sheep farming, however, land is not cultivated; it is pasture. We might, however, expect a *dāmos*, or village, that had cultivated land to also have uncultivated land when it lay fallow, and that this was used as pasture to graze sheep given that sheep were such an important part of the Late Bronze Age Cretan economy. Consequently, I think it is not unexpected that one of the

---

6. Michael Ventris & John Chadwick, *Documents in Mycenaean Greek* (2nd Ed.)(Cambridge: Cambridge University Press, 1973), pp232–233

The Translations 133

categories of land and landholders represented in Column Zero is the pasture grounds of the villages and, as we are inferring that the heading "tax" applies to all groups listed in Column Zero, that this translates as "[tax from the] pasture grounds [of the] villages".

Subheading Two: Transcription Column Zero, Row Two, Symbols One and Two:

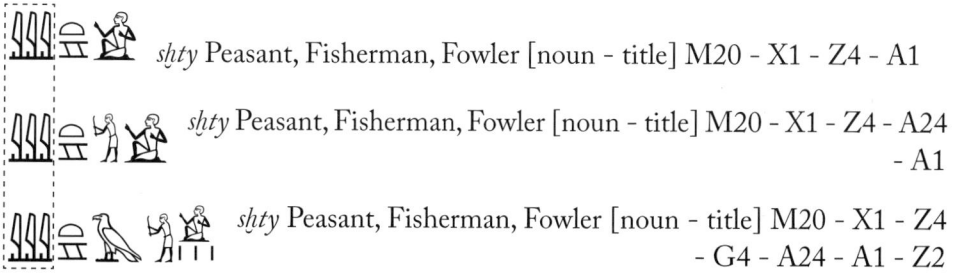

Hieroglyph M2 / rotated / reversed / Linear A symbol L64
This Linear A symbol is Hieroglyph M2 rotated by 180 degrees then reversed. Again, as we are dealing with landholder groups and their landholdings, here this symbol represents the last hieroglyph in the word:

3ḥt arable land, meadow, tilled land [noun] M8 - N23 - M2

Hieroglyph M20 / rotated / simplified / Linear A symbol L82
This Linear A symbol is Hieroglyph M20 rotated by 180 degrees and simplified. Incising this symbol in its rotated and simplified form was easier and quicker (7 strokes rather than at least 10 being required). Again, as we are dealing with landholder groups, here this symbol represents the first hieroglyph in the word:

šḥty Peasant, Fisherman, Fowler [noun - title] M20 - X1 - Z4 - A1

šḥty Peasant, Fisherman, Fowler [noun - title] M20 - X1 - Z4 - A24 - A1

šḥty Peasant, Fisherman, Fowler [noun - title] M20 - X1 - Z4 - G4 - A24 - A1 - Z2

134   The Decipherment of Linear A

These two symbols therefore mean "[tax from the] meadows [of the] peasants" (we can infer that the word tax still applies but, being common across all categories of land and landholders listed, the scribe has not bothered to write it). This is the second category of land on which tax is owed.

Subheading Three: Transcription Column Zero, Row Three: Symbols One and Two:

Note: I believe that the lacuna that precedes the first identified symbol on Brice's tabulated transcription here was, in fact, part of the deficit value for the previous debtor category on Row Two.

Hieroglyph V28 / rotated / simplified / Linear A symbol L31
This Linear A symbol is Hieroglyph V28 rotated by 180 degrees and simplified for ease of inscription. Again, as we are dealing with landholder groups and their landholdings, here this symbol represents the first hieroglyph in the word:

    ḥnbwt margin (of arable land), measured land, confines (of district) [noun] V28 - M2 - N35 - D58 - X1 - N23 - Z2

    ḥnb margin (of arable land), measured land [noun] V28 - M2 - N35 - D58 - Z7 - N23 - Z1

Margins (of arable land) are the strips of land lying between the field boundary and a crop being grown (such as vines).

Hieroglyphs D28 - Z1 / simplified / modified / Linear A symbol L55
Linear A symbol L55 is formed from Hieroglyphs D28 - Z1. Here they are simplified (the detail of the hands on Hieroglyph D28 is dispensed with) and then joined together to

form one Linear A symbol, for ease of inscription. Again, as we are dealing with landholder groups, here this symbol represents the first hieroglyphs in the word:

 *k3ny* vintner, vine grower [noun - title] D28 - Z1 - N35 - M17 - M17 - M43 - A1

It is not a coincidence that this word appears (abbreviated) after the word for the margins (of arable land) appears (abbreviated), which would be applicable to the land around which vines were grown. These two symbols therefore mean "[tax from the] margin (of arable land) [of the] vintners".

Ruth Palmer notes that animal husbandry complemented arable farming; in the case of viticulture, because the prunings from the vines after harvest could be used for livestock feed and the livestock manure could fertilise the soil.[7] Moreover, as she points out, the ability to produce wine and livestock was the mark of an aristocrat in all periods since it implied basic subsistence needs had already been met, and that this ethos developed in the Bronze Age.[8] Vintners is here, therefore, used as something of a metonym for aristocrats; this category refers to the aristocrat's sheep (rams, explicitly, and ewes, implicitly) and the resulting wool taxation obligation arising thereon. Moreover, we can also infer something of the social structure of contemporary society, and the split of ownership of the island's livestock (and land) resources between its different social classes.

---

7. Ruth Palmer, "Bridging the Gap: the Continuity of Greek Agriculture from the Mycenaean to the Historical Period", in David W. Tandy (Ed.), *Prehistory and History: Ethnicity, Class and Political Economy* (Montreal: Black Rose Books, 2001), p51, citing Hamish Forbes, "The identification of pastoral sites within the context of estate-based agriculture in ancient Greece", *Annual of the British School at Athens* (90)(1995), p329, and Paul Halstead, "Counting sheep in Neolithic and Bronze Age Crete", in Ian Hodder (Ed.), *Pattern of the past: Studies in honour of David Clarke* (Cambridge: Cambridge University Press, 1981), pp314–315, 319
8. Ruth Palmer, "Bridging the Gap: the Continuity of Greek Agriculture from the Mycenaean to the Historical Period", in David W. Tandy (Ed.), *Prehistory and History: Ethnicity, Class and Political Economy* (Montreal: Black Rose Books, 2001), p60

136   The Decipherment of Linear A

Subheading Four: Transcription Column Zero, Row Four: Symbols One and Two:

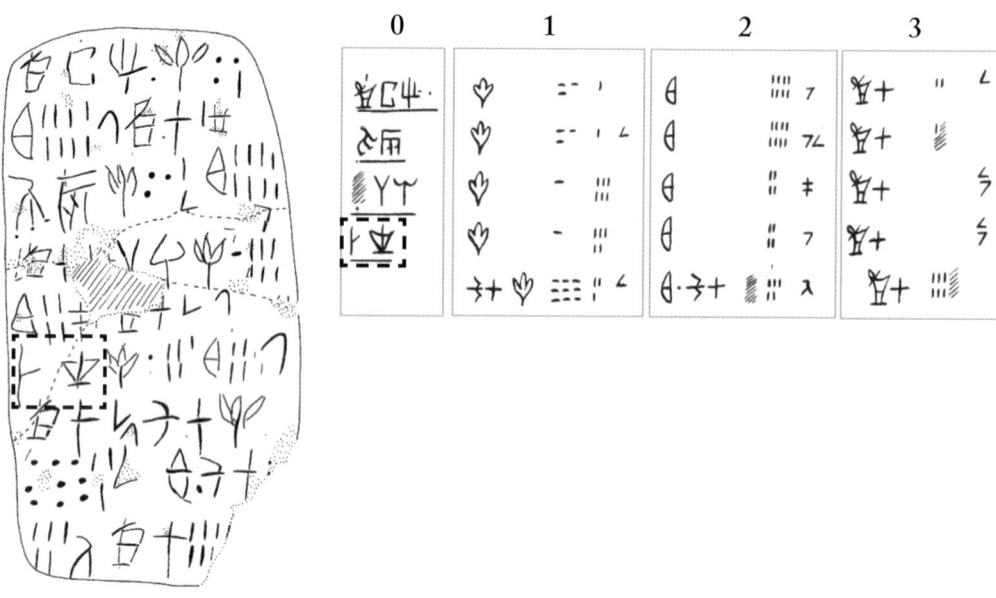

Hieroglyph T14 ⎞ replaced by AA26 (or J26) ⎛ / reversed ⎠ / Linear A symbol L30 ⎡
Sir Alan Gardiner, in his eponymous list of hieroglyphs, noted that Hieroglyph T14 was often replaced by Hieroglyph AA26 (or, as some would identify it, J26).[9] The interchangeability between Hieroglyph T14 and Hieroglyph AA26 (or J26) has been utilised here.

Hieroglyph T14 ⎞ looks extremely similar to Hieroglyph T15 ⎠ (which, as we shall see later in this chapter, is represented by Linear A symbol L69). Probably for this reason Hieroglyph T14 was, in effect, replaced by Hieroglyph AA26 (or J26) in the spelling of the words that might be represented by it in Linear A. It is, therefore, this hieroglyph that was then represented by Linear A symbol L30.

Given the context in which it appears on this tablet, this symbol represents the (replaced) first hieroglyph in the word:

⎟ ʿwt small cattle, goats, herds [noun - ani.] T14

⎟ ʿwt small cattle, herds, flocks, goats [noun - ani.] T14 - G43 - E28 - Z2

⎟ ʿwt small cattle, herds, flocks, goats [noun - ani.] T14 - G43 - X1 - E1 - Z2

---

9. A. H. Gardiner, *Egyptian Grammar: Being an Introduction to the Study of Hieroglyphs* (3rd Ed.)(Oxford: Griffith Institute, 1957), pp513, 544

The Translations 137

'wt small cattle, herds, flocks, goats [noun - ani.] T14 - G43 - X1 - E8 - Z2

'wt small cattle, herds, flocks, goats [noun - ani.] T14 - Z7 - X1 - E28 - F27 - Z3A

'wt small cattle, herds, flocks, goats [noun - ani.] T14 - Z7 - X1 - E28 - Z2

'wt small cattle, herds, flocks, goats [noun - ani.] T14 - Z7 - X1 - Z5 - Z2

<u>Hieroglyph R7</u> / modified / Linear A symbol L6

The principal difficulty in identifying this symbol is that it appears in differing styles according to the handwriting preferences of the scribe in question. If we look at pictures of how it appears on two other tablets, however, we will be able to identify the hieroglyph that it represents more easily:

Extract of photograph of Tablet HT 98A

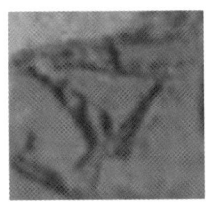

Extract of photograph of Tablet HT 112A

Brice and Godart & Olivier rightly recognised these two depictions as being the same symbol as the one we are considering on Tablet HT 123A, namely Linear A symbol L6, despite the obvious differences:

- The vertical line extends through the trapezium of the symbol on Tablet HT 123A, rather that stopping at the trapezium's top edge as it does in both of the above examples; and
- The bottom line of the trapezium extends beyond the points where it meets the side lines of the symbol on Tablet HT 123A, as it does in the example on Tablet HT 112A but not in the example on Tablet HT 98A.

We have, therefore, to take differing handwriting styles into account when we are looking to identify the hieroglyph that a Linear A symbol represents. Moreover, given the very limited numbers of tablets that have survived, we cannot infer which style is the more correct based simply on the number of occurrences within the very limited surviving corpus. We therefore have to consider all iterations of a symbol when seeking to identify the hieroglyph that it represents.

138 The Decipherment of Linear A

Therefore, while appearing less frequently, the style of representation seen on Tablet HT 98A and Tablet HT 112A is more correct, and from these we can see that the symbol represents Hieroglyph R7. Again, as we are dealing with landholder groups and their landholdings, here this symbol represents the first hieroglyph in the word:

bkyt precinct, temenos, temple area [noun - arch.] R7 - G29
- D28 - Z1 - M17 - M17 - X1 - O1

bkyt precinct, temenos, temple area [noun - arch.] R7 - G29
- Z1 - D28 - Z1 - M17 - M17 - X1 - O1

The plural for temenos is *temenē*, which is therefore used as the translation for this symbol and the word it represents.

This symbol, together with the symbol preceding it, therefore mean "[tax on the] flocks [in the] *temenē*". Whereas the other categories are described by way of a land type followed by the land owner or operator, here the owners or operators are the temples and consequently the scribe, who worked in one of these temples, did not feel the need to state the owner or operator explicitly but, instead, chose to refer to the temples' flocks by their location (on temple land) only.

Category One: Transcription Column One, Rows One to Four, Symbol One, and Row Five, Symbol Three:

Hieroglyph F155 ⟨glyph⟩ / simplified / Linear A symbol L49 ⟨glyph⟩ or modified further ⟨glyph⟩ (as here)
From the analysis in Chapter Two we know that this symbol represents a word that means sheep and, in particular, male sheep i.e. rams.

The Linear A symbol is, in fact, derived from Hieroglyph F155, one which seems to have caused the scribes significant difficulty when writing it, leading to significant variation when it was used (not all of which clearly exhibit the characteristics of the original hieroglyph). We are fortunate that Brice and Godart & Olivier correctly identified its differing representations as all being one and the same symbol.

It is probably easiest to see the derivation of Linear A symbol L49 from Hieroglyph F155 in the two instances that it appears on Tablet HT 14, which we first saw in Chapter Three and which we will again see later in this chapter. The overall form of the horns is maintained and while the box drawn between them on the hieroglyph is retained, it is much reduced (almost to a dash):

Hieroglyph F155		Linear A symbol L49
⟨glyph⟩	clearly becomes	⟨glyph⟩ ⟨glyph⟩
		HT 14 (2 instances)

While the transition is clear here and the Linear A symbol is clearly a representation of Hieroglyph F155, the scribe of Tablet HT 123A departs even further from the original hieroglyph:

Hieroglyph F155		Linear A symbol L49
⟨glyph⟩	also becomes	⟨glyphs⟩
		HT 123A (5 instances)

We are fortunate that the scribe of Tablet HT 14 wrote as precisely as he did, or we might never have been able to identify the symbol as representing Hieroglyph F155. This is a particularly rare hieroglyph and, as noted previously, we can therefore be confident that it represents the first hieroglyph in the word:

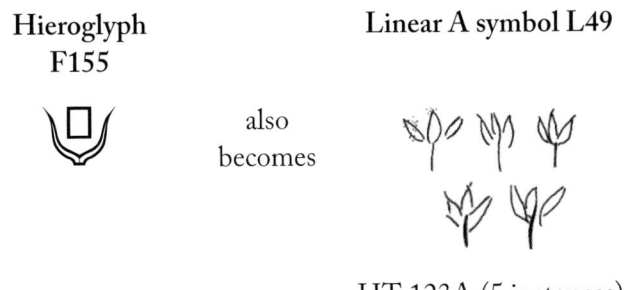 *wp* horned cattle [noun - ani.] F155 - E1 - Z3

Instead of writing male sheep, a collective noun has been used and we are reliant on the context given by the other information on the tablet to inform us that it represents sheep (rams) (which it clearly does).

Is the use of such collective nouns to be expected? Yes, based on our knowledge of and from Linear B. In the Linear B corpus the word "quadruped" (*qe-to-ro-po-pi*), which Ventris and Chadwick in *Documents in Mycenaean Greek* arguably mis-translated as "cattle", was used as a collective noun for goats and sheep but, more importantly, could refer to either *just* goats or *just* sheep.[10] In fact, the same is true when we meet the word for quadrupeds in the Linear A corpus later in this chapter.

In the Linear A corpus the Middle Egyptian word *wp* with its meaning of "horned cattle" is another such collective noun that can be used in a general way (covering many animal types) as well as, by implication, in a specific way (covering a single animal type). When *wp* was used here, it was intended to convey a specific meaning, in particular a specific animal type. Here, given the 4:1 ratio we determined in Chapter Two, we know from the Dk series of Linear B tablets that it was meant to convey that the animals in question were sheep (rams).

The meaning of this word is also why, despite representing a male animal, this symbol never has a male = symbol joined to it as would otherwise be expected, for the males of the breed of sheep in question evidently had horns whereas the females did not (or, at least, those of the females were so indistinct as to not be a defining characteristic). As Chadwick observed was typically the case with the Dk series of Linear B tablets,[11] female sheep are not recorded here on Tablet HT 123A. As discussed in the analysis after the translation of this tablet, aside from the total numbers of sheep (of both genders) being too large to feasibly record on this or any other tablet, this was most likely because referring to just the numbers of male sheep was a practical proxy for the much larger number of sheep that were present and on which the wool tax obligation was payable (and it was evidently used as such in that calculation).

Analysis of the fractions (and what turned out not to be fractions) on the tablet (in Chapter Two) allowed us to be certain of the numbers recorded on this tablet, and analysis of the numbers on the tablet allowed us to identify and be certain of what was recorded on it, namely sheep (rams). Now we can confirm this analysis was correct through analysis of the symbols themselves. Knowing that we are dealing with Middle Egyptian written in shorthand using hieroglyphs, we can identify the hieroglyph that the Linear A symbol represented. Having identified the symbol that was used, we can further determine its precise meaning by identifying the only word that it can reasonably have been an abbreviation for. Indeed, we are lucky that the symbol represents such a rarely used hieroglyph (a common hieroglyph, after all, could represent a number of

---

10. For further discussion of the use of the term "quadrupeds" in the Linear A (and Linear B) corpus, see page 196. Linear B tablet PY Ae 134, by implication of referring to a shepherd tending quadrupeds, only refers to sheep, and Linear B tablet PY Ae 108, by implication of referring to a goatherd tending quadrupeds, only refers to goats (Michael Ventris & John Chadwick, *Documents in Mycenaean Greek* (2nd Ed.)(Cambridge: Cambridge University Press, 1973), pp169,170).
11. John Chadwick, *The Decipherment of Linear B* (2nd Ed.)(Cambridge: Cambridge University Press, 1967), p122

The Translations 141

words). That there was only one word that can reasonably have been represented by a symbol representing the hieroglyph that it started with, and it had the same ultimate practical meaning as that determined by our mathematically driven analysis had already indicated it would have, gives us two independent routes to the same conclusion, that the tablet records sheep (rams). This is the mathematical "proof" of the nature of Linear A in action.

Transcription Column One, Rows Two and Five, and Column Three, Row One fraction symbols: Linear A fraction symbol J: ∠

	0	1	2	3
	☥C⊬·	♡	⸗ ⌐ ⎿	ᘯ	ᴵᴵᴵᴵ 7	¥+	⎿⎿ ∠
	ᘉ⊓	♡	⸗ ⎿ ⎿	ᘯ	ᴵᴵᴵᴵ 7∠	¥+	⎿
	⋎ꝨꞳ	♡	- ⎾⎾	ᘯ	ᴵᴵ ⨹	¥+	⁵⁄₇
	⊢Ψ	♡	- ⎾⎾	ᘯ	ᴵᴵ 7	¥+	⁵⁄₇
	⫟+♡	⁝⁝⁝ ⎿⎿ ∠	ᘯ·⫟+	ᴵᴵᴵ λ	¥+	⎾⎾⎾

Note: in contrast to Brice's transcription, the first instance of the fraction symbol here (in Column Three, Row One of the transcript), Godart & Olivier interpreted this to be a "#" symbol (following a single tally mark). The upper horizontal line of the purported "#" symbol is, however, a scuff mark, and the lower horizontal line extends less to the left and further to the right to form the base of the ∠ symbol (following two tally marks). This can be seen below in an extract of the photograph of the tablet in Brice:

Extract of photograph of   Extract of photograph of
Tablet HT 123A from Brice   Tablet HT 123A from Brice
                                   (tally marks and fraction
                                   symbol highlighted)

 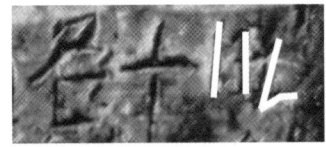

Extract of photograph of
Tablet HT 123A from Brice
(scuff mark highlighted)

Brice's transcription is, therefore, correct.

142   The Decipherment of Linear A

Knowing that Linear A is Middle Egyptian written in shorthand (using hieroglyphs) directs us to the value of this symbol.

As historian of mathematics Annette Imhausen has written, from their earliest days in the Old Kingdom (c.2700 BC–2200 BC) certain fractions in Ancient Egypt were written using a number of special signs in hieroglyphs and hieratic. These were used initially as fractions of specific things, such fractions of a finger length or fractions of an area of land, but later they were used as fractions in a more abstract sense.[12] While the script of Linear A is based on hieroglyphs, a number of its fraction symbols are taken from hieratic, the Egyptian script of administration and commerce.

The symbol ⋋ was a hieratic "special sign" that had a value of ½. As we have seen with numerous symbols in the Linear A corpus already, and we will continue to see throughout the corpus, certain Linear A symbols are reversed versions of the hieroglyphs that they represent. Here, the hieratic special sign is reversed to become Linear A fraction symbol J, thus the hieratic special sign ⋋ becomes the Linear A fraction symbol ∠ ; it still, however, represents the value of ½.

Why were the Linear A symbols reversed compared to the hieroglyphs they represented (or, here, hieratic special sign)? In certain cases and, indeed, in this case this was presumably so that it would be easier for a right-handed scribe to incise the Linear A symbol in clay (in much the same way as in our own time, or at least when I was at school, left-handed teachers wrote ticks as ⋎ with the tail drawn towards their writing hand rather than the more common ✓ with the tail pushed away from their writing hand).

There is, perhaps, mathematical evidence that supports this being the correct value. Given that, as we saw in Chapter Two on Tablet HT 123A, the Column One value on any row should be four times the Column Two value on the same row, then taking Row Two, we have 31 ½ in Column One which means that Column Two should equal 7⅞. We have, however, 8 recorded, plus a fraction symbol ⎜∠ (Linear A fraction symbol EJ). This symbol must equal –0.125 or –⅛. Does this, another negative fraction, make sense?

Looking at the composition of this symbol we have:

- Linear A fraction symbol J, namely ∠ , which we have deduced, above, to have had a value of ½ or 0.5; and
- Linear A fraction symbol E, namely 7, which was algebraically proven in Chapter Two to have had a value of –¼ or –0.25.

Of course, multiplying these two values together (i.e. –0.25 x 0.5), gives us –0.125 as the value of Linear A fraction symbol EJ, ⎜∠. It can be no coincidence that the component symbols of Linear A fraction symbol EJ, with their deduced and proven values, when multiplied together gives us the very value that leads, on Row Two, to the Column One and Column Two values having a 4:1 ratio which our analysis in Chapter Two suggested

---

12. Annette Imhausen, *Mathematics in Ancient Egypt: A Contextual History* (Princeton and Woodstock: Princeton University Press, 2016), p53 and Table 3

The Translations 143

they would have (and as already observed on all the other rows). Indeed, this evidences the deduced value of Linear A fraction symbol J is correct.

Despite this mathematical logic, the natural question, of course, is how can half a sheep (ram) be recorded in Column One, Row Two? This is considered further in the notes to the translation of this tablet on page 156.

Column Two, Rows One to Four (only symbol) & Row Five, First Symbol:

Hieroglyphs X1 - Z4 / rotated / modified / simplified / Linear A symbol L90

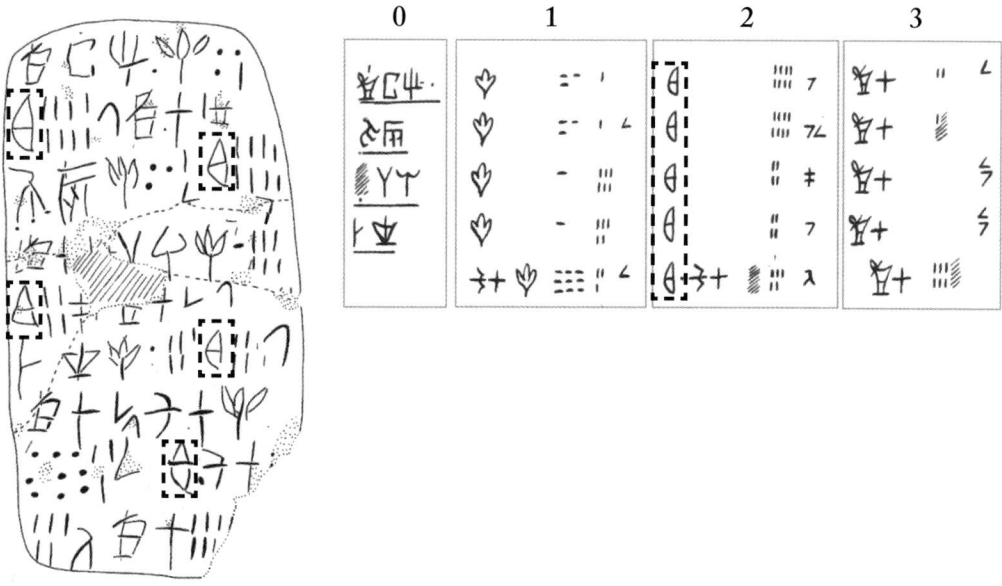

As we saw in Chapter Two, we were able to deduce, mathematically, that Linear A symbol L90 represented wool. The Middle Egyptian word for wool written in hieroglyphs is:

šnw hair, wool [noun - bod.] V49 - X1 - Z4 - D3

This form of the word *šnw* and its component hieroglyphs are discussed further in Appendix 3 to which the reader could now usefully refer. As discussed subsequently in this chapter, Hieroglyph V49 (being likely a fair representation of the hieroglyph that represented the hieratic symbol) is similar to Hieroglyph M12 which can have a meaning of the value 1,000, so this would be a poor choice to represent the word for wool as it would risk being mistaken for the count of the item previously recorded in any list. Moreover, Hieroglyph D3 (represented by Linear A symbol L89) is used throughout the corpus to represent "grass (cattle fodder)" and, while symbols can have more than one meaning (because, after all, this is shorthand), if a different symbol could be chosen to represent this commonly recorded item (which we can infer wool originally was, not that that is wholly reflected in the surviving corpus) that would make sense.

144   The Decipherment of Linear A

    This guides us to the conclusion that it is Hieroglyphs X1 - Z4 that are represented by Linear A symbol L90. Hieroglyphs X1 - Z4 have been rotated by 90 degrees, the effect of which is, again, so that (in its finished form) the Linear A symbol takes up less space horizontally. Then Hieroglyph Z4, having been simplified to a single stroke, has been placed inside the semi-circle of Hieroglyph X1 so as not to be mistaken for tally marks on the tablet (or, indeed, Linear A symbol L47 which the symbol would otherwise appear similar to). This then leaves a semi-circle with a single diagonal line within it, namely:

⌒\\\\   is rotated 90 degrees to become

⊂≥   which is simplified to

⊂⁻   and the now single line of Hieroglyph Z4 is moved inside the X1 semi-circle, becoming

⌐   Linear A symbol L90

We can again see something of the effect of the different scribes' handwriting styles in how the symbol was then written for, if we look again at the instances we referred to in Chapter Two where this symbol appears at Khania (KH), we can see that the single line within the rotated semi-circle is not uniformly written:

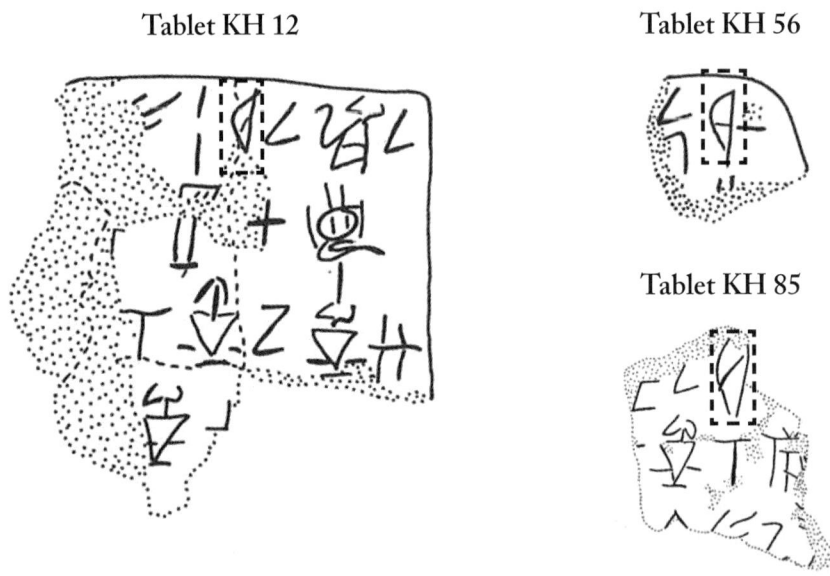

Tablet KH 12

Tablet KH 56

Tablet KH 85

In the case of Tablet KH 12 and Tablet KH 85, the line is slanted upwards reflecting the slant of Hieroglyph Z4. In the case of Tablet KH 56 the scribe has not bothered and has simply written the line horizontally.

Column Two, Row One and Three, fraction symbols: Linear A fraction symbol E: 𐄷

	0	1	2	3
	⚹Ϲ⇞·	❦	꞊ˎ ι	ᑫ	꞉꞉꞉꞉ [𐄷]	ϒ+	ˮ ⌐
	ⵊ⵲	❦	꞊ˎ ι ⌐	ᑫ	꞉꞉꞉ 𐄸	ϒ+	⦚
	ⵊϒϒ	❦	‐ ꞉꞉꞉	ᑫ	꞉꞉ ⧧	ϒ+	⇄
	⊢⋎	❦	‐ ꞉꞉꞉	ᑫ	꞉꞉ [𐄷]	ϒ+	⇄
	⇞+❦	꞊꞊꞊ ꞉꞉ ⌐	ᑫ·⇞+	⧧꞉꞉ ⋋	ϒ+	꞉꞉꞉

As set out in Chapter Two, this symbol has a value of -0.25 or -¼.

Column Two, Row Two, fraction symbols: Linear A fraction symbol EJ: 𐄸

	0	1	2	3
	⚹Ϲ⇞·	❦	꞊ˎ ι	ᑫ	꞉꞉꞉꞉ 𐄷	ϒ+	ˮ ⌐
	ⵊ⵲	❦	꞊ˎ ι ⌐	ᑫ	꞉꞉꞉ [𐄸]	ϒ+	⦚
	ⵊϒϒ	❦	‐ ꞉꞉꞉	ᑫ	꞉꞉ ⧧	ϒ+	⇄
	⊢⋎	❦	‐ ꞉꞉꞉	ᑫ	꞉꞉ 𐄷	ϒ+	⇄
	⇞+❦	꞊꞊꞊ ꞉꞉ ⌐	ᑫ·⇞+	⧧꞉꞉ ⋋	ϒ+	꞉꞉꞉

Note: Brice's transcription and Godart & Olivier's diagram disagree here. Brice appears to be correct: the smaller first half of the symbol appears to have followed the straight lines of the right extremity of the tablet break; the second half of the fraction symbol, clearly visible on the photograph, can be seen to be incorrectly drawn by Godart & Olivier, with the bottom horizontal line of the symbol missing. I have therefore followed Brice.

Extract of photograph of Tablet HT 123A from Brice

Extract of photograph of Tablet HT 123A from Brice

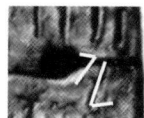

As discussed previously this symbol has a value of -0.125 or -⅛.

146   The Decipherment of Linear A

Column Two, Rows Three Fraction Symbol: Linear A fraction symbol A / Linear A symbol L2 ǂ

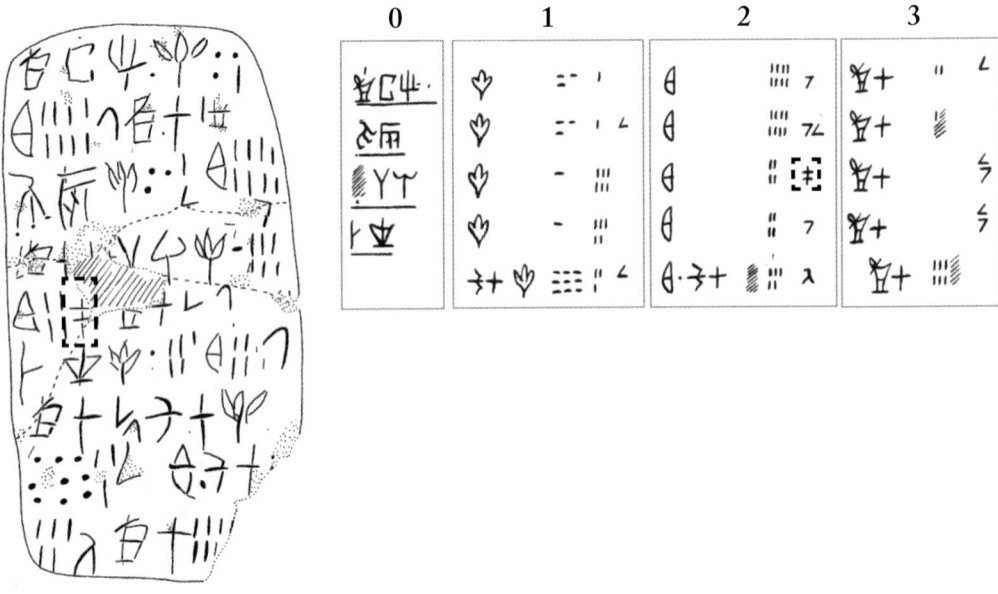

As set out in Chapter Two, this symbol has a value of zero (or, here, a zero value of fractional units). As noted previously, both Brice and Godart & Olivier were uncertain but they believed there might originally have been another symbol after the ǂ symbol highlighted. I do not (and it is, therefore, not shown on the transcription).

Column Two, Fifth Row, Final Symbol: Hieroglyph U32 ↓ simplified / Linear A fraction symbol H: λ

Mathematics, accounting, and logic, can direct us, again, to the meaning of this symbol. Consider the items listed on the broken Tablet HT 23A (an extract of Brice's transcription of which is set out below):

Extract of transcript of Tablet HT 23A

On this tablet, the first item recorded has a quantity of zero. In Chapter Two, when referring to Tablet HT 91A where there were nine items all of a zero quantity, the fact that there were such numerous occurrences of the same value at the same time for different commodities (including one known to be an animal) evidenced the fact that Linear A symbol L2 could only mean zero. That meaning was certain given the use of that symbol on Tablet HT 21B.

Yet here we have five commodities that are also recorded as having the same value at the same time. Does this mean there was a flaw in the logic that identified Linear A symbol L2? No, because of the use of Linear A symbol L2 on Tablet HT 21B. So what of the five items recorded on Tablet HT 23A with the same value represented by Linear A fraction symbol H? They cannot be zero amounts, and yet they are unlikely to represent the same value at the same point in time, so what value might they represent?

The only other "value" that might be represented by the same symbol across many commodities on the same tablet (so, at the same time) would, in modern parlance, be *de minimis*. This "value" does not even have to be the same when listed in more than one instance, it is simply an amount smaller than the smallest fraction being used to count the commodity in question. *De minimis*, of course, is a Latin expression; thinking

148   The Decipherment of Linear A

as to how that expression and concept might have been conveyed in Middle Egyptian, mathematics, accounting, and logic guides us to the word "remainder":

mn the remainder is, remainder, balance, due, remains U32

smn remainder [noun] U32 - Y1

A remainder, in a mathematical sense, is a *de minimis* amount that cannot be apportioned completely into a number of the lowest value units that are being counted. It is a fraction too small to be recorded with a meaningful numerical value but, nonetheless, there is a value and it is worth recording (as opposed to simply showing zero).

For example, if we were working in a system of fractions where the smallest fraction value was one eighth and we wanted to know how many eighths were in 11.3, simple arithmetic would give us the answer 90 but we would be left with a remainder with a value (in our decimal system) of 0.05 (i.e. $1/20$). With a system of fractions that only went as low as one eighth, what could we call the 0.05 that is left over other than call it a "remainder"? It is an amount that is physically present, so not "zero", but is too small to count using the smallest value fraction in the system of fractions in use. That is, therefore, how this symbol should be interpreted. This is why it appears a number of times on the same tablet for a number of commodities but is not zero (which, fortunately, is also present on Tablet HT 23A (as, indeed, both symbols are on Tablet HT 123A), so we know that these two symbols have different values).

Thus:

Hieroglyph
U32

is modified (the bottom detail is removed) to become

Linear A fraction symbol "H"

This is not quite the end of the story, however. With this "value" now determined and, similarly, the value of all the fraction symbols in Columns One and Two also now determined, can we check our findings against the totals of those two columns? Let us set out the values we have determined for the values in Columns One and Two, recalculate the column totals, and then compare these to the column totals recorded on the tablet:

	Column One: Sheep (rams)	Column Two: Wool
Row One	31	7¾
Row Two	31½	7⅞
Row Three	16	4 + 0
Row Four	15	3¾
Total (recalculated)	93½	23⅜
Total (per Tablet HT 123A)	93½	[2]5λ

Knowing the values of the fraction symbols we can recalculate the Column One and Column Two totals on Tablet HT 123A as 93 ½ and 23⅜, respectively, yet for the latter the tablet itself records 25 λ.

Portraying 23⅜ as 25λ (where λ would have to be a negative remainder balance) is technically correct, given that a remainder is a value that does not fit into the fraction system in use (the missing fraction is −1⅜). However, I think it more likely that the total was recorded in this way due to the arithmetic skills of the scribe (or limits thereof). If we put ourselves in the scribe's position, I think that, when adding up the value of the four Column Two fraction symbols (including the zero), he assumed that, together with the whole unit tally marks he could see (7 + 7 + 4 +3 = 21), when he then added the four fractions to that total (well, three, because one was zero) that the closest whole number was 25. He was incorrect and, being unable or not bothering to work out the correct total for Column Two values he simply wrote 25 plus a remainder symbol (which can have any value outside of the fraction system being used).

We can also infer something of the accounting that led to this occurring, and the relative experience of the temple staff involved. As noted in the analysis section after the translation of this tablet, this tablet represents an ad hoc report on the status of wool tax receipts at a specific point in time after the start of the year. This tablet did not form part of the accounting system itself. To produce an ad hoc report, the values had to be taken from the temple's permanent accounting ledgers. The scribe of this tablet would have copied down the values in Rows One to Four from different debtors' ledgers which had already been totalled (presumably by more experienced scribes) and then, having written down those values, he had to total them on his report. The scribe could copy accurately, but he could not add as accurately as we (and, presumably, his superior) would want, thus he has had to obfuscate; he is not, perhaps, wrong in what he wrote, but he is not as right as he might have been.

150   The Decipherment of Linear A

Column Three, Rows One to Five, Symbol One:

Hieroglyph G1 / simplified / Linear A symbol L103

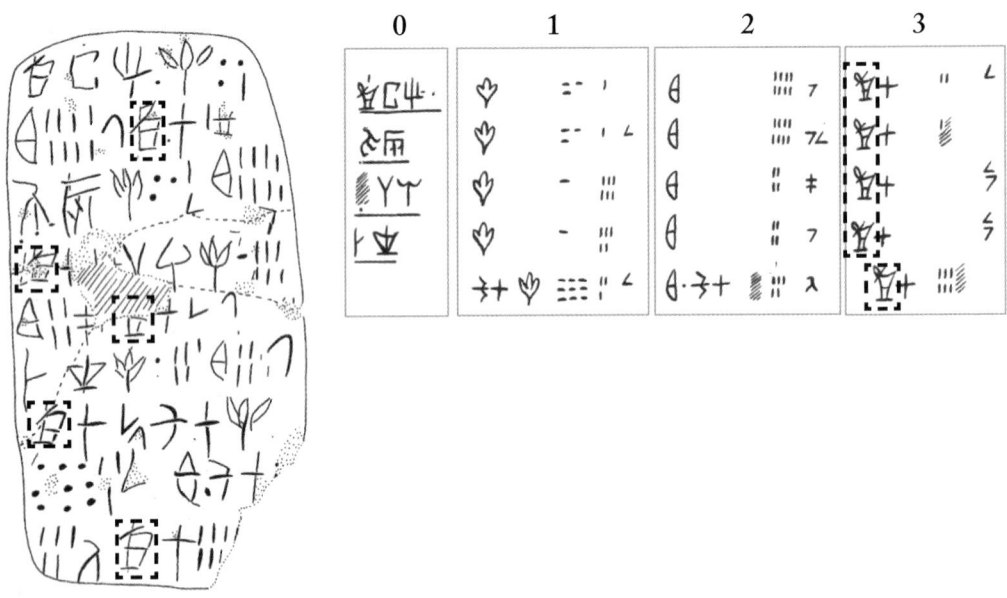

As noted previously, Linear A symbol L103 is, in fact, a simplified representation of Hieroglyph G1. This is difficult to see as the Linear A depiction is a particularly abstract one and seems to have posed some difficulties for the scribes; the symbol itself, like others we have seen, varies widely from tablet to tablet and from scribe to scribe (or even on the same tablet when written by the same scribe a number of times, as we shall see here).

The derivation is most clearly seen if we look at how the symbol was written on Tablet HT 118, and compare this to Hieroglyph G1:

           Hieroglyph G1   Linear A symbol L103
                                   on Tablet HT 118

Hieroglyph G1 was a particularly complex one meaning that it was difficult to write in clay without significant simplification. However, we see the key components of it nonetheless in the representation here: the beak of the bird is present here (as it always is); the two feet and legs of the bird are present beneath the body (as they always are); and the body and closest wing (though not separately detailed) are present and distinct (as they always are). Indeed, the rise of the symbol to the top right is presumably the shoulder of the bird.

The scribe for Tablet HT 123A evidently had difficulty with the portrayal and could not decide whether the bird should have a separate head or not. In the five times the symbol is used on Tablet HT 123A, three times the depiction has no separate head, one time it has a head, and in one instance we cannot tell because the tablet is damaged. An example of how the symbol was portrayed with and without a head on this tablet is shown below:

Differing depictions of Linear A symbol L103 on Tablet HT 123A

If this was all we had to go on, we might never have identified the hieroglyph that the symbol represents; we are, therefore, fortunate that the scribe of Tablet HT 118 wrote as he did, where the depiction is at least a little clearer. Moreover, we are fortunate that, in what it records, Tablet HT 123A mirrors the Dk series of Linear B tablets, thus helping us identify its meaning (and ultimately confirm our identification of the hieroglyph on which this symbol was based).

As we have seen in Chapter Two, Linear A symbol L103 was used to represent a word with the general meaning of "deficit" (reflecting what was recorded on the Dk series of Linear B tablets). With this in mind, and now knowing that Linear A symbol L103 represented Hieroglyph G1, we can determine the word that was represented. There are, however, no Middle Egyptian words that begin or end with this hieroglyph and which mean "deficit". We are, therefore, guided to the word:

gbi deficiency, deprivation, damage, uneven [noun] W11 - G1 - D58 - G37 - Z9

This, therefore, might be considered to be an example of the shorthand method being used where, as Milne stated it could be, a word is abbreviated to "distinctive letter or syllable (from the body of the word in question, not being the first or the last)". It is very difficult, if not impossible, for us to conjecture which hieroglyphs were particularly distinctive for the Egyptians. However, I would suggest more practical reasons also seem likely, based on our limited evidence, to have determined why this particular choice was made.

The Middle Egyptian word *gbi* could not be abbreviated to its first hieroglyph, Hieroglyph W11. This is because, as we shall see later in this chapter, Hieroglyph W11, would be represented by a symbol similar to Linear A symbol L14 (i.e. I) (and we can tell this because of how this hieroglyph was represented when joined to Hieroglyph Z1 in Linear A symbol L39). Linear A symbol L14, however, represented Hieroglyph M12, the first hieroglyph of the Middle Egyptian word *ḥrps* meaning "loaves" (of bread), and was likely commonly used as such. Although we do not see this in the surviving corpus from Hagia Triada, which primarily concerns cattle and livestock, if Linear A symbol L14 represented a commodity, such as loaves of bread, that was likely frequently recorded, it would not make sense to use a similar Linear A symbol to represent another word that was also frequently represented in the original (although not surviving) corpus.

Further, Hieroglyph Z9 is a poor candidate to abbreviate a word to given that it looks like, and could be confused for, Linear A fraction symbol B, as well as Linear A symbol L22 (which represents Hieroglyph N14), both of which are represented by a cross symbol, i.e. + (although, as we will see it is used to represent another word later in this chapter, so perhaps that is another reason why it was not used here). Coming second in the word, Hieroglyph G1 is, therefore, perhaps the most logical choice to represent it (as well, Milne would argue, as being distinctive).

Of course, the charge might be levelled here that I am biased and only accepting what I want to see in the evidence in order to prove my hypothesis, rather than even-handedly assessing the evidence and letting the facts speak for themselves. However, there are three points to remember in how we arrived at this translation for the symbol:

- First, we have correctly identified the hieroglyph that the symbol represents, and this is clear from the other words that it represents in the corpus (for example, the word for "cow", $3ht$, is abbreviated to this symbol representing its first hieroglyph, Hieroglyph G1).
- Second, the meaning of the word abbreviated here has been determined through comparison with the Dk series of Linear B tablets, which seems conclusive.
- Third, in the entirety of this work we have a body of evidence that Linear A is Middle Egyptian written in shorthand using hieroglyphs, and the shorthand method used was one that, being reflected in the later Greek method of shorthand, words could be abbreviated to a "distinctive letter or syllable (from the body of the word in question, not being the first or the last)" (or, as I would have it, for more practical reasons). No one has challenged this as being a characteristic of the Greek shorthand method when it is used in Greek, and, as Linear A demonstrates the same characteristics, we would expect to see words abbreviated on this basis in Linear A (and, indeed, it would be suspicious if we did not). This word being abbreviated to this symbol, in fact, evidences that the shorthand method we are using to derive translations is the correct one.

Therefore, the proposed translation cannot be considered a contentious one. Nonetheless, it is certainly the case that only by understanding the symbol's context on the tablet (by reference to the Dk series of Linear B tablets) that we can feel assured that this is the correct translation.

Moreover, as we now know (and as evidenced) that Hieroglyph G1 could be used to represent a word in shorthand in preference to Hieroglyph W11 (when that hieroglyph preceded it), we can, therefore, be more certain that the first word on this tablet was correctly identified, namely the word $g3w / g3wt$, meaning "tax". Again, with that word, we determined its likely meaning first: we identified that the tablet concerned a tax, and administrative convention then dictated that the first word on the tablet would most likely say that. One of the Middle Egyptian words for tax is *g3w* / *g3wt*, and applying the same rule of the shorthand method to the same hieroglyphs when written in the same order (Hieroglyph G1 following Hieroglyph W11) that word was similarly abbreviated to the same hieroglyph (or, rather, Linear A symbol representing that same hieroglyph) as we saw with the word for deficiency, *gbi*. This is no coincidence and it supports the identification of both words being correct as well as that the shorthand method is correctly applied.

Totals: Columns One, Two, and Three

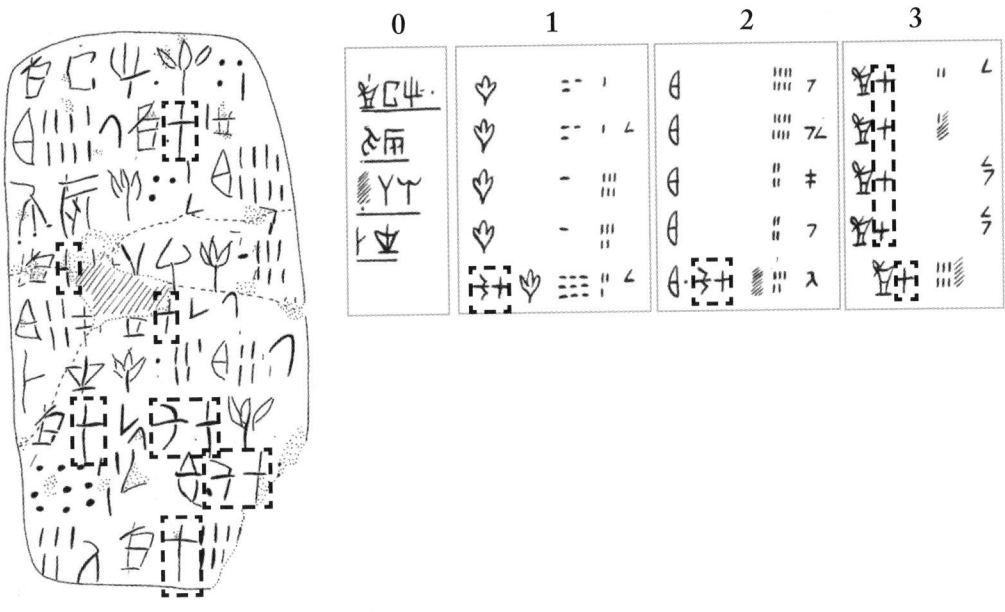

We have already discussed these symbols in Chapter Two. However, for completeness, they are:

Hieroglyph F14  / rotated / simplified / Linear A symbol L98

As we have seen previously, this symbol represents the first hieroglyph in the word:

wpt rnpt New Year's Day (and its festivals) [noun] F14 - W3

wpt rnpt New Year's Day (and its festivals) [noun] F15 - W3 - N5

As to why this symbol is rotated (it does not serve the purpose of saving space horizontally), it is so that it is not confused with Linear A symbol L49 (Hieroglyph F155) when, in particular, it was written in the more correct manner that we saw on Tablet HT 14.

154   The Decipherment of Linear A

Hieroglyph N14 ✶ / modified / Linear A symbol L22 ✚
As we have seen previously, this symbol represents the first hieroglyph in the word:

✶⛥ *dmḏ sm3* grand total [noun] N14 - F36

It is perhaps also worth noting, if we consider over time that a consistent lexicon of words would have been used by Egyptian scribes, that this word written with this spelling (in hieratic) was used in the late 4th or early 5th Dynasty Gebelein papyri concerning provincial administration.[13]

When this symbol appears in Column Three, this symbol means "grand total". When this symbol appears at the bottom of Column One and Two with the preceding symbol in front of it, together they mean "[on] New Year's Day, grand total".

Column Three, Rows Three and Four Fraction Symbol: Linear A fraction symbol J_E: ∠⁄7

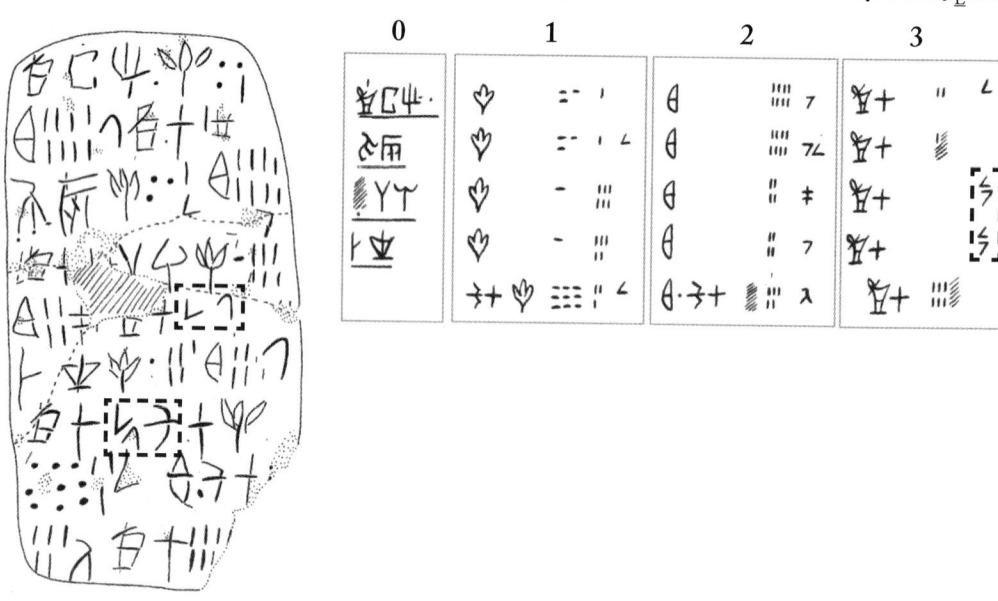

This fraction symbol is made up of two Linear A fraction symbols:

- Linear A fraction symbol J, namely ∠, which we have deduced, above, had a value of 0.5 or ½.
- Linear A fraction symbol E, namely 7, which was proven algebraically in Chapter Two to have had a value of −0.25 or −¼.

---

13. Hana Vymazalová, *The accounting documents from the papyrus archive of Neferre and their specific terminology* (PhD: Charles University in Prague, 2005), pp15–16, 175

These were also the two components of Linear A fraction symbol EJ, i.e. 𐝄, where we saw that these two symbols, when placed next to each other, should be multipied together. Here, however, they are one on top of the other; they are not, therefore, multiplied together. Realising this guides us to what is actually happening; in fact, they add together.

The value of symbol J_E is:

0.5 + (−0.25) = 0.25 or ½ + (−¼) = ¼

As we shall see later in this chapter, there was another fraction symbol that represented ¼ or 0.25, namely Linear A fraction symbol B, i.e. + . That being the case, why would the scribe have added two different symbols together here to get a value that he could have recorded with a single symbol already known to him? The answer is quite simple. When Linear A fraction symbol B, i.e. + , is written it is the same as Linear A symbol L22, i.e. + , which, as we have seen, also represents the word meaning "grand total". This could cause confusion (especially if one was next to the other, as could have been the case with the two examples here). Therefore, the scribe here has arrived at the same numerical value by a different route, using two fraction symbols added together instead.[14]

Therefore, taking the tabulation of HT 123A:

We are now in a position to translate the tablet in full:

---

14. Conversely, the scribe of Linear A Tablet ZA 8 from Zakros, having used Linear A symbol L22 to signify "grand total", and then writing 4 single unit tally marks, then wrote two Linear A fraction symbol Bs to represent a total fraction value of one half (so, 0.25 + 0.25) rather than simply using Linear A fraction symbol J (so, 0.5). Presumably the separation of Linear A symbol L22 from the two Linear A fraction symbol Bs by the 4 single unit tally marks meant the scribe felt no confusion would arise.

156 The Decipherment of Linear A

		Transcription Column 0	Transcription Column 1	Transcription Column 2 (Note 1)	Transcription Column 3
Transcript Row 1	Category One:	Tax [from the] pasture grounds [of the] villages	Sheep (rams) – 31	Wool – 7¾	Deficiency Grand Total – 2½
Transcript Row 2	Category Two:	[tax from the] meadows [of the] peasants	Sheep (rams) – 31½ (Note 2)	Wool – 7⅞	Deficiency, Grand Total – 4 (?)
Transcript Row 3	Category Three:	[tax from the] margin (of arable land) [of the] vintners	Sheep (rams) – 16	Wool – 4	Deficiency, Grand Total – ¼
Transcript Row 4	Category Four:	[tax on the] flocks [in the] temenē	Sheep (rams) – 15	Wool – 3¾	Deficiency, Grand Total – ¼
Transcript Row 5	Category Five:		[On] New Year's Day, Grand Total [of] sheep (rams) – 94⅛	Wool, [on] New Year's Day, Grand Total – 25 + remainder	Deficiency, Grand Total – 7 (?)

Note 1: Of course, if the calculation that gave rise to the wool tax payment obligation is exactly the same on Linear A Tablet HT 123A as in the Dk series of Linear B tablets (as it was), then the units of measure of the obligations once calculated (which were units of measure of weight) were also the same. We know from Ventris' and Chadwick's analysis that the units of measure of weight for the wool tax payment was a weight of 6.4 pounds or 2.90 kilograms, and that this was not an Egyptian measure of weight.[15] We might reasonably expect that the wool tax obligation was calculated by reference to units of measure of weight that were familiar to the taxpayer. Thus, given that this tax was being paid by Minoans (both during the period that Linear A was in use, when it was levied by the Egyptians, as well as during the period that Linear B was in use, when it was levied by the Mycenaeans), the most likely explanation is that this was a Minoan measure of weight. We see further evidence of this Minoan system of weights in the tithe-like tax paid to the temple which is considered subsequently in this chapter.

Note 2: One very obvious question that arises from the above is how can you have half a sheep (ram), which appears on Row Two. This is not, after all, an inventory where an animal might have been slaughtered and part consumed or have reflected partial ownership. As we shall see in the subsequent analysis, I estimate that typical flock ratios were on average 350 ewes to every 1 ram, and this typical ratio was at least implicit in the calculation of the annual wool tax obligation. The calculation on Tablet HT 123A uses male sheep (rams) as a proxy for the size of the whole flock e.g. if there were 700 ewes and 2 rams in

---

15. Michael Ventris & John Chadwick, *Documents in Mycenaean Greek* (2nd Ed.)(Cambridge: Cambridge University Press, 1973), pp56–57

a flock, the flock would be represented by just the 2 rams. What, then, if there were 175 ewes and no rams in a flock owned by a poorer farmer? The flock would be represented by a notional ½ ram in the tax calculation. The number of rams on the tablet, which is an ad hoc report, is, therefore, a notional number (which can include fractions) as well as a proxy, and it is no coincidence that the fraction value of rams is recorded under the peasant farmer heading given that, even today, poorer farmers who do not own (valuable) rams hire them to cover their ewes in the breading season. While the calculation no doubt started with a real number of rams, the number ultimately listed in the report on Tablet HT123A was not a real number in all cases; the wool tax was, to all intents and purposes, payable only on the ewes' wool, and if rams were used as a proxy for flock size, adjustment would have to be made when there were no rams in the flock in question.

Note 3: The reverse of the tablet (Tablet HT 123A) is, I believe, unrelated to this side of the tablet (reflective of this side of the tablet's use for an ad hoc report). It is too heavily damaged to be translated in this work.

As noted already, given the degree of summarisation, as well as the arithmetical skill of the scribe, we can see that this tablet does not form part of the day-to-day ledgers of the temple. It is an ad hoc report produced in response to a request for up to date information on the level of tax received based on the information contained within the day-to-day ledgers. This evidences the point for the Linear A corpus as a whole; the Linear A tablets were not a part of the state's (or temple's) accounts themselves, they were the peripheral workings, calculations, side notes, raw data, and ad hoc reports produced by scribes outside the processing of day-to-day accounting entries.

Before moving on, it is worth considering what else Tablet HT 123A, probably the most important tablet in the Linear A corpus, can tell us. Four further aspects are considered below.

Analysis

1. Evidence regarding the Egyptian administration on Crete

Tablet HT 123A tells us something about the Egyptian administration on Crete. As previously noted, we know that in the New Kingdom, in the 18th Dynasty, the state increasingly used the larger temples as its agents, in addition to (i.e. supplementing) or instead of (i.e. replacing) provincial administrators that had been used in Old Kingdom and Middle Kingdom Egypt.[16] Further, we know that in the New Kingdom the temples were, in particular, used by the king as royal agents to collect royal revenues on behalf of the king and that the temples kept accounts of state revenues, as well as producing and collecting their own temple revenues which the king was also known to tax (indeed, as we have seen on this tablet, the final category on the tablet records the temples paying tax to

---

16. Brian P. Muhs, *The Ancient Egyptian Economy 3000–30 BCE* (Cambridge: Cambridge University Press, 2016), pp115–116

the state in relation to their own flocks).¹⁷ We know from records found in Egypt that, during the 18th Dynasty, the scribes of the granary and the treasury recorded the arrival of shipments of harvests and harvest taxes at the royal granaries.¹⁸ On Crete, during the period that it was part of Egypt's empire, a "harvest tax" was evidently paid in wool, and we see record of this on Tablet HT 123A. As in Egypt, in collecting that tax, the temple was acting as agent for and on behalf of the state, supplementing the administration of the Egyptian governors (such as General Djehuty).

In the light of our knowledge of Egypt, and the information on this tablet, we can also infer something of the mechanics of the administration of the tax regime. The tax on sheep (that was to be paid in wool) was based on the number of sheep (rams) (as a proxy for total flock size) on New Year's Day. For the number of sheep (rams) (and, indeed, total flock size) to be known on New Year's Day, there must have been a census of livestock at that date. We know that in the late 18th Dynasty, after the period we are considering and after the tumult of the Amarna Revolution, the Decree of Horemheb tells us that the Overseer of Cattle was required to conduct a census of cattle (called an *irt irw iḥw*) for the apparent purpose of collecting a cattle tax or levy.¹⁹ Given that Horemheb's reign continued (or, at least, portrayed itself as continuing) the restoration of pre-Amarna practices we might infer this was a pre-Amarna practice in Egypt. Indeed, this is supported by Tablet HT 123A indicating an annual census of sheep was undertaken on Crete for the purposes of taxation when the island was part of Egypt's empire. The temple, as agent of the state, held the records of the state (including the sheep flock sizes of taxpayers) and recorded the tax received from taxpayers as they paid their taxes. As we shall see on the next tablet that we consider, Tablet HT 102, the detailed records of animal numbers that were held were not restricted to just sheep and were updated more frequently than annually.

2. Evidence for the size of Hagia Triada's area of administrative responsibility

As already noted, numbers of sheep (rams) were used as a proxy for the wider sheep flock size in the wool tax obligation calculation. If we can determine the total number of sheep implied by Tablet HT 123A, by comparison to archaeologists' estimates as to the number of sheep on Crete in the period, we can infer something of the size of the region that Hagia Triada had administrative responsibility for (at least in respect of the wool tax) and, therefore, its relative importance. To do this, first we need to determine how many sheep were implied by Tablet HT 123A.

Historian J. T. Killen wrote in 1964 that (contemporary) flocks of sheep in England were usually comprised of 50 or 60 ewes to 1 ram. He noted, however, that, in Medieval England, the number of breeding ewes serviced by a single ram was perhaps much

---

17. Brian P. Muhs, *The Ancient Egyptian Economy 3000–30 BCE* (Cambridge: Cambridge University Press, 2016), p96
18. Brian P. Muhs, *The Ancient Egyptian Economy 3000–30 BCE* (Cambridge: Cambridge University Press, 2016), pp115–116
19. Brian P. Muhs, *The Ancient Egyptian Economy 3000–30 BCE* (Cambridge: Cambridge University Press, 2016), p109

higher.[20] Today, ratios are unchanged from when Killen wrote, at roughly 50 (ewes) to 1 (ram), but it is known that rams can "cope" with many more ewes than this; one New Zealand researcher studied 40 flocks of 200–300 ewes each joined to a single ram.[21]

We also need to take into account the fact that the number of rams in Egyptian (and Mycenaean) Crete was used to calculate a tax liability, and the imposition of taxation tends to alter taxpayer behaviour. A good example of this is the Window Tax that was payable in England from 1696 to 1851. Above a minimum number of windows, the greater the number of windows on a building, the greater the amount of tax that had to be paid by the building owner. The number of windows was, therefore, a proxy for the value of the property in question and, in turn, the wealth of the taxpayer owner (and his or her ability to pay). As taxes do, this prompted a change in the behaviour of the taxpayers and, in an effort to avoid the tax, windows were blocked up, leaving lower numbers to be counted and included in the calculation of the relevant taxpayers' liabilities, which were correspondingly reduced. (Of course, tax authorities react to such avoidance; rates and thresholds on the Window Tax changed over time, and adding notional ram numbers into the tax calculation for a flock with too few rams would achieve the same.)

The same, I think it safe to say, will have been true in Late Bronze Age Crete. Here, the number of rams was a proxy for the flock size as a whole and the value of that flock and, in turn, the wealth of the flock-owning taxpayer liable to taxation. Again, the tax being calculated on this basis would have prompted a change in the behaviour of the taxpayers and, to avoid the tax, as few rams as possible would have been retained in the flocks so that lower numbers of rams were included in the calculation of the taxpayers' liabilities, which will have been correspondingly reduced. What ratio of ewes to rams should we therefore choose?

If a 300:1 ewe to ram ratio is one that can be coped with, it seems likely that the tax-avoiding flock owners would have tried to manage with even fewer rams, relatively, and had flocks with an even higher ewe to ram ratio. Perhaps, therefore, we can assume a 350:1 ratio of ewes to rams applied to the Cretan flocks. If we assume this, we can extrapolate an estimate for the number of sheep in the flocks implied by Tablet HT 123A as a whole, namely:

- Belonging to the village: 31 rams + 10,850 ewes
- Belonging to the peasants: 31 ½ (say 32) rams + 11,025 ewes
- Belonging to the vintners: 16 rams + 5,600 ewes
- Belonging to the temples (by implication of being in the *temenē*): 15 rams + 5,250 ewes

Thus, a combined total of 32,819 sheep, excluding lambs, is implied as recorded on Tablet HT 123A. These are clearly large numbers, far larger than anything explicitly recorded

---

20. J. T. Killen, "The Wool Industry of Crete in the Late Bronze Age", *Journal of the British School at Athens* (59) (1964), p2 footnote 9
21. Peter Hanrahan, *Agriculture Notes: Ram Percentage* (February 2003): https://www.vgls.vic.gov.au/client/en_AU/search/asset/1280773/0 (accessed 31 July 2022)

in the surviving Linear A corpus (and, indeed, writing such large numbers in full on a clay tablet would have been impractical if not impossible hence, perhaps, the need for a proxy when writing Tablet HT 123A let alone in order to make the wool tax obligation calculation itself much simpler). From these numbers, Tablet HT 123A clearly does not deal with a single village, peasant, vintner aristocrat, and temple. Rather, the inferred numbers demonstrate that Hagia Triada was a regional administrative centre and, as this tablet gives an aggregation of sheep (rams) by landholder group, underlying these numbers must have been the individual counts of sheep for the individual taxpayers within Hagia Triada's administrative region.

How big was this region? From the tablets that relate to the temple acting as principal in its dealings, as a religious institution, we might infer the extent of this area from the place names mentioned in the corpus (where tablets record transactions and balances): Tablet HT 2 and Tablet HT 86 (and Tablet HT 97A) refer to Knossos; Tablet HT 21A refers to Phaistos; and Tablet HT 13 refers to Amnisos. We might also use the total (implied) number of sheep on Tablet HT 123A to indicate the likely extent of the region administered from Hagia Triada when it acted in its capacity as agent of the state (i.e. here, collecting the wool tax). To do this, we need to include an estimate of the number of lambs.

Today, sheep litter sizes vary from 1 (at the end of a ewe's first year) to typically 2 (or more) thereafter up to the age of 10 (when ewes are slaughtered),[22] giving an average litter size of 1.9 (or more). However, the propensity for having 2 (or more) lambs per litter is something that has been increased in modern times through selective breading. Taking into account stillbirths, losses to predators, disease etc., and a lower rate of twin births, we might expect an average of 1.5 lambs per litter for the ewes recorded on Tablet HT 123A. While these lambs may have been slaughtered by the time that Tablet HT 123A was written (some time after New Year's Day which, as we will see, was mid to late August), at the flocks' peak sizes immediately after lambing, based on the ewes recorded on Tablet HT 123A, there would have been approximately 49,088 lambs in those flocks, giving a combined sheep total (rams, ewes, and lambs) of 81,907. Gerald Cadogan estimated that something of the order of 500,000 sheep were on Crete in Minoan times.[23] Therefore the sheep implied as recorded on Tablet HT 123A at Hagia Triada were approximately ⅙ of the estimated total on the island.

With this broad estimate to guide us, as well as the place names in the corpus, it would seem likely that the wool tax was administered from Hagia Triada for an area that we might sensibly see as including the high ground above the valleys of the Geropotamos river, and its tributary the Koutsoulidi, which enters the sea near Hagia Triada, and the high ground above the valleys of the Karteros, Giofyros, and Galanos rivers, in the north of the island around Knossos and Amnisos (though, of course, the sheep would have been

---

22. https://www.provicorural.com.au/what-is-the-gestation-period-for-sheep-what-to-know-when-raising-sheep/ (accessed 31 July 2022)
23. Gerald Cadogan, *Palaces of Minoan Crete* (London: Barrie & Jenkins Ltd, 1976), p13

in the hills above the valleys (to the south), not near the (north) coast). Together, this is roughly ⅙ of the island.

Why would Hagia Triada, rather than Knossos, have been the centre of administration for the wool tax for this region? Well, it is perhaps self-evident that if the tax was administered from here, and the receipts were recorded here, then, importantly, this is where the wool was physically received (after all, with the sheep in the Karteros, Giofyros, and Galanos valleys in the hills to the south, away from the north coast, a journey to a northern port might not have taken that much longer than a journey to Hagia Triada). Hagia Triada is close to the southern port of Kommos and the wool that had been collected from the tax at Hagia Triada could easily have been transported to Kommos and loaded onto ships for transport to Egypt; and from here, not having to sail round the island, and travelling with the prevailing winds and currents, those ships could reach Egypt in the quickest time possible.

3. <u>The interaction between the Egyptian calendar and the shearing season on Crete</u>
The Egyptian Civil Calendar had a 365-day year. This was divided into three seasons of four months each (in order, $Ꜣḥt$, Prt, and $Šmw$). When written, each month was numbered by reference to the season in which it fell (i.e. 1 to 4). Each month had 30 days and the twelfth month (4 $Šmw$) was followed by an intercalary month of five days. Not having leap years, New Year's Day in the Egyptian Civil Calendar moved forward roughly one day in every four years relative to what would have been New Year's Day in our own Gregorian Calendar. In the period that we are considering, where Crete was part of the Egyptian empire, in 1455 BC New Year's Day would have been on or around 22 August, and in 1424 BC, New Year's Day would have been on or around 14 August. While these are approximate dates, they are sufficiently accurate for the following discussion.

In Crete today, sheep are sheared every year from mid-May to mid-June.[24] It would seem likely that this is substantially unchanged since ancient times. Further, we can infer that Tablet HT 123A was written a reasonably significant period after shearing (indeed, from its Column One and Column Two totals, we know it was written after New Year's Day, the date the wool tax was actually assessed); only 7 units of wool (it seems) remained to be received out of a total obligation of 23⅜ units (i.e. 70% had been received) and, as we have seen, that wool was received from across a wide area (so the tablet was probably written towards the end of the first month of the New Year, 1 $Ꜣḥt$). If, therefore, the tax was determined by reference to the number of animals on New Year's Day, perhaps two months after shearing took place, how could the correct tax have been calculated? An enterprising flock owner might shear his sheep, keep the wool, but then sell all of his sheep before they were counted on New Year's Day in order to avoid the tax (although the purchaser that the tax liability then fell upon would have had to have been ignorant of the tax he now had to pay which, given that this tax appears to have affected all sheep owners, appears unlikely). Beyond relying on prospective taxpayers being informed as to their obligations, there seem two possible legislative ways that could have prevented this.

---
24. http://www.wondergreece.gr/v1/en/Articles/Architecture/8721-Mitata_in_Crete (accessed 31 July 2022)

In the Petra Papyri, from the 6th Century AD, there were a number of documents called *epistalmata tou somatismou*, "requests for transfer of taxation". These were drawn up for taxpayers transferring their tax liability to the name of another person as a result of, for example, the sale of the property on which that tax was being levied (and, presumably, the new owner not yet being recorded by the state as owning the property, which remained in the name of the former owner).[25] The incentive here was for the vendor to ensure state records were accurate.

I think a similar approach was probably adopted with rams. As we have seen, rams were used as a proxy for whole flock numbers in the wool tax obligation calculation. The starting point for calculating the value of that proxy would have been the actual number of rams (and the imposition of a tax calculated on the basis of ram numbers would have prompted their numbers to have been as low as possible within the flocks, as we have already discussed). If a farmer with 350 ewes and 1 ram sold or transferred his ram to a new owner between shearing and New Year's Day (and given the high value of rams, due to their lower numbers, but their importance to the sustainability of the overall flock, it would have been onerous to prevent such sales) the use of ram numbers as a proxy in the wool tax obligation calculation would no longer have worked (because the vendor now had 350 ewes and no rams). As noted previously, the number of rams in the wool tax calculation was not, in all circumstances, a real number. A notional 1 ram would, therefore, have been added back in to the farmer's total flock size of (now, only) 350 ewes to then be included in the calculation (which would, in turn, then be based on the right number of implied sheep (ewes)). As to the new owner of the ram, he would not have had to have paid tax based on this same animal now notionally included in the former owner's tax calculation. The incentive here, however, was for the purchaser to ensure state records were accurate. By registering the recent purchase of the ram, when the wool tax obligation was then calculated, it would be known not to include this ram in the new owner's tax calculation (especially if census officers could not attend all landowners on New Year's Day) and instead to leave the tax liability with the vendor. Consequently, rams could still change hands and on Tablet HT 13 we see rams being received by the temple in this period.

This would infer detailed records were maintained throughout, so it would seem likely that the census date on New Year's Day may, in reality, have been one of many days throughout the year when numbers of sheep were recorded (and, while the records concerning this have not survived, the style of record and calculation that this would have resulted in would have been the same as that on Tablet HT 102, which, as we will see subsequently, considers changes in numbers of goats in a herd in the month before New Year's Day).

For ewes, whose wool almost entirely paid the wool tax, a similar approach to rams would have had to have been adopted. Peasant farmers may have had no rams (having to hire rams to cover their ewes), so their taxation calculation could only initially have been

---

25. Marja Vierros, "Scribes and other writers in the Petra Papyri", in Rodney Ast, Malcolm Choat, Jennifer Cromwell, Julia Lougovaya, and Rachel Yuen-Collingridge (Eds.), *Observing the Scribe at Work: Scribal Practice in the Ancient World* (Leuven, Paris, Bristol, CT: Peeters, 2021), p103

based on the number of ewes. From the number of ewes, notional ram numbers would have been derived (using the relevant ratio of rams to ewes), and the tax obligation payable would have been calculated based on that derived notional number of rams. This would have necessitated a similar restriction on sales and transfers of ownership between shearing time and New Year's Day (perhaps except by prior permission, as also hypothesised with rams, subject to the exception noted in the analysis of Tablet HT 89).

Of course, the cause of the difficulty here is that the date the tax was assessed by reference to the animals in question was after the date when the material with which the tax payment obligation would be met was separated from those animals. Why, then, was the date of the census not undertaken earlier, before the date of shearing? Presumably this was because New Year's Day was when taxes were levied in Egypt proper and, I imagine, Egypt's imperial territories, such as Crete in this period, followed the administrative practices followed in Egypt. At a procedural level we will see evidence of Egyptian administrative practices being followed when we consider Tablet HT 86A and Tablet HT 86B.

4. Evidence regarding continuity between the Egyptian and Mycenaean regimes and the Dk series of Linear B tablets

That the same approach to recording sheep (i.e. males only) and calculating the wool tax obligation payable thereon on Tablet HT 123A was used as the Dk series of Linear B tablets attests to a significant degree of administrative continuity between the Egyptian and Mycenaean regimes (and perhaps even the Minoan regime before that given that Minoan units of measure of weight appear to have been used to weigh the wool tax obligation that was calculated). For the taxation system to have been administered in the same way it seems likely that at least some of those involved in the Egyptian administration served on under the Mycenaean regime. This is not particularly surprising given that, although it is not completely understood how, Linear B was related to Linear A, and we now know Linear A is Middle Egyptian written in shorthand using modified and simplified hieroglyphs. There is further evidence of this continuity if we reconsider the Dk series of Linear B tablets and, in particular, the phrase highlighted at (1), below, as it appears on Linear B Tablet Dk 1072 (which we noted in Chapter Two exhibits a 4:1 ratio of sheep (rams) to wool):

Linear B Tablet Dk 1072[26]

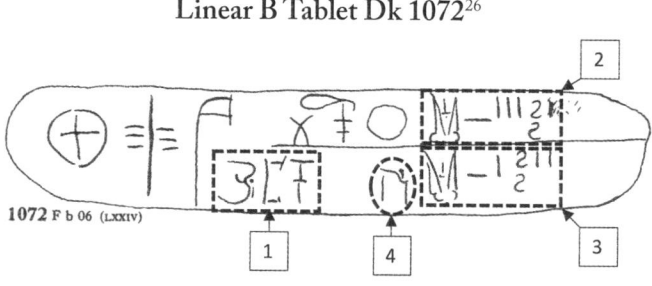

1072 F b 06 (LXXIV)

---

26. Sir Arthur Evans, *Scripta Minoa: The Written Documents of Minoan Crete, with special reference to the archives of Knossos, Volume II* (Oxford: Clarendon Press, 1952), p205

Ventris and Chadwick noted five tablets where the 4:1 sheep (rams) to wool ratio appears (Dk 1070–Dk 1074).[27] As we have seen, the wool amount in that ratio is made up of a combination of amounts received and to be received (i.e. the deficit). In the example of Tablet Dk 1072 above, in a standard format adopted across this series, the amount of wool already received is recorded above the line (top right of the tablet, highlighted at (2)), and the deficit amount to be received is recorded below the line (bottom right of the tablet, highlighted at (3)).

In each of Ventris and Chadwick's five examples the phrase highlighted at (1) precedes Linear B ideogram *61, which means deficit, highlighted at (4), as it also does on seven similar tablets exhibiting the 4:1 sheep (rams) to wool ratio, Tablets Dk 1064 - Dk 1069, and Tablet Dk 1075,[28] although not in the similar tablets also exhibiting the 4:1 sheep (rams) to wool ratio, Tablet Dk 1076 and Tablet Dk 1077. Twelve out of fourteen similar tablets (86%) is more than a high enough correlation to indicate that the phrase highlighted at (1) and Linear B ideogram *61 are synonymous (especially if we can understand the two exceptions).

In *Documents in Mycenaean Greek*, Ventris and Chadwick transcribed this phrase phonetically, according to the Linear B script's phonetic values, as *ku-ta-to*, which they believed to be a place name.[29] The thing about a place name (indeed virtually any name) is that it cannot be translated into a word or have any other meaning in the context it is written other than as that name. This, I think was their logic; the word could not be translated so it had to be a place name (they thought) and that, for them, was where the matter rested. In fact, it can be translated because it is Linear A. So, what do the Linear A symbols say? That they are both the same and are both next to the Linear B symbol for deficit indicates, again, a similar meaning.

Linear B Tablet Dk 1072[30]

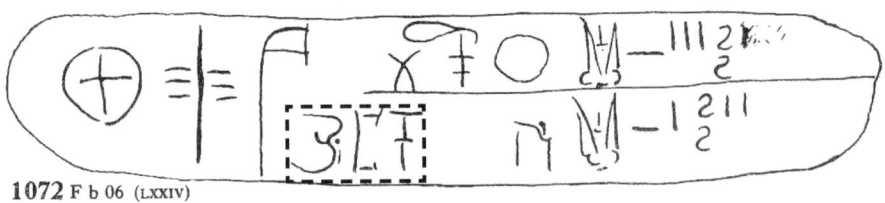

1072 F b 06 (LXXIV)

---

27. Michael Ventris & John Chadwick, *Documents in Mycenaean Greek* (2nd Ed.)(Cambridge: Cambridge University Press, 1973), p204
28. In the case of Dk 1068 the three symbols appear above the line, against the amounts (presumably) already received, rather than against the amounts, below the line, that, appearing in the same format, and with Linear B ideogram *61 to indicate so, are a deficit. I put this down to simple scribal error and include this tablet in tablets agreeing to this general rule.
29. Michael Ventris & John Chadwick, *Documents in Mycenaean Greek* (2nd Ed.)(Cambridge: Cambridge University Press, 1973), p204
30. Sir Arthur Evans, *Scripta Minoa: The Written Documents of Minoan Crete, with special reference to the archives of Knossos, Volume II* (Oxford: Clarendon Press, 1952), p205

The Translations

Hieroglyph F14 ⊍ / rotated ⌒ / simplified / Linear A symbol L98 ⇁ (NOT Linear B symbol *81 ("ku") ⇁)

As we have seen previously, this symbol represents the first hieroglyph in the word:

⊍ ▽ *wpt rnpt* New Year's Day (and its festivals) [noun] F14 - W3

⊍ ⊙ *wpt rnpt* New Year's Day (and its festivals) [noun] F15 - W3 - N5

Hieroglyph O1 ⊏⊐ / rotated ⊔ / Linear A symbol L74 ⊔ (NOT Linear B symbol *59 ("ta") ⊔)

As we have seen previously, Linear A symbol L74 represents Hieroglyph O1. As we will frequently see in the Linear A corpus, this symbol represents the last hieroglyph in the word(s):

🦉 ⎯⎯ △ ⊏⊐ *mḫr* storehouse, barn [noun - arch.] G17 - D36 - T28 - D21 - M17 - O1

🦉 ⎯⎯ △ ⊏⊐ *mḫr* storehouse, barn [noun - arch.] G17 - D36 - T28 - D21 - M17 - X1 - O1

🦉 ⎯⎯ △ ⊏⊐ *mḫr* storehouse, barn [noun - arch.] G17 - D36 - T28 - D21 - O1

⎯ 🦉 ⎯⎯ ⊏⊐ *šmyt / šmy* storehouse, barn ambulatory [noun - arch.] N37 - G17 - M17 - M17 - X1 - O1

Hieroglyph W11 - Z1 ⌷ / simplified / Linear A symbol L39 ⊤ (NOT Linear B symbol *05 ("to") ⊤)

The derivation of this Linear A symbol is discussed later in this chapter on page 446. As we will see, here it represents the first hieroglyphs in the word:

⌷ *gb* deficiency [noun] W11 - Z1 - D58

The three symbols therefore mean "[on] New Year's Day [in the] storehouse / barn – deficiency".

It is inconceivable, given the extremely high degree of correlation (86%), that it was anything other than intentional that both the Linear A term for "deficiency" and Linear B term for "deficit" were used, so why might this be? Something that is a deficit in a set of accounts is going to be labelled as such in order to be understood as such by the person that reads it (after all, one of the core characteristics of accounts today, which will have

166   The Deciperment of Linear A

always been the case, is that they should be comprehensible to their users[31]). We can infer, therefore, that there were people who used the Dk series of Linear B tablets who could only read Linear B, and there were some who used the Dk series of Linear B tablets who could only read Linear A.

What about the subheadings on the other two tablets, Linear B Tablet Dk 1076 and Tablet Dk 1077 (which are both the same)?

Linear B Tablet Dk 1076[32]

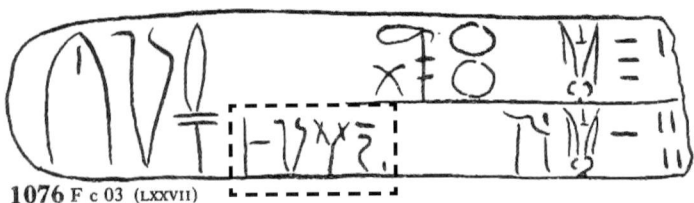

1076 F c 03 (LXXVII)

Hieroglyph T14 ⌐ replaced by AA26 (or J26) ¥ / reversed ⌐ / Linear A symbol L30 ⌐ (NOT Linear B symbol *01 ("da") ⌐)

As we have seen previously, this symbol represents the (replaced) first hieroglyph used in the word:

'wt small cattle, goats, herds [noun - ani.] T14

'wt small cattle, herds, flocks, goats [noun - ani.] T14 - G43 - E28 - Z2

'wt small cattle, herds, flocks, goats [noun - ani.] T14 - G43 - X1 - E1 - Z2

'wt small cattle, herds, flocks, goats [noun - ani.] T14 - G43 - X1 - E8 - Z2

'wt small cattle, herds, flocks, goats [noun - ani.] T14 - Z7 - X1 - E28 - F27 - Z3A

'wt small cattle, herds, flocks, goats [noun - ani.] T14 - Z7 - X1 - E28 - Z2

'wt small cattle, herds, flocks, goats [noun - ani.] T14 - Z7 - X1 - Z5 - Z2

---

31. Financial Accounting Standards Board, *Statement of Financial Accounting Concepts Statement No. 1: Objectives of Financial Reporting by Business Enterprises* (Norwalk (Conn.): Financial Accounting Standards Board, November 1978), Paragraph 34
32. Sir Arthur Evans, *Scripta Minoa: The Written Documents of Minoan Crete, with special reference to the archives of Knossos, Volume II* (Oxford: Clarendon Press, 1952), p205

The Translations 167

Hieroglyph D36 ⌐⎯◖ / modified / simplified / Linear A symbol L76 (NOT Linear B symbol *73 ("mi"))

The derivation of this symbol is discussed on page 196. As we shall see throughout the Linear A corpus, it represents the first hieroglyph in the word:

iw'w quadrupeds, animals [noun – ani.] D36 - D36 - F28 - Z3

Hieroglyph T25 / rotated / simplified / Linear A symbol L60 (NOT Linear B symbol *30 ("ni"))

This Linear A symbol represents Hieroglyph T25 which has been rotated by 180 degrees and simplified, both for ease of incision. As we shall see throughout the Linear A corpus, it is the first hieroglyph (or, in one instance, the last hieroglyph) in the word:

db3w payments, reward, compensation, bribes [noun] T25 - D58

db3w payments, reward, compensation, bribes [noun] T25 - D58 - G1 - Z7 - Y1 - Z2

db3w payments, reward, compensation, bribes [noun] T25 - D58 - G43 - Y1 - Z2

db3w payments, rewards [noun] T25 - D58 - N33 - N33 - N33 - G43

db3 reward, payment [noun] T25 - D58 - Z7 - Y1

db3 reward, payment [noun] D46 - D58 - T25

Hieroglyph U19 / rotated / reversed / Linear A symbol unrecognised by Brice (NOT Linear B symbol *36 ("jo"))

The derivation of this symbol is discussed on page 446. Here, it represents the second hieroglyph in the word:

nwi to gather, to collect, to assemble, return, bring back, come back [verb] N35 - U19 - W24 - G43 - M17 - M17 - D54

nwi fix, bring order to (equipment), care for, take care of, collect, assemble [verb] N35 - U19 - W24 - G43 - V1 - D40

168 The Decipherment of Linear A

𓈖𓏤𓂓𓀁 *nwi* to gather, to collect, to assemble [verb] N35 - U19 - W24 - Z4 - A24

𓈖𓏤𓏭𓏭𓏴𓂢𓏫 *nwi* to gather, to collect, to assemble [verb] N35 - U19 - W24 - Z4 - M17 - M17 - Z9 - D40 - Z3A

𓈖𓏤𓂓𓂡 *nwi* to gather, to collect, to assemble [verb] N35 - U19 - W24 - Z7 - D40

𓈖𓅱𓏭𓏭𓏏𓀁𓀀𓏥 *nwi* to gather, to collect, to assemble [verb] N35 - U19 - W24 - Z7 - M17 - M17 - X1 - Y1 - A24 - A1 - Z2

𓈖𓅱𓏭𓏭𓏴𓂢𓏫 *nwi* to gather, to collect, to assemble [verb] N35 - U19 - Z7 - M17 - M17 - Z9 - D40 - Z3A

As we will see, when this word is used on Linear A Tablet KH 11, it is represented by its second, rather than its first, hieroglyph. The most likely reason for this is that Hieroglyph N35, by itself, spells the Middle Egyptian word *n*, a preposition meaning "to", "for", or "because of". If a symbol representing just this hieroglyph were to appear then it would be confusing for the reader; it could represent the preposition or another word intended to be conveyed by it. Consequently, the second hieroglyph is chosen to represent the word (and, indeed, Hieroglyph N35 is not, apparently, represented by a Linear A symbol because it is not represented in the corpus).

These four symbols therefore mean "[from the] flock [of] quadrupeds, payments to [be] gather[ed]" and, in practical effect, without explicitly stating it, this is a deficit. Again, therefore, this is Linear A, and its meaning clearly makes sense in the context indicated by Linear B.

There is further evidence of Linear A being used on the Dk series of Linear B tablets. Returning to Tablet Dk 1072, we can also translate its heading highlighted below:

Linear B Tablet Dk 1072[33]

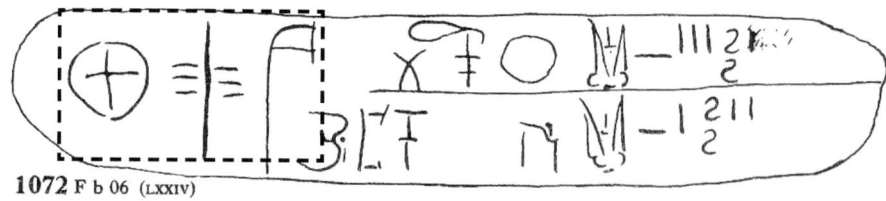

1072 F b 06 (LXXIV)

---

33. Sir Arthur Evans, *Scripta Minoa: The Written Documents of Minoan Crete, with special reference to the archives of Knossos, Volume II* (Oxford: Clarendon Press, 1952), p205

The Translations 169

<u>Hieroglyph O49</u> ⊗ / simplified / Linear A symbol L29 ⊕ (NOT Linear B symbol *77 ("ka") ⊕)

This Linear A symbol represents Hieroglyph O49 simplified. As we shall see, throughout the Linear A corpus, it represents the word:

⊗ *niwt* city, town [noun] O49

Of the fourteen tablets of the Dk series of Linear B tablets that we are considering now, six are damaged so we cannot see their first symbol. However, of the remaining eight, three begin with the Linear A symbol L29, representing Hieroglyph O49 and the word *niwt* meaning "city". As we have noted, as a matter of administrative convention we would expect tablets to begin with a place name and, therefore, as we shall see throughout the Linear A corpus, this symbol frequently appears at the start of Linear A tablets.

<u>Hieroglyph V16</u> / rotated / simplified / Linear A symbol L92 (NOT Linear A symbol *04 ("te"))

The derivation of this symbol is discussed on pages 193 to 194. As we shall see throughout the Linear A corpus, and as discussed in Appendix 4, the symbol that follows the symbol for "city" represents the name of that city. Unfortunately, we know the names of relatively few Cretan city names in Middle Egyptian and we do not know of any Cretan city names that could be abbreviated to a symbol representing Hieroglyph V16. The place name represented here is, therefore, unknown.

<u>Hieroglyph M17</u> / reversed / Linear A symbol L97 (NOT Linear A symbol *10 ("u"))

As we will see throughout the Linear A corpus, this Linear A symbol represents (reversed) Hieroglyph M17. Here, it represents the first hieroglyph in the word:

ipw payments, tax [noun] M17 - Q3 - G43 - Y1 - Z2

ipw payments, tax [noun] M17 - Q3 - G43 - Y1V

The three symbols at the start of Tablet Dk 1072 therefore mean "[from the] city of [unknown place name], tax". Ventris and Chadwick had believed this to be a personal name.[34] It is not.

This is not the place to translate all of the headings and subheadings of the Dk series of Linear B tablets, but far from being names written in Linear B that could not be translated, these tablets show us that Linear A was still being used alongside Linear B

---
34. Michael Ventris & John Chadwick, *Documents in Mycenaean Greek* (2nd Ed.)(Cambridge: Cambridge University Press, 1973), p204

perhaps a century after the Egyptians had left Crete. Graph 4.1 in Chapter Four was wrong, and deliberately so, for it shows the received wisdom on the subject (until now). The administrative use of Linear A demonstrably survived on into the Mycenaean period.

Conclusion

So, why would Egyptian accounting terminology and narrative be used in Mycenaean tax records? The answer is simple. An Egyptian temple in Knossos, left over from the time when Crete was part of the Egyptian empire (and, indeed, from before that), continued to function. As Sultan Mehmet II had permitted the Greek Orthodox Church to continue to function after the fall of Constantinople in AD 1453, so too this Egyptian temple at Knossos (where the Dk series of Linear B tablets was found) continued to function long after the Mycenaean conquest of Crete. Here, however, it also continued to function in its capacity as agent of the state, administering the collection of taxes, as it had done when Crete was part of Egypt's empire.

Given that Hagia Triada's area of administrative responsibility for the wool tax included Knossos, in line with Crete's changing trading patterns after the period of Egyptian rule (discussed in Chapter Four), in the Mycenaean period a portion of that area of responsibility (presumably at least for Knossos) was instead administered at Knossos, reflecting state trade being directed northwards, towards Greece, rather than, as previously, the wool tax being exported southwards to Egypt.

Tablet HT 102

Tablet HT 102 records the highest number explicitly recorded on any tablet found at Hagia Triada (1,060, the end total), and from Chapter One we know that it records cattle or livestock. As might be expected, therefore, it records one of the two most common cattle or livestock animals on Crete during the period, goats.

It seems most likely that the record of herd numbers would have been created for the purposes of taxation (for why else would the Egyptian temple, other than as agent of the state, be interested in the size of a third party's goat herd?) For that reason, it is included in this section of the chapter.

Heading: Row One, Symbols One and Two

Hieroglyph O49 ⊗ / simplified / Linear A symbol L29 ⊕
As we have seen previously, this symbol represents the word:

⊗ *niwt* city, town [noun] O49

Hieroglyph F35 ͡/ simplified / Linear A symbol L2 ✝
As set out in Appendix 4, the name of a city follows the word for "city". Unfortunately, as we do not know of any Cretan town names that could be abbreviated to a symbol representing Hieroglyph F35, the name of the city that this symbol represents is unknown.

Stating the city name is unknown is not, however, to fall into the same trap as Ventris and Chadwick as abbreviations of three major place names that we would expect to see represented in the corpus at the start of tablets appear this way (i.e. following the symbol representing the word for "city") (see Appendix 4). What the place names of Crete were called in Middle Egyptian are, in the majority of cases, unknown, so we would expect unknown place names to feature in the translations of the tablets.

With our current knowledge, therefore, we can only say that the first two symbols of this tablet mean "[in the] city [of] [unknown place name]".

Category One: Row One, Symbols Three to Five:

Hieroglyph V28 ⟨⟩ / rotated ⟨⟩ / simplified / Linear A symbol L31 Y

In Chapter One we determined that the third of the three symbols considered in Category One (i.e. Symbol Five on Row One, the symbol discussed after next) represented an animal because it could be written with the male = sign (as it is later on this tablet). This animal type is the subject of this category (and indeed, the tablet as a whole). That it represents an animal (the one that appears in the greatest number in the corpus) helps us identify the meaning to be attributed to the other symbols on the tablet. The determination of the meaning of this symbol is set out in Appendix 5, which the reader should consult.

As we shall see with the receipts recorded on Tablet HT 114A and Tablet HT 121 which follow in the next section of this chapter and where these same three symbols in succession are also used, this first symbol can represent the Middle Egyptian verb *ḥtr*, which means "to provide (a temple with)". Here, however, the numbers recorded under this category of livestock (976) evidently do not deal with a delivery in the month. We have here, therefore, a demonstration of the principal problem with deciphering shorthand, namely that the same symbol can mean two or more different things. We can only tell from a symbol's context, in this case provided by the count of items in the category, what its most likely meaning is.

Given the heading of the tablet, from which we know the record relates to a whole city, and given the numbers in question, as on Tablet HT 123A, this symbol most likely represents the word:

ḥnbwt margin (of arable land), measured land, confines (of district) [noun] V28 - M2 - N35 - D58 - X1 - N23 - Z2

ḥnb margin (of arable land), measured land [noun] V28 - M2 - N35 - D58 - Z7 - N23 - Z1

While the same Middle Egyptian word as was used on Tablet HT 123A, because we are dealing with the herds of a city (rather than just the aristocratic vintners), a different (attested) meaning in English should be inferred when it is used here, namely "[in the] confines (of the district)".

Hieroglyphs Z5 - Z5\\/ Linear A symbol L58
This symbol, representing two hieroglyphs, is used in the Linear A corpus in the context of dates (see, for example, Tablet HT 1A in Appendix 8). Here, therefore, the symbol represents the following word:

ꜣbd month [noun] N14 - N11 - Z5 - Z5 - N5

The scribe's choice to abbreviate this spelling of the word *ꜣbd* here appears to have been a deliberate one, for the spelling of the word using a representation of Hieroglyph N11, which by itself can also spell the word *ꜣbd*, is used elsewhere (e.g. on Tablet HT 19 and Tablet HT 17, which are considered later in this chapter). Nonetheless the choice not to use a symbol representing the simpler iteration of the word having been made, the word could not be abbreviated to its first hieroglyph (as this represented the word *dmḏ smꜣ* meaning "grand total" when abbreviated to a symbol representing its first hieroglyph, Hieroglyph N14, and this was used on the final row of this tablet), and it could not be abbreviated to its last hieroglyph (which, as we will see when discussing Linear A symbol L26, would simply become a dot in Linear A and thus be confused with a section break dot, as appears after headings and subheadings, or a count mark for 10). Having additionally decided not to abbreviate the word to a symbol representing Hieroglyph N11, this therefore left Hieroglyphs Z5 - Z5.

These two symbols therefore mean "[in the] confines (of the district) [in the] month". The reference to "[in the] month" reflects the fact that these animals were there throughout the month-long period covered by the tablet and additions to or deductions from the herd did not affect this number (i.e. this was an opening balance at the start of the month). This also suggests that the record of herd numbers was updated every month.

Hieroglyph F27 / partially rotated / simplified / modified / Linear A symbol L42
As noted, the derivation of this Linear A symbol from the hieroglyph it represents, and the identification of its meaning, is considered in Appendix 5 which the reader should consult. For now, however, this symbol represents the last hieroglyph in the word:

ꜥr goat [noun - ani.] D36 - D21 - E31 - F27

This symbol is not joined to a male = sign (as it is later on this tablet), so we know these are female goats (i.e. nanny goats).

174   The Decipherment of Linear A

These three symbols therefore mean "[in the] confines (of the district), [in the] month, [female] goats". They are followed by a count of 976.

<u>Category Two: Row Two, Symbols One to Three:</u>

Hieroglyph O43 𓎼 / rotated 𓎼 / simplified / Linear A symbol L1 𐙀
This symbol is a representation of Hieroglyph O43 rotated by 90 degrees to take up less space horizontally, and simplified, removing some of the intricate detail that could not be incised in clay. Here this symbol represents the first hieroglyph in the word:

𓌉 ooo šsp to receive [verb] O43 - U30 - D40 - M33

Hieroglyph T25 𓌉 / rotated 𓌉 / simplified / Linear A symbol L60 Y
This Linear A symbol represents Hieroglyph T25 which has been rotated by 180 degrees and simplified, both for ease of incision. As we have seen previously, this symbol represents the first hieroglyph (or, in one instance, last hieroglyph) in the word:

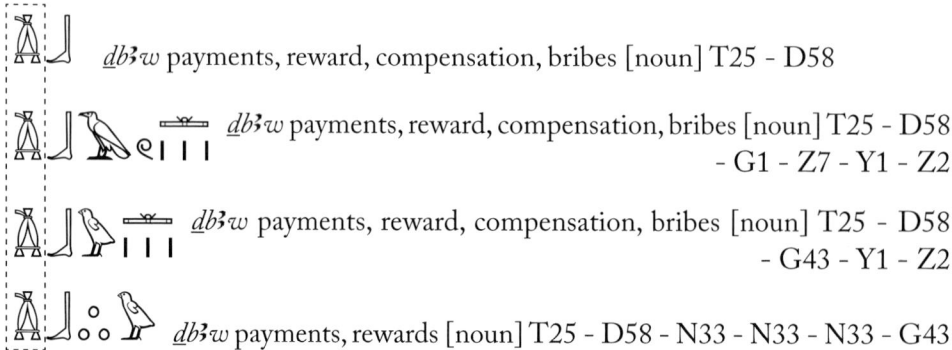

The Translations 175

db3 reward, payment [noun] T25 - D58 - Z7 - Y1

db3 reward, payment [noun] D46 - D58 - T25

Hieroglyph F27 / partially rotated / simplified / modified / Linear A symbol L42
(plus male = symbol)
As we have seen previously, this symbol represents the last hieroglyph in the word:

ꜥr goat [noun - ani.] D36 - D21 - E31 - F27

In this instance, however, the symbol has the male = symbol joined to it, crossing its stem. As we saw in Chapter One, with Linear B, when the = symbol is joined to a symbol that represents an animal, it indicates that animal was a male animal. This is also the case in Linear A. Here, therefore, we have male (i.e. billy) goats.

These three symbols therefore mean "received [for] payment, male [billy] goats". On the undamaged portion of the tablet, it records 33 animals as having been received. However, the damage here has, Godart & Olivier concedes, possibly destroyed additional tally marks originally recorded here. Indeed, in order for the tablet to reconcile to its total, I believe that the original total here was 35 (with the first symbol of the following category being written slightly below and to the right of these missing tally marks). The layout of the count of 5 single tally marks, only 3 of which have survived, would match that seen on Category Seven, with 3 above and 2 below.

At this stage it is worth considering the = male symbol further as it is, in fact, also derived from a hieroglyph (although it has not previously been recognised as such). Excursus 5.1, below, discusses this in more detail.

Excursus 5.1: The male = symbol

In both Linear A and Linear B, where the = symbol is joined to a symbol that represents an animal it indicates that animal was male. The shorthand method we are using shows us where this symbol originates from.

If we look at the following nouns which mean "male":

ḥ3wty warrior, male, man [noun] D34 - G1 - Z7 - X1 - Z4 - A24

ḥ3wty warrior, male, man [noun] D34 - G45 - X1 - Z4

176 The Decipherment of Linear A

ꜣwty warrior, male, man [noun] D34 - Z4 - G43 - X1 - A7 - Z3

ꜣy male [noun] G47 - G1 - Z7 - Z4 - D52 - Y1 - A1 - Z2

All of these contain the hieroglyph Z4 \\. If we take the second word above, in particular, and apply the shorthand method, it could be abbreviated to a symbol representing its last hieroglyph, namely Hieroglyph Z4:

ꜣwty warrior, male, man [noun] D34 - G45 - X1 - Z4

If we take this hieroglyph and rotate it by 90 degrees, i.e.:

\\ is rotated by 90 degrees to become ╱ which is the male = symbol

This is the Linear A and Linear B = symbol that means male when it is joined to another symbol that represents an animal. It appears twice on Tablet HT 102:

The Translations   177

Category Three: Row Two, Symbol Four & Row Three, Symbols One & Two:

Hieroglyph D46 ⌒ / rotated ⎵ / simplified / Linear A symbol L100 Ψ

Although the tablet is damaged, Brice's transcription indicates that this symbol was Linear A symbol L100. I agree. As we have seen previously, this symbol represents Hieroglyph D46 rotated by 90 degrees to save space horizontally, and then simplified and written as a "stick" hand.

From the context in which it appears on this tablet (as will become clear, the tablet is a record of the movements on the numbers of goats in the city's herd during the last month of the year), here the symbol represents the first hieroglyph in the word:

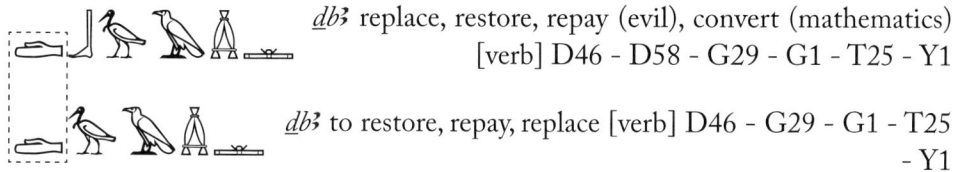

      ḏbꜣ replace, restore, repay (evil), convert (mathematics) [verb] D46 - D58 - G29 - G1 - T25 - Y1

      ḏbꜣ to restore, repay, replace [verb] D46 - G29 - G1 - T25 - Y1

Hieroglyph A59 🯅 / reversed 🯅 / simplified / Linear A symbol L99 ⁊

While the tablet is again damaged, here this symbol is nonetheless Linear A symbol L99, a simplified (and reversed) representation of Hieroglyph A59. This is the first hieroglyph in the word:

      mniw herdsmen [plural noun - title] A59 - M17 - M17 - Z7 - D40 - A1 - Z2

178   The Decipherment of Linear A

Hieroglyph F27 ⧗ (+ Hieroglyph Z4 ⟍ rotated) / partially rotated / simplified / modified / Linear A symbol L42 ⧙ (plus male = symbol)

As we have seen previously, this symbol represents the joined last hieroglyphs in the words:

⟨image⟩ ꜥr goat [noun - ani.] D36 - D21 - E31 - F27

⟨image⟩ ḥꜣwty warrior, male, man [noun] D34 - G45 - X1 - Z4

Here, therefore, this joined symbol means "male goats".
   These three symbols therefore mean "replaced [by the] herdsmen, male goats". They are followed by a count of 33.
   The Linear B records show that shepherds tending palatial flocks could swap their own (mostly adult) sheep for fat wethers (for consumption) or ewes (for breeding).[35] It would seem logical to presume that similar arrangements existed for herdsmen when they tended (here, the city's) goat herds, as the shepherds tending palatial sheep flocks, and the effect of those similar arrangements, in terms of their ability to swap animals from personal flocks with animals in the city's flock, is what is seen here. The herdsmen are making repayment of 33 (male) goats, presumably indicating that number of animals had been taken from the herd previously, necessitating the repayment that was now being made and which was recorded here.

Category Four: Row Three, Symbols Three to Five:

---

35. Paul Halstead, "Missing Sheep: On the Meaning and Wider Significance of O in Knossos Sheep Records", *The Annual of the British School at Athens*, 94(1999), p166 and Dimitri Nakassis, "The Extractive Systems of the Mycenaean World", in Jonathan Valk and Irene Soto Marín (Eds.), *Ancient Taxation: The Mechanics of Extraction in Comparative Perspective* (New York: New York University Press, 2021), p102

The Translations   179

Hieroglyphs Z5 - Z2 ιιι / rotated \ / modified / Linear A symbol L51

As we saw in Chapter Three, Linear A symbol L51 represents Hieroglyphs Z5 - Z2 that were rotated by 180 degrees and modified to have a line drawn over them so that they were not confused with tally marks:

Hieroglyphs Z5 - Z2 ιιι

is rotated to become \ and

modified to become \ which is Linear A symbol L51

This symbol represents the last hieroglyphs in the Middle Egyptian word meaning "small cattle":

'wt small cattle, herds, flocks, goats [noun - ani.] T14 - Z7 - X1 - Z5 - Z2

An alternative here might, however, have been:

rnn young ones, younglings, calves [noun – ani.] D21 - N35 - N35 - Z5 - Z1

When Michael Ventris determined the syllabic values of Linear B symbols this could be tested by applying them to the Linear B corpus as a whole. Given the very different nature of Linear A we cannot do the same (as the example in Chapter Three noted, A can stand for apples as well as avocados). In certain instances, however, we can do something similar as regards the meanings of words. In this instance, for example, we can rely on a degree of administrative consistency having been present, and a consistency in meanings being conveyed, across the Linear A corpus as a whole in order to determine which of these two words is the correct one to infer was abbreviated here:

- Tablet HT 2 (which we shall review later in this chapter) records fodder for quadrupeds followed by fodder for "small cattle" using the Middle Egyptian word 'nḫ rather than 'wt as here;
- Tablet HT 14 (which we shall also review later in this chapter), which has a similar layout to Tablet HT 2, records fodder for quadrupeds followed by fodder for what could be either small cattle ('wt) or young cattle (rnn) represented by Linear A symbol L51 (representing Hieroglyphs Z5 - Z1).
- Given the similar layout of Tablet HT 14 to Tablet HT 2, assuming the categorisation of commodities was consistent in terms of meanings, a reasonable assumption within the accounts of one institution (despite different scribes within that institution choosing to convey that same meaning with different Middle Egyptian words represented in

shorthand), we can infer that "small cattle", rather than "young cattle", was meant, and that Linear A symbol L51 (on Tablet HT 14) represented the middle Egyptian word 'wt.
- Here, therefore, for consistency across the corpus as a whole, "small cattle" is the more appropriate meaning for this symbol.

Thus, the symbol here represents the last hieroglyphs in the word:

'wt small cattle, herds, flocks, goats [noun - ani.] T14 - Z7 - X1 - Z5 - Z2

Of course, we have already seen this word when it was abbreviated to a symbol representing its first hieroglyph (or, rather, the hieroglyph that replaced its first hieroglyph) on Tablet HT 123A. As we noted in Chapter Three, depending on the choices of the scribe in question (governed, no doubt, by the scribe's professional background, immediate necessity, and institutional convention), one scribe might abbreviate a word to a symbol representing its first hieroglyph(s) whereas another might abbreviate the word to a symbol representing its last hieroglyph(s). As the simplistic example in Chapter Three also stated, avocado can be abbreviated to either A or O.

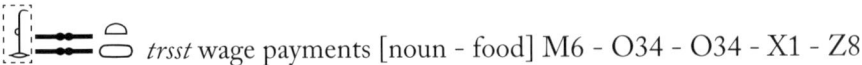
Hieroglyph M6 / reversed / simplified / Linear A symbol L72/94 ₹ or ₹ (as here)
Here Hieroglyph M6 has been reversed for ease of incision (for a right-handed scribe it would be easier to write in the same manner as our number 2, from top to bottom, than if it were not reversed). It has also been simplified (the base is written as a straight line, and the circle half way up the stem is written as a dot (as here) or, occasionally, as a straight line). Here, therefore, from the context on the tablet, it represents the first hieroglyph in the word:

trsst wage payments [noun - food] M6 - O34 - O34 - X1 - Z8

Hieroglyphs N5 - Z1 / simplified / modified / Linear A symbol L26
Hieroglyphs N5 - Z1 became Linear A symbol L26 in two steps. First, Hieroglyph N5, a dot in the centre of a circle, has been simplified for ease of incision to become merely a dot:

Leaving the symbol as this would, however, potentially be confusing as it might be mistaken as a count of 11 made up of a vertical tally mark (representing a count of 1) and a dot (which sometimes replaces the horizontal tally mark, representing a count of 10). Therefore, as we saw previously with Hieroglyphs Z5 - Z2 and the process of modification they went through to become Linear A symbol L51 (and for the same reason), a second step was undertaken and the symbol was modified further to have a bar added to the top of it:

The Translations   181

i becomes ī

Hieroglyphs Z5 - Z1 are, therefore, represented by Linear A symbol L26. These hieroglyphs appear last in the word:

wnwt duty, service, hour [noun] E34 - N35 - W24 - G43 - X1
  - N14 - N5 - Z1

These three symbols therefore mean "[less] small goats [for] wage payments [for] services". They are followed by a count of 10. We can infer that this is a deduction from the accumulating total given both the translation (wages are an expense) and the end total for the tablet (which needs to correctly add up).

Commodity Four: Row Three, Symbol Six and Row Four, Symbol One

The first symbol here, Row Three, Symbol Six, is Linear A symbol L95. This, however, is a combination of two Linear A symbols, Linear A symbol L55 and Linear A symbol L91. How they are joined together is set out in Appendix 6, to which the reader should refer.

Hieroglyphs D28 - Z1 / simplified / modified / Linear A symbol L55
As we have previously seen, this symbol represents Hieroglyphs D28 - Z1. Here it represents the word:

k3w food, bounty [noun - food] D28 - Z1

182   The Decipherment of Linear A

joined to Hieroglyph Z4B - Z4B - W24 ☰ ⊙/ modified (four dashes as dots inside / adjoining circle) / Linear A symbol L91 ⊙

As set out in Appendix 6, this symbol, representing Hieroglyphs Z4B - Z4B - W24, represents the ordinal:

☰ ⊙ *fdnw* fourth Z4B - Z4B - W24

becomes Linear A symbols L55 + L91 / Linear A symbol L95 ⊕

As stated in Appendix 6, we would normally expect the all four dashes of Hieroglyphs Z4B - Z4B to be written inside Hieroglyph W24 when Linear A symbol L91 was written. However, here the scribe has realised that not all four dashes (or, dots that the scribe has turned them into) could fit into the circle given that the symbol is, in turn, joined to Linear A symbol L55. The scribe has, therefore, put two of the dots inside the circle and has put the other two above the circle touching the arms of Linear A symbol L55 (presumably to highlight that they relate to this combined symbol and are not related to the count of the previous category). This is shown below, on an extract of a photograph of the tablet.

Extract of photograph from
Godart & Olivier
of Tablet HT 102
Row Three, Symbol Six

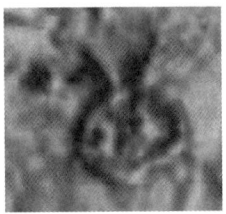

Extract of photograph from
Godart & Olivier
of Tablet HT 102
Row Three, Symbol Six
with ordinal dots highlighted

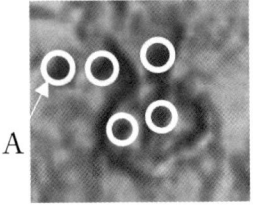

On the left-hand side of the second picture, the first dot in a white circle (labelled "A"), which is not joined to the symbol we are considering, represents the count of 10 small goats from the previous category recorded on the tablet, which were wage payments for services. To the right of this there are a further four highlighted in white circles: there are two dots inside the symbol main body of Linear A symbol L55 (i.e. Hieroglyph W24 circle) and two dots outside but attached to its arms (i.e. Hieroglyphs D28 - Z1). The two dots attached to the arms of Linear A symbol L55 were omitted from Godart & Olivier's sketch diagram and represent the two dashes from Hieroglyph Z4B that would not fit into the Hieroglyph W24 circle.

The Translations 183

Hieroglyph W19 ⚱ / rotated ⚱ / simplified / Linear A symbol L3 ⚱
Hieroglyph W19 has been rotated by 180 degrees and, it appears (despite the damage on the tablet), its stem has been simplified to become Linear A symbol L3. It represents the first hieroglyph in the word:

miswt horned animals [noun - ani.] W19 - G17 - O34 - X1 - E28 - E28 - E28

These two symbols therefore mean "[less] food [in the] fourth [month of] horned animals". These appear to be male goats (i.e. billy goats) that were eaten during the month (presumably by the city dwellers). They are followed by a count of 3.

It is interesting that the term *miswt* "horned animals" is used here, meaning (we can infer from the context) "(male) [billy] goats". Yet another symbol, Linear A symbol L42 with the male = symbol, has also been used twice on this tablet with the same implied meaning in Category Two and Category Three. The difference, however, is that animals in these two other categories of animals were not being eaten. English has different terms for meat types and the animals they come from (the different terms coming from Norman French and Anglo Saxon, respectively). Perhaps the different Middle Egyptian terms used on this tablet were similarly meant to convey different intended purposes (i.e. here for eating rather than herding)?

<u>Category Six: Row Four, Symbol Two:</u>

Hieroglyph F31 ⚱ / simplified / Linear A symbol L9 ⚱ or L28 ⚱ (as here)
Linear A symbol L28 is a straightforward simplified version of Hieroglyph F31. Here, it represents the first hieroglyph in the word:

184   The Decipherment of Linear A

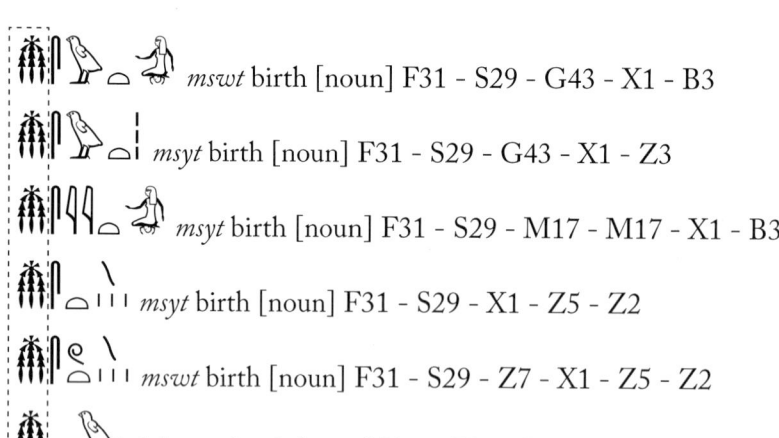

This symbol therefore means "births", and the surviving portion of the tablet records that there were 10 in the period by the single dot that appears after the symbol.

In the area of damage, given the total of the tablet and this being the only category where an additional unit of 10 could have appeared on the tablet (and this being required for the tablet to add up), it is likely that there was another unit of 10 recorded here (i.e. another dot, below the one that survives).

This still leaves us 4 short as regards the total for the tablet. These four single unit tally marks were most likely written next (two on top and two below) after the two units of 10 (the dot counting 10 that survives and the dot counting 10 that did not). There was certainly space for them if they were written around the same size, say, of the first single unit tally mark on the second row of single unit tally marks in Category One, and we can see this if, for illustrative purposes, we superimpose four of these into the damaged area here, giving us an approximation of how the tablet was most likely originally incised:

There were, therefore, 24 births in the period that were originally recorded on the tablet.

The Translations   185

Category Seven: Row Four, Symbols Three and Four:

Hieroglyph D46 ⌐/ rotated ⌐ / simplified / Linear A symbol L100 ᵠ
As we have seen previously, this symbol represents the first hieroglyph in the word:

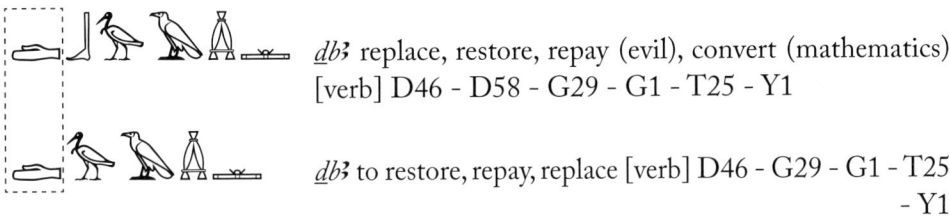

db3 replace, restore, repay (evil), convert (mathematics) [verb] D46 - D58 - G29 - G1 - T25 - Y1

db3 to restore, repay, replace [verb] D46 - G29 - G1 - T25 - Y1

Hieroglyph O49 ⊗/ simplified / Linear A symbol L29 ⊕
As we have previously seen, this symbol represents the word:

⊗ *niwt* city, town [noun] O49

These two symbols therefore mean "repaid [to the] city". They are followed by a count of 5.

Here it appears that goats had previously been borrowed from the herd and, in the month that this tablet records (month four of, by implication, the third season of the year, which was the last month of the year), they were repaid to the city (and replaced into the herd) by, as we shall see, New Year's Day. One wonders whether this was for the borrower's animal husbandry purposes (perhaps billy goats being used to cover nanny goats in another herd) or whether this was more what we would consider to be a financing arrangement, albeit in a pre-monetary economy (for example, perhaps borrowing four goats because the borrower needed them to purchase something with them and then, later, the borrower repaid five goats). If elements of the wealth of the city were stored in its animal herd and a borrower needed access to that wealth for his own commercial purposes, then he might borrow from the city and make repayment later on the terms agreed. The point will, I feel, have to remain an open one.

Summation: Row Five, Symbols One and Two:

Hieroglyph F14 ⋃ / rotated ⋺ / simplified / Linear A symbol L98 ⋺
As we have seen previously, this symbol represents the first hieroglyph in the word:

⋃⋺ *wpt rnpt* New Year's Day (and its festivals) [noun] F14 - W3

⋃⊙ *wpt rnpt* New Year's Day (and its festivals) [noun] F15 - W3 - N5

Hieroglyph N14 ✶ / modified / Linear A symbol L22 ✚
As we have seen previously, this symbol represents the first hieroglyph in the word:

✶⊤ *dmḏ sm3* grand total [noun] N14 - F36

The two symbols on Row Five therefore again mean "[on] New Year's Day, grand total", which is followed by a count of 1,060.

The Translations 187

Total: Row Five, Linear A symbol for 1,000:

Hieroglyph N65 ☒ / Linear A numerical symbol ☉

This symbol is acknowledged by Brice and Godart & Olivier to represent the number 1,000, of which there is one here (plus a further six dots, representing units of ten, making a total on the tablet of 1,060). The symbol is, in fact, a representation of Hieroglyph N65.

The symbol's use to represent the number 1,000 seems to have arisen from some abstract thinking by the Egyptians when creating a symbol for use in Linear A, as evidenced by the fact that Hieroglyph N65 is the final hieroglyph in the word:

𓊃𓂋𓇼 *sꜣr* (constellation) [noun - astro.] S29 - D36 - D21 - N65

What obvious thing was there that was readily visible in the Late Bronze Age and that there were thousands of? The stars! This, therefore, is why this symbol has been chosen to represent the number 1,000. However, Hieroglyph M12 by itself spelled the word for 1,000:

𓆼 *ḫꜣ* 1,000 [adjective + noun] M12

So why was a Linear A symbol representing just this hieroglyph not used? We do not have a lot of information from the surviving Linear A tablets to help us, but it seems that the most likely reason, based on what has survived, is that if this hieroglyph were represented by a Linear A symbol, that symbol could have also represented the likely commonly recorded commodity of loaves (of bread), representing the first hieroglyph in the word:

𓆼𓄿𓂋𓊪𓋴𓐠 *ḥrps* loaves, pastry [noun - food] M12 - G1 - E23 - Q3
- Z7 - J18 - Z1 - X1 - Z8

188   The Decipherment of Linear A

If Hieroglyph M12 were represented as a Linear A symbol, our experience thus far has suggested that the detail at the top and bottom of the hieroglyph would be simplified to horizontal lines. The hieroglyph would thereby become Linear A symbol L14:

ꟿ becomes I

And, while we do not have the whole tablet, the commodity represented by this symbol, which I believe is most likely ḥrps, appears to have been recorded on Tablet HT 132[36]:

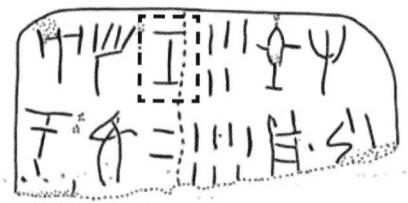

If Linear A symbol L14, representing Hieroglyph M12, represented such a likely commonly recorded commodity as loaves of bread (although that commonality is not reflected in the limited surviving Linear A corpus which is skewed towards cattle and livestock records), then also representing the value of 1,000 with that same symbol representing that same hieroglyph would clearly cause confusion. As the word ḥȝ was a one-hieroglyph word, another symbol, drawn from more abstract thinking, had to be chosen to represent the value of 1,000. This is an interesting point to finish this section on as, in an apparent departure from the Greek shorthand methodology that we are applying to decipher Linear A, we see a symbol representing a hieroglyph used to represent a word that was not part of that word's spelling when it was written out in full in hieroglyphs. While we have been able to get this far in our translations using the characteristics of the Greek shorthand method, identifying the fact that the symbol for 1,000 was based on Hieroglyph N65 required us to think more abstractly, as a Late Bronze Age Egyptian would have. From the perspective of the 21st Century AD there are limits to our ability to do so. I suspect this symbol was an exception to the rule, so this is not, ultimately, too problematic, but if there were any more such exceptions, we might never be able to decipher Linear A in its absolute entirety.

---

36. Although we cannot be certain, as the tablet only partially survives, what does survive most likely states: Title: Sustenance provisions: loaves – 5; [plus] Gifts [of] food – Linear A fraction symbol F (value: ⅔ or 0.67); [from the] festival of the half moon – 27; Subtitle: To [be] receive[d]; [at] daily services (assuming the final, partially complete, symbol is Linear A symbol L88) – 1. See also footnote 3 in Appendix 3 regarding the use of the word ḥrps.

For now, however, we can translate this tablet in full:

Row One	Heading:	[In the] city [of] [unknown place name]
	Category One:	[In the] confines (of the district) [in the] month, [female] goats – 976
Row Two	Category Two:	Received [in] payment, male [billy] goats – 3[5]
	Category Three:	Replaced
Row Three		[by the] herdsmen, male goats – 33
	Category Four:	[Less] small goats [for] wage payments [for] services – (10)
		[Less]
	Category Five:	Food [in the] fourth [month]
		[of] horned animals – (3)
	Category Six:	Births – 2[4]
Row Four	Category Seven:	Repaid [to the] city – 5
	Total:	[On] New Year's Day, grand total – 1,060

Part II: Tablets reflecting the Hagia Triada temple acting as principal, as a religious institution

The majority of the extant Hagia Triada tablets fall into this category and they are considered in the following groupings:

1. Records of goods received, to be received, and issued;
2. Inventories;
3. End of period accounting; and
4. Forecasts (and evidence thereof).

The tablets will be considered in this order.

1. <u>Records of goods received, to be received, and issued</u>
These tablets deal with goods (animals and fodder) that fall into four groups:

   a) Accounts of goods (i) partially received and partially to be received (in the form of an ad hoc report), and (ii) wholly received (akin to what we would call goods receipts notes). These tablets exhibit certain characteristics of the Mc series of Linear B tablets and relate to a tax, similar to a tithe, that was payable in animals (and their fodder) to the temple.
   b) Accounts that show goods (animals and fodder, again) partially received and partially to be received (again, in the form of an ad hoc report). These do not appear to relate to the tithe-like tax payable to the temple.
   c) Accounts of the receipt of goods from a particular source, and then issued as remuneration to the phyle of priests. Again, these do not appear to relate to the tithe-like tax payable to the temple.
   d) Accounts of the issue of goods during one month periods to the phyle (of priests) in the temple.

The translations are set out in the above order. Interestingly, the translations in Section 1(a) and 1(b) indicate that certain items received and to be received were described by their future intended application or recipient, not simply by what they were (e.g. "small cattle [for the] Chief of the Phyles [for] food"). For an item to be described as such, it indicates that the temple had a detailed forecast of what supplies it would be using, what it would be using them for, and when it was going to be using them (that also presumably showed that it would have sufficient materials at the right time in order to pay for those supplies, if it needed to buy from third parties). The existence of a temple forecast being prepared at Hagia Triada is further evidenced in Section 4 (and it is similarly evidenced at the temple at Khania in Part III of this chapter).

Double entry bookkeeping, invented in the Middle Ages, recognises two current effects of a single transaction, and an entry in one account is described by the name of the other account simultaneously affected (e.g. for a temple receiving a donation of stock, the stock account is debited to show stock increasing (a current effect), this entry labelled "donations", and the donations account is credited to show income being received (another current effect), this entry labelled "stock"). The Egyptian temples on Crete did not use double entry bookkeeping, but described some transactions as having two effects: one current effect (e.g. a tablet listing stock receipts, thus showing stock increasing), and one future effect (how that stock was to be used in the future). That there were two effects noted hints at the use of concepts not too far removed from double entry bookkeeping.

1(a). Goods wholly and partially received exhibiting certain characteristics of the Mc series of Linear B tablets

Tablet HT 14

This tablet is a record of animals and fodder received and to be received. The proportionality of certain of the items to each other, some of which are in the same proportion to each other as when they are recorded on the Mc series of Linear B tablets, indicates, as we shall see, that the amounts relate to a tithe-like tax payable to the temple. The tablet records the tax paid and payable by one of the classes of tax payer recorded on Tablet HT 123A and, like Tablet HT 123A, given the size of the related deliveries recorded on Tablets HT 114A and Tablet HT 121, which follow in this chapter, it seems likely that this tablet records the total annual tax that was payable by this class of taxpayer.

As a record of goods received and to be received, the tablet is, like Tablet HT 123A, an ad hoc report, but relates to a single class of debtor. As the temple's phyle of priests is listed as the beneficiary (by virtue of the first subheading of the tablet), the tablet is included here as a record of the temple rather than in Part I of this chapter as a record of the state. However, I suspect that distinction was not perceived in such a clear-cut way by the temple itself given that the class of taxpayer is listed as the payer, rather than the king (i.e. the state) which would perhaps have been more correct given the agency relationship held by the temple from the state. As we shall see, from the similar proportionality observed on Tablet HT 114A in particular, we know that not only were these animals and fodder for the phyle (of priests), they were for their remuneration.

192   The Decipherment of Linear A

Heading: Row One, Symbols One and Two

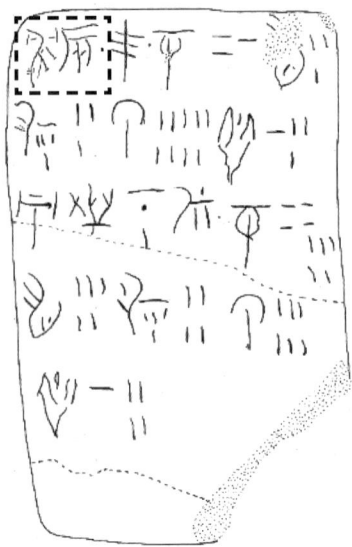

Hieroglyph M2 / rotated / reversed / Linear A symbol L64 [37]
As we have seen previously, this symbol represents the last hieroglyph in the word:

ꜣḥt arable land, meadow, tilled land [noun] M8 - N23 - M2

Hieroglyph M20 / rotated / simplified / Linear A symbol L82
As we have seen previously, this symbol represents the first hieroglyph in the word:

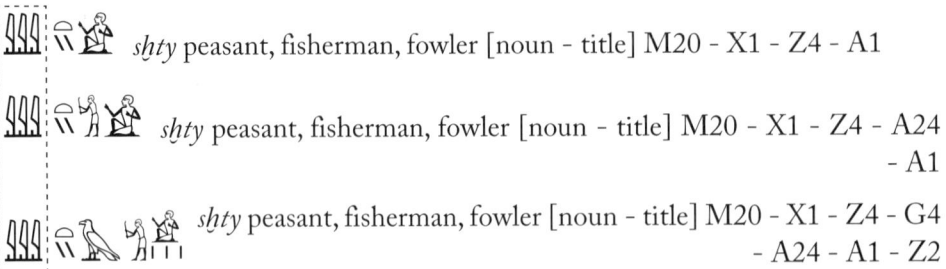

shty peasant, fisherman, fowler [noun - title] M20 - X1 - Z4 - A1

shty peasant, fisherman, fowler [noun - title] M20 - X1 - Z4 - A24
  - A1

shty peasant, fisherman, fowler [noun - title] M20 - X1 - Z4 - G4
  - A24 - A1 - Z2

These two symbols therefore mean "[from the] meadows [of the] peasants" and it is no coincidence that this class of taxpayer is the same as one of the four listed on the wool tax debtor summary Tablet HT 123A. This reflects the fact that, as the proportionality of the items recorded on the tablet will also indicate, these are the proceeds of a tax and that the payer is a class of taxpayer.

---

37. The first symbol appears to have originally been Linear A symbol L52 and presumably meant "sustenance" as it does in the second subheading on this tablet.

By virtue of the numbers of animals (explicitly) recorded on this tablet, compared to the (implicily) recorded numbers on Tablet HT 123A, and the fact that no location is specifically stated, we must assume that the peasants referred to here were from the Hagia Triada area. After all, if there were a tithe-like cattle and livestock tax payable to a temple, we would expect it to be one that was paid primarily by the local populace to its local temple.

<u>Subheading One: Row One, Symbol Three:</u>

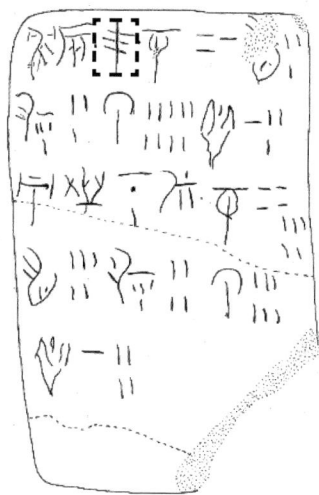

Hieroglyph V16 / rotated / simplified / Linear A symbol L92

This Linear A symbol represents Hieroglyph V16 that has been rotated by 90 degrees, to save space horizontally, and simplified. The hieroglyph is a looped cord; it has four loops on either side of the central "spine" and one loop at each end. The Linear A symbol has been simplified to have three loops (themselves simplified to a straight line) on each side and no end loops.

To demonstrate that this Linear A symbol and Hieroglyph V16 are one and the same, in one example, on the damaged Tablet HT 98A, we see the symbol written closer to the hieroglyph that it represents with four loops on either side, as set out in an extract of the photograph of that tablet, below:

194 The Decipherment of Linear A

Extract of photograph of Tablet HT 98A from Godart & Olivier

From the limited number of possible words that this symbol, representing Hieroglyph V16, might represent, here (and throughout the extant Linear A corpus) this symbol represents the first hieroglyph in the word:

𓎙𓀀𓏥 *s3* phyle (of priests), company, regiment (of troops), troop (of animals) [noun]
V16 - A1 - Z2

Here, it means "[for the] phyle (of priests)".

The "phyle (of priests)" is a term that we will encounter frequently in the corpus, so at this stage it is worth having a brief excursus to say what this was.

Excursus 5.2: What was a phyle?

In Egyptian temples, lower levels of the priesthood were arranged into groups called phyles, which performed part time service in temples. From at least the 12th Dynasty in the Middle Kingdom, and during the period we are considering here (indeed up until the Ptolemaic Dynasty), four phyles operated in the temples.[38] During the year, the phyles rotated in monthly service in the temple, so that each phyle served three times.[39] They were paid in kind for their service.[40]

In contrast to the Old Kingdom, where the phyles were named, from the Middle Kingdom onwards they were identified by number, being referred to as the "first phyle", "second phyle", "third phyle", and "fourth phyle".[41]

---

38. Ann Macy Roth, *Egyptian Phyles in the Old Kingdom: The Evolution of a System of Social Organisation – Studies in Ancient Oriental Civilization No. 48* (The Oriental Institute of the University of Chicago: Chicago, 1991), pp2–3
39. Ann Macy Roth, *Egyptian Phyles in the Old Kingdom: The Evolution of a System of Social Organisation – Studies in Ancient Oriental Civilization No. 48* (The Oriental Institute of the University of Chicago: Chicago, 1991), p3
40. Antony Spalinger, "Further Remarks on the Old Kingdom Phyle System", *Orientalia* 83(3)(2013), p163
41. Ann Macy Roth, *Egyptian Phyles in the Old Kingdom: The Evolution of a System of Social Organisation – Studies in Ancient Oriental Civilization No. 48* (The Oriental Institute of the University of Chicago: Chicago, 1991), p9

Category One: Row One, Symbol Four:

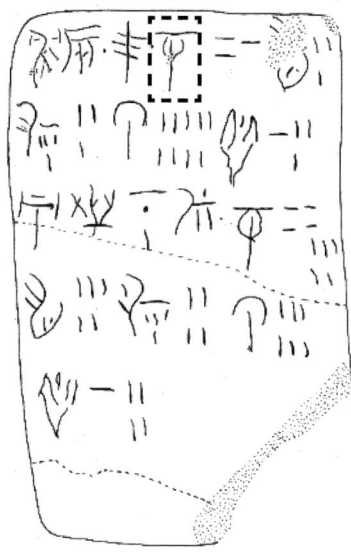

Hieroglyph F27 ⌂/ partially rotated / simplified / modified / Linear A symbol L42 ⊤
As we have seen previously, this symbol represents the last hieroglyph in the word:

⟨goat image⟩ ꜥr goat [noun - ani.] D36 - D21 - E31 - F27

Here, therefore, the symbol means "goats". This is followed by a count of 30.

Category Two: Row One Symbol Five joined to Symbol Six:

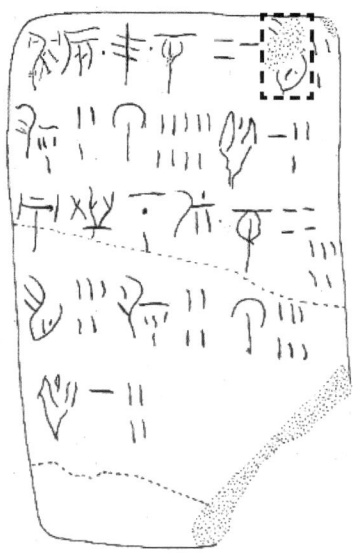

Hieroglyph D3 / rotated / reversed / Linear A symbol L89

As we saw in Chapter Three, this Linear A symbol represents Hieroglyph D3 that has been rotated by 90 degrees, to save space horizontally, and reversed, so that it is easier for a right-handed scribe to incise in clay. It represents the last hieroglyph in the word:

šnw grass (cattle fodder) [noun - flora] V7 - N35 - W24 - Z7 - D3

joined to Hieroglyph D36 / modified / simplified / Linear A symbol L76

Linear A symbol L76 is a modified version of Hieroglyph D36.[42] If one imagines the arm of Hieroglyph D36 being shown as bent rather than straight, one can see how the hieroglyph became the Linear A symbol L76:

would become which, if bent further and simplified, becomes

As with those symbols that are hieroglyphs rotated by 90 degrees, the purpose of bending the arm of Hieroglyph D36 is also so that it takes up less space horizontally. We already know from the fact that on this tablet we have three categories of animals listed (two specific animal types and one a collective noun that can represent a specific animal type) but only two categories of fodder, the fodder categories will, consequently, be described by reference to a collective noun. Here, therefore, Linear A symbol L76 represents the first hieroglyph in the word:

iwʿw quadrupeds, animals [noun - ani.] D36 - D36 - F28 - Z3

The use of the word quadrupeds is worthy of note as it is also used in the Linear B corpus.[43] As historian Anna Judson has noted, the word "quadruped" (*qe-to-ro-po-pi*) is recorded on three Linear B tablets at Pylos which indicate that it had a meaning that included both goats and sheep collectively.[44] The word was, however, translated as "cattle" by Ventris and Chadwick.[45] On this tablet, as we shall see, in addition to goats, cows are also recorded and, by implication, both goats and cows could also be described by the collective noun of "quadrupeds" (*iwʿw*) in Linear A. I shall not follow Ventris and Chadwick in translating the term as "cattle"; rather, I shall use the more correct term "quadrupeds" in the translations in this work.

These two joined symbols therefore mean "grass (cattle fodder) [for the] quadrupeds". They are followed by a count of 3.

---

42. It is worth noting that Ventris and Chadwick saw this Linear A symbol as based upon a hieroglyph that was a bent arm (though a Cretan Hieroglyph, rather than an Egyptian Hieroglyph)(Michael Ventris & John Chadwick, *Documents in Mycenaean Greek* (2nd Ed.)(Cambridge: Cambridge University Press, 1973), p33, Figure 6).
43. John Chadwick, *The Decipherment of Linear B* (2nd Ed.)(Cambridge: Cambridge University Press, 1967), p92
44. See https://itsallgreektoanna.wordpress.com/2020/02/07/queries-about-quadrupeds-in-linear-b/ (accessed 30 January 2021), referring to tablets PY Ae 108, PY Ae 134, and PY Ae 489
45. Michael Ventris & John Chadwick, *Documents in Mycenaean Greek* (2nd Ed.)(Cambridge: Cambridge University Press, 1973), pp169 (PY Ae 134), 170 (PY Ae 108)

The Translations   197

Category Three: Row Two, Symbols One and Two:

Hieroglyph D3 / rotated / reversed / Linear A symbol L89
As we have seen previously, this symbol represents the last hieroglyph in the word:

šnw grass (cattle fodder) [noun - flora] V7 - N35 - W24 - Z7 - D3
joined to Hieroglyphs Z5 - Z2 / rotated / modified / Linear A symbol L51
As we have seen previously, this symbol represents the last hieroglyphs in the word:

ʿwt small cattle, herds, flocks, goats [noun - ani.] T14 - Z7 - X1 - Z5 - Z2

These two joined symbols therefore mean "grass (cattle fodder) [for the] small cattle". They are followed by a count of 3.

That there was separate fodder for small (and, by implication, but not expressly stated, young) animals and quadrupeds (who, by further implication, were not small, and not young, animals so, therefore, were mature) is not unexpected. On this tablet goats and, as we shall see, cows are recorded. Young goats require their grain to be processed if they are younger than six weeks because they do not have a functioning rumen.[46] Similarly, for cows, calves' rumens do not function in their first few weeks of life.[47] Consequently, there are some feeds that mature goats and cows can eat which kids and young calves cannot. This, therefore, explains the different categories of fodder here. We can infer, therefore, that

---

46. https://www.tractorsupply.com/tsc/cms/life-out-here/the-barn/animal-medication-for-goats/nutritional-requirements-for-goats (accessed 30 January 2021)
47. https://extension.umn.edu/dairy-nutrition/ruminant-digestive-system (accessed 30 January 2021)

198   The Decipherment of Linear A

the fodder for the small (young) animals, evidently from a grass crop, has been processed in some way whereas the fodder for the (mature) quadrupeds has not.⁴⁸

<u>Category Four: Row Two, Symbol Three</u>

Hieroglyph F45 ⏺ / simplified / Linear A symbol L67 ⏺
This Linear A symbol is a simplified representation of Hieroglyph F45. We know it represents an animal becaue, as we saw in Chapter One, on Tablet HT 100 it appears with the male = symbol across the stem (becoming Linear A symbol L10). The only animal type the word for which begins or ends with Hieroglyph F45 is a cow,⁴⁹ which was spelled:

idt cow [noun - ani.] F45 - M17 - N42 - X1

idt cow [noun - ani.] F45 - X1 - Z1 - E1

idt cow [noun - ani.] N41 - X1 - F45

Here, therefore, this symbol means "cows". This is followed by a count of 9.

---

48. The same is, incidentally, true for sheep (which are also ruminants): http://www.sheep101.info/201/feedinglambs.html (accessed 30 January 2021).
49. The only other word for an animal whose spelling has Hieroglyph F45 in it is *idt* meaning "mother pig", which is spelled N41 - X1 - F45 - E12 so could not be abbreviated to a symbol representing this hieroglyph.

The Translations

Category Five: Row Two, Symbol Four:

Hieroglyph F155 ⌑ / simplified / Linear A symbol L49 ⋎ (as here) or modified further ⋎

As we have seen previously, this symbol represents the first hieroglyph in the word:

⌑ 🐂 *wp* horned cattle [noun - ani.] F155 - E1 - Z3

This symbol therefore means "horned cattle". This is followed by a count of 13.

Subheading Two: Row Three, Symbols One to Four:

Hieroglyph S34 ⚲/modifed (loop replaced by horizontal bar) / Linear A symbol L52 T̄
As we will see later in this chapter:

⚲ Hieroglyph S34 (the Ankh, as we pronounce it), can be written as

⚲ Linear A symbol L23, with which it is practically identical.

In addition, however, the hieroglyph can be modified to become Linear A symbol L52, as it is here.

In Chapter Two we saw how Hieroglyph F35 was simplified to become Linear A symbol L2:

The way in which Hieroglyph S34 is modified to become Linear A symbol L52 is very similar. A horizonal line replaced the oval (and the finer detail within it) at the bottom of Hieroglyph F35 for the reason that a line was easier to incise in clay. With Hieroglyph S34, the loop at the top of the symbol is replaced by a horizontal line for the same reason, giving us Linear A symbol L52:

⚲ becomes T̄

Thus the line, or "accent bar", sometimes seen above Linear A symbol L52 is formed in this way. Whether it was actually written, however, seems to have been down to the scribe's preference, and the symbol can simply appear as:

T

More commonly, as the arms of Hieroglyph S34 splayed outwards, the horizontal extremes of the arms of the Linear A symbol are typically, although not always (and especially not when used in subscript), written with vertical strokes (or, "side bars"), giving us Linear A symbol L52 as it appears here, namely:

┬┤

Knowing that Linear A symbol L52 represents Hieroglyph S34, and that appearing in the subheading it would likely repesent a word that referred to all of the things in the list that followed it, we can determine that the symbol represents the first hieroglyph in the word:

[hieroglyphs] ꜥnḫ sustenance [noun - food] S34 - Z1 - X4 - Z2

[hieroglyphs] ꜥnḫ sustenance [noun - food] S34 - Z1 - Z8

Hieroglyph M16 [glyph] / simplified / Linear A symbol L34 [glyph]

Hieroglyph M16 (a clump of papyrus) has also been simplified for ease of inscription, with Linear A symbol L34 having horizontal lines replacing the plant's bulbs and its base. This symbol represents the first hieroglyph in the word:

[hieroglyphs] ḥꜣw ḥrt 'deficit, deficiency, arrears [noun] M16 - D2 - D36

This word has been translated as "arrears" in the mid-5th Dynasty papyrus archive of the funerary temple of King Neferirkare found at Abusir, where it was used to refer to the difference between the actual amount of goods received (i.e. those goods that had been delivered to the temple) and those goods that were anticipated to be received (i.e. those goods that remained to be delivered to the temple).[50] The word, therefore, as can also be seen above, means "deficiency", which is the translation used here. This is also seemingly confirmed by the fact that other Middle Egyptian words that also have this meaning are used in similar subheadings in the corpus. For example, as we shall see, the subheading on Tablet HT 2 uses the Middle Egyptian word gbi which we saw previously on Tablet HT 123A, namely:

[hieroglyphs] gbi deficiency, deprivation, damage, uneven [noun] W11 - G1 - D58 - G37 - Z9

"Deficiency" being the translation here (as well as in the subheading on Tablet HT 2) thus infers a degree of consistency across the corpus as a whole when a consistent layout was used, even if different Middle Egyptian words were used (or, indeed, represented) by different scribes. In my own profession, simply by their layout, an accountant could pick up a set of accounts, identify the Profit and Loss Account (or Income Statement), and know that the first item listed would be Turnover (or Sales) regardless, even, of the language used. Such an approach guides us here.

Is it reasonable to expect that different words would be used to convey the same meaning? Yes. If there was more than one way of saying something in Middle Egyptian, it was because different people used different ways to say the same thing. By extension, people could write that same thing in different ways. Historian Hana Vymazalová believes that, when alternative forms of the word ḥꜣw ḥrt' were used, for example, this represented different bureacratic

---

50. Hana Vymazalová, *The accounting documents from the papyrus archive of Neferre and their specific terminology* (PhD: Charles University in Prague, 2005), pp147, 153–154

202 The Decipherment of Linear A

traditions.[51] Where different forms of the same word are used, therefore, we might infer that the scribes are not only different, but that they had different professional backgrounds. By extension, we can infer the same thing when different words meaning the same thing (in English) are used in modern accounting: for example, one man's Turnover is another man's Sales, and both have the same practical meaning. Nonetheless, the terminology used can, and does, infer something of that professional's background.

Perhaps surprisingly, this is a relatively common feature in the Hagia Triada corpus (it is also seen, for example, with the word *'wt* on this Tablet HT 14 and *'nḫ* on Tablet HT 2 each meaning "small cattle", and in the interchangability between *wp* meaning "horned cattle" and the words *iw'w* and *ḥꜣwty* for "male quadrupeds", which we will see through comparison of this Tablet HT 14 with Tablet HT 114A and Tablet HT 121 or, indeed, the different spellings of the word *ꜣbd* meaning "month" in dates (see Appendix 8)). From this we can infer, given the limited size of the corpus, that there was most likely a large staff at the temple at Hagia Triada coming from diverse backgrounds in Egypt (and its territories) who thus used a wider range of vocabulary. The large size of the phyle (of priests) would, perhaps, seem to be borne out by the amounts recorded as having been paid or issued to its members that we see set out on the tablets in this chapter. That differences prevailed suggests that the scribes did not become wholly institutionalised and adopt a wholly uniform instutional lexicon; this is perhaps reflective of the part time nature of the priestly duties they undertook.

Hieroglyphs N5 - Z1 ☉̇ / simplified / modified / Linear A symbol L26 ī

As we have seen, Linear A symbol L26 represents Hieroglyphs N5 - Z1. Here it represents the last hieroglyphs in the word:

🦉 🦅 𓈖 𓉐 𓏏 ☉̇ *m tꜣ wnwt* now, immediately, at once G17 - X1 - G1 - E34
                                                           - N35 - W24 - X1 - N2 - N5 - Z1

🦉 🦅 𓈖 𓉐 ✱ ☉̇ *m tꜣ wnwt* now, immediately, at once G17 - X1 - G1 - E34
                                                           - N35 - W24 - X1 - N14 - N5 - Z1

🦉 🦅 \\ 𓈖 𓉐 ✱ ☉̇ *m tꜣ wnwt* now, immediately, at once G17 - X1 - G1 - Z4
                                                              - E34 - N35 - W24 - X1 - N14 - N5 - Z1

While this symbol represented the word for "services" on Tablet HT 102, as we are dealing with shorthand, the same symbol can represent more than one word and we have to look at its context to determine its meaning. Here, the tablet records the deficit at the moment in time when the scribe wrote; for the scribe, when he wrote, it was "now", much as a modern accountant would write of a deficit now being "current".

---

51. Hana Vymazalová, *The accounting documents from the papyrus archive of Neferre and their specific terminology* (PhD: Charles University in Prague, 2005), p155

The Translations 203

Hieroglyph A24 / simplified / modified / Linear A symbol L93

This symbol is a simplified version of Hieroglyph A24. However, to avoid confusion with Linear A symbol L99 (which represents Hieroglyph A59) and which is also a man holding a stick (but facing the other way), the man's stick, here, is exaggerated. Importantly, and particularly clear here, the stick held by the man is shown curved, reflecting the stick held by the man portrayed in Hieroglyph A24; it is not straight, as it would have been if, say, the symbol had represented Hieroglyph A21, Hieroglyph A22, or Hieroglyph A23. As we saw in Chapter Three, Milne noted that it was the distinctive part of a letter that was taken to produce the symbol used in shorthand,[52] and we see that being the case here.

Given the context in which it appears, here the symbol represents the last hieroglyph in the word:

sm3 take part in, receive [verb] F36 - G1 - G17 - Z7 - Z4 - Y1 - A24

These four symbols therefore mean "sustenance deficiency now, to [be] receive[d]".

Category Six: Row Three, Symbol Five:

Hieroglyph F27 / partially rotated / simplified / modified / Linear A symbol L42

As we have previously seen, this symbol represents the last hieroglyph in the word:

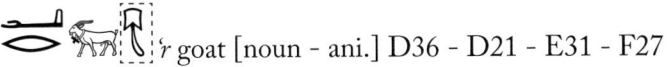

ʿr goat [noun - ani.] D36 - D21 - E31 - F27

Here, therefore, the word means "goats". This is followed by a count of 45.

---
52. H. J. M. Milne, *Greek Shorthand Manuals: Syllabary and Commentary* (London: Egypt Exploration Society, 1934), p2

204   The Decipherment of Linear A

Category Seven: Row Four Symbol One joined to Symbol Two:

Hieroglyph D3 / rotated / reversed / Linear A symbol L89
As we have seen previously, this symbol represents the last hieroglyph in the word:

šnw grass (cattle fodder) [noun - flora] V7 - N35 - W24 - Z7 - D3

joined to Hieroglyph D36 / modified / simplified / Linear A symbol L76
As we have seen previously, this symbol represents the first hieroglyph in the word:

iw'w quadrupeds, animals [noun - ani.] D36 - D36 - F28 - Z3

These two joined symbols therefore mean "grass (cattle fodder) [for the] quadrupeds". They are followed by a count of 5.

The Translations

Category Eight: Row Four, Symbols Three joined to Symbol Four:

Hieroglyph D3 / rotated / reversed / Linear A symbol L89

As we have seen previously, this symbol represents the last hieroglyph in the word:

šnw grass (cattle fodder) [noun - flora] V7 - N35 - W24 - Z7 - D3

joined to Hieroglyphs Z5 - Z2 / rotated / modified / Linear A symbol L51

As we have seen previously, this symbol represents the last hieroglyphs in the word:

ʿwt small cattle, herds, flocks, goats [noun - ani.] T14 - Z7 - X1 - Z5 - Z2

These two joined symbols therefore mean "grass (cattle fodder) [for the] small cattle". They are followed by a count of 4.

206 The Decipherment of Linear A

Category Nine: Row Four, Symbol Five:

Hieroglyph F45 ⌇ / simplified / Linear A symbol L67 ⌇
As we have previously seen, this symbol represents the first (or, in one case, last) hieroglyph in the word:

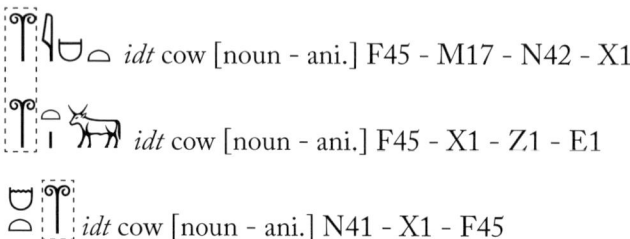

Here, therefore, this symbol means "cows". This is followed by a count of 6.

The Translations

Category Ten: Row Five, Symbol One:

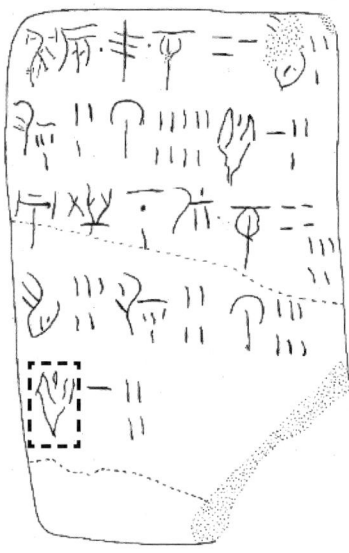

Hieroglyph F155 ⌵ / simplified / Linear A symbol L49 ⩔ (as here) or modified further ⩔.

As we have seen previously, this symbol represents the first hieroglyph in the word:

⌵ 🐂 *wp* horned cattle [noun - ani.] F155 - E1 - Z3

This symbol therefore means "horned cattle". It is followed by a count of 14.

We can now translate the tablet in full:

Row 1	Heading:	[From the] meadows [of the] peasants
	Subheading:	[for the] phyle (of priests)
	Category One:	(Female) goats – 30
	Category Two:	Grass (cattle fodder) [for the] quadrupeds – 3
Row 2	Category Three:	Grass (cattle fodder) [for the] small cattle – 3
	Category Four:	(Female) cows – 9
	Category Five:	Horned cattle – 13
Row 3	Subheading:	Sustenance deficiency now, to [be] receive[d]
	Category Six:	Goats – 45
Row 4	Category Seven:	Grass (cattle fodder) [for the] quadrupeds – 5
	Category Eight:	Grass (cattle fodder) [for the] small cattle – 4
	Category Nine:	Cows – 6
Row 5	Category Ten:	Horned cattle – 14

208   The Decipherment of Linear A

Analysis

As noted, this tablet, like Tablet HT 123A, appears to shows us what this class of taxpayers' total obligation was, by implication, for an entire year. We can see what the total obligation was by adding the amounts received to the amounts to be received, namely:

- (Female) goats: 75
- (Female) cows: 15
- Grass (cattle fodder) for the quadrupeds: 8
- Grass (cattle fodder) for the small cattle: 7
- Horned cattle: 27

Importantly, the ratio between the total of the horned cattle (male animals) and the total of the female animals (goats and cows) is 30%. This ratio is significant as it appears in the Linear B corpus, in the Mc series of Linear B tablets, and we shall also see it on Tablet HT 114A which is considered next.

Tablet HT 114A

Tablet HT 114A is a record of a specific receipt of animals and fodder from a specific (unnamed) debtor relating, given the proportionality of the items recorded, to the tithe-like tax we saw previously on Tablet HT 14.

Heading: Row One, Symbols One to Three:

Hieroglyph G1 / simplified / Linear A symbol L103
As was the case with the heading on Tablet HT 123A, here this symbol most likely represents the word:

g3wt tax, tribute [noun] W11 - G1 - M17 - M17 - X1 - Y1

g3wt tax, tribute [noun] W11 - G1 - O37 - M2 - Z3A

The same proportionality observed on Tablet HT 14 between certain items in the total of the amounts received and the amounts to be received is, as we shall see, seen on this tablet, not only indicating that all the amounts due have been received from this particular debtor (and that there is no deficiency, so that is not the meaning of this symbol here) but also indicating that we are dealing with a tax, giving us the meaning of this symbol here.

In particular, we know from Tablet HT 14 that, when all amounts were received, the number of "horned cattle" (i.e. male animals) would be 30% of the number of female animals (goats and cows). Here, while there are no cows recorded, we can see that there are 10 goats, recorded in the first category on the tablet (as noted below), and in the final category (which we can already see records a male animal by virtue of the male = symbol) 3 male animals are recorded (i.e. 30%). As will also be seen, the symbol representing the animals recorded in the final category is equivalent to "horned cattle".

Hieroglyph M6 / reversed / simplified / Linear A symbol L72/94 (as here) or

As we have previously seen, this symbol represents the first hieroglyph in the word:

trsst wage payments [noun - food] M6 - O34 - O34 - X1 - Z8

Hieroglyphs D28 - Z1 / simplified / modified / Linear A symbol L55

As we have previously seen, this symbol represents the word:

k3w food, bounty [noun - food] D28 - Z1

joined to Hieroglyphs Z4B - Z4B - W24 / modified (four dashes as dots inside enclosed arms) / Linear A symbol L91

As set out in Appendix 6, this symbol, representing Hieroglyphs Z4B - Z4B - W24, represents the ordinal:

fdnw fourth Z4B - Z4B - W24

becomes Linear A symbols L55 + L91 / Linear A symbol L86

As set out in Appendix 6, Linear A symbol L55 combined with Linear A symbol L91 produces Linear A symbol L87. This symbol therefore means "food [in the] fourth [month]".

The first three symbols therefore mean "tax [for] wages [of] food [in the] fourth [month]".

210   The Decipherment of Linear A

Subheading: Row One, Symbol Four, and Row Two, Symbol One:

Hieroglyph V28 ⌇ / rotated ⌇ / simplified / Linear A symbol L31 Y

Here, given that we know we are looking at the goods delivered to an Egyptian temple arising from a tax and, in particular, a specific delivery fulfilling a taxpayer's obligations, this symbol represents the first hieroglyph in the word:

ḥtr tax, levy, provide (a temple with) [verb + noun] V28 - V13 - D21 - M17 - M5B

ḥtr tax, levy, provide (a temple with) [verb + noun] V28 - V13 - D21 - M17 - M6

ḥtr tax, levy, provide (a temple with) [verb + noun] V28 - V13 - D21 - M17 - M7A - A2

ḥtr tax, levy, provide (a temple with) [verb + noun] V28 - X1 - D21 - M6 - Y1V

ḥtr tax, levy, provide (a temple with) [verb + noun] V28 - X1 - D21 - M7A - A2

ḥtr tax, levy, provide (a temple with) [verb + noun] V28 - X1 - D21 - Y1

Hieroglyphs Z5 - Z5\\/ Linear A symbol L58

As we have seen previously, this symbol represents the word:

★ ⌇ ☉ 3bd month [noun] N11 - N14 - Z5 - Z5 - N5

These two symbols therefore mean "provided [(with) for the] month". These are, therefore, amounts that have been received in the (current) month.

Category One: Row Two, Symbol Two:

Hieroglyph F27 ⌐⌐/ partially rotated / simplified / modified / Linear A symbol L42 ⌐

As we have seen previously, this symbol represents the last hieroglyph in the word:

🌿🐐⌐ ꜥr goat [noun - ani.] D36 - D21 - E31 - F27

Here this symbol means "goats". This is followed by a count of 10.

Category Two: Row Two, Symbol Three:

Hieroglyph D3 ⌐/ rotated ⌐ / reversed ⌐ / Linear A symbol L89 ⌐

As we have seen previously, this symbol represents the last hieroglyph in the word:

⌐⌐⌐ šnw grass (cattle fodder) [noun - flora] V7 - N35 - W24 - Z7 - D3

Here this symbol means "grass (cattle fodder)". This is followed by a count of 7.

Category Three: Row Three, Symbol One:

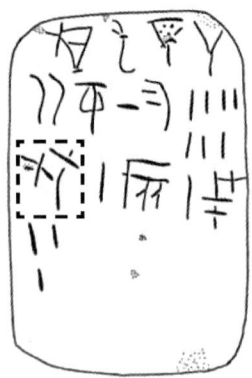

Hieroglyph T25 / rotated / simplified / Linear A symbol L60

As we have seen previously, this symbol represents the first hieroglyph (or, in one instance, last hieroglyph) in the word:

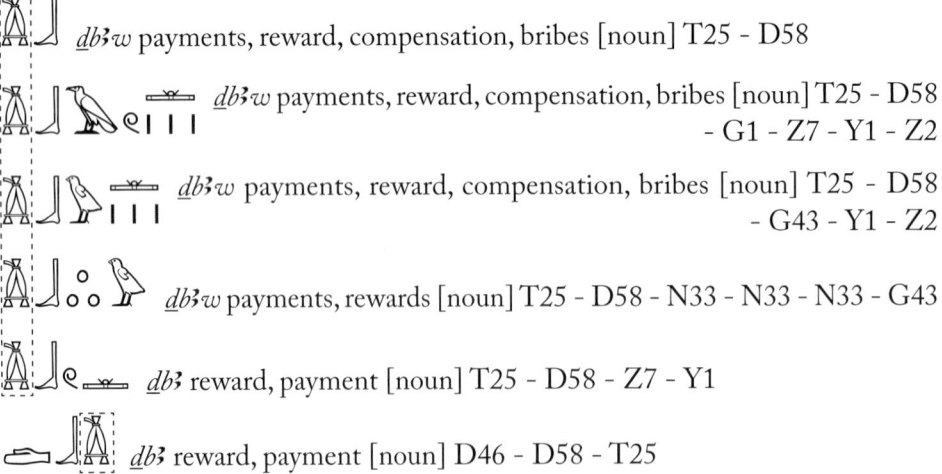

This symbol therefore means "[for] payments". This is followed by a count of 1. As we shall see, often in the corpus an item is described not by what it is (that much must have been clear to the scribe already), but by its future intended use or its future intended recipient. Here we see our first example of that in this work. As to why there has been a change in the style of how this category was recorded, while like the previous category this was a unit of fodder received from the tithe-like tax ostensibly for the remuneration of the phyle (of priests) (presumably that was the intention of the tithe-like tax being levied in the first place), the amount was instead going to be used (in the future) for the purchase of goods or services from third parties (as indicated by its use on Tablet HT 86, which is discussed later in this chapter).

Category Four: Row Three, Symbol Two:

Hieroglyph M20 𓍱 / rotated 𓍲 / simplified / Linear A symbol L82 𐘅

As we have seen previously, this symbol represents the first hieroglyph in the word:

    shty peasant, fisherman, fowler [noun - title] M20 - X1 - Z4 - A1

    shty peasant, fisherman, fowler [noun - title] M20 - X1 - Z4 - A24 - A1

    shty peasant, fisherman, fowler [noun - title] M20 - X1 - Z4 - G4 - A24 - A1 - Z2

This symbol therefore means "[for the] peasants". This is followed by a count of 1. Again, while this unit of fodder was received from the tithe-like tax ostensibly for the remuneration of the phyle (of priests) (presumably that was the intention of the tithe-like tax being levied in the first place), this amount was instead going to be paid (in the future) to the peasants who, presumably, tended the temple's lands (as indicated by its use on Tablet HT 86, which is discussed later in this chapter).

Category Five: Row Three, Symbol Three:

214   The Decipherment of Linear A

Hieroglyph D36 ⊸ / Linear A symbol L76 ⟅ / rotated ⟆ / reversed ⟆ / simplified / modified + male = symbol / Linear A symbol L2' ⟊

When discussing Tablet HT 14 we saw how Hieroglyph D36 became Linear A symbol L76. Two further sets of significant changes have then happened to that symbol in order for it to become Linear A symbol L2'; it has been rotated by 180 degrees and then reversed (and the male = sign added). This is considered in the excursus below.

Excursus 5.3: Linear A symbol L76 to Linear A symbol L2' (+ male = symbol)

On the following page (where extracts of photographs of tablets are taken from Godart & Olivier):

- Column A – shows pictures of:
    - Linear A symbol L2' on Tablet HT 121 (where the symbol is clearer);
    - Linear A symbol L76 on Tablet HT 95B; and
    - Linear A symbol L76 on Tablet HT 47A.

  It can be clearly seen that handwriting styles played a significant part in how Linear A symbol L76 was incised, the dot in the "shoulder" of the symbol on Tablet HT 47A, for example, is missing in the "shoulder" of the symbol on Tablet HT 95B.

- Column B – shows Linear A symbol L76 on Tablet HT 95B and Tablet HT 47A rotated by 180 degrees.

- Column C – shows Linear A symbol L76 on Tablets HT 95B and HT 47A reversed to match Linear A symbol L2' on Tablet HT 121 (which is unchanged from Column A).

- Column D – shows Linear A symbol L2' on Tablet HT 121 and Linear A symbol L76 on Tablet HT 95B highlighted for clarity.

- Column E – shows the highlighted symbols from Column D with the photograph removed.

- Column F – shows the addition of the dot, which was present in the "shoulder" of Linear A symbol L76 on Tablet HT 47A, to the symbol from Tablet HT 95B (where it was missing).

- Column G – shows the effect of adding the male = symbol to the symbol from Tablet HT 95B (including the dot omitted by the scribe). This is now the same as Linear A symbol L2' on Tablet HT 121 (and Tablet HT 114A).

The Translations 215

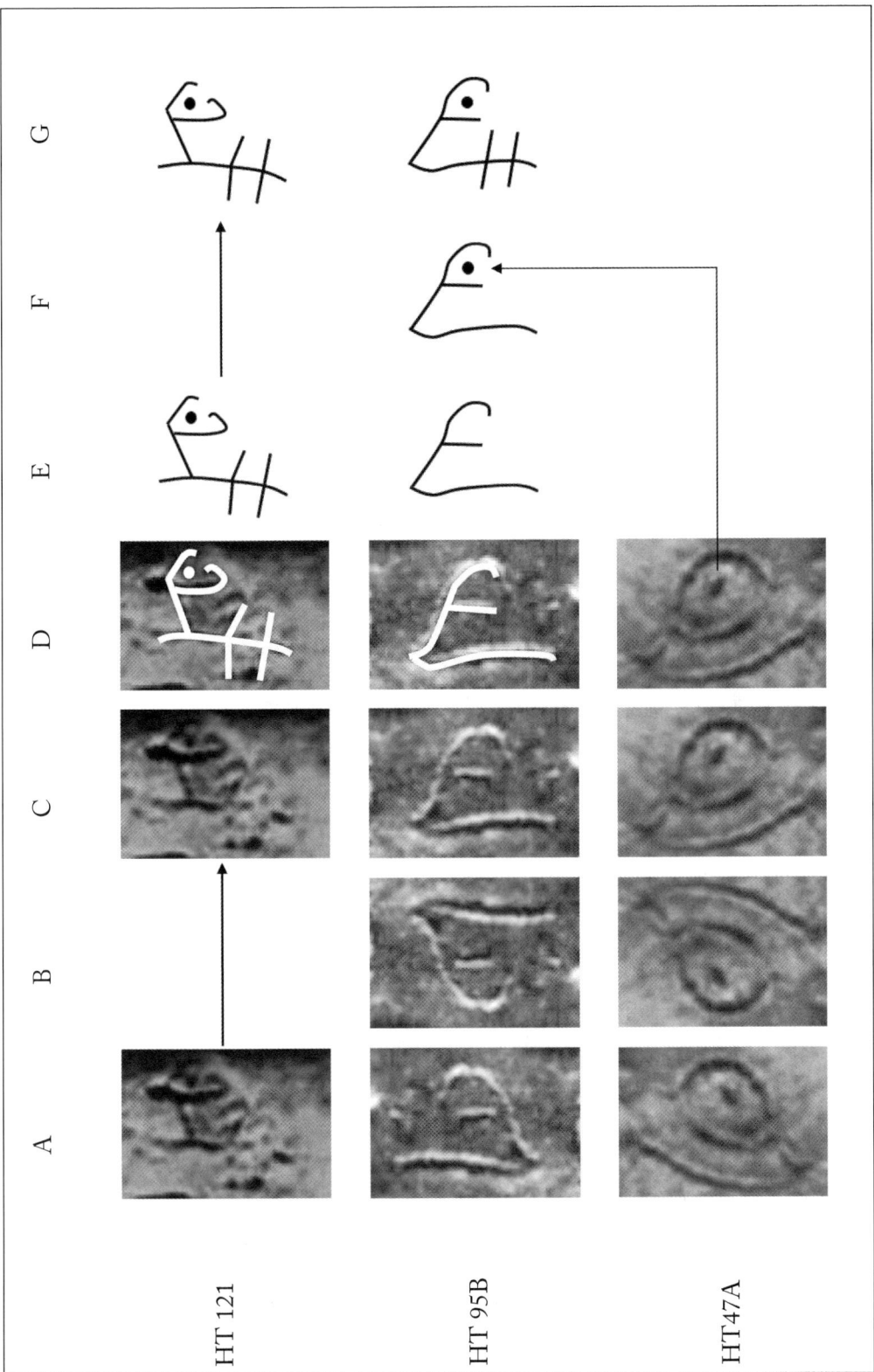

Having demonstrated that Linear A symbol L2' is, in fact, a rotated and reversed Linear A symbol L76 with a male = symbol joined to it, it is clear that this symbol (again) represents the first hieroglyph in the word:

iw'w quadrupeds, animals [noun - ani.] D36 - D36 - F28 - Z3

joined to the male = symbol which, as we have seen, represents the last hieroglyph in the word:

ḥꜣwty warrior, male, man [noun] D34 - G45 - X1 - Z4

Thus, these joined symbols (Linear A symbol L2') mean "male quadrupeds". As a matter of scribal preference, the scribe has chosen to use this word rather than the word for "horned cattle", which was used on Tablet HT 14. It is, or they are, followed by a count of 3.

We are now in a position to translate this tablet in full:

Row One:	Heading:	Tax, [for] wages [of] food [in the] fourth [month]
	Subheading:	Provided [(with) in the] month
	Category One:	(Female) goats – 10
	Category Two:	Grass (cattle fodder) – 7
Row Two:	Category Three:	[Grass (cattle fodder) for] payments – 1
	Category Four:	[Grass (cattle fodder) for the] peasants – 1
	Category Five:	Male quadrupeds –
Row Three:		3

Note: Given the significant space left on this side of the tablet, I believe that the brief record on the reverse side is not connected to the information recorded on this side of the tablet. Accordingly, the translation of the reverse of this tablet is not included in this work.

The identification of Hieroglyph D36 and Hieroglyph Z4 as being represented by Linear A symbol L2' is of particular importance in demonstrating one of the principal aspects of the multifaceted relationship between Linear A (and Middle Egyptian written in hieroglyphs) and Linear B. At this juncture, therefore, we shall have another excursus to consider what we can now infer regarding this relationship.

Excursus 5.4: Certain aspects of the relationship between Middle Egyptian, Linear A, and Linear B

Given that Linear A was Middle Egyptian written in shorthand using hieroglyphs, and given the complexities of Middle Egyptian itself, written in hieroglyphs, with its syllabic symbols, phonetic compliments, ideograms, and determinatives, the relationship with Linear B, with its mixture of ideograms, syllabic symbols, and special (and unknown) symbols, was clearly a multifaceted one. Those aspects immediately evident from the decipherment of Linear A thus far are set out below.

<u>Ideograms</u>
Linear B ideograms evidently drew from Linear A symbols. If we consider Linear A symbol L2' with the male = symbol attached to it which, as we know, means "male quadrupeds":

This is evidently the basis for Linear B ideogram 109a (meaning "ox" or "bull") and Linear B ideogram 108a (meaning "boar"), which we saw previously in Chapter One:

It also seems likely to be the basis for Linear B ideogram 106a (meaning "ram"), reversed:

The additions to the original Linear A symbol L2' in Linear B were presumably made so that the different iterations of the symbol could be used to record specific (male) animal types in Linear B rather than the more generic (male) quadrupeds in Linear A. As we shall see on Tablet HT 2, a version of Linear A symbol L2' existed without the male = symbol, representing female quadrupeds; the Linear B ideograms for the female varieties of the above animals (i.e. meaning "cow", "sow", and "ewe") are, similarly, variations of that Linear A symbol, with the additional gender identifying characteristic of a bifurcated stem.

218 The Decipherment of Linear A

Linear A symbol L2' without male = symbol	Linear B ideogram 109b ("cow")	Linear B ideogram 108b ("sow")	Linear B ideogram 106b ("ewe") (reversed)
⊢	𓃻	𓃾	𓃱

Unfortunately, with the limited surviving Linear A corpus, we may never determine the origins of all Linear B ideograms. That said, however, Linear A was not the only source for Linear B ideograms, which were also evidently drawn directly from Egyptian hieroglyphs. Linear B ideogram *34, (correctly) believed by Ventris to mean "month",[53] is Hieroglyph N11 (which, by itself, spells the Middle Egyptian word *3bd* meaning "month") rotated by 90 degrees:

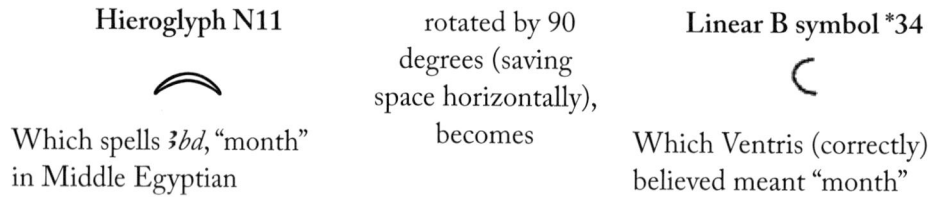

Hieroglyph N11	rotated by 90 degrees (saving space horizontally), becomes	Linear B symbol *34
Which spells *3bd*, "month" in Middle Egyptian		Which Ventris (correctly) believed meant "month"

Syllabic signs
While the syllabic comparative school of attempted decipherment of Linear A incorrectly believed that those Linear A symbols that were visually similar to Linear B symbols had the same phonetic values in Linear A as they had in Linear B, we have shown, however, that this is incorrect: X does not equal X, and Y does not equal Y. Certain of the symbols at least are, however, related.

Syllabic symbols in the Egyptian hieroglyphic script were derived from pictographs, symbols that were a picture of an object representing the word for that object. If the word represented by that pictograph were transliterated, however, by a process of acrophony (which means "initial sound"), the sound of the first letter of the transliteration was, henceforth, taken to be represented by that symbol, the former pictograph (and used to spell other words that included that sound). To take a simple example, in the Egyptian hieroglyphic script, Hieroglyph D21 ⊂⊃ was the pictograph for a mouth. We would transliterate this as *r* (and, indeed, "r" was how it was pronounced, or "r" followed by any vowel). By acrophony, therefore, the sound of first letter in this transliteration (indeed, the only letter in its transliteration), "r" (or "r" followed by a vowel), was represented by this hieroglyph henceforth in the

---

53. Michael Ventris & John Chadwick, *Documents in Mycenaean Greek* (2nd Ed.)(Cambridge: Cambridge University Press, 1973), p170 (narrative to Tablet Am 819), and p213

hieroglyphic script.[54] Interestingly, in addition to Egyptian hieroglyphic script, acrophony is also evidenced in the creation of the first alphabet, the Proto-Sinaitic script. This script, a precursor of the later 10th Century BC Phoenician alphabet that in turn gave rise to the Greek and Latin alphabets, is first evidenced in c.1700 BC in the turquoise mines at Serabit al-Khadim in Sinai. It used the first letter of the transliteration of the Semitic word for an original pictograph as the sound for that symbol when it was used thereafter.[55]

A similar process can clearly be seen with certain Linear B symbols. We have already seen that Hieroglyph S34 became Linear A symbol L52:

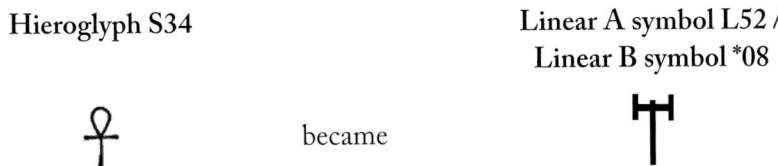

Hieroglyph S34 became **Linear A symbol L52 / Linear B symbol *08**

Linear A symbol L52 is, however, identical to the Linear B symbol *08, which had the syllabic sound "a". Hieroglyph S34 spells the word 'nḫ, meaning life; we would pronounce this "ankh". The Linear B symbol, by a process of acrophony, came to represent the sound of the first letter of "ankh", and is therefore pronounced "a". This acrophonic relationship can be seen most obviously in the following Linear B symbols (especially given that vowel sounds are uncertain in Middle Egyptian):

Hieroglyph		Meaning of word when sole hieroglyph	Transliteration of word	Linear B symbol from (simplified) hieroglyph	Pronunciation from Linear B
A6		Pure	w'b	*40	"wi"
A38		Cusae (place name)	Ḵsy	*44	"ke"
O44		Office	i3wt	*28	"i"

---

54. John F. Healey, *The Early Alphabet* (Berkeley & Los Angeles: University of California Press, 1990), p16
55. John F. Healey, *The Early Alphabet* (Berkeley & Los Angeles: University of California Press, 1990), pp17–18. Healey believes that the Semitic symbols' similarity to Egyptian hieroglyphs and the acrophonic principle itself (which had no parallel outside of Egyptian usage) suggest an Egyptian inspiration behind the invention. The subsequent invention of Linear B, in part using a similar principle, suggests Healey is correct.

The Decipherment of Linear A

Hieroglyph	Meaning of word when sole hieroglyph	Transliteration of word	Linear B symbol from (simplified) hieroglyph	Pronunciation from Linear B
P5	Wind	ꜣw	*05	"to" [56]
T9 rotated	Bow	pdt	*72	"pe"
U38	Balance	mꜣḫt	*80	"ma"

It is clear that the start of the pronunciation of the words spelled with the individual hieroglyphs (in the transliteration, above) was used as the pronunciation of the respective Linear B symbols based on those hieroglyphs. As clear as this is, however, this cannot be the whole story for there are many more Linear B syllabic symbols than just these. However, one further thing is worth noting:

- Hieroglyph O1, which alone can spell the Middle Egyptian word ḥwt (meaning "place") which <u>ends</u> in a "t" and clearly, rotated, represents Linear B symbol *59 pronounced "ta"; and
- Hieroglyph U21, which alone spells the Middle Egyptian word stp (meaning "chosen") <u>ends</u> in a "p" and clearly, rotated and reversed, represents Linear B symbol *11 which is pronounced "po".

In the same way that Linear A shorthand abbreviated words to a symbol representing their first hieroglyph(s) or last hieroglyph(s) (or significant hieroglyph(s) coming from the body of the word), could it be that, while some Linear B syllabic symbols took their pronunciations from the start of the transliteration of the Egyptian words spelled using just the hieroglyph on which those Linear B symbols were based, certain other Linear B syllabic symbols took their pronunciations from the end of the transliteration of the Egyptian words spelled using just the hieroglyph on which those Linear B symbols were based? To me the evidence suggests this was the case.

With these aspects of the evident link between Linear A shorthand and longhand Middle Egyptian and Linear B thus demonstrated, it will be for a panel of experts in Middle Egyptian (and Linear A) and Mycenaean Greek (and Linear B) to determine the further intricacies of the relationship between scripts. For now, however, we can

---

56. Although identical in appearance, Linear B symbol *05 (the pronunciation of which was based on Hieroglyph P5) was unrelated to Linear A symbol L39 (which represented Hieroglyphs W11 - Z1).

The Translations   221

safely conclude that the relationship between Middle Egyptian and Linear A and its successor script Linear B is one that is wholly consistent with our conclusions regarding the Linear A script, and it is one that reflects the historic relationship between Egypt and Crete set out in this work.

Tablet HT 121

This tablet represents another record of animals and fodder received but it is not as straightforward as that on Tablet HT 114A as there is already fodder in store received from this debtor that was deposited in the prior month (so, there was a split delivery, and what has been delivered to date has been recorded before the record of what was received in the current month, presumably so that the scribe recording what was received this month did not think that this month's delivery was short). The ratio between male and female animals that we saw on Tablet HT 14 and HT 114A is again present, to the nearest whole animal (i.e. as close as it could be). On the face of it there is more fodder compared to animals on this tablet than on Tablet HT 114A; however, the units of measure are not stated and may be different (I believe they are), so we cannot be certain that we are comparing like with like (I believe we are not).

Heading: Row One, Symbols One to Three:

Hieroglyph G1 / simplified / Linear A symbol L103

As we have seen previously, this symbol represents the word:

g3wt tax, tribute [noun] W11 - G1 - M17 - M17 - X1 - Y1

g3wt tax, tribute [noun] W11 - G1 - O37 - M2 - Z3A

222 The Decipherment of Linear A

Hieroglyph M6 ∫ / reversed ∫ / simplified / Linear A symbol L72/94 ζ (as here) or ζ
As we have seen previously, this symbol represents the first hieroglyph in the word:

∫▬▬◯ *trsst* wage payments [noun - food] M6 - O34 - O34 - X1 - Z8

Hieroglyphs D28 - Z1 ∪ / simplified / modified / Linear A symbol L55 Y
As we have seen previously, this symbol represents the word:

∪ *k3w* food, bounty [noun - food] D28 - Z1

joined to Hieroglyphs Z4B - Z4B - W24 ≡◯ / modified (four dashes as dots inside enclosed arms) / Linear A symbol L91 ⊙
As set out in Appendix 6, this symbol, representing Hieroglyphs Z4B - Z4B - W24, represents the ordinal:

≡◯ *fdnw* fourth Z4B - Z4B - W24

becomes Linear A symbols L55 + L91 / Linear A symbol L86 ⚰
As set out in Appendix 6, Linear A symbol L55 combined with Linear A symbol L91 produces Linear A symbol L86. These joined symbols therefore mean "food [in the] fourth [month]".

The first three symbols therefore mean "tax, [for] wages [of] food [in the] four [month]".

Category One: Row One, Symbols Four to Six:

Hieroglyph D3 ⩘ / rotated ⨍ / reversed ⫠ / Linear A symbol L89 ⨍
As we have seen previously, this symbol represents the last hieroglyph in the word:

⨎◯◉ ⩘ *šnw* grass (cattle fodder) [noun - flora] V7 - N35 - W24 - Z7 - D3

The Translations   223

joined to <u>Hieroglyphs Z2 - W24 ○ / rotated ○ / modified (three dashes as dots inside circle) / Linear A symbol L91 ⊙</u>

As set out in Appendix 6, this symbol, representing Hieroglyphs Z2 - W24, represents the ordinal:

○ *ḫmt nw* third [ordinal number] Z2 - W24

joined to <u>Hieroglyphs Z5 - Z2 ııı / rotated \ / modified / Linear A symbol L51 ııı</u>
As we have seen previously, this symbol represents the last hieroglyphs in the word:

ꜥwt small cattle, herds, flocks, goats [noun - ani.] T14 - Z7 - X1 - Z5 - Z2

Appendix 8 discusses dates that appear next to the first item on a list. These indicate amounts brought forward from the prior month and available for use in the current month. Here, therefore, these three symbols mean "grass (cattle fodder) [for the] small cattle [from the] third [month]". They are followed by a count of 10.

The tablet then progresses on to goods received, by implication, in month four.

<u>Subheading: Row Two, Symbols One and Two:</u>

Hieroglyph V28 / rotated / simplified / Linear A symbol L31 Y
As we have seen previously, this symbol represents the first hieroglyph in the word:

ḥtr tax, levy, provide (a temple with) [verb + noun] V28 - V13 - D21 - M17 - M5B

ḥtr tax, levy, provide (a temple with) [verb + noun] V28 - V13 - D21 - M17 - M6

224   The Decipherment of Linear A

ḥtr tax, levy, provide (a temple with) [verb + noun] V28 - V13 - D21 - M17 - M7A - A2

ḥtr tax, levy, provide (a temple with) [verb + noun] V28 - X1 - D21 - M6 - Y1V

ḥtr tax, levy, provide (a temple with) [verb + noun] V28 - X1 - D21 - M7A - A2

ḥtr tax, levy, provide (a temple with) [verb + noun] V28 - X1 - D21 - Y1

<u>Hieroglyphs Z5 - Z5 \\ / Linear A symbol L58</u>
As we have seen previously, this symbol represents the word:

⭐ \\ ☉ *3bd* month [noun] N14 - N11 - Z5 - Z5 - N5

These two symbols therefore mean "provided [(with) in the] month".

<u>Category Two: Row Two, Symbol Three:</u>

<u>Hieroglyph F27 / partially rotated / simplified / modified / Linear A symbol L42</u>

As we have seen previously, this symbol represents the last hieroglyph in the word:

ʿr goat [noun - ani.] D36 - D21 - E31 - F27

This symbol again, therefore means "goats". This is followed by a count of 5.

The Translations   225

Category Three: Row Two, Symbol Four:

Hieroglyph D3 〰/ rotated / reversed / Linear A symbol L89
As we have seen previously, this symbol represents the last hieroglyph in the word:

šnw grass (cattle fodder) [noun - flora] V7 - N35 - W24 - Z7 - D3

This symbol again, therefore, means "grass (cattle fodder)". This is followed by a count of 4.

Category Four: Row Three, Symbol One:

Hieroglyph T25 / rotated / simplified / Linear A symbol L60
As we have seen previously, this symbol represents the first hieroglyph (or, in one instance, the last hieroglyph) in the word:

ḏbꜣw payments, reward, compensation, bribes [noun] T25 - D58

ḏbꜣw payments, reward, compensation, bribes [noun] T25 - D58
    - G1 - Z7 - Y1 - Z2

226   The Decipherment of Linear A

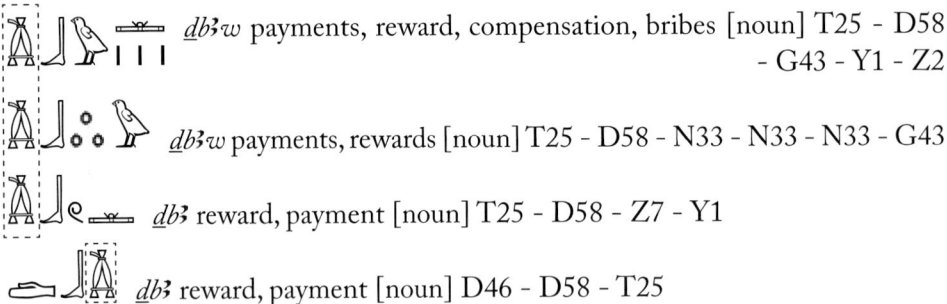

ḏbȝw payments, reward, compensation, bribes [noun] T25 - D58 - G43 - Y1 - Z2

ḏbȝw payments, rewards [noun] T25 - D58 - N33 - N33 - N33 - G43

ḏbȝ reward, payment [noun] T25 - D58 - Z7 - Y1

ḏbȝ reward, payment [noun] D46 - D58 - T25

As we saw on Tablet HT 114A, this symbol again means "[for] payments". It is followed by a count of 2. Again, while these 2 units of fodder were received from the tithe-like tax ostensibly for the remuneration of the phyle (of priests) (presumably that was the intention of the tithe-like tax being levied in the first place), these amounts appear instead to have been allocated to be used in the future to pay for the purchase of goods or services instead from third parties (as indicated by its use on Tablet HT 86, which is discussed later in this chapter).

<u>Category Five: Row Three, Symbol Two:</u>
Hieroglyph M20 / rotated / simplified / Linear A symbol L82

As we have seen previously, this symbol represents the first hieroglyph in the word:

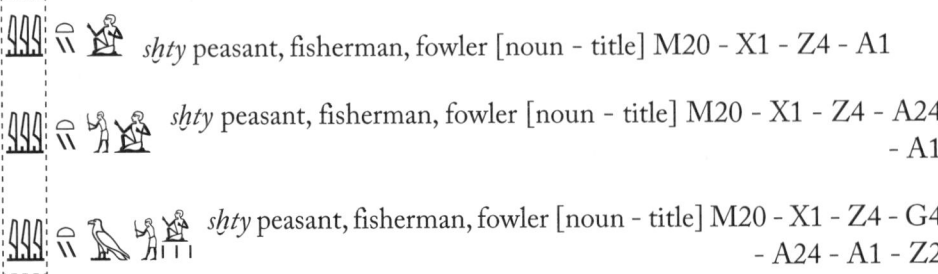

šty peasant, fisherman, fowler [noun - title] M20 - X1 - Z4 - A1

šty peasant, fisherman, fowler [noun - title] M20 - X1 - Z4 - A24 - A1

šty peasant, fisherman, fowler [noun - title] M20 - X1 - Z4 - G4 - A24 - A1 - Z2

This symbol therefore means "[for the] peasants". It is followed by a count of 3. Again, while these 3 units of fodder were received from the tithe-like tax ostensibly for the remuneration of the phyle (of priests) (presumably that was the intention of the tithe-like tax being levied in the first place), this amount was instead going to be paid (in the future) to the peasants who, presumably, tended the temple's lands (as indicated by its use on Tablet HT 86, which is discussed later in this chapter).

<u>Category Six: Row Three, Symbol Three:</u>

Hieroglyph D36 / Linear A symbol L76 / rotated / reversed / simplified / modified + male = symbol / Linear A symbol L2'

As discussed in Excursus 5.3 in this chapter, this symbol represented Hieroglyph D36 with the male = symbol added, and it represents the first hieroglyph in the word:

iw'w quadrupeds, animals [noun - ani.] D36 - D36 - F28 - Z3

joined to the last hieroglyph in the word:

ḥꜣwty warrior, male, man [noun] D34 - G45 - X1 - Z4

These joined symbols therefore mean "male quadrupeds". The tablet is damaged at this point, but, it appears, it records 2 such animals (as noted, tablets were reused and it appears that after the first two single unit tally marks noted on the sketch diagram, anything else on this row of the tablet is the residual imprint of what was previously recorded on the tablet and not intended to be counted again).

We are now in a position to fully translate the tablet:

Row One	Heading:	Tax [for] wages [of] food [in the] fourth [month]
	Category One:	Grass (cattle fodder) [for the] small / young cattle [from the] third [month] – 10
Row Two	Subheading:	Provided [(with) in the] month
	Category Two:	Goats – 5
	Category Three:	Grass (cattle fodder) – 4
Row Three	Category Four:	[For] payments – 2
	Category Five:	[For the] peasants – 3
	Category Six:	Male quadrupeds –
Row Four		2

As discussed, unlike Tablet HT 114A, this tablet records what was received (from a debtor) across (at least) two months and (at least) two deliveries. Although Tablet HT 114A and Tablet HT 121 record receipts from debtors, those debtor's names are not stated. However, given the process for the use of tablets, we might not expect them to be. Given the institutional similarities between Hagia Triada, which we are considering, and Knossos, which Ventris and Chadwick considered, we might infer that broadly similar processes were adopted. Ventris and Chadwick, described them thus:

"After writing, the tablets were dried (not baked) and then generally filed away in boxes of gypsum or wood, or in wicker baskets, and stacked on shelves in rooms set aside for the purpose. The boxes and baskets were secured with cord and sealed with prismatic lumps of clay impressed with seal-stones and inscribed with personal names or with a reference to the itemized [sic] commodities. The name of the responsible scribe, which never seems to occur on the tablets themselves, may sometimes have been recorded here."[57]

This does not relate the process of transferral of information from the temporary tablets to the permanent ledgers, the existence of which was implied by Tablet HT 123A (although that tablet did not record information to be entered into the temple accounts but was, rather, a summary of information drawn from them). After entering such information in the permanent ledgers of the temple accounts, presumably the tablets used to temporarily record that information were stored in an ordered manner for a set period of time before reuse. Rather than the name of the scribe, it would probably have made more sense for tablets to be ordered (and stored) by transaction counterparty.

In more modern times, assuming that such things are not done electronically, when businesses issue invoices and statements of account to their customers (their debtors), copies of these are retained on file. Invoices today always list the customer (debtor) name, thus copies for all customers (debtors) are generally simply filed in date order. Sometimes,

---

57. Michael Ventris & John Chadwick, *Documents in Mycenaean Greek* (2nd Ed.)(Cambridge: Cambridge University Press, 1973), p114

however, a copy is also placed on an order file (which might be considered a debtor file, giving details of the order fulfilled and the debt arising therefrom). These order (debtor) files would be listed by order number, but, hypothetically, if there were no such system of ordering, they would presumably be filed by customer (i.e. debtor) name (and then by period, so that it was known when they could be destroyed). Similarly, if a business received a cash payment from a debtor and a receipt were given by the business to that debtor to confirm the cash amount that had been received, a copy of that receipt would, again, be retained on the order (debtor) file.

We are dealing with goods, not money, but this is what would have happened here when a debtor paid the temple in goods. In the first instance the goods receipt note would have been used as the basis of the accounting entries made in the permanent ledgers: in the stock account, showing the receipt of goods, and in the debtor's account, showing that this portion of the debt was no longer outstanding. However, additionally, I imagine that a copy of what had been recorded as received on the goods receipt note (but in a more permanent form i.e. not on a clay tablet) would have been given to the debtor, in the same manner as a receipt, for the debtor to evidence (should it ever be required) that he or she had paid the amounts in question. With items being received by the temple from individual taxpayer debtors, it would seem most likely that the goods receipt note (which the receipt had copied), once its details had been entered into the permanent ledgers, would then have been stored according to the debtors' names (rather than the names of the scribes as Ventris and Chadwick suggested). In line with Ventris and Chadwick's description, however, no name was written on the tablet itself and one would have labelled the basket in which the tablet was stored (but this would have been the debtor's name).

The Mc series of Linear B tablets records four commodities (three believed to be types of animals or parts of animals counted by number, and one commodity counted by weight). They appear in proportion to each other, and Tablet HT 14, Tablet HT 114A, and Tablet HT 121 are directly comparable to them, as discussed in the following analysis.

Analysis

1. The tithe-like tax payable to Egyptian temples on Crete and the Mc series of Linear B tablets

The Mc series of Linear B tablets records four commodities, three of which are counted by number (and are believed to be animals or parts of animals), and one of which is counted by weight.[58] Their Linear B symbols are:

---

58. Michael Ventris & John Chadwick, *Documents in Mycenaean Greek* (2nd Ed.)(Cambridge: Cambridge University Press, 1973), pp301–302

The Decipherment of Linear A

Symbol	Commodity / Symbol No.	Meaning (believed)
	G / *150	Unknown (animal recorded by number)
	H / *107b	She-goat
	I / *142	Unknown (recorded in weight)
	J / *151	Horns of agrimi goat

Ventris and Chadwick noted that the Mc series of Linear B tablets recorded these in the ratio of 5 : 3 : 2 : 4 (although, with less rounding, the ratio is more accurately 4.6 : 2.8 : 2 : 4.4).[59] Of most relevance now is the final commodity, represented by Linear B symbol *151 (commodity J), which has been believed to record the number of horns of the agrimi goat. From the Linear B tablet data, if we:

- Divide the number of horns by two we get the total number of animals. We can presume these are male given that, like the "male quadrupeds" on Tablet HT 114A and Tablet HT 121 and the "horned cattle" recorded on Tablet HT 14 (which we saw from Tablet HT 123A were male), this is the last recorded category on the tablet, always after fodder. This number of animals is set out in column "B" in the table below.
- Compare this number of male animals to the total of:
  - The number of she-goats, represented by Linear B symbol *107b (commodity H), plus
  - The number of the other (unknown) animal, which we can presume were also female given that, like the she-goats, it also appeared on the Linear B tablets before fodder, and the first two animals that appear on Tablet HT 14 were female. It is represented by Linear B symbol *150 (commodity G).

  (Indeed, the key thing, at least in so far as our analysis goes now, was that these two animal types were female, not what type of animal they were).

This comparison indicates a ratio of 30% male to female animals. This is set out on the tablet below:

---

59. Michael Ventris & John Chadwick, *Documents in Mycenaean Greek* (2nd Ed.)(Cambridge: Cambridge University Press, 1973), p303

Table 5.1: Analysis of the Mc series of Linear B tablets' data[60]

Linear B Tablet	Meaning:	?	She-goat	Total	?	Horns of agrimi goats	No. of male animals	Ratio
	Commodity:	"G"	"H"	"A"	"I"	"J"	"B"	
	Linear B symbol:	*150	*107b	("G"+"H")	*142	*151	"J" / 2	"B"/"A"
	Measured in:	(No.)	(No.)	(No.)	(KG)	(No.)	(No.)	(%)
Mc5098		345	208	553	154	345	172.5	31%
Mc0462 + 5792 + 5808		62	30	92	24	52	26	28%
Mc0454 + 0458		30	17	47	13	26	13	28%
Mc0455		28	17	45	12	24	12	27%
Mc0453 + 5798		28	17	45	12	24	12	27%
Mc5118		0	15	15	0	20	10	67%
Mc0459		23	15	38	10	20	10	26%
Mc0456 + 0477		16	10	26	7	14	7	27%
Mc1508 + 1528 + 1564		16	10	26	6	12	6	23%
Mc0460		14	8	22	6	12	6	27%
Mc0464		12	0	12	6	0	0	0%
Totals		574	347	921	250	549	274.5	30%
Ventris and Chadwick observed ratio:		5	3		2	4		
Key relevant ratio:				921			274.5	30%

The number of male animals (the number of horns, "J", divided by two) in Column B is, therefore, 30% of the total number of (believed) female animals represented by the total of "G" and "H" in Column A. As noted, we see this same ratio in certain of the Linear A tablets: the total of the amounts received and to be received on Tablet HT 14 (the best for this analysis, as the numbers are sufficiently large not to be distorted by rounding), and what was actually received in the period recorded on Tablet HT 114A and (taking into account rounding) Tablet HT 121. These tablets record four categories of goods (with the term for one being capable of being expressed in two different ways, as "horned cattle" or "male quadrupeds"). These categories of goods are:

Symbol	Symbol No.	Meaning
Ψ	L42	Female (and young) goats
↑	L67	Female (and young) cows
⟩	L89	Fodder (various types)
(symbol)	L49	Horned cattle (interchangeable with male quadrupeds)
‡	L2'	Male quadrupeds (interchangeable with horned cattle)

---

60. Michael Ventris & John Chadwick, *Documents in Mycenaean Greek* (2nd Ed.)(Cambridge: Cambridge University Press, 1973), p302 (the Column "H" count for Tablet Mc 0459 has been corrected to 15 (see photograph of tablet on page 235)). While it was noted that all of the tablets, other than Tablet Mc 5098, had an even number of horns, it was not discussed as to why this was the case (we now know this was because horn numbers were being used as a proxy for animal numbers) or why, in the case of Tablet Mc 5098, an odd number was recorded (345). As we shall see later in this chapter, on Tablet HT 120 in particular, there is evidence that some animals were only part owned by the temple (presumably with the herdsmen who tended them). Here, therefore, the tax payment that was recorded on Tablet Mc 5098 was the result of a calculation that involved 172 ½ male animals being payable (the last half corresponding to one horn in the proxy measure being used, making this an odd number, rather than two).

Given that "horned cattle" and "male quadrupeds" are synonymous, it is no coincidence that the resulting four (rather than five) categories of goods are, like their Linear B counterparts,[61] ones where three would be recorded by number (goats, cows, and horned cattle / male quadrupeds) and one (fodder of various types) would be recorded by weight. The numbers and amounts recorded on these three tablets is set out below:

Table 5.2: Analysis of certain Linear A tablets' data

Linear A Tablet	Heading	Female Goats	Female Cows	Total ("A")	Fodder for small cattle	Fodder for quadrupeds	Horned cattle	Male quadrupeds	Total ("B")	Ratio ("B"/"A")
	Linear A symbol	L42	L67	L42+L67			L45	L2'	(L45 or L2')	(%)
HT 14	"[from the] meadows [of the] peasants"	75	15	90	8	7	27	0	27	30%
HT 114A	"tax, [for] wages [of] food [in the] third [month]"	10	0	10	0	9	0	3	3	30%
HT 121	"tax, [for] wages [of] food [in the] fourth [month]"	5	0	5	10	9	0	2	2	40%
		90	15	105	18	25	27	5	32	30%

Notes:
1. Tablets HT 14 data includes both amounts received and to be received (i.e. the completed obligation that, at the time the tablet was written, had not yet been fulfilled).
2. Tablet HT 121 fodder data includes amounts delivered in the previous month. Tablet HT 114A and Tablet HT 121 fodder values include amounts that, while ostensibly received from the tithe-like tax levied in order to pay the remuneration of the priests, were instead allocated to make payments (presumably for goods and services received by the temple from third parties) and pay the peasants (presumably working the temple's lands), as these were still part of the original tax obligation that had to be paid.
3. The number of male quadrupeds on Tablet HT 121 is counted as 2, whereas Brice and Godart & Olivier count it as 3. As noted previously, tablets were reused and it appears that, after the first two single unit tally marks, anything else on this row of the tablet is the residual imprint of what was previously recorded on the tablet and not intended to be counted again. The ratio is slightly higher due to rounding, as discussed below.

As with the Mc series of Linear B tablets, the above table shows us that a ratio of 30% was present between the (male) horned cattle or male quadrupeds and the total number of female animals (goats and cows) on Tablet HT 14 and Tablet HT 114A. That there was not on Tablet HT 121 was evidently because, in this instance, only whole animals were being dealt with (and the obligation, as regards male quadrupeds, had been rounded up to the closest whole number of animals, i.e. 2). As such, therefore, these Linear A tablets (from Hagia Triada) are directly comparable to the Mc series of Linear B tablets (from Knossos). What does this tell us?

First, that we have (male) horned cattle or male quadrupeds (i.e. male animals) recorded in the same ratio to female animals in Linear A tablets as male animals to female animals

---
61. Michael Ventris & John Chadwick, *Documents in Mycenaean Greek* (2nd Ed.)(Cambridge: Cambridge University Press, 1973), p202

(assumed or presumed) in the Linear B tablets indicates that the identified meanings of (male) "horned cattle" for Linear A symbol L49 and "male quadruped" for Linear A symbol L2' are, beyond reasonable doubt, correct (although, of course, we have already proved the former through analysis of Tablet HT 123A).

Second, this constant ratio between male and female animals being evident at two sites on opposite sides of the island (Hagia Triada and Knossos) perhaps a century apart indicates that the obligation was no mere local contractual commitment (such as rent). For such an obligation to have been imposed supra-regionally it was imposed by a supra-regional body. This was a tax imposed by the state, administered from Hagia Triada (for part of the island, to benefit the temple there) during the period when Crete was part of Egypt's empire, and, after the Mycenaean conquest, administered from Knossos (presumably for part of the island, presumably to benefit the temple there).

As with the tax on sheep that resulted in the wool payment obligations recorded on Tablet HT 123A, another tax obligation existed here akin, as we would understand it, to a tithe payable to the temples. It was primarily intended to be used for the priests' remuneration (as the subheading for Tablet HT 14 explicitly tells us and as we might infer from the heading of Tablet HT 114A and HT 121 because these indicate that the amounts in question were for wages). From Tablet HT 14 it appears, at least, that this tithe-like tax was levied on the peasants (presumably different peasants to those paid by the temple, the future recipients of fodder on Tablet HT 114A and HT 121, who presumably worked on the temple's land). Tablet HT 14 deals with one of the classes of taxpayer that was recorded on Tablet HT 123A, recording its entire annual obligation and the amounts that have been paid or remain payable at that point in time; it is, therefore, another ad hoc report. Presumably, as the tax benefitted just the temple, it was levied across a smaller area than the wool tax recorded on Tablet HT 123A. Presumably the other classes of taxpayer listed on Tablet HT 123A were also required to pay this tithe-like tax, other than the temple itself of course (it seems illogical for the wool tax to have been applied to all strata of society, and the tithe-like tax to have only been levied upon the lowest strata of society). Tablet HT 114A and Tablet HT 121 are the records of the payments received from two individual debtors in a particular month (month four) against their individual obligations (with the latter also showing an amount received in the prior month).

Finally, while the decipherment of Linear A has relied on Linear B in certain important aspects (as discussed at the start of this chapter), that favour can now be returned to a very small extent. In particular, Linear B symbol *142 (commodity "I") would seem most likely to represent a type of fodder. Unfortunately, we cannot help further in this regard due to the fact that the (female) goats and cows on these Linear A tablets do not follow the same 4.6 : 2.8 relationship of female animals as exhibited by commodities "G" and "H" on the Mc series of Linear B tablets (although, of course, as the Linear B tablets Mc 5118 and Mc 0464 demonstrate, this ratio was not always present there anyway).

That we can see that yet another tax that was levied during the period of Egyptian rule which continued to be levied in the Mycenaean period demonstrates yet another degree of administrative continuity that has not previously been appreciated. Moreover, as with the

234   The Decipherment of Linear A

Dk series of Linear B tablets, this is also reflected in the use of Linear A alongside Linear B on the Mc series of Linear B tablets. We shall consider this after briefly considering the units of measure of weight on the Linear A tablets.

2. Minoan units of measure of weight
Tablet HT 114A is the only one of the three Linear A tablets we are considering where there is only one type of fodder recorded (as with the Mc series of Linear B tablets). We are, therefore, able to undertake some analysis concerning the units of measure of weight that were used on it. We know that:

- The total of the Mc series of Linear B tablets records 1,167.5 animals and 250 units of fodder.
- From Ventris and Chadwick's analysis, we know that the units of measure used to record the weight of fodder on the Mc series of Linear B tablets weighed 0.967 Kilograms.[62] In contrast to the unit of measure used to weigh the wool tax obligation, I presume this was a Mycenaean unit of measure. The 250 units of fodder therefore had a total weight of 241 Kilograms.
- On Tablet HT 114A there were 13 animals recorded and 9 units of fodder recorded (including those labelled as being "for payments" and "for the peasants"). If this were scaled up, so that there were 1,167.5 animals instead of 13, there would have been 808.3 units of fodder instead of 9.
- Given that the 30% male to female animals ratio was present on this tablet (and Tablet HT 14), as it was on the Mc series of Linear B tablets, we can assume that the same amount of fodder (by weight) would be represented by the 808.3 units of fodder on the scaled-up Tablet HT 114A as was represented by the 250 units of fodder in the total of the Mc series of Linear B tablets, i.e. 241 Kilograms.
- As a result, we know that each unit of fodder on Tablet HT 114A weighed 0.298 Kilograms.

As we have seen, on Tablet HT 123A, the wool tax obligation was recorded in units of measure of 2.90 Kilograms. It is no coincidence that, but for an insignificant 2.7% margin of error, the units of measure for recording weight on this tablet are one tenth of the units of measure for recording weight on Tablet HT 123A. Such regularity suggests these two units of measure of weight were related and part of the same system of units of measure of weight, and given that this was not an Egyptian system of measures of weight, it was most likely Minoan. That the ratio between animals and fodder is different on Tablet HT 114A to the Mc series of Linear B reflects the fact that fodder recorded on the Mc series of Linear B tablets was not recorded in the same units of measure of weight (and that it was only the wool tax obligations recorded on the Dk series of Linear B tablets

---

62. Michael Ventris & John Chadwick, *Documents in Mycenaean Greek* (2nd Ed.)(Cambridge: Cambridge University Press, 1973), p57

that continued to be recorded in Minoan units of measure of weight in the Mycenaean period, Mycenaean units of measure of weight being used otherwise).[63]

We cannot replicate this analysis for Tablet HT 14 or Tablet HT 121 for two reasons. First, it appears from the numbers recorded that different orders of units of measure were used to record the weight of fodder (i.e. as if Kilograms instead of Grams, or Grams instead of Milligrams). Here we do not know the order of magnitude between the different units of measure used (in the case of Tablet HT 14 they appear to be higher, and in the case of Tablet HT 121 they appear to be lower). Secondly, in a difference to the Mc series of Linear B tablets which only has one type of fodder, there are two fodder types on Tablet HT 14 and Tablet HT 121, with both fodder for small (young) cattle and fodder for (mature) quadrupeds. The fodder for small (young) cattle has, presumably, been processed to aid digestion by immature animals without developed rumens and the act of processing it would result, presumably, in the processed fodder having a reduced volume and weight (as waste material was removed). The processed fodder would therefore presumably have had a higher value per volume / weight because of the labour hours required to process it. If meeting a tax obligation, such as here, required the same value to be transferred, the volume / weight of fodder that was required to be paid would be reduced. We do not know, however, by what factor this portion of the obligation would have been reduced. As a result of these two factors, we cannot, therefore, calculate the units of weight used to record for fodder on Tablet HT 14 or Tablet HT 121.

3. The use of Linear A on the Mc series of Linear B tablets

Returning to the use of Linear A on the Mc series of Linear B tablets, let us consider an example.

Example: Linear B Tablet Mc 4459 [0459] + 5786 + frr.(4)[64]

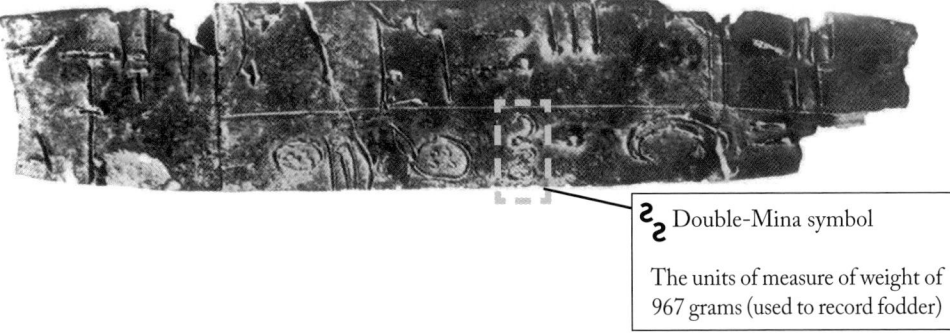

2_2 Double-Mina symbol

The units of measure of weight of 967 grams (used to record fodder)

---

63. Wool was recorded in units of measure of weight of just under 3 Kilograms (Michael Ventris & John Chadwick, *Documents in Mycenaean Greek* (2nd Ed.)(Cambridge: Cambridge University Press, 1973), p57); fodder was recorded in units of measure of weight denoted by the "double-mina" symbol, 2_2 (Lydia Baumbach, "The Dilemma of the Horns – An Analysis of the Knossos Mc Tablets", *Acta Classica* 14(1971), pp2–4; José L. Melena, "Mycenaean Writing" in Yves Duhoux & Anna Morpurgo Davies (Eds.), *A Companion to Linear B Mycenaean Greek Texts and their World* (Louvain-La-Neuve & Walpole, MA: Peeters, 2014), p155). This weighed 967 grams (Michael Ventris & John Chadwick, *Documents in Mycenaean Greek* (2nd Ed.)(Cambridge: Cambridge University Press, 1973), p57).

64. https://liber.cnr.it/tablet/view/4483 (accessed 1 January 2022) © Hellenic Ministry of Culture (HCRMDO)

236 The Decipherment of Linear A

On this tablet:

- The first row records: 23 of the first type of animal (presumed to be female) denoted by Linear B symbol G (*150), and 15 of the second type of animal, believed to be she-goats, denoted by Linear B symbol H (*107b); and
- The second row records: 10 units of the commodity denoted by Linear B symbol I (*142), with the units of measure of the double-mina highlighted above, and 20 of what are believed to be horns of the agrimi goat, denoted by Linear B symbol J (*151).

These are recorded in Linear B. However, if we look, we can see that Linear A is used for the heading and subheadings on the tablet.

A. Heading ("*ta-to*")
It has been believed that the heading for this tablet was a place name written in Linear B.[65] It is not. Moreover, it is written in Linear A.

⌐ Linear B symbol *59 ("ta")
T Linear B symbol *05 ("to")

Hieroglyph O1 ⊏⊐/ rotated ⌐/ Linear A symbol L74 ⌐ (NOT Linear B symbol *59 ("ta") ⌐)

As we will frequently see in the Linear A corpus, this symbol represents the last hieroglyph in the word(s):

🦉 ⎯ ⏃ ⎝⌐⌐⌐⎠ *mḫr* storehouse, barn [noun - arch.] G17 - D36 - T28
                                                      - D21 - M17 - O1

🦉 ⎯ ⏃ ⎝⌐⌐⌐⎠ *mḫr* storehouse, barn [noun - arch.] G17 - D36 - T28
                                                      - D21 - M17 - X1 - O1

🦉 ⎯ ⏃ ⌐⌐⌐ *mḫr* storehouse, barn [noun - arch.] G17 - D36 - T28
                                                      - D21 - O1

  🦉 ⎯ ⏃ ⎝⌐⎠ *šmyt / šmy* storehouse, barn ambulatory [noun - arch.] N37
                                                      - G17 - M17 - M17 - X1 - O1

---

65. José L. Melena, "On the Knossos Mc Tablets", *Minos* 13(1972), p35

The Translations 237

Hieroglyph W11 - Z1 ▣| / simplified / modified / Linear A symbol L39 ⊤ (NOT Linear B symbol *05 ("to") ⊤)

As we have seen previously, this symbol represents the first hieroglyphs in the word:

▣|⌐ *gb* deficiency [noun] W11 - Z1 - D58

Here the syllabic values of the Linear B symbols are irrelevant because we are not dealing with Linear B (and this is not a place name). These two symbols are written in Linear A and mean "[in the] storehouse / barn – deficiency".

B(i). First subheading ("*a-ko-ta*")[66]

It has been believed that this subheading was the name of a collector of taxes.[67] It is not. Moreover, it is written in Linear A.

⊤ Linear B symbol *08 ("a")

ϙ Linear B symbol *70 ("ko")

⌐ Linear B symbol *59 ("ta")

Hieroglyph S34 ⚲ / modifed (loop replaced by horizontal bar) / Linear A symbol L52 ⊤ (NOT Linear B symbol *08 ("a") ⊤)

As we have seen, this symbol represents the first hieroglyph in the word:

⚲|||| *'nḫ* sustenance [noun - food] S34 - Z1 - X4 - Z2

⚲|⌐ *'nḫ* sustenance [noun - food] S34 - Z1 - Z8

---

66. The first subheading has previously been transcribed as "*a-ko-ro-ta*" (Lydia Baumbach, "The Dilemma of the Horns – An Analysis of the Knossos Mc Tablets", *Acta Classica* 14(1971), p2). As discussed in the following footnote, I do not, however, see the "ro" symbol here.

67. José L. Melena, "On the Knossos Mc Tablets", *Minos* 13(1972), p35. Instead of "*a-ko-ta*" (not that that is actually what is being conveyed here), it had also been believed that the tablet recorded "*a-ko-ro-ta*" (which is not being conveyed either). I do not, however, see the "ro" symbol (the "+" sign of Linear B symbol 2, and Linear A symbol L22). I believe the vertical line of what is believed to be the + is simply the vertical line that divides the heading section of the tablet (on the left) from the section of the tablet that records the list of items (on the right), along which the tablet broke, and the final symbol of this phrase has simply been written to the right of this line because it could not fit to the left of it.

238   The Decipherment of Linear A

It is interesting that the "accent" horizontal bar is present on the symbol, as it was in Linear A.

Hieroglyph F36 ⎍/ rotated ⎍ / simplified / Linear A symbol L45 ⎍ (NOT Linear B symbol *70 ("ko") ⎍)

This Linear A symbol is Hieroglyph F36 rotated by 180 degrees, with its stem simplified, for ease of incision.

   This word we saw on Tablet HT 14, where it was abbreviated to Linear A symbol L93 representing its last hieroglyph, Hieroglyph A24. As we see elsewhere in the Linear A corpus, one scribe will abbreviate a word to a symbol representing its last hieroglyph while another will abbreviate it to a symbol representing its first hieroglyph. As the simplistic example in Chapter Three stated, A can stand for avocado as easily as O can stand for avocado. Here, the scribe chose not to represent the word with a symbol representing its last hieroglyph as in the surviving Linear A corpus; instead, the symbol represents the first hieroglyph in the word:

   smꜣ take part in, receive [verb] F36 - G1 - G17 - Z7 - Z4 - Y1 - A24

Hieroglyph O1 ⎍/ rotated ⎍/ Linear A symbol L74 ⎍ (NOT Linear B symbol *59 ("ta") ⎍)

As we will see frequently in the Linear A corpus, this symbol represents the last hieroglyph in the word:

   mḫr storehouse, barn [noun - arch.] G17 - D36 - T28 - D21 - M17 - O1

   mḫr storehouse, barn [noun - arch.] G17 - D36 - T28 - D21 - M17 - X1 - O1

   mḫr storehouse, barn [noun - arch.] G17 - D36 - T28 - D21 - O1

   šmyt / šmy storehouse, barn ambulatory [noun - arch.] N37 - G17 - M17 - M17 - X1 - O1

Here the syllabic values of the Linear B symbols are irrelevant because we are not dealing with Linear B (and this is not a person's name). These three symbols are written in Linear A and mean "sustenance to [be] receive[d] [in the] storehouse / barn". As the heading and subheading show, none of the items listed have yet been received. In contrast to Linear A

The Translations   239

Tablet HT 14, Tablet HT 114A, and Tablet HT 121, this tablet is an individual debtor's account showing the full value of the debt and no amounts had been received when it was created and the record incised.

B(ii). Second subheading ("*qe-wa-ra*")
This series of symbols has been labelled by historians as an "additional entry", but no meaning has been discerned (for if not a place name and not a person's name, what else could it be that could not be translated?).[68] Again, it is written in Linear A.

☺ Linear B symbol *78 ("qe")
冊 Linear B symbol *54 ("wa")
Ŀ Linear B symbol *60 ("ra")

Hieroglyphs Z4B - Z4B - W24 ≡ ○/ modified (four dashes as dots inside enclosed arms) / Linear A symbol L91 ☺ (NOT Linear B symbol *78 ("qe") ☺)
As set out in Appendix 6, this symbol, representing Hieroglyphs Z4B - Z4B - W24, represents the ordinal:

≡ ○ *fdnw* fourth Z4B - Z4B - W24

Hieroglyph O20 🏛 / simplified / Linear A symbol L75 冊 (NOT Linear B symbol *54 ("wa") 冊)
As we will see on Tablet HT 86A, this symbol represents the last hieroglyph in the word:

🏺🏛 *ḥwt nṯr* temple [noun – arch.] R8 - O20

Hieroglyph I12 / simplified / Linear A symbol L53 ⌐/ reversed ⌐ (NOT Linear B symbol *60 ("ra") Ŀ)
As we will see on Tablet HT 17 and Tablet HT 19, this symbol represents the last hieroglyph in the word:

---
68. José L. Melena, "On the Knossos Mc Tablets", *Minos* 13(1972), p35

240   The Decipherment of Linear A

ntrt goddess [noun - div.] R8 - D21 - X1 - I12

ntrt goddess [noun - div.] R8 - D21 - X1 - J2 - I12

ntrt goddess [noun - div.] R8 - D21 - X1 - Z5 - I12

ntrt goddess [noun - div.] R8 - X1 - D21 - M17 - M17 - X1 - J2 - I12

ntrt goddess [noun - div.] R8 - X1 - D21 - X1 - I12

ntrt goddess [noun - div.] R8 - X1 - D21 - X1 - J2 - I12

ntrt goddess [noun - div.] R8 - X1 - I12

ntrt goddess [noun - div.] R8 - X1 - J2 - I12

ntrt goddess [noun – div.] R8 - Z5 - Z5 - Z5 - I12

Given that the symbol written after this on both Tablet HT 17 and Tablet HT 19 referred to the Goddess Hathor, and given that the tablets here were written in Linear A (i.e. Middle Egyptian written in shorthand using hieroglyphs), it seems likely that the goddess being referred to here was (still) Hathor. (It is also no coincidence that this symbol, referring to the same goddess, begins the first subheading on Linear B Tablet Mc 4462.)

Here the syllabic values of the Linear B symbols are irrelevant because we are not dealing with Linear B. These three symbols are written in Linear A and mean "[in the] fourth [month], [for the] temple [of the] Goddess [Hathor]". This was the recipient of the items in question, when they were received.

Conclusion

In 1956, in *Documents in Mycenaean Greek*, Ventris and Chadwick wrote that the Mc series of Linear B tablets were "too fragmentary to be worth transcribing".[69] By the time Chadwick published the second edition of *Documents in Mycenaean Greek* in 1973 and additional joins of tablet fragments had been discovered, this was clearly no longer the case. I suspect that, because Chadwick was still unable to translate the tablet headings and subheadings revealed by the newly joined portions of the tablets, despite them being written (he wrongly thought) in Linear B, he decided that discretion was the better part of valour and simply omitted any reconsideration of the tablets from the second edition. In the light of the headings and subheadings on the Mc series of Linear B tablets being written in Linear A, and, as discussed previously, there being Linear A headings and

---

69. Michael Ventris & John Chadwick, *Documents in Mycenaean Greek* (2nd Ed.)(Cambridge: Cambridge University Press, 1973), p302

subheadings on the Dk Series of Linear B tablets rather than, in both cases, undecipherable names of people or places written in Linear B, Ventris and Chadwick's assertion that at least 65 per cent of the recorded Mycenaean words in the Linear B corpus were proper names clearly needs significant reassessment (in particular when that assertion relates to Crete, and especially when those names do not bear comparison with known legendary or historical Greek names).[70] What is already clear, however, is that Linear A continued to be used alongside Linear B on Crete, there was continuity of two key components of the taxation regime, and Linear B was derived from Linear A and Middle Egyptian written in hieroglyphs. All these reflect the survival of aspects of the Egyptian administration on Crete well into the Mycenaean period.

As we have already seen, an Egyptian temple continued to operate at Knossos after the Egyptian withdrawal. That it should have done so is not, perhaps, surprising given that, after Constantinople fell to the Ottoman Turks in AD 1453, even Sultan Mehmet II allowed the Greek Orthodox church to persist. Linear B tablet Mc 4459 [0459], which we examined above, has been dated to the Late Minoan III A2 period (1375–1300 BC),[71] so the Egyptian temple at Knossos persisted for a considerable time (50 to 125 years at least) after the withdrawal.

As we have also already seen, the nature of the temple's role remained unchanged. We have already seen evidence of this with the Dk series of Linear B tablets which were found at Knossos. With their Linear A headings and subheadings, we know that the wool tax, payable to the (Mycenaean) state, was administered by the Egyptian temple at Knossos in the same way that the Egyptian temple at Hagia Triada had previously administered the wool tax for the (Egyptian) state (and, indeed, some of the area that the temple at Knossos had administrative responsibility for evidently encapsulated some of the area that the temple at Hagia Triada had previously had administrative responsibility for). For undertaking this role, the temples evidently received the benefit of a tithe-like tax (the Mycenaean state, and its people, with different gods and goddesses, would hardly grant the benefit of a tithe-like tax to an Egyptian temple at Knossos worshipping an Egyptian goddess for doing nothing), and the purpose of this tax, specifically noted to be for the benefit the Egyptian temple at Knossos on the Mc series of Linear B tablets (where the Mc series of Linear B tablets was found), was unchanged from that at the Egyptian temple at Hagia Triada during the period of Egyptian administration, and which we know from Tablet HT 14, Tablet HT 114A, and Tablet HT 121 was for the remuneration of the phyle (of priests). That an Egyptian temple at Knossos continued to benefit from the same tax in the Mycenaean period as had the Egyptian temple at Hagia Triada previously when Crete was part of Egypt's empire, therefore reflects the Egyptian temple at Knossos continuing to function as agent of the state and being paid for doing so. As the Egyptian temples in Egypt were agents of the state in 18th Dynasty Egypt, and as they have now been shown to have been at Hagia Triada during the period that

---

70. Michael Ventris & John Chadwick, *Documents in Mycenaean Greek* (2nd Ed.)(Cambridge: Cambridge University Press, 1973), p92
71. https://liber.cnr.it/tablet/view/4483 (accessed 1 January 2022)

Crete was part of Egypt's empire, the Egyptian temple at Knossos continued to function as agent of the state after the Mycenaean conquest of the island.

That an Egyptian temple continued to function well into the Mycenaean period then begs the question of who worshipped there? After all, that the Dk series of Linear B tablets and Mc series of Linear B tablets included accounting terms written in Linear A demonstrates that those who wrote the records of state still used Linear A in administration (which we know to be Middle Egyptian written in shorthand using hieroglyphs) in preference to Linear B, despite Linear B being the language of the Mycenaean regime. This was not the temple of Egyptian traders who had returned to Crete (for the place of worship of transient traders would not likely be allowed to act as agent of the state collecting its taxes). The most likely answer, therefore, is that the temple was used either by Cretans descended from those who had adopted the Egyptian faith during the period Crete was part of Egypt's empire (or before) and whose faith persisted after the Egyptian withdrawal, and / or descendants of Egyptians who had been left behind by the withdrawal. There is, after all, written evidence of the presence of the latter for, as we have already seen, one Linear B tablet found at Knossos records that a man in charge of a flock of sheep was called *a3-ku-pi-ti-jo*, meaning "Memphite" or "Egyptian" in Mycenaean Greek.[72]

---

72. Eric Cline, "The Nature of the Economic Relations of Crete with Egypt and the Near East during the Late Bronze Age", in Angelos Chaniotis (Ed.), *From Minoan Farmers to Roman Traders: Sidelights on the Economy of Ancient Crete* (Franz Steiner Verlag: Stuttgart, 1999), pp126–127, citing Linear B Tablet Db 1105

The Translations 243

1(b). Other goods wholly and partially received

The records of goods partially and wholly received that are recorded on the tablets in this section, by virtue of the absence of the ratios noted in the previous section, do not appear to relate to the tithe-like tax received by the temple but, rather, relate to other deliveries of goods received by the temple.

Tablet HT 13

This tablet shows amounts received (and one amount to be received) by the temple from the city of Amnisos. The amounts are recorded by a description of both what they are and their future intended application or recipient. The nature of the transaction is not stated but, not being the result of the tithe-like tax, it is more likely than not that the tablet record reflects a purchase.

<u>Heading: Row One, Symbols One and Two:</u>

<u>Hieroglyph O49 ⊗ / simplified / Linear A symbol L29 ⊕</u>
As we have seen previously, this symbol represents the word:

⊗ *niwt* city, town [noun] O49

As before, and as set out in Appendix 4, after the word "city" follows the name of that city.

<u>Hieroglyph M17 / reversed / Linear A symbol L97</u>
As we have seen previously, this symbol represents Hieroglyph M17 reversed. Place names are discussed in Appendix 4 and we know from the list of Aegean place names in

244   The Decipherment of Linear A

the mortuary temple of Amenhotep III at Kom el-Hetan that the name for the city of Aminos was written in hieroglyphs as:

⸻ 'mni-s3 Amnisos [noun - loc.] M17 - A2 - D38 - N35 - Z4
- M8

Here, as highlighted above, the name of the city has been abbreviated to the Linear A symbol representing its first hieroglyph. Thus, the first two symbols mean "[from the] city [of] Amnisos".

Subheading: Row One, Symbols Three and Four, and Row Two, Symbol One:

Hieroglyph V17 / simplified / Linear A symbol L102
Linear A symbol L102 is a straightforward simplified representation of Hieroglyph V17. Here it could represent the first hieroglyph in the noun:

s3 protection [noun] V17

s3 protection, magical protection, safe conduct, amulet [noun - clo.] V17
- Z1 - Y1 - Z2

s3 protection [noun] V17 - Z1 - Z2

s3 protection [noun] V17 - Z3A

Alternatively, it could represent the first hieroglyph in the verb:

s3 n ḥ s3 protect [verb] V17 - Y1 - Z2 - N35 - M16 - G1 - D1

This symbol therefore means either "[for] protection" or "[being] protect[ed]", depending on whether the scribe wanted this symbol to represent a noun or a verb. For the purposes of our translation here, there is little practical difference between the two.

Hieroglyph O1 ⌑ / rotated ⌑ / Linear A symbol L74 ⌑

As we have seen previously, this symbol represents the last hieroglyph in the word(s):

mḫr storehouse, barn [noun - arch.] G17 - D36 - T28 - D21 - M17 - O1

mḫr storehouse, barn [noun - arch.] G17 - D36 - T28 - D21 - M17 - X1 - O1

mḫr storehouse, barn [noun - arch.] G17 - D36 - T28 - D21 - O1

šmyt / šmy storehouse, barn, ambulatory [noun - arch.] N37 - G17 - M17 - M17 - X1 - O1

Hieroglyph M20 / rotated / simplified / Linear A symbol L82

As we have seen previously, this symbol represents Hieroglyph M20. Here, this symbol represents the first hieroglyph in the word:

sḥtyw cattle [noun - ani.] M20 - G4 - E1 - N33A

This is not a widely attested word in what has survived of the written usage of Middle Egyptian (not that that is necessarily reflective of how widespread its use actually was, which may have been more extensive) and there is some uncertainty as to its precise meaning.[73] However, its believed meaning, "cattle", is sufficiently correct for our purposes here (and, I believe, correct in so far as that goes). It is worth stating at this juncture, however, that as well as being the collective noun "cattle", like the collective nouns *'nḫ* and *'wt*, I believe this word could also be used as the name of specific animals. From this tablet, and the specific animals referred to under this subheading, we can infer what these specific animals most probably were, which will be of relevance later in this chapter.

For now, however, these three symbols mean "[for] protection / [being] protect[ed] [in the] storehouse / barn, cattle".

---

73. https://aaew.bbaw.de/tla/servlet/GetWcnDetails?u=guest&f=0&l=0&wn=141870&db=0 (accessed 25 March 2022)

246   The Decipherment of Linear A

Subheading: Row Two, Symbol Two:

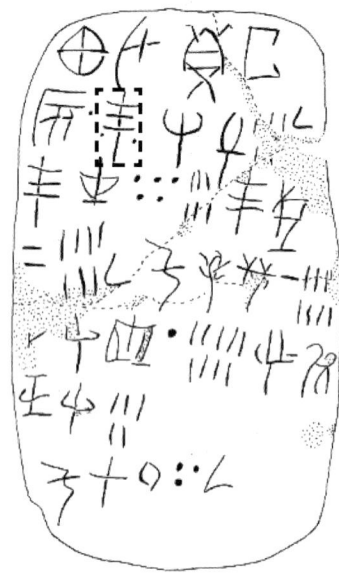

Hieroglyph V16 / rotated / simplified / Linear A symbol L92
As we have seen previously, this symbol represents the first hieroglyph in the word:

    s3 phyle (of priests), company, regiment (of troops), troop (of animals) [noun]
                                                          V16 - A1 - Z2

Here, this means "[for the] phyle (of priests)".

Category One: Row Two, Symbols Three and Four:

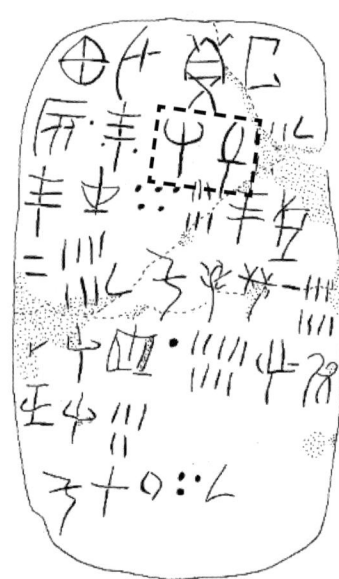

The Translations 247

Hieroglyphs D28 - Z1 ⊔ / simplified / modified / Linear A symbol L54 Ψ

We have already seen that Hieroglyphs D28 - Z1 are represented by Linear A symbol L55 Υ.

Linear A symbol L54, however, also represents those hieroglyphs. It differs slightly in style: the central stem of Linear A symbol L55 (which represents Hieroglyph Z1) has simply been written elongated so that it began above the arms of the symbol (which represent Hieroglyph D28):

Linear A symbol L55 Υ represents the same hieroglyphs as

Linear A symbol L54 Ψ

In certain cases, both appear on a tablet the different symbols, representing the same hieroglyphs but representing different words, such as on Tablet HT 2 and Tablet HT 7A, for example. That is not the case here, where the scribe has simply chosen Linear A symbol L54, apparently as a result of personal preference. Here, this symbol represents the word:

⊔ *k3w* food, bounty [noun - food] D28 - Z1

Hieroglyph S34 ☥ / simplified / Linear A symbol L23 ☥

As we will see on the next tablet, Tablet HT2, the Middle Egyptian word *'nḫ* was used to record "small cattle". Here, that word is again represented by a Linear A symbol representing its first hieroglyph:

☥ 🐐 *'nḫ* goat, small cattle [noun - ani.] S34 - E31

☥ 🐐||| *'nḫ* goat, small cattle [noun - ani.] S34 - G43 - E31 - Z2

☥ *'nḫ* goat, small cattle [noun - ani.] S34 - N35 - J1 - Z7 - F28 - Z3

There are, however, two differences here. First, Hieroglyph S34 is represented by Linear A symbol L23, rather than being modified further to be represented by Linear A symbol L52 (as it is on Tablet HT 2). Second, the word has the meaning "goats", rather than "small cattle" (as it does on Tablet HT 2).

Thus, in these two symbols we have "[for] food, goats". This is followed by a count of 5½ (the half being represented by Linear A fraction symbol J), meaning that at least one of the animals had already been slaughtered and half a carcass was now being delivered.

At this stage, despite the subheading, the scribe then felt that he had to state that the next two categories of items recorded were specifically for the phyle (of priests). Indeed,

248   The Decipherment of Linear A

the scribe seems to have been premature (or overzealous) in writing the subheading as after the next two categories of items recorded the further categories of items recorded were not for the phyle (of priests).

Category Two: Row Three, Symbols One and Two:

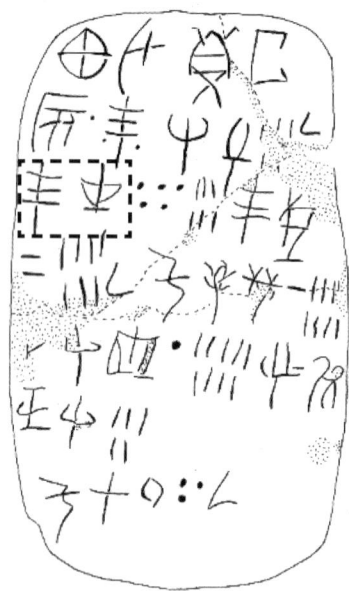

Hieroglyph V16 ⚟ / rotated ⚟ / simplified / Linear A symbol L92 ⚟
As we have seen previously, this symbol represents the first hieroglyph in the word:

    s3 phyle (of priests), company, regiment (of troops), troop (of animals) [noun]
                                                              V16 - A1 - Z2

Hieroglyph R7 ⚟ / modified / Linear A symbol L6 ⚟
As we have seen previously, this symbol represents Hieroglyph R7. Here, this symbol represents the first hieroglyph in the word:

    b3 sacred ram, ram, Ba, soul [noun - ani.] R7 - E10

These symbols therefore mean "[for the] phyle (of priests), rams". They are followed by a count of 56.

    As we have seen, given the timing of the wool tax perhaps two months after shearing, it is likely that sales or transfers of ownership of rams were permitted if they were registered with state. Here, both as a party to the transaction and as agent of the state, the temple would also know to make the necessary amendments to its own and the vendor's or transferor's records to record the change of ownership and correctly calculate each party's wool tax payment obligation appropriately thereafter.

The count is recorded using a dot to represent units of 10, rather than a horizonal tally mark (which are also used on this tablet). Dots are also used to count Category Five (and the total). This indicates that these two categories differ from the others on the tablet. In particular, it infers that these two categories record the same specific type of animal. For the tablet's ultimate total, being a combination of both animals and non-animals, the scribe had to choose one way (dots) or the other (horizontal tally marks), and he chose the former (but he could equally have chosen the latter).

Category Three: Row Three, Symbols Three and Four:

Hieroglyph V16 / rotated / simplified / Linear A symbol L92

As we have seen previously, this symbol represents the first hieroglyph in the word:

s3 phyle (of priests), company, regiment (of troops), troop (of animals) [noun]
V16 - A1 - Z2

Hieroglyph G1 / simplified / Linear A symbol L103

As we have seen previously, this symbol represents Hieroglyph G1. It does not represent the word meaning "deficiency" here (*gbi*), which is perhaps unsurprising as it does not come at the end of a list (where a deficiency might be expected to be recorded). Rather, as it does on Tablet HT 91 (where the context in which it appears allows us to draw this conclusion), here this symbol represents the first hieroglyph in the word:

250   The Decipherment of Linear A

𓄿ḫt cow [noun - ani.] G1 - O4 - X1 - E1

These two symbols therefore mean "[for the] phyle (of priests), cows". They are followed by a count of 27½ (the half being represented by Linear A fraction symbol J), again meaning that, because there is a fraction of an animal, at least one animal has been slaughtered and half a carcass was now being delivered.

Category Four: Row Four, Symbols One to Three:

Hieroglyph F14 / rotated / simplified / Linear A symbol L98
As we have seen previously, this symbol represents the first hieroglyph in the word:

    wpt rnpt New Year's Day (and its festivals) [noun] F14 - W3
    wpt rnpt New Year's Day (and its festivals) [noun] F15 - W3 - N5

Hieroglyph M34 / simplified / Linear A symbol L101 (as here) / modified
Linear A symbol L101 (here) is a simplified representation of Hieroglyph L101. As set out in the analysis in Appendix 7, it represents the last hieroglyph in the word:

    pḥ3 grain, seed [noun - flora - food] Q3 - J1 - M34

While the word for "grain" is used, it is not stated which cereal is being referred to. This characteristic was also noted by historian Hana Vymazalová in her review of the Abusir papyrus archive of the 5th Dynasty king, King Neferefre.[74]

---

74. Hana Vymazalová, *The accounting documents from the papyrus archive of Neferre and their specific terminology* (PhD: Charles University in Prague, 2005), p187

Hieroglyph T25 𓌫 / rotated 𓋿 / simplified / Linear A symbol L60 𐘂

As we have seen previously, this symbol represents the first hieroglyph (or, in one instance, last hieroglyph) in the word:

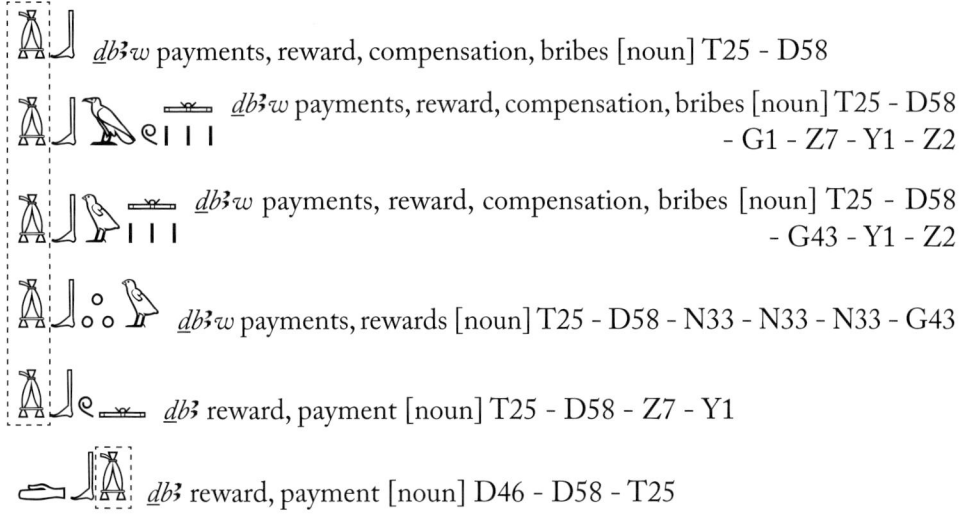

ḏbȝw payments, reward, compensation, bribes [noun] T25 - D58

ḏbȝw payments, reward, compensation, bribes [noun] T25 - D58 - G1 - Z7 - Y1 - Z2

ḏbȝw payments, reward, compensation, bribes [noun] T25 - D58 - G43 - Y1 - Z2

ḏbȝw payments, rewards [noun] T25 - D58 - N33 - N33 - N33 - G43

ḏbȝ reward, payment [noun] T25 - D58 - Z7 - Y1

ḏbȝ reward, payment [noun] D46 - D58 - T25

These three symbols therefore mean "[for the] New Year's Day grain payment". As noted previously, and as we will be able to infer from Tablet HT 86 which is discussed later in this chapter, payments labelled as such appear to represent the temple paying for goods and services from third parties (not, for example, the remuneration of the phyle (of priests)). This is followed by a count, according to Brice, of 17½ (the half being represented by Linear A fraction symbol J, where the tablet is damaged, circled above).

It seems likely that payments would have commonly been made on New Year's Day. In the modern day, businesses have their monthly payment run to pay their suppliers at the start of the month. More archaically, commercial leases in the UK are often still paid quarterly on the rental quarter dates. Due dates for making payments to meet obligations fall on specifically defined dates in the calendar; New Year's Day is one of the most obvious (in our own calendar as well as that of Ancient Egypt), and, as we have already seen, that the wool tax obligation was calculated by reference to that date on Tablet HT 123A indicates that date certainly had financial significance (or however that would be termed in a pre-monetary economy). In addition, in a pre-monetary economy it is unsurprising to find payments being made in grain, as here.

252   The Decipherment of Linear A

Category Five: Row Five, Symbols One to Three:

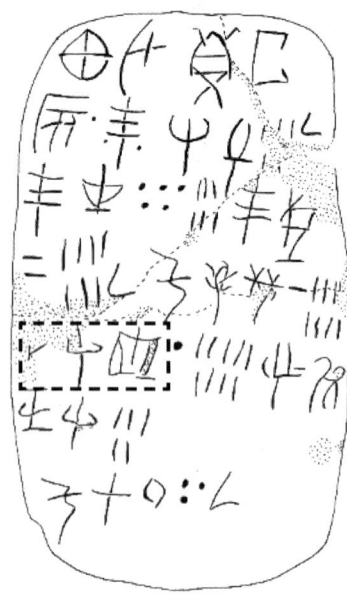

Hieroglyph T14 ⸢ replaced by AA26 (or J26) ⸢ / reversed ⸣ / Linear A symbol L30 ⸢
As we have seen previously, this symbol represents the (replaced) first hieroglyph in the word:

'wt small cattle, goats, herds [noun - ani.] T14

'wt small cattle, herds, flocks, goats [noun - ani.] T14 - G43 - E28 - Z2

'wt small cattle, herds, flocks, goats [noun - ani.] T14 - G43 - X1
                                                        - E1 - Z2

'wt small cattle, herds, flocks, goats [noun - ani.] T14 - G43 - X1
                                                        - E8 - Z2

'wt small cattle, herds, flocks, goats [noun - ani.] T14 - Z7 - X1 - E28
                                                        - F27 - Z3A

'wt small cattle, herds, flocks, goats [noun - ani.] T14 - Z7 - X1 - E28
                                                        - Z2

'wt small cattle, herds, flocks, goats [noun - ani.] T14 - Z7 - X1 - Z5 - Z2

As with the rams recorded in the earlier Category Two on this tablet, the units of 10 that this category is counted in are dots, not horizontal dashes. Horizontal dashes were used to count Categories Three and Four on the tablet, so the choice not to use them in Category Two and now here in Category Five was a conscious one that inferred something i.e. that the animals that were being counted in these two categories were of the same type and the "small cattle" here were (young) rams.

Hieroglyph R1 / simplified / Linear A symbol L57

Linear A symbol L57 is a simplified representation of Hieroglyph R1. Here, given the context in which it appears, it represents the last hieroglyph in the word:

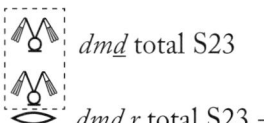 *wdḥw* offering table, offerings [noun - furn.] G43 - D46 - V28 - G43 - R1

Hieroglyph AA6 (or J6) or S23 / simplified / modified / Linear A symbol L85

Linear A symbol L85 is a simplified representation of Hieroglyph AA6 (or J6) or Hieroglyph S23, which Gardiner believed were one and the same.[75] Here it represents the word, or the first hieroglyph in the word:

dmḏ total S23

dmḏ r total S23 - D21

Both of these words appear with these spellings (in hieratic) in the accounts of the Abusir papyri from the mid-5th Dynasty archives of the funerary temples of King Neferirkare, King Neferefre, and Queen Khentkaus II, where they are used in accounting documents and inventory listings.[76] In the 12th Dynasty Kahun accounting records, which relate to the administration of a pyramid town, *dmḏ* is used as a column heading for records of cattle.[77]

These three symbols therefore mean "small cattle (rams) [for] offerings – total". They are followed by a count of 19.

As discussed under the next category recorded on this tablet, the word "total" is used on this penultimate category because this was the last item in store when the tablet was written (i.e. that had been received). The items recorded under the final category on the tablet were yet to be received (so was presumably owed by the city of Amnisos to the temple at Hagia Triada). While all the preceding items on the tablet are items received into inventory, this final category on the tablet is, therefore, a debt.

---

75. A. H. Gardiner, *Egyptian Grammar: Being an Introduction to the Study of Hieroglyphs* (3rd Ed.)(Oxford: Griffith Institute, 1957), p539
76. Hana Vymazalová, *The accounting documents from the papyrus archive of Neferre and their specific terminology* (PhD: Charles University in Prague, 2005), pp7, 168
77. Hana Vymazalová, *The accounting documents from the papyrus archive of Neferre and their specific terminology* (PhD: Charles University in Prague, 2005), pp134–135, 169

254   The Decipherment of Linear A

Category Six: Row Five, Symbols Four and Five, and Row Six, Symbols One and Two:

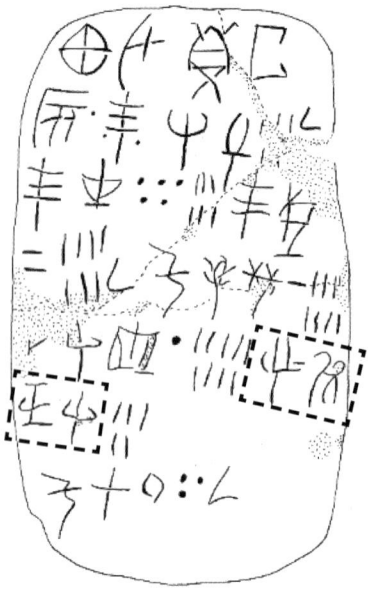

Hieroglyph D46 ⌒ / rotated / simplified / modified / Linear A symbol L100 Ψ
As we have seen previously, this symbol represents Hieroglyph D46. Here, this symbol represents the first hieroglyph in the word:

drpw offerings, provisions, meal, sustenance [noun - food] D46 - D21 - Q3 - Z7 - N37 - Z2

Hieroglyph A24 / simplified / modified / Linear A symbol L93
As we have seen previously, this symbol represents the last hieroglyph in the word:

sm³ take part in, receive [verb] F36 - G1 - G17 - Z7 - Z4 - Y1 - A24

In Appendix 8 we see that when the last item on a list has an ordinal (representing a numbered month), it indicates that item is for use in that next numbered month (i.e. the next month in the future). However, on this tablet, Tablet HT 36 and Tablet HT 19, the final category on the list includes this symbol, indicating the verb "to receive" (and, in the case of this tablet, and Tablet HT 36, the penultimate category finishes with Linear A symbol L85). Given that in each case Linear A symbol L93 appears next to the last item on the list, as with ordinals when they appear, we can infer that it also relates to the future. Consequently, the future tense should be inferred for this verb (as, indeed, it is when it is used in subheadings on Tablet HT 14, Tablet HT 86A and Tablet HT 95).

The Translations 255

Hieroglyph AA8 (or J8) ⊢⊣ / rotated ⊥ / Linear A symbol L61 ⊥

Linear A symbol L61 is a straightforward representation of Hieroglyph AA8 (or J8) rotated by 90 degrees to save space horizontally. Here it represents the first hieroglyph in the word:

ḳn first quality, best quality [noun] J8 - N35 - Y1

Hieroglyph R1 / simplified / Linear A symbol L57

As we have seen previously, this symbol represents the last hieroglyph in the word:

wdḥw offering table, offerings [noun - furn.] G43 - D46 - V28 - G43 - R1

These four symbols therefore mean "provisions to [be] receive[d of the] best quality [for] offerings". They are followed by a count of 5.

Total: Row Seven, Symbols One and Two:

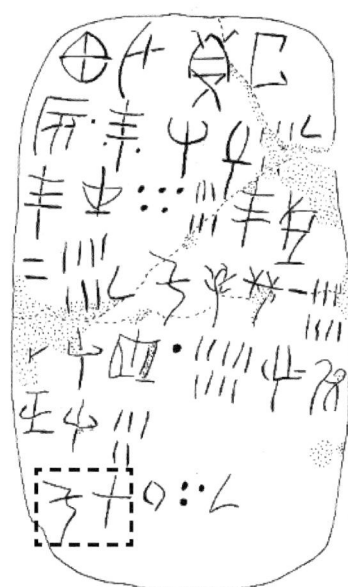

Hieroglyph F14 / rotated / simplified / Linear A symbol L98

As we have seen previously, this symbol represents the first hieroglyph in the word:

wpt rnpt New Year's Day (and its festivals) [noun] F14 - W3
wpt rnpt New Year's Day (and its festivals) [noun] F15 - W3 - N5

Hieroglyph N14 ✶ / modified / Linear A symbol L22 ✚

As we have seen previously, this symbol represents the first hieroglyph in the word:

✶ *dmḏ sm3* grand total [noun] N14 - F36

These two symbols therefore mean "[on] New Year's Day, grand total". They are followed by a count of 130½.

We are, therefore, now in a position to fully translate this tablet:

Row 1	Heading:	[From the] city [of] Amnisos
	Subheading One:	[for] protection / [being] protect[ed] [in the] storehouse / barn,
Row 2		cattle
	Subheading Two:	[For] the Phyle(s) (of priests)
	Category One:	[For] food, goats – 5½
Row 3	Category Two:	[For the] phyle (of priests), rams – 56
	Category Three:	[For the] phyle (of priests), cows
Row 4		– 27½
	Category Four:	[For the] New Year's Day grain payment – 17½
Row 5	Category Five:	Small cattle ((young) rams) [for] offerings – total – 19
	Category Six:	Provisions to [be] receive[d]
Row 6		of the] best quality [for] offerings – 5
Row 7	Total:	[On] New Year's Day, grand total: 130½

The Translations

Tablet HT 2
This tablet is another partial receipt, this time of animal fodder from the city of Knossos. In layout it is similar to Tablet HT 14 (so, is another ad hoc report), with amounts received thus far followed, after a subheading with similar terminology, by amounts to be received in the future.

Heading: Row One, Symbols One to Three:

Hieroglyph S34 ⚲ / modifed (loop removed) / Linear A symbol L52 ⊤

As we have seen previously, this symbol represents the first hieroglyph in the word:

⚲ 'nḫ sustenance [noun - food] S34 - Z1 - X4 - Z2

⚲ 'nḫ sustenance [noun - food] S34 - Z1 - Z8

Hieroglyph O49 ⊗ / simplified / Linear A symbol L29 ⊕

As we have seen previously, this symbol represents the word:

⊗ niwt city, town [noun] O49

Hieroglyphs D28 - Z1 ⊔ / simplified / modified / Linear A symbol L55 ⚲

As we have seen previously, Linear A symbol L55 represents Hieroglyphs D28 - Z1. Place names are considered in Appendix 4, and we know from the list of Aegean place names in the mortuary temple of Amenhotep III at Kom el-Hetan that the name for the city of Knossos was written in hieroglyphs as:

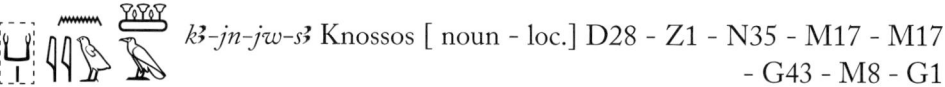

k3-jn-jw-s3 Knossos [noun - loc.] D28 - Z1 - N35 - M17 - M17 - G43 - M8 - G1

258   The Decipherment of Linear A

Here, as highlighted above, the name for the city was abbreviated to the Linear A symbol representing its first hieroglyphs.

The first three symbols on this tablet therefore mean "sustenance [from the] city [of] Knossos".

Category One: Row One, Symbols Four and Five (joined):

Hieroglyph D3 / rotated / reversed / Linear A symbol L89
As we have seen previously, this symbol represents the last hieroglyph in the word:

šnw grass (cattle fodder) [noun - flora] V7 - N35 - W24 - Z7 - D3

joined to Hieroglyph D36 / Linear A symbol L76 / rotated / reversed / simplified / modified / Linear A symbol L2' (without the male = symbol)

Where this symbol appears on the first row, the tablet has been damaged. As a result, the sketch, above, is not completely accurate. It is, however, more clearly seen where the symbol appears again, in Category Four below. This can be seen from an extract of the photograph of the tablet:

Extract of photograph of Tablet HT 2 from Godart & Olivier	Extract of photograph of Tablet HT 2 from Godart & Olivier with symbols highlighted	Highlighted symbols with extract of photograph of Tablet HT 2 removed
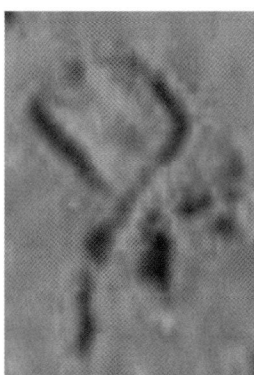	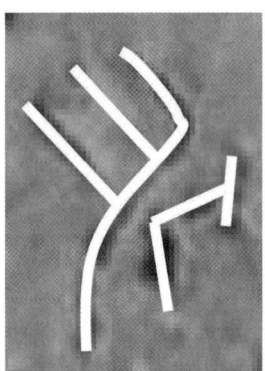	

The second symbol is, in fact, Linear A symbol L2' ⊥ but without the male = symbol, i.e. ⌐. This has not, to date, been recognised as a variant of Linear A symbol L2' (but which we should, in reality, consider to be the truer form of the symbol).

As we saw with Tablet HT 114A and Tablet HT 121, Linear A symbol L2' is a modified and simplified version of Hieroglyph D36 (although when used on those tablets it had the male = sign added). Here, again, this symbol therefore represents the first hieroglyph in the word:

iw'w quadrupeds, animals [noun - ani.] D36 - D36 - F28 - Z3

That there is no male = sign indicates that these are female quadrupeds that are being referred to. Consequently, these two joined symbols mean "grass (cattle fodder) [for the female] quadrupeds". They are followed by a count the value of which has been lost due to the tablet being damaged.

260   The Decipherment of Linear A

Category Two: Row Two, Symbols One and Two:

Hieroglyph D3 / rotated / reversed / Linear A symbol L89
As we have seen previously, this symbol represents the last hieroglyph in the word:

šnw grass (cattle fodder) [noun - flora] V7 - N35 - W24 - Z7 - D3

joined to Hieroglyph S34 / modifed (loop removed) / Linear A symbol L52
Here, this symbol represents the first hieroglyph in the word:

ʿnḫ goat, small cattle [noun - ani.] S34 - E31

ʿnḫ goat, small cattle [noun - ani.] S34 - G43 - E31 - Z2

ʿnḫ goat, small cattle [noun - ani.] S34 - N35 - J1 - Z7 - F28 - Z3

On Tablet HT 14, the category "grass (cattle fodder) [for the] quadrupeds" is recorded; this was the previous category of fodder recorded on this tablet (although the form on Tablet HT 14 was not one that was applied to specific genders of animals, as appears to be the case here). The other category of fodder recorded on Tablet HT 14 was "grass (cattle fodder) [for the] small cattle"; this is the category recorded here now, although rather than using the Middle Egyptian word ʿwt as was used on Tablet HT 14, this tablet uses the Middle Egyptian word ʿnḫ.

The word ʿwt has broadly similar meanings to ʿnḫ: the former is attested to mean "sheep" and "goats" in the specific, and "small cattle" in the general; the latter, as noted above, is attested to mean "goats" in the specific and "small cattle" in the general. As with the translation on Tablet HT 14, where the general meaning was used, the general meaning "small cattle" should also be used here (especially in the light of the meaning of the next symbol).

These two joined symbols therefore mean "grass (cattle fodder) [for the] small cattle". They are followed by a count of 18.

Category Three: Row Two, Symbols Three and Four:

Hieroglyph D3 ⟋ / rotated ⟋ / reversed ⟋ / Linear A symbol L89 ⟋
As we have seen previously, this symbol represents the last hieroglyph in the word:

⟋ šnw grass (cattle fodder) [noun - flora] V7 - N35 - W24 - Z7 - D3

joined to Hieroglyph S29 ⟋ + Hieroglyph Z4 ⟋ (rotated) / modified / Linear A symbol L44 ⟋

Here, Linear A symbol L44 (which also appears in this form on Tablet HT 21A, which is considered later in this chapter), is Hieroglyph S29 written in a slightly modified form, its two legs being joined at a point (as if written as an inverted V rather than an inverted U), presumably because this was easier to incise. The male = symbol was then added.

Making matters difficult for us is the fact that the two arms of Hieroglyph S29 have been drawn to a similar length rather than one being notably longer than the other. Consequently, when with the male = sign is added to create Linear A symbol L44 this looks like Hieroglyph N11 horizontally compressed with the male = sign added which has also been seen to be Linear A symbol L44, as we shall see later in this chapter.

Here, however, it represents the first hieroglyph in the word:

⟋ siwt sheep [noun - ani.] S29 - M17 - Z7 - X1 - F27 - Z3A

joined to the male = symbol, which represents the last hieroglyph in the word:

⟋ ḥꜣwty warrior, male, man [noun] D34 - G45 - X1 - Z4

We saw on Tablet HT 123A that the Middle Egyptian word wp, which means "horned cattle", was used to refer to sheep (rams); here, however, the scribe has decided to be explicit.

These two joined Linear A symbols (the second representing two hieroglyphs) therefore mean "grass (cattle fodder) [for the] male sheep". They are followed by a count the exact value of which has been lost due to the tablet being damaged. It was, however, at least 31.

262   The Decipherment of Linear A

Subheading: Row Three, Symbols One to Four:

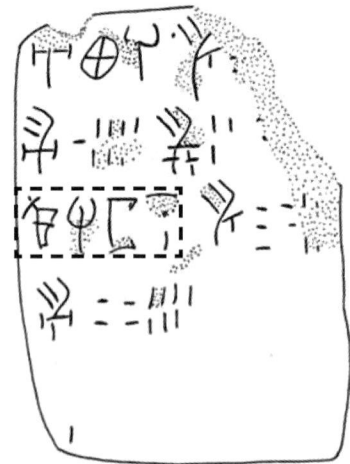

Hieroglyph G1 / simplified / Linear A symbol L103
As we have seen previously, this symbol represents the word:

gbi deficiency, deprivation, damage, uneven [noun] W11 - G1
- D58 - G37 - Z9

Hieroglyphs D28 - Z1 / simplified / modified / Linear A symbol L54
As we have seen previously, Linear A symbol L54 is a stylised version of Linear A symbol L55. Both represent Hieroglyphs D28 - Z1.

We have already seen Linear A symbol L55 used on this tablet; in the same manner as on Tablet HT 86A, where there are two different Linear A symbols that represent Hieroglyph S34 because two different words beginning with (and so abbreviated to) that hieroglyph are represented, so too here two different words are represented that we know can be (and are) abbreviated to Hieroglyphs D28 - Z1.

As we have seen previously, this symbol represents Hieroglyphs D28 - Z1. Here it represents the word:

k3w food, bounty [noun - food] D28 - Z1

The first two symbols therefore mean "deficiency [of] food".

As we have noted previously, the second subheading on the similarly formatted Tablet HT 14 also includes a symbol representing the Middle Egyptian word ḥ3w ḥrt ', meaning "deficiency". This symbol was written second in that subheading, after a symbol representing the Middle Egyptian word 'nḥ, meaning "sustenance". Here a symbol representing the Middle Egyptian word gbi, meaning "deficiency", appears first in the subheading, and it is followed by a symbol representing the Middle Egyptian word k3w, meaning "food" (which is clearly synonymous with 'nḥ, meaning "sustenance"). As we have discussed, and as we know from our own language when it is used in an administrative context, word order can change significantly, and in numerous ways, away from the more grammatically correct usage seen used in a literary context. The Linear A tablets represent administrative not literary use of the Middle Egyptian language and, thus, we should perhaps expect similar changes to the use of the Middle Egyptian language and where those changes occur that it reflects usage by different scribes. Moreover, in addition to it being reflected in the changed word order, as we have seen previously and as it does here, vocabulary also changes from one scribe to the next.

Hieroglyph O1 ⌷/ rotated ⌷/ Linear A symbol L74 ⌷

As we have previously seen, this symbol represents the last hieroglyph in the word(s):

mḫr storehouse, barn [noun - arch.] G17 - D36 - T28 - D21 - M17 - O1

mḫr storehouse, barn [noun - arch.] G17 - D36 - T28 - D21 - M17 - X1 - O1

mḫr storehouse, barn [noun - arch.] G17 - D36 - T28 - D21 - O1

šmyt / šmy storehouse, barn, ambulatory [noun - arch.] N37 - G17 - M17 - M17 - X1 - O1

Hieroglyphs N5 - Z1 ⊙/ simplified / modified / Linear A symbol L26 ｜

As we have seen previously, this symbol represents Hieroglyphs N5 - Z1. As with the similarly formatted Tablet HT 14, where it also appears in the equivalent setting, here it also represents the last hieroglyphs in the word:

m ẞ wnwt now, immediately, at once G17 - X1 - G1 - E34 - N35 - W24 - X1 - N2 - N5 - Z1

m ẞ wnwt now, immediately, at once G17 - X1 - G1 - E34 - N35 - W24 - X1 - N14 - N5 - Z1

m ẞ wnwt now, immediately, at once G17 - X1 - G1 - Z4 - E34 - N35 - W24 - X1 - N14 - N5 - Z1

These four symbols therefore mean "deficiency [of] food [in the] storehouse / barn now". The amounts recorded after this reflect, therefore, a "current deficit" (in modern accounting parlance), as did the amounts recorded after the second subheading on Tabet HT 14.

264   The Decipherment of Linear A

Category Four: Row Three, Symbols Five and Six:

Hieroglyph D3 / rotated / reversed / Linear A symbol L89
As we have seen previously, this symbol represents the last hieroglyph in the word:

šnw grass (cattle fodder) [noun - flora] V7 - N35 - W24 - Z7 - D3

joined to Hieroglyph D36 / Linear A symbol L76 / rotated / reversed / simplified / modified / Linear A symbol L'2 (without the male = symbol)
As we have seen previously, this symbol represents the first hieroglyph in the word:

iw'w quadrupeds, animals [noun - ani.] D36 - D36 - F28 - Z3

As we have seen, these two joined symbols therefore mean "grass (cattle fodder) [for the female] quadrupeds". They are followed by a count the exact value of which has been lost due to the tablet being damaged. It was, however, at least 54.

The Translations 265

Category Five: Symbols One and Two:

Hieroglyph D3 / rotated / reversed / Linear A symbol L89

As we have seen previously, this symbol represents the last hieroglyph in the word:

šnw grass (cattle fodder) [noun - flora] V7 - N35 - W24 - Z7 - D3

joined to Hieroglyph S34 / modifed (loop removed) / Linear A symbol L52

As we have seen previously, this symbol represents the first hieroglyph in the word:

'nḫ goat, small cattle [noun - ani.] S34 - E31
'nḫ goat, small cattle [noun - ani.] S34 - G43 - E31 - Z2
'nḫ goat, small cattle [noun - ani.] S34 - N35 - J1 - Z7 - F28 - Z3

These two joined symbols therefore mean "grass (cattle fodder) [for the] small cattle". This is followed by a count of 47.

We are, therefore, now in a position to fully translate this tablet:

Row One	Heading:	Sustenance [from the] city [of] Knossos
	Category One:	Grass (cattle fodder) [for the female] quadrupeds – [?]
Row Two	Category Two:	Grass (cattle fodder) [for the] small cattle – 17
	Category Three:	Grass (cattle fodder) [for the] male sheep – 31[?]
Row Three	Subheading:	Deficiency [of] food [in the] storehouse / barn now
	Category Four:	Grass (cattle fodder) [for the female] quadrupeds – 54[?]
Row Four	Category Five:	Grass (cattle fodder) [for the] small cattle – 47

266   The Decipherment of Linear A

Tablet HT 86A
As on the previous tablet, Tablet HT 86A records goods (here, animals only) received and to be received. Even more explicitly than Tablet HT 13, it records them by their future intended application or recipient.

Heading: Row One, Symbols One to Three:

Hieroglyph S34 ⚱/ modifed (loop removed) / Linear A symbol L52 ⵟ
As we have seen previously, this symbol represents the first hieroglyph in the word:

⚱‖⏃ 'nḫ sustenance [noun - food] S34   Z1   X4 - Z2

⚱∣◯ 'nḫ sustenance [noun - food] S34 - Z1 - Z8

Hieroglyph O49 ⊗/ simplified / Linear A symbol L29 ⊕
As we have seen previously, this symbol represents the word:

⊗ niwt city, town [noun] O49

Hieroglyphs D28 - Z1 ⎵ / simplified / modified / Linear A symbol L55 Y
As we have seen previously, this symbol represents the first hieroglyphs in the place name:

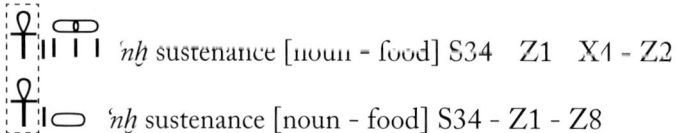 k3-jn-jw-s3 Knossos [noun - loc.] D28 - Z1 - N35 - M17 - M17
                                                              - G43 - M8 - G1

As on Tablet HT 2, these three symbols mean "sustenance [from the] city [of] Knossos".

Category One: Row One, Symbols Four and Five, and Row Two, Symbols One to Four:

Hieroglyph F14 / rotated / simplified / Linear A symbol L98
As we have seen previously, this symbol represents the first hieroglyph in the word:

wpt rnpt New Year's Day (and its festivals) [noun] F14 - W3
wpt rnpt New Year's Day (and its festivals) [noun] F15 - W3 - N5

Hieroglyph T25 / rotated / simplified / Linear A symbol L60
As we have seen previously, this symbol represents the first hieroglyph (or, in one instance, last hieroglyph) in the word:

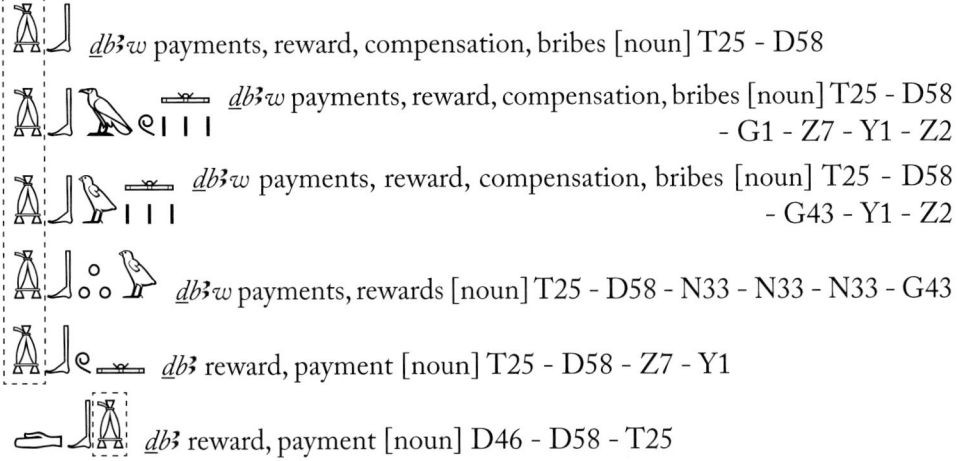

The first two symbols therefore mean "[for the] New Year's Day payments".

Hieroglyph O4 ⌂ / rotated ⊏ / Linear A symbol L59 ⊏ or ⊏

Linear A symbol L59 clearly represents Hieroglyph O4 rotated by 90 degrees to save space horizontally.

The meaning of this symbol here has been inferred from the final three categories of payee on Tablet HT 89 which lists the types of payments made by the temple. The three categories of payee listed there are: the Priests of Hathor (i.e. temple staff), peasants (presumably in return for working on the temple's land, so remuneration of sorts), and "payments", using the word _dbꜣ_ / _dbꜣw_ as used in this category.

Two out of three of those categories are used on this tablet. The Priests of Hathor are recorded on the tablet but under the separate categories of the phyle (of priests) and the chief of the phyles. The payment would not be to them therefore (in addition to their wages not being termed as payments in any event, as we have already seen). Peasants are not recorded on the tablet (and amounts allocated to them are not termed payments, as we will see). So who would these payments be to?

With the priests' future remuneration (in its different guises) having been recorded under different categories on this tablet, and future payments to peasants apparently being outside the scope of this tablet's subject matter, we can infer from the nature of the temple's operations and what would likely be its principal outgoings (which were really like any service industry business), that the "payments" would most likely be for goods and services received from third parties. This symbol therefore most likely represents a category of supplier.

Knowing that this category records payments to be made to a type of supplier, and that this type of supplier is represented in shorthand by a symbol representing Hieroglyph O4, we can determine that the symbol most likely represents the word _ḥꜣy_ / _ḥꜣw_, abbreviated to a symbol representing its first hieroglyph, meaning, for arguments sake, "[to the] corvee / labourers":

ḥꜣw corvee [noun] O4 - G1 - A9

ḥꜣw corvee, compulsory labour, faction (operating within the temple) [noun] O4 - G1 - G43 - A24

ḥꜣw bonded labourers [plural noun - title] O4 - G1 - G43 - A24 - A1 - Z2

ḥꜣw bonded labourers [plural noun - title] O4 - G1 - M17 - M17 - G43 - D40 - Z2

ḥꜣy / _ḥꜣw_ corvee, compulsory labour, faction (operating within temple) [noun] O4 - G1 - M17 - M17 - X1 - Y1 - A24 - A1 - Z2

ḥꜣy (labour) service [noun] O4 - G1 - M17 - M17 - Z5 - Z5 - A24 - A1 - Z2

Hieroglyph F27 / partially rotated / simplified / modified / Linear A symbol L42
As we have seen previously, this symbol represents the last hieroglyph in the word:

ꜥr goat [noun - ani.] D36 - D21 - E31 - F27

Hieroglyph S34 / modifed (loop removed) / Linear A symbol L52 (without sidebars)
Here, this symbol appears in subscript, as a descriptor to the word it follows. It represents the first hieroglyph in the word:

'nḫt nanny goat, small domestic animal [noun - ani.] S34 - N35 - J1 - F27

'nḫt nanny goat, small domestic animal [noun - ani.] S34 - N35 - J1 - X1 - E31

'nḫt nanny goat, small domestic animal [noun - ani.] S34 - N35 - J1 - X1 - E31 - Z2

'nḫt nanny goat, small domestic animal [noun - ani.] S34 - X1 - F27

While it may appear superfluous to include an additional note that these were female animals (as, after all, the male = sign is not added), we know from Tablet HT 120, which is considered later in this chapter, that some scribes felt that this clarification was necessary. On that tablet, the male animals were denoted by the male = sign and the other animals that do not have the male = sign had this symbol next to them as a subscript descriptor, as here. Not being male, by implication the symbol indicates these other animals were female. As apparently superfluous as it was, therefore, this is the meaning of this symbol here (i.e. these were nanny goats).

Hieroglyph V19 / rotated / Linear A symbol L47
Linear A symbol L47 is a straightforward representation of Hieroglyph V19 that has been rotated by 90 degrees. Here it represents the word:

mḏt byre, cow shed, pen, enclosure [noun – arch.] V19

The reason that the symbol has been rotated (and thereby taking up *more* room horizontally than it would otherwise have, against the trend that we have observed thus far) is probably because otherwise it would have looked too similar to Linear A symbol L44.

These six symbols therefore mean "[for the] New Year's Day payments [to the] corvee / labourers, goats (nanny goats) [from the] enclosure". Presumably, having been delivered from Knossos, these animals were held nearby in an enclosure before being used to make a payment. They are followed by a count of 20.

270 The Decipherment of Linear A

Category Two: Row Two, Symbols Five and Six:

Hieroglyph V28 / rotated / simplified / Linear A symbol L31
As we have seen, Linear A symbol L31 represents Hieroglyph V28. Here we can infer from the context of the symbol and how animals would have been used by the temple that this symbol represents the first hieroglyph in the word:

ḥbyt festival offerings, festival court [noun] V28 - D58 - M17 - M17 - X1 - W4

ḥbyt festival offerings, festival court [noun] V28 - D58 - M17 - M17 - X1 - Y24 - Z3A

ḥbyt festival offerings [noun] V28 - D58 - W4 - M17 - M17 - X1 - Z2

ḥbyt festival offerings [noun] V28 - D58 - X1 - W3

Hieroglyphs D28 - Z1 / simplified / modified / Linear A symbol L55
As we have seen previously, this symbol represents the word:

k3w food, bounty [noun - food] D28 - Z1

These two symbols therefore mean "[for] festival offerings [of] food". Presumably, as a different animal is not stated, these are also female goats. They are followed by a count of 20.

The Translations 271

<u>Category Three: Row Three, Symbols One to Three:</u>

Hieroglyphs Z5 - Z2 ⌇⌇⌇/ rotated \ / modified / Linear A symbol L51 ⁝⁝⁝

As we have seen previously, this symbol represents the last hieroglyphs in the word:

ꜥwt small cattle, herds, flocks, goats [noun - ani.] T14 - Z7 - X1 - Z5 - Z2

Hieroglyph V17 / simplified / Linear A symbol L102

As we have seen previously, this symbol represents Hieroglyph V17. Given the fact that we have the phyle (of priests) recorded later on this tablet as going to receive (older) quadrupeds (for food, no doubt), it seems appropriate that if (younger, tastier) small cattle were to be issued for food, they would be issued to the phyle's superiors.

Here, therefore, this symbol represents the last hieroglyph in the word:

ḥry sꜣ Chief of the Phyles [noun - title] D2 - D21 - V17

Hieroglyphs D28 - Z1 / simplified / modified / Linear A symbol L55

As we have previously seen, this symbol represents the word:

kꜣw food, bounty [noun - food] D28 - Z1

These three symbols therefore mean "small cattle [for the] Chief of the Phyles [for] food". They are followed by a count of 20.

272 The Decipherment of Linear A

<u>Category Four: Row Three, Symbols Four to Six:</u>

<u>Hieroglyph AA27 (or J27)</u> / simplified / Linear A symbol L62
Linear A symbol L62 is a straightforward simplified representation of Hieroglyph AA27 (or J27). Here it represents the first hieroglyph in the word:

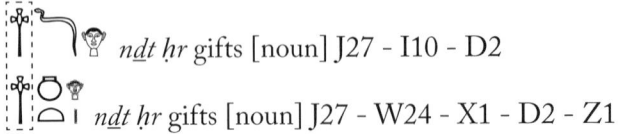

n<u>d</u>t ḥr gifts [noun] J27 - I10 - D2

n<u>d</u>t ḥr gifts [noun] J27 - W24 - X1 - D2 - Z1

Given that Tablet HT 118 records gifts of cows to the Goddess Hathor, I presume these gifts are future sacrifices.

<u>Hieroglyphs Z5 - Z5</u> / Linear A symbol L58
As we have previously seen, this symbol represents Hieroglyphs Z5 - Z5. While we see this symbol used in dates, given the context in which the symbol appears on this tablet (where all categories deal with animals, and this is the last category listed which, as we saw Tablet HT 14, Tablet HT 114A, and Tablet HT 121, would suggest it is a male animal), here this symbol represents the last hieroglyphs in the word:

k3 bull [noun – ani.] D28 - Z5 - Z5

<u>Hieroglyph O20</u> / simplified / Linear A symbol L75
Linear A symbol L75 is a straightforward simplified representation of Hieroglyph O20. Here it represents the last hieroglyph in the word:

ḥwt n<u>t</u>r temple [noun - arch.] R8 - O20

These three symbols therefore mean "gifts [of] bulls [for the] temple". They are followed by a count of 10.

The Translations 273

<u>Subheading One: Row Four, Symbols One and Two:</u>

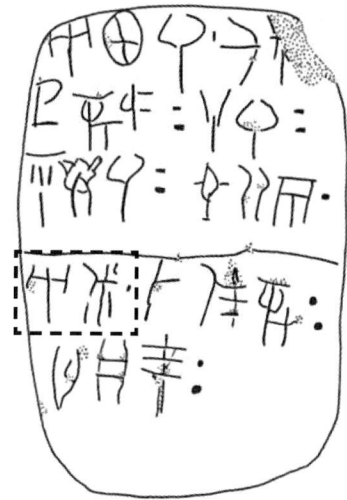

Hieroglyph S34 ⚲ / modifed (loop removed) / Linear A symbol L52 ⊤

As we have seen previously, this symbol represents the first hieroglyph in the word:

ꜥnḫ sustenance [noun - food] S34 - Z1 - X4 - Z2

ꜥnḫ sustenance [noun - food] S34 - Z1 - Z8

Hieroglyph A24 / simplified / modified / Linear A symbol L93

As we have seen previously, this symbol represents the last hieroglyph in the word:

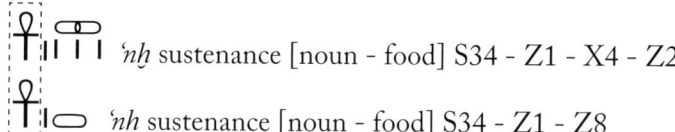 sm³ take part in, receive [verb] F36 - G1 - G17 - Z7 - Z4 - Y1
 - A24

These two symbols therefore mean "sustenance to [be] receive[d]". As was discussed in Chapter Three, this appears to be shorthand for "sustenance [deficit now,] to [be] receive[d]". From the category descriptions that follow, and, in particular, coming after an atypical line dividing the top half of the tablet (the goods received from Knossos) from the bottom half (goods to be received, that were a shortfall, but which were not, now, going to be delivered from Knossos in time) it appears that the deficiency was to be made good from the temple's own herds.

274   The Decipherment of Linear A

Category Five: Row Four, Symbols Three and Four:

Hieroglyph T14 ⎤ replaced by AA26 (or J26) ⎦/ reversed ⎣ / Linear A symbol L30 ⊦

As we have seen previously, the last hieroglyphs on the last below listed iteration of the Middle Egyptian word '*wt*, Hieroglyphs Z5 - Z2 (highlighted in the dashed circle, below, and represented by Linear A symbol L51), have already been used on this tablet to represent that word with the meaning of "small cattle".

Here, however, while the same Middle Egyptian word is used by the scribe, it is abbreviated instead to Linear A symbol L30 representing its first hieroglyph, Hieroglyph T14 (as replaced by Hieroglyph AA26 (or J26)):

'*wt* small cattle, goats, herds [noun - ani.] T14

'*wt* small cattle, herds, flocks, goats [noun - ani.] T14 - G43 - E28 - Z2

'*wt* small cattle, herds, flocks, goats [noun - ani.] T14 - G43 - X1 - E1 - Z2

'*wt* small cattle, herds, flocks, goats [noun - ani.] T14 - G43 - X1 - E8 - Z2

'*wt* small cattle, herds, flocks, goats [noun - ani.] T14 - Z7 - X1 - E28 - F27 - Z3A

'*wt* small cattle, herds, flocks, goats [noun - ani.] T14 - Z7 - X1 - E28 - Z2

'*wt* small cattle, herds, flocks, goats [noun - ani.] T14 - Z7 - X1 - Z5 - Z2

The Translations   275

The reason for this is that, rather than "small cattle", a different attested meaning of the same word was being referred to. Moreover, as a specific animal type is conveyed by the symbol after next, we can infer a more collective meaning of this symbol (but not "small cattle"). Here, therefore, the symbol has the meaning "herds".

Hieroglyph A24 / simplified / modified / Linear A symbol L93 + male = symbol / modified / Linear A symbol L84/48

This tablet is particularly important because it helps demonstrate clearly how this Linear A symbol has been derived from the hieroglyphs that it represents (and why).

As can be clearly seen, the symbol was incised in a similar manner to the second symbol o ause both are based on the same (initial) hieroglyph. This symbol, however, has been modified further. The man character has only one leg drawn rather than two because it has the male = sign attached to it and it would not have been possible for two legs to have been incised in clay then crossed by the male = sign without the symbol's legs losing integrity as the clay moved more with each successive incision. Thereafter, when this symbol is used elsewhere in the corpus, scribal handwriting preference played a part in how the symbol was portrayed and the single leg became shorter and shorter, no longer reaching the ground, to the point where it became a stub. This is the Linear A symbol L84/48 we more typically see (and, without its atypical representation here, its relationship to Hieroglyph A24 would probably have been impossible to ascertain).

In contrast to the male = symbol indicating that an animal was male, as we have seen it used thus far, here it was added to indicate that the meaning of the symbol to which it was added was a type of man or men (we will see the symbol used in this way again when Linear A symbol L44 represents "*3bd* Priests in their month of duty", on Tablet HT 91, for example). Here, that this symbol related to a man had to be explicitly stated so that the reader did not think that the symbol, again, meant "to be received" as it did in the subheading. The symbol therefore represents the last hieroglyph (or, in one instance, first hieroglyph) in the word:

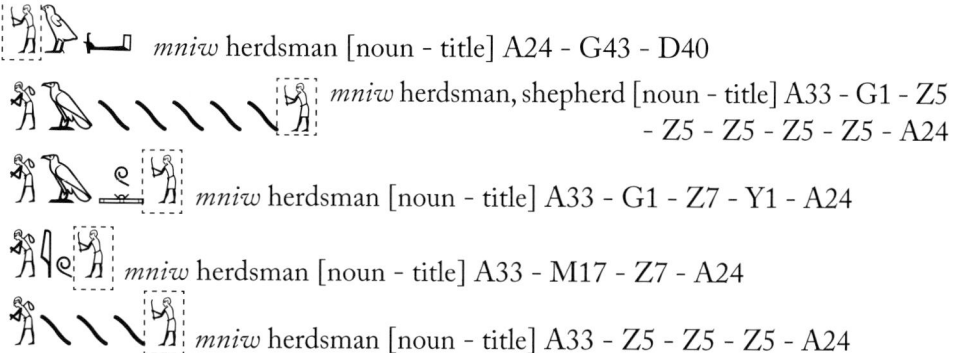

mniw herdsman [noun - title] A24 - G43 - D40

mniw herdsman, shepherd [noun - title] A33 - G1 - Z5 - Z5 - Z5 - Z5 - Z5 - A24

mniw herdsman [noun - title] A33 - G1 - Z7 - Y1 - A24

mniw herdsman [noun - title] A33 - M17 - Z7 - A24

mniw herdsman [noun - title] A33 - Z5 - Z5 - Z5 - A24

This is not, however, the only way this word is represented in the corpus, and Linear A symbol L99, representing Hieroglyph A59, is also used to represent the word *mniw*

276 The Decipherment of Linear A

when it is spelled differently (as we saw on Tablet HT 102 or as we will see more clearly on Tablet HT 7A, for example). In respect of the use of this word, if not spelling, there was consistency across the corpus. Therefore, while the Middle Egyptian word *nr*, which also meant "herdsman", and which could also have been abbreviated to Linear A symbol L84/48 representing its last hieroglyph:

nr herdsman [noun - title] N35 - D21 - A24

given the presumed consistency of terminology across the corpus, this is discounted as a possible meaning for the symbol on this tablet (although given that it means the same thing, in English, as *mniw*, perhaps the point is moot).

As a final note, given that Linear A symbol L84/48 was created, it seems, avoid confusion with Linear A symbol L93, it seems reasonable to question why, with the shorthand method that we are using, did the scribe not simply use a symbol based on the first hieroglyph in the word *mniw*, Hieroglyph A33 (which, as we will see, is represented by Linear A symbol L125), to represent that word? The answer, it seems, is that this appears to be a convention adopted by the institution (a symbol representing Hieroglyph A33 being used to represent another word that likely originally frequently occurred, but does not in the surviving corpus). This apparent convention helps us in our subsequent analysis of Tablet HT 89 later in this chapter.

Hieroglyph F27 / partially rotated / simplified / modified / Linear A symbol L42
As we have seen previously, this symbol represents the last hieroglyph in the word:

ꜥr goat [noun - ani.] D36 - D21 - E31 - F27

Subscript Hieroglyph S34 / modifed (loop removed) / Linear A symbol L52 (without sidebars)
As previously noted, and as we will see, this symbol is only used with non-male (i.e. female) animals on Tablet HT 120. From this, we can infer that it explicitly states that the animals in question were female and, thus, represents the first hieroglyph in the word:

ʿnḫt nanny goat, small domestic animal [noun - ani.] S34 - N35 - J1 - F27

ʿnḫt nanny goat, small domestic animal [noun - ani.] S34 - N35 - J1 - X1 - E31

ʿnḫt nanny goat, small domestic animal [noun - ani.] S34 - N35 - J1 - X1 - E31 - Z2

ʿnḫt nanny goat, small domestic animal [noun - ani.] S34 - X1 - F27

These symbols therefore mean "[from the] herd [for the] herdsmen, goats (nanny goats)". They are followed by a count of 20.

The Translations 277

As we have already noted, the Linear B records show shepherds tending palatial flocks.[78] Here, herdsmen appear to be tending the temple's herd (in the same manner as the herd of the city recorded on Tablet HT 102 was also tended by herdsmen who received remuneration for undertaking that task). The female goats here, already in the temple herd (and not coming from Knossos, as they are recorded beneath the line break in the tablet), were to be paid to the herdsmen.

<u>Category Six: Row Five, Symbols One to Three:</u>

<u>Hieroglyph D36</u> ⌒ / modified / simplified / Linear A symbol L76 ৬
As we have previously seen, this symbol represents the first hieroglyph in the word:

⌒ 𓃀 *iw'w* quadrupeds, animals [noun - ani.] D36 - D36 - F28 - Z3

<u>Hieroglyph N23</u> ⚏ / rotated ⌶ / Linear A symbol L25/7 ⌶
Linear A symbol L25/7 is a straightforward representation of Hieroglyph N23 rotated by 90 degrees to save space horizontally. As to its meaning, we are guided by the context in which it appears.

It follows Category Six which relates how animals from the temple's herd (presumably, therefore, far away grazing on the unenclosed hills), were yet to be received. If the animals far away have been considered in the tablet, then the animals closer by (on the enclosed land) remained to be considered. With that logic in mind, it is most likely that Hieroglyph N23, represented by Linear A symbol L25/7, represents a word meaning "field" and, as with the previous category of animals, these animals belonged to the temple, were in fields presumably belonging to the temple, but they had not yet been received by the temple when the tablet was written.

---

78. Paul Halstead, "Missing Sheep: On the Meaning and Wider Significance of O in Knossos Sheep Records", *The Annual of the British School at Athens*, 94(1999), p166 and Dimitri Nakassis, "The Extractive Systems of the Mycenaean World", in Jonathan Valk and Irene Soto Marín (Eds.), *Ancient Taxation: The Mechanics of Extraction in Comparative Perspective* (New York: New York University Press, 2021), p102

On this basis, this symbol most likely represents the last hieroglyph in the word:

3ḥt field, arable land, earth, mound area (geometry) [noun] G1 - V28 - X1 - N23

3ḥt field, arable land, earth, mound area (geometry) [noun] V28 - G1 - X1 - N23

Hieroglyph V16 / rotated / simplified / Linear A symbol L92
As we have seen previously, this symbol represents the first hieroglyph in the word:

s3 phyle (of priests), company, regiment (of troops), troop (of animals) [noun] V16 - A1 - Z2

These three symbols therefore mean "quadrupeds [from the] fields [for the] phyle (of priests)". Coming after the line break in the tablet we, again, know that this element of the deficit was not going to be delivered from the city of Knossos. They are followed by a count of 20.

We are now in a position to translate the tablet in full:

Row One	Heading: Category One:	Sustenance [from the] city [of] Knossos [For the] New Year's Day payments
Row Two		[to the] corvee / labourers, goats (nanny goats) [from the] enclosure – 20
	Category Two:	[For] festival offerings [of] food – 20
Row Three	Category Three: Category Four:	Small cattle [for the] Chief of the Phyles [for] food – 20 Gifts [of] bulls [for the] temple – 10
Row Four	Subheading One:	Sustenance [deficit now,] to [be] receive[d]
	Category Five:	[From the] herd, [for the] herdsmen, goats (nanny goats) – 20
Row Five	Category Six:	Quadrupeds [from the] fields [for the] phyle (of priests) – 20

Analysis

1. Evidence of contemporary Egyptian administrative practice at Hagia Triada
In addition to informing us about the workings of the temple and how its cattle and livestock provisions were sourced, this side of the tablet (Side A), and its reverse (Side B), tells us about the administrative practices that the temple adopted, and how they reflect contemporary administrative practice in Egypt (as we would expect them to, given that we are dealing with an Egyptian temple).

The hieratic papyrus Louvre E. 3226, which probably came from Thebes, dates from between Year 28 and Year 34 of Thutmose III's reign (i.e. c.1452 BC–c.1446 BC),[79] within the period that we have determined that Crete was part of Egypt's empire. The papyrus preserves two running accounts of a branch of the royal double granary. The first text on that papyrus ("Text A") is an account of dated deliveries of grain (from named ships, places,

---

79. https://collections.louvre.fr/ark:/53355/cl010003433 (accessed 1 January 2022)

and other granaries) with periodic totals. The second text on the papyrus ("Text B") is an account of dated deliveries with periodic totals. The rectos of Texts A and B were written by the scribe, Hapu, of the overseer of the double granary, Minnakht. The versos of Texts A and B were written by the scribe, My, of the overseer of the double granary, Tjenuna. The rectos and versos are virtually identical parallel texts and historian Brian Muhs believes that this is because one was being used as a check on the other.[80] This is seen on Tablet HT 86A and HT 86B, which are pictured below, where front (A) and rear (B) appear to have been duplicate counts of the first four categories of items (above the line) that had been delivered from Knossos, which were undertaken by separate individuals (although the second, checking, count appears not to have been completed beyond Category Three).

Tablet HT 86A photograph

Tablet HT 86B photograph

Tablet HT 86A sketch diagram

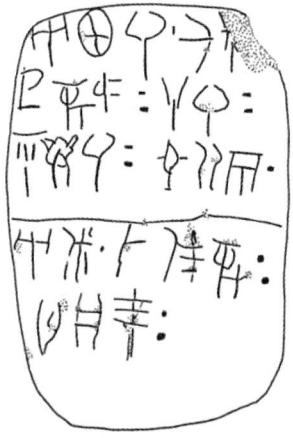

Tablet HT 86B sketch diagram

---

80. Brian P. Muhs, *The Ancient Egyptian Economy: 3000–30 BCE* (Cambridge: Cambridge University Press, 2016), p116

280　The Decipherment of Linear A

We can see that each side of the tablet was written by a different scribe from the fourth symbol on the second line: on Tablet HT 86A Linear A symbol L47 ⴲ uses dashes for its right-hand extremities whereas on Tablet HT 86B the scribe (perhaps to save space horizontally) it uses dots.

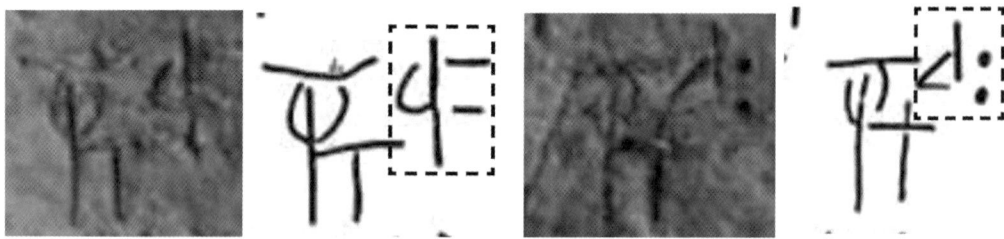

For us, the change in style is fortunate because it shows that different scribes wrote on each side of the tablet. The same administrative process of checking undertaken at Thebes in Egypt was also being undertaken by the scribes at Hagia Triada in Crete. They did so because Crete, at this time, was part of the Egyptian empire, and the administrative practices of Egyptian temples in Egypt were the same as the administrative practices of the Egyptian temples on Crete.

The Translations 281

Tablet HT 95A

Tablet HT 95 is written on the front (A) and back (B). The front shows cattle and livestock that have already been received. The back, as we will see subsequently, shows cattle and livestock that are yet to be received. As with Tablet HT 13 and Tablet HT 86A, the cattle and livestock are described by reference to their future intended application or recipient.

Heading: Row One, Symbols One to Four:

Hieroglyph T14 ⎮ replaced by AA26 (or J26) ⎮ / reversed ⎮ / Linear A symbol L30 ⎮

As we have seeen previously, this symbol represents the (replaced) first hieroglyph in the word:

'wt small cattle, goats, herds [noun - ani.] T14

'wt small cattle, herds, flocks, goats [noun - ani.] T14 - G43 - E28 - Z2

'wt small cattle, herds, flocks, goats [noun - ani.] T14 - G43 - X1 - E1 - Z2

'wt small cattle, herds, flocks, goats [noun - ani.] T14 - G43 - X1 - E8 - Z2

'wt small cattle, herds, flocks, goats [noun - ani.] T14 - Z7 - X1 - E28 - F27 - Z3A

'wt small cattle, herds, flocks, goats [noun - ani.] T14 - Z7 - X1 - E28 - Z2

'wt small cattle, herds, flocks, goats [noun - ani.] T14 - Z7 - X1 - Z5 - Z2

As we will see, this word is also represented in Category Five of this tablet, but in that instance it is abbreviated to a symbol, Linear A symbol L51, representing its final hieroglyphs, Hieroglyphs Z5 - Z2. That the same word appears twice on the same tablet but is abbreviated to different symbols representing different hieroglyphs indicates that the word conveyed different meanings each time it was used.

All but the last category recorded on this tablet were recorded on Tablet HT 86A, so we therefore know their meanings: they are animals, with their specific types being described (as well as their future intended application or recipient). This, therefore, is how the word ꜥwt was used when it was represented in Category Five, i.e. to convey a specific, not general, meaning. Conversely, in the tablet heading we can infer that the word was used in a more general manner because it relates to all of the animals described in all of the categories. We therefore know that here it means "herds".

Hieroglyph A24 / simplified / modified / Linear A symbol L93
As we have seen previously, this symbol represents the last hieroglyph in the word:

    sm3 take part in, receive [verb] F36 - G1 - G17 - Z7 - Z4 - Y1
                                                                                                                 - A24

Hieroglyphs D28 - Z1 / simplified / modified / Linear A symbol L55
As we have seen previously, this symbol represents the word:

    k3w food, bounty [noun - food] D28 - Z1

joined to Hieroglyphs W24 - Z4A / rotated / modified (two dashes inside circle as dots) / Linear A symbols L91
As set out in Appendix 6, this symbol, representing Hieroglyphs W24 - Z4A, represents the ordinal:

    snnw the second (one), the other, twin, equal, comrade [noun] W24 - Z4A

becomes Linear A symbol L55 + L91 / Linear A symbol L95
As set out in Appendix 6, this symbol therefore means "[for] food [in the] second [month]".

Hieroglyph O1 / rotated / Linear A symbol L74
As we have seen previously, this symbol represents the last hieroglyph in the word(s):

    mḫr storehouse, barn [noun - arch.] G17 - D36 - T28 - D21
                                                                                                                  - M17 - O1

    mḫr storehouse, barn [noun - arch.] G17 - D36 - T28 - D21
                                                                                                     - M17 - X1 - O1

    mḫr storehouse, barn [noun - arch.] G17 - D36 - T28 - D21
                                                                                                               - O1

    šmyt / šmy storehouse, barn, ambulatory [noun - arch.] N37 - G17
                                                                     - M17 - M17 - X1 - O1

The first five symbols therefore mean "[from the] herds, receive[d] [for] food [in the] second [month], [in the] storehouse / barn".

Category One: Row One, Symbol Six, Row Two, Symbols One and Two:

Hieroglyph F27 ⛨ / partially rotated / simplified / modified / Linear A symbol L42 ⍦
As we have seen previously, this symbol represents the last hieroglyph in the word:

⌇ 'r goat [noun - ani.] D36 - D21 - E31 - F27

Hieroglyph T14 ⎮ replaced by AA26 (or J26) ⎮ / reversed ⎮ / Linear A symbol L30 ⎮
As we have seen previously, this symbol represents the (replaced) first hieroglyph in the word:

⎮ 'wt small cattle, goats, herds [noun - ani.] T14

⎮ 'wt small cattle, herds, flocks, goats [noun - ani.] T14 - G43 - E28
- Z2

⎮ 'wt small cattle, herds, flocks, goats [noun - ani.] T14 - G43 - X1
- E1 - Z2

⎮ 'wt small cattle, herds, flocks, goats [noun - ani.] T14 - G43 - X1
- E8 - Z2

⎮ 'wt small cattle, herds, flocks, goats [noun - ani.] T14 - Z7 - X1 - E28
- F27 - Z3A

⎮ 'wt small cattle, herds, flocks, goats [noun - ani.] T14 - Z7 - X1 - E28
- Z2

⎮ 'wt small cattle, herds, flocks, goats [noun - ani.] T14 - Z7 - X1 - Z5 - Z2

284   The Decipherment of Linear A

Hieroglyph A24 / simplified / modified / Linear A symbol L93 + male = symbol / modified / Linear A symbol L84/48

As we have seen previously, this symbol represents the last hieroglyph, or in one instance first hieroglyph, in the word:

mniw herdsman [noun - title] A24 - G43 - D40

mniw herdsman, shepherd [noun - title] A33 - G1 - Z5 - Z5 - Z5 - Z5 - Z5 - A24

mniw herdsman [noun - title] A33 - G1 - Z7 - Y1 - A24

mniw herdsman [noun - title] A33 - M17 - Z7 - A24

mniw herdsman [noun - title] A33 - Z5 - Z5 - Z5 - A24

joined to the male = symbol, which represents the last hieroglyph in the word:

ḥꜣwty warrior, male, man [noun] D34 - G45 - X1 - Z4

These three symbols therefore mean "goats [from the] herds [for the] herdsmen". They are followed by a count of 10.

Category Two: Row Two, Symbols Three to Five:

Hieroglyph D36 / modified / simplified / Linear A symbol L76

As we have seen previously, this symbol represents the first hieroglyph in the word:

iwʿw quadrupeds, animals [noun - ani.] D36 - D36 - F28 - Z3

The Translations   285

Hieroglyph N23 ⊥/ rotated H / Linear A symbol L25/7 H
As we have seen previously, this symbol represents the last hieroglyph in the word:

𓄿𓐍𓏏𓇿 *ꜣḥt* field, arable land, earth, mound area (geometry) [noun] G1 - V28 - X1
— N23

𓐍𓄿𓏏𓇿 *ꜣḥt* field, arable land, earth, mound area (geometry) [noun] V28 - G1 - X1
— N23

Hieroglyph V16 / rotated / simplified / Linear A symbol L92
As we have seen previously, this symbol represents the first hieroglyph in the word:

sꜣ phyle (of priests), company, regiment (of troops), troop (of animals) [noun]
V16 - A1 - Z2

These three symbols therefore mean "quadrupeds [from the] fields [for the] phyle (of priests)". They are followed by a count of 10.

Category Three: Row Two, Symbols Three to Five:

Hieroglyph V28 / rotated / simplified / Linear A symbol L31 Y
As we have seen previously, this symbol represents the first hieroglyph in the word:

ḥbyt festival offerings, festival court [noun] V28 - D58 - M17 - M17
- X1 - W4

ḥbyt festival offerings, festival court [noun] V28 - D58 - M17 - M17
- X1 - Y24 - Z3A

ḥbyt festival offerings [noun] V28 - D58 - W4 - M17 - M17 - X1
- Z2

ḥbyt festival offerings [noun] V28 - D58 - X1 - W3

286   The Decipherment of Linear A

Hieroglyphs D28 - Z1 ⊔ / simplified / modified / Linear A symbol L55 Y
As we have seen previously, this symbol represents the word:

⊔ k3w food, bounty [noun - food] D28 - Z1

These two symbols therefore mean "[for] festival offerings [of] food". Presumably these were also "quadrupeds", as per the prior category in the list (on Tablet HT 86A they were nanny goats). They are followed by a count of 20.

Category Four: Row Three, Symbols Three to Five:

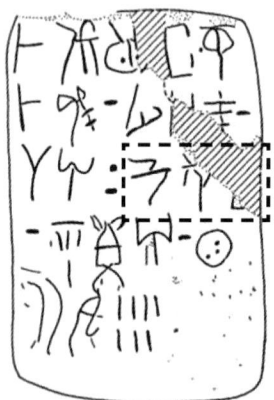

Hieroglyph F14 ⩎ / rotated ⟩ / simplified / Linear A symbol L98 ⤴
As we have seen previously, this symbol represents the first hieroglyph in the word:

⩎ wpt rnpt New Year's Day (and its festivals) [noun] F14 - W3
⩎ wpt rnpt New Year's Day (and its festivals) [noun] F15 - W3 - N5

Hieroglyph T25 ⩕ / rotated ⩔ / simplified / Linear A symbol L60 Y
As we have seen previously, this symbol represents the first hieroglyph (or, in one instance, the last hieroglyph) in the word:

⩕ db3w payments, reward, compensation, bribes [noun] T25 - D58
⩕ db3w payments, reward, compensation, bribes [noun] T25 - D58
                                                        - G1 - Z7 - Y1 - Z2
⩕ db3w payments, reward, compensation, bribes [noun] T25 - D58
                                                        - G43 - Y1 - Z2
⩕ db3w payments, rewards [noun] T25 - D58 - N33 - N33 - N33 - G43

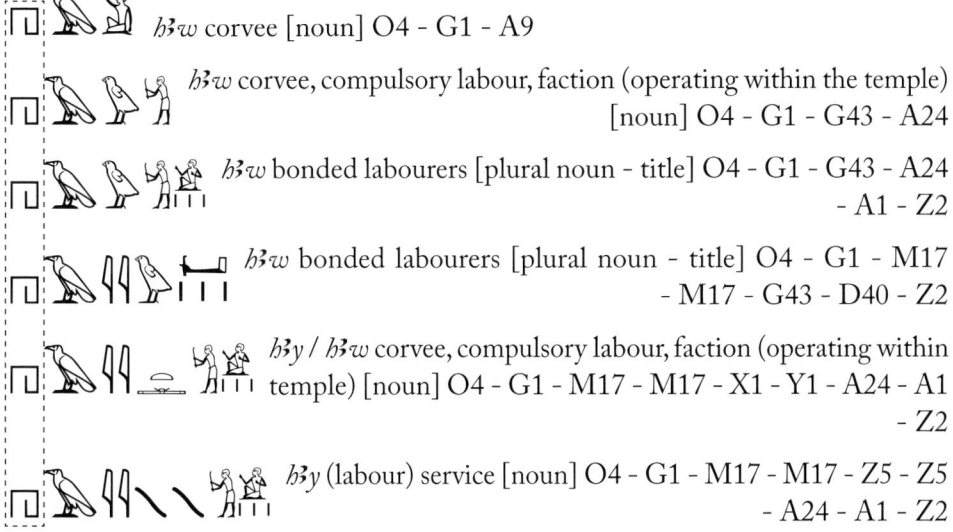

ḏbꜣ reward, payment [noun] T25 - D58 - Z7 - Y1

ḏbꜣ reward, payment [noun] D46 - D58 - T25

Hieroglyph O4 / rotated / Linear A symbol L59 or

This portion of the tablet is damaged, but both Brice and Godart & Olivier transcribe it as Linear A symbol L59 (aided, perhaps, by the fact that on the reverse side of this tablet, which records all the same categories as this side, the symbol is undamaged and clear to read). As we have seen previously, this symbol represents the first hieroglyph in the word:

hꜣw corvee [noun] O4 - G1 - A9

hꜣw corvee, compulsory labour, faction (operating within the temple) [noun] O4 - G1 - G43 - A24

hꜣw bonded labourers [plural noun - title] O4 - G1 - G43 - A24 - A1 - Z2

hꜣw bonded labourers [plural noun - title] O4 - G1 - M17 - M17 - G43 - D40 - Z2

hꜣy / *hꜣw* corvee, compulsory labour, faction (operating within temple) [noun] O4 - G1 - M17 - M17 - X1 - Y1 - A24 - A1 - Z2

hꜣy (labour) service [noun] O4 - G1 - M17 - M17 - Z5 - Z5 - A24 - A1 - Z2

These three symbols therefore mean "[for the] New Year's Day payment [to the] corvee / labourers". They are followed by a count of 10.

Category Five: Row Four, Symbols One to Three:

288   The Decipherment of Linear A

Hieroglyphs Z5 - Z2 ∣∣∣/ rotated \ / modified / Linear A symbol L51 ⫶

As we have seen previously, this symbol represents the last hieroglyphs in the word:

'wt small cattle, herds, flocks, goats [noun - ani.] T14 - Z7 - X1 - Z5 - Z2

We have, of course, seen this word used previously on the tablet (the first symbol of the tablet's heading, for example) where it was represented by Linear A symbol L30 (representing its (replaced) first hieroglyph). That the same word is represented on the tablet with two different symbols reflects the fact that each time it represents a different attested meaning of the word (as, for example, was the case on Tablet HT 86A). Here, as was also the case when this category of animal was recorded on Tablet HT 86A, this symbol means "small cattle".

Hieroglyph V17 ⚱/ simplified / Linear A symbol L102 ⚛

As we have seen previously, this symbol represents the last hieroglyph in the word:

ḥry s3 Chief of the Phyles [noun - title] D2 - D21 - V17

Hieroglyphs D28 - Z1 ⎵ / simplified / modified / Linear A symbol L55 Y

As we have seen previously, this symbol represents the word:

k3w food, bounty [noun - food] D28 - Z1

These three symbols therefore mean "small cattle [for the] Chief of the Phyles [for] food". They are followed by a count of 10.

Category Six: Row Four, Symbol Four, and Row Five, Symbols One and Two:

Hieroglyphs Z2 - W24 ⊙ / rotated / modified (three dashes as dots inside circle) / Linear A symbol L91 ⊙

As set out in Appendix 6, this symbol, representing Hieroglyphs Z2 - W24, represents the ordinal:

ḥmt nw third [ordinal number] Z2 - W24

Hieroglyphs Z5 - Z5 \\ / Linear A symbol L58

As we have seen previously, this symbol represents the last hieroglyphs in the word:

k3 bull [noun – ani.] D28 - Z5 - Z5

Hieroglyphs X1 - D17 / modified (hieroglyphs joined) / simplified / Linear A symbol L88 (reversed)

Both Brice and Godart & Olivier believe this is Linear A symbol L97, which represents Hieroglyph M17; this is incorrect. The symbol is, in fact, the Hieroglyphs X1 - D17 joined to create Linear A symbol L88 (reversed). The steps in this process are set out below:

A	B	C

- Column A shows:
  - Top: extract of photograph of Tablet HT 95A showing the Linear A symbol; and
  - Bottom: Hieroglyphs X1 - D17.
- Column B shows:
  - Top: extract of photograph of Tablet HT 95A showing the Linear A symbol highlighted; and
  - Bottom: Hieroglyphs X1 - D17 joined, with left had part of D17 simplified to a vertical stroke.
- Column C shows:
  - Top: highlighted Linear A symbol with picture of Tablet HT 95A removed; and

o Bottom: Linear A symbol, being the combined and simplified Hieroglyphs X1 - D17, (partially rotated to align with the Linear A symbol as written, for better comparison).

The symbol, as it was written, was, therefore, Linear A symbol L88 (reversed). This symbol therefore represents Hieroglyphs X1 - D17 which are the final hieroglyphs in the word:

imny (daily) service, offerings, portion, ration [noun] M17 - Y5 - N35 - X1 - D17

These three symbols therefore mean "[for the] third [month], bulls [for] daily services". They are followed by a count of 7.

We can now, therefore, translate this side of the tablet in full:

Row One	Heading:	[From the] herds, received [for] food [in the] second [month], [in the] storehouse
	Category One:	Goats
Row Two		[from the] herds [for the] herdsmen – 10
	Category Two:	Quadrupeds [from the] fields [for the] phyle (of priests) – 10
Row Three	Category Three:	[For] festival offerings [of] food – 10
	Category Four:	[For the] New Year's Day payment [to the] corvee / labourers – 10
Row Four	Category Five:	Small cattle [for the] Chief of the Phyles [for] food – 10
	Category Six:	[For the] third [month],
Row Five		bulls [for] (daily) services – 7

The Translations   291

Tablet HT 95B
As noted, the reverse side of this tablet deals with the animals that were yet to be received.

Heading: Row One, Symbols One and Two:

Hieroglyph S34 ⚱/modifed (loop removed) / Linear A symbol L52 ⊤
As we have seen previously, this symbol repesents the first hieroglyph in the word:

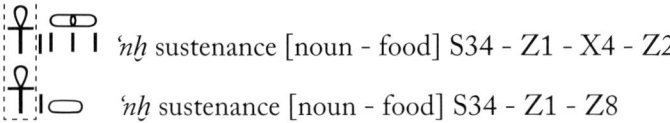

Hieroglyph A24 / modified / simplified / Linear A symbol L93
As we have seen previously, this symbol represents the last hieroglyph in the word:

 sm₃ take part in, receive [verb] F36 - G1 - G17 - Z7 - Z4 - Y1
                                                                                    - A24

These two symbols therefore mean "sustenance to [be] receive[d]".

Category One: Row One, Symbols Three and Four:

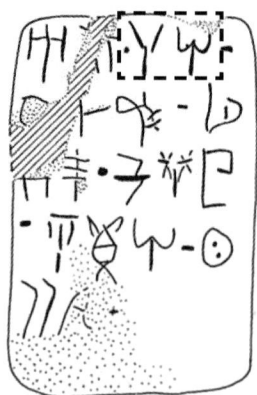

Hieroglyph V28 ⦗ / rotated ⦘ / simplified / Linear A symbol L31 Y
As we have seen previously, this symbol represents the first hieroglyph in the word:

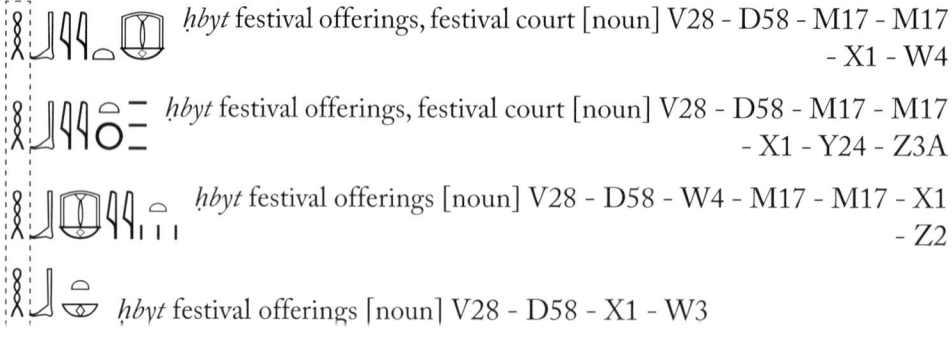

ḥbyt festival offerings, festival court [noun] V28 - D58 - M17 - M17 - X1 - W4

ḥbyt festival offerings, festival court [noun] V28 - D58 - M17 - M17 - X1 - Y24 - Z3A

ḥbyt festival offerings [noun] V28 - D58 - W4 - M17 - M17 - X1 - Z2

ḥbyt festival offerings [noun] V28 - D58 - X1 - W3

Hieroglyphs D28 - Z1 ⊔ / simplified / modified / Linear A symbol L55 Y
As we have seen previously, this symbol represents the word:

k3w food, bounty [noun - food] D28 - Z1

These three symbols therefore mean "[for] festival offerings [of] food". This is followed by a count of 10. It is perhaps interesting to note that the animal in question is not specified and, this category not following another where an animal was specified, cannot be inferred. We can, however, look to the front side of the tablet, i.e. on Tablet HT 95A, as all of its categories are repeated on this side, i.e. on Tablet HT 95B. As a result we can infer that this category, again, records "quadrupeds" (although that, in turn, is perhaps not all that helpful for us!).

Category Two: Row Two, Symbols One to Three:

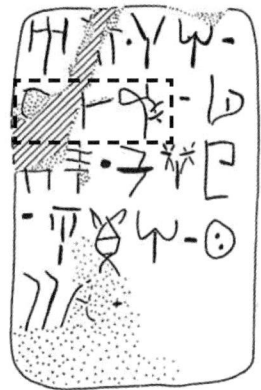

Hieroglyph F27 ⵂ / partially rotated / simplified / modified / Linear A symbol L42 ⵀ
While this symbol is damaged, both Brice and Godart & Olivier believe it to be Linear A symbol L42. As we have seen previously, this symbol represents the last hieroglyph in the word:

◯🐐 ʿr goat [noun - ani.] D36 - D21 - E31 - F27

Hieroglyph T14 ⎮ replaced by AA26 (or J26) ⵀ / reversed ⵀ / Linear A symbol L30 ⵀ
As we have seen previously, this symbol represents the (replaced) first hieroglyph in the word:

⎮ ʿwt small cattle, goats, herds [noun - ani.] T14

⎮🐐🏹 ⎮⎮⎮ ʿwt small cattle, herds, flocks, goats [noun - ani.] T14 - G43 - E28 - Z2

⎮🐐◯🏹 ⎮⎮⎮ ʿwt small cattle, herds, flocks, goats [noun - ani.] T14 - G43 - X1 - E1 - Z2

⎮🐐◯🏹 ⎮⎮⎮ ʿwt small cattle, herds, flocks, goats [noun - ani.] T14 - G43 - X1 - E8 - Z2

⎮🐐🏹 ʿwt small cattle, herds, flocks, goats [noun - ani.] T14 - Z7 - X1 - E28 - F27 - Z3A

⎮🐐🏹 ⎮⎮⎮ ʿwt small cattle, herds, flocks, goats [noun - ani.] T14 - Z7 - X1 - E28 - Z2

⎮ \ ⎮⎮⎮ ʿwt small cattle, herds, flocks, goats [noun - ani.] T14 - Z7 - X1 - Z5 - Z2

As on the front (A) side of this tablet, here this symbol means "herds".

294 The Decipherment of Linear A

Hieroglyph A24 𓀗 / simplified / modified / Linear A symbol L93 + male = symbol / modified / Linear A symbol L84/48

As we have seen previously, this symbol represents the word:

mniw herdsman [noun - title] A24 - G43 - D40

mniw herdsman, shepherd [noun - title] A33 - G1 - Z5 - Z5 - Z5 - Z5 - Z5 - A24

mniw herdsman [noun - title] A33 - G1 - Z7 - Y1 - A24

mniw herdsman [noun - title] A33 - M17 - Z7 - A24

mniw herdsman [noun – title] A33 - Z5 - Z5 - Z5 - A24

joined to the male = symbol, which represents the last hieroglyph in the word:

ḥꜣwty warrior, male, man [noun] D34 - G45 - X1 - Z4

These three symbols therefore mean "goats [from the] herd [for the] herdsmen". They are followed by a count of 10.

Category Three: Row Two, Symbol One, and Row Two, Symbols One and Two:

Hieroglyph D36 / modified / simplified / Linear A symbol L76

As we have seen previously, this symbol represents the first hieroglyph in the word:

iwʿw quadrupeds, animals [noun - ani.] D36 - D36 - F28 - Z3

Hieroglyph N23 ⟂ / rotated H / Linear A symbol L25/7 H
As we have seen previously, this symbol represents the last hieroglyph in the word:

ꜣḥt field, arable land, earth, mound area (geometry) [noun] G1 - V28 - X1
- N23

ꜣḥt field, arable land, earth, mound area (geometry) [noun] V28 - G1 - X1
- N23

Hieroglyph V16 / rotated / simplified / Linear A symbol L92
As we have seen previously, this symbol represents the last hieroglyph in the word:

sꜣ phyle (of priests), company, regiment (of troops), troop (of animals) [noun]
V16 - A1 - Z2

These three symbols therefore mean "quadrupeds [in the] fields [for the] phyle (of priests)". They are followed by a count of 10.

Category Four: Row Three, Symbols Three to Five:

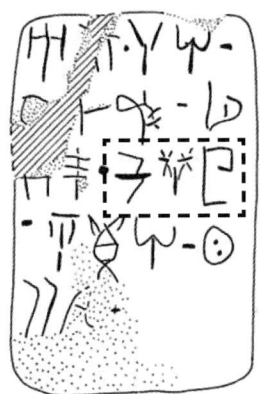

Hieroglyph F14 / rotated / simplified / Linear A symbol L98
As we have seen previously, this symbol represents the first hieroglyph in the word:

wpt rnpt New Year's Day (and its festivals) [noun] F14 - W3

wpt rnpt New Year's Day (and its festivals) [noun] F15 - W3 - N5

296   The Decipherment of Linear A

Hieroglyph T25 / rotated / simplified / Linear A symbol L60
As we have seen previously, this symbol represents the first hieroglyph (or, in one instance, the last hieroglyph) in the word:

db3w payments, reward, compensation, bribes [noun] T25 - D58

db3w payments, reward, compensation, bribes [noun] T25 - D58
  - G1 - Z7 - Y1 - Z2

db3w payments, reward, compensation, bribes [noun] T25 - D58
  - G43 - Y1 - Z2

db3w payments, rewards [noun] T25 - D58 - N33 - N33 - N33 - G43

db3 reward, payment [noun] T25 - D58 - Z7 - Y1

db3 reward, payment [noun] D46 - D58 - T25

Hieroglyph O4 / rotated / Linear A symbol L59 or
As we have seen previously, this symbol represents the first hieroglyph in the word:

h3w corvee [noun] O4 - G1 - A9

h3w corvee, compulsory labour, faction (operating within the temple)
  [noun] O4 - G1 - G43 - A24

h3w bonded labourers [plural noun - title] O4 - G1 - G43 - A24
  - A1 - Z2

h3w bonded labourers [plural noun - title] O4 - G1 - M17
  - M17 - G43 - D40 - Z2

h3y / h3w corvee, compulsory labour, faction (operating within temple) [noun] O4 - G1 - M17 - M17 - X1 - Y1 - A24 - A1
  - Z2

h3y (labour) service [noun] O4 - G1 - M17 - M17 - Z5 - Z5
  - A24 - A1 - Z2

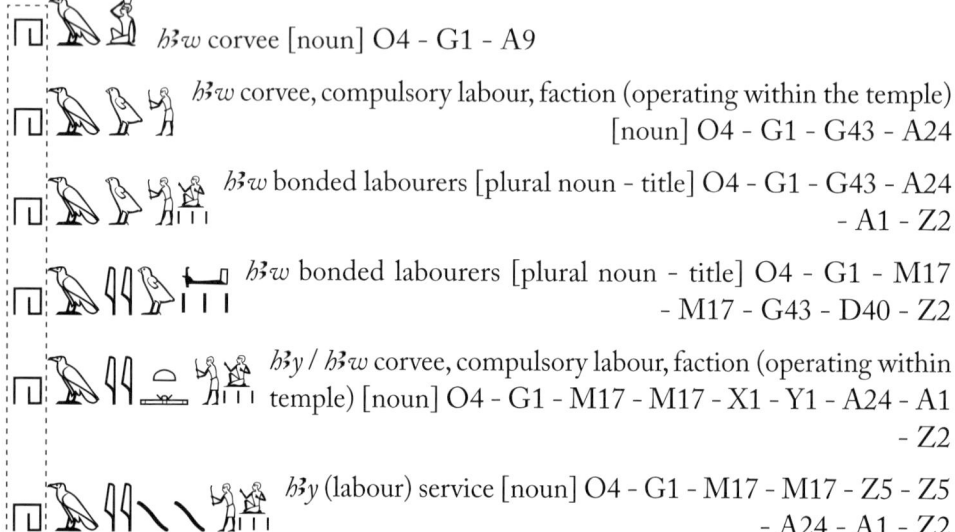

These three symbols therefore mean "[for the] New Year's Day payment [to the] corvee / labourers". They are followed by a count of 10.

Category Five: Row Four, Symbols One to Three:

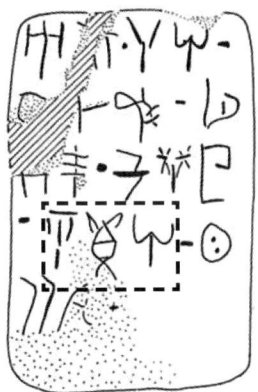

Hieroglyphs Z5 - Z2 ⋮⋮⋮/ rotated \ / modified / Linear A symbol L51 ⫶
As we have seen previously, this symbol represents the last hieroglyphs in the word:

ꜥwt small cattle, herds, flocks, goats [noun - ani.] T14 - Z7 - X1 - Z5 - Z2

Hieroglyph V17 / simplified / Linear A symbol L102
As we have seen previously, this symbol represents the last hieroglyph in the word:

ḥry sꜣ Chief of the Phyles [noun - title] D2 - D21 - V17

Hieroglyphs D28 - Z1 / simplified / modified / Linear A symbol L55
As we have seen previously, this symbol represents the word:

kꜣw food, bounty [noun – food] D28 - Z1

These three symbols therefore mean "small cattle [for the] Chief of the Phyles [for] food". They are followed by a count of 10.

298   The Decipherment of Linear A

Category Six: Row Four, Symbol Four, and Row Five Symbols One and Two:

Hieroglyphs Z2 - W24 ⊙ / rotated ○ ⹀ / modified (three dashes as dots inside circle) / Linear A symbol L91 ☻

The sketch diagram for this tablet indicates two dots (representing two of the three dashes of Hieroglyph Z2) within the circle (representing Hieroglyph W24); these are identified by the arrows on the left of the extract of the photograph of the tablet below. In addition, however, and not included on the sketch diagram, there is a third dot (representing the third dash of Hieroglyph Z2). This dot is adjacent to the line of the circle, so it was missed off the sketch diagram of the tablet; it is identified with an arrow at the bottom of the extract of the photograph of the tablet below:

Extract of photograph of Tablet HT 95B from Godart & Olivier

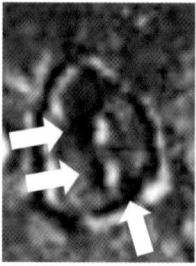

Here, therefore, as set out in Appendix 6, this symbol, representing Hieroglyphs Z2 - W24, represents the ordinal:

⊙ ḥmt nw third [ordinal number] Z2 - W24

Hieroglyphs Z5 - Z5 \\\/ Linear A symbol L58

As we have seen previously, this symbol represents the last hieroglyphs of the word:

𓃾 \\\ *k3* bull [noun - ani.] D28 - Z5 - Z5

Hieroglyphs X1 - D17 / modified (hieroglyphs joined) / Linear A symbol L88 (reversed)

As we have seen previously, this symbol represents the last hieroglyphs of the word:

imny (daily) service, offerings, portion, ration [noun] M17 - Y5 - N35 - X1 - D17

These three symbols therefore mean "[for the] third [month], bulls [for] daily services". Both Brice and Godart & Olivier believe that the count for this is 10 represented by a single horizontal tally mark. The tablet is, however, damaged and the original count here may have been higher.

We are now in a position to translate the tablet in full:

Row One	Heading:	Sustenance to [be] receive[d]
	Category One:	[For] festival offerings [of] food – 10
Row Two	Category Two:	Goats [from the] herds [for the] herdsmen – 10
	Category Three:	Quadrupeds
Row Three		[in the] fields [for the] phyle (of priests) – 10
	Category Four:	[For the] New Year's Day payment [to the] corvee labourers – 10
Row Four	Category Five:	Small cattle [for the] Chief of the Phyles [for] food – 10
	Category Six:	[For the] third [month],
Row Five		bulls [for] (daily) services – 10(?)

300 The Decipherment of Linear A

Tablet HT 36
On this tablet we see record of a (historic) receipt of goats and the outstanding (future) receipt of grain. The animals appear to be from the temple's own herd; by implication of being recorded on the same tablet, it would appear likely that the grain was from the temple's own land. The tablet therefore records historic and future internal stock transfers, in modern parlance, presumably as these animals and this grain was to be used in the near future.

Heading: Row One, Symbols One to Three:

Hieroglyph D54 ⌒ / reversed / modified / Linear A symbol L81 X
Hieroglyph D54, if it were reversed, and incised in clay, would be written as:

⌒ reversed would become ⌒

If incised in clay this would be ∧

As we have seen a number of times now, in becoming a Linear A symbol the hieroglyph is compressed, to save space horizontally. When that occurs here, the legs of the symbol overlap each other. Hieroglyph D54 thus becomes Linear A symbol L81:

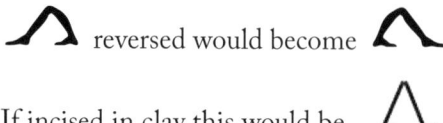

Given, as we shall see, that Category Two on this tablet records amounts to be received, it seems most likely that this symbol represents the first hieroglyph in the word:

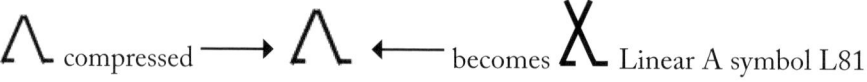 *iw* delivered, come, return D54 - Z7

The Translations   301

Hieroglyphs Z5 - Z2 ııı / rotated \ / modified / Linear A symbol L51 ııı
As we have seen previously, this symbol represents the last hieroglyph in the word:

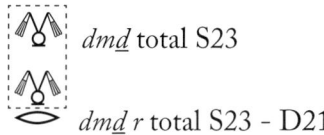 ꜥwt small cattle, herds, flocks, goats [noun - ani.] T14 - Z7 - X1 - Z5 - Z2

As it is written in a subheading on the tablet, as with Tablet HT 95A, we can infer that it conveys a more general meaning and, given the animals that are specifically referred to in Category One, this was most likely "herd".

Hieroglyph AA6 (or J6) ⋀ or S23 / simplified / modified / Linear A symbol L85
As we have seen previously, Linear A symbol L85 represents Hieroglyph S23 (or AA6 / J6). Where this symbol was written the tablet is damaged. Moreover, the symbol is modified further (being further compressed horizontally) so its derivation is not so immediately obvious as it was on Tablet HT 13, for example.

This further modification to the symbol is set out in the discussion of Tablet HT 21A (on page 363), where this can be more clearly seen. For now, however, this symbol represents either the word or the first hieroglyph in the word:

⋀ dmḏ total S23

⋀ dmḏ r total S23 - D21

These three symbols therefore mean "delivered [from the] herd, total".

Category One: Row One, Symbols Four and Five:

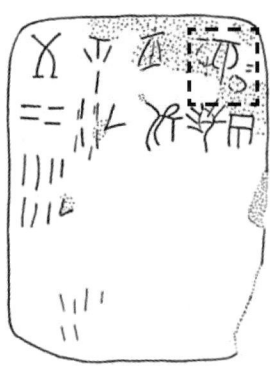

Hieroglyph F27 / partially rotated / simplified / modified / Linear A symbol L42
As we have seen previously, this symbol repesents the last hieroglyph in the word:

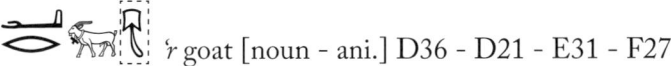 ỉr goat [noun - ani.] D36 - D21 - E31 - F27

302   The Decipherment of Linear A

Subscript Hieroglyph Z4B - Z4B - W24 ☱⊙ / modified (four dashes inside circle as dots) / Linear A symbol L91 ⊙
As set out in Appendix 6, this symbol, representing Hieroglyphs Z4B - Z4B - W24, represents the ordinal "fourth":

☱ ⊙ *fdnw* fourth Z4B - Z4B - W24

Here, however, the ordinal is not represented by a single Linear A symbol L91; in fact, there are two. While this is detail missing from the sketch drawing of the tablet, above, we can see this if we look at an extract of the photograph of the tablet from Brice, below:

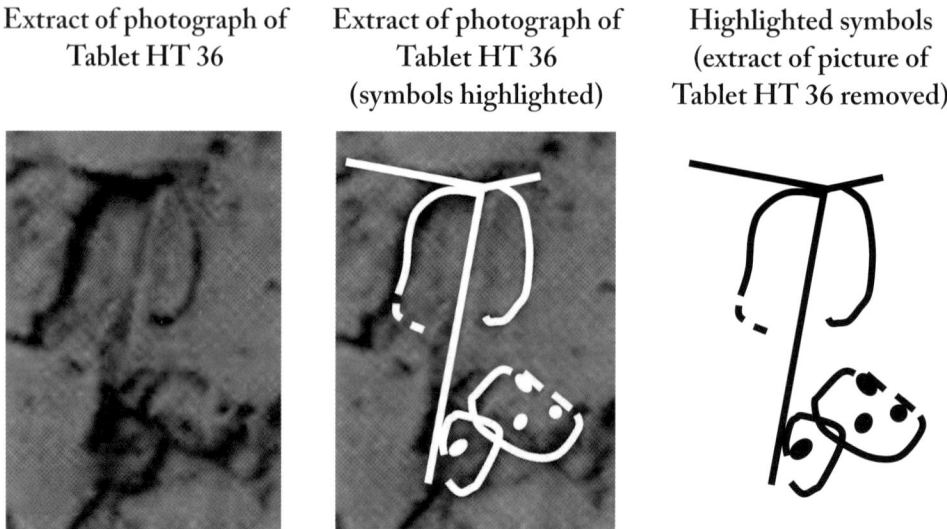

| Extract of photograph of Tablet HT 36 | Extract of photograph of Tablet HT 36 (symbols highlighted) | Highlighted symbols (extract of picture of Tablet HT 36 removed) |

As can be seen, there are, in fact, two circles at the bottom right of Linear A symbol L42: the circle to the right was included in Godart & Olivier's sketch diagram of the tablet, and this contained three dots (to represent the ordinal "third"), and a second circle lower down containing a single dot. It appears, having written the first circle and written three dots in it, the scribe determined that a fourth would have been too difficult to include and so wrote another circle with one dot in it.

As set out in Appendix 8, an ordinal next to the first item on a list indicates that this amount was brought forward from the prior month. Here, therefore, these symbols mean "goats [from the] fourth [month]". The tablet was, therefore, written in the first month of the following season which, given the references throughout the corpus to New Year's Day, we can assume was the first month in the New Year).

This is then followed by a count of 44 ½ (the fraction value being indicated by Linear A fraction symbol J).

As to how half an animal could be received as an internal transfer of stock, as we will see with Tablet HT 120, and as we saw with Linear B Tablet Mc 5098 (on page 231), there is some evidence of part ownership of animals (with, most likely, the herdsmen). This would seem to be such an example.

The Translations 303

Category Two: Row Two, Symbols One to Three:

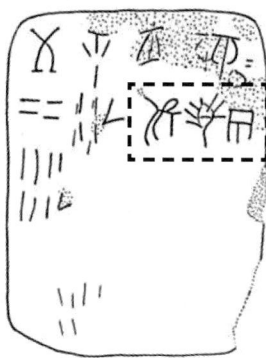

Hieroglyph A24 / modified / simplified / Linear A symbol L93

As we have seen previously, this symbol represents the last hieroglyph in the word:

smȝ take part in, receive [verb] F36 - G1 - G17 - Z7 - Z4 - Y1 - A24

As we saw previously on Tablet HT 13, and as we will see subsequently on Tablet HT 19, this verb being written in the final category on a tablet should be inferred to be in the future tense.

Hieroglyph M34 / Linear A symbol L101 (as here) or

As set out in Appendix 7, this symbol represents the last hieroglyph in the word:

pḥȝ grain, seed [noun - flora - food] Q3 - J1 - M34

Hieroglyph O20 / simplified / Linear A symbol L75

As we have seen previously, this symbol represents the last hieroglyph in the word:

ḥwt nṯr temple [noun - arch.] R8 - O20

These three symbols therefore mean "to [be] receive[d], grain, [at the] temple". They are followed by a count of 7 ½ (the fraction value again being indicated by Linear A fraction symbol J).

We are, therefore, now in a position to translate the tablet:

Row One	Heading:	Delivered [from the] herd, total
	Category One:	Goats [from the] fourth [month] –
Row Two		44 ½
	Category Two:	To [be] receive[d], grain, [at the] temple –
Row Three		7 ½

304   The Decipherment of Linear A

1(c). Receipts of goods from a certain source, and their subsequent issue during the same period

Tablet HT 91
This tablet was referred to previously in Chapter Two, where we noted seven of its categories of items under the first subheading were recorded with a zero amount (in fact there is an eighth that is too). This tablet might be seen to largely represent something of an exercise in pointless bureaucracy, listing items that were not received. However, that they were listed suggests these categories of items were expected to be received.

After listing the receipts (such as they were) the tablet records who they were issued to. While the tablet then breaks off, it appears to do so where the contents are complete. Therefore, this tablet is included in this work.

Heading: Row One, Symbols One and Two:

Hieroglyph D46 ⌒ / rotated / simplified / Linear A symbol L100 Ψ
As we have previously seen, this symbol represents the first hieroglyph in the word:

drpw offerings, provisions, meal, sustenance [noun - food] D46 - D21 - Q3 - Z7 - N37 - Z2

The Translations 305

Hieroglyph O49 ⊗ / simplified / Linear A symbol L29 ⊕
As we have seen previously, this symbol represents the word:

⊗ *niwt* city, town [noun] O49

The first two symbols therefore mean "provisions [from the] city".

Subheading: Row One, Symbol Three:

Hieroglyphs D28 - Z1 ᵾ / simplified / modified / Linear A symbol L54 ψ
Brice and Godart & Olivier believe this symbol to be Linear A symbol L67:

↑

It is not. As we saw previously on Tablet HT 2, the central stem of this symbol, Linear A symbol L54, has been written elongated above the point where its two arms join the stem. On top of this, the extremities of the two arms of the symbol have then been incised so that they touch at the apex. The result is a heavily stylised version of Linear A symbol L54. Yes, the scribe appears to have written the arms of the symbol from the top down and one (on the right) does not appear to quite reach the stem at the bottom, but this symbol is, nonetheless, Linear A symbol L54, rather than Linear A symbol L67.
Here, therefore, the symbol represents the word:

 k3w food, bounty [noun - food] D28 - Z1

This, therefore, means "[for] food".

306   The Decipherment of Linear A

<u>Category item one: Row One, Symbol Four:</u>

Hieroglyph F27 ⌂/ partially rotated / simplified / modified / Linear A symbol L42 ⊤
As we have seen previously, this symbol represents the last hieroglyph in the word:

⟨image⟩ 'r goat [noun - ani.] D36 - D21 - E31 - F27

The fraction symbol that follows it, believed by Godart & Olivier to be **#**, is more correctly considered by Brice to be **‡‡** i.e. two consecutive representations of Linear A symbol L2 / fraction symbol A which, as we have seen, represented Hieroglyph F35 and meant zero. Why would there be two consecutive "zeros"? Looking at the damage to the tablet, it appears that, when the first "zero" was incised, it was the one at the extreme right of the tablet and, being too close to the edge, the act of incising it caused the edge of the tablet to partly break away leaving the damage we see today (and a symbol that was not entirely clear). This meant that, to be clear, the scribe needed to incise the zero symbol again, and he did so closer to Linear A symbol L42, leaving us with the two "zeroes" that we see today.

Ignoring the repetition, therefore, the tablet records "goats". This is followed by a count of zero (represented by Linear A symbol L2 / fraction symbol A).

The Translations 307

<u>Category Two: Row Two, Symbol One:</u>

Hieroglyph F45 ↑ / simplified / Linear A symbol L67 ↑
As we have seen previously, this symbol represents the first (or, in one case, last) hieroglyph in the word:

idt cow [noun - ani.] F45 - M17 - N42 - X1

idt cow [noun - ani.] F45 - X1 - Z1 - E1

idt cow [noun - ani.] N41 - X1 - F45

This symbol means "cows". This is followed by a count of zero (represented by Linear A symbol L2 / fraction symbol A).

<u>Category Three: Row Two, Symbols Three and Four:</u>

308   The Decipherment of Linear A

Hieroglyph D3 / rotated / reversed / Linear A symbol L89
As we have seen previously, this symbol represents the last hieroglyph in the word:

šnw grass (cattle fodder) [noun - flora] V7 - N35 - W24 - Z7 - D3

joined to Hieroglyph G1 / simplified / Linear A symbol L103
As we first saw on Tablet HT 123A, Linear A symbol L103 represents Hieroglyph G1. There it represented the word for "deficiency", but that is not what it represents here, for one because it would interrupt the typical order of categories recorded (goat, cows (normally), fodder (various types), cows (sometimes), horned cattle / male quadrupeds). Here, therefore, it represents the first hieroglyph in the word:

ȝḥt cow [noun - ani.] G1 - O4 - X1 - E1

Given that this is a type of fodder, and given that we have cows recorded immediately before it, it seems reasonable to conclude that, for some reason for this category the word ȝḥt for cow was used, rather than idt. Perhaps joining Linear A symbol L89 and Linear A symbol L103 was a linguistic faux pas? Or perhaps, as in English, where you might say bovine feed or cow feed, there may, in fact, be no significance to this beyond the contemporary customary use of language that then prevailed (as happens in our own language).

These joined symbols therefore mean "grass (cattle fodder) [for] cows". They are followed by a count of zero (represented by Linear A symbol L2 / fraction symbol A).

Category Four: Row Two, Symbols Four and Five:

Hieroglyph D3 / rotated / reversed / Linear A symbol L89
As we have seen previously, this symbol represents the last hieroglyph in the word:

šnw grass (cattle fodder) [noun - flora] V7 - N35 - W24 - Z7 - D3

joined to Hieroglyph V4 ⟨glyph⟩ / reversed ⟨glyph⟩ / simplified / (incorrectly) Linear A symbol L97 ⟨glyph⟩

Hieroglyph V4 has been reversed and simplified to become the Linear A symbol that was used here. Brice and Godart & Olivier, however, incorrectly identified it as Linear A symbol L97 (and, in fact, it has not been given a separate identification previously). As the symbol is joined here to Linear A symbol L89, it is easier to see how this Linear A symbol was derived when it was not joined to another Linear A symbol on Tablet HT 120, which is considered later in this chapter (see page 352).

Accepting, for now, that this symbol represents Hieroglyph V4, and knowing that this symbol represents a type of animal, there are two animals that it might represent. First:

⟨hieroglyphs⟩ wȝpw sheep [noun - ani.] V4 - G1 - M17 - M17 - Q3 - G43 - E10

⟨hieroglyphs⟩ wȝpt sheep [noun – ani.] V4 - G1 - Q3 - X1

Or, second:

⟨hieroglyphs⟩ iwȝ ox, long horned cattle [noun - ani.] M17 - V4

In choosing between these, we first must consider the fact that there are three types of animal and three types of fodder recorded here. The symbol as it appears here was preceded by joined symbols that mean "grass (cattle fodder) for cows", and it is followed by joined symbols that mean "grass (cattle fodder) for quadrupeds" (and quadrupeds, as we know, from Tablet HT 14, include goats, at least in so far as fodder was concerned). The last-mentioned animal before these three categories was cows and, before that, goats, so the known fodder types before and after this category were probably for these types of animal. The next mentioned animal after these three fodder categories is, however, "horned cattle" which, by a process of elimination, must therefore relate to the animal type this category of fodder is for. As we know, "horned cattle" were male animals so this category of fodder was for male animals (of the type we are trying to determine); moreover, that these animals were male evidently did not need to be indicated with the addition of a male = symbol (because one is not present). This, then, helps us determine the animal type: an "ox" is male animal and a symbol representing that word would not need a male = symbol to indicate that animal was male; a "sheep" can be either male or female and a symbol representing that word would need a male = symbol to indicate that animal was male (i.e a ram). The symbol here has no male = sign so cannot mean male sheep. We cannot always take the meaning of "horned cattle" at face value; on Tablet HT 123A, as the reader will recall, the use of that collective noun inferred sheep (rams). On this tablet, however, it seems most likely that we should take "horned cattle", when it subsequently

310   The Decipherment of Linear A

appears, at face value and here infer as a result that the meaning of this symbol is "ox". That way, there are three types of feed that can be matched to the same three types of animals.

These joined symbols therefore mean "grass (cattle fodder) [for the] oxen". They are followed by a count of zero (represented by Linear A symbol L2 / fraction symbol A).

Category Five: Row Three, Symbols One and Two:

Hieroglyph D3 / rotated / reversed / Linear A symbol L89
As we have seen previously, this symbol represents the last hieroglyph in the word:

šnw grass (cattle fodder) [noun - flora] V7 - N35 - W24 - Z7 - D3

Joined to Hieroglyph D36 / modified / simplified / Linear A symbol L76
As we have seen previously, this symbol represents the first hieroglyph in the word:

iw'w quadrupeds, animals [noun - ani.] D36 - D36 - F28 - Z3

These joined symbols therefore mean "grass (cattle fodder) [for the] quadrupeds". They are followed by a count of zero (represented by Linear A symbol L2 / fraction symbol A).

The Translations 311

<u>Category Six: Row Three, Symbol Three:</u>

<u>Hieroglyph F155</u> ⛉ / simplified / <u>Linear A symbol L49</u> (as here) or modified further

As we have seen previously, this symbol represents the first hieroglyph in the word:

⛉ 🐂 *wp* horned cattle [noun - ani.] F155 - E1 - Z3

This symbol means "horned cattle". As discussed previously, we can infer, here, that these are, in fact, oxen. It is followed by a count of zero (represented by Linear A symbol L2 / fraction symbol A).

As we saw on Tablet HT 114A and Tablet HT 121, where certain categories of items received were not to be used for their originally intended recipient or purpose, the following three categories on the tablet represent "horned cattle" (i.e. oxen) that were to have been received but which, after receipt, will be issued to, and are described by, alternative intended recipients.

Moreover, the future intended recipients in Category Seven, Category Eight, and Category Nine match the categories of payee listed on Tablet HT 89 (and Tablet HT 27A). The "*3bd* priests in their month of service" is synonymous with the payee category "Priests of Hathor" that appears on Tablet HT 89 (and Tablet HT 27A). As we know this is a temple dedicated to Hathor (not least by the explicit heading on Tablet HT 17 and Tablet HT 19 which we will see later in this chapter), we can safely assume that the priests in their month of service were Priests of Hathor. Similarly the categories "[for] payments" (to the temple's suppliers) and "[for the] peasants" are also listed here as well as on Tablet HT 89 (and Tablet HT 27A).

Category Seven: Row Three, Symbol Four:

Hieroglyph T25 / rotated / simplified / Linear A symbol L60

As we have seen previously, this symbol represents the first hieroglyph (or, in one instance, last hieroglyph) in the word:

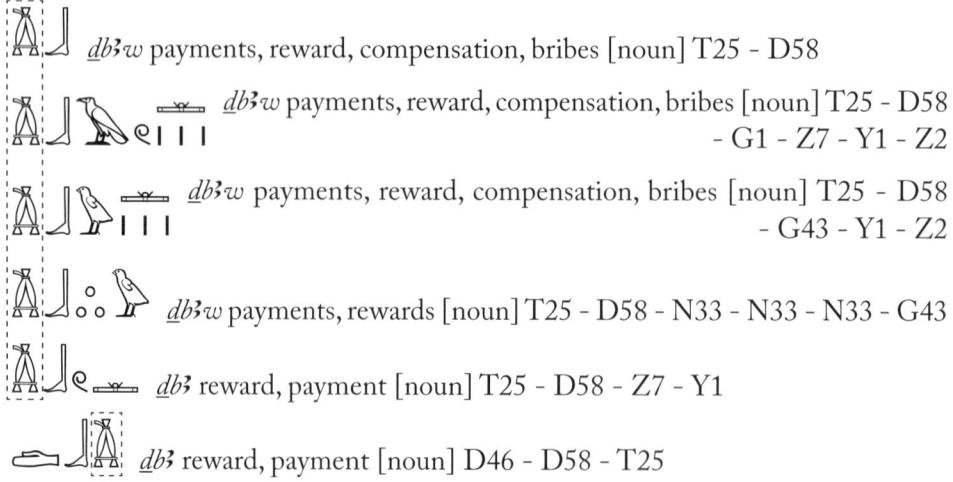

This symbol therefore means "[for] payments". This is followed by a count of zero (represented by Linear A symbol L2 / fraction symbol A).

As discussed previously, these future payments would presumably be for goods and services to be purchased by the temple (for example, as we have seen, on Tablet HT 86A, what was labelled as a payment was made to the corvee / labourers). If there had been a value, it would have represented "horned cattle" (i.e. oxen), the same animal type being referred to in the previous category. These were now intended to be paid to alternative recipients (a third party or third parties) in the future.

Category Eight: Row Four, Symbol One:

Hieroglyph M20 𓆰𓆰𓆰 / rotated / simplified / Linear A symbol L82

As we have seen previously, this symbol represents the first hieroglyph in the word:

shty peasant, fisherman, fowler [noun - title] M20 - X1 - Z4 - A1

shty peasant, fisherman, fowler [noun - title] M20 - X1 - Z4 - A24 - A1

shty peasant, fisherman, fowler [noun - title] M20 - X1 - Z4 - G4 - A24 - A1 - Z2

This symbol therefore means "[for the] peasants". This is followed by a count of zero (represented by Linear A symbol L2 / fraction symbol A).

As discussed previously, these would presumably have been peasants working on the temple's lands. Again, if there had been a value, it would have represented horned cattle (i.e. oxen), the same animal type being referred to in Category Six. These were now intended to be issued to alternative recipients (the peasants) in the future.

314   The Decipherment of Linear A

<u>Category Nine: Row Two, Symbol Two:</u>

<u>Hieroglyph N11 + Hieroglyph Z4 / modified (horizontally compressed) + male = symbol /</u>
<u>Linear A symbol L44</u> 𐘺
This Linear A symbol is formed, first, from Hieroglpyh N11. This hieroglyph has been modified by being compressed horizontally in order to save space:

In its own right, this is Linear A symbol L78, as we will see later in this chapter. To this, the male = symbol (which, as we have seen, represents Hieroglyph Z4) is then added. This gives us Linear A symbol L44.

This symbol therefore represents the first hieroglyph in the word:

joined to the male = symbol, which represents the last hieroglyph in the word:

ḥ3wty warrior, male, man [noun] D34 - G45 - X1 - Z4

The addition of the male = symbol is interesting because, as was the case with Linear A symbol L84/48 which we considered previously, it is not being used to highlight that the thing represented by the symbol to which it was joined was male in gender (and not that, without the male symbol joined to it, it would otherwise mean the same thing but, by implication, be female). Rather, the male = symbol is used here to denote that the symbol to which it is joined indicates a category of men (rather than anything else that Hieroglyph N11 or, rather, Linear A symbol L78 representing it, might represent).

The Translations 315

This symbol therefore means "[for the] *3bd* Priests (in their month of service)", who were evidently part of the phyle (of priests) on duty for the month. This mirrors the category of payee of "Priests of Hathor" that, as we shall see, appears on Tablet HT 89. This is followed by a count of 5. Again, these are "horned cattle" (i.e. oxen), the same animal type being referred to in Category Six. These are now intended to be issued to an alternative recipient (the *3bd* Priests) in the future.

At this stage, having dealt with goods (animals and fodder) received (such as they were), the tablet deals with their issue. As the category descriptions under the first heading indicates, the only future intended recipients were the "*3bd* priests in their month of service" (who were part of the phyle (of priests)). We therefore see them being the only recipient in the following section of the tablet.

<u>Subheading Two: Row Five, Symbols One and Two:</u>

<u>Hieroglyph V16</u> / rotated / simplified / Linear A symbol L92
As we have seen previously, this symbol represents the first hieroglyph in the word:

s3 phyle (of priests), company, regiment (of troops), troop (of animals) [noun]
V16 - A1 - Z2

<u>Hieroglyph M6</u> / reversed / simplified / Linear A symbol L72/94 or
As we have seen previously, this symbol represents the first hieroglyph in the word:

trsst wage payments [noun - food] M6 - O34 - O34 - X1 - Z8

These two symbols therefore mean "[for the] phyle (of priests), wage payments".

316   The Decipherment of Linear A

Category Ten: Row Five, Symbols Three and Four:

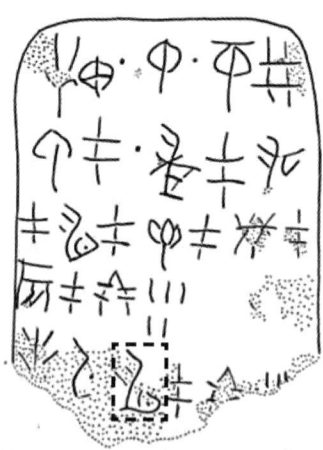

Hieroglyph D3 / rotated / reversed / Linear A symbol L89
As we have seen previously, this symbol represents the last hieroglyph in the word:

šnw grass (cattle fodder) [noun - flora] V7 - N35 - W24 - Z7 - D3

joined to Hieroglyph D36 / modified / simplified / Linear A symbol L76
As we have seen previously, this symbol represents the first hieroglyph in the word:

iw'w quadrupeds, animals [noun - ani.] D36 - D36 - F28 - Z3

These symbols therefore mean "grass (cattle fodder) [for the] quadrupeds". This is followed by a count of zero (represented by Linear A symbol L2 / fraction symbol A).

Category Eleven: Row Five, Symbol Five:

Hieroglyph N11 + Hieroglyph Z4 / modified / Linear A symbol L44 ⚶ + male = symbol

As we have seen previously, these joined symbols represent the first hieroglyph in the word:

3bd Priest (in his month of service) [noun - title] N11 - N14 - W3 - A1

joined to the male = symbol, which represents the last hieroglyph in the word:

h3wty warrior, male, man [noun] D34 - G45 - X1 - Z4

While only a count of 3 has survived, it is, perhaps, reasonable to believe that the tally here was originally five, being all of those "horned cattle" (i.e. oxen) recorded as having been received in the top half of the tablet.

We can now translate the tablet in full:

Row One	Heading:	Provisions [from the] city
	Subheading One:	[for] food
	Category One:	Goats – 0
Row Two	Category Two:	Cows – 0
	Category Three:	Grass (cattle fodder) [for] cows – 0
	Category Four:	Grass (cattle fodder) [for] oxen
Row Three		– 0
	Category Five:	Grass (cattle fodder) [for the] quadrupeds – 0
	Category Six:	Horned cattle (oxen) – 0
	Category Seven:	[Horned cattle (oxen)] [For] payments – 0
Row Four	Category Eight:	[Horned cattle (oxen)] [For the] peasants – 0
	Category Nine:	[Horned cattle (oxen)] [For the] *3bd* Priests (in their month of service) – 5
Row Five	Subheading Two:	[For the] phyle (of priests), wage payments
	Category Ten:	Grass (cattle fodder) [for the] quadrupeds – 0
	Category Eleven:	[For the] *3bd* Priests (in their month of service) – 5(?)

318   The Decipherment of Linear A

1(d). Issue of goods (animals) to the phyle of priests
The following two tablets, which are of similar size and have similar content, concern the issue of goods (animals) to the phyle of priests in, it appears most likely, consecutive months.

Tablet HT 19
Heading: Row One, Symbols One to Three:

Hieroglyph I12 / simplified / Linear A symbol L53
As we have seen previously, Linear A symbol L53 is a straightforward simplified representation of Hieroglyph I12. Here, it represents the last hieroglyph in the word:

ntrt goddess [noun - div.] R8 - D21 - X1 - I12

ntrt goddess [noun - div.] R8 - D21 - X1 - J2 - I12

ntrt goddess [noun - div.] R8 - D21 - X1 - Z5 - I12

ntrt goddess [noun - div.] R8 - X1 - D21 - M17 - M17 - X1 - J2 - I12

ntrt goddess [noun - div.] R8 - X1 - D21 - X1 - I12

ntrt goddess [noun - div.] R8 - X1 - D21 - X1 - J2 - I12

ntrt goddess [noun - div.] R8 - X1 - I12

ntrt goddess [noun - div.] R8 - X1 - J2 - I12

ntrt goddess [noun – div.] R8 - Z5 - Z5 - Z5 - I12

The Translations 319

Hieroglyph O10 🦅/ simplified / Linear A symbol L43 ⊠ or ꗃ (as, erroneously, here)
The representation of Hieroglyph O10 on this tablet merits comparison with a similar portrayal on Tablet HT 17, where it also appears. Taking an extract of the photograph of this tablet and stretching it so that it is of similar dimensions to that on Tablet HT 17, we see as follows:

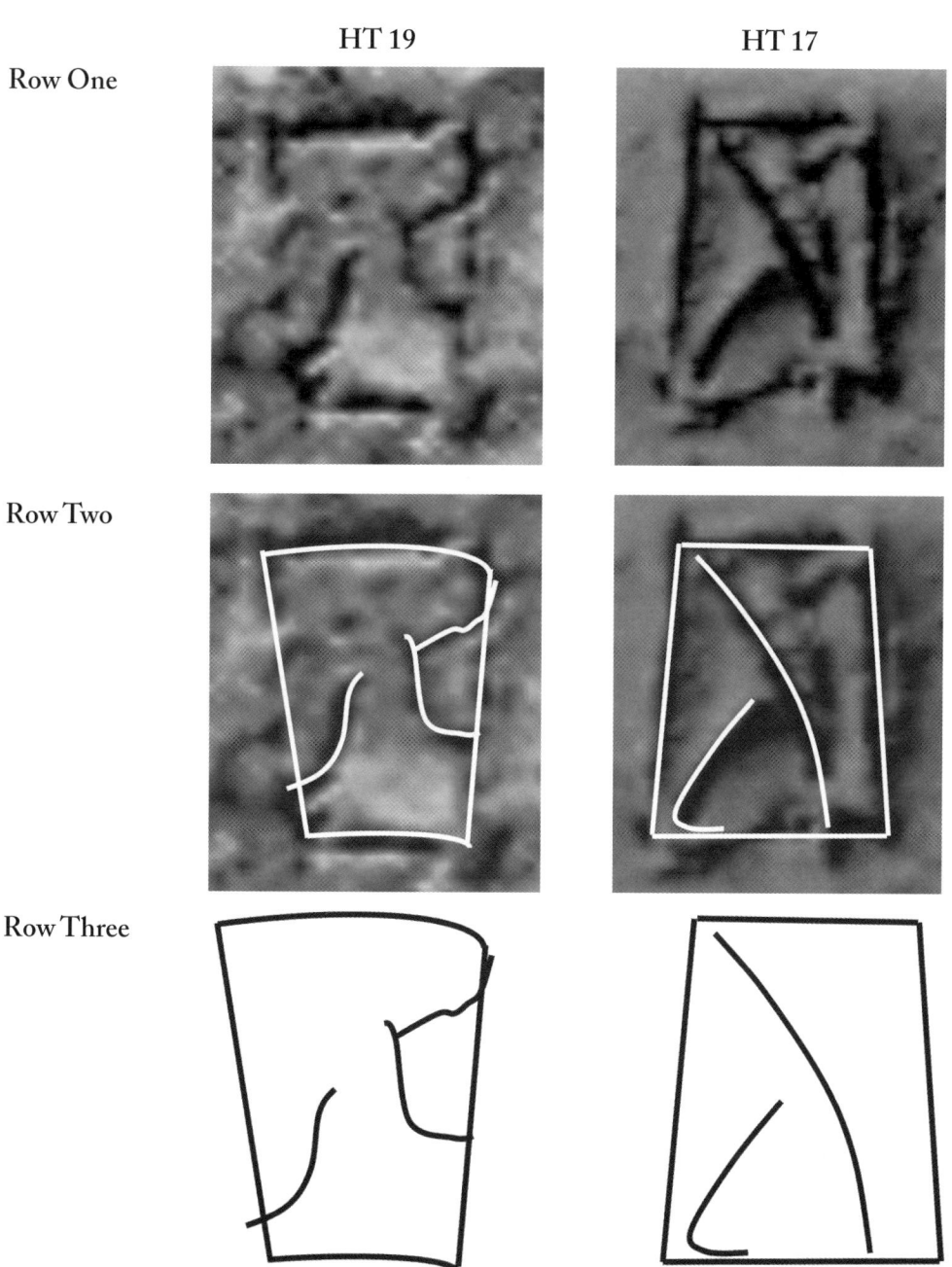

320 The Decipherment of Linear A

Row Four

HT 19

HT 17

As we can see:

- On Row One we have the picture of the symbol as it was used on this tablet and the similar symbol on Tablet HT 17.
- On Row Two we see the symbols highlighted in white.
- On Row Three we see the highlighted symbols, in black, with the background photographs removed.
- On Row Four we see Hieroglyph O10. In the case of Tablet HT 19, but not Tablet HT 17, the symbol has been reversed (indicating, for one, that different scribes wrote the two tablets).

On Tablet HT 19, within the square outline of the symbol, the line that extends from bottom left to top right is broken, but it clearly mirrors the symbol on Tablet HT 17 which extends from bottom right to top left. Once we identify this, we can see that both portray the same hieroglyph but the symbol on Tablet HT 19 has been reversed. Both symbols clearly represent a simplified Hieroglyph O10. Significantly, this hieroglyph is only used when writing the name of the Goddess Hathor:

ḥwt ḥr Hathor [noun - div.] O10

As we have already noted, Hathor is the very goddess we would expect an Egyptian temple to be dedicated to if it were outside of Egypt. That she appears so explicitly in the Linear A corpus is, therefore, not a coincidence.

Hieroglyph N11 / modified / Linear A symbol L78
As we have seen previously, when analysing Linear A symbol L44, Linear A symbol L78 represents Hierolgyph N11 that has been compressed in order to save space horizontally:

Here it represents the word:

◠ *3bd* month [noun] N11

These three symbols therefore mean "[from the] Goddess Hathor, [in the] month".

Subheading: Row One, Symbol Four:

Hieroglyph V16 / rotated / simplified / Linear A symbol L92

As we have seen previously, this symbol represents the first hieroglyph in the word:

s3 phyle (of priests), company, regiment (of troops), troop (of animals) [noun]
V16 - A1 - Z2

This symbol therefore means "[to the] phyle (of priests)".

Category One: Row Two, Symbol One:

322   The Decipherment of Linear A

Hieroglyph M20 𓆰 / rotated 𓆱 / simplified / Linear A symbol L82 ⚏

As we have seen previously, this symbol represents Hieroglyph M20. Here, it represents the first hieroglyph in the word:

𓆰 𓅓 𓃾 *šṯyw* cattle [noun - ani.] M20 - G4 - E1 - N33A

As we have seen, this is not a widely attested word in what has survived of the written usage of Middle Egyptian (not that that is necessarily reflective of how widespread its use actually was, which may have been much more extensive) and there is some uncertainty as to its precise meaning. From its use in the heading of Tablet HT 13, however, and the list of animals that followed it there we know that it encapsulated goats, cows, and rams.

As with other collective nouns seen in the corpus, it seems reasonable to believe that this collective noun could be used in both the general and the specific. Tablet HT 133, which is discussed later in this chapter, indicates that in a forecast (i.e. standard) month, the phyle (of priests) was to receive 55 goats. The amount here is some way from that forecast number, but is nonetheless the largest number of animals recorded on the tablet as to be issued in the month (and, as we know, forecasts always represent the ideal and do not always fully eventuate).

Therefore, while this word does have the general meaning of "cattle", and that was the meaning when used in the heading of Tablet HT 13, for the purposes of the translation of this tablet it seems reasonable to infer that the word also had the specific meaning of "goats" and to use that meaning here. This is followed by a count of 30.

Category Two: Row Two, Symbols Two and Three:

Hieroglyph V28 𓍯 / rotated 𓍰 / simplified / Linear A symbol L31 Y
As we have seen previously, this symbol represents the first hieroglyph in the word:

The Translations 323

ḥbyt festival offerings, festival court [noun] V28 - D58 - M17 - M17 - X1 - W4

ḥbyt festival offerings, festival court [noun] V28 - D58 - M17 - M17 - X1 - Y24 - Z3A

ḥbyt festival offerings [noun] V28 - D58 - W4 - M17 - M17 - X1 - Z2

ḥbyt festival offerings [noun] V28 - D58 - X1 - W3

<u>Hieroglyph Z9 ✗ / (incorrectly) Linear A symbol L22 ✚</u>
Here, this Linear A symbol is a diagonal-diagonal cross and the bulge to its bottom left is simply due to how it was incised. The symbol is not, however, Linear A symbol L22, which represents Hieroglyph N14, as that cross was vertical-horizontal. In fact, it represents Hieroglyph Z9 and here it represents the first hieroglyph in the word:

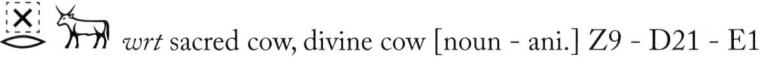 *wrt* sacred cow, divine cow [noun - ani.] Z9 - D21 - E1

These two symbols therefore mean "[from the] festival offerings, sacred cows". They are followed by a count of 5 ½. Presumably, therefore, at least one sacred cow that was a festival offering has been half consumed, or liturgically used in some way (presumably at the festival), or, indeed, allocated to another recipient, leaving the half that was issued to the phyle (of priests) and recorded here.

Tablet HT 133, as we will see, indicates that in a standard month no cows would be issued to the phyle (of priests); conversely, Tablet HT 92 indicates that 12 would be issued during the entire year, presumably as an exceptional rather than regular occurrence given that they were not issued in a standard month. Given that 5 ½ were recorded as issued in this month, this appears to be an exceptional month. Indeed, that the animals are labelled as sacred, and were received as festival offerings, also indicates this issue was exceptional (dependent on voluntary donations, which were variable, rather than regular allocations).

Although a similar value, the number of cows received does not agree to the one month recorded on Tablet HT 118, so this tablet does not relate to the final month of the year as portrayed on that tablet.

324   The Decipherment of Linear A

Category Three: Row Three, Symbol One to Three:

Hieroglyph A24 𓀀 / modified / simplified / Linear A symbol L93 𓀀
As we have seen previously, this symbol represents the last hieroglyph in the word:

sm3 take part in, receive [verb] F36 - G1 - G17 - Z7 - Z4 - Y1
                                                              - A24

As we saw on Tablet HT 13 and Tablet HT 36, given that this is the final category recorded, we can infer that this verb should be in the future tense as it indicates an amount to be received in the future. The amount in question had, therefore, not yet been issued to the phyle (of priests) but would be received by the phyle (of priests) from the herdsmen subsequently (the animals, therefore, presumably coming from the temple's herds that were in the herdsmen's care).

Hieroglyph A24 𓀀 / simplified / modified / Linear A symbol L93 𓀀 + male = symbol / modified / Linear A symbol L84/48 𓀀
As the reader will recall, on Tablet HT 86A, Linear A symbol L84/48 (representing Hieroglyph A24 joined to Hieroglyph Z4) was written in a demonstrably similar way to Linear A symbol L93 (but with only one leg, and with a male = symbol crossing it). Although written less precisely, here the symbol nonetheless represents the last hieroglyph (or, in one instance, first hieroglyph) in the word:

mniw herdsman [noun - title] A24 - G43 - D40

mniw herdsman, shepherd [noun - title] A33 - G1 - Z5
                                         - Z5 - Z5 - Z5 - Z5 - A24

mniw herdsman [noun - title] A33 - G1 - Z7 - Y1 - A24

mniw herdsman [noun - title] A33 - M17 - Z7 - A24

mniw herdsman [noun - title] A33 - Z5 - Z5 - Z5 - A24

joined to the male = symbol, which represents the last hieroglyph in the word:

ḥꜣwty warrior, male, man [noun] D34 - G45 - X1 - Z4

Hieroglyphs Z5 - Z2 ⅢⅠ/ rotated \ / modified / Linear A symbol L51 Ⅲ
As we have seen previously, this symbol represents the last hieroglyphs in the word:

ꜥwt small cattle, herds, flocks, goats [noun - ani.] T14 - Z7 - X1 - Z5 - Z2

These three symbols therefore mean "to [be] receive[d] [from the] herdsman, small cattle". Presumably these animals were to come from the temple's own herd, hence the scribe can be certain they would be received and issued to the phyle (of priests) during the month even though they had not been when the tablet was written. They are followed by a count of 43 ½.

As to how half an animal could be delivered by the herdsmen, it would seem most likely that the other half was to be allocated to another recipient (and that half, which was recorded elsewhere, plus this half equalled a whole animal that was to be received).

We are now in a position to fully translate this tablet:

Row One	Heading:	[From the] Goddess Hathor, [for the] month
	Subheading:	[to the] phyle (of priests)
Row Two	Category One:	Cattle (goats) – 30
	Category Two:	[From the] festival offerings, sacred cows – 5 ½
Row Three	Category Three:	To [be] receive[d] [from the] herdsman, small cattle – 43 ½

Analysis

<u>1. Further evidence that Linear A is Middle Egyptian (written in shorthand)</u>
As noted, perhaps the most important aspect of this tablet is that, like Tablet HT 17 which follows, it contains a very explicit reference to the Goddess Hathor in its first two symbols. The second symbol is particularly significant because the hieroglyph that it so clearly represents, Hieroglyph O10, is only used in the name of the Goddess Hathor. As noted in Chapter Four, if an Egyptian temple were found overseas from and outside of Egypt (and the reconstructed history indicates that we would expect such temples to have been found on Crete), we would expect it to have been dedicated to the Goddess Hathor. Here, we see that explicitly stated. Moreover, given the extreme rarity of Hieroglyph O10,

326 The Decipherment of Linear A

in that it is used for no other purpose other than to convey the name of the Goddess Hathor in Middle Egyptian, it is inconceivable to think that this hieroglyph, specifically and above all others, would have been used to create a letter in a Minoan alphabet. This is again evidence that Linear A is not Minoan. It is again evidence that Linear A is Middle Egyptian (written in shorthand using hieroglyphs).

Tablet HT 17

The tablet bears obvious similarities to Tablet HT 19 and, similarly, records an issue of animals to the phyle (of priests). In this case, however, all the animals have been received and issued and none are outstanding.

The tablet also relates to a different month than Tablet HT 19 as the "small cattle" in the final category are from offerings that have been made (as well as the animals in the other two categories having different values). The different abbreviation for "small cattle" in that final category indicates that this tablet was written by a different scribe to Tablet HT 19.

Heading: Row One, Symbols One to Three:

Hieroglyph I12 / simplified / Linear A symbol L53
As we have seen previously, this symbol represents the last hieroglyph in the word:

  ntrt goddess [noun - div.] R8 - D21 - X1 - I12

  ntrt goddess [noun - div.] R8 - D21 - X1 - J2 - I12

  ntrt goddess [noun - div.] R8 - D21 - X1 - Z5 - I12

  ntrt goddess [noun - div.] R8 - X1 - D21 - M17 - M17 - X1 - J2 - I12

The Translations 327

𓏲𓂋𓏏𓆗 *ntrt* goddess [noun - div.] R8 - X1 - D21 - X1 - I12

𓏲𓂋𓏏𓏤𓆗 *ntrt* goddess [noun - div.] R8 - X1 - D21 - X1 - J2 - I12

𓏲𓏏𓆗 *ntrt* goddess [noun - div.] R8 - X1 - I12

𓏲𓏤𓆗 *ntrt* goddess [noun - div.] R8 - X1 - J2 - I12

𓏲𓏤𓏤𓏤𓆗 *ntrt* goddess [noun - div.] R8 - Z5 - Z5 - Z5 - I12

Hieroglpyph O10 𓊁 / modified / Linear A symbol L43  (in a transcription error, as here) or

In identifying this symbol we are not helped by a rare transcription error by Brice which was then duplicated by Godart & Olivier.

Brice and Godart & Olivier thought this symbol should be written as . However, an examination of a picture of this portion of the tablet reveals that this is incorrect:

Extract of photograph of Tablet HT 17

As can be seen above, there is no "spoke" from the centre of the symbol to its top right-hand corner (if there is a dot in the top right hand corner, it would appear to represent the square in the top right hand corner of Hieroglyph O10). Moreover, the spoke that goes from the centre to the bottom left-hand corner of the symbol turns in on itself, like (and because it represents) a foot. Noting this, we can see that Linear A symbol L43 (corrected for this error) is, in fact, a simplified Hieroglyph O10:

328   The Decipherment of Linear A

Hieroglyph O10   becomes   Linear A symbol L43

As we have seen, and of particular significance for us, this hieroglyph is only used when writing the name of the Goddess Hathor:

 ḥwt ḥr Hathor [noun - div.] O10

Hieroglyph N11 ⌒ / modified / Linear A symbol L78 ∧
As we have seen previously, this symbol represents the word:

⌒ *3bd* month [noun] N11

These three symbols therefore mean "[from the] Goddess Hathor, [in the] month".

Subheading: Row One, Symbol Four:

Hieroglyph V16 / rotated / simplified / Linear A symbol L92
As we have seen previously, this symbol represents the first hieroglyph in the word:

s3 phyle (of priests), company, regiment (of troops), troop (of animals) [noun] V16 - A1 - Z2

This symbol therefore means "[to the] phyle (of priests)".

Category One: Row One, Symbol Five:

Hieroglyph M20 ꧁꧁꧁ / rotated ꧁꧁꧁ / simplified / Linear A symbol L82 ⍓
As we saw on Tablet HT 19, this symbol represents the first hieroglyph on the word:

꧁꧁꧁ 🦅 🐂 *sḥtyw* cattle [noun - ani.] M20 - G4 - E1 - N33A

As we have previously discussed, while this word has the general meaning of "cattle", we can infer it has the specific meaning of "goats" here. This is followed by a count of 38.

Category Two: Row Two, Symbols One and Two:

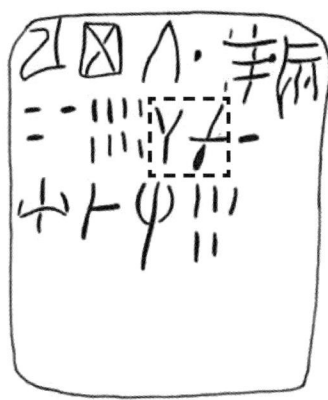

Hieroglyph V28 ⟨ / rotated ⟨ / simplified / Linear A symbol L31 Y
As we have seen previously, this symbol represents the first hieroglyph in the word:

330   The Decipherment of Linear A

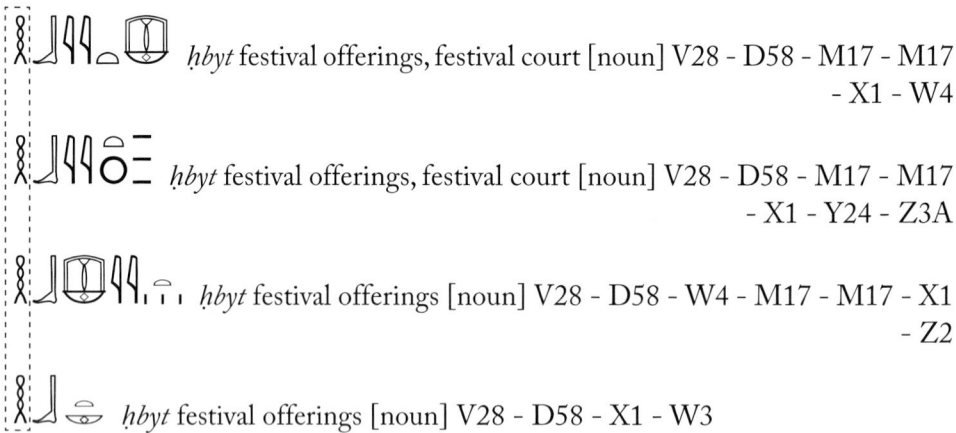

ḥbyt festival offerings, festival court [noun] V28 - D58 - M17 - M17 - X1 - W4

ḥbyt festival offerings, festival court [noun] V28 - D58 - M17 - M17 - X1 - Y24 - Z3A

ḥbyt festival offerings [noun] V28 - D58 - W4 - M17 - M17 - X1 - Z2

ḥbyt festival offerings [noun] V28 - D58 - X1 - W3

Hieroglyph Z9 ✕ / (incorrectly) Linear A symbol L22 ✢
As we have seen previously, this symbol represents the first hieroglyph in the word:

wrt sacred cow, divine cow [noun - ani.] Z9 - D21 - E1

These two symbols therefore mean "[from the] festival offerings, sacred cows". They are followed by a count of 10. Again, the number of cows does not agree to the one month recorded on Tablet HT 118, so this tablet does not relate to the final month of the year as portrayed on that tablet.

Category Three: Row Three, Symbols One to Three:

Hieroglyph R1 / simplified / Linear A symbol L57
As we have seen previously, this symbol represents the last hieroglyph in the word:

wdḥw offering table, Offerings [noun - furn.] G43 - D46 - V28 - G43 - R1

Hieroglyph T14 ⸯ replaced by AA26 (or J26) 𓏺 / reversed 𓏺 / Linear A symbol L30 𐘀

As we have seen previously, this symbol represents the (replaced) first hieroglyph in the word:

ꜥwt small cattle, goats, herds [noun - ani.] T14

ꜥwt small cattle, herds, flocks, goats [noun - ani.] T14 - G43 - E28 - Z2

ꜥwt small cattle, herds, flocks, goats [noun - ani.] T14 - G43 - X1 - E1 - Z2

ꜥwt small cattle, herds, flocks, goats [noun - ani.] T14 - G43 - X1 - E8 - Z2

ꜥwt small cattle, herds, flocks, goats [noun - ani.] T14 - Z7 - X1 - E28 - F27 - Z3A

ꜥwt small cattle, herds, flocks, goats [noun - ani.] T14 - Z7 - X1 - E28 - Z2

ꜥwt small cattle, herds, flocks, goats [noun - ani.] T14 - Z7 - X1 - Z5 - Z2

As noted, Tablet HT 17 and Tablet HT 19 are clearly related and, while their headings, subheadings, and first two categories are identical, the third category, which can reasonably be expected to represent the same item being recorded on both tablets (although not the same source of that item), is not. In fact, while the same Middle Egyptian word is used on each, namely ꜥwt, meaning "small cattle", on this tablet it is abbreviated to a symbol representing its (replaced) first hieroglyph, represented by Linear A symbol L30, whereas on Tablet HT 19 it was abbreviated to a symbol representing its final two hieroglyphs in one iteration of its spelling, Hieroglyphs Z5 - Z2 (highlighted in the dashed circle above), represented by Linear A symbol L51. The nature of this shorthand method is that, when used by different scribes, the same word might be abbreviated differently. As noted a number of times now, to refer again to the simplistic example in Chapter Three, A can stand for avocado as easily as O can stand for avocado (the choice of the scribe being driven, amongst other things, by what he was used to writing, not necessarily just his immediate need). The meaning here, as on Tablet HT 19, is, therefore, "small cattle".

As also noted we can, therefore, additionally infer that Tablet HT 19 and Tablet HT 17 were incised by different scribes, presumably because the phyle (of priests) on duty changed between Tablet HT 19 being incised and Tablet HT 17 being incised when one month ended and the next began, and the scribe from each phyle allocated to recording this information had changed.

Hieroglyphs D28 - Z1 ⊔ / simplified / modified / Linear A symbol L54 Ψ
As we have seen previously, this symbol represents the word:

⊔ *k3w* food, bounty [noun - food] D28 - Z1

These three symbols therefore mean "[from the] offerings, small cattle [for] food". There is then a count of 5.

We can now, therefore, translate the tablet in full:

Row One	Heading: Subheading: Category One:	[From the] Goddess Hathor, [in the] month [to the] phyle (of priests) Cattle (goats) – 38
Row Two	Category Two:	[From the] festival offerings, sacred cows – 10
Row Three	Category Three:	[From the] offerings, small cattle [for] food – 5

2. Inventories

There are three types of inventory records in the Hagia Triada corpus (at least in so far as it is translated in this work). All concern animals and their fodder. They are:

a) The inventory (animals and some fodder) belonging to the temple and held "on hand" i.e. at or near the Hagia Triada temple.
b) The inventory (animals and some fodder) belonging to the temple but with the herdsmen, being grazed on the margins of land of the temple's vineyard, or in a storehouse / barn.
c) The inventory (animals and fodder) belonging to the temple but held at nearby Phaistos.

We shall consider these in turn.

2(a). Inventory (animals and some fodder) belonging to the temple and held "on hand"

Tablet HT 7A

This tablet records inventory (animals and some fodder) presumably at the beginning of the stated month, including certain future anticipated receipts (which presumably are planned receipts from the temple's herds held remotely). This inventory was held "on hand" (i.e close by, in and around the Hagia Triada temple) and the animals in question included bulls and rams only.

Heading: Row One, Symbols One and Two:

Hieroglyph Z4B - Z4B - W24 ⲞΞ/ modified (dashes inside circle) / Linear A symbol L91 ⊙

As set out in Appendix 6, this symbol, representing Hieroglyphs Z4B - Z4B - W24, represents the ordinal:

Ξ Ⲟ *fdnw* fourth Z4B - Z4B - W24

334   The Decipherment of Linear A

Hieroglyph N11 ⌒ / modified / Linear A symbol L78 ∧
As we have seen previously, this symbol represents the word:

⌒ *3bd* month [noun] N11

The first two symbols of this tablet therefore mean "[in the] fourth month".

Subheading One: Row One, Symbol Three:

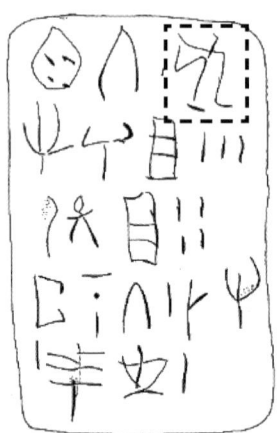

Hieroglyph A59 / reversed / simplified / Linear A symbol L99
As we have seen previously, this symbol represents the first hieroglyph in the word:

mniw herdsmen [plural noun - title] A59 - M17 - M17 - Z7 - D40 - A1 - Z2

This symbol therefore means "[from the] herdsmen".

The Translations   335

Category One: Row Two, Symbols One to Three:

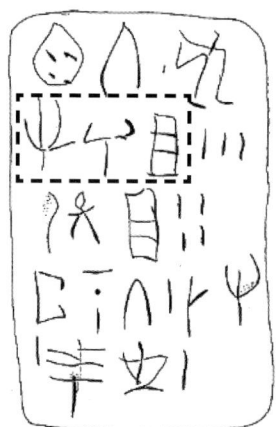

Hieroglyph D46 ▱ / rotated / simplified / Linear A symbol L100 Ψ
As we have seen previously, this symbol represented the first hieroglyph in the word:

drpw offerings, provisions, meal, sustenance [noun - food] D46 - D21 - Q3 - Z7 - N37 - Z2

Hieroglyphs D28 - Z1 / simplified / modified / Linear A symbol L55
As we have seen previously, this symbol represents Hieroglyphs D28 - Z1. Here, this symbol represents the first hieroglyphs in the word:

k3 bull [noun - ani.] D28 - Z1 - E1

Hieroglyph O11 / simplified / Linear A symbol L32
Linear A symbol L32 is a straightforward simplified representation of Hieroglyph O11. Here it represents the first hieroglyph in the word:

ḥ palace, temple, cabin [noun - arch.] O11

ḥ palace, temple, cabin [noun - arch.] O11 - D36 - O1

ḥ palace, temple, cabin [noun - arch.] O11 - D36 - X1 - O1

ḥ palace, temple, cabin [noun - arch.] O11 - G36 - D21 - O1

ḥ palace, temple, cabin [noun - arch.] O11 - O1

ḥ palace, temple, cabin [noun - arch.] O11 - Z1 - D36 - O1 - G7

These three symbols therefore mean "provisions [of] bulls [in the] temple". They are followed by a count of 3.

336   The Decipherment of Linear A

Category Two: Row Three, Symbols One and Two:

Hieroglyph A24 / modified / simplified / Linear A symbol L93
As we have seen previously, this symbol represents the last hieroglyph in the word:

smꜣ take part in, receive [verb] F36 - G1 - G17 - Z7 - Z4 - Y1
                                                              - A24

Hieroglyph O11 / simplified / Linear A symbol L32
As we have seen previously, this symbol represents the first hieroglyph in the word:

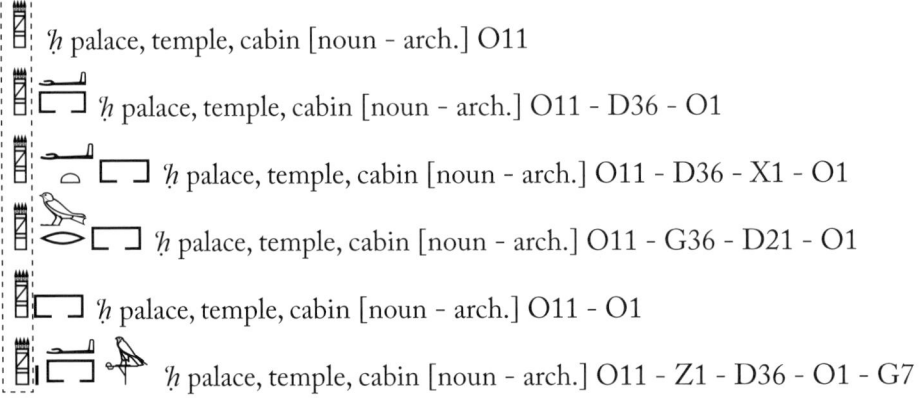

ḥ palace, temple, cabin [noun - arch.] O11

ḥ palace, temple, cabin [noun - arch.] O11 - D36 - O1

ḥ palace, temple, cabin [noun - arch.] O11 - D36 - X1 - O1

ḥ palace, temple, cabin [noun - arch.] O11 - G36 - D21 - O1

ḥ palace, temple, cabin [noun - arch.] O11 - O1

ḥ palace, temple, cabin [noun - arch.] O11 - Z1 - D36 - O1 - G7

These two symbols therefore mean "to [be] receive[d by the] temple". They are followed by a count of 4. Again, these are from the herdsmen and, again, following on from the previous category given that no other animal is mentioned, these were, presumably, bulls.

The Translations   337

Subheading Two: Row Four, Symbols One:

Hieroglyph O1 ⊏⊐/ rotated ⊔/ Linear A symbol L74 ⊔
As we have seen previously, this symbol represents the last hieroglyph in the word(s):

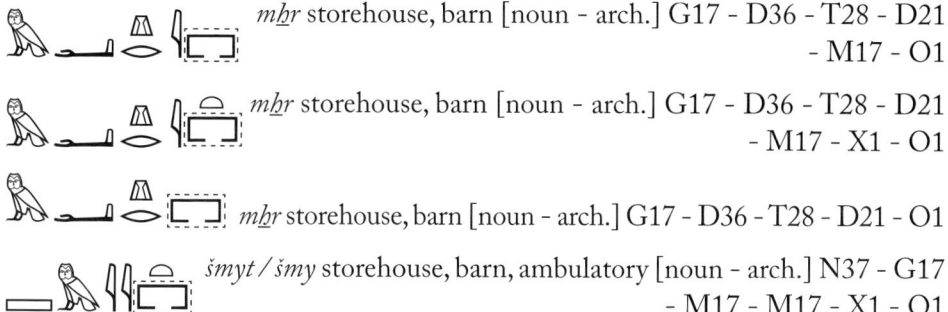

mḫr storehouse, barn [noun - arch.] G17 - D36 - T28 - D21
 - M17 - O1

mḫr storehouse, barn [noun - arch.] G17 - D36 - T28 - D21
 - M17 - X1 - O1

mḫr storehouse, barn [noun - arch.] G17 - D36 - T28 - D21 - O1

šmyt / šmy storehouse, barn, ambulatory [noun - arch.] N37 - G17
 - M17 - M17 - X1 - O1

This symbol therefore means "[in the] storehouse / barn". In reality, the way this scribe has written this tablet, while this probably was not a discrete subheading and instead formed part of the description of Category Four which follows, it also then applied, by implication, to the categories thereafter but was not explicitly repeated. For the convenience of the reader, however, it has been transcribed as a separate subheading.

338   The Decipherment of Linear A

Category Four: Row Four, Symbols Two and Three:

Hieroglyphs N5 - Z1 ☉/ simplified / modified / Linear A symbol L26
As we have seen previously, Linear A symbol L26 represents Hieroglyphs N5 - Z1. Here it represents the last hieroglyphs in the word:

 ḫrt ꜣbd daily needs [noun] T28 - D21 - X1 - O4 - D21 - G43 - N5 - Z1

Hieroglyph N11 ⌒ / modified / Linear A symbol L78 ∧
As we have seen previously, this symbol represents the word:

⌒ ꜣbd month [noun] N11

These two symbols therefore mean "[for] daily needs [in the] month". They are followed by a count of 1. As no different type of animal has been mentioned since Category One, these were, presumably, (still) bulls.

The Translations 339

Category Four: Row Four, Symbols Four and Five:

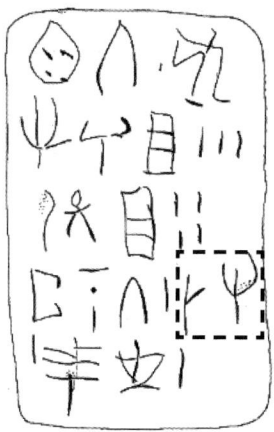

<u>Hieroglyph T14</u> ⎫ replaced by AA26 (or J26) ⋎ / reversed ⋏ / Linear A symbol L30 ⊦
As we have seen previously, this symbol represents the world:

⎫ ꜥwt small cattle, goats, herds [noun - ani.] T14

⎫ 🐐 ℐℐℐ ꜥwt small cattle, herds, flocks, goats [noun - ani.] T14 - G43 - E28 - Z2

⎫ ◯ 🐐 ℐℐℐ ꜥwt small cattle, herds, flocks, goats [noun - ani.] T14 - G43 - X1
    - E1 - Z2

⎫ ◯ 🐐 ℐℐℐ ꜥwt small cattle, herds, flocks, goats [noun - ani.] T14 - G43 - X1
    - E8 - Z2

⎫ 🐐 ℷ ꜥwt small cattle, herds, flocks, goats [noun - ani.] T14 - Z7 - X1 - E28
    - F27 - Z3A

⎫ 🐐 ℐℐℐ ꜥwt small cattle, herds, flocks, goats [noun - ani.] T14 - Z7 - X1 - E28
    - Z2

⎫ \ ℐℐℐ ꜥwt small cattle, herds, flocks, goats [noun - ani.] T14 - Z7 - X1 - Z5 - Z2

<u>Hieroglyphs D28 - Z1</u> ⋃ / simplified / Linear A symbol L54 ψ
As we have seen previously, this symbol represents Hieroglyphs D28 - Z1. As we have also seen previously, Linear A symbol L55 (which was used in the second line of this tablet) also represents Hieroglyphs D28 - Z1. As we saw on Tablet HT 2, when both symbols appeared, both symbols represented the same hieroglyphs but they represented different words (in the same way that two different styles of Linear A symbol L52, both representing Hieroglyph S34, represented words with different meanings on Tablet

340   The Decipherment of Linear A

HT 86A). Here, therefore, while representing the same hieroglyphs, Linear A symbol L54 has a different meaning to the word represented by Linear A symbol L55. In fact, this symbol represents the word:

k3w food, bounty [noun - food] D28 - Z1

These two symbols therefore mean "small cattle [for] food". They are followed by a count of 1. Again, as no different type of animal has been mentioned since Category One, these were presumably (young) bulls.

Category Five: Row Five, Symbols One and Two:

Hieroglyph V16 / rotated / simplified / Linear A symbol L92
As we have seen previously, this symbol represents the first hieroglyph in the word:

s3 phyle (of priests), company, regiment (of troops), troop (of animals) [noun]
V16 - A1 - Z2

Hieroglyph R7 / modified / Linear A symbol L6
As we have seen previously, this symbol represents the first hieroglyph in the word:

b3 sacred ram, ram, Ba, soul [noun - ani.] R7 - E10

These two symbols therefore mean "[for the] phyle (of priests), rams". They are followed by a count of 1.

The Translations   341

Table HT 7B

Category Six: Row One, Symbols One to Three:

Hieroglyph N13 ✲ / Linear A symbol L79 ⋔

Here, as set out further in the excursus below, Linear A symbol represents Hieroglyph N13. This is a rarely used hieroglyph (it can represent a day half way through the month, or the festival of the half month). Given that no specific recipient is noted (and only when a specific distribution on a specific day is noted in the corpus, the specific recipient is noted or inferred too e.g. on Tablet HT 86A, where a payment of goats was to be made to the corvee / labourers on New Year's Day), the symbol most likely represents the first hieroglyph in the word:

✲ *smdt / md dint* festival of the half month (15th day) [noun] N13

The rarity of this hieroglyph in Middle Egyptian is further evidence that we are correct to view Linear A as Middle Egyptian written in shorthand using hieroglyphs. As with Linear A symbol L43 representing Hieroglyph O10, it is inconceivable that this rarely used hieroglyph, Hieroglyph N13, represented here by Linear A symbol L79, which is only used in four words in Middle Egyptian (well, two words each spelled two different ways), meaning either a date in the Egyptian calendar or an Egyptian festival on that day, could have been used by anyone other than the Egyptians.

342 The Decipherment of Linear A

Excursus 5.5: The many Linear A representations of Hieroglyph N13

Hieroglyph N13 appears to have caused some difficulty for the scribes and it appears in a number of guises in the Linear A script. Hieroglyph N13 is, itself, a combination of two hieroglyphs:

Hieroglyph N11 ⌒
Hieroglyph N14 ✶

The arc of Hieroglyph N11 was written from the lefthand extremity of the point of the star, to the topmost extremity of the point of the star to create:

Hieroglyph N13 ✣

In clay, this has proved difficult for the scribe resulting, firstly, in Linear A symbol L79:

Linear A symbol L79 ⑂

The scribes clearly had difficulty writing this symbol, as we can see from its varying quality in the corpus, resulting in another iteration, Linear A symbol L48:

Linear A symbol L48 ⑃

To solve this problem, a solution we have seen elsewhere in the corpus was also adopted. As we have seen, the five-pointed star of Hieroglyph N14 was represented in the corpus by Linear A symbol L22, a four-pointed star:

Linear A symbol L22 +

When Hieroglyph N11 was added to this simplified representation of Hieroglyph N14 in the same manner as before, joining the lefthand extremity of the (now) cross, to the topmost extremity of the (now) cross, Linear A symbol L48' resulted:

Linear A symbol L48' ⌐+

This appears on Tablet HT 38 (which is broken and, therefore, not translated in this work):

Thus, Linear A symbol L48, Linear A symbol L48', and Linear A symbol L79 are all representations of the same hieroglyph, Hieroglyph N13.

The Translations 343

<u>Hieroglyph R7 ⛉ / modified / Linear A symbol L6 ⛉</u>
As we have seen previously, this symbol represents the first hieroglyph in the word:

⛉ 🐏 *bꜣ* sacred ram, ram, Ba, soul [noun - ani.] R7 - E10

<u>Hieroglyph AA8 (or J8) ⊢┼⊣ / rotated Ŧ / Linear A symbol L61 Ŧ</u>
As we have seen previously, this symbol represents the first hieroglyph in the word:

⊢┼⊣ *kn* first quality, best quality [noun] J8 - N35 - Y1

These three symbols therefore mean "[for the] festival of the half month, rams [of the] best quality". They are followed by a count of 1. Again, this animal is in the storehouse / barn.

<u>Subheading Three: Row Two, Symbols One and Two</u>

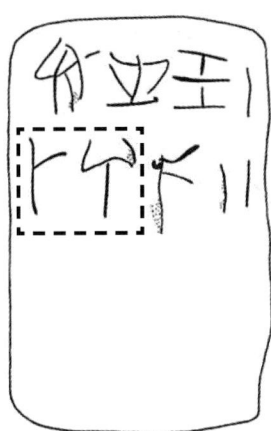

<u>Hieroglyph T14 ╲ replaced by AA26 (or J26) Ÿ / reversed ↱ / Linear A symbol L30 ↱</u>
As we have seen previously, this symbol represents the first hieroglyph in the words:

╲ *'wt* small cattle, goats, herds [noun - ani.] T14

╲🐏 I I *'wt* small cattle, herds, flocks, goats [noun - ani.] T14 - G43 - E28 - Z2

╲◯🐂 I I I *'wt* small cattle, herds, flocks, goats [noun - ani.] T14 - G43 - X1
                                                    - E1 - Z2

╲◯🐂 I I I *'wt* small cattle, herds, flocks, goats [noun - ani.] T14 - G43 - X1
                                                    - E8 - Z2

╲ ◌🐏 ⫶ *'wt* small cattle, herds, flocks, goats [noun - ani.] T14 - Z7 - X1 - E28
                                                    - F27 - Z3A

344   The Decipherment of Linear A

⟨image⟩ '*wt* small cattle, herds, flocks, goats [noun - ani.] T14 - Z7 - X1 - E28 - Z2

⟨image⟩ '*wt* small cattle, herds, flocks, goats [noun - ani.] T14 - Z7 - X1 - Z5 - Z2

Hieroglyphs D28 - Z1 ⨆ / simplified / modified / Linear A symbol L55 Y
As we have seen previously, this symbol represents the word:

⨆ *k3w* food, bounty [noun - food] D28 - Z1

These two symbols therefore mean "[for the] small cattle, [for] food".

It is interesting to note that Linear A symbol L55 is used to represent this word, rather than Linear A symbol L54 (as it was on the front of the tablet). On the front of this tablet, as on Tablet HT 2, when both symbols appeared, Linear A symbol L55 appeared first and Linear A symbol L54 appeared second. Given that Linear A symbol L55 was the more correct representation of the Hieroglyphs D28 - Z1, perhaps it was the scribes' intention to use this first, then use the less correct representation of Linear A symbol L54 afterwards, and that order began again each time a new side of a tablet was started, irrespective of prior use on the other side of the tablet?

It is also interesting to note that on this tablet, here on the back (B) and previously front (A), we have the same two symbols used: here, in Subheading Three, meaning "[for the] small cattle, [for] food", and in Category Four, where they meant "small cattle [for] food". Because of their different contexts (subheading or category description), we can be certain that they have different meanings despite the same symbols appearing. The different meanings would, of course, be clear if the Middle Egyptian grammar and vocabulary were fully represented, but because this is shorthand, they are not.

Category Seven: Row Two, Symbol Three:

Hieroglyph T19 / reversed / simplified / Linear A symbol L33

Linear A symbol L33 is a simplified representation of reversed Hieroglyph T19. Here it represents the last hieroglyph in the word:

wšm ear of corn, awn [noun - flora] G43 - N37 - G17 - T19

This symbol therefore means "ears of corn". This is followed by a count of 2. The units of measure are not given.

We are now in a position to translate the tablet as a whole:

Side A		
Row One	Heading: Subheading One:	[In the] fourth month [From the] herdsmen
Row Two	Category One:	Provisions [of] bulls [in the] temple – 3
Row Three	Category Two:	To [be] receive[d] [by the] temple – 4
Row Four	Subheading Two: Category Three: Category Four:	[In the] storehouse / barn [For] daily needs [in the] month – 1 (bull?) Small cattle [for] food – 1 ((young) bull?)
Row Five	Category Five:	[For the] phyle (of priests), rams – 1

Side B		
Row One	Category Six:	[For the] festival of the half month, rams [of the] best quality – 1
Row Two	Subheading Three: Category Seven:	[For the] small cattle, [for] food Ears of corn – 2

346 The Decipherment of Linear A

<u>2(b). Inventory (animals and some fodder) belonging to the temple held by the herdsmen, grazed on the margin of the temple's vineyard, and in the storehouse / barn</u>

Tablet HT 120
This tablet records the location of temple's cattle and livestock, away from the temple itself, in the fourth month of the season and final month of the year.

<u>Heading: Row One, Symbols One to Three:</u>

<u>Hieroglyph T14) replaced by AA26 (or J26) ↑ / reversed ↑ / Linear A symbol L30 ⊢</u>
As we have seen previously, this symbol represents the first hieroglyph in the word:

'wt small cattle, goats, herds [noun - ani.] T14

'wt small cattle, herds, flocks, goats [noun - ani.] T14 - G43 - E28 - Z2

'wt small cattle, herds, flocks, goats [noun - ani.] T14 - G43 - X1
 - E1 - Z2

'wt small cattle, herds, flocks, goats [noun - ani.] T14 - G43 - X1
 - E8 - Z2

'wt small cattle, herds, flocks, goats [noun - ani.] T14 - Z7 - X1 - E28
 - F27 - Z3A

'wt small cattle, herds, flocks, goats [noun - ani.] T14 - Z7 - X1 - E28
 - Z2

'wt small cattle, herds, flocks, goats [noun - ani.] T14 - Z7 - X1 - Z5 - Z2

Hieroglyph Z4B - Z4B - W24 ⟨Z4B-Z4B-W24⟩ / modified (dashes inside circle as dots) / Linear A symbol L91 ⟨L91⟩

As set out in Appendix 6, this symbol, representing Hieroglyphs Z4B - Z4B - W24, represents the ordinal:

⟨Z4B-Z4B-W24⟩ *fdnw* fourth Z4B - Z4B - W24

Although the sketch diagram above appears to show five dots in the circle of this symbol, Godart & Olivier's transcription of the tablet (correctly) includes only four.

Hieroglyph I12 ⟨I12⟩ / simplified / Linear A symbol L53 ⟨L53⟩

As we have seen previously, this symbol represents the last hieroglyph in the word:

⟨R8-D21-X1-I12⟩ *nṯrt* goddess [noun - div.] R8 - D21 - X1 - I12

⟨R8-D21-X1-J2-I12⟩ *nṯrt* goddess [noun - div.] R8 - D21 - X1 - J2 - I12

⟨R8-D21-X1-Z5-I12⟩ *nṯrt* goddess [noun - div.] R8 - D21 - X1 - Z5 - I12

⟨R8-X1-D21-M17-M17-X1-J2-I12⟩ *nṯrt* goddess [noun - div.] R8 - X1 - D21 - M17 - M17 - X1 - J2 - I12

⟨R8-X1-D21-X1-I12⟩ *nṯrt* goddess [noun - div.] R8 - X1 - D21 - X1 - I12

⟨R8-X1-D21-X1-J2-I12⟩ *nṯrt* goddess [noun - div.] R8 - X1 - D21 - X1 - J2 - I12

⟨R8-X1-I12⟩ *nṯrt* goddess [noun - div.] R8 - X1 - I12

⟨R8-X1-J2-I12⟩ *nṯrt* goddess [noun - div.] R8 - X1 - J2 - I12

⟨R8-Z5-Z5-Z5-I12⟩ *nṯrt* goddess [noun – div.] R8 - Z5 - Z5 - Z5 - I12

These three symbols therefore mean "[in the] herd [in the] fourth [month], [for the] goddess".

348   The Decipherment of Linear A

Subheading One: Row One, Symbol Four and Five:

Hieroglyph T14 ⎱ replaced by AA26 (or J26) ⎱ / reversed ⎱ / Linear A symbol L30 ⎱
As we have seen previously, this symbol represents the (replaced) first hieroglyph in the word:

  ʿwt small cattle, goats, herds [noun - ani.] T14

  ʿwt small cattle, herds, flocks, goats [noun - ani.] T14 - G43 - E28 - Z2

  ʿwt small cattle, herds, flocks, goats [noun - ani.] T14 - G43 - X1
  - E1 - Z2

  ʿwt small cattle, herds, flocks, goats [noun - ani.] T14 - G43 - X1
  - E8 - Z2

  ʿwt small cattle, herds, flocks, goats [noun - ani.] T14 - Z7 - X1 - E28
  - F27 - Z3A

  ʿwt small cattle, herds, flocks, goats [noun - ani.] T14 - Z7 - X1 - E28
  - Z2

  ʿwt small cattle, herds, flocks, goats [noun - ani.] T14 - Z7 - X1 - Z5 - Z2

Hieroglyph A24 / simplified / modified / Linear A symbol L84/48
As we have seen previously, this symbol represents the last hieroglyph (or, in one instance, first hieroglyph) in the word:

  mniw herdsman [noun - title] A24 - G43 - D40

  mniw herdsman, shepherd [noun - title] A33 - G1 - Z5
  - Z5 - Z5 - Z5 - Z5 - A24

The Translations   349

𓀠 𓅃 𓂝 𓀠 *mniw* herdsman [noun - title] A33 - G1 - Z7 - Y1 - A24

𓀠 𓇋 𓏲 𓀠 *mniw* herdsman [noun - title] A33 - M17 - Z7 - A24

𓀠 𓏭 𓏭 𓏭 𓀠 *mniw* herdsman [noun – title] A33 - Z5 - Z5 - Z5 - A24

joined to the male = symbol, which represents the last hieroglyph in the word:

𓂡 𓅓 𓏏 𓏭 *ḥꜣwty* warrior, male, man [noun] D34 - G45 - X1 - Z4

These two symbols therefore mean "[in the] herd [with the] herdsmen".

<u>Category One: Row Two, Symbols One to Three:</u>

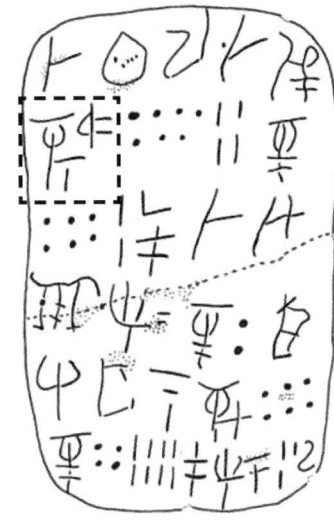

<u>Hieroglyph F27</u> 𓄜/ partially rotated / simplified / modified / Linear A symbol L42 𐘌
As we have seen previously, this symbol represents the last hieroglyph in the word:

𓂋 𓃝 𓄜 *ꜥr* goat [noun - ani.] D36 - D21 - E31 - F27

Subscript <u>Hieroglyph S34</u> 𓋹/ modifed (loop removed) / Linear A symbol L52 𐘚
(without sidebars)
This symbol is only used with non-male (i.e. female) animals on this tablet. From this, we can infer that it indicates that the animals in question were female and the symbol, therefore, represents the first hieroglyph in the word:

350   The Decipherment of Linear A

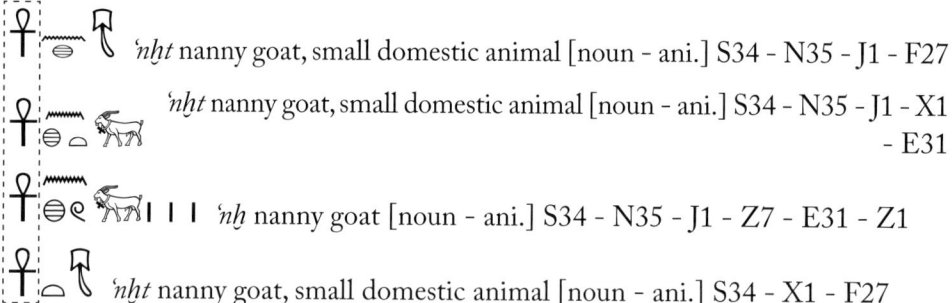

'nḫt nanny goat, small domestic animal [noun - ani.] S34 - N35 - J1 - F27

'nḫt nanny goat, small domestic animal [noun - ani.] S34 - N35 - J1 - X1 - E31

'nḫ nanny goat [noun - ani.] S34 - N35 - J1 - Z7 - E31 - Z1

'nḫt nanny goat, small domestic animal [noun - ani.] S34 - X1 - F27

Hieroglyph V19 / rotated / Linear A symbol L47
As we have seen previously, this symbol represents the word:

mdt byre, cow shed, pen, enclosure [noun - arch.] V19

These symbols therefore mean "goats (nanny goats) [in the] enclosure". They are followed by a count of 74.

Category Two: Row Two, Symbol Four:

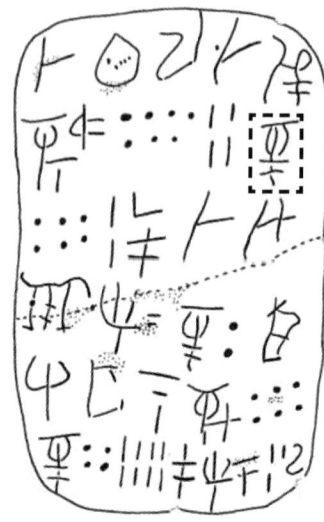

Hieroglyph F27 + Hieroglyph Z4 (rotated) / partially rotated / simplified / modified / Linear A symbol L42 + male = symbol

As we have seen previously, this symbol represents the joined last hieroglyph in the words:

'r goat [noun - ani.] D36 - D21 - E31 - F27

joined to the male = symbol, which represents the last hieroglyph in the word:

ḥȝwty warrior, male, man [noun] D34 - G45 - X1 - Z4

This symbol therefore means "male goats". This is followed by a count of 62½. The symbol for half (i.e. Linear A fraction symbol J) is on top of a symbol for zero (or, as we saw on Tablet HT 123A, a zero value of fraction units) (i.e. Linear A symbol L2 / fraction symbol A). This seems slighlty unnecessary and, presumably, was as much to act as a space filer beneath Linear A fraction symbol J as anything else.

That half a male goat is recorded is, however, more interesting. This animal, not being in a storehouse / barn, cannot have been part consumed. The implication must be, therefore, that the animal was partly owned by the temple and partly owned by another party (most likely one or a number of the herdsmen). This mirrors Linear B tablet Mc 5098, where half an animal was owed to the temple at Knossos as a result of the tithe-like tax payable to it during the Mycenaean period (the tablet records an odd number of horns); here, again, only half an animal was owned by the temple. We, of course, cannot tell how many animals were jointly rather than wholly owned by the temple, but it would presumably be unlikely to have been just one.

<u>Subheading Two: Row Three, Symbols One and Two, and Row</u>

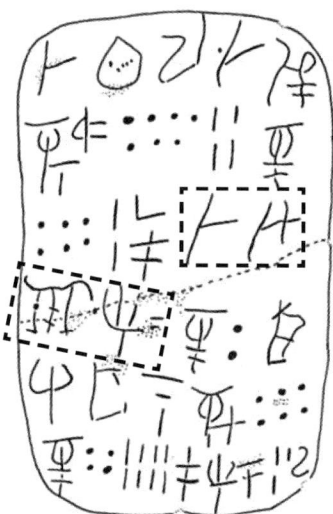

<u>Hieroglyph T14 replaced by AA26 (or J26) / reversed / Linear A symbol L30</u>
As we have seen previously, this symbol represents the (replaced) first hieroglyph in the word:

'wt small cattle, goats, herds [noun - ani.] T14

'wt small cattle, herds, flocks, goats [noun - ani.] T14 - G43 - E28 - Z2

'wt small cattle, herds, flocks, goats [noun - ani.] T14 - G43 - X1 - E1 - Z2

'wt small cattle, herds, flocks, goats [noun - ani.] T14 - G43 - X1 - E8 - Z2

'wt small cattle, herds, flocks, goats [noun - ani.] T14 - Z7 - X1 - E28 - F27 - Z3A

'wt small cattle, herds, flocks, goats [noun - ani.] T14 - Z7 - X1 - E28 - Z2

'wt small cattle, herds, flocks, goats [noun - ani.] T14 - Z7 - X1 - Z5 - Z2

Hieroglyph V4 / reversed / simplified / (incorrectly) Linear A symbol L97

As we saw previously on Tablet HT 91, this Linear A symbol, which has (incorrectly) been identified as Linear A symbol L97, represents Hieroglyph V4. This can be seen more clearly in this instance as it is not joined to another symbol (as it was on Tablet HT 91).

Hieroglyph V4		Hieroglyph V4 (reversed)		Linear A symbol
	reversed →		simplified →	

The hieroglyph represents a lasso, which has been reversed and simplified. As we have seen previously, a common way that hieroglyphs were modified to become Linear A symbols, as was the case with Hieroglyph F35 when it became Linear A symbol L2 (and, indeed, as is the case with the next symbol on this tablet), is for a circle or oval feature on the hieroglyph (here, the noose of the lasso) to be replaced with a line (which this time is vertical). Curved lines being more difficult to incise in clay, the general loop of the rest of the lasso is then also straightened, to a joined vertical line, and horizontal line for the lasso knot, the latter of which then intersects with the vertical line that represents the lasso noose.

As we have seen previously, this symbol represents the last hieroglyph in the word:

iw3 ox, long horned cattle [noun - ani.] M17 - V4

While this word had the specific meaning of "oxen" on Tablet HT 91, here the word has the more general meaning of "long horned cattle" as it is used in a subheading under which the category of male goats is recorded, as we shall see.

The Translations 353

Hieroglyph M43 🍇 / simplified / Linear A symbol L120 ⵯ

The derivation of Linear A symbol L120 is best seen by a side-by-side comparison with the hieroglyph that it represents, Hieroglyph M43:

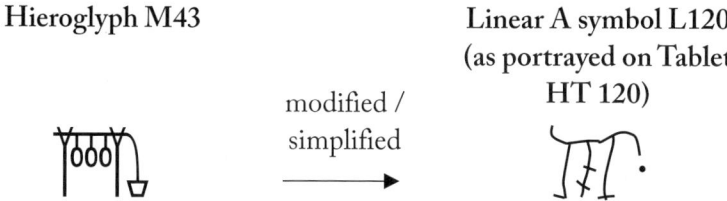

Hieroglyph M43

Linear A symbol L120
(as portrayed on Tablet HT 120)

modified / simplified

Hieroglyph M43 is a vine on props. It has been modified and simplified to become Linear A symbol L120, in that the ovals that the three bunches of grapes hanging from the cord between the props are modified to become two horizontal lines on one vertical line (i.e. in total, three lines) suspended from the cord (in a similar way that the oval on Hieroglyph F35 was simplified to become a horizontal line on Linear A symbol L2 or the lasso loop on Hieroglyph V4 was simplified to become a straight line on the Linear A symbol that represented it). The vessel or basket at the end of the vine is also simplified to become merely a dot.

As we have seen, animal husbandry complemented arable farming; in the case of viticulture, the prunings from the vines after harvest could be used for livestock feed and the livestock manure could fertilise the soil.[81] Here, therefore, this symbol represents the last hieroglyph in the word:

k3nw vineyard [noun] D28 - M43

Hieroglyph D46 / rotated / simplified / Linear A symbol L100

While previously we have seen that this symbol represents the first hieroglyph in the word:

drpw offerings, provisions, meal, sustenance [noun - food] D46 - D21 - Q3 - Z7 - N37 - Z2

here the symbol represents the first hieroglyph in the related verb:

drp offer to (god), feed (someone), present (dues), to make offerings [transitive verb] D46 - D21 - Q3 - D40

---

81. Ruth Palmer, "Bridging the Gap: the Continuity of Greek Agriculture from the Mycenaean to the Historical Period", in David W. Tandy (Ed.), *Prehistory and History: Ethnicity, Class and Political Economy* (Montreal: Black Rose Books, 2001), p51, citing Hamish Forbes, "The identification of pastoral sites within the context of estate-based agriculture in ancient Greece", *Annual of the British School at Athens*, 90(1995), p329, and Paul Halstead, "Counting sheep in Neolithic and Bronze Age Crete", in Ian Hodder (Ed.), *Pattern of the past: Studies in honour of David Clarke* (Cambridge: Cambridge University Press, 1981), pp314–315, 319

354   The Decipherment of Linear A

These four symbols therefore mean "[in the] herd [of] long horned cattle [in the] vineyard, being fed".

As we saw on Tablet HT 123A, the aristocratic vintners grazed their sheep on the margins of arable land next to their vines. Here, the implication is that the temple itself also had its own vineyard (religious institutions are, after all, rarely poor, and they are often staffed by aristocrats – as, indeed was the case in Egypt, as evidenced by the later Restoration Stela of Tutankhamun).

Category Three: Row Four, Symbol Three:

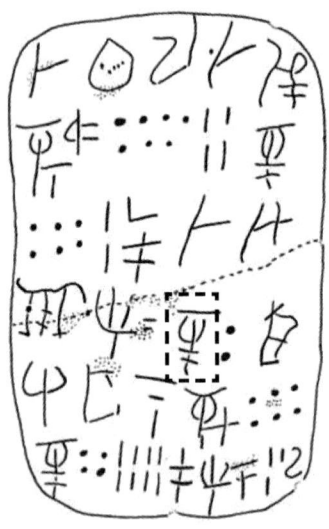

Hieroglyph F27 + Hieroglyph Z4 (rotated) / partially rotated / simplified / modified / Linear A symbol L42 + male = symbol

As we have seen previously, this symbol represents the joined last hieroglyphs of the word(s):

ꜥr goat [noun - ani.] D36 - D21 - E31 - F27

joined to the male = symbol, which represents the last hieroglyph in the word:

ḥꜣwty warrior, male, man [noun] D34 - G45 - X1 - Z4

This symbol therefore means "male goats". This is followed by a count of 20.

The Translations 355

Category Four: Row Four, Symbol Four:

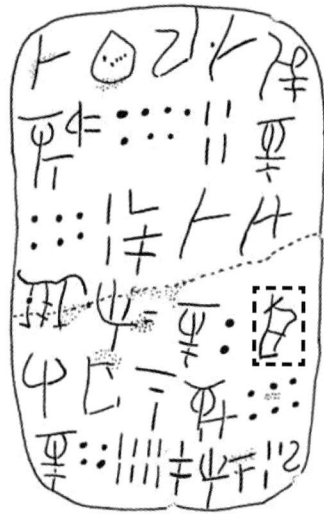

Hieroglyph G1 / simplified / Linear A symbol L103
As we have seen previously, this symbol represents the first hieroglyph in the word:

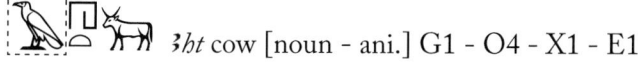

Missing from the sketch diagram of the tablet is a dot, a count mark for 10, that touches the bottom right of this symbol. This can be seen highlighted on an extract of a photograph of the tablet below:

          Extract of photograph of   **Extract of photograph of**
                 Tablet HT 120   **Tablet HT 120**
            from Godart & Olivier   **from Godart & Olivier**
                                                 (count mark highlighted)

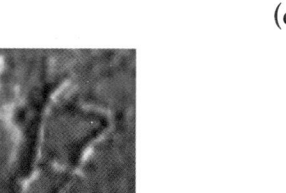 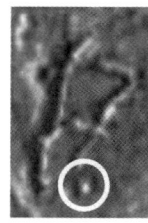

This symbol therefore means "cows". This is followed by a count of 10.

356　The Decipherment of Linear A

Category Five: Row Five, Symbol One:

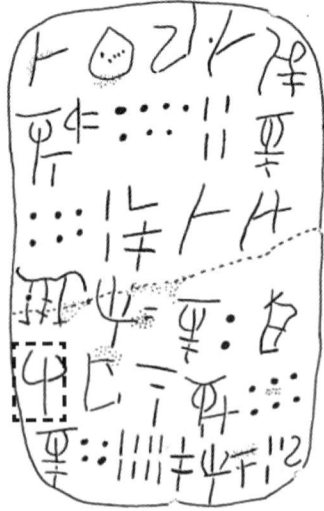

Hieroglyphs D28 - Z1 ⊍ / simplified / modified / Linear A symbol L54 Ψ
As we have seen previously, this symbol represents the word:

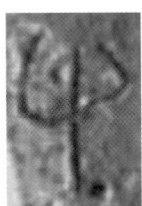 *k3* bull [noun – ani.] D28 - Z1 - E1

Again, missing from the sketch diagram of the tablet is a dot, a count mark for 10, that this time almost touches the bottom right of this symbol. This can be seen highlighted on an extract of a photograph of the tablet below:

| Extract of photograph of Tablet HT 120 from Godart & Olivier | Extract of photograph of Tablet HT 120 from Godart & Olivier (count mark highlighted) |

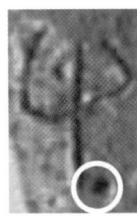

This symbol therefore means "bulls". This is followed by a count of 10.

The Translations 357

Subheading Three: Row Five, Symbols Two and Three:

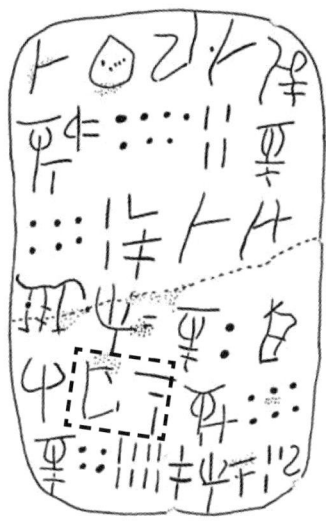

Hieroglyph O1 ⌑/ rotated ⌑/ Linear A symbol L74 ⌑

As we have seen previously, this symbol represents the last hieroglyph in the word(s):

mḫr storehouse, barn [noun - arch.] G17 - D36 - T28 - D21 - M17 - O1

mḫr storehouse, barn [noun - arch.] G17 - D36 - T28 - D21 - M17 - X1 - O1

mḫr storehouse, barn [noun - arch.] G17 - D36 - T28 - D21 - O1

šmyt / šmy storehouse, barn ambulatory [noun - arch.] N37 - G17 - M17 - M17 - X1 - O1

Hieroglyphs N5 - Z1 ⊙/ simplified / modified / Linear A symbol L26 |

As we have seen previously, this symbol represents the last hieroglyphs in the word:

m ꜣ wnwt now, immediately, at once G17 - X1 - G1 - E34 - N35 - W24 - X1 - N2 - N5 - Z1

m ꜣ wnwt now, immediately, at once G17 - X1 - G1 - E34 - N35 - W24 - X1 - N14 - N5 - Z1

m ꜣ wnwt now, immediately, at once G17 - X1 - G1 - Z4 - E34 - N35 - W24 - X1 - N14 - N5 - Z1

These four symbols therefore mean "[in the] storehouse / barn now".

358   The Decipherment of Linear A

Category Six: Row Five, Symbols Four and Five:

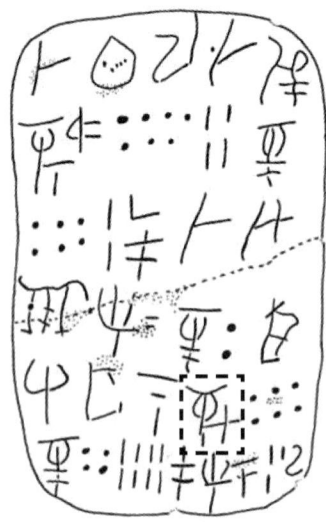

Hieroglyph F27 / partially rotated / simplified / Linear A symbol L42
As we have seen previously, this symbol repesents the last hieroglyph in the word:

ꜥr goat [noun - ani.] D36 - D21 - E31 - F27

Subscript Hieroglyph S34 / modifed (loop removed) / Linear A symbol L52
As we have seen previously, this symbol represents the first hieroglyph in the word:

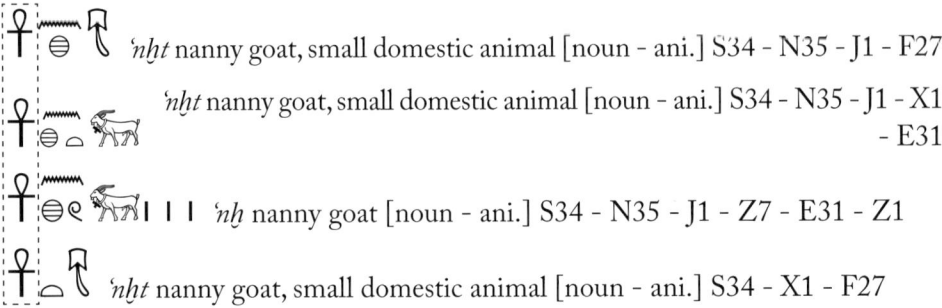

'nḫt nanny goat, small domestic animal [noun - ani.] S34 - N35 - J1 - F27

'nḫt nanny goat, small domestic animal [noun - ani.] S34 - N35 - J1 - X1 - E31

'nḫ nanny goat [noun - ani.] S34 - N35 - J1 - Z7 - E31 - Z1

'nḫt nanny goat, small domestic animal [noun - ani.] S34 - X1 - F27

These symbols therefore mean "goats (nanny goats)". They are followed by a count of 60.

Category Seven: Row Six, Symbol One:

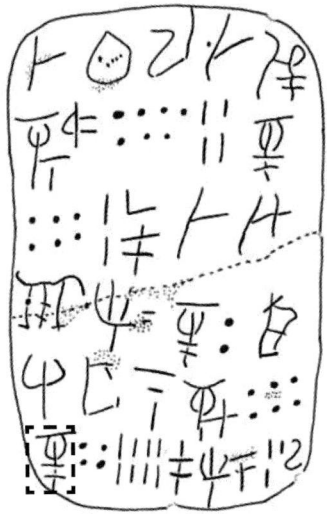

Hieroglyph F27 + Hieroglyph Z4 (rotated) / partially rotated / simplified / modified / Linear A symbol L42 + male = symbol

As we have seen previously, this symbol represents the joined last hieroglyphs of the words:

ꜥr goat [noun - ani.] D36 - D21 - E31 - F27

joined to the male = symbol, which represents the last hieroglyph in the word:

ḥꜣwty warrior, male, man [noun] D34 - G45 - X1 - Z4

Again, this symbol therefore means "male goats". This is followed by a count of 48. That count is also followed by a symbol for zero or, as we have seen, a zero value of fractional units (represented by Linear A symbol L2 / fraction symbol A). It would be superfluous unless, perhaps, it were to indicate that none of the animals were part owned.

360   The Decipherment of Linear A

<u>Category Eight: Row Five, Symbols Two and Three:</u>

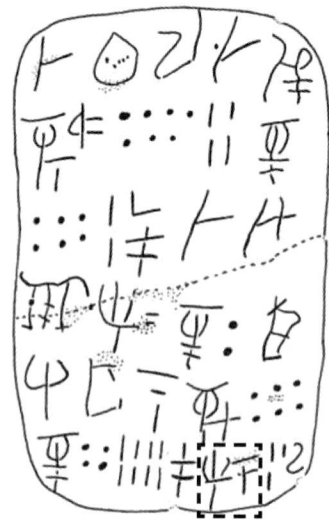

<u>Hieroglyph D46 ⌒ / rotated ⌒ / simplified / Linear A symbol L100 Ψ</u>
As we have seen previously, this symbol represents the first hieroglyph in the word:

⌒▯ℓ| | | *drpw* offerings, provisions, meal, sustenance [noun - food] D46 - D21
                                                          - Q3 - Z7 - N37 - Z2

<u>Hieroglyphs N5 - Z1 ⊙ / simplified / modified / Linear A symbol L26 ⎯|</u>
While this symbol appears to be Linear A symbol L39 (which is derived from Hieroglyphs W11 - Z1), it is, in fact, Linear A symbol L26 representing Hieroglyphs N5 - Z1. As we can see on the row above on this tablet, the scribe wrote the dot in Linear A symbol L26 as a horizontal line. As space has become more constrained towards the end of this tablet, he has not been able to form the symbol wholly accurately (the stem of the symbol crosses the horizontal line representing the dot above it and continues until it almost reaches to the top vertical line).

Having identified this symbol correctly, it again represents the last hieroglyphs in the word:

𓅓𓏏𓁹𓏺𓇳 *m ꜣ wnwt* now, immediately, at once G17 - X1 - G1 - E34
                                                          - N35 - W24 - X1 - N2 - N5 - Z1

𓅓𓏏𓁹𓏺𓇳 *m ꜣ wnwt* now, immediately, at once G17 - X1 - G1 - E34
                                                          - N35 - W24 - X1 - N14 - N5 - Z1

𓅓𓏏𓁹𓏺𓇳 *m ꜣ wnwt* now, immediately, at once G17 - X1 - G1 - Z4
                                                          - E34 - N35 - W24 - X1 - N14 - N5 - Z1

These two symbols therefore mean "provisions now", i.e. these are the provisions in the storehouse / barn when this tablet was written. This was presumably animal feed, although the units of measure are not given so we cannot say whether this was a large or small amount.

Linear A fraction symbol D: ᘒ

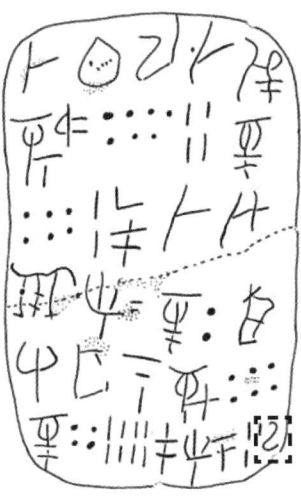

Given that we have so firmly established that Linear A is Middle Egyptian written in shorthand using hieroglyphs, even though for some fraction symbols an insufficient number of surviving tablets means we cannot mathematically prove their value, we can now infer that a symbol that was used in Middle Egyptian records in Egypt had the same value as when it was written in Linear A. As set out in Appendix 2, this symbol, Linear A fraction symbol D, is, therefore, one of a number of special symbols written in hieratic which has a value of ⅓. The count of the "provisions now" (as noted, presumably animal feed) is, therefore, 3⅓.

We are now in a position to translate the tablet in full:

Row One:	Heading:	[In the] herds, [in the] fourth [month], [for the] goddess
	Subheading One:	[In the] herd [with the] herdsmen
Row Two:	Category One:	Goats (nanny goats) [in the] enclosure – 74
	Category Two:	Male goats – 62½
Row Three:	Subheading Two:	[In the] herd [of] long horned cattle
Row Four:		[in the] vineyard, [being] fed
	Category Three:	Male goats – 20
	Category Four:	Cows – 10
Row Five:	Category Five:	Bulls – 10
	Subheading Three:	[In the] storehouse / barn now
	Category Six:	Goats (nanny goats) – 60
Row Six:	Category Seven:	Male goats – 48
	Category Eight:	Provisions now – 3⅓

362 The Decipherment of Linear A

2(c). Inventory (animals and fodder) belonging to the temple but held at nearby Phaistos

Table HT 21A
This tablet records an inventory of animals and fodder. The use of fractions of animals in this tablet indicates either that some have been slaughtered and part consumed (in contrast to the part animals recorded on the previous tablet where this could not be the case as they were still with the herd) or partial ownership.

While the tablet heading indicates the items in question are in the storehouse / barn at the city of Phaistos, the subheading reveals nonetheless that these are the temple's animals (and fodder) that were to be issued to the phyle (of priests). That the temple used a storehouse / barn in Phaistos is, perhaps, not surprising given that Phaistos is only a little over 2 miles from Hagia Triada and we might assume that some of its peasants, performing services for the temple, tended its flocks and herds.

Heading: Row One, Symbols One to Four:

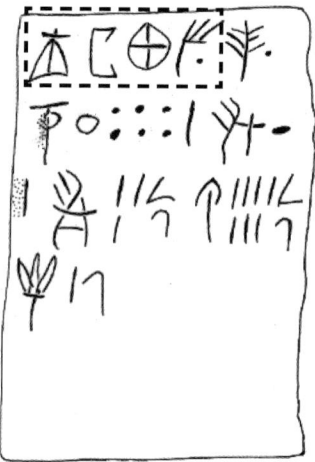

Hieroglyph AA6 (or J6) or S23 / simplified / modified / Linear A symbol L85
Brice and Godart & Olivier see this symbol to be Linear A symbol L56:

The reader will recall from Tablet HT 102 that this represented Hieroglyph F31. This is, however, not the symbol represented here. It is, instead, Linear A symbol L85 which represents a simplified and modified Hieroglyph AA6 (or J6) or S23 (which, as we have seen previously, Gardiner believed to be one and the same[82]). The symbol has, however,

---

82. A. H. Gardiner, *Egyptian Grammar: Being an Introduction to the Study of Hieroglyphs* (3rd Ed.)(Oxford: Griffith Institute, 1957), p539

been modified further so its appearance differs to that on Tablet HT 13, being compressed further in order to save space horizontally. This is demonstrated below:

	A	B	C	D	E
1. Tablet HT 21A			▲	▲	▲
2. Tablet HT 24B		▲	▲		
3. Linear A symbol L85 / Hieroglyph AA26 (or J26) or S32 (simplified)	▲▲	→ ▲ ←	→ ▲ ←		

On Row One in the table above:

- Column E: shows how the symbol appears on Tablet HT 21A in an extract from a photograph of this tablet;
- Column D: shows the symbol highlighted; and
- Column C: shows the symbol by itself with the background photograph removed.

On Row Three in the table above:

- Column A: shows Linear A symbol L85 (which, as we have seen, represents Hieroglyph AA6 (J6) / S23);
- Column B: shows Linear A symbol L85 with the triangles on that symbol moved closer together; in Row Two above, it shows how the symbol appears the first time it is used on Tablet HT 24B; and
- Column C: shows the triangles on Linear A symbol L85 now overlapping. Linear A symbol L85 is now the same as it appears on Tablet HT 21A (shown on Row One) and virtually the same as it appears the second time it is used on Tablet HT 24B (in Row Two above it).

Having identified the correct Linear A symbol and, therefore, the hieroglyph that it represents, as we have seen previously, this symbol represents the word or first hieroglyph in the word:

364   The Decipherment of Linear A

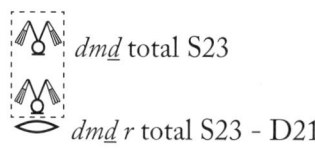 *dmd* total S23

dmd r total S23 - D21

Hieroglyph O1 ▭ / rotated ▯ / Linear A symbol L74 ▯
As we have seen previously, this symbol represents the last hieroglyph in the word(s):

mḫr storehouse, barn [noun - arch.] G17 - D36 - T28 - D21 - M17 - O1

mḫr storehouse, barn [noun - arch.] G17 - D36 - T28 - D21 - M17 - X1 - O1

mḫr storehouse, barn [noun - arch.] G17 - D36 - T28 - D21 - O1

šmyt / šmy storehouse, barn ambulatory [noun - arch.] N37 - G17 - M17 - M17 - X1 - O1

Hieroglyph O49 ⊗ / simplified / Linear A symbol L29 ⊕
As we have seen previously, this symbol represents the word:

niwt city, town [noun] O49

Hieroglyph D58 ⌋ / rotated ⌈ / modified / Linear A symbol L77 ⊔⊔⊔
This Linear A symbol is Hieroglyph D58 that has been rotated and then simplified by being written as a "stick" foot (in the same way that Linear A symbol L100 was a "stick" hand representation of a rotated Hieroglyph D46).

Place names are discussed in Appendix 4 and we know from the list of Aegean place names in the mortuary temple of Amenhotep III at Kom el-Hetan that the name for the city of Phaistos was written in hieroglyphs as:

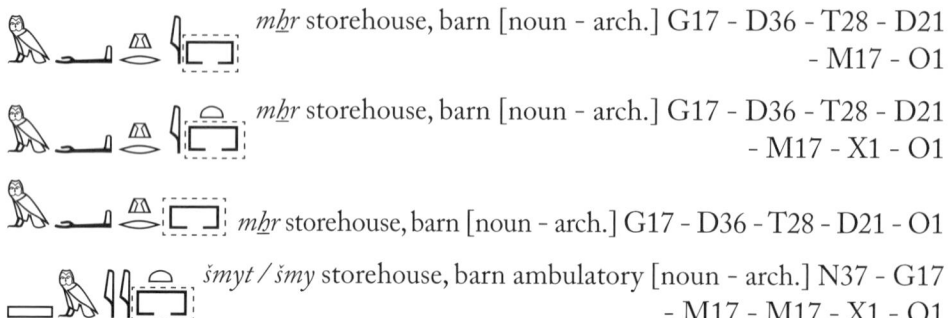 *b3-jj-ss-tj* Phaistos [noun - loc.] D58 - G29 - M17 - M17 - M8

Here, as highlighted above, the name of the city has been abbreviated to the Linear A symbol representing its first hieroglyph.

These four symbols therefore mean "total [in the] storehouse / barn [at the] city [of] Phaistos". Given the first symbol on the tablet has already been noted to be used when amounts have already been received, and the number of animals in question, the tablet records animals (and fodder) stored at Phaistos, not animals (and fodder) that has been delivered from Phaistos (as other tablets with a place name in their heading have been).

The Translations 365

Subheading: Row One, Symbol Five:

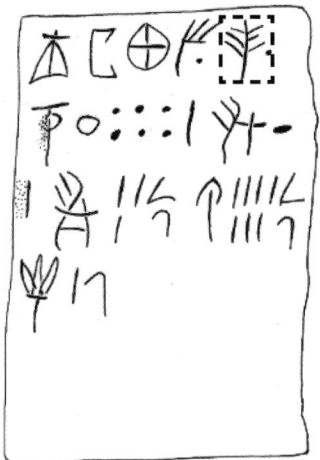

Hieroglyph V16 🪢 / rotated ⚕ / simplified / Linear A symbol L92 ⚚
As we have seen previously, this symbol represents the first hieroglyph in the word:

    s3 phyle (of priests), company, regiment (of troops), troop (of animals)
                                                        [noun] V16 - A1 - Z2

Here, this symbol means "[for the] phyle (of priests)".

Category One: Row Two, Symbol One:

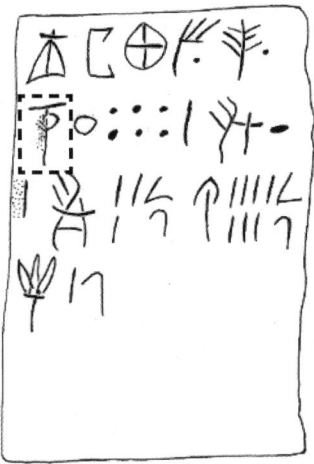

Hieroglyph F27 / partially rotated / simplified / modified / Linear A symbol L42
As we have seen previously, this symbol represents the last hieroglyph in the word:

366   The Decipherment of Linear A

⟨hieroglyphs⟩ ỉr goat [noun - ani.] D36 - D21 - E31 - F27

This symbol therefore means "goats". This is followed by a count of 161.

Category Two: Row Two, Symbol Two jointed to Symbol Three:

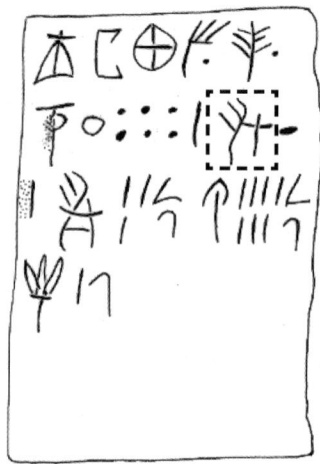

Hieroglyph D3 ⟨sym⟩ / rotated ⟨sym⟩ / reversed ⟨sym⟩ / Linear A symbol L89 ⟨sym⟩
As we have seen previously, this symbol represents the last hieroglyph in the word:

⟨hieroglyphs⟩ šnw grass (cattle fodder) [noun - flora] V7 - N35 - W24 - Z7 - D3

joined to Hieroglyph D36 ⟨sym⟩/ Linear A symbol L76 ⟨sym⟩ / rotated ⟨sym⟩/ reversed ⟨sym⟩ / simplified / modified / Linear A symbol L2' ⟨sym⟩ (without the male = symbol)
As we have seen previously, this symbol represents the first hieroglyph in the word:

⟨hieroglyphs⟩ iwʿw quadrupeds, animals [noun - ani.] D36 - D36 - F28 - Z3

These joined symbols therefore mean "grass (cattle fodder) [for the] quadrupeds". There is no male = sign, so the fodder is for female quadrupeds. They are followed by a count of 11.

Category Three: Row Three, Symbol One joined to Symbol Two:

Hieroglyph D3 ⋒/ rotated / reversed / Linear A symbol L89
As we have seen previously, this symbol represents the last hieroglyph in the word:

šnw grass (cattle fodder) [noun - flora] V7 - N35 - W24 - Z7 - D3

joined to Hieroglyph S29 + Hieroglyph Z4 (rotated) / modified / Linear A symbol L44
As we have seen previously, this symbol represents the first hieroglyph in the word:

siwt sheep [noun - ani.] S29 - M17 - Z7 - X1 - F27 - Z3A

joined to the male = symbol, which represents the last hieroglyph in the word:

ḥȝwty warrior, male, man [noun] D34 - G45 - X1 - Z4

These two symbols therefore mean "grass (cattle fodder) [for the] male sheep". There is then a count of 3 plus a fraction value. The fraction value is represented by Linear A fraction symbol J$_E$ that, as we saw in our analysis of Tablet HT 123A, has a value of ¼.

368   The Decipherment of Linear A

Category Four: Row Three, Symbol Three:

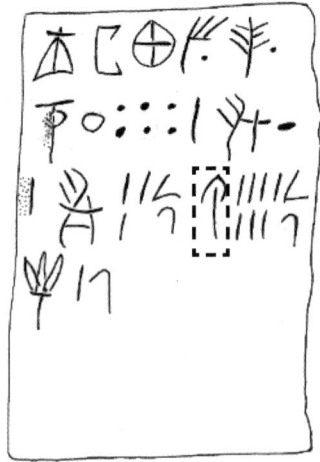

Hieroglyph F45 / simplified / Linear A symbol L67
As we have previously seen, this symbol represents the first (or, in one case, last) hieroglyph in the word:

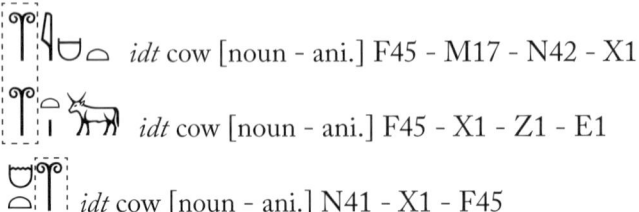

This symbol therefore means "cows". It is followed by a count of 7 plus a fraction. The fractional value is, again, represented by Linear A fraction symbol J_E that, as we have seen, has a value of ¼. Here, the fraction value may represent (at least) one animal having been slaughtered and part consumed or it may represent part ownership by the temple.

Category Five: Row Four, Symbol One:

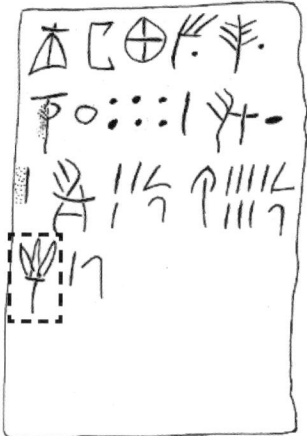

Hieroglyph F155 ⌂/ simplified / Linear A symbol L49 ⋎ (as here) or modified further ⋎

As we have seen previously, this symbol represents the first hieroglyph in the word:

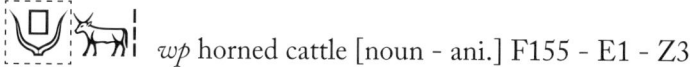 *wp* horned cattle [noun - ani.] F155 - E1 - Z3

As we have seen, this symbol means "horned cattle". Given that we have "grass (cattle fodder) for the male sheep" recorded on the tablet we can infer that rams are referred to here.

This symbol is followed by a count of 1 plus Linear A fraction symbol E, which was mathematically proved in Chapter Two to equal −0.25 or -¼ (i.e. together with the count of 1 giving a total 0.75 or ¾). Again, the fraction value may represent (at least) one animal having been slaughtered and part consumed or it may represent part ownership of (at least) one animal by the temple.

We are now in a position to translate this tablet in full:

Row One	Heading	Total [in the] storehouses [at the] city [of] Phaistos
	Subheading	[for the] phyle
Row Two	Category One	Goat – 161
	Category Two	Grass (cattle fodder) [for the] quadrupeds – 11
Row Three	Category Three	Grass (cattle fodder) [for the] male sheep – 3 ¼
	Category Four	Cows – 7 ¼
Row Four	Category Five	Horned cattle (rams) – ¾

Tablet HT21B
As we saw in Chapter Two, Tablet HT 21B had the symbol for zero written on it, which meant, in modern parlance, "this page is intentionally left blank". We are lucky that it did.

We might infer from this that the scribe who completed the tablet was not the one who then entered the information recorded on it into the temple's ledgers and so needed to inform the ultimate user of the tablet of the fact that there was no additional information to be conveyed. In the more common cases where the reverse of tablets were left blank, we might infer that it was more likely to be the scribe who completed the tablet that then entered the information recorded on them into the temple's ledgers.

The Translations

3. End of month accounting

Here we see the scribes of the temple accounting for its income and expenditure at the end of the month. The first tablet, Tablet HT 89, records goods (most likely sheep (ewes)) received and how some will of them were to be used for expenditure in the future. The second tablet, Tablet HT 118, accounts for cattle during the final month of the year showing how those animals have been issued to the temple staff and used for offerings as well as the overall deficiency in supply that the institution suffered and how this was allocated across the different categories of desired expenditure. The third tablet, Tablet HT 18, concerns a discrete element of the cattle and livestock (and related fodder) held by the temple at the start of a month and additional animals received during that month.

Tablet HT 89

As noted, this tablet deals with assets / income received (most likely sheep (ewes)), how (and when) the temple came into possession of them, and how they were to be used for expenditure after New Year's Day.

Heading: Row One, Symbols One to Three:

Hieroglyph S34 ⚚ / modifed (loop removed) / Linear A symbol L52 ⊤

As we have seen previously, this symbol represents the first hieroglyph in the word:

⚚ı ı ı 'nḫ sustenance [noun - food] S34 - Z1 - X4 - Z2

⚚ı ⊂ 'nḫ sustenance [noun - food] S34 - Z1 - Z8

Hieroglyph V28 ⟨glyph⟩ / rotated ⟨glyph⟩ / simplified / Linear A symbol L31 ⟨glyph⟩

As we have seen previously, Linear A symbol L31 represents Hieroglyph V28. Here this symbol represents the first hieroglyph in the word:

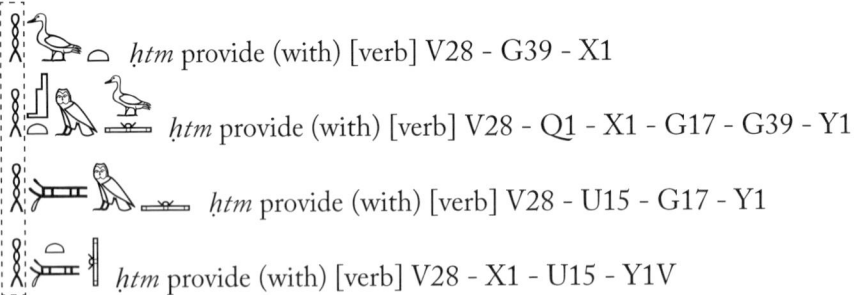

ḥtm provide (with) [verb] V28 - G39 - X1

ḥtm provide (with) [verb] V28 - Q1 - X1 - G17 - G39 - Y1

ḥtm provide (with) [verb] V28 - U15 - G17 - Y1

ḥtm provide (with) [verb] V28 - X1 - U15 - Y1V

It is perhaps worth noting, in addition to the above, that the word ḥtmt written (in hieratic) as ⟨glyph⟩ appears in account table headings in the mid-5th Dynasty Abusir papyri of the funerary temple of King Neferefre. One of the potential meanings that Hana Vymazalová ascribes to this is "provided with".[83] If this were abbreviated to just one hieroglyph (its first, Hieroglyph V28) it would also be written in Linear A using Linear A symbol L31.

Hieroglyphs Z5 - Z5 ⟨glyph⟩ / Linear A symbol L58 ⟨glyph⟩

As we have seen previously, this symbol represents the word:

⟨glyph⟩ 3bd month [noun] N11 - N14 - Z5 - Z5 - N5

These three symbols therefore mean "sustenance provided (with) [for the] month".

---

83. Hana Vymazalová, *The accounting documents from the papyrus archive of Neferre and their specific terminology* (PhD: Charles University in Prague, 2005), p179

Subheading One: Row One, Symbol Four:

Hieroglyph AA6 (or J6) 🜨 or S23 🜨 / modified / simplified / Linear A symbol L85 △△

This symbol has been transcribed by Brice and Godart & Olivier as Linear A symbol L56:

However, a review of an extract of the photograph of the tablet showing this symbol (taken from Brice, where the symbol is clearer) indicates that, due to the extensive damage the tablet has suffered, it has been transcribed incorrectly and is, in fact, Linear A symbol L85:

Extract of photograph of Tablet HT 89	**Extract of photograph of Tablet HT 89 (symbol highlighted)**	**Highlighted symbol (extract of picture of Tablet HT 89 removed)**

As we have seen previously, this symbol represents Hieroglyph S23. Again, therefore, this symbol represents the word or the first hieroglyph of the word:

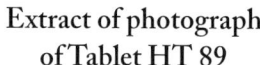 *dmd* total S23

 dmd r total S23 - D21

374   The Decipherment of Linear A

This symbol therefore means "total". As we have seen, that this word for total is used indicates that all the amounts that follow it have been received.

Category One: Row One, Symbol Five:

Hieroglyphs X1 - D17 ⌒⌒/ reversed ⌒⌒/ modified (hieroglyphs joined) / simplified / Linear A symbol L88 ⅄

This symbol has been transcribed as Linear A symbol L66:

ε

However, a review of an extract of the photograph of the tablet showing this symbol (taken from Brice, where the symbol is clearer) indicates that, due to the extensive damage the tablet has suffered, it has been transcribed incorrectly and is, in fact, Linear A symbol L88:

Extract of photograph of Tablet HT 89	**Extract of photograph of Tablet HT 89 (symbol highlighted)**	**Highlighted symbol (extract of picture of Tablet HT 89 removed)**
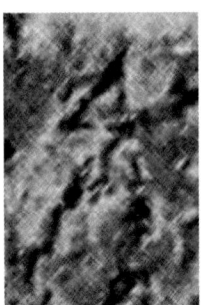		

As can be seen above, however, this is, in fact, Linear A symbol L88:

⅄

As we have seen previously, this symbol represents Hieroglyphs X1 - D17 (reversed). Again, therefore, this symbol represents the last hieroglyphs in the word:

imny (daily) service, offerings, portion, ration [noun] M17 - Y5 - N35 - X1 - D17

This symbol therefore means "[from] (daily) services". This is followed by a count of 23. As discussed below, given that the following category is dated (as indeed is the one after that), these animals were received before the current period.

<u>Category Two: Row Two, Symbols One to Three:</u>

Hieroglpyph O10 / reversed / simplified / Linear A symbol L68/96
Here, Hieroglyph O10 is reversed and then simplified to Linear A symbol L68/96 (in order to be easier to incise):

 is reversed to become

 which is simplified to become

 Linear A symbol L68/96

While, as we have seen, Linear A symbol L43 represented Hieroglyph O10, here the Linear A symbol representing this hieroglyph is simplified even further (omitting three sides of its box outline). The symbol nonetheless represents the same hieroglyph (reversed).

This symbol, therefore, again represents the name of the Goddess Hathor:

ḥwt ḥt Hathor [noun - div.] O10

joined to Hieroglyph R1 ⛩ / simplified / Linear A symbol L57 ⇓
If we look at Godart & Olivier's sketch of just this symbol, it is easier to see that it is Linear A symbol L57 (bearing, perhaps, an even closer resemblance to the hieroglyph that it represents):

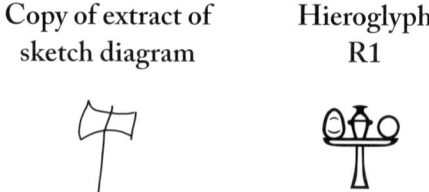

| Copy of extract of sketch diagram | Hieroglyph R1 |

In addition to the central stem and the two curved arms of Linear A symbol L57 as it is usually drawn, here the scribe has drawn a line from the top of the curved arms back to the top of the central stem. Hieroglyph R1 represents a table with loaves and a jug on it. In incising the additional lines, the scribe has simply enclosed the entire area representing the loaves and jug (without incising them in detail, which he would not be able to in clay).

Therefore, this symbol is Linear A symbol L57 which, again, represents Hieroglyph R1 and the last hieroglyph in the word:

𓅱𓍘𓈙𓏏𓐎 *wdḥw* offering table, offerings [noun - furn.] G43 - D46 - V28
                                                                     - G43 - R1

Subscript Hieroglyph Z4B - Z4B - W24 ☰Ⓞ/ modified (four dashes inside circle as dots) / Linear A symbol L91 ⁝⁝

Although Godart & Olivier's sketch has three dots within this subscript symbol, a closer examination of an extract of a photograph of the tablet from Brice indicates there are four:

| Extract of photograph of Tablet HT 89 | Extract of photograph of Tablet HT 89 (symbol highlighted) | Highlighted symbol (extract of photograph of Tablet HT 89 removed) |

As set out in Appendix 6, therefore, this symbol, representing Hieroglyphs Z4B - Z4B - W24, represents the ordinal:

☰ ○ *fdnw* fourth Z4B - Z4B - W24

As noted in Appendix 8 (dating Type Two), when an ordinal appears next to the first category on a list it refers to the items in question being brought forward from the previous month (i.e. they were already in store at the start of the current period, having been received in a prior period) and subsequent categories that were received in the current month are not dated. Here the dating symbol appears next to the second category of item on the list, the method of recording the date (though not what was being conveyed) is apparently reversed (dating Type Two(A) in Appendix 8). It would seem that items recorded in Category One were received in the prior month but, rather than stating this, Category Two (and, as we shall see, Category Three) were explicitly stated to have been received in the current month instead. Given that we know (from the total description) that this tablet records the final month of the year, it is unsurprising that the current month referred to is the fourth month (of the season), the final month of the year.

These three symbols therefore mean "[from the] offerings [to] Hathor [in the] fourth [month]". They are followed by a count of 22.

Category Three: Row Two, Symbols Three to Six:

Hieroglyph V28 ⏀ / rotated ⏀ / simplified / Linear A symbol L31 Y
As we have seen previously, this symbol represents the first hieroglyph in the word:

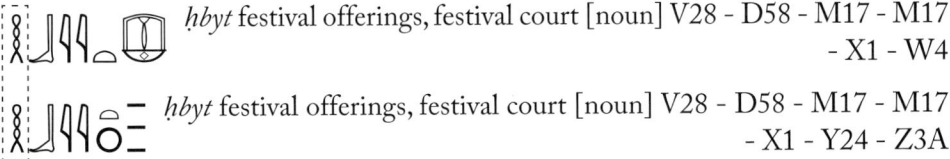

378   The Decipherment of Linear A

![symbols] ḥbyt festival offerings [noun] V28 - D58 - W4 - M17 - M17 - X1 - Z2

![symbols] ḥbyt festival offerings [noun] V28 - D58 - X1 - W3

joined to Hieroglyph Z4B - Z4B - W24 ≡⊙ / modified (four dashes inside circle as dots) / Linear A symbol L91 ⊙
Although Godart & Olivier's sketch has two dots within this symbol, a closer examination of an extract of a photograph of the tablet from Brice indicates there are four (although unlike Tablet HT 102, two of the dots have not been incised adjoining the "ears" of the symbol):

Extract of photograph of Tablet HT 89	Extract of photograph of Tablet HT 89 (symbol highlighted)	Highlighted symbol (extract of photograph of Tablet HT 89 removed)

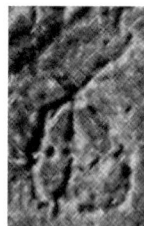 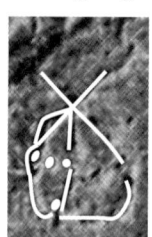

Again, as set out in Appendix 6, this symbol, representing Hieroglyphs Z4B - Z4B - W24, represents the ordinal:

≡ ⊙ fdnw fourth Z4B - Z4B - W24

becomes Linear A symbols L31 + L91 / Linear A symbol L95
As set out in Appendix 6, these joined symbols therefore mean "[from the] festival offerings [in the] fourth [month]".
   As with the previous category, it had to be explicitly stated that the items recorded as received under this category were received in the current month, month four.

Hieroglyph D46 ▱ / rotated ▯ / simplified / modified / Linear A symbol L100 Ψ
As we have seen previously, this symbol represents the first hieroglyph in the word:

drpw offerings, provisions, meal, sustenance [noun - food] D46 - D21 - Q3 - Z7 - N37 - Z2

The Translations 379

<u>Hieroglyph D36 ⟶ / modified / simplified / Linear A symbol L76</u>
As we have seen previously, this symbol represents the first hieroglyph in the word:

iw'w quadrupeds, animals [noun - ani.] D36 - D36 - F28 - Z3

These three symbols therefore mean "[from the] festival offerings [in the] fourth [month], provisions [of] quadrupeds". They are followed by a count of 24.

<u>Category Four: Row Three, Symbol One:</u>

<u>Hieroglyph A33 / reversed / simplified / Linear A symbol L125</u>
This symbol is a simplified representation of a reversed Hieroglyph A33, where the bag carried by the man is simplified to a straight line and the bent arm he uses to carry it is given a wide sweep. The symbol could represent the first hieroglyph in the word:

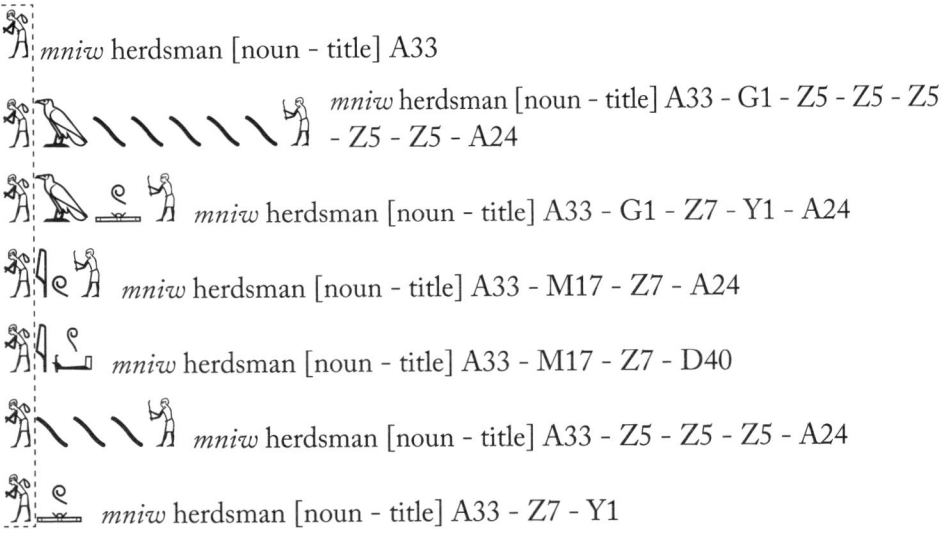

mniw herdsman [noun - title] A33

mniw herdsman [noun - title] A33 - G1 - Z5 - Z5 - Z5 - Z5 - Z5 - A24

mniw herdsman [noun - title] A33 - G1 - Z7 - Y1 - A24

mniw herdsman [noun - title] A33 - M17 - Z7 - A24

mniw herdsman [noun - title] A33 - M17 - Z7 - D40

mniw herdsman [noun - title] A33 - Z5 - Z5 - Z5 - A24

mniw herdsman [noun - title] A33 - Z7 - Y1

380   The Decipherment of Linear A

However, I think this meaning is unlikely here, given that we already have two Linear A symbols representing the word *mniw* and meaning "herdsmen" used at Hagia Triada:

- Linear A symbol L84/48 representing Hieroglyph A24, its last hieroglyph (in four iterations of the spelling above), with the male = symbol added for additional clarity (as we saw on Tablet HT 86A and Tablet HT 120); and
- Linear A symbol L99 representing Hieroglyph A59 (as we saw in the iteration of the spelling of the word represented on Tablet HT 102 and Tablet HT 7A).

Indeed, as we saw on Tablet HT 86A, there appears to have been something of a preference, at Hagia Triada, for spelling the word in the second, third, fourth, and sixth iterations, above, as represented by a Linear A symbol representing its final hieroglyph, Hieroglyph A24, suggesting that a Linear A symbol representing its first hieroglyph, Hieroglyph A33, was used to represent something else that was likely originally frequently recorded (but where, perhaps, this is not reflected in the limited surviving corpus). Given this, I think a symbol that represented the first hieroglyph in all of the above iterations of the spelling of the word *mniw* was used to represent those who tended the most common animal on the island sheep (i.e. the shepherds) and, in particular, it represented the first hieroglyph in the (evidently related) word:

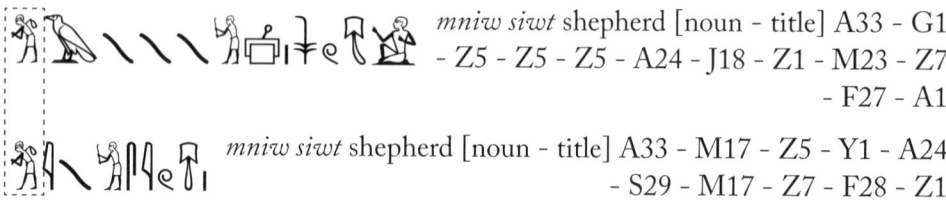

mniw siwt shepherd [noun - title] A33 - G1 - Z5 - Z5 - Z5 - A24 - J18 - Z1 - M23 - Z7 - F27 - A1

mniw siwt shepherd [noun - title] A33 - M17 - Z5 - Y1 - A24 - S29 - M17 - Z7 - F28 - Z1

This symbol therefore means "[from the] shepherds". These were shepherds tending the temple's own flocks, and this entry on the tablet represents an internal stock transfer to the temple from those flocks (to become "stock on hand"). This is followed by a count of 13. While the tablet does not explicitly state it, the tablet, therefore, records sheep. Given the overall numbers recorded, we can be confident that these were ewes.

The Translations   381

Category Five: Row Three, Symbols Two and Three:

Hieroglyph O1 ⌐⌐/ rotated ⌐/ Linear A symbol L74 ⌐
As we have seen previously, this symbol represents the last hieroglyph in the word(s):

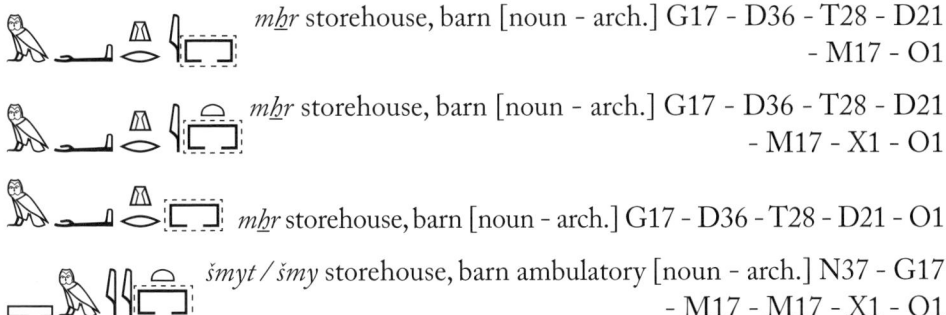

       mḫr storehouse, barn [noun - arch.] G17 - D36 - T28 - D21
                      - M17 - O1

       mḫr storehouse, barn [noun - arch.] G17 - D36 - T28 - D21
                      - M17 - X1 - O1

      mḫr storehouse, barn [noun - arch.] G17 - D36 - T28 - D21 - O1

     šmyt / šmy storehouse, barn ambulatory [noun - arch.] N37 - G17
                      - M17 - M17 - X1 - O1

Hieroglyph I12 / simplified / Linear A symbol L53
As we have seen previously, this symbol represents the last hieroglyph in the word:

   nṯrt goddess [noun - div.] R8 - D21 - X1 - I12

   nṯrt goddess [noun - div.] R8 - D21 - X1 - J2 - I12

   nṯrt goddess [noun - div.] R8 - D21 - X1 - Z5 - I12

   nṯrt goddess [noun - div.] R8 - X1 - D21 - M17 - M17 - X1 - J2
                     - I12

   nṯrt goddess [noun - div.] R8 - X1 - D21 - X1 - I12

   nṯrt goddess [noun - div.] R8 - X1 - D21 - X1 - J2 - I12

382   The Decipherment of Linear A

𐦀 *ntrt* goddess [noun - div.] R8 - X1 - I12

𐦀 *ntrt* goddess [noun - div.] R8 - X1 - J2 - I12

𐦀 *ntrt* goddess [noun – div.] R8 - Z5 - Z5 - Z5 - I12

These two symbols therefore mean "[from the] storehouse / barn [of the] goddess". They are followed by a count of 5. This is, therefore, a withdrawal of stock from the temple's storehouse / barn with the animals held on hand for future use (i.e. another internal stock transfer).

Total: Row Four, Symbols One and Two:

Hieroglyph F14 ⋃ / rotated ⌒ / simplified / Linear A symbol L98 ⊐
As we have seen previously, this symbol represents the first hieroglyph in the word:

⋃ ⌣ *wpt rnpt* New Year's Day (and its festivals) [noun] F14 - W3

⋃ ☉ *wpt rnpt* New Year's Day (and its festivals) [noun] F15 - W3 - N5

Hieroglyph N14 ✶ / modified / Linear A symbol L22 +
As we have seen previously, this symbol represents the first hieroglyph in the word:

✶ ⍭ *dmd sm3* grand total [noun] N14 - F36

As we have seen, these two symbols have a meaning of "[on] New Year's Day, grand total". They are followed by a count of 87.

The Translations   383

The following three categories, coming after total income, represent future expenditure. As noted previously, it is particularly important that they have been recorded in this manner on this tablet (and similarly on Tablet HT 27 which, being badly damaged, is not translated here) as it indicates to us the three principal classifications of outgoings of the temple. If we think who exactly a temple would pay in the ordinary course of its activities (other than taxation which, from Tablet HT 123A we also know it paid, and as distinct from items used within the temple during the conduct of its religious activities), it is these three categories of payee. In addition to being the ones we would expect if listed all in one place, these categories of payee are, as we have seen, evident across the corpus.

<u>Category Six: Row Five, Symbol One:</u>

<u>Hieroglyph A28</u> 𓀠 / reversed 𓀠 / simplified / modified (bowing, slightly) / Linear A symbol L71

Linear A symbol L71 is a simplified "stick man" representation of reversed Hieroglyph A28. As we know this tablet reflects certain aspects of the activities of a temple dedicated to the Goddess Hathor. It seems reasonable to assume, therefore, that amongst the principal outgoings of the institution would be the remuneration of the priests (paid in kind in this pre-monetary era). This symbol, therefore, represents the last hieroglyph in the word:

𓏺𓀠 *i̓3s* (a Priest of Hathor) [noun - title] M17 - S29 - A28

This symbol therefore means "[to the] *i̓3s* (Priests of Hathor)". This is then followed by a count of 2 plus a fraction value represented by Linear A fraction symbol J_E. As we saw with the analysis of Tablet HT 123A, this has a value of ¼ (giving a total of 2 ¼). Presumably (at least) one animal would, therefore, be slaughtered and butchered prior to a portion being used to make this payment.

384   The Decipherment of Linear A

Category Seven: Row Five, Symbol Two:

Hieroglyph T25 / rotated / simplified / Linear A symbol L60
As we have seen previously, this symbol represents the first hieroglyph (or, on one occasion, last hieroglyph) in the word:

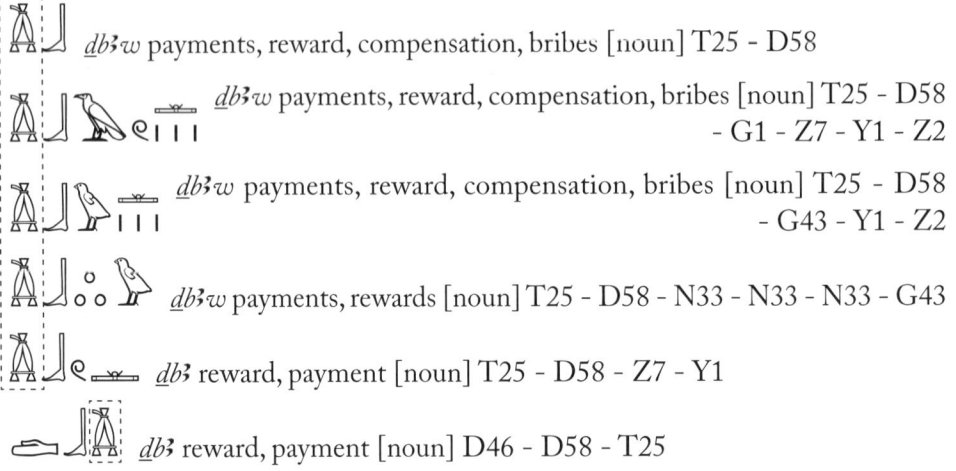

Here, this symbol therefore means "[for] payments" (i.e. for goods or services obtained by the temple). This is then followed by a count of 2 plus a fraction value represented by Linear A fraction symbol E. As we saw with the analysis of Linear A Tablet HT 123A, this has a value of -¼ (giving a total of 1 ¾). Presumably (at least) one animal would, therefore, again be slaughtered and butchered prior to a portion being used to make this payment.

Category Eight: Row Five, Symbol Three:

Hieroglyph M20 / rotated / simplified / Linear A symbol L82

As we have seen previously, this symbol represents the first hieroglyph in the word:

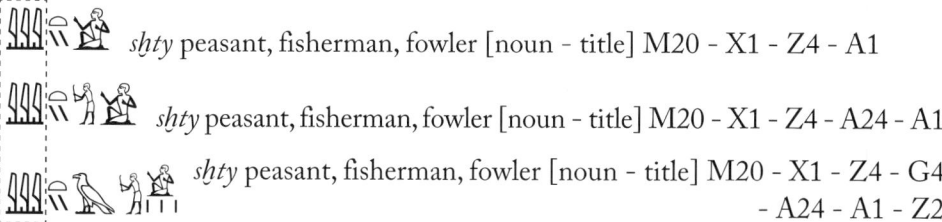

This symbol, representing the first hieroglyph in the above word, therefore translates as "[to the] peasants", who were presumably working on the temple's lands. This is then followed by a count which is on part of the tablet that has been too badly damaged to be determined.

We are now in a position to translate this tablet in full:

Row One	Heading:	Sustenance provided (with) [in the] month
	Subheading One:	Total
	Category One:	[From the] (daily) services – 23
Row Two	Category Two:	[From the] offerings [to] Hathor [in the] fourth [month] – 22
Row Three	Category Three:	[From the] festival offerings [in the] fourth [month], provisions [of] quadrupeds – 24
Row Four	Category Four:	[From the] shepherds – 13
	Category Five:	[From the] storehouse [of the] goddess – 5
Row Five	Total:	[On] New Year's Day, grand total – 87
Row Six	Category Six:	[To the] i3s (Priests of Hathor) – 2½
	Category Seven:	[For] payments – 1¾
	Category Eight:	[To the] peasants – [unknown value]

Analysis

1. The timing of temple receipts and payments using sheep (ewes)
This tablet concerns month four given the total being on New Year's Day and the dates against the second and third categories of items recorded. Amounts held at the start and income received in the current period (the first three categories) plus internal stock transfers (the final two income categories) totalled 87 sheep (ewes), and expenditure was to be at least 4¼ sheep (ewes). Importantly, expenditure was to be undertaken after New Year's Day, after the current period.

That this tablet concerns the final month of the year (mid-late July to mid-late August) means that it relates to the period, we inferred from our analysis of Tablet HT 123A, that sales or transfers of ownership of sheep (ewes) were not permitted (falling during the period between shearing, which was completed in mid-June, and New Year's Day, when the wool tax obligation was assessed on flock owners). It seems offerings were an exception; the temple, administering the taxation system, would be aware of these, and where the animals in question had come from, so could consequently ensure they were correctly accounted for and the correct wool tax obligation calculated (which would remain payable by the prior owners). Moreover, the temple itself also benefitted from this exception, and offerings to Hathor were not be delayed through such earthly trivialities as taxation, and perhaps this was the point.

As to expenditure, therefore, this would seem to be the most likely reason as to why there was no expenditure of sheep (ewes) in the period recorded (month four), for that would reduce the potential for offerings to Hathor, and the expenditure of at least 4¼ sheep (ewes) is recorded as going to take place after New Year's Day.

The Translations 387

Tablet HT 118

This tablet accounts for how a specific type of animal (cows) have been expended in the period in question (which is not stated but which was presumably a month) to certain categories of recipient, the deficiency in supply evidently suffered by the institution, and how that was allocated across the different categories of recipient. The deficit is not stated as "to be received", thus this is not a record of goods received and to be received.

As with Tablet HT 123A, we will approach this tablet's translation in the order of its two columns on Brice's transcription.

Heading: Transcription Column One, Row One, Symbols One and Two:

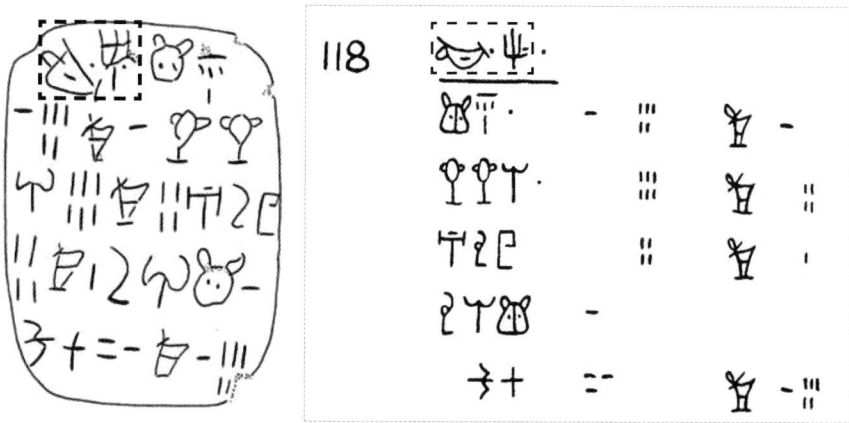

Hieroglyph F1 / reversed / Linear A symbol L112

This hieroglyph has been reversed and simplified for ease of incision to become Linear A symbol L112. Here it represents one of the two following words (representing either the only, or the last, hieroglyph):

k3 cow [noun - ani.] F1

šsr beef cattle, sacrificial bull [noun - ani.] N37 - S29 - D21 - T11 - F1

Given the simplicity of the first of the above words, the likelihood must be that this is the word represented here. For this reason, this is the meaning inferred.

Hieroglyph D46 / rotated / simplified / modified / Linear A symbol L100

As we have seen previously, this symbol represents the first hieroglyph in the word:

drpw offerings, provisions, meal, sustenance [noun - food] D46 - D21 - Q3 - Z7 - N37 - Z2

The first two symbols, therefore, mean "cows [for] sustenance"

388   The Decipherment of Linear A

Category One: Transcription Column One, Row Two, Symbols One and Two:

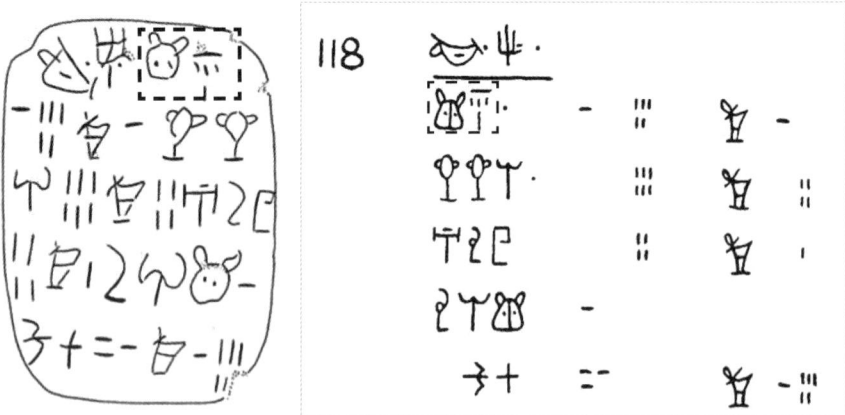

Hieroglyph D2 / simplified / Linear A symbol L95 (with no central partitioning line) This Linear A symbol is very similar in appearance to the "combined ordinals" discussed in Appendix 6. However, the lack of central partitioning line on this symbol (which is correctly absent from Godart & Olivier's sketch diagram but, erroneously, is included on Brice's transcription) shows that this is a different symbol. This can be seen below, in an extract of the photograph of the tablet, when it appears more clearly in Category Four:

**Extract of photograph of Tablet HT 118
From Godart & Olivier**

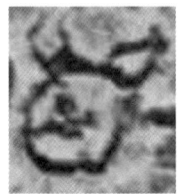

In fact, this symbol represents Hieroglyph D2, which has been simplified and, while the size of the symbol means that the facial details were evidently still too difficult for the scribe to accurately incise, the result is still clear enough for us to correctly identiy the hieroglyph that is being represented (and discount those that are not). Here, therefore, this symbol represents the first hieroglyph in the word:

 ḥry s3 Chief of the Phyles [noun - title] D2 - D21 - V17

This word was represented on Tablet HT 86A, Tablet HT 95A and Tablet HT 95B but, as we have seen a number of times with a number of words now (not least the next word on this tablet) it was instead abbreviated there to a symbol representing its last hieroglyph.

The Translations   389

Hieroglyphs Z5 - Z2 \|\|\| / rotated \ / modified / Linear A symbol L51 ⸗

As we have seen previously, this symbol represents the last hieroglyphs in the word:

ꜥwt small cattle, herds, flocks, goats [noun - ani.] T14 - Z7 - X1 - Z5 - Z2

Here, these three symbols therefore mean "[for the] Chief of the Phyles, small cattle". This category mirrors that on Tablet HT 86A, Tablet HT 95A, and Tablet HT 95B which records small cattle being given to the Chief of the Phyles for food. They are followed by a count of 15.

Category Three: Transcription Row Three, Symbols One to Three:

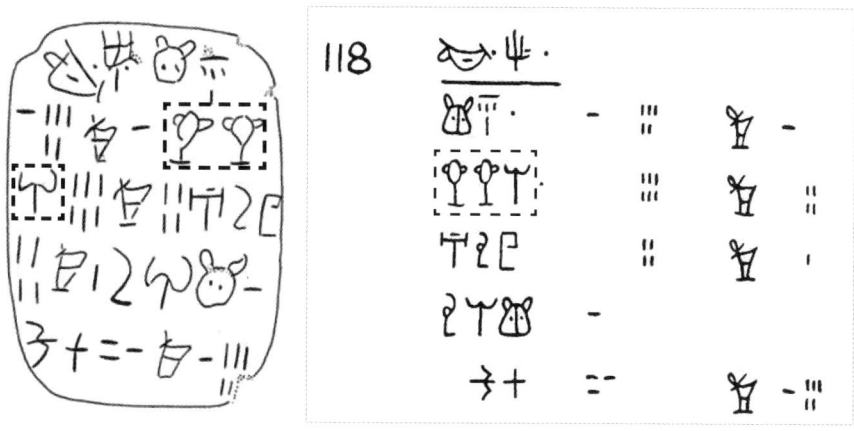

Hieroglyph AA27 (or J27) ⚱ / simplified / Linear A symbol L62 ⚱

Linear A symbol L62 is a straightforward simplified representation of Hieroglyph AA27 (or J27). Here it represents the first hieroglyph in the word:

ndt ḥr gifts [noun] J27 - I10 - D2

ndt ḥr gifts [noun] J27 - W24 - X1 - D2 - Z1

Hieroglyph AA27 (or J27) ⚱ / simplified / Linear A symbol L62 ⚱

Here, the symbol represents the first hieroglyph in the word:

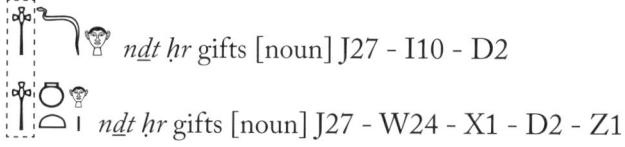

ndtt Protectress, Avenger [feminine noun - title] J27 - W24 - X1 - X1

390 The Decipherment of Linear A

It will interest the reader to note that "Protectress" is an epithet (or, rather, part of an epithet) of the Goddess Hathor.[84]

Hieroglyphs D28 - Z1 ⎵ / simplified / modified / Linear A symbol L55 ⋎

As we have seen previously, this symbol represents the word:

⎵ k3w food, bounty [noun - food] D28 - Z1

These three symbols therefore mean "gifts [to the] Protectress [of] bulls". Again this mirrors the category on Tablet HT 86A that records "gifts of bulls for the temple" and the category on Tablet HT 95A and Tablet HT 95B of "bulls for (daily) services". They are followed by a count of 6.

Category Three: Transcription Row Four, Symbols One to Three:

Hieroglyph S34 ⊥ / modifed (loop replaced by accent bar) / Linear A symbol L52 ⊤

As we have seen previously, this symbol represents the first hieroglyph in the word:

⊥ 'nḫ sustenance [noun - food] S34 - Z1 - X4 - Z2

⊥ 'nḫ sustenance [noun - food] S34 - Z1 - Z8

---

84. The Goddess Hathor was known as the Protectress of various things. For example, at the Temple of Deir El Bahari, on the Eastern Wall of the Anteroom, Hathor is described as "Protectress of Thebes" (Stefan Bergdoll, *The Temple of Deir El Bahari* (Berlin: epubli, 2013), p135). Hathor also had the epithet "Protectress for her Brother", in allusion to Osiris, as well as being referred to as "Protectress" of her father Re (Barbara Ann Richter, *The Theology of Hathor of Dendera: Aural and Visual Scribal Techniques in the Per-Wer Sanctuary* (PhD: University of California, Berkeley, 2012), pp90, 258–259, 360, 426). We do not know the full title that was intended to be conveyed by the shorthand reference here, and which one of Hathor's epithets was intended to be conveyed, so the translation here simply states "[the] Protectress".

Hieroglyph M6 ↧/ reversed ↥/ simplified / Linear A symbol L72/94 ⟅ or ⟆

As we have seen previously, this symbol represents the first hieroglyph in the word:

⬚ ⬚ ⬚ *trsst* wage payments [noun - food] M6 - O34 - O34 - X1 - Z8

Hieroglyph O4 ⬚/ rotated ⬚/ Linear A symbol L59 ⊏ or ⊐

In determining the meaning of this symbol on this tablet we have to rely on the consistent use of accounting terminology across the corpus by the temple's scribes.

On Tablet HT 86A, Tablet HT 95A, and Tablet HT 95B, the term "payment" (*ḏbꜣw*) was used in respect of the animals issued to the corvee / labourers. Here, therefore, given that we have the term "wage payments" (*trsst*) being used next to a symbol that has previously been translated as "corvee / labourers" (*ḥꜣw / ḥꜣy*), as the "corvee / labourers" received "payments" and not "wage payments", if this symbol were translated as "corvee / labourers", there would be a conflict in the terminology being used.

However, as we have seen from the first subheading on Tablet HT 14, which indicated that the amounts in question were to be received by the phyle (of priests), and Tablet HT 114A and Tablet HT 121, which had a similar proportionality of items recorded (thus inferring that the amounts were for the same purpose and recipient as Tablet HT 14) and which indicated that the goods for the phyle (of priests) (animals and related fodder) were termed "wage payments" (*trsst*) (i.e. remuneration), we know that if issues of food were termed "wage payments" they were issued to the phyle (of priests). (As an aside, I suspect other issues of food to the phyle (of priests) were made, perhaps to feed them while they performed their duties in the temple; I suspect these animals could not be taken away from the temple so, perhaps, were not strictly part of the priests' remuneration and, therefore, were not termed "wage payments".)

Given that this category reflects "wage payments" (*trsst*), this symbol cannot represent a word meaning "corvee / labourers" and, instead, it represents the first hieroglyph in the word:

⬚ ⬚ ⬚ ⬚ ⬚ ⬚ *ḥꜣtyw* duty phyle, phyle on duty [plural noun] O4 - G1 - X1 - D54 - A1 - A1 - A1

Translating these three symbols as "sustenance wage payments [for the] phyle on duty" is therefore based on the assumption that the accounting terminology used by the scribes was consistent. They are followed by a count of 4.

392   The Decipherment of Linear A

Category Four: Transcription Row Four, Symbols One to Three:

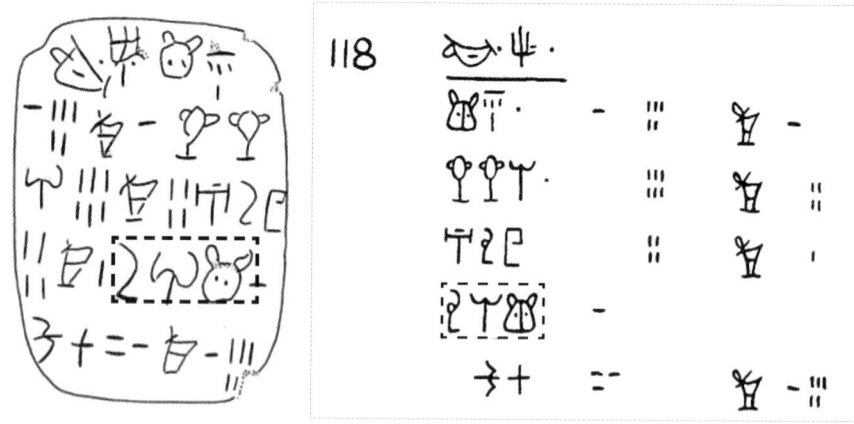

Hieroglyph M6 ⌠/ reversed ⌡/ simplified / Linear A symbol L72/94 ⟨ or ⟩
As we have seen previously, this symbol represents the first hieroglyph in the word:

⌠═○ *trsst* wage payments [noun - food] M6 - O34 - O34 - X1 - Z8

Hieroglyphs D28 - Z1 ⋃ / simplified / modified / Linear A symbol L55 Y
As we have seen previously, this symbol represents Hieroglyphs D28 - Z1. Given the theme of the categories on this tablet, here it represents the word:

⋃ 🐂 *k3* bull [noun - ani.] D28 - Z1 - E1

Hieroglyph D2 / simplified / Linear A symbol L95 (with no central partitioning line)
As discussed previously, this symbol represents the first hieroglyph in the word:

ḥry s3 Chief of the Phyles [noun - title] D2 - D21 - V17

These three symbols therefore mean "wage payments [of] bulls [for the] Chief of the Phyles". They are followed by a count of 10.

Total: Transcription Row Five, Symbols One and Two:

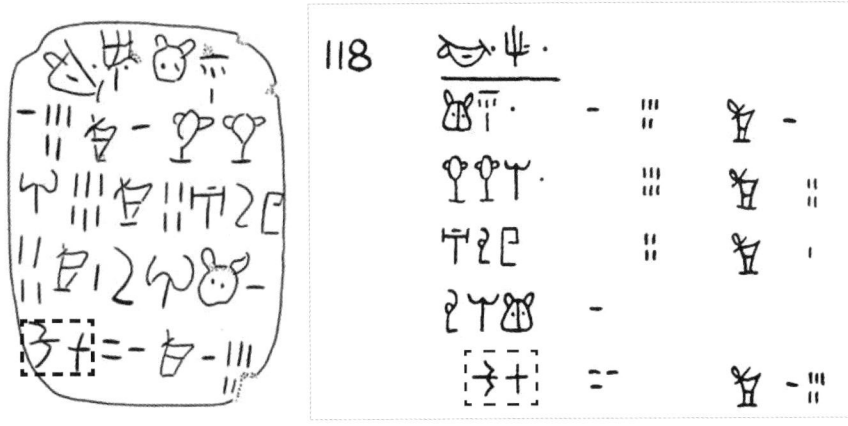

Hieroglyph F14 ⚋ / rotated ⚌ / simplified / Linear A symbol L98 ⊐

As we have seen previously, this symbol represents the first hieroglyph in the word:

⚋⚊ *wpt rnpt* New Year's Day (and its festivals) [noun] F14 - W3

⚋⊙ *wpt rnpt* New Year's Day (and its festivals) [noun] F15 - W3 - N5

Hieroglyph N14 ✶ / modified / Linear A symbol L22 +

As we have seen previously, this symbol represents the first hieroglyph in the word:

✶⚊ *dmḏ smȝ* grand total [noun] N14 - F36

These two symbols therefore mean "[on] New Year's Day, grand total". They are followed by a count of 30.

Deficiencies: Transcript Column Two, all Row Two to Four and Six:

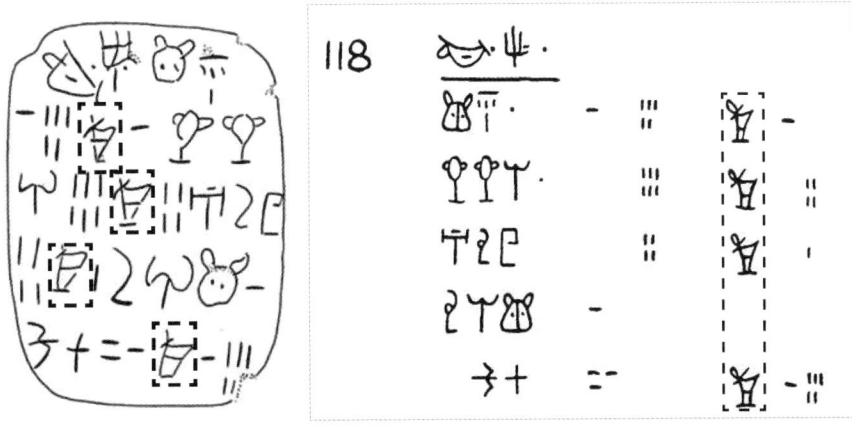

Hieroglyph G1 / simplified / Linear A symbol L103
As we have seen previously, this symbol represents the word:

gbi deficiency, deprivation, damage, uneven [noun] W11 - G1 - D58 - G37 - Z9

This symbol therefore means "deficiency". This is followed by a count of 10 (Transcript Row Two), 4 (Transcript Row Three), 1 (Transcript Row Four), and 15 (Transcript Row Six).

We are now in a position to translate the tablet in full:

Transcript Row One	Heading: Category One:	Cows [for] sustenance [For the] Chief of the Phyles, small cattle –	
Transcript Row Two		15	Deficiency – 10
	Category Two:	Gifts, [to the] Protectress,	
Transcript Row Three		[of] bulls – 6	Deficiency – 4
	Category Three:	Sustenance wage payments [for the] phyle on duty – 4	
Transcript Row Four	Category Four:	Wage payments [of] bulls [for the] Chief of the Phyles – 10	Deficiency – 1
Transcript Row Five	Total:	On New Year's Day, grand total – 30	
	Total deficiency:		Deficiency – 15

The Translations 395

Tablet HT 18

As this tablet involves the record of an amount brought forward as well as the amounts provided in the month, it is included in this section concerning end of month accounting for the activities of the temple. There is limited information on the tablet, but it appears to concern a discrete element of the cattle and livestock (and related fodder) held for use by the temple, perhaps in a certain field or enclosure.

Heading: Row One, Symbols One and Two:

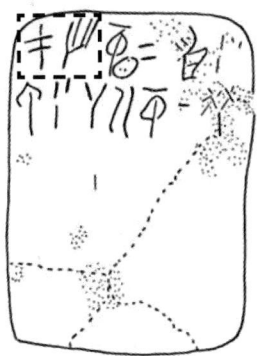

Hieroglyph F35 / simplified / Linear A symbol L2

As we have previously seen, Linear A symbol L2 represents Hieroglyph F35. Here, given the contents of the tablet, we can infer that it most likely represents the first hieroglyph in the word:

nfrt cattle [noun - ani.] F35 - D21 - X1 - E1 - Z2

nfrt cattle [noun - ani.] F35 - I9 - D21 - X1 - E1 - Z2

nfrt cattle [noun - ani.] F35 - X1 - E1 - Z2

nfrt cattle [noun - ani.] F35 - X1 - Z2

Hieroglyph D58 / rotated / simplified / Linear A symbol L77

As we have seen previously, this symbol represents Hieroglyph D58. Here, given the contents of the tablet, we can infer that it most likely represents the first hieroglyph in the word:

b't nourishment, food [noun - food] D58 - D36 - X1 - X2 - Z2

The first two symbols on this tablet therefore mean "cattle [for] food".

396   The Decipherment of Linear A

Category One: Row One, Symbol Three:

Hieroglyph F27 ⌂/ partially rotated / simplified / Linear A symbol L42 ⌶
As we have seen previously, this symbol represents the final hieroglyph in the word:

ꜥr goat [noun - ani.] D36 - D21 - E31 - F27

Subscript Hieroglyphs Z2 - W24 / rotated / modified (three dashes as dots inside circle) / Linear A symbol L91
As set out in Appendix 6, this symbol, representing Hieroglyphs Z2 - W24, represents the ordinal:

ḫmt nw third [ordinal number] Z2 - W24

As set out in Appendix 8, when an ordinal appears next to the first category of item on a list, it indicates the amount in question was brought forward from the prior month (i.e. it had been received before the start of the current month). These two symbols therefore mean "goats [from the] third [month]" (i.e. the current month was, therefore, month four). They are followed by a count of 20.

The Translations 397

Category Two: Row One, Symbols Five and Six:

Hieroglyph D3 / rotated / reversed / Linear A symbol L89
As we have seen previously, this symbol represents the last hieroglyph in the word:

šnw grass (cattle fodder) [noun - flora] V7 - N35 - W24 - Z7 - D3

joined to Hieroglyph G1 / simplified / Linear A symbol L103
As we have seen previously, this symbol represents the first hieroglyph in the word:

ȝḥt cow [noun - ani.] G1 - O4 - X1 - E1

These joined symbols therefore mean "grass (cattle fodder) [for] cows". They are followed by a count of 2.

Category Three: Row Two, Symbol One:

Hieroglyph F45 / simplified / Linear A symbol L67
As we have seen previously, this symbol represents the first hieroglyph (or, in one instance, last hieroglyph) in the word:

398   The Decipherment of Linear A

𓏏𓇋𓄿𓃙 *idt* cow [noun - ani.] F45 - M17 - N42 - X1

𓏏𓏏𓃒 *idt* cow [noun - ani.] F45 - X1 - Z1 - E1

𓈉𓏏 *idt* cow [noun - ani.] N41 - X1 - F45

This symbol therefore means "cows". This is followed by a count of 3.

As we saw on Tablet HT 91, it is again interesting to note that the word for cows (*ȝht*) was used in the previous category, to specify that the fodder was for cows only, and that a different word is used to describe the cows themselves (*idt*). As noted previously, this was presumably the result of linguistic convention.

<u>Subheading: Row Two, Symbols Two and Three:</u>

Hieroglyph V28 𓎛 / rotated 𓎛 / simplified / Linear A symbol L31 𐘀
As we have previously seen, this symbol represents the first hieroglyph in the word:

𓎛𓅓𓏏 *ḥtm* provide (with) [verb] V28 - G39 - X1

𓎛𓏇𓏏𓇋𓅓𓏛 *ḥtm* provide (with) [verb] V28 - Q1 - X1 - G17 - G39 - Y1

𓎛𓃀𓇋𓏛 *ḥtm* provide (with) [verb] V28 - U15 - G17 - Y1

𓎛𓏏𓃀𓏛 *ḥtm* provide (with) [verb] V28 - X1 - U15 - Y1V

<u>Hieroglyphs Z5 - Z5\ \/ Linear A symbol L58</u> 𐘁
As we have seen previously, this symbol represents the word:

★𓈖𓇳 *ȝbd* month [noun] N14 - N11 - Z5 - Z5 - N5

The Translations 399

These two symbols therefore mean "provided [in the] month". This indicates the following categories of items were received in the current month (when the tablet was written) and were added to the amounts already held that had been brought forward from the prior month.

Category Four: Row Two, Symbol Four:

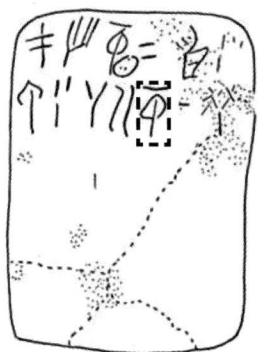

Hieroglyph F27 / partially rotated / simplified / modified / Linear A symbol L42
As we have seen previously, this symbol represents the last hieroglyph in the word:

ꜥr goat [noun - ani.] D36 - D21 - E31 - F27

This symbol therefore means "goats". This is followed by a count of 10.

Category Five: Row Two, Symbol Five:

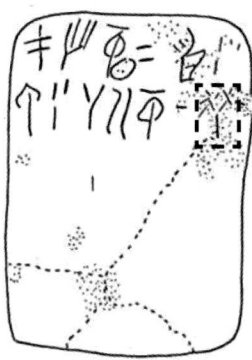

Hieroglyph T25 / rotated / simplified / Linear A symbol L60
As we have seen previously, this symbol represents the first hieroglyph (or, in one instance, last hieroglyph) in the word:

ꞏ *ḏbꜣw* payments, reward, compensation, bribes [noun] T25 - D58

ꞏ *ḏbꜣw* payments, reward, compensation, bribes [noun] T25 - D58
- G1 - Z7 - Y1 - Z2

ꞏ *ḏbꜣw* payments, reward, compensation, bribes [noun] T25 - D58
- G43 - Y1 - Z2

ꞏ *ḏbꜣw* payments, rewards [noun] T25 - D58 - N33 - N33 - N33 - G43

ꞏ *ḏbꜣ* reward, payment [noun] T25 - D58 - Z7 - Y1

ꞏ *ḏbꜣ* reward, payment [noun] D46 - D58 - T25

This symbol therefore means "[for] payments". This is followed by a count of 10. Following on from the previous category, these were, presumably, goats but, although received ostensibly for food, they were going to be used, instead, for payments (presumably to third parties providing goods and services to the temple).

We are now in a position to translate the tablet:

Row One	Heading:	Cattle [for] food
	Category One:	Goats [from the] third [month] – 20
	Category Two:	Grass (cattle fodder) [for] cows [from the third month] – 2
Row Two	Category Three:	Cows [from the third month] – 30
	Subheading:	Provided [in the] month
	Category Four:	Goats – 10
	Category Five:	[For] payments – 10

The Translations

4. Forecasts

The final section of tablets, at least in so far as this work is concerned, deals with forecasts. It considers:

a) Two tablets that, together, evidence annual forecasts for cattle and livestock use being prepared in the temple at Hagia Triada; and
b) Forecasts for cattle and livestock use in future periods (at Hagia Triada and, in Part III of this chapter, at Khania).

We shall consider these in turn.

4(a). Evidence of annual forecasts being prepared in the temple at Hagia Triada

Tablet HT 92 & Tablet HT 133

The next two tablets are clearly related. As we can see, the first three symbols on each tablet are the same but are written in a different order (i.e. A.BC vs BC.A), most likely because each tablet was written by a different scribe (Tablet HT 133 is the more conventional layout) and each evidently had his own preference (but did not seek to convey a different meaning). We can also infer the tablets had different scribes from the different handwriting styles, which is particularly noticeable on the stick held by the man in Linear A symbol L93 and in the use of dashes or dots for units of 10.

As will become evident, Tablet HT 92 is an annual forecast of amounts of goats and cows that were to be issued to the phyle (of priests) from a particular source or particular sources (and, indeed, in respect of a particular purpose). Tablet HT 133 represents a standard monthly number of goats that it seems were regularly to be given to the phyle; it does not include cows which, it would seem, while planned to be given during the year, were not part of the regular monthly issue (suggesting, therefore, they were to be given in respect of special occasions).

That we see evidence of forecasts being prepared is unsurprising for if items being received were described by their future intended application or recipient (which, as we have seen, they were), that implies that there was a forecast that indicated what those future applications or who those future recipients would be. That a number of scribes worked to prepare that forecast is no different from a number of accountants working on a large project today.

402   The Decipherment of Linear A

Tablet HT 92
Heading: Row One, Symbols Two and Three:

Tablet HT 133
Heading: Row One, Symbols One and Two:

Hieroglyph S34 / modifed (loop removed) / Linear A symbol L52
As we have seen previously, this symbol represents the first hieroglyph in the word:

'nḥ sustenance [noun - food] S34 - Z1 - X4 - Z2

'nḥ sustenance [noun - food] S34 - Z1 - Z8

Hieroglyph A24 / modified / simplified / Linear A symbol L93
As we have seen previously, this symbol represents the last hieroglyph in the word:

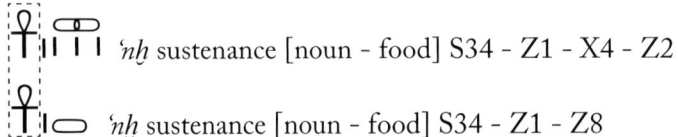 smȝ take part in, receive [verb] F36 - G1 - G17 - Z7 - Z4 - Y1 - A24

These symbols therefore mean "sustenance to [be] receive[d]".

Subheading: Row One, Symbol One:

Subheading: Row One, Symbol Three:

Hieroglyph V16 / rotated / simplified / Linear A symbol L92
As we have seen previously, these symbols represent the first hieroglyphs in the word:

sȝ phyle (of priests), company, regiment (of troops), troop (of animals) [noun]
V16 - A1 - Z2

This symbol therefore means "[for the] phyle (of priests)".

The Translations

Category One: Row One, Symbol Four: Category One: Row One, Symbol Four:

Hieroglyph F27 / partially rotated / simplified / Linear A symbol L42
As we have seen previously, these symbols represent the last hieroglyphs in the word:

ʾr goat [noun - ani.] D36 - D21 - E31 - F27

This symbol therefore means "goats". On Tablet HT 92 this is followed by a count of 680. On Tablet HT 133 this is followed by a count of 55.

Category Two: Row Two, Symbol Two

Hieroglyph F45 / simplified / Linear A symbol L67
As we have seen previously, this symbol represents the first hieroglyph (or, in one instance, last hieroglyph) in the word:

idt cow [noun - ani.] F45 - M17 - N42 - X1
idt cow [noun - ani.] F45 - X1 - Z1 - E1
idt cow [noun - ani.] N41 - X1 - F45

This symbol therefore means "cows". On Tablet HT 92 this is followed by a count of 12. It does not appear on Tablet HT 133 so, presumably, these were animals that were to be allocated on special, but nonetheless planned, occasions during the year, i.e. not in the standard monthly amounts issued. The most likely explanation would seem to be that these were special payments arising from festivals.

We are now in a position to translate both tablets:

		HT 92	HT 133
Row One	Subheading / Heading:	[For the] Phyle	Sustenance [to be] received
	Heading / Subheading:	Sustenance [to be] received	[For the] Phyle
	Category One:	Goats – 680	Goats – 55
Row Two	Category Two:	Cows – 12	

Analysis
As we have seen previously, the heading / subheading "sustenance to be received", appearing frequently as it does when deficits are stated (such as on Tablet HT 14, for example), is a future looking statement; we are, therefore, looking at elements of a forecast on these tablets (and the future recipient is the phyle (of priests)).

As we have noted previously, the Egyptian calendar was made up of 365 days, comprising of 12 months of 30 days plus 5 intercalary days. If the 680 goats and 12 cows on Tablet HT 92 represented one year's food supply, then one month's food, on average, would be 55.9 goats and 1.0 cows (both to 1 decimal place). As cows seem to be for special, but nonetheless planned, occasions they do not appear in the standard forecast month on Tablet HT 133 which, therefore, records only 55 goats (rounded down to the nearest whole animal).

As with all forecasts, what actually happened could vary; thus, in the months recorded on Tablet HT 17 and Tablet HT 19, the number and mix of animals historically allocated to the phyle (of priests) was different, with more cows, some small cattle from (variable) offerings, and some small cattle drawn from the wider temple herd supplementing the lesser numbers of goats that was issued compared to the numbers forecast to be issued in future months. If so, this would perhaps also reflect the various shortfalls in receipts noted throughout the corpus. As with many forecasts created in modern businesses today, the ones being created here were, perhaps, more aspirational than realistic.

The Translations 405

4(b). Forecast for cattle and livestock use in future period

Tablet HT 116A

This tablet considers cattle and livestock and fodder received and to be received in a particular storehouse / barn and sets out the future recipients of these animals and this fodder after New Year's Day (this is, therefore, a forecast of the first month in the New Year).

Heading: Row One, Symbols One to Three:

Hieroglyph T15) / reversed (/ Linear A symbol L69 (

Linear A symbol L69 is a straightforward representation of reversed Hieroglyph T15. As we have previously noted, this hieroglyph is virtually identical to Hieroglyph T14 (necessitating, the reader will recall, that the Linear A symbol that represented Hieroglyph T14 was based upon its replacement, Hieroglyph AA26 (or J26), with which Gardiner noted it could be interchangeable).

Here, therefore, the symbol represents the last hieroglyph in the word:

mtn allocate, assign [verb] G17 - V13 - N35 - T15

Hieroglyph O1 ▭/ rotated ▯/ Linear A symbol L74 ▯

As we have seen previously, this symbol represents the last hieroglyph in the word(s):

🦉 — △ 𓎛 ▭ *mhr* storehouse, barn [noun - arch.] G17 - D36 - T28 - D21 - M17 - O1

🦉 — △ 𓎛 ▭ *mhr* storehouse, barn [noun - arch.] G17 - D36 - T28 - D21 - M17 - X1 - O1

🦉 — △ ▭ *mhr* storehouse, barn [noun - arch.] G17 - D36 - T28 - D21 - O1

— 🦉 𓏥 ▭ *šmyt / šmy* storehouse, barn ambulatory [noun - arch.] N37 - G17 - M17 - M17 - X1 - O1

Hieroglyph N14 ✶/ modified / Linear A symbol L22 +

As we have seen previously, this symbol represents the first hieroglyph in the word:

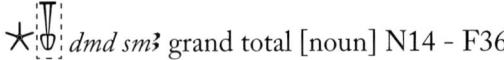 *dmd sm3* grand total [noun] N14 - F36

The three symbols therefore mean "to [be] allocate[d] [from the] storehouse / barn, grand total".

Subheading: Row One, Symbol Four:

The Translations 407

<u>Hieroglyph V16</u> 𓍢 / rotated / simplified / Linear A symbol L92

As we have seen previously, this symbol represents the first hieroglyph in the word:

s3 phyle (of priests), company, regiment (of troops), troop (of animals) [noun]
V16 - A1 - Z2

This symbol therefore means "[for the] phyle (of priests)".

<u>Subheading Two: Row One, Symbols Five to Seven:</u>

<u>Hieroglyph F14</u> / rotated / simplified / Linear A symbol L98

As we have seen previously, this symbol represents the first hieroglyph in the word:

wpt rnpt New Year's Day (and its festivals) [noun] F14 - W3

wpt rnpt New Year's Day (and its festivals) [noun] F15 - W3 - N5

<u>Hieroglyph F35</u> / simplified / Linear A symbol L2

As we have seen previously, this symbol represents the first hieroglyph in the word:

nfrt cattle [noun - ani.] F35 - D21 - X1 - E1 - Z2

nfrt cattle [noun - ani.] F35 - I9 - D21 - X1 - E1 - Z2

nfrt cattle [noun - ani.] F35 - X1 - E1 - Z2

nfrt cattle [noun - ani.] F35 - X1 - Z2

Hieroglyph O11 / simplified / Linear A symbol L32
As we have seen previously, this symbol represents the first hieroglyph in the word:

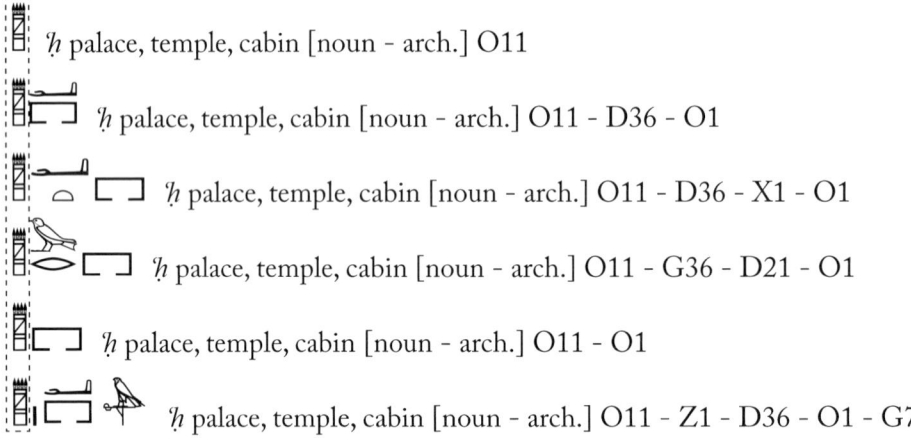

ḥ palace, temple, cabin [noun - arch.] O11

ḥ palace, temple, cabin [noun - arch.] O11 - D36 - O1

ḥ palace, temple, cabin [noun - arch.] O11 - D36 - X1 - O1

ḥ palace, temple, cabin [noun - arch.] O11 - G36 - D21 - O1

ḥ palace, temple, cabin [noun - arch.] O11 - O1

ḥ palace, temple, cabin [noun - arch.] O11 - Z1 - D36 - O1 - G7

These three symbols therefore mean "[on] New Year's Day, cattle [from the] temple."

Category One: Row One, Symbol Eight:

Hieroglyph F27 / partially rotated / simplified / modified / Linear A symbol L42
As we have seen previously, this symbol represents the last hieroglyph in the word:

The Translations

ȝr goat [noun - ani.] D36 - D21 - E31 - F27

This symbol therefore means "goats". This is followed by a count of 16.

<u>Subheading Three: Row One, Symbol Eight:</u>

<u>Hieroglyph M2 / rotated / reversed / Linear A symbol L64</u>
As we have seen previously, this Linear A symbol represents Hieroglyph M2. Given the context in which it appears, here it represents the word:

 ii follow [verb] M2 - M2

<u>Hieroglyphs Z5 - Z5 \ \ / Linear A symbol L58</u>
As we have seen previously, this symbol represents the word:

ȝbd month [noun] N14 - N11 - Z5 - Z5 - N5

These two symbols therefore mean "to follow [in the] month".

410   The Decipherment of Linear A

Category Two: Row Two, Symbol Three:

Hieroglyph F27 ⍼/ partially rotated / simplified / modified / Linear A symbol L42 ⍦
As we have seen previously, this symbol represents the last hieroglyph in the word:

⎯⎯ 🐐 ⍼ *ꜥr* goat [noun - ani.] D36 - D21 - E31 - F27

This symbol therefore means "goats". This is followed by a count of 40. Together with the goats in the previous category, they total 56 goats, 1 more than the standard month's food allocation forecast on Tablet HT 133 (although the standard forecast allocation was, technically, 55.9, so this month it seems they rounded up!)

Category Three: Row Two, Symbols Four and Five:

The Translations 411

Hieroglyph D3 ⋓/ rotated / reversed / Linear A symbol L89
As we have seen previously, this symbol represents the last hieroglyph in the word:

šnw grass (cattle fodder) [noun - flora] V7 - N35 - W24 - Z7 - D3

joined to Hieroglyphs Z5 - Z2 ııı/ rotated / modified / Linear A symbol L51
As we have seen previously, this symbol represents the last hieroglyphs in the word:

ꜥwt small cattle, herds, flocks, goats [noun - ani.] T14 - Z7 - X1 - Z5 - Z2

These two joined symbols therefore mean "grass (cattle fodder) [for the] small cattle". They are followed by a count of 5.

Subheading Four: Row Three, Symbols One and Two:

Hieroglyph R1 / simplified / Linear A symbol L57
As we have seen previously, this symbol represents the last hieroglyph in the word:

wdḥw offering table, offerings [noun - furn.] G43 - D46 - V28 - G43 - R1

joined to Hieroglyph D58 / rotated / modified / Linear A symbol L77
As we have seen previously, this Linear A symbol represents Hieroglyph D58. Here it represents the first hieroglyph in the word:

412   The Decipherment of Linear A

⌐⊐ θ
⊔ ⌒ ׀׀׀   *bꜣt* nourishment, food [noun - food] D58 - D36 - X1 - X2 - Z2

These two joined symbols therefore mean "[from] offerings [of] food".

<u>Category Four: Row Three, Symbol Three:</u>

Hieroglyph F27 ⋂/ partially rotated / simplified / modified / Linear A symbol L42 ⌐⊓
As we have seen previously, this symbol represents the last hieroglyph in the word:

⌐⊐ 🐐 ⌂   *ꜥr* goat [noun - ani.] D36 - D21 - E31 - F27

This symbol therefore means "goats". This is followed by a count of 16.

Category Five: Row Three, Symbols Four and Five:

Hieroglyph D3 / rotated / reversed / Linear A symbol L89
As we have seen previously, this symbol represents the last hieroglyph in the word:

šnw grass (cattle fodder) [noun - flora] V7 - N35 - W24 - Z7 - D3

joined to Hieroglyph G1 / simplified / Linear A symbol L103 (reversed)
As we have seen previously, this symbol represents the first hieroglyph in the word:

ȝḥt cow [noun - ani.] G1 - O4 - X1 - E1

The symbol here has, however, been reversed (due to it also being joined to Linear A symbol L89), so the beak points to the right. These two joined symbols therefore mean "grass (cattle fodder) [for the] cows". They are followed by a count of 1.

414   The Decipherment of Linear A

Category Six: Row Three, Symbols Six and Seven:

Hieroglyph D3 / rotated / reversed / Linear A symbol L89
As we have seen previously, this symbol represents the last hieroglyph in the word:

šnw grass (cattle fodder) [noun - flora] V7 - N35 - W24 - Z7 - D3

joined to Hieroglyph D36 / modified / simplified / Linear A symbol L76
As we have seen previously, this symbol represents the first hieroglyph in the word:

iwʿw quadrupeds, animals [noun - ani.] D36 - D36 - F28 - Z3

These two joined symbols therefore mean "grass (cattle fodder) [for the] quadrupeds". They are followed by a count of 6. In this instance, the fodder most likely relates to the previously listed goats.

Category Seven: Row Four, Symbol One:

Hieroglyph F155 ⛎ / simplified / Linear A symbol L49 ⚘ (as here) or modified further ⚘

As we have seen previously, this symbol represents the first hieroglyph in the word:

⛎ 🐂 *wp* horned cattle [noun - ani.] F155 - E1 - Z3

This symbol therefore means "horned cattle". This is followed by a count of 3. Given that we have fodder for cows recorded under this subheading (and the goats are female, so cannot have been described as horned cattle), the horned cattle were, presumably, male cows (i.e. bulls).

In addition, given that this food came from (variable) offerings that could not be planned, or forecasted, perhaps this accounts for these amounts not being included in the standard monthly forecast on Tablet HT 133 (but, that said, it could equally be the case that there was a forecast for offerings that were likely to be received and distributed, which would have matched the entries on this tablet, but that the separate tablet it was recorded on, if it existed, has simply not survived).

416   The Decipherment of Linear A

Subheading Five: Row Four, Symbols Two to Four:

Hieroglyph AA6 (or J6) ⋀ or S23 ⋀ / modified / simplified / Linear A symbol L85 ⋀⋀
As we have seen previously, this symbol represents the word or first hieroglyph in the word:

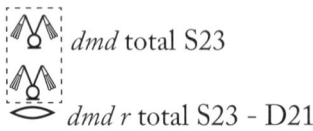

dmd total S23

dmd r total S23 - D21

The use of the word for "total" here suggests that up to and including this point the animals and fodder in question have been received into the storehouse / barn already and await issue whereas the amounts recorded from the next subheading, Subheading Six, onwards had not yet been received when the tablet was written (but would be, and would then be issued, in the future).

Hieroglyph T15) / reversed (/ Linear A symbol L69 (
As we have seen previously, this symbol represents the last hieroglyph in the word:

mtn allocate, assign [verb] G17 - V13 - N35 - T15

To note, the dot at the apex of the curve does not appear to be anything other than this being where the scribe had to adjust his angle of incision when he was incising this symbol on the tablet which led to a slight scuffing of the clay at this point.

The Translations 417

Hieroglyph V16 𓎙 / rotated 𓎙 / simplified / Linear A symbol L92 ⚹

As we have seen previously, this symbol represents the first hieroglyph in the word:

𓎙𓀀𓏼 s3 phyle (of priests), company, regiment (of troops), troop (of animals) [noun]
V16 - A1 - Z2

These three symbols therefore mean "total – to [be] allocate[d] [to the] phyle (of priests)".

Category Eight: Row Four, Symbols Two to Four:

Hieroglyph F27 / partially rotated / simplified / modified / Linear A symbol L42

As we have seen previously, this symbol represents the last hieroglyph in the word:

𓂝𓂋𓃠 ꜥr goat [noun - ani.] D36 - D21 - E31 - F27

This symbol therefore means "goats". This is followed by a count of 5.

418 The Decipherment of Linear A

<u>Category Nine: Row Five, Symbols One and Two:</u>

<u>Hieroglyph D3</u> 〰/ rotated ⌇ / reversed ⌇ / <u>Linear A symbol L89</u> ⌇
As we have seen previously, this symbol represents the last hieroglyph in the word:

⌇ *šnw* grass (cattle fodder) [noun - flora] V7 - N35 - W24 - Z7 - D3

joined to <u>Hieroglyph R7</u> ⌇ / modified / <u>Linear A symbol L6</u> ⌇
As we have seen previously, this symbol repesents the first hieroglyph in the word:

⌇ *b3* sacred ram, ram, Ba, soul [noun - ani.] R7 - E10

These two joined symbols mean "grass (cattle fodder) [for the] rams". They are followed by a count of 5.

Category Ten: Row Five, Symbols Three and Four:

Hieroglyph D3 〰/ rotated / reversed / Linear A symbol L89

As we have seen previously, this symbol represents the last hieroglyph in the word:

𓃀 𓏥 šnw grass (cattle fodder) [noun - flora] V7 - N35 - W24 - Z7 - D3

joined to Hieroglyph D36 ⟶ / modified / simplified / Linear A symbol L76

As we have seen previously, this symbol represents the first hieroglyph in the word:

iw'w quadrupeds, animals [noun - ani.] D36 - D36 - F28 - Z3

These two joined symbols therefore mean "grass (cattle fodder) [for the] quadrupeds". They are followed by a count of 1.

420   The Decipherment of Linear A

<u>Category Eleven: Row Five, Symbols Five and Six:</u>

Hieroglyph F155 ⛝ / simplified / Linear A symbol L49 ⚶ (as here) or modified further ⚶

As we have seen previously, this symbol represents the first hieroglyph in the word:

⛝ 🐂 *wp* horned cattle [noun - ani.] F155 - E1 - Z3

joined to Hieroglyph R7 ⛉ / modified / Linear A symbol L6 ⚴
As we have seen previously, this symbol represents the first hieroglyph in the word:

⛉ 🐏 *b3* sacred ram, ram, Ba, soul [noun - ani.] R7 - E10

On this tablet we have already seen the use of Linear A symbol L49, representing the collective noun "horned cattle", where it implied a meaning of male cows (i.e. bulls). Here, to indicate that same symbol had a different meaning, it is joined to the symbol meaning "rams", namely Linear A symbol L6 representing Hieroglyph R7, the first hieroglyph in the Middle Egyptian word *b3*. The symbol for male sheep that we saw on Tablet HT 2 and Tablet HT 21A, Linear A symbol L44 (Hieroglyph S29 + male = symbol) has not been used, presumably simply as a matter of scribal preference or, perhaps, linguistic convention, as in both of those examples that symbol was joined to the symbol for "grass (cattle fodder)".

These two joined symbols here therefore mean "horned cattle (rams)". They are followed by a count of 2.

It is perhaps also interesting to note that the issue to the phyle of 2 male animals (rams) and 5 female animals (goats) under Subheading Five is in the same proportion (allowing for low numbers and rounding to the nearest whole animal) that we saw on Tablet HT 14, Tablet HT 114A, and Tablet HT 121. Here, male animals are 40% of female animals, but if only one ram had been issued, the ratio would have been 20%; thus, it was not possible to achieve exactly the 30% ratio seen paid in the tithe-like tax that the temple received without slaughtering a ram and using half, which was clearly not the intention here. As we have seen, these tablets concerned the remuneration of the priests (termed "wages" (*trsst*)). Perhaps not coincidentally, the number and type of animals are the same as recorded on Tablet HT 121 (if we assume that the male quadrupeds on Tablet HT 121 were, in fact, rams).

Although not being expressly termed as "wages" (*trsst*), therefore, it seems more likely than not that this issue to the phyle (of priests) represents remuneration being paid, hence the amount is recorded under a different subheading from those previously. Not being expressly termed as wages (*trsst*) either, however, it seems more likely than not that Category One and Two on the tablet, totalling 56 goats, were animals to be issued to the phyle (of priests) as food while on duty in their month of service (i.e. eaten at the temple). It is perhaps no coincidence again that the 56 goats recorded in those two categories equals the number of goats implied as issued each month by Tablet HT 92 (55.9 goats per month, rounded up) (one more than the standard 55 goats per month forecasted on Tablet HT 133, again due to rounding). At least at the start of the year the standard monthly issue was, therefore, to be made (despite previous months' apparent shortfalls). This suggests that Tablet HT 92 and Tablet HT 133 recorded goats (and cows) issued as food for the phyle (of priests) while on duty in their month of service, not remuneration, in the strictest sense.

<u>Subheading Six: Row Five, Symbols Seven and Eight, and Row Six, Symbol One:</u>

Hieroglyph R1 / simplified / Linear A symbol L57

As we have seen previously, this symbol represents the last hieroglyph in the word:

 *wdhw* offering table, offerings [noun - furn.] G43 - D46 - V28 - G43 - R1

Hieroglyph G1 / simplified / Linear A symbol L103

As we have seen previously, Linear A symbol L103 represents a simplified Hieroglyph G1. In contrast to its previous use on this tablet in describing the items recorded under Category Five, given its context in a subheading here, here this symbol represents the last hieroglyph in the word:

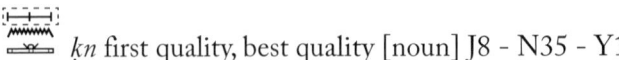 *fk3* reward, present [verb] I9 - N29 - G1

Hieroglyph AA8 (or J8) / rotated / Linear A symbol L61

Godart & Olivier sees this as Linear A symbol as L61; Brice sees this as Linear A symbol L92. I agree with Godart & Olivier. As we have seen previously, this Linear A symbol represents Hieroglyph AA8 (or J8) rotated. Here it represents the word:

kn first quality, best quality [noun] J8 - N35 - Y1

These three symbols therefore mean "[for] offerings to [be] present[ed of the] best quality".

As noted when discussing the previous subheading, these animals have not yet been received into the storehouse / barn (but, implicitly, they were forecasted to be). While the tablet does not expressly state from whom these animals would be received or why (as it concerns outgoings only), the forecasted future outgoings after they were received is stated here.

Category Twelve: Row Six, Symbol Two:

Hieroglyph F27 ⌂/ partially rotated / simplified / modified / Linear A symbol L42 ⟁
As we have seen previously, this symbol represents the word:

⌐⌐ ꜥr goat [noun - ani.] D36 - D21 - E31 - F27

This symbol therefore means "goats". This is followed by a count of 12.

Category Thirteen: Row Seven, Symbol Three:

424   The Decipherment of Linear A

Hieroglyph F45 ⚘ / simplified / Linear A symbol L67 ⋀
As we have seen previously, this symbol represents the first (or, in one case, last) hieroglyph in the word:

idt cow [noun - ani.] F45 - M17 - N42 - X1

idt cow [noun - ani.] F45 - X1 - Z1 - E1

idt cow [noun - ani.] N41 - X1 - F45

This symbol means "cows". This is followed by a count of 12.

Subheading Seven: Row Six, Symbols Four to Six:

Row Six, Symbol Four
The tablet is heavily damaged here. Brice sees this symbol as Linear A symbol L6; Godart & Olivier sees this symbol as Linear A symbol L62 (shown on the sketch diagram). I see it as neither.

In fact there is and was no separate symbol here. If one reviews an extract of the photograph of the tablet that appears in Godart & Olivier, while the surface damage as it extends to the right has the outline drawn by Godart & Olivier, that line, delineating the extreme right of the area of damage, was never the result of a symbol being incised. Rather, the area of damage between the count marks after Symbol Three on this row (i.e. Category Twelve) and Symbol Five on this row (considered next) was never incised, because it formed a brief space between the tally marks that recorded the number of animals falling under Category Twelve and Subheading Three.

Extract of photograph of Tablet HT 116A

Extract of photograph of Tablet HT 116A (space between Category Twelve count and Subheading Seven highlighted)

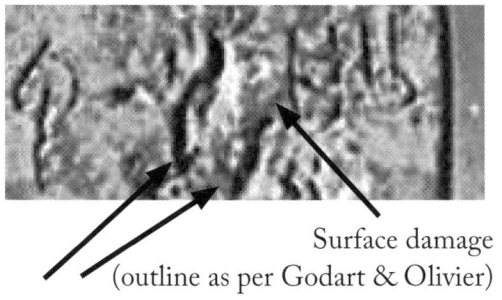

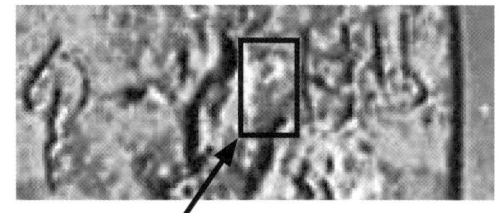

Surface damage (outline as per Godart & Olivier)

Area that never contained a symbol

Deep scores damaging tablet

We shall, therefore, move on to the next symbol, which was incised by the scribe.

<u>Hieroglyph N23 ⛝ / rotated 𓈈 / Linear A symbol L25/7 H</u>
As we have seen previously, this symbol represents the last hieroglyph in the word:

     ꜣḥt field, arable land, earth, mound area (geometry) [noun] G1 - V28 - X1 - N23

     ꜣḥt field, arable land, earth, mound area (geometry) [noun] V28 - G1 - X1 - N23

<u>Hieroglyph V28 𓎛 / rotated 𓎛 / simplified / Linear A symbol L31 Y</u>
As we have seen previously, this symbol represents the first hieroglyph in the word:

     ḥbyt festival offerings, festival court [noun] V28 - D58 - M17 - M17 - X1 - W4

     ḥbyt festival offerings, festival court [noun] V28 - D58 - M17 - M17 - X1 - Y24 - Z3A

     ḥbyt festival offerings [noun] V28 - D58 - W4 - M17 - M17 - X1 - Z2

     ḥbyt festival offerings [noun] V28 - D58 - X1 - W3

joined to Hieroglyphs W24 - Z4A 𓏮 / rotated ⊖ / modified (two dashes inside circle as dots) / Linear A symbols L91 ☺

As set out in Appendix 6, this symbol, representing Hieroglyphs W24 - Z4A, represents the ordinal:

𓏮 *snnw* the second (one), the other, twin, equal, comrade [noun] W24 - Z4A

becomes Linear A symbols L31 + L91 / Linear A symbol L95 ⊕

As set out in Appendix 6, these joined symbols therefore mean "[for] festival offerings [in the] second [month]".

These two symbols therefore mean "[to the] fields, [for] festival offerings [in the] second [month]". It seems these animals had not yet been received into the storehouse / barn (but, implicitly, they were forecasted to be). While the tablet does not expressly state from whom these animals would be received or why (as it concerns outgoings only), the future transfer of the animals in month one so that they would be kept in the fields until their use as festival offerings in the following month, month two, is recorded here. As we will see on the reverse, the tablet is totalled after the categories of items under this subheading. Consequently, this subheading is the final subheading on the tablet and, given that the animals are to be carried forward into a future period for future use, that fact is noted with the addition of a complex ordinal referring to that following month, month two (as discussed in Appendix 8). Presumably the fields were those of the temple, and these animals were to be the temple's contribution to the festival in month two.

Category Fourteen: Row Seven, Symbol One:

Hieroglyph F27 / partially rotated / simplified / modified / Linear A symbol L42

As we have seen previously, this symbol represents the last hieroglyph in the word:

ꜥr goat [noun - ani.] D36 - D21 - E31 - F27

This symbol therefore means "goats". This is followed by a count of 20.

Category Fifteen: Row Seven, Symbol Two:

Hieroglyph F45 / simplified / Linear A symbol L67

As we have seen previously, this symbol represents the first (or, on one case, last) hieroglyph in the word:

idt cow [noun - ani.] F45 - M17 - N42 - X1

idt cow [noun - ani.] F45 - X1 - Z1 - E1

idt cow [noun - ani.] N41 - X1 - F45

This symbol therefore means "cows". This is followed by a count of 3.

We are now in a position to translate the tablet in full:

Row One	Heading: Subheading One:	To [be] allocate[d], [from the] storehouse, grand total [For the] phyle (of priests)
	Subheading Two: Category One:	[On] New Year's Day, cattle [from the] temple Goats
Row Two		– 16
	Subheading Three: Category Two: Category Three:	To follow [in the] month Goats – 40 Grass (cattle fodder) [for the] small cattle – 5
Row Three	Subheading Four: Category Four: Category Five: Category Six:	[From] offerings [of] food Goats – 16 Grass (cattle fodder) [for the] cows – 1 Grass (cattle fodder) [for the] quadrupeds – 6
Row Four	Category Seven:	Horned cattle (bulls) – 3
	Subheading Five: Category Eight:	Total [i.e. final amount in store] – to [be] allocate[d] [to the] phyle (of priests) Goats – 5
Row Five	Category Nine: Category Ten: Category Eleven:	Grass (cattle fodder) [for the] rams – 5 Grass (cattle fodder) [for the] quadrupeds – 1 Horned cattle (rams) – 2
	Subheading Six:	*[to be received, then subsequently issued]* [For] offerings to [be] present[ed]
Row Six		[of the] best quality
	Category Twelve: Category Thirteen:	Goats – 12 Cows – 12
	Subheading Seven:	[To the] fields, [for] festival offerings [in the] second [month]
Row Seven	Category Fourteen: Category Fifteen:	Goats – 20 Cows – 3

The total of the above is on the reverse of the tablet, Tablet HT 116B, which is considered overleaf.

Tablet HT 116B

<u>Total: Row One, Symbols One and Two:</u>

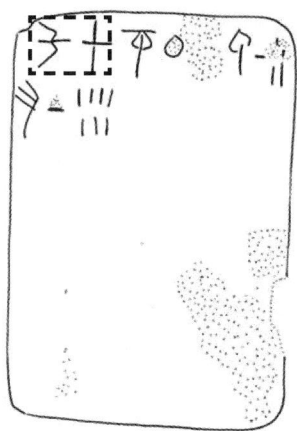

<u>Hieroglyph F14 ⍾ / rotated ⌒/ simplified / Linear A symbol L98 ⤴</u>
As we have seen previously, this symbol represents the first hieroglyph in the word:

⍾⌒ *wpt rnpt* New Year's Day (and its festivals) [noun] F14 - W3

⍾⊙ *wpt rnpt* New Year's Day (and its festivals) [noun] F15 - W3 - N5

<u>Hieroglyph N14 ✶/ modified / Linear A symbol L22 +</u>
As we have seen previously, this symbol represents the first hieroglyph in the word:

✶⌇ *dmd sm3* grand total [noun] N14 - F36

These two symbols therefore mean "[on] New Year's Day, grand total".

430   The Decipherment of Linear A

Category Sixteen: Row One, Symbol Three:

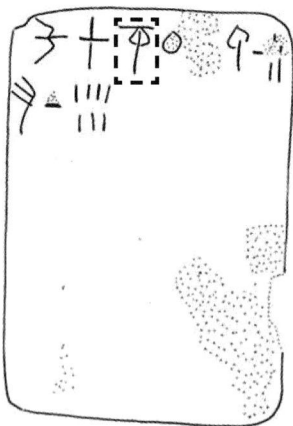

Hieroglyph F27 ⌂/ partially rotated / simplified / modified / Linear A symbol L42 ⍦
As we have seen previously, this symbol represents the last hieroglyph in the word:

ꜥr goat [noun - ani.] D36 - D21 - E31 - F27

This symbol therefore means "goats". This is followed by a count of at least 100 but the full original total is lost due to the tablet being damaged. However, given that this appears to be the total of Categories One (16), Two (40), Four (16), Eight (5), Twelve (12), and Fourteen (20), it would be reasonable to infer that the original count shown here was 109.

Category Two: Row One, Symbol Four:

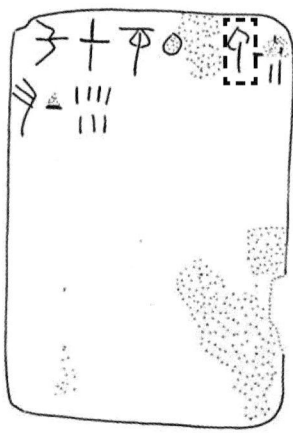

The Translations 431

Hieroglyph F45 / simplified / Linear A symbol L67
As we have seen previously, this symbol represents the first (or, in one case, last) hieroglyph in the word:

idt cow [noun - ani.] F45 - M17 - N42 - X1
idt cow [noun - ani.] F45 - X1 - Z1 - E1
idt cow [noun - ani.] N41 - X1 - F45

This symbol therefore means "cows". This is followed by a count of at least 12 but the full original total is lost due to the tablet being damaged. However, given that this appears to be the total of Categories Thirteen (12) and Fifteen (3), it would be reasonable to infer that the original count shown here was 15.

<u>Category Three: Row Two, Symbol One:</u>

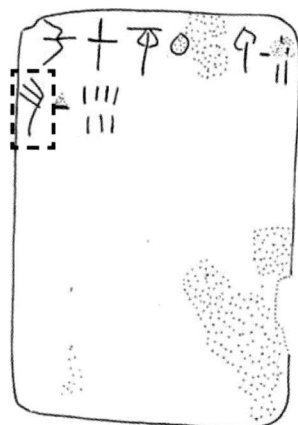

Hieroglyph D3 / rotated / reversed / Linear A symbol L89
As we have seen previously, this symbol represents the last hieroglyph in the word:

šnw grass (cattle fodder) [noun - flora] V7 - N35 - W24 - Z7 - D3

This symbol therefore means "fodder" (of all types). It is followed by a count of 17. It is the total of Categories Three (5), Five (1), Six (6), Nine (5), and Ten (1). This, of course, totals 18. It seems, therefore, that the scribe made an arithmetical error here.

432   The Decipherment of Linear A

We are now in a position to translate this side of the tablet:

Row One	Total: Category One: Category Two:	On New Year's Day, grand total: Goats – [109] Cows – [15]
Row Two	Category Three:	Grass (cattle fodder) – 17 [should be 18]

The question is, then, what has happened to the "horned cattle" (from Categories Seven and Eleven on the front of the tablet)? While the other categories on the front side of the tablet all added to totals on this side of the tablet, why would the "horned cattle" have disappeared? The implied meaning of the collective noun of "horned cattle" is dependent on its context, and we had two different meanings on the front of the tablet, bulls and rams, so, presumably, to present a combined total would have been inappropriate. Why did the scribe not, therefore, present two separate totals? Perhaps, using the symbol for "horned cattle" to present a total for just bulls using Linear A symbol L49, divorced from the context conveyed on the front side of the tablet, would have been too confusing. By why not even write a total for rams, using Linear A symbol L49 joined to Linear A symbol L6 as on the front of the tablet? Perhaps the answer therefore lies in the human factor, and the scribe simply did not complete his count of the final category (or categories). Perhaps, it is appropriate for us to finish his task now, almost three and a half thousand years later. The final two categories should be, in order:

The Translations 433

Part III – Tablet from the temple at Khania, acting as principal, as a religious institution

Tablet KH 11

At the start of this chapter I indicated that, due to the inherent risks entailed in attempting to translate any incomplete shorthand text, I would not translate any damaged tablets where all the symbols had not survived. I am, however, going to break this rule for this tablet, but only because there is sufficient information from those parts of the damaged symbols that do survive that, together with their context on the tablet, we can restore them without undue risk.

This tablet is from Khania (to the north west rather than south of the island) and, as were the tablets from Hagia Triada we have reviewed thus far, it is dated to the Late Minoan IB period. As with the tablets from Hagia Triada, as will become evident this tablet is also the temporary administrative output of a temple of Hathor.

This tablet deals predominantly with animals not yet in the possession of the temple but which were to be issued to certain parties once received, the animal feed for some of those parties that needed to be gathered and issued once it was, and the animal feed already in the possession of the temple or on its property. As the tablet mainly deals with future payments of animals and animal feed to specific parties, it is shown here as a forecast.

<u>Subheading One: Row One, Symbols One to Four</u>

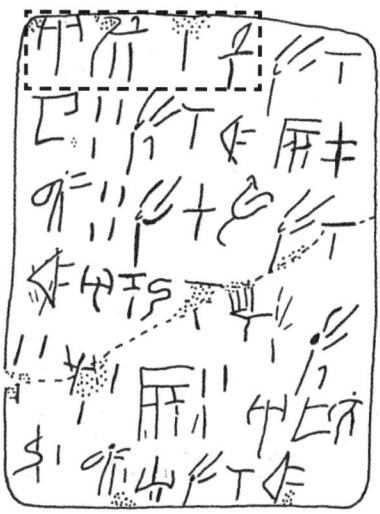

Hieroglyph S34 ☥ /modifed (loop removed) / Linear A symbol L52 ⊤
As we have seen previously, this symbol represents the first hieroglyph in the word:

☥ ||| ⟅ '*nḥ* sustenance [noun - food] S34 - Z1 - X4 - Z2

☥ ⟅ '*nḥ* sustenance [noun - food] S34 - Z1 - Z8

Hieroglyph A24 / modified / simplified / Linear A symbol L93
As we have seen previously, this symbol represents the last hieroglyph in the word:

smꜣ take part in, receive [verb] F36 - G1 - G17 - Z7 - Z4 - Y1 - A24

These two symbols therefore mean "sustenance to [be] receive[d]".

(restored) Hieroglyphs W11 - Z1 / simplified / Linear A symbol L39 ⊤
The derivation of this Linear A symbol from the hieroglyphs it represents is most clearly seen when it next appears on this tablet (which is considered below). For now, however, Linear A symbol L39 represents Hieroglyphs W11 - Z1. Here it represents the first hieroglyphs in the word:

gb deficiency [noun] W11 - Z1 - D58

The reason for restoring this symbol, only the bottom half of which survives, is that, when the phrase "sustenance to be received" was used in the second subheading on Tablet HT 14, it was also explicitly stated that this related to a deficiency. Here, again, it seems likely that when the subheading "sustenance to be received" was used, there was a deficiency, and that this is the most likely meaning of this symbol. The word order is different compared to Tablet HT 14, but we are not dealing with literary Middle Egyptian and, as we saw with the subheading on Tabet HT 2 in comparison, word order can vary. As discussed in Chapter Three, in English, when used in an administrative context, we can just as easily write "apples to be received from the supplier" as "to be received from the supplier, apples". We see the same here.

Finally, it seems that the gap in front of this symbol is larger than one might expect, perhaps suggesting something of a section break, despite a section break dot not being written. For this reason, therefore, I shall insert a hyphon before this word in the translation.

The Translations

Hieroglyph S34 ⚚ / simplified / Linear A symbol L23 ⚚

As we have seen previously, when the word for goats is represented, it is typically represented by Linear A symbol L42 reprsenting Hieroglyph F27, the last hieroglyph in the Middle Egyptian word:

🝆 𓌳 𓃗 ꜥr goat [noun - ani.] D36 - D21 - E31 - F27

Here, however, the scribe has used Linear A symbol L23, representing Hieroglyph S34, to represent the first hieroglyph in the word:

⚚ 𓃗 ꜥnḫ goat, small cattle [noun - ani.] S34 - E31

⚚ 𓅂 𓃗 ||| ꜥnḫ goat, small cattle [noun - ani.] S34 - G43 - E31 - Z2

⚚ ⌇ ꜥ 𓃘 ꜥnḫ goat, small cattle [noun - ani.] S34 - N35 - J1 - Z1 - F28 - Z3

As with the word ꜥr, ꜥnḫ can represent goats of either gender. As we shall see, therefore, the scribe subsequently had to additionally specify which gender of animal he was referring to as he recorded the different categories on the tablet.

These four symbols therefore mean "[from the] sustenance to [be] receive[d] – [for the] deficiency [of] goats".

Category One: Row One, Symbols Five and Six:

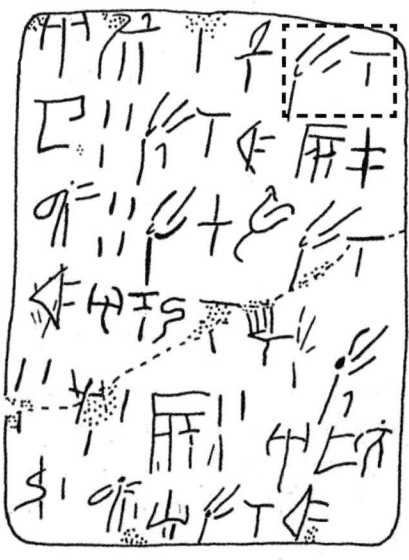

Hieroglyph A28 [glyph] / reversed [glyph] / simplified / modified (bowing slightly) / Linear A symbol L71 [glyph]

As we have seen previously, this symbol represents the last hieroglyph in the word:

[glyph] *i3s* (a Priest of Hathor) [noun - title] M17 - S29 - A28

This symbol therefore means "[for the] *i3s* (Priests of Hathor)".

Hieroglyph S34 [glyph] / modifed (loop removed) / Linear A symbol L52 [glyph] (without sidebars)

While the symbol that follows here has been considered to be a fraction symbol, Linear A fraction symbol K (i.e. T), it is not. As we have discussed, Tablet HT 120 indicated that this symbol specifically related to female animals (where it was used as a subscript descriptor of the noun it related to, also goats). It was determined that it related to female animals because all of the other animals recorded on that tablet, that were not accompanied by this symbol, had the male = sign.

Here, the symbol is not used in subscript, so it is not describing a noun that it relates to; instead, it is the noun. The symbol, therefore, represents the first hieroglyph in the word:

[glyph] *'nht* nanny goat, small domestic animal [noun - ani.] S34 - N35 - J1 - F27

[glyph] *'nht* nanny goat, small domestic animal [noun - ani.] S34 - N35 - J1 - X1 - E31

[glyph] *'nh* nanny goat [noun - ani.] S34 - N35 - J1 - Z7 - E31 - Z1

[glyph] *'nht* nanny goat, small domestic animal [noun - ani.] S34 - X1 - F27

Instead of recording a count of 1 after the more typical symbol for (nanny) goats (i.e. Linear A symbol L42 without the male = sign), in this instance the scribe has wanted to be more specific and, under the subheading indicating that the items recorded after it concerned a deficiency of goats (whose gender is not defined), he has then explicitly stated that this category of recipient was to receive "[a] nanny goat". The result is that the symbol, here, has been confused with a fraction symbol, which it is not.

These two symbols, therefore, mean "[for the] *i3s* (Priests of Hathor) – [a] nanny goat".

The Translations   437

Category Two: Row Two, Symbol Two:

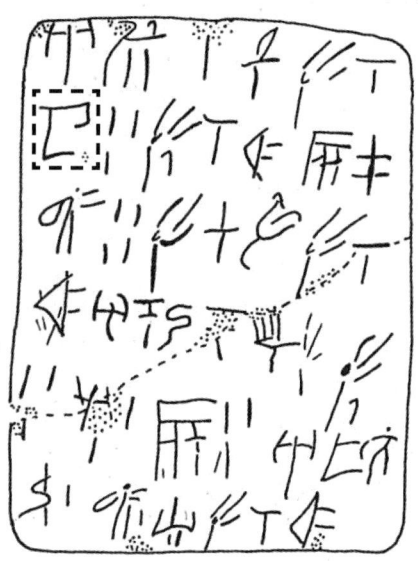

Hieroglyph O4 ⌐⌐/ rotated ⌐/ Linear A symbol L59 ᒉ or ᒉ

The *i3s* Priests of Hathor have already been listed so this symbol could not represent the word *h3tyw* which, as we saw on Tablet HT 118, meant "[the] phyle on duty". As we have seen previously, therefore, this symbol represents the first hieroglyph in the word:

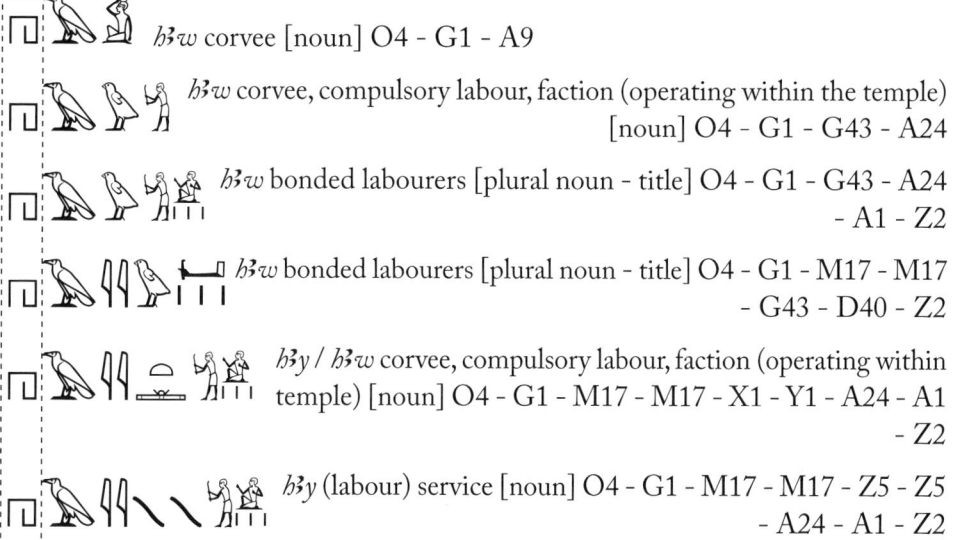

This symbol therefore means "[for the] corvee / labourers". This is followed by a count of 3. As to why it is not expressly stated that this is to be paid in female goats, it is because, as we have seen previously, the category before it recorded a nanny goat and, thus, the items being counted in the category after it, not having been specified to be otherwise, continued to be nanny goats. Moreover, it was impossible to state "three nanny goats" with one symbol using this shorthand method.

438   The Decipherment of Linear A

Category Three: Row Two, Symbols Two to Four

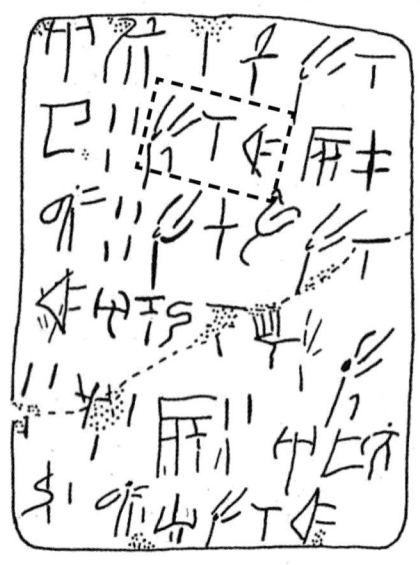

Hieroglyph C11 ᵾ / reversed ᵾ / simplified / unrecognised Linear A symbol ᚠ
This symbol has been misinterpreted by Brice and Godart & Olivier to be Linear A symbol L71 followed by Linear A fraction symbol E, i.e.:

ᚠ followed by 7

This is, however, incorrect although perceiving this is difficult because, in this instance, the front leg of the kneeling stick man is drawn some way in front of his body. In fact, the two parts of the symbol should be joined, i.e.:

ᚠ

This is a Linear A symbol in its own right, and it represents Hieroglyph C11 (reversed). This is considerably clearer when the component parts of the symbol are joined up as, for example, they are on Tablet HT 12, a copy of the extract of the sketch diagram of which is shown below, alongside the hieroglyph that it represents:

Tablet HT 12: Hieroglyph C11
copy of extract of (reversed)
sketch diagram
(extract)

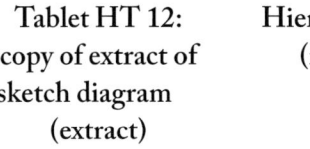

Hieroglyph C11 is a relatively rarely used hieroglyph. In the circumstances, it can, conceivably, only represent the word:

ḥḥ Heh (section of a Phyle) [noun - title] C11

This symbol therefore means "[for the] *Heh* (section of a Phyle)".

Hieroglyph S34 / modifed (loop removed) / Linear A symbol L52 (without sidebars)
As previously noted, this is not a fraction symbol. It is Linear A symbol L52, which represents the first hieroglyph in the word:

ʿnḫt nanny goat, small domestic animal [noun - ani.] S34 - N35 - J1 - F27

ʿnḫt nanny goat, small domestic animal [noun - ani.] S34 - N35 - J1 - X1 - E31

ʿnḫ nanny goat [noun - ani.] S34 - N35 - J1 - Z7 - E31 - Z1

ʿnḫt nanny goat, small domestic animal [noun - ani.] S34 - X1 - F27

These two symbols therefore mean "[for the] *Heh* (section of a Phyle) – [a] nanny goat".

Hieroglyph V19 / rotated / Linear A symbol L47
The next symbol has been seen to be Linear A fraction symbol L2. It is, however, Linear A symbol L47. As we saw on Tablet HT 86A, this is a straightforward representation of Hieroglyph V19 that has been rotated by 90 degrees in order not to be confused with Linear A symbol L44. Again, this symbol represents the word:

mdt byre, cow shed, pen, enclosure [noun - arch.] V19

These three symbols therefore mean "[for the] *Heh* (section of a Phyle), [a] nanny goat [from the] enclosure".

440 The Decipherment of Linear A

Category Four: Row Two, Symbol Five

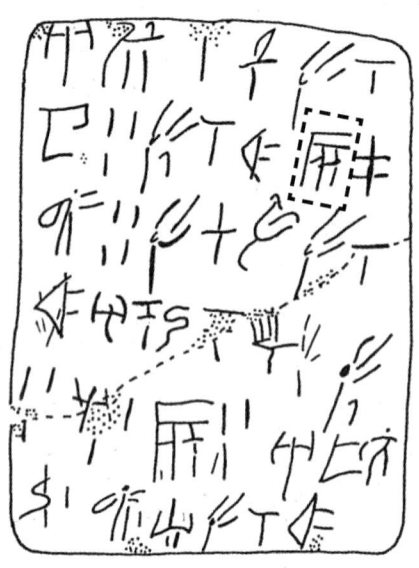

Hieroglyph M20 / rotated / simplified / Linear A symbol L82
As we have seen previously, this symbol represents the first hieroglyph in the word:

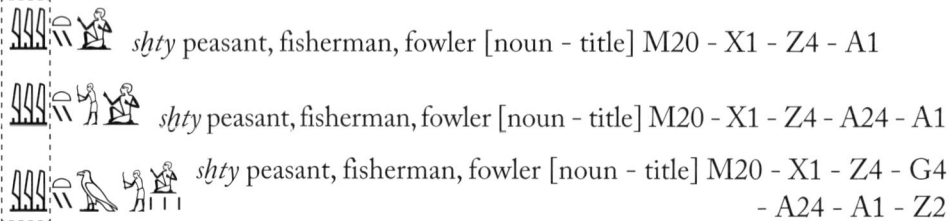

This symbol therefore means "[for the] peasants". This is followed by a count of zero, represented by Linear A fraction symbol A. Thus, presumably, the peasants had already received their allocation of goats when this tablet was written, or why else would this category be included?

The Translations 441

Category Five: Row Three, Symbol One

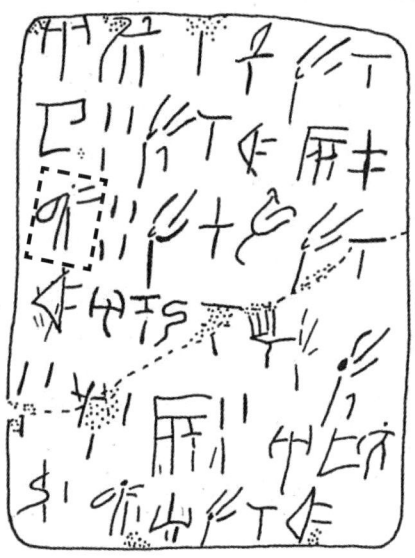

Hieroglyph A1 / reversed / simplified / Linear A symbol unrecognised by Brice

This Linear A symbol is a straightforward simplified representation of Hieroglyph A1. We have frequently seen the Middle Egyptian word *mniw*, meaning "herdsmen" in the corpus of tablets from Hagia Triada. As we have also seen, there were a number of iterations as to how it could be spelled, with those different spellings being capable of abbreviation to a number of hieroglyphs represented by a number of Linear A symbols. Here, further iterations of the spelling of the word are abbreviated to the Linear A symbol representing the last hieroglyph in the words:

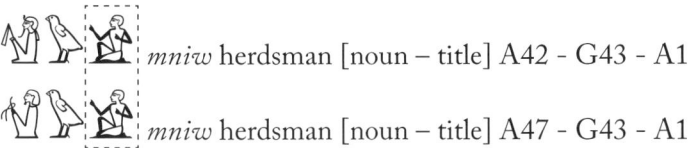

mniw herdsman [noun – title] A42 - G43 - A1

mniw herdsman [noun – title] A47 - G43 - A1

This symbol therefore means "[for the] herdsmen". Presumably this relates to future payment of remuneration to the herdsmen for tending the temple's herds (rather than a future intended transfer into the herdsmen's care of animals that the temple was yet to receive). This is followed by a count of 4. Continuing with the theme of the list, we can again infer that these are nanny goats.

Of course, we have noted previously there appeared to have been a convention at Hagia Triada of representing the word *mniw* with Linear A symbol L84/48 representing Hieroglyph A24 (its last hieroglyph in certain spellings of that word) or Linear A symbol L99 representing Hieroglyph A59 (its first hieroglyph in another spelling of that word). The temple at Khania, while dedicated to the worship of the same goddess, Hathor,

442   The Decipherment of Linear A

seems to have had slightly different shorthand practices, such as recording single animals on this tablet by their animal type (i.e. "a (nanny) goat") rather than stating the animal type in the subheading or category and using a single tally mark to count it (i.e."|"). Similarly, while both the temple at Khania and the temple at Hagia Triada were temples to the Goddess Hathor, even if practices had been the same, as we have noted previously, the vocabulary that scribes used could also have been determined by their different professional backgrounds. Consequently, it is not unexpected that the scribe at Khania used this symbol to represent a different hieroglyph from a different spelling of the word *mniw* compared to those that we have seen at Hagia Triada.

Category Six: Row Three, Symbol Two and Three

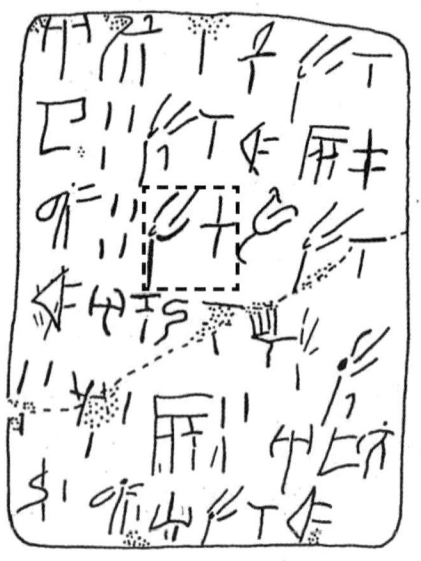

Hieroglyph A28 / reversed / simplified / modified (bowing slightly) / Linear A symbol L71

As we have seen previously, this symbol represents the last hieroglyph in the word:

i3s (a Priest of Hathor) [noun - title] M17 - S29 - A28

Here this symbol means "[for the] *i3s* (Priests of Hathor)". Ordinarily it would be unexpected for the same category to appear twice in a list under the same subheading. That it happens here on a list of forecast distributions by future recipient indicates that what was to be paid to this future recipient when listed for the second time differs to what was to be paid to this future recipient when listed for the first time, which we shall see is the case from the next symbol.

The Translations 443

Hieroglyph Z11 ⟊ / simplified / Linear A symbol L22 †
So far, when one item to be distributed was recorded on this tablet, the scribe used an abbreviation of the word for the item in question. Here, therefore, while this may appear to be Linear A fraction symbol B (i.e. +), in this instance it is not (because that would not explain the second occurrence of this future recipient on this list of future recipients). In fact, it represents the first hieroglyph in the word:

⟊𓀁𓅱𓃾 *wnmw* (cattle) feed [noun] Z11 - A2 - G43 - E186

We therefore have "[for the] *i3s* (Priests of Hathor) – cattle feed [1 unit]".

<u>Category Seven: Row Three, Symbols Four to Six, and Row Four, Symbol One</u>

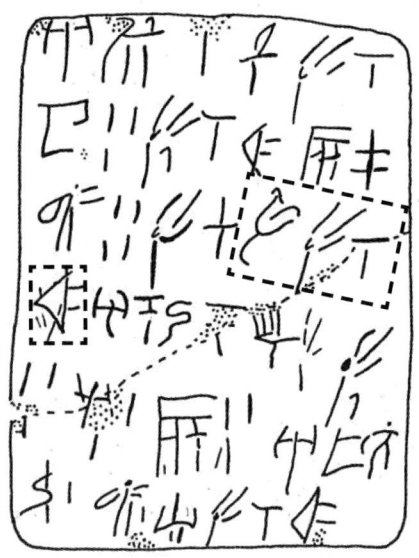

Hieroglyph F22 𓄘 / rotated ℓ / Linear A symbol ℰ unrecognised by Brice
This Linear A symbol is Hieroglyph F22 rotated, presumably to save space horizontally. In his attempt to draw the symbol, the scribe has not, however, managed to join the two curved lines that would form the contained space at the centre of the hieroglyph, but we can see the hieroglyph represented by it nonetheless. Here, it represents the first hieroglyph in the word:

𓄘𓌳𓏏𓏲 *ph spdt* 22nd day of the month [noun] F22 - M44 - X1 - W3

This therefore means "[on the] 22nd day of the month".

444   The Decipherment of Linear A

Hieroglyph A28 𓀠 / reversed 𓀡 / simplified / modified (bowing slightly) / Linear A symbol L71

As we have seen previously, this symbol represents the first hieroglyph in the word:

𓅓𓀠 *i3s* (a Priest of Hathor) [noun - title] M17 - S29 - A28

Hieroglyph S34 ☥ / modifed (loop removed) / Linear A symbol L52 † (without sidebars)
As previously noted, this is not a fraction symbol. It is Linear A symbol L52 representing the first hieroglyph in the word:

☥ 〜 𓃶 *'nḫt* nanny goat, small domestic animal [noun - ani.] S34 - N35 - J1 - F27

☥ 〜 𓃶 *'nḫt* nanny goat, small domestic animal [noun - ani.] S34 - N35 - J1 - X1 - E31

☥ 〜 𓃶 ||| *'nḫ* nanny goat [noun - ani.] S34 - N35 - J1 - Z7 - E31 - Z1

☥ 𓃶 *'nḫt* nanny goat, small domestic animal [noun - ani.] S34 - X1 - F27

Hieroglyph V19 ⊓ / rotated ⊏ / Linear A symbol L47
As we have seen previously, this symbol represents the word:

⊓ *mdt* byre, cow shed, pen, enclosure [noun – arch.] V19

These four symbols therefore mean "[on the] 22nd day of the month, [for the] *i3s* (Priests of Hathor) – [a] nanny goat [from the] enclosure".

The *i3s* (Priests of Hathor) were recorded in Category One as being owed a nanny goat (and Category Six as being owed feed); here they are recorded again receiving a nanny goat in the future. Here, however, while the animal is also yet to be received by the temple, so cannot be paid out, it is due to be paid out later in the month (hence it is recoded last in the list under this subheading). Like a typical Australian business' payroll, which is paid fortnightly, rather than a typical British business' payroll, which is paid monthly, the remuneration paid to the *i3s* (Priests of Hathor) here seems to have been split. Presumably this was because the date of the future outgoing payment was matched to the anticipated date of the receipt of the animal needed to meet that payment obligation (indeed, this must have been forecasted). As to why it is only the *i3s* (Priests of Hathor) at this temple whose remuneration is split during the month, perhaps, in the extreme, like a struggling private business today where owner-managers might defer their salary to help their business' cashflow so that the rest of the bills can be paid on time, the priests were prepared to defer their remuneration here. This is not to say that this temple was necessarily struggling to find the resources necessary to meet its obligations; but it was matching the timing of its most controllable payments to the timing of the receipts that it needed to pay them with.

Subheading Two: Row Four, Symbols Two to Six

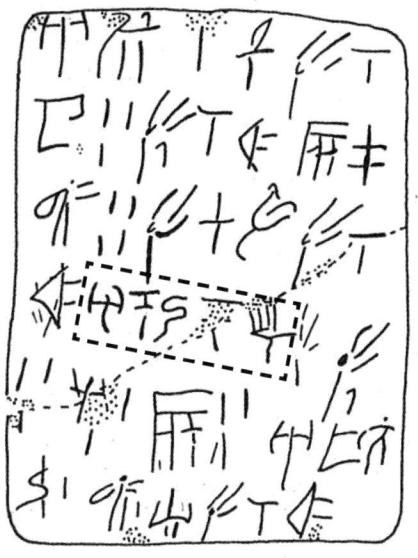

Hieroglyph S34 ⚱ / modifed (loop removed) / Linear A symbol L52 ⊤

As we have seen previously, this symbol represents the first hieroglyph in the word:

⚱ | | | | ⌒ 'nḫ sustenance [noun - food] S34 - Z1 - X4 - Z2

⚱ | ⌒ 'nḫ sustenance [noun - food] S34 - Z1 - Z8

Hieroglyph W11 - Z1 ▣ / modified / simplified / Linear A symbol L39 ⊤

This Linear A symbol is derived from two component hieroglyphs that are joined. This is most clearly seen here because the scribe has written the representation of the component hieroglyphs separately (one of them simplified). This can be seen by a comparison of Hieroglyphs W11 - Z1 with Linear A symbol L39 how it is written here and how it is most commonly written, which is set out below:

446   The Decipherment of Linear A

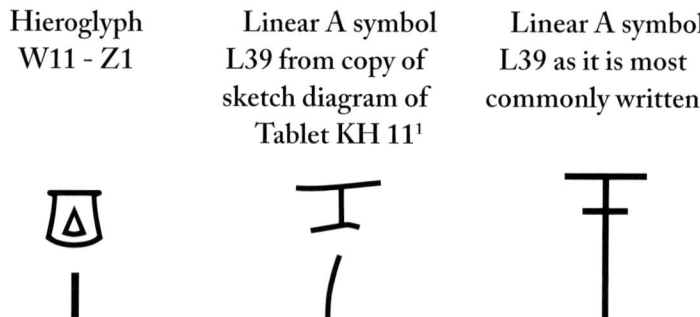

Here again, therefore, this symbol represents the first hieroglyphs in the word:

gb deficiency [noun] W11 - Z1 - D58

Hieroglyph U19 ↶ / rotated ↷ / reversed ↶ / Linear A symbol unrecognised by Brice
This Linear A symbol is derived from the hieroglyph it represents by rotating it clockwise in order to save space horizontally (then reversed for ease of inscription by a right-handed scribe). From its context on the tablet, it appears most likely that the symbol represents the word:

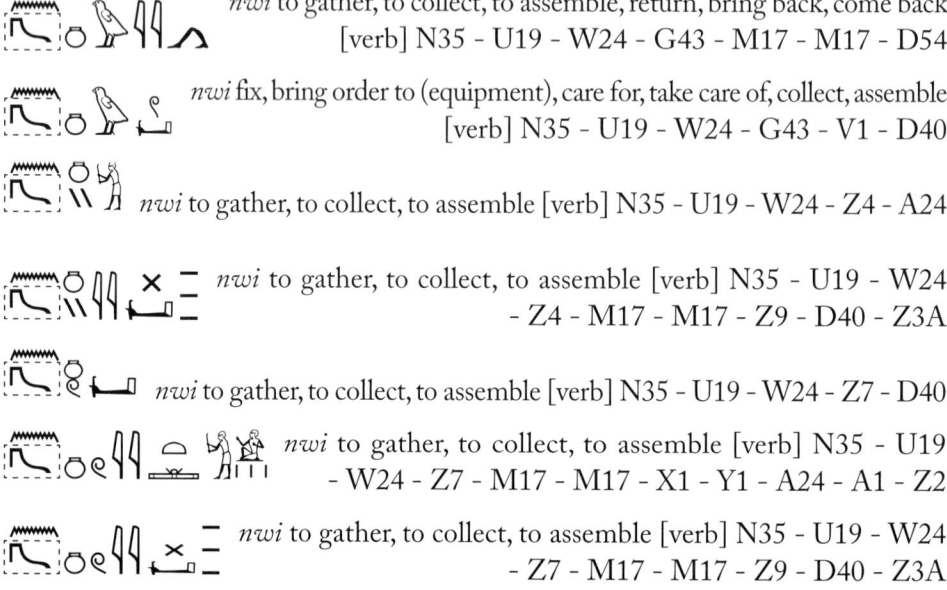

nwi to gather, to collect, to assemble, return, bring back, come back [verb] N35 - U19 - W24 - G43 - M17 - M17 - D54

nwi fix, bring order to (equipment), care for, take care of, collect, assemble [verb] N35 - U19 - W24 - G43 - V1 - D40

nwi to gather, to collect, to assemble [verb] N35 - U19 - W24 - Z4 - A24

nwi to gather, to collect, to assemble [verb] N35 - U19 - W24 - Z4 - M17 - M17 - Z9 - D40 - Z3A

nwi to gather, to collect, to assemble [verb] N35 - U19 - W24 - Z7 - D40

nwi to gather, to collect, to assemble [verb] N35 - U19 - W24 - Z7 - M17 - M17 - X1 - Y1 - A24 - A1 - Z2

nwi to gather, to collect, to assemble [verb] N35 - U19 - W24 - Z7 - M17 - M17 - Z9 - D40 - Z3A

---

1. As noted, and as can be seen above, when simplified, Hieroglyph W11 appears similar to Linear A symbol L14 which, as we have seen, represents Hieroglyph M12. Given that the word for loaves, *ḥrps*, was abbreviated to Linear A symbol L14 (representing its first hieroglyph, Hieroglyph M12), the word represented on this tablet was not abbreviated to a symbol representing just its first hieroglyph, Hieroglyph W11 (similarly other words that begin with Hieroglyph W11 were also not abbreviated to a symbol representing that hieroglyph e.g. the Middle Egyptian word *gbi*, meaning "deficiency", was abbreviated to its second hieroglyph, Hieroglyph G1). Here, therefore, Hieroglyph W11 is added to Hieroglyph Z1 and then simplified, resulting in the distinct Linear A symbol L39.

Here this symbol means "to be collected". Of course, this symbol does not represent the first or last hieroglyph in the word that it represents; it represents its second hieroglyph. As we saw when analysing Linear B Tablet DK 1076, the most likely reason for this is that Hieroglyph N35, by itself, spells the Middle Egyptian word *n*, a preposition meaning "to", "for", or "because of". If a symbol representing just this hieroglyph were to appear then it would be confusing for the reader as to whether the preposition or another word was intended to be conveyed by it. Consequently, the second hieroglyph is chosen to represent the word (and, indeed, Hieroglyph N35 is not, apparently represented by any Linear A symbol because it is not represented in the corpus).

(restored) Hieroglyphs N5 - Z1 / simplified / modified / Linear A symbol L26

As we have seen previously, when a deficiency is noted in a subheading, it is noted, in modern parlance, to be a "current" deficit and, in Linear A parlance, it is noted to be a deficit "now". This is seen, for example, on Tablet HT 14 and Tablet HT 2. For that reason, restoring this symbol as Linear A symbol L26 appears reasonable and, indeed, this fits with the surviving elements of the symbol, as can be seen below:

Extract of photograph of Tablet KH 11 from Godart & Olivier	Extract of photograph of Tablet KH 11 from Godart & Olivier with existing and restored symbol elements highlighted	Restored symbol as it is believed to have originally appeared on Tablet KH 11
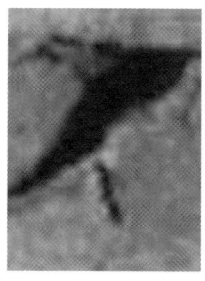	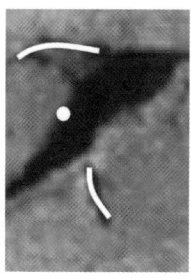	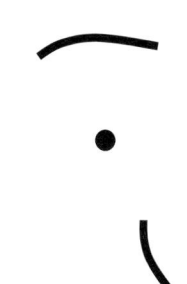

As discussed on Tablet HT 102, Hieroglyphs N5 - Z1 are simplified and modified to become Linear A symbol L26. Here this symbol represents the last hieroglyphs in the word:

m ꜣ wnwt now, immediately, at once G17 - X1 - G1 - E34 - N35 - W24 - X1 - N2 - N5 - Z1

m ꜣ wnwt now, immediately, at once G17 - X1 - G1 - E34 - N35 - W24 - X1 - N14 - N5 - Z1

m ꜣ wnwt now, immediately, at once G17 - X1 - G1 - Z4 - E34 - N35 - W24 - X1 - N14 - N5 - Z1

448   The Decipherment of Linear A

Hieroglyph D46 ⊂⊃ / rotated / simplified / Linear A symbol L100 Ψ
While previously we have seen that this symbol represents the first hieroglyph in the word:

     drpw offerings, provisions, meal, sustenance [noun - food] D46 - D21
                                                                                             - Q3 - Z7 - N37 - Z2

here, however, as we saw on Tablet HT 120, this symbol represents the first hieroglyph in the related verb:

     drp offer to (god), feed (someone), present (dues), to make offerings
                                                                                        [transitive verb] D46 - D21 - Q3 - D40

These five symbols therefore mean "sustenance deficit to [be] gather[ed] now, [for] feed[ing]". This section therefore appears to deal with animal fodder. As we will see, this is also suggested by how certain of the amounts are recorded (in particular, for Category Nine).

Category Eight: Row Four, Symbol Seven:

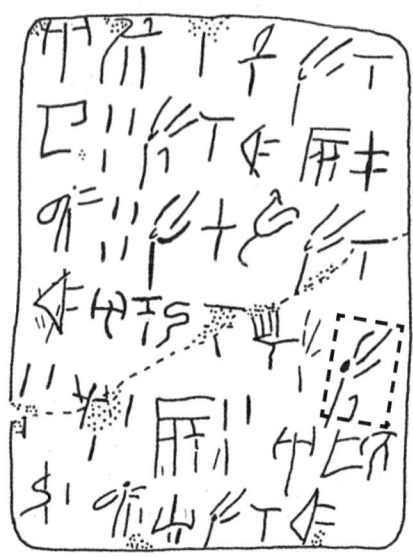

Hieroglyph C11 / reversed / unrecognised Linear A symbol
As we have seen previously, this symbol represents the word:

     ḥḥ Heh (section of a Phyle) [noun - title] C11

This symbol therefore means "[for the] *Heh* (section of a Phyle)". This is followed by a count of 3. Given that the following category records a value of 1, rather than a single animal by animal type, we can infer that this amount (and, similarly, amounts recorded under Category Ten) is an amount of fodder (i.e. sustenance for animals).

Category Nine: Row Five, Symbol One

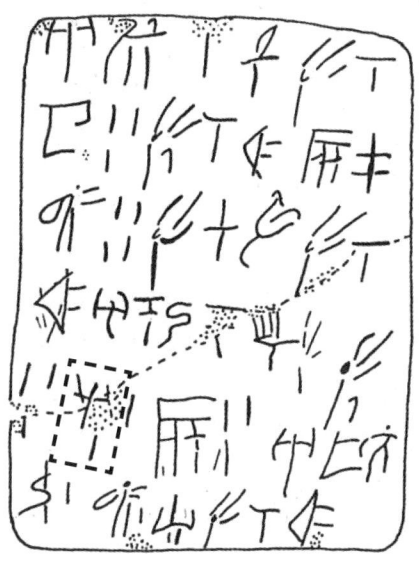

Hieroglyph T25 / rotated / simplified / Linear A symbol L60
As we have seen previously, this symbol represents the first (or, in one instance, last) hieroglyph in the word:

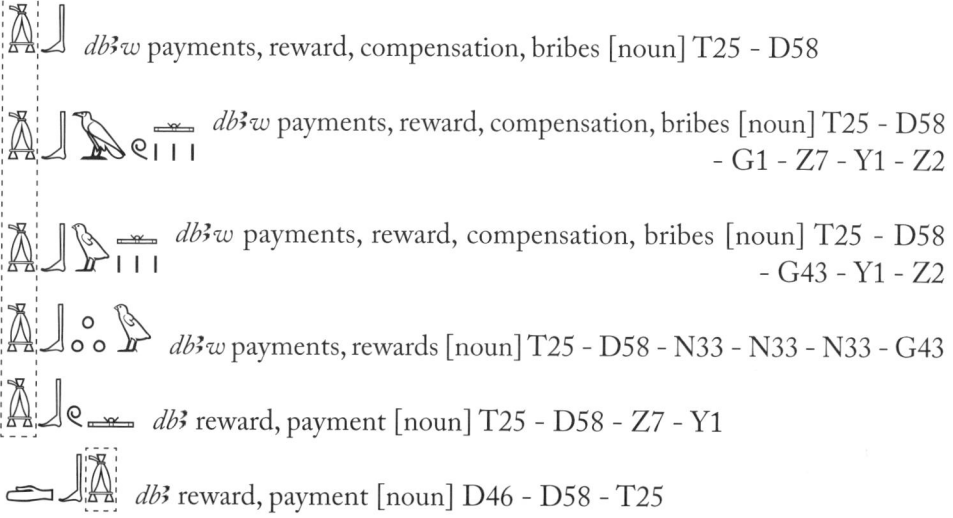

db3w payments, reward, compensation, bribes [noun] T25 - D58

db3w payments, reward, compensation, bribes [noun] T25 - D58 - G1 - Z7 - Y1 - Z2

db3w payments, reward, compensation, bribes [noun] T25 - D58 - G43 - Y1 - Z2

db3w payments, rewards [noun] T25 - D58 - N33 - N33 - N33 - G43

db3 reward, payment [noun] T25 - D58 - Z7 - Y1

db3 reward, payment [noun] D46 - D58 - T25

450   The Decipherment of Linear A

This symbol therefore means "[for] payments". This is followed by a count of 1. Here, a count of 1 indicates that we are not dealing with animals under Subheading Two (as we were, almost exclusively, under Subheading One) and this is not a reference to a singular animal but, rather, we are dealing with units of fodder (i.e. sustenance for animals), as Subheading Two suggests.

Category Ten: Row Five, Symbol Two

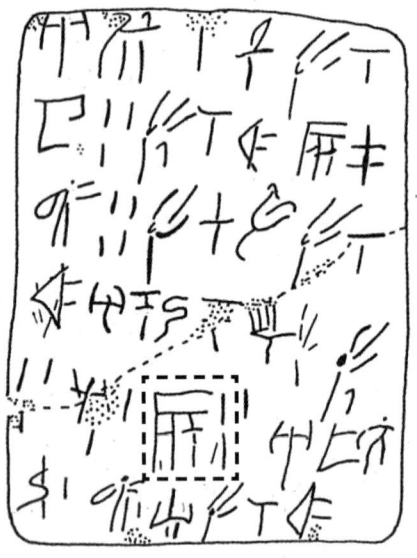

Hieroglyph M20 ![M20] / rotated ![rotated] / simplified / Linear A symbol L82 ![L82]
As we have seen previously, this symbol represents the first hieroglyph in the word:

  ![gly1] *shty* peasant, fisherman, fowler [noun - title] M20 - X1 - Z4 - A1

  ![gly2] *shty* peasant, fisherman, fowler [noun - title] M20 - X1 - Z4 - A24 - A1

  ![gly3] *shty* peasant, fisherman, fowler [noun - title] M20 - X1 - Z4 - G4
                                                                    - A24 - A1 - Z2

This symbol therefore means "[for the] peasants". This is followed by a count of 3 which, as noted, refers to units of fodder. We know that the peasants have animals as, even though they were not due to receive any from the temple, they were still listed in Category Four under Subheading One (so, presumably, they had already received the animals they were due when the tablet was incised). Here, they are to be allocated fodder for those animals.

Subheading Three: Row Five, Symbols Three

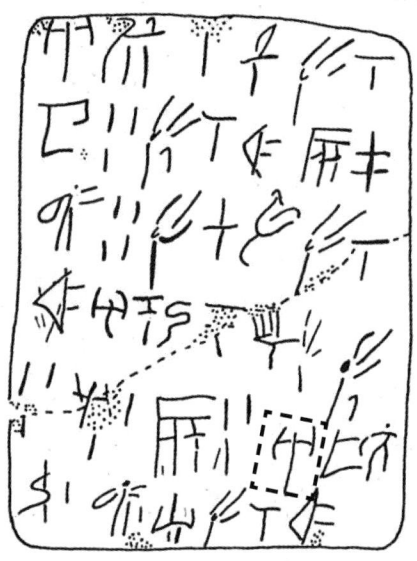

Hieroglyph S34 ⚚ / modifed (loop removed) / Linear A symbol L52 ⊤

As we have seen previously, this symbol represents the first hieroglyph in the word:

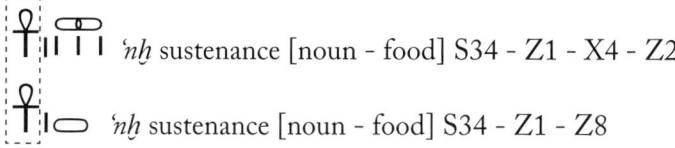

'nḥ sustenance [noun - food] S34 - Z1 - X4 - Z2

'nḥ sustenance [noun - food] S34 - Z1 - Z8

This subheading therefore simply means "sustenance". As will be seen, this section of the tablet records fodder already in hand, by location.

452   The Decipherment of Linear A

Category Eleven: Row Five, Symbol Four

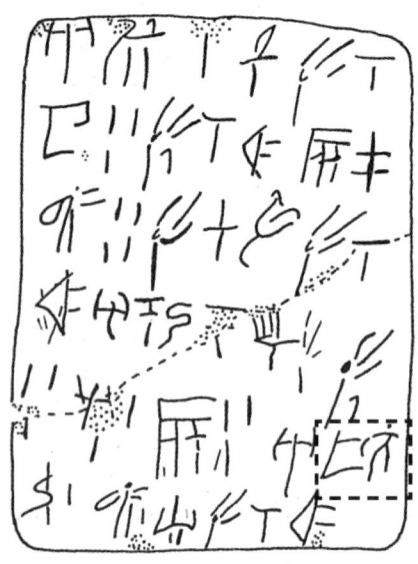

Hieroglyph O1 ⌑/ rotated ⌑/ Linear A symbol L74 ⌑

As we have seen preivously, this first symbol represents the last hieroglyph in the word(s):

mhr storehouse, barn [noun - arch.] G17 - D36 - T28 - D21 - M17 - O1

mhr storehouse, barn [noun - arch.] G17 - D36 - T28 - D21 - M17 - X1 - O1

mhr storehouse, barn [noun - arch.] G17 - D36 - T28 - D21 - O1

šmyt / šmy storehouse, barn ambulatory [noun - arch.] N37 - G17 - M17 - M17 - X1 - O1

This symbol therefore means "[in the] storehouse / barn". This is followed by a count represented by Linear A fraction symbol H (i.e. λ), highlighted second above. As we have seen, represents the word:

mn the remainder is, remainder, balance, due, remains U32

smn remainder [noun] U32 - Y1

Given that the next two categories under Subheading Three record counts of 1, rather than relating to singular animals described by animal type, this *de minimis* value refers, again, to an amount of fodder.

Category Twelve: Row Six, Symbol One

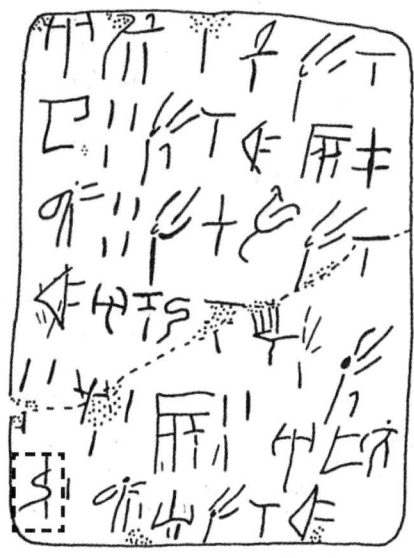

Hieroglyph I14B ⟨symbol⟩ / rotated ⟨symbol⟩/ modified (less curves) / (incorrectly) Linear A symbol L88 ⟨symbol⟩ (reversed)/ ⟨symbol⟩

While this symbol appears similar to the Linear A representation of Hieroglyphs X1 - D17, here it represents Hieroglyph I14B, which has been rotated by 90 degrees, so that it takes up less space horizontally, and simplified so that the snake has less curves (which would have been difficult to incise in clay). This is a rare hieroglyph, which helps us identify its meaning here, namely:

⟨symbol⟩ *β* land [noun] I14B

This symbol therefore means "[on the] land". It is followed by a count of 1. Given that tablet records a count of 1 rather than a singular animal by animal type, we can, again, infer than this is a unit of fodder.

Category Thirteen: Row Six, Symbol Two

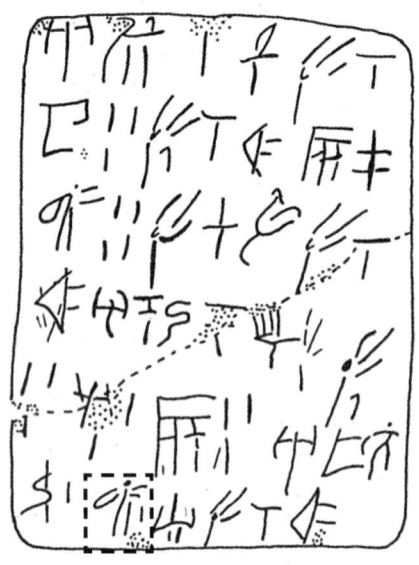

Hieroglyph A1 / reversed / simplified / Linear A symbol unrecognised by Brice

As we have seen previously, this symbol represents the last hieroglyph in the word:

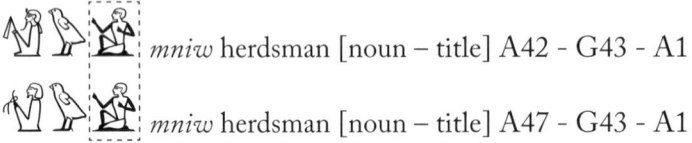

 mniw herdsman [noun – title] A42 - G43 - A1

 mniw herdsman [noun – title] A47 - G43 - A1

This symbol therefore means "[with the] herdsmen". This is followed by a count of 1. Given that the tablet records a count of 1 rather than a singular animal by animal type, we can, again, infer that this is a unit of fodder.

The three categories under Subheading Three, of which this is the third, therefore all deal with fodder: in the storehouse; in the field; and, finally, with the herdsmen.

The Translations   455

Category Fourteen: Row Six, Symbols Three to Six
This category is standalone, showing an animal (a nanny goat) received by the temple as an offering and held for the *i3s* (Priests of Hathor) in the enclosure. This would presumably be used to meet the obligation listed under Category One of the tablet.

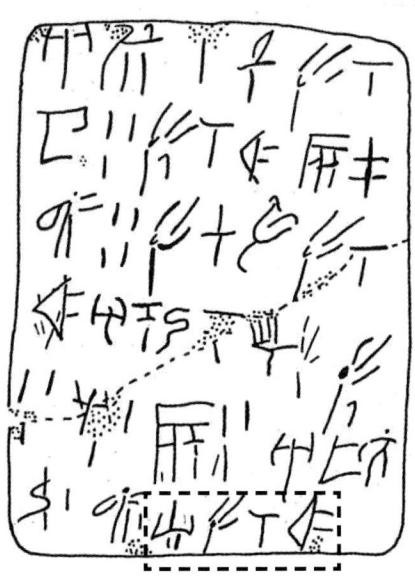

Hieroglyph R1 / simplified / Linear A symbol L57
As we have seen previously, this symbol represents the last hieroglyph in the word:

wdḥw offering table, offerings [noun - furn.] G43 - D46 - V28
— G43 - R1

Hieroglyph A28 / reversed / simplified / modified (bowing slightly) / Linear A symbol L71
As we have seen previously, this symbol represents the last hieroglyph in the word:

i3s (a Priest of Hathor) [noun - title] M17 - S29 - A28

Hieroglyph S34 / modifed (loop removed) / Linear A symbol L52 (without sidebars)
As previously noted this is not a fraction symbol. It is Linear A symbol L52 representing the first hieroglyph in the word:

[hieroglyphs] *'nḥt* nanny goat, small domestic animal [noun - ani.] S34 - N35 - J1 - F27

[hieroglyphs] *'nḥt* nanny goat, small domestic animal [noun - ani.] S34 - N35 - J1 - X1 - E31

[hieroglyphs] *'nḥ* nanny goat [noun - ani.] S34 - N35 - J1 - Z7 - E31 - Z1

[hieroglyphs] *'nḥt* nanny goat, small domestic animal [noun - ani.] S34 - X1 - F27

Hieroglyph V19 [symbol] / rotated [symbol] / Linear A symbol L47 [symbol]

As we have seen previously, this symbol represents the word:

[hieroglyph] *mdt* byre, cow shed, pen, enclosure [noun - arch.] V19

These four symbols therefore mean "[from the] offerings, [for the] *i3s* (Priests of Hathor) – [a] nanny goat [in the] enclosure".

We are now in a position to translate this tablet in full:

Row One	Subheading One:	[From the] sustenance to [be] receive[d] – [for the] deficiency [of] goats
	Category One:	[For the] *i3s* (Priests of Hathor) – [a] nanny goat
Row Two	Category Two:	[For the] corvee / bonded labourers – 3
	Category Three:	[For the] *Heh* (section of a Phyle) – [a] nanny goat
	Category Four:	[For the] peasants – 0
Row Three	Category Five:	[For the] herdsmen – 4
	Category Six:	[For the] *i3s* (Priests of Hathor) – cattle feed [1 unit]
	Category Seven:	[On the] 22nd of the month, [for the] *i3s* (a Priest of Hathor) – [a] nanny goat
Row Four		[from the] enclosure
	Subheading Two:	Sustenance deficit to [be] gather[ed] now, [for] feed[ing]
	Category Eight:	[For the] *Heh* (section of a Phyle)
Row Five		– 3 [units of feed / fodder]
	Category Nine:	[For] payments – 1 [unit of feed / fodder]
	Category Ten:	[For the] peasants – 3 [units of feed / fodder]
	Subheading Three:	Sustenance
	Category Eleven:	[In the] storehouse / barn – remainder [units of feed / fodder]
Row Six	Category Twelve:	[On the] land – 1 [unit of feed / fodder]
	Category Thirteen:	[With the] herdsmen – 1 [unit of feed / fodder]
	Category Fourteen:	[From the] offerings, [for the] *i3s* (Priests of Hathor) – [a] nanny goat [in the] enclosure

Chapter 6

The End of the Beginning?

"He came in here and he trashed the place, and it's not his place to trash"
(David Broder, *Washington Post* (1998))[1]

Linear A is Middle Egyptian written in shorthand using hieroglyphs. Its origins most likely reflect the initial phase of Egypt's involvement in Crete which was probably commercially driven, when Egyptian traders on Crete had significant influence but not control of the island (or, rather, parts of it). Reflective of this influence, it seems that the Egyptian expatriates were allowed their own temples. Most likely in relation to their trading (of which evidence does not survive), but also for the operation of their temples (of which evidence does survive), these Egyptian traders wished to keep their dealings beyond the purview of the Cretans and therefore used Linear A.

After the collapse of Minoan power, Egypt's involvement in Crete transformed and in 1455 BC (most of) Crete and (certain of) the Aegean Islands, including Thera, which had constituted the Minoan Empire, voluntarily became part of Egypt's empire as a protectorate. Egypt's extant temple institutions, in common with the prevailing style of government in Egypt, became agents of the Egyptian state, administering certain state taxes. They continued to use Linear A as there was no need to change; after all, "if it ain't broke, don't fix it". After the Mycenaeans (who had, it seems, been allowed to settle on Crete by the Egyptians) rebelled in c.1424 BC, Egypt withdrew from those remaining territories it still controlled. In Knossos, however, an Egyptian temple still functioned and it continued to act as agent of the (new) state, still administering the same taxes as the temples had previously, and still enjoying at least some of the same privileges for doing so. Surely it was evidence of this agency relationship, between temple and state, which existed in both the Egyptian and Mycenaean periods, that led Sir Arthur Evans to call the rulers of Crete "priest-kings"?

Of the decipherment of Linear B, John Chadwick wrote that "most of the archaeologists were predjudiced against the Greek solution."[2] To paraphrase Mandy Rice-Davies, they would be, wouldn't they? The archaeological evidence now seen as demonstrating the Mycenaean occupation of Crete was not always seen that way; it had to be reassessed in the light of, and to concur with, the decipherment of Linear B. As in the 1950s, so now. The archaeological evidence will have to be reassessed again in light of the decipherment of Linear A. I am sure some academics will have great difficulty in accepting this. I am

---

1. https://www.washingtonpost.com/wp-srv/politics/special/clinton/stories/quinn110298.htm. With thanks to my friend Marco Soto for this quote.
2. John Chadwick, *The Decipherment of Linear B* (2nd Ed.)(Cambridge: Cambridge University Press, 1967), p68

sure for that reason the conclusions of this work will never be accepted by some academics. In the 1950s, however, written Linear B evidence quickly prevailed in the academics' deliberations over extrapolations from (partial) archaeological evidence; the better form of evidence prevailed. As regards Linear A, archaeologists will have to be careful they are now on the right side of history when publishing their views.

I imagine prejudice, to use John Chadwick's word again, will also extend to some ancient historians, in particular those who, in order to support their own narratives, have ignored evidence of Egyptian rule of Crete such as, most obviously, the Golden Bowl of General Djehuty. This has simply been omitted from most modern histories of Late Bronze Age Crete despite explicitly recording that this Egyptian general was governor of the island. When those historians challenge this work the reader may find it amusing to review those historians' previously published works to see the extent of their omissions and draw their own conclusions as to the motivations behind their opposition. One would suggest to this group that discretion is probably the better part of valour. Some might even accuse me of the same style of omissions; I have not, after all, mentioned Cretan hieroglyphs. Put simply, however, I have not needed to. This book concerns Egypto-Cretan relations, not, other than indirectly, a history of Crete. Moreover, I do not want to fall into the same trap that Ventris and Chadwick (and everyone else) did with Linear A by (incorrectly) guessing as to the nature of Cretan hieroglyphs. That said, we are fast running out of written scripts from Bronze Age Crete that might be Minoan. That must be the working assumption but, given that cleverer people than me have been shown to be wrong in the past on similar matters, I shall remain circumspect.

However, let me extend an olive branch to both the archaeologists and the ancient historians. Inherent in the Egyptian solution to Linear A are strong elements of continuity that accord with their views. The broad conclusion of academics was that the evidence suggested that Mycenaean Crete's economy was managed in much the same way as it had been previously (in the Egyptian period). They were right, and I have endeavoured to highlight the evidence from the Egyptian solution that supports how they were right. Perhaps, therefore, this will smooth the path towards acceptance.

Finally, I am sure, too, that some of those who have attempted decipherment before me (who are not named in this book), and have failed, will be prejudiced, to use John Chadwick's word a final time, against the solution set out here only because they did not work it out for themselves. There is no getting around this but, as one of my best bosses used to say, "you aren't doing your job properly if you aren't falling out with some people." He was right. Then again, perhaps this is unfair. I don't think that the (successful) approach adopted here could have been undertaken by anyone who was not a forensic accountant (and very few historians are also forensic accountants). Ultimately one hopes for magnanimity from this group (and, indeed, all the others) although one suspects one will not (immediately) get it; but that is not a reason not to publish and advance our collective knowledge.

Personally, I think the conclusions set out in this book suggest exciting new avenues for study of the Minoans, the Egyptians, and the Mycenaeans in the Late Bronze Age.

Indirectly we can now determine more about the Minoans. Elusive from history as they still frustratingly remain, now knowing that, before the Mycenaeans' arrival, Crete had two cultures rather than one will allow us to better understand each and get closer to the truth regarding both. The archaeologists who reasses the evidence in light of this will have their work cut out for them, but the path ahead is now much clearer.

We can also now better assess the achievements and legacy of Thutmose III. The empire he created was inherently unstable at its peak, with almost perpetual rebellion in Syria-Palestine and, we now know, weakness in Crete that, under his successor Amenhotep II, led to rebellion and the loss of the island. This was an undeniable part of Thutmose III's legacy which, in doctoring the Annals, Amenhotep II concealed in order that he might save face when he could not maintain the empire he inherited. Knowing this, we can now better understand both the conduct of international relations thereafter, with Egypt coming to realise the limits of her power and this realisation being acknowledged under Amenhotep III and Akhenaten in a treaty-based relationship with Mycenaean Crete (and Greece), and us better understand how those relations were portrayed in Egypt, with Egyptian propaganda nonetheless depicting the new status quo as continuing Egyptian domination.

The Egyptian administration of Crete did, nonetheless, enjoy some practical success. Attesting to its efficiency, key aspects of the Egyptian administration on Crete were subsequently adopted by the Mycenaeans at Knossos. Indeed, the extent to which the Mycenaeans assumed the form and style of the earlier Egyptian administration is now worthy of further thought as this, in turn, will indicate the extent to which, and for how long, the Mycenaeans were simply another imperial power occupying the island (before its people become one).

The conclusions set out in this book also give us an insight into aspects of Egyptian society that have previously been unknown. Shorthand, for example, was previously unknown prior to the Graeco-Roman period, yet it now seems that Greaco-Roman shorthand was derived from the Egyptian form of shorthand that we have seen in this work which had evidently existed in Egypt for over a millennia. Another obvious example is the use of clay tablets. The use of clay tablets has not typically been seen as a mainstream Egyptian practice, but this view needs to be revised in the light of extensive (and, now, recognised) finds, for example:

- From the end of the Old Kingdom period (between 2200 BC and 2000 BC), 530 clay tablets from Balat in the Dakhleh Oasis in southern Egypt, written in hieratic, and used in provincial administration[3];

---

3. Laure Pantalacci, "Balat, A Frontier Town and its Archive", in Juan Carlos Moreno García (Ed.), *Ancient Egyptian Administration* (Leiden & Boston: Brill, 2013), pp197–198; and Laure Pantalacci, "Between Old and Middle Kingdom: paleography of the clay documents from Balat", in S. A. Gülden, K. van der Moezel, and U. Verhoeven (Eds.), *Ägyptologische "Binsen" – Weisheiten III Formen und Funktionen von Zeichenliste und Paläographie. Akten der internationalen und interdisziplinären Tagung in der Akademie der Wissenschaften und der Literatur Mainz im April 2016* (Stuttgart: Franz Steiner Verlag, 2018), p217

- From the end of the Middle Kingdom period, when used by certain Egyptian temples on Crete, and later in the New Kingdom period (between 1455–c.1424 BC), when those temples also acted as agents of the state administering Crete as an Egyptian protectorate, 324 clay tablets, written in Middle Egyptian in shorthand using hieroglyphs (i.e. Linear A);
- Again, in the New Kingdom period, during the latter part of the reign of Amenhotep III (1379–1342 BC) and on into the reign of Akhenaten (1341–1325 BC), 377 tablets of the Amarna Correspondence, mostly written in Akkadian cuneiform (with some also written in the language of the ruler being addressed e.g. Hittite), used by the Egyptian Foreign Office[4]; and
- From the Graeco-Roman period, 4 tablets written in Greek, again from the Dakhleh Oasis,[5] and all dealing with accounts.[6] (Not all have been published but one, dated to the 3rd or 4th Century AD, deals with the issue of grain, perhaps by officialdom,[7] and another, dated to the 4th Century AD, accounts for doum fruit provisions.[8])

The surviving evidence may never allow us to make a wholly accurate assessment, but the use of clay tablets in Egypt (and in its overseas interests and possessions) was evidently much more widespread and enduring than previously thought.

The story as regards Linear A is also not over. Unashamedly this work has focussed on the easiest tablets to translate, and the remaining Linear A tablets not in this work might also yield up more insights to us regarding Egypt's involvement in Crete. For some of the tablets that are damaged a more panel-based approach with forensic accounting, Mycenaean Crete, and Egyptian temple administration expertise combined may be able to produce yet more robust translations. Similarly, the future reassessment of (incorrectly) believed place names and individuals' names that appear on the Linear B tablets that are, in fact, Middle Egyptian words written in shorthand using hieroglyphs (i.e. Linear A), will surely tell us more about the Mycenaean period.

Now knowing the starting point (Middle Egyptian written in hieroglyphs and Linear A) and the ending point (Mycenaean Greek and Linear B), we will also be better able to understand how Linear B was created. While this work advances our knowledge further in this regard, highlighting the multifaceted nature of that indirect relationship (including

---

4. James M. Weinstein, Eric H. Cline, Kenneth A. Kitchen, and David O'Connor, "The World Abroad", in David O'Connor and Eric H. Cline (Eds.), *Amenhotep III: Perspectives on His Reign* (Ann Arbor: The University of Michigan Press, 201), p225 and footnote 7
5. Olaf E. Kaper, "The Western Oases", in Christina Riggs (Ed.) *The Oxford Handbook of Roman Egypt* (Oxford: Oxford University Press, 2012), pp727–728
6. Anna Lucille Boozer, *Amheida II: A Late Romano-Egyptian House in the Dakhla Oasis / Amheida House B2* (New York: New York University Press, 2016), p361
7. Klaas A. Worp & Colin A. Hope, "A Greek Account on a Clay Tablet from the Dakhleh Oasis", in Rudolf De Smet, H. M. Melaerts, & Cecilia Saerens (Eds.), *Papyri in Honorem: Johannis Bingen Octogenarii* (Leuven: Uitgeverij Peeters, 2000), pp473–474, referring to tablet P.Bingen 116 found at Kellis.
8. Anna Lucille Boozer, *Amheida II: A Late Romano-Egyptian House in the Dakhla Oasis / Amheida House B2* (New York: New York University Press, 2016), p361, referring to tablet O.Trim. 1.24 found at Amheida (Trimithis). Another tablet, O.Trim. 1.62, is fragmentary but appears to deal with festival offerings.

the more direct, at times acrophonic, relationship between Middle Egyptian hieroglyphs and Linear B syllabic symbols), to fully understand all facets of that relationship will require the collaboration of a panel of experts in both languages and both scripts. Given the greater certainty regarding vowel sounds in Mycenaean Greek than Middle Egyptian, the same experts can perhaps work backwards to recreate a more accurate picture of the vowel sounds of Middle Egyptian.

Beyond this, I believe that the Byblos Script merits closer review.[9] Egypt's lengthy involvement in Byblos in the Levant even by the time of the New Kingdom is well known and there was a temple there to the Egyptian Goddess Hathor, for Egyptian traders, from at least 2800 BC.[10] It seems to me that the Byblos Script, which is conventionally dated to the 18th to the 15th Century BC,[11] might also be Middle Egyptian written in shorthand using hieroglyphs. After all, we have the same historical ingredients as witnessed in Middle Bronze Age Crete that gave rise to Linear A from the 18th Century BC: relatively weak native city states, the presence of long established traders from a relatively strong Egypt, and evidence of a similar dynamic between the two in the concession of a local temple of Hathor. Perhaps this will be my next project, but if that is not in the near future I hope the reader will forgive me for having a break. Deciphering one ancient script, in some respects, has proved more of a mammoth undertaking than I appreciated it would be at the outset.

I am, however, optimistic; I think the future is bright for the study of ancient history. For now though it is time to end my current contribution. Intentionally this has not been too big a book for, as Callimachus wrote, "big book, big problem" (μέγα βιβλίον μέγα κακόν, or *mega biblion, mega kakon*), and I have constantly had this in mind. I hope, however, that you, the reader, have enjoyed the journey that this book set out to relate. Historian Jan Driessen had faith enough to write that someone would decipher Linear A. That someone was me.

---

9. Juan-Pablo Vita & José-Ángel Zamora, "The Byblos Script", in Silvia Ferrara and Miguel Valério (Eds.), *Paths into Script Formation in the Ancient Mediterranean* (Rome: Edizioni Quasar, 2018), pp75–102
10. Susan Tower Hollis, "Hathor and Isis in Byblos in the Second and First Millennia BCE", *Journal of Ancient Egyptian Interconnection* 1(2)(2009), p2
11. Juan-Pablo Vita & José-Ángel Zamora, "The Byblos Script", in Silvia Ferrara and Miguel Valério (Eds.), *Paths into Script Formation in the Ancient Mediterranean* (Rome: Edizioni Quasar, 2018), p89

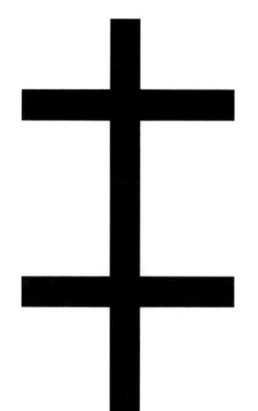

Appendix 1

Identified Linear A Symbols

Hieroglyph		Rotated?	Reversed?	Simplified?		Modified?		Linear A symbol		Why?	Analysis on page
A1								Unrecognised by Brice		Ease of incision	441
A24			Yes	Yes		Stick exaggerated		L93		Ease of incision	203
A24 + Z4	N/A			Yes		Single leg (shortened)		L84/48		Exaggerated stick differentiates from Hieroglyph A59	275
A28			Yes	Yes		Bowing slightly		L71		Combined to demonstrate meaning	383
A33			Yes	Yes				L125		Ease of incision	379
A59			Yes	Yes				L99		Ease of incision	177
C11			Yes	Yes				Unrecognised by Brice		Ease of incision	438
D2				Yes				L95 (incorrect-no central line)		Ease of incision	388
D3		90 degrees		Yes				L89		To save space, horizontally	32
D28 - Z1				Yes		Central line extended		L54		Ease of incision (stylised version of, and to distinguish itself from, L55)	247
D28 - Z1				Yes		Central line joined		L55		Ease of incision	134
D36				Yes		Arm bent		L76		To save space, horizontally	196
D36		180 degrees	Yes	Yes				L2' (no male = sign)		Ease of incision	258
D36		180 degrees	Yes	Yes		Arm bent [(+ male = sign)]		L2' [(+ male = sign)]		Ease of incision	214
D46		90 degrees		Yes				L100		To save space, horizontally	131
D54			Yes	Yes		Compressed horizontally		L81		Ease of incision	300
D58		180 degrees	Yes	Yes				L77		Ease of incision	364
F1			Yes	Yes				L112		Ease of incision?	387
F14		90 degrees		Yes				L98		To avoid confusion with Linear A symbol L49 / Hieroglyph F155	20
F22		90 degrees		Yes				Unrecognised by Brice		To save space horizontally	443

Hieroglyph	Rotated?	Reversed?	Simplified?	Modified?	Linear A symbol	Why?	Analysis on page
F27	Partially?					Partially rotated so symbol "stem" is vertical? Ease of incision (simplification)	173 / 481
F31			Yes	Top bar added	L42	To avoid being mistaken as a number count (modification)	184
F35			Yes		L9 or L28	Ease of incision	18
F36	180 degrees		Yes		L2	Ease of incision	238
F45			Yes		L45	Ease of incision	198
F45 + Z4	N/A				L67	Ease of incision	5
F155			Yes		L10	Combined to demonstrate meaning	139
G1			Yes	Stylised	L49	Ease of incision (both simplified and further modified versions used)	150
I12			Yes		L103	Ease of incision (difficulty in incision still led to significant variation)	318
114B	90 degrees		Yes		L53	Ease of incision	453
AA6 (J6) / S23			Yes	Central pivot removed	L88 (incorrectly)	To save space horizontally	253
AA8 (J8)	90 degrees		Yes		L85	Ease of incision	255
AA26 (J26) (replacing T14)		Yes	Yes		L61	To save space, horizontally	136
AA27 (J27)			Yes		L30	To avoid confusion with Hieroglyph T15 (replacing T14 with AA26 (J26)	272
M2	180 degrees	Yes	Yes		L62	Ease of incision?	133
M6		Yes	Yes		L64	Ease of incision? (circle on stem replaced by bar as on L72)	180
M12			Yes		L72/94	Ease of incision	187
M16			Yes		L14	Ease of incision	201
M17		Yes	Yes		L34	Ease of incision	169 / 243
M20	180 degrees		Yes		L97	Ease of incision	133
					L82		

Hieroglyph	Rotated?	Reversed?	Simplified?	Modified?	Linear A symbol	Why?	Analysis on page
M34			Yes	Sometimes stalk removed		Ease of incision	250
M43			Yes	Stylised?	L101	Ease of incision	353
N5 - Z1			Yes	Top bar added	L120	To distinguish from count / tally marks	180
N11			Yes	Compressed horizontally	L26	To save space, horizontally	320
N11 + Z4	N/A				L78	To save space horizontally Combined to demonstrate meaning	314
N13				Stylised?	L44	Ease of incision (difficulty in incision led to significant variation)	341
N13				Stylised	L79	Ease of incision	342
N13				From five to four points	L48	Ease of incision	342
N14				From five to four points	L48'	Ease of incision	21
N23	90 degrees		Yes		L22	Ease of incision	277
O1	90 degrees				L25/7	To save space, horizontally	131
O4	90 degrees			Stylised (occasionally)	L74	To save space, horizontally	268
O10		[occasionally]	Yes		L59	To save space, horizontally	319
O10		Yes	Yes		L43 (corrected)	Ease of incision	375
O11			Yes		L68/96	Ease of incision	335
O20			Yes		L32	Ease of incision	272
O43	90 degrees		Yes		L75	To save space, horizontally Ease of incision	174
O49			Yes		L1	Ease of incision	171
R1			Yes		L29	Ease of incision	253
R7				Stylised	L57	Handwriting style	137
					L6		

Hieroglyph	Rotated?	Reversed?	Simplified?	Modified?	Linear A symbol	Why?	Analysis on page
R8	180 degrees				L11	Unknown	n/a
S23 (see AA6 (J6))					N/A	N/A	n/a
S29 + 24	N/A				L44	Combined to demonstrate meaning	261
S34				Bar replaces loop	L52	Ease of incision (accent bar often omitted; sidebars sometimes omitted, especially in subscript)	200
S34			Yes		L23	Ease of incision	247
T8	180 degrees		Yes		L36	Ease of incision	n/a
T14 (replaced by Hieroglyph AA26 (J26))					N/A	N/A	136
T15		Yes			L69	Ease of incision	405
T19		Yes	Yes		L33	Ease of incision	345
T25	180 degrees		Yes		L60	Ease of incision	167 / 174
U19	90 degrees	Yes			Unrecognised by Brice	To save space, horizontally	167 / 466
V4		Yes	Yes		L97 (incorrectly)	Ease of incision	352
V16	90 degrees		Yes		L92	To save space, horizontally	193
V17			Yes		L102	Ease of incision	244
V19	90 degrees				L47	To avoid confusion with L44	269
V28	180 degrees		Yes		L31	Ease of incision	134
W11 - 21			Yes	Symbols joined	L39	Ease of incision	446
W19	180 degrees		Yes		L3	Ease of incision?	183
X1 - D17	[partially?]	Yes (often, not always)	Yes	Symbols joined	L88	To save space, horizontally	289
X1 - 24	90 degrees			Z4 merged, then placed inside X1	L90	To avoid (1) Hieroglyph Z4 being mistaken as tally marks; and (2) being mistaken for alternative version meaning; and to save space, horizontally	38 / 143

Hieroglyph	Rotated?	Reversed?	Simplified?	Modified?	Linear A symbol		Why?	Analysis on page
Z4	90 degrees		Yes	=	male = sign	=	To cross other symbols (to indicate the animal is male or the symbol denotes a type of man)	175
Z5 - Z2	180 degrees		Yes	Top bar added	L51		To distinguish the symbol from tally marks	31
Z5 - Z5					L58		N/A	173
Z9			Yes	X	L22 (awry)	X	Ease of incision	323
Z11			Yes	+	L22	+	Ease of incision	443
Various (see Appendix 6)	N/A				L86			
Various (see Appendix 6)	N/A				L91			
Various (see Appendix 6)	N/A				L95			

Note 1

At this stage, given that so many of the Linear A symbols are rotated so as to save space horizontally (and so many others are compressed horizontally so as to save space horizontally), the question is, why? After all, in the case of rotating symbols to save space horizontally is to lose space vertically, if a tall symbol replaces a wide symbol.

The reason, I believe, lies in the fact that papyrus scrolls, as were typically used in record keeping, were typically many times wider than they were tall. Similarly, when inscribed on buildings, hieroglyphs were meant to be read by those at ground level so the inscriptions could not be too high up and, therefore, the building that displayed a large amount of text written in hieroglyphs could not be too tall, but it could be wide, relatively speaking. The opposite, however, is true with Linear A, where tablets are taller than they are wide.

When hieroglyphs were written on papyrus scrolls or inscribed on buildings, hieroglyphs' widths would not have been so much of a constraining factor (relatively) in determining the amounts that could be written. If, however, hieroglyphs were written on tablets, without modification, their width ultimately could have been a constraining factor in determining the amounts that could be written.

Therefore, it seems likely that the style of the symbols used in the Linear A script took this into account and, if wide hieroglyphs needed to be used, they had to be rotated (or compressed) so that they took up less space horizontally, and while that meant that they instead took up more space vertically, that way there was (relatively) more space to spare.

Note 2

Of course, these are not all of the Linear A symbols. They are, however, the vast majority and most frequently occurring symbols in the corpus. In 1956, when Ventris and Chadwick published *Documents in Mycenaean Greek*, Linear B symbols also remained undeciphered.[1] Some of them are still undeciphered today (as we saw with the Mc series of Linear B tablets). No academic sensibly suggested in 1956, or suggests now, that because all of the Linear B symbols had not been or are not deciphered that Linear B was not or is not Mycenaean Greek. One hopes today's academics are as sensible as their forefathers and that a similar evidentiary threshold, and burden of proof requirement, is applied to this work as it was to that work, and that Linear A is rightly agreed to be Middle Egyptian written in shorthand using hieroglyphs.

---

1. See, for example, in the area of livestock and agricultural produce, Michael Ventris & John Chadwick, *Documents in Mycenaean Greek* (2nd Ed.)(Cambridge: Cambridge University Press, 1973), p200 (regarding Linear B symbol *75), p220 (regarding Linear B symbols 125, 132, and ME), p223 (regarding Linear B symbols 157 and 131b), p226 (regarding Linear B symbols PE and MI), where symbols' meanings are uncertain or entirely unknown.

Appendix 2

Identified Linear A Number and Fraction Symbols

A. Numbers

Number	Middle Egyptian word	Hieroglyph	Linear A	Symbol / Based on	Page
0	nfr	F35		Linear A symbol L2 / Hieroglyph F35 (modified)	18
1	wʿ	Z1		Hieroglyph Z1 / vertical tally mark	N/A
10	mḏ	V20		Horizontal tally mark	N/A
100	šnt	V1		N/A	N/A
1000	ḫꜣ	M12		Hieroglyph N65	187

B. Fractions

Four things have prevented the correct identification of the values of believed fraction symbols in Linear A: some fraction symbols do not actually represent fractions but nonetheless have a numerical value; some fraction symbols have negative values; one fraction value has two fraction symbols representing it; and, some believed fraction symbols appear not to be fractions at all. The first three of these are listed below. The fourth group is referred to in the body of this work, where relevant.

i) (Incorrectly) believed Linear A fraction symbols from hieroglyphs

Fraction value	Middle Egyptian word	Hieroglyph	Linear A	Symbol	Page
0	nfr	F35	L2 (fraction "A")		18
"remainder" (de minimis)	mn	U32	Fraction "H" (modified hieroglyph - removed bottom detail)		146

ii) Linear A fraction symbols from hieratic special status fraction symbols²

Fraction value	Middle Egyptian word	Hieratic symbol	Linear A	Symbol	Page
0.25 or ¹/₄	r-fdw	×	Fraction "B" (partially rotated hieractic sign)	+	155
0.33 or ¹/₃	r-ḥmtw		Fraction "D" (hieratic sign written as reverse "S")	ƨ	361
0.5 or ¹/₂	gś		Fraction "J" (reversed hieratic sign)	∠	141
0.67 or ²/₃	r.wj		Fraction "F" (partially rotated hieratic sign)	㇁	188

iii) Bespoke fraction symbols created for Linear A

Fraction value	Middle Egyptian word	Linear A	Symbol	Page
-0.25 or -$^1/_4$	N/A (Linear A innovation, mathematically proven)	Fraction "E"	7	13-16
-0.125 or -$^1/_8$	N/A (Linear A innovation, mathematically proven)	Fraction "EJ"	7L	142
0.25 or $^1/_4$	N/A (Linear A innovation, inferred)	Fraction "^J_E"	∠/7	154

---

2. For Middle Egyptian words, see: Helena Lopez Palma, "Egyptian Fractional Numerals: The grammar of Egyptian NPs and statements with fractional number expressions", *LingAeg* 23(2015), p211. For Hieratic symbols, see: Paul Benoit, Karine Chemla, and Jim Ritter, *Histoire de fractions, fractions d'histoire* (Basel, Boston, & Berlin: Birkhäuser Verlag, 1992), p6, and Annette Imhausen, *Mathematics in Ancient Egypt: A Contextual History* (Princeton & Woodstock: Princeton University Press, 2016), p53.

Appendix 3

The forms of Egyptian words we need to consider

What has survived of the use of any language in the ancient world, necessarily in writing, is fragmentary and, like any other form of archaeological evidence, the date of surviving written texts only provide us with the dates *after* which we know with certainty that their particular component words were used. Any surviving text is highly unlikely to contain the first written use of a word (or it would represent an extraordinarily fortuitous survival of evidence); it is therefore accepted that the first written use of a word will almost certainly predate the earliest evidence of that word being used. This is something that we have to bear in mind throughout the decipherment of Linear A.[3]

In considering this, the period of time between the actual date of a word's first use and the date of the first archaeological evidence of the use of that word might be significant; for example, the Vindolanda Tablets, wooden tablets dating from the 1st and 2nd Centuries AD that were found in the 1970s and 1980s near to Hadrian's Wall, have revealed the use of Latin words in the 1st and 2nd Centuries AD that were not previously known to have been used until the Middle Ages, approximately a millennium later.[4]

Consequently, there are two iterations of the Middle Egyptian word for wool, for example, that we should consider in relation to the Linear A corpus:

šnꜥw hair, wool [noun - bod.] V49 - X1 - Z4 - D3

šnw hair, [wool] [noun - bod.] V6 - N35 - X1 - Z4 - D3

Historian Jac J. Janssen determined that the word *šnw*, which meant "hair" (and, as we also see, "grass (cattle fodder)"), could also mean "wool" from the 19th Dynasty (1292–1189 BC),

---

3. Such as, for example, the word *ḥrps* referred to on page 187 is first attested just over 200 years after the date of the Hagia Triada Linear A tablets, during the reign of Seti II (1203 BC–1197 BC) in the 19th Dynasty (Leonard H. Lesko (Ed.), *A Dictionary of Late Egyptian: Volume I* (2nd Ed.)(Providence RI: BC Scribe Publications, 2002), p373, citing Alan H. Gardener, *Late Egyptian Miscellanies* (Bruxelles: Édition de la Fondation Egyptologique Reine Elisabeth, 1937), p50 (Papyrus Anastasi IV, 50.6a)). See also Alan H. Gardener, *Late Egyptian Miscellanies* (Bruxelles: Édition de la Fondation Egyptologique Reine Elisabeth, 1937), p xv. It is not unreasonable for us to assume this word's first actual use was before the date it is first attested to have been used in a surviving written text (in a similar manner as that set out here for *šnw*) and that it too enjoyed contemporary usage when these Linear A tablets were written.
4. J. N. Adams, "The Latin of the New Vindolanda Tablets", *Britannia* 50(2019), p261, referring to the Latin words *scissorius* and *inacundiola*, which were unknown in Latin before the medieval period; J. N. Adams, "The Latin of the New Vindolanda Tablets", *The Classical Quarterly*, 53(2)(2003), p562, referring to *braciarius*, which was also not previously attested until the medieval period.

and he cited two different spellings of šnw in three different contexts to demonstrate this general change of meaning.⁵ It is not unreasonable to believe that this word, in its many different spellings, had this meaning in the 18th Dynasty (1539–1292 BC), if not before (which period corresponds to the date of the Linear A tablets we are considering), but that, simply, evidence of this has not survived. Leonard H. Lesko agreed with Janssen as regards the change of meaning and, in his Late Egyptian dictionary (Late Egyptian being the more vulgar form of the Egyptian language that began to be used from c.1350 BC), he ascribed the first iteration of the spelling of the word, above, the meaning of "wool" (as well as "hair").⁶ This iteration of the spelling of the word was also first attested in the 19th Dynasty, during the reign of Merneptah (1213 BC–1203 BC), in a hieratic text.⁷ Again, it is not unreasonable to believe that this spelling of the word *in particular* had been used and, given Janssen's general findings, had this meaning in the 18th Dynasty, if not before.

The second iteration of the spelling of the word, above, is attested at an even closer date to that of the Linear A tablets we are considering. It appears in the London Medical Papyri,⁸ which dates to c.1325 BC (in the late 18th Dynasty).⁹ Again, it is not unreasonable to believe that this form of the word had been used earlier in the 18th Dynasty, if not before. While the second iteration is only attested to have meant "hair", it has been hypothesised that it also had other meanings.¹⁰ Given the general change of meaning that Janssen noted for the word šnw, *irrespective of spelling*, and Lesko's ascription of the meaning of "wool" to the first iteration of the word, above, in particular, it is not, perhaps, unlikely that the similarly spelled second iteration of the word, above, therefore also meant "wool" at that same time. As with the word for month which we see used in dates (see Appendix 8), there could be many different ways of spelling the same (spoken) word with the same meaning at the same time in hieroglyphs. However, rather than relying on (I think) a well-founded theory concerning potential alternate meanings of the second iteration of the spelling of the word, for the sake of prudence and given its specifically attested meaning, in this work the first iteration of the spelling of the word šnw, above, is taken as the one from which

---

5. Jac J. Janssen, *Commodity Prices from the Ramessid Period: an economic study of the village of necropolis workmen at Thebes* (2nd Ed.)(Leiden: E. J. Brill, 1975), pp443–444. He cites both [hieroglyphs] (Papyrus Bologna 1094.I.I, and Ostraka Michaelides 8.6), and [hieroglyphs] (Papyrus Leiden I.352.11) as having the changed meaning, specifically, but also thus demonstrates the changed meaning of the word, generally. While previously known to have meant hair, and subsequently also wool, wool is simply a certain type of animal hair, so the distinction may ultimately exist more in our language, rather than Middle Egyptian, and this is simply the first surviving evidence of something that, naturally, had existed for quite some time.
6. Leonard H. Lesko (Ed.), *A Dictionary of Late Egyptian: Volume II* (2nd Ed.)(Providence RI: BC Scribe Publications, 2004), p128, citing Jac J. Janssen, *Commodity Prices from the Ramessid Period: an economic study of the village of necropolis workmen at Thebes* (2nd Ed.) (Leiden: E. J. Brill, 1975), p444
7. Leonard H. Lesko (Ed.), *A Dictionary of Late Egyptian: Volume II* (2nd Ed.)(Providence RI: BC Scribe Publications, 2004), p128, citing Alan H. Gardiner, *Late-Egyptian Stories* (Bruxelles: Édition de la Fondation Egyptologique Reine Elisabeth, 1932), p20 (D'Orbiney Papyrus: 2.10.9)
8. https://aaew.bbaw.de/tla/servlet/DzaBrowser?u=guest&f=0&l=0&wn=156340 (accessed 22 December 2023)
9. https://web.archive.org/web/20111227072625/http://www.bridgemanart.com/image/Egyptian-18th-Dynasty-c-1567–1320-BC/London-Medical-Papyrus-New-Kingdom-c-1325-BC-papyrus/e35c48d76a244423a930cb0723adf68c (accessed 22 December 2023)
10. https://aaew.bbaw.de/tla/servlet/DzaBrowser?u=guest&f=0&l=0&wn=156340 (accessed 22 December 2023)

the Linear A symbol for wool is derived (and represents). It could, however, be derived from (and represent) both!

One final point to note relating to this first iteration of the spelling of the word *šnw* concerns its first hieroglyph, Hieroglyph V49. Hieroglyph V49 is, in fact, a modern construct used to give hieroglyphic form to what has only been recorded to date in hieratic[11]:

⟨glyph⟩ was the modern hieroglyph construct corresponding to the

⟨glyph⟩ hieratic symbol, which has the value *šn*

In its (albeit day-to-day) use writing the Egyptian language, the hieratic script was structurally the same as the hieroglyphic script; each hieratic symbol corresponded to a hieroglyph. Hieratic symbols were derived from their hieroglyphic antecedents; they were visually similar to hieroglyphs, but typically they were simplified. When he was compiling his sign list, Gardiner was searching for the hieroglyph that matched the above hieratic symbol but discovered that an example of it had not been found. Knowing the structures of the respective scripts, however, he effectively anticipated its discovery and form and constructed Hieroglyph V49, as it now appears, as an approximation of the elusive hieroglyph.[12] As an approximation it remains in use and continues to be accepted by Egyptologists to this day as Hieroglyph V49 has still not been discovered, but we (like Gardiner) can be reasonably assured it existed and that it had this approximate appearance, given our knowledge of the respective scripts.

That a hieroglyph remains absent from the archaeological record is, perhaps, not entirely unexpected. Indeed, to use another analogy from what survives of the use of Latin, there are still instances of Latin words known to us from only one surviving text and if that one text had not survived then knowledge of that word would have been lost.[13] Perhaps the loss of a whole Latin word is more likely to have occurred than the loss of a single Egyptian hieroglyph, but, I think, this illustrates the point. Gardiner was right to construct Hieroglyph V49 as a fair representation of the hieroglyph that he thought corresponded to this hieratic symbol. Even though the hieroglyph has not been found, it almost certainly existed, and it was used, amongst other things, in spelling this iteration of the word *šnw*, with the meaning of "wool" that we can also safely infer.[14]

---

11. Alan H. Gardiner, "The Transcription of New Kingdom Hieratic", *The Journal of Egyptian Archaeology* 15(1)(1929), p53
12. Alan H. Gardiner, "The Transcription of New Kingdom Hieratic", *The Journal of Egyptian Archaeology* 15(1)(1929), p53
13. For example, the Latin word "eoigena", an adjective that referred to the sun, signifying "one born in the east", is only known to us from a single epigraph found in Castellammare di Stabia (ancient Stabiae) (*Oxford Latin Dictionary* (Oxford: Clarendon Press, 1968), p611 citing Corpus Inscriptionum Latinarum 10.8131).
14. This hieroglyph (and the hieratic symbol it corresponds to) are clearly very similar to Hieroglyph M12, which has further implications that are discussed on page 143.

Appendix 4

Place names

In *Documents in Mycenaean Greek*, Ventris and Chadwick identified five of the most important cities in Crete that appeared in the Linear B corpus:

- Amnisos;
- Knossos;
- Lyktos;
- Phaistos; and
- Tylissos.[15]

As set out in Chapter Two, the decipherment of Linear A has been approached on the basis that the economic transactions and how they were recorded in Linear B would be similar to the economic transactions and how they were recorded in Linear A (and, indeed, we have found this to be the case in a number of instances).

Of course, the destruction that occurred at the end of the period of Egyptian rule and the consequent abandonment of certain sites means that we cannot say that the relative importance of Crete's cities during the Mycenaean period when Linear B was the principal script used necessarily reflects the relative importance of those same cities during the earlier Egyptian period when Linear A was the principal script used (or, even, before that). Nonetheless, Knossos' importance as a political centre predated the period of Egyptian rule; it was important throughout (and, as we have seen, it is recorded numerous times in the Linear A corpus). If it was important throughout, then so too would have been its port, Amnisos (and, as we have seen, it too is recorded in the Linear A corpus).

In addition to the destruction and abandonment of certain sites, we also have significantly less Linear A tablets than we have Linear B tablets; it is possible, if not, in fact, likely, that sites will not be as equally represented in the Linear A corpus as they are in the Linear B corpus. Nonetheless, with the apparent similar administrative functions undertaken at Hagia Triada during the Egyptian period as at Knossos during the Mycenaean period, as administrative centres of similar importance, we might infer a similar geographic reach of each.

Therefore, while not wholly directly comparable, it is reasonable to expect that at least some of the major place names in the Linear B tablets will also be recorded in the Linear A tablets (and, indeed, they are).

---

15. Michael Ventris & John Chadwick, *Documents in Mycenaean Greek* (2nd Ed.)(Cambridge: Cambridge University Press, 1973), p22

476 The Decipherment of Linear A

From the list of place names in the mortuary temple of Amenhotep III (1386–1349 BC) at Kom el-Hetan, which we discussed in Chapter Four, we know what the Egyptians called some of the cities of Crete. Whilst that list dates to perhaps to 75 years after the period in which Crete was part of Egypt's empire, we can safely assume that the Egyptians would have still used the same names for the cities listed as they had previously. Of Ventris and Chadwick's list of the five most important cities in Crete recorded in the Linear B corpus, therefore, we know four of their Egyptian names from Amenhotep III's mortuary temple list:

Place	Hieroglyphic name	Transliteration	Linear B name
Amnisos	M17 - A2 - D38 - N35 - Z4 - M8	ꜣmni-sꜣ ('a-m-ni-ša)	a-mi-ni-so
Knossos	D28 - Z1 - N35 - M17 - M17 - G43 - M8 - G1	kꜣ-jn-jw-sꜣ (ku-nu-ša)	ko-no-so
Lyktos	D21 - Z4 - V31 - G1 - U33 - M17	rj-kꜣ-tj (ri-ki-ta)	ru-ki-to
Phaistos	D58 - G29 - M17 - M17 - M8	bꜣ-jj-sꜣ-tj (bi-ja-š-ta)	pa-i-to
Tylissos	Unknown	Unknown	tu-li-so

For these four major cities where their names are known in Egyptian, if we assume these were abbreviated to a Linear A symbol representing their first hieroglyph, we see what is most likely to be the names of three of these cities represented in the Hagia Triada corpus of Linear A tablets (each time in a heading, as administrative convention would dictate, and each time after the symbol representing the word for "city"). The (likely) appearance of these city names is no coincidence; for the reasons set out above, certainly two of them we would have expected to see.

Amnisos:

As we saw in Chapter Five, Amnisos appears on Tablet HT 13, represented by a Linear A symbol (L97) that in turn represented the place name's first hieroglyph, reversed. This is the only instance in the Hagia Triada corpus of Linear A tablets where it does so:

Place names 477

Tablet HT 13

Knossos:

As we saw in Chapter Five, Knossos also appears in the Hagia Triada corpus of Linear A tablets represented by a Linear A symbol (L55) that in turn represented the place name's first two hieroglyphs. It does so four times (on three tablets):

Tablet HT 2

Tablet HT 86A

Tablet HT 86B

Tablet HT 97A

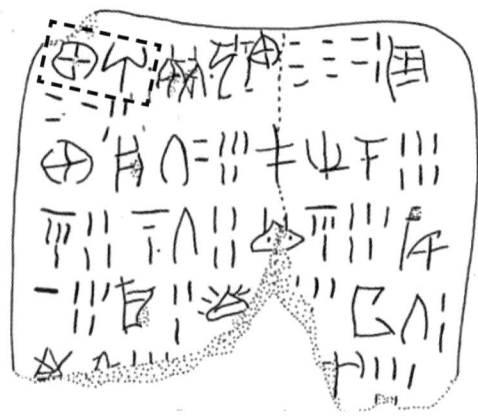

Knossos is the most frequently occurring place name in the Hagia Triada corpus of Linear A tablets; given the city's importance, this is no coincidence. Moreover, for Knossos to be recorded more times than any other city in the Hagia Triada corpus of Linear A tablets, given its relative importance, is further evidence that the approach adopted to translation, and Linear A being Middle Egyptian written in shorthand using hieroglyphs, is correct.

However, so that the reader does not think I am trying to present a skewed picture of the evidence, it would be proper of me to highlight that in the list of place names in the mortuary temple of Amenhotep III there is another Cretan city recorded, Kydonia, and it also begins with Hieroglyphs D28 - Z1:

$k3 - tw - n3 - jj$ D28 - Z1 - X1 - G43 - N35 - G1 - M17 - M17

Kydonia was considerably further away from Hagia Triada than Knossos, which makes it less likely that it was being referred to in the Hagia Triada corpus of Linear A tablets. However, it is also worth considering the workings of the Linear A shorthand method here, and how we can, perhaps, reach that same conclusion by another route.

If there were two cities that appeared in the records of the same institution and both place names began with the same hieroglyph(s) but one was more important than the other, it would seem logical to presume that the name of the more important place would be abbreviated to a symbol representing its first hieroglyph(s) and the name of the place of lesser importance that began with the same hieroglyph(s) would not be and, instead, it would be abbreviated to a symbol representing its last hieroglyph(s). Hieroglyphs D28 - Z1 appear first in the place names of Knossos and Kydonia. Linear A symbol L55 (representing Hieroglyphs D28 - Z1) therefore most likely represents the more important city, Knossos. Following the Linear A shorthand method, Kydonia could have been abbreviated to a symbol representing its last hieroglyph, Hieroglyph M17 (Linear A symbol L97). However, a Linear A symbol representing its last hieroglyph had already been used as the abbreviation for Amnisos (which was referred to on Tablet HT 13, and which was also probably more important than Kydonia, as well as being closer to Hagia Triada and so more likely to have been mentioned in its records). This would suggest, therefore, that whatever Kydonia was abbreviated to, it was not its first or its last hieroglyph. If it ever was ever recorded at Hagia Triada, what it was abbreviated to must remain a mystery unrevealed by the limited surviving corpus of Linear A tablets.

Phaistos:

Finally, as we saw in Chapter Five, Phaistos appears on Tablet HT 21 represented by a Linear A symbol (L77, a simplified "stick foot") that represented its first hieroglyph, rotated and simplified. This is the only instance in the Hagia Triada corpus of Linear A tablets where it does so:

Tablet HT 21A

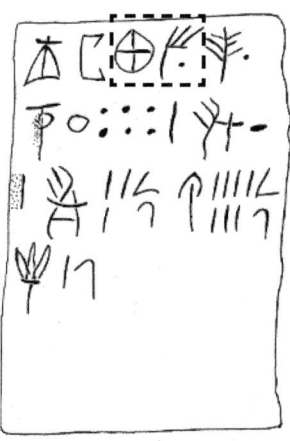

It is perhaps interesting to note that in Linear B (i.e. Mycenaean Greek), Phaistos is written (phonetically) as Pa-i-to, whereas the Egyptians would have pronounced the name of the town as bi-ja-š-ta. The Egyptian Ba sound, derived from Hieroglyph D58, has become "Pa" in Pa-i-to. This is because, in Linear B, the "p" consonant could be pronounced as either "pa" or "ba".[16] However, Bi-ja-š-ta had four syllables but Pa-i-to had only had three; the "š" (pronounced "sh", but which we might assume became a simple "s") having been somehow lost in Linear B, only to subsequently reappear in Classical Greek. Given that the "š" syllable (or, at least the "s") returns to the name of the town when it is recorded in Classical Greek, could it be that one of the Linear B consonants' range of pronunciations needs to be reassessed?

---

16. John Chadwick, *The Decipherment of Linear B* (2nd Ed.)(Cambridge: Cambridge University Press, 1967), p75

Appendix 5

Goats

Linear A symbol L42 is derived from Hieroglyph F27 (actually a representation of a cow skin and tail, not that that is relevant for what it ultimately represents in Linear A). How the Linear A symbol was derived from the hieroglyph that it represented is best seen beginning with its second representation on Tablet HT 18 which is examined below:

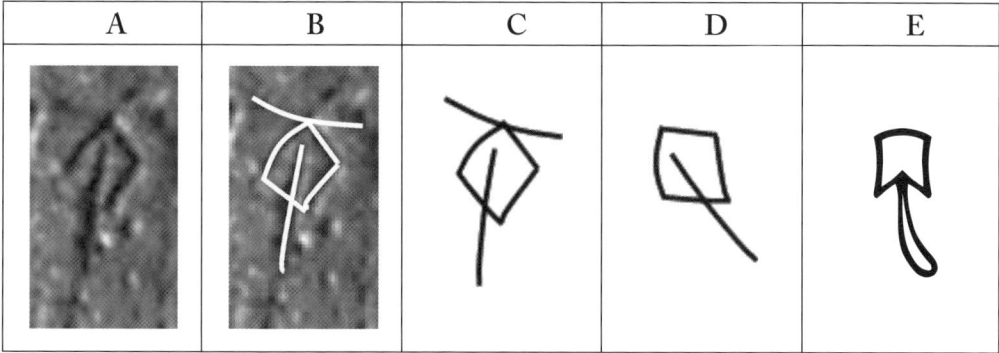

The table shows:

- <u>Column A</u>: Linear A symbol L42 as it appears in an extract of the photograph of Tablet HT 18;
- <u>Column B</u>: Linear A symbol L42 highlighted;
- <u>Column C</u>: the photograph of the tablet is removed, leaving just Linear A symbol L42 as it was written;
- <u>Column D</u>: the horizontal line at the top of the symbol is removed (i.e. the modification to the hieroglyph is reversed) and the symbol partially rotated, anti-clockwise, by 45 degrees (so that it is portrayed how Hieroglyph F27 is orientated); and
- <u>Column E</u>: Hieroglyph F27, to reach which from the symbol now in Column D, the simplification of the symbol has undergone is reversed: the tail is written as two tapering lines, joined by a curve furthest away from the body, and meeting at a point where they met the main body, which itself was indented at this point. The symbol thus becomes Hieroglyph F27.

The changes that Hieroglyph F27 had undergone to become Linear A symbol L42 are, therefore (progressing back from Column E to A):

- The tail of the symbol is written as an simplified single line rather than as two tapering lines that meet when the touch the body of the symbol (and in a curved join at the other end). The indentation on the body of the symbol where the tail met it is also dispensed with.
- The hieroglyph is partially rotated (clockwise, by 45 degrees) because it is easier to write a vertical straight line than a curved angled line.
- A horizontal line is added at the top of the hieroglyph to prevent being mistaken as a count marks (otherwise the skin, the main body of the symbol, might have been mistaken as the circular symbol for a count of 100 and the tail might be mistaken as a vertical tally mark counting 1). This type of modification is one which, for exactly the same reason, we see elsewhere in the corpus e.g. Hieroglyphs N5 - Z1 when they become Linear A symbol L26, and Hieroglpyphs Z5 - Z2 when they become Linear A symbol L51.

On Tablet HT 18 the (broadly) square cow skin, the main body of the symbol, is clear. However, in most instances when this symbol is written it appears, and has been recorded by Brice and Godart & Olivier, as a circle, presumably because it was formed from two arced strokes joining at the top and bottom as this was quicker than incising the four lines of the square (although this necessitated the addition of the top horizontal line, for the reasons set out above, the symbol was still, overall, formed from less lines).

As we saw in Chapter One, this symbol represents an animal, as it can be incised with the male = symbol joined to it (although we have since seen that is not wholly definitive, that remains the case here). Having now also identified the hieroglyph this symbol represents, and knowing the method of shorthand used, we can determine which animal it represented.

There are four possibilities, based on the Linear A shorthand method alone. These are listed below, together with the principal reasons for discounting (or selecting) them:

1. Bulls / Cows
The symbol might represent bulls / cows, representing the hieroglyph that appears last in the word:

ḥnrt cows, cattle [noun - ani.] U31 - X1 - F27

k3t cows [noun - ani.] U31 (reversed) - X1 - F27

However, as we have seen cows are represented by two other symbols, depending on the context:

- Linear A symbol L67, representing Hieroglyph F45 in the Middle Egyptian word *idt* (as we saw on Tablet HT 116A, for example):

idt cow [noun - ani.] F45 - M17 - N42 - X1

idt cow [noun - ani.] F45 - X1 - Z1 - E1

idt cow [noun - ani.] N41 - X1 - F45

- Linear A symbol L103 𒀀, representing Hieroglyph G1 𓄿 in the Middle Egyptian word *3ht* (as we also saw on Tablet HT 116A, for example):

𓄿 𓉐 𓃾 *3ht* cow [noun - ani.] G1 - O4 - X1 - E1

It seems unlikely that with two ways of recording cows, a third would be necessary. It appears unlikely, therefore, that this symbol represents cows.

2. <u>Sheep</u>
The symbol might potentially represent sheep, representing the hieroglyph that appears last in the word:

𓊃 𓂋 𓅱 *srw* (an animal, sheep?) [noun - ani.] O34 - D21 - G43 - F27

This is not a particularly common way of writing sheep in Middle Egyptian, if that is the word this symbol represents (for its meaning is, ultimately, uncertain). Indeed, the known use of the word *srw* does not suggest itself as likely to have been used in a context such as this. The Thesaurus Lingae Aegyptiae tells us that this word was used in medical contexts, which is clearly not the context here, and when it was used the word represented male sheep (i.e. rams).[17] We know that Linear A symbol L42 appears with the male = symbol specifically to indicate that the animal in those instances was male; if Linear A symbol L42 represented the word *srw* then appearing with a male = sign would be an unnecessary tortology, suggesting *srw* is not the word represented by this symbol.

Moreover, as we have seen, male sheep (if specifically stated as such) is represented by Linear A symbol L44 𓏤, representing Hieroglyph S23 𓋬 (plus the male = symbol) (as we saw on Tablet HT 21A, for example) representing the first hieroglyph in the word:

𓋴 𓇋 𓏲 𓏏 𓏥 *siwt* sheep [noun - ani.] S29 - M17 - Z7 - X1 - F27 - Z3A

Other than, perhaps, linguistic convention, there would be nothing preventing this being used without the male = symbol if female sheep needed to be represented. As such, it seems unlikely that another way of recording sheep was necessary.

Overall, therefore, it appears unlikely that this symbol represents sheep.

---

17. https://aaew.bbaw.de/tla/servlet/GetWcnDetails?u=guest&f=0&l=0&wn=139250&db=0 referencing, in particular, Adolf Erman and Hermann Grapow, *Worterbuch der Aegyptischen Sprachen* (Volume 4) (J. C. Hinrich'sche Buchhandlung: Leipzig, 1930), 193.6 states that the term is believed to be a medical one.

3. Pigs
The symbol might represent pigs, representing the hieroglyph that appears last in the word:

𓃘 𓅊 𓃟 *šꜣ* pig, swine [noun - ani.] M8 - G1 - F27

𓃘 𓅊 𓇋𓃟 *šꜣi* pig [noun - ani.] M8 - G1 - M17 - F27

We know from Tablet HT 14, however, that (collectively) the males of both the animal represented by Linear A symbol L42 and Linear A symbol L67 (cows) had horns (there were 30% the number of (male) "horned cattle" (*wp*) to the total number of females of these two animal types, and with the numbers of the two genders of animals in proportion it seems more likely than not that the male animals were the same animal type to one of the female animals). Male pigs do not have horns, however. Therefore, it seems likely that Linear A symbol L42 does not represent pigs (and for other previously stated reasons we have discounted cows).

4. Goats
By a process of elimination in the first instance, the symbol seems most likely to represent goats, representing the hieroglyph that appears last in the word:

𓂝𓂋𓃀𓃟 *ꜥr* goat [noun - ani.] D36 - D21 - E31 - F27

In addition to this word, there are many other words for types of goat (by differing age and gender) that end with this hieroglyph:

𓇋𓃀𓃘𓃟 *ib* kid goat [noun - ani.] M17 - D58 - E8 - F27

𓋴𓈖𓏭𓃟 *ꜥnḫt* nanny goat, small domestic animal [noun - ani.] S34 - N35 - J1 - F27

𓋴𓏏𓃟 *ꜥnḫt* nanny goat, small domestic animal [noun – ani.] S34 - X1 - F27

𓋴𓈖𓏭𓏤𓃟 *ꜥnḫ* billy goat [noun - ani.] S34 - N35 - J1 - Z7 - F27

Linear A symbol L42 represents Hieroglyph F27, the final hieroglyph in all of these words. However, we know that the symbol is used in a general sense, as a generic representation of "goats", with such additional clarification provided as to type when necessary (gender, in particular, not age, because the term "small cattle" was used for young animals) by the male = sign or subscript descriptors. From the male = symbol or subscript descriptors being used to indicate when the animal in question is male or female, we can infer that the word that is being abbreviated is gender neutral in meaning. This would suggest that the first word above, *ꜥr*, is the correct meaning of the symbol (rather than a word for a more specific type of goats by gender). Linear A symbol L42, representing Hieroglyph F27, therefore represents the last hieroglyph in the word:

ꜥr goat [noun - ani.] D36 - D21 - E31 - F27

We can use archaeological evidence to check this conclusion.

The large numbers of sheep on Crete in the Late Bronze Age have already been referred to earlier in this work, both as regards Gerald Cadogan's estimate of 500,000 being on the island in Minoan times,[18] and as suggested by the analysis of Tablet HT 123A. It is difficult to distinguish between sheep and goats in the archaeological record but, when it is possible, sheep generally (with a few exceptions) outnumber goats. With these few exceptions in mind, therefore, I think it reasonable to state that, for there to have been those few exceptions, if not numbering quite as many as sheep, there must have been large numbers of goats on Crete in the Late Bronze Age too; indeed historian Jennifer Moody even believes that the ratio of sheep to goats on Crete would have been about 1:1 during the Late Minoan IB period that we are considering.[19]

With the large number of sheep implicitly recorded on Tablet HT 123A, and knowing why large numbers of sheep are not otherwise explicitly recorded (because of the prohibition on sales or other transfers of sheep during the period between shearing and New Year's Day, which period the majority of tablets appear to date to), it would seem most likely that the largest number of animals that are explicitly recorded in the Linear A tablets were, therefore, goats (and not sheep).

---

18. Gerald Cadogan, *Palaces of Minoan Crete* (Barrie & Jenkins Ltd: London, 1976), p13
19. Jennifer Moody, "Hinterlands and hinterseas: resources and production zones in Bronze Age and Iron Age Crete", *British School at Athens Studies*, 20(2012), p237

Appendix 6

Ordinals

Pure ordinals

We have seen a number of instances of ordinals in the corpus. Representing the ordinals "second", "third", and "fourth", we have seen that:

- The symbol for "second" is derived from the Middle Egyptian word:

  𓏥𓏌 *snnw* the second (one), the other, twin, equal, comrade [noun] W24 - Z4A

  Hieroglyphs W24 - Z4A:

  Which is then rotated:

  And Z4A dashes are placed inside W24 (sometimes as dots) to become Linear A symbol L91:

- The symbol for "third" is derived from the Middle Egyptian word:

  ḥmt nw third [ordinal number] Z2 - W24

  Hieroglyphs Z2 - W24:

  Which is then rotated:

  And Z2 dashes are placed inside W24 (sometimes as dots) to become Linear A symbol L91:

- The symbol for "fourth" is derived from the Middle Egyptian word:

  fdnw fourth Z4B - Z4B - W24

  Hieroglyphs Z4B - Z4B - W24:

  And Z4B - Z4B dashes are placed inside W24 (sometimes as dots) to be Linear A symbol L91

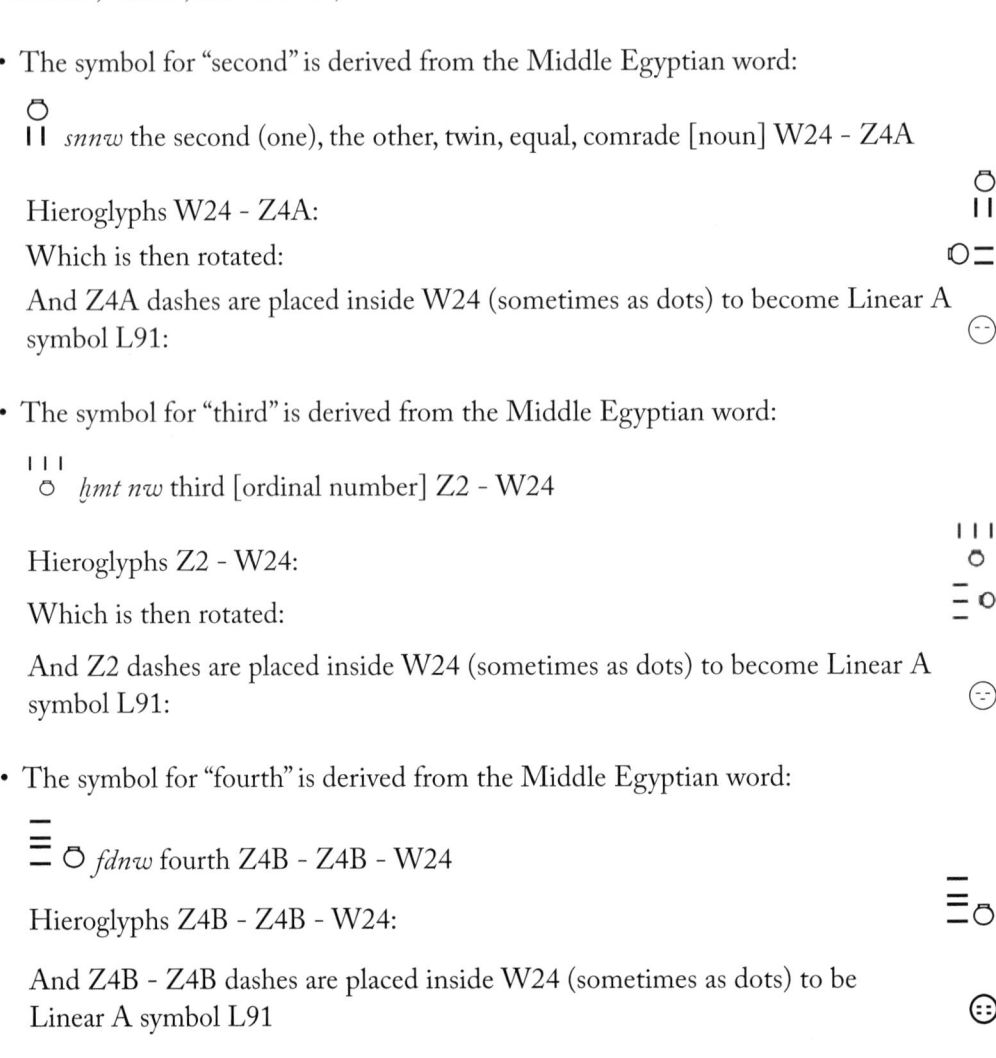

In each case, the dashes of Hieroglyphs Z4A, Z2, or Z4B - Z4B are placed inside the circle of Hieroglyph W24 as horizontal dashes (as they appear) or dots (i.e. modified). In each case this is so that they are not mistaken for tally marks or units of ten. The number of horizontal dashes or dots within the circle therefore tells us the ordinal number, whether second, third or fourth.

In the context of dates, these three ordinals are considered further in Appendix 8 (together with the ordinal for "first", again, when used in the context of dates).

Combined ordinals

Linear A symbol L86 is an example of what we might call a "combined ordinal", where Linear A symbol L91, i.e. a pure ordinal of the type listed above, is joined with another Linear A symbol to then become a different, combined, Linear A symbol. Combined ordinals do not, therefore, represent a single hieroglyph or hieroglyphs from a single Middle Egyptian word but, rather, represent two hieroglyphs or groups of hieroglyphs from two Middle Egyptian words that are combined in one Linear A symbol. The steps in how this took place are set out in the examples below.

<u>Example One: derivation of Linear A symbol L86</u>
<u>(Linear A symbol L91 within arms of Linear A symbol L55)</u>
In Linear A shorthand, two words would be required to be represented if one wanted to write "food [in the] fourth [month]": the word for "food", and the word for "fourth" (as we will see in Appendix 8, when a date is referred to in this manner the word for "month" is frequently omitted). How the single symbol representing these two words is created is set out as follows:

488   The Decipherment of Linear A

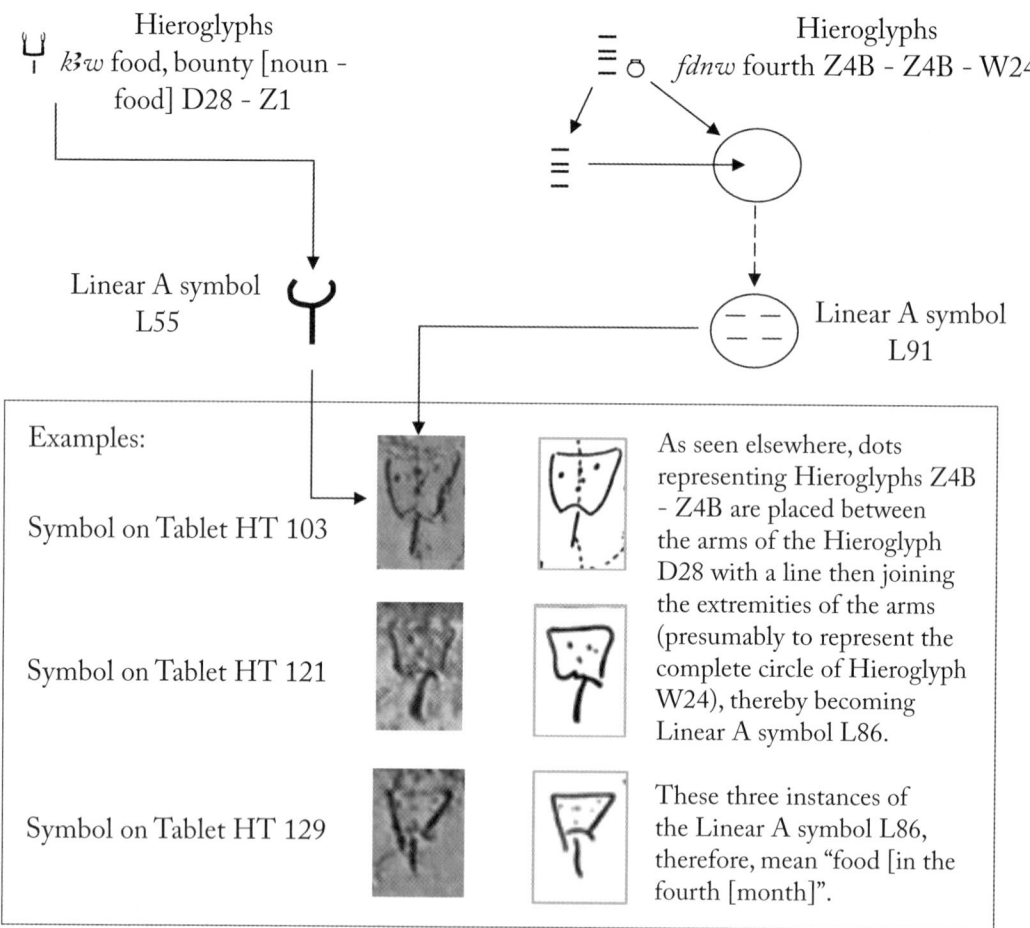

Linear A symbol L86 is not, however, the only combined ordinal; so too is Linear A symbol L95:

Example Two: derivation of Linear A symbol L95
(Linear A symbol L55 superimposed on Linear A symbol L91)
If we wished to write "food [in the] second [month]" in Linear A, two words would be required to be represented: the word for "food" and the word for "second". How the single symbol representing these two words is created is set out as follows:

Ordinals 489

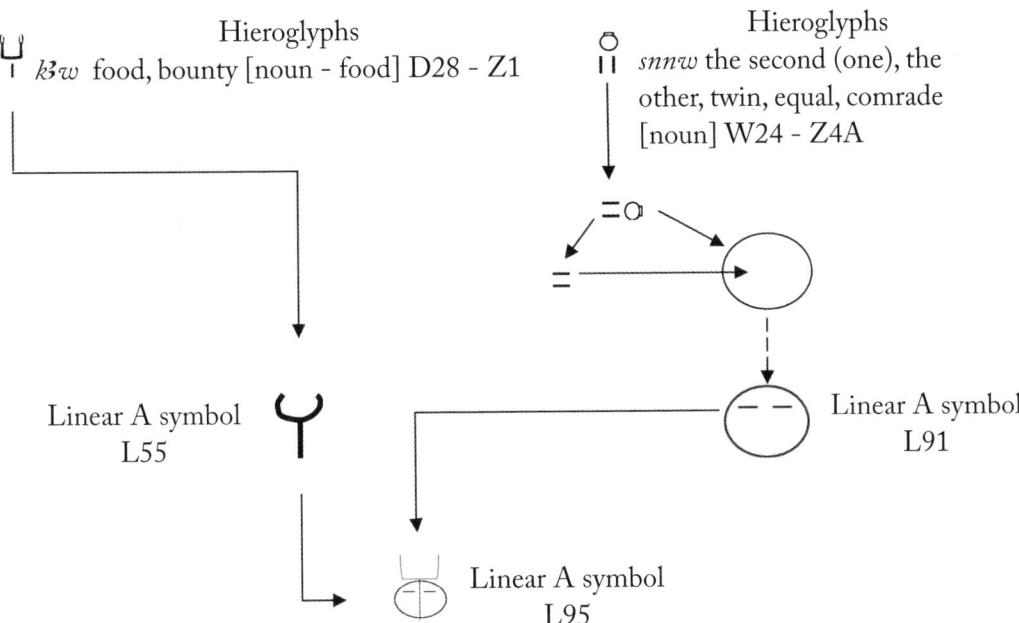

This is most clearly seen on Tablet HT 95A (despite the symbol being partly damaged):

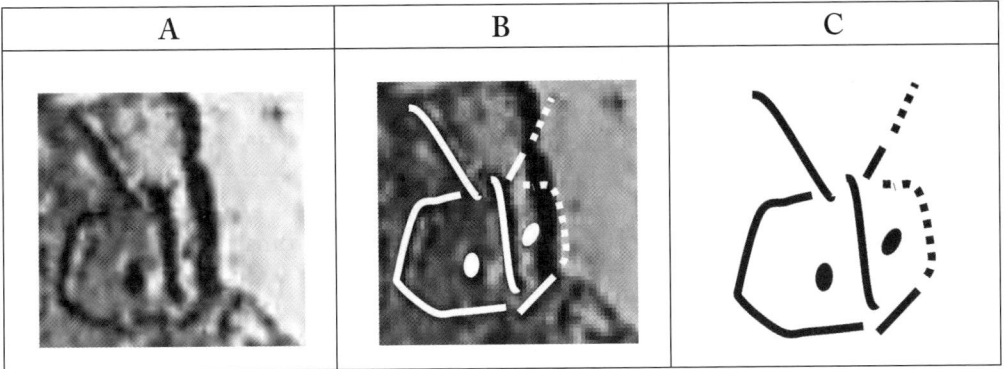

In the above table:

- Column A: shows an extract from the picture of Tablet HT 95A. The right portion has been lost through damage.
- Column B: the picture is darkened to more clearly show the two component Linear A symbols:
  - Liner A symbol L55 as the Y figure, formed of the central vertical line and two arms above, where the restored right arm is formed of a dotted line as this portion of the tablet is damaged;
  - Linear A symbol L91 (with two dots, rather than dashes, representing "second") is the remainder, again with the right portion restored and shown in a dotted line.
- Column C: shows the combined symbol in its entirety with the picture removed.

490   The Decipherment of Linear A

Although the scribe of Tablet HT 95A wrote the symbol from its two component parts (i.e. its two component Linear A symbols), so we are able to see what it actually (originally) represented, the symbol was frequently stylised, so it could be written as:

This is, for example, seen on Tablet HT 102. In that instance, however, the scribe wanted to write "food [in the] fourth [month]". Being written in clay, however, it was difficult to put all four Hieroglyph Z4B - Z4B dashes inside the Hieroglyph W24 circle, even as dots. The scribe for that tablet, therefore, having incised two dots inside the circle, one on either side of the central partitioning line, used the solution of joining two of the dots to the two "ears" of the symbol (highlighted below):

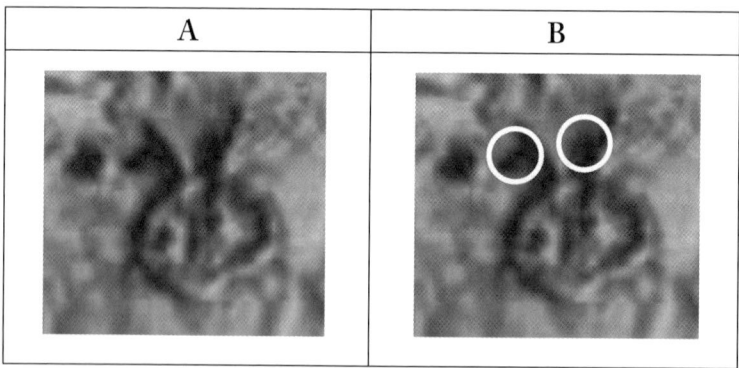

This has posed a problem for would be decipherers due to its similarity to how Hieroglyph D2 would be portrayed (which, as we have seen, is also erroneously represented by Linear A symbol L95, despite it not having a central partitioning line).

Example Three: derivation of Linear A symbol L95
(Linear A symbol L31 superimposed on Linear A symbol L91)
It is not just Linear A symbol L55 that is combined with an ordinal. In addition, Linear A symbol L31, representing Hieroglyph V28, is also joined to pure ordinals in a similar way, set out as follows:

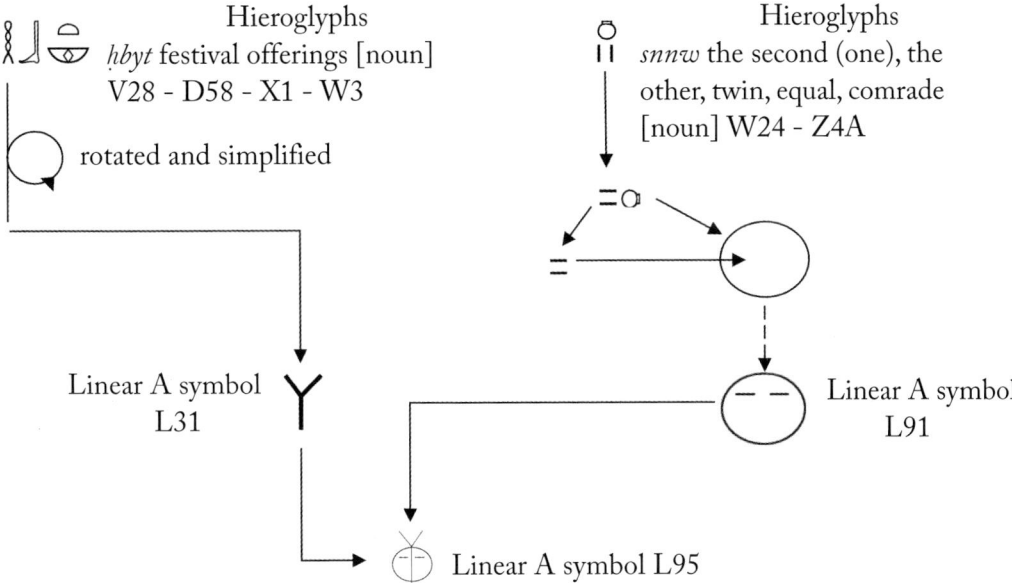

This symbol would therefore mean "festival offerings [in the] second [month]". We saw this, for example, on Tablet HT 116A, an extract of the photograph of which is set out below:

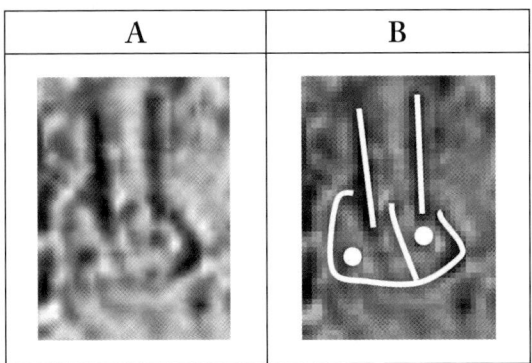

While similar in appearance to the picture of the first Linear A symbol shown in Example Two above, the meaning is, in fact, somewhat different and, given that it is so similar to the Linear A symbol from Tablet HT 102 that we saw above in Example Two, for example, we have to rely on the context of the tablet to indicate its meaning, such as if the tablet is a record of state (completed by the temple acting as its agent) or a record of a temple acting as principal in its dealings (i.e. as a religious institution).

Appendix 7

Grain

As we saw on Tablet HT 13:

Linear A symbol L101 was a simplified representation of

Hieroglyph M34

Having identified the hieroglyph that the symbol represented, in the context in which it appeared, there were three potential words that it might have represented. The process for determining the most likely of these is discussed in this appendix.

Option One: *bdt / bty* (emmer)
The first possible meaning is "emmer", where Hieroglyph M34, being represented by Linear A symbol L101, is the first hieroglyph in that word:

bdt emmer [noun - flora - food] M34 - D46 - X1

bdt emmer [noun - flora - food] M34 - D46 - X1 - U9 - Z2

bdt emmer [noun - flora - food] M34 - M33A

bdt emmer [noun - flora - food] M34 - X1

bdt emmer [noun - flora - food] M34 - X1 - Z1 - U10 - Z2

bdt emmer [noun - flora - food] M34 - X1 - Z4 - U9

bdt / bty emmer [noun - flora - food] M34 - X1 - Z5 - U10 - Z2

bdt / bty emmer [noun - flora - food] M34 - U10 - Z2

bdt / bty emmer [noun - flora - food] M34 - X1 - Z4 - U10 - Z2

bdt / bty emmer [noun - flora - food] M34 - X1 - Z5 - U10 - Z2 *bdt / bty* emmer [noun - flora - food] M34 - U10 - Z2

bdt / bty emmer [noun - flora - food] M34 - X1 - Z4 - U10 - Z2

Archaeologist Julie M. Hansen notes, however, that no emmer has been discovered at any of the six Late Bronze Age sites in Crete that she considered in her study of archaeological data on Aegean agriculture. Bread wheat and 6-row barley were recorded at Knossos (6-row barley was also discovered at Myrtos Pyrgos and Sklavakambos).[20] Emmer is, therefore, unlikely to have been recorded on a Linear A tablet.

There is little contemporary evidence to help us decied between the next two options:

Option Two: *it* (barley, corn)
The next possible meaning is "barley", where Hieroglyph M34, being represented by Linear A symbol L101, is the last hieroglyph in that word:

it barley, corn [noun - flora - food] M33A - M34

Option Three: *pḥ3* (grain, seed)
The final possible meaning is "grain", where Hieroglyph M34, being represented by Linear A symbol L101, is, again, the last hieroglyph in that word:

pḥ3 grain, seed [noun - flora - food] Q3 - J1 - M34

The accounts of grain preserved in the mid-5th Dynasty papyrus archives of the Abusir funerary temple of King Neferefre use this word with this spelling (in hieratic).[21] Conversely, in that corpus, barley is frequently recorded using the word *šm'*,[22] not *it*, and *šm'* is written in hieroglyphs as:

šm' Upper Egyptian barley [noun - flora - food] M26 - U9

šm' Upper Egyptian barley [noun - flora - food] M26 - U9 - Z2

šm' Upper Egyptian barley [noun - flora - food] M27 - U9

---

20. Julie M. Hansen, "Agriculture in the Prehistoric Aegean: Data versus Speculation", *American Journal of Archaeology* 92(1)(1988), p43
21. Hana Vymazalová, *The accounting documents from the papyrus archive of Neferre and their specific terminology* (PhD: Charles University in Prague, 2005), pp186–187
22. Hana Vymazalová, *The accounting documents from the papyrus archive of Neferre and their specific terminology* (PhD: Charles University in Prague, 2005), pp71, 73, and 76

The 5th Dynasty ruled in Egypt 900 years before the period we are considering, thus the papyrus archive of the funerary temple complex of King Neferefre was certainly not contemporary with the Linear A records that we are considering. Nonetheless, we have worked on the assumption thus far that the lexicon of words used in the administration of Egypt's temples of the 5th Dynasty would more likely than not to have been consistent with that used in the Egyptian temples of the 18th Dynasty and, indeed, we have found numerous instances, highlighted throughout this work, where this is the case. As a result, this symbol is therefore most appropriately translated as the Middle Egyptian word *pḥ3* meaning "grain".

Having identified this symbol's meaning as being "grain", a final excursus is required.

Excursus 7A.1: The expected recording of wheat

In Chapter Two it was noted that Ruth Palmer ascribed certain Linear A symbols their believed meanings on the basis of a comparison of their appearance to Linear B symbols. On the basis of these believed meanings Palmer was, however, surprised by the lack of any record of sheep at Khania on the surviving Linear A tablets.[23] Using this same comparative approach, the symbol for wool had not been identified. However, the symbol identified as meaning wool in Chapter Two was recorded at Khania, indicating that Palmer was correct to believe that there must have been sheep there (as, by implication of the presence of wool, there must have been).

In a similar way, Ilse Shoep notes the absence of wheat being recorded at Zakros but believed this was most likely due to accidental gaps in the evidence.[24] While that is a constant handicap we have to face with the limited surviving corpus of Linear A tablets, Schoep did not consider the alternative possibility that the symbol she believed to be wheat, Linear A symbol L71 (i.e. A303 in Godart & Olivier's nomenclature), had been incorrectly identified (which, indeed, it was). As we have seen, grain is represented by Linear A symbol L101 (Egyptian hieroglyph M34). Shoep was correct to expect this to be recorded at Zakros for, indeed, it is:

---

23. Ruth Palmer, "Linear A commodities: a comparison of resources", in Robert Laffineur and Wolf-Dietrich Niemeier (Eds.), *Politea: Society and State in the Aegean Bronze Age: proceedings of the 5th International Aegean Conference/5e Rencontre égéenne internationale, University of Heidelberg, Archäologisches Institut, 10–13 April, 1994* (Bruxelles & Austin: Université de Liège & University of Texas at Austin, 1994), p146
24. Ilse Shoep, "Tablets and Territories? Reconstructing Late Minoan IB Political Geography through Undeciphered Documents", *American Journal of Archaeology* 103(2)(1999), p208

Grain 495

Tablet ZA 4A[25]

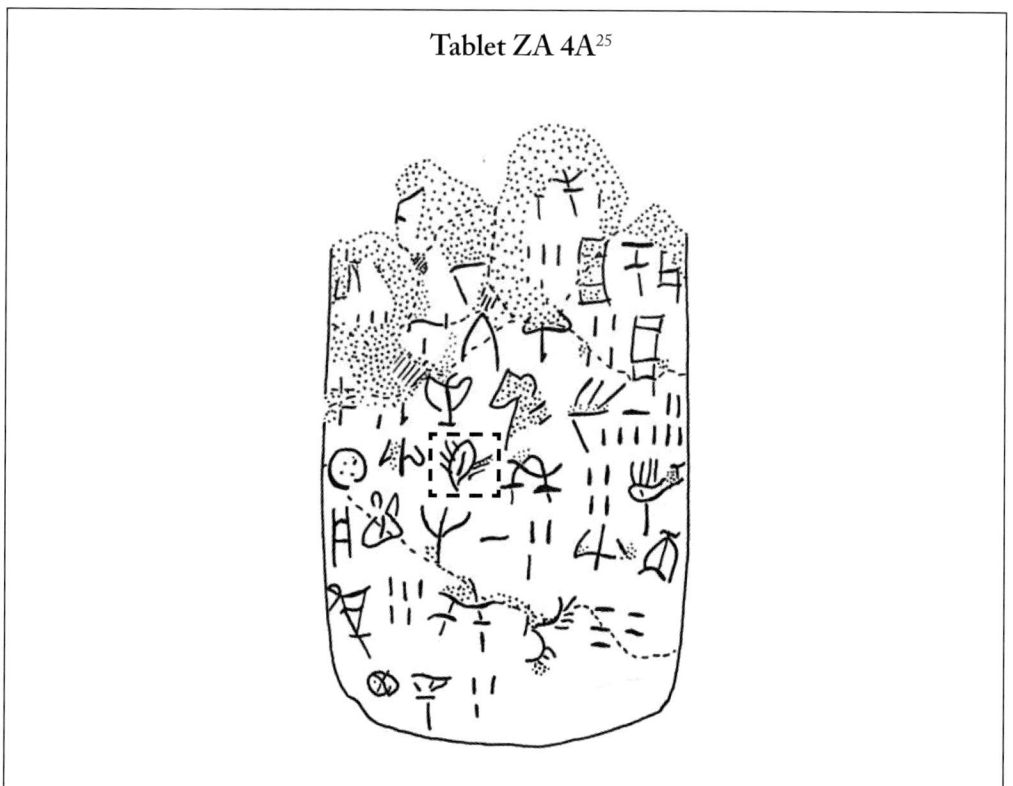

---
25. This tablet is not translated in this work as it is too heavily damaged, but this category translates as "[in the] fourth [month], offerings [of] grain [for the] *3bd* priests (in their month of service) – 4".

Appendix 8

Dates

Dates appear in four places on Linear A tablets:

1. In tablet headings;
2. As a subscript note next to the first item on a list (or, in one case, next to the second and subsequent, but not first, items on a list);
3. As part of the description of the last item on a list, or as a subscript note (or in one case superscript note) next to the last item on a list; and
4. Next to the grand total (in particular when a date in the heading was not given).

We shall consider these in turn. The reader may wish to refer to Appendix 6 as regards the ordinals "second", "third", and "fourth" that are included within dates.

Of course, as we have already seen (on Tablet HT 86A and Tablet HT 120, for example), it is important to note that not all subscript notations next to the first or last item on a list represent dates, and only dates are considered here (with other subscript notations, which are descriptors, being considered in the main body of this work when they arise).

<u>Type One: In tablet headings</u>
As a matter of administrative convention we would expect dates to be written in tablets' headings, and for the contents of the tablets set out thereafter to relate to that date (if a specific day) or period (if longer than a day).

Three examples, for successive months, are set out below:

<u>Example 1: Tablet heading of the third month (believed to be the month of 3 Šmw, the penultimate month of the year)</u>
Our first example of this type concerns the first two symbols on Tablet HT 1A:

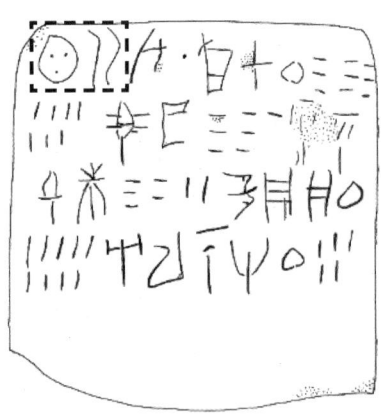

Dates 497

Hieroglyphs Z2 - W24 ◯ / rotated ◯ / modified (dashes as dots inside circle) / Linear A symbol L91 ⊙

As we have seen previously (and as set out in Appendix 6), this symbol, representing Hieroglyphs Z2 - W24, represents the ordinal:

◯ ḫmt nw third [ordinal number] Z2 - W24

Hieroglyphs Z5 - Z5 \\/ Linear A symbol L58

As we have seen previously, this symbol represents the word:

★ ⌒⌒ ⊙ ꜣbd month [noun] N11 - N14 - Z5 - Z5 - N5

These two symbols therefore mean "[in the] third month" (which, by virtue of the repeated reference to New Year's Day found throughout the corpus we can infer is the third month (out of four) of the final four-month season of the year in the Egyptian calendar, Šmw).

Example 2: Tablet heading of the fourth month (believed to be the month of 4 Šmw, the final month of the season and the year)

Our next example concerns the first two symbols on Tablet HT 7A:

Hieroglyph Z4B - Z4B - W24 ◯ / modified (dashes inside circle) / Linear A symbol L91 ⊙

As we have seen previously (and as set out in Appendix 6), this symbol, representing Hieroglyphs Z4B - Z4B - W24, represents the ordinal:

◯ fdnw fourth Z4B - Z4B - W24

Hieroglyph N11 ⌒ / modified / Linear A symbol L78 ∧

As we have seen previously, this symbol represents the word:

498   The Decipherment of Linear A

⌒ *3bd* month [noun] N11

These two symbols therefore mean "[in the] fourth month".

Example 3: Tablet heading of the first month of the year (believed to be the month of 1 *3ht*, the first month of the first season of the year)
  Our final example of this type concerns the first two symbols on Tablet HT 35:

Hieroglyph N11 ⌒ / modified / Linear A symbol L78 ⋀
As we have seen previously, Linear A symbol L78 represents Hieroglyph N11. Here, this symbol represents the ordinal (when used in dates):

⌒ *3bd* 1st [used in dates] N11

Hieroglyph N11 ⌒ / modified / Linear A symbol L78 ⋀
As we have seen previously, this symbol represents the word:

⌒ *3bd* month [noun] N11

These two symbols therefore mean "[in the] first month".

Type Two: As a subscript note next to the first item on a list
In addition to appearing in headings, dates are expressed as an ordinal (without the word for month) when they appear within lists. The first type we shall consider is next to the first category of item recorded on lists.
  The reason as to why a date would appear next to the first category of item recorded on a list is similar to modern accounts. When a ledger account deals with how a balance (be that stock, debtors, cash, creditors, whatever) moves during a defined period, such as one month, then if there is a balance existing at the start of the period of account, because it was there at the end of the previous accounting period, it is recorded in the current

period as having been "brought forward" from that previous accounting prior into the current accounting period.

This is not the moment to teach ancient historians double entry book keeping (which, of course, did not exist in the ancient world). However, a simple example is set out below of a T-account, showing the movement of stock on the ledger of a business in January 2022 beginning with a balance brought forward from the previous month (shown on the left hand side of the T-account, as it is an asset balance), one purchase is made during the month (adding to the asset balance on the left hand side of the T-account), four sales are made during the month (with the cost of the items sold, to be deducted from the total value of stock held, shown on the right hand side of the T-account), and the month ends on 31 January 2022 with no stock (the balance carried forward to the next month is zero) (because the total of the assets or additions thereto on the left equals the total of the deductions on the right):

ABC Limited - Stock account

	£		£
1/01/2022 Balance brought forward	100		
2/01/2022 Purchases	250		
		5/01/2022 Cost of Sales	100
		12/01/2022 Cost of Sales	125
		23/01/2022 Cost of Sales	50
		29/01/2022 Cost of Sales	75
		31/01/2022 Balance carried forward	0
	350		350
1/02/2022 Balance brought down	0		

Similarly, on the Linear A tablets, if in the current month being recorded a balance was brought forward from the prior month, then next to that item is a subscript note indicating that fact with an ordinal indicating the number of the prior month. We see this in the following example:

500   The Decipherment of Linear A

<u>Example 4: Subscript reference to fourth month (believed to be 4 *Šmw*, the final month of the year) next to first item on list</u>
In this example, a subscript ordinal appears next to the first item recorded on Tablet HT 36:

Hieroglyph F27 ⌂/ partially rotated / simplified / modified / Linear A symbol L42 ⌶
As we have seen previously, this symbol repesents the last hieroglyph in the word:

⚊🐐⌂ *ỉr* goat [noun - ani.] D36 - D21 - E31 - F27

Subscript Hieroglyph Z4B - Z4B - W24 ⚌⊙/ modified (four dashes inside circle as dots) / Linear A symbol L91 ⊙
To summarise our analysis of this symbol set out in Chapter 5 (there is one circle with three dots and another with one dot, presumably because all four dots would not fit in the same circle), as we have seen previously (and as out in Appendix 6), this symbol (if all four dots had been written in one circle), representing Hieroglyphs Z4B - Z4B - W24, represents the ordinal "fourth":

⚌⊙ *fdnw* fourth Z4B - Z4B - W24

These symbols therefore mean "goats [from the] fourth [month]".

Dates   501

Example 5: Subscript reference to third month (believed to be 3 Šmw, the penultimate month of the year) next to first item on list

In this example, a subscript ordinal has been incised next to the first item recorded on Tablet HT 18:

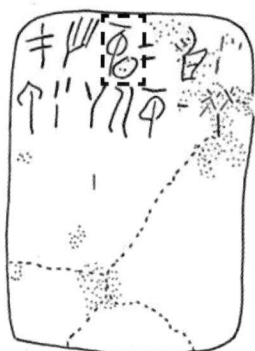

Hieroglyph F27 ⌒/ partially rotated / simplified / modified / Linear A symbol L42 ⚇

As we have seen previously, this symbol represents the last hieroglyph in the word:

ꜥr goat [noun - ani.] D36 - D21 - E31 - F27

Subscript Hieroglyphs Z2 - W24 ⦿ / rotated ⊖/ modified (dashes as dots inside circle) / Linear A symbol L91 ☺

As we have seen previously (and as set out in Appendix 6), this symbol, representing Hieroglyphs Z2 - W24, represents the ordinal:

ḫmt nw third [ordinal number] Z2 - W24

As we have seen on this tablet, these symbols mean "goats [from the] third [month]" (they were provisions left over from month three that were to be used in the current month, month four).

In the case of this tablet, however, we can also make the further inference that both of first two categories of items were from the prior month as they are both recorded before the subheading on Row Two (which, we have seen, means "provided in the month" inferring that, unlike the categories of items that preceded it, those items that followed were received in the current month when it was written (i.e. month four)).

The layout of the tablet and specifically its subheading on Row Two segmenting the categories of items in question, allows us to make this assumption. The scribe of the tablet in the next example, however, follows a different (in fact the opposite) approach (yet showing essentially the same information).

502   The Decipherment of Linear A

<u>Type Two(A): As a subscript note next to the second (and third) but not first items on a list</u>

<u>Example 6: Subscript reference to third month (believed to be 3 Šmw, the penultimate month of the year) next to second item on list (relating, therefore, to both the first and second items)</u>

In this example there was no subscript ordinal incised next to the first item listed, but there was a subscript ordinal incised next to the second item (and a combined ordinal with the first symbol of the third item) listed on Tablet HT 89:

Hieroglpyph O10 / reversed / simplified / Linear A symbol L68/96
As we have seen previously, this symbol represents the name of the goddess:

ḥwt ḥt Hathor [noun - div.] O10

joined to Hieroglyph R1 / simplified / Linear A symbol L57
As we have seen previously, this symbol represents Hieroglyph R1 and the last hieroglyph in the word:

 *wdḥw* offering table, offerings [noun - furn.] G43 - D46 - V28
　　　　　　　　　　　　　　　　　　　　　　　　　　　　　　　　　　　- G43 - R1

Subscript Hieroglyph Z4B - Z4B - W24 / modified (four dashes inside circle as dots) / Linear A symbol L91
As we have seen previously, this symbol, representing Hieroglyphs Z4B - Z4B - W24, represents the ordinal:

fdnw fourth Z4B - Z4B - W24

These three symbols therefore mean "[from the] offerings [to] Hathor [in the] fourth [month]".

The detailed analysis of the photograph of tablet concerning the next category should be consulted on pages 377 to 379. Space constraints preclude the duplication of that analysis here. However, it suffices to say here that the combined ordinal included within the first symbol of the next category also indicates fourth [month].

While an ordinal appearing next to the first category of item on a list typically indicates that those goods were brought forward from the previous month (i.e. they were already in store at the start of the current month), here the symbol appears next to the second item on the list (and within the first symbol of the third item on the list, as a combined ordinal). As we have seen, it seems likely that the first item recorded had been received prior to the current month but instead of specifying that the scribe decided to specify that the two categories that followed it were received in the current month (month four), the opposite of the apparently standard approach, but having the same effect in terms of information conveyed.

Type Three: Written within the description of, or a subscript (or, occasionally, superscript) note next to, the last item on a list

Again we can turn to modern accounting to guide us as to the meaning of a date (as expressed solely by an ordinal) when it appears within the description, or next to the description in subscript (or superscript), of a final item on a list.

When an account records the movements on a balance during a certain period of, say, a month, if at the end of the period the account balance is not zero and an amount remains, it is recorded as carried forward to the next period.

Taking the same example as before, and a T-account, showing the movement of stock on the ledger of a business in January 2022, but assuming a second purchase had been made on the penultimate day of the month, and this stock was unused at the end of the month on 31 January 2022, we see that this stock is carried forward to be used in the next period (i.e. February):

	ABC Limited - Stock account		
	£		£
1/01/2022 Balance brought forward	100		
2/01/2022 Purchases	250		
		5/01/2022 Cost of Sales	100
30/01/2022 Purchases	100		
		12/01/2022 Cost of Sales	125
		23/01/2022 Cost of Sales	50
		29/01/2022 Cost of Sales	75
		31/01/2022 Balance carried forward	100
	450		450
1/02/2022 Balance brought down	100		

Similarly, in the Linear A tablets, if in the current month being recorded an amount that was to be carried forward to the next month, then that item was listed last and an ordinal indicating that next month was included within the description of that item or next to that item's description written in subscript (or superscript). We see this in the following examples:

Example 7: Reference to third month (3 Šmw) written within the description of the last item on list:
In this example, an ordinal is added to the description of the final item on Tablet HT 95B:

Hieroglyphs Z2 - W24 ¹¹¹ₒ / rotated ᵒ⁼ / modified (three dashes as dots inside circle) / Linear A symbol L91 ☺

To summarise our analysis of this symbol set out in Chapter 5 (there are three dots rather than two in the circle), as we have seen previously (and as out in Appendix 6), this symbol, representing, representing Hieroglyphs Z2 - W24, represents the ordinal:

¹¹¹ₒ ḥmt nw third [ordinal number] Z2 - W24

Hieroglyphs Z5 - Z5 \\ / Linear A symbol L58 ⑊
As we have seen previously, this symbol represents the last hieroglyphs of the word:

⊔\\ k3 bull [noun - ani.] D28 - Z5 - Z5

Hieroglyphs X1 - D17 ⌒~ / modified (hieroglyphs joined) / Linear A symbol L88 ᴿ (reversed)
As we have seen previously, this symbol represents the last hieroglyphs of the word:

𓇋𓏺𓈖𓏏𓂋 imny (daily) service, offerings, portion, ration [noun] M17 - Y5 - N35 - X1 - D17

These three symbols therefore mean "[for the] third [month], bulls [for] daily services".

Dates 505

Example 8: Reference to third month (3 Šmw) next to last item on list:
In this example, a subscript ordinal is incised next to the final item listed on Tablet HT 99A:

Hieroglyph F27 / partially rotated / simplified / Linear A symbol L42
As we have seen previously, this symbol represents the last hieroglyph in the word:

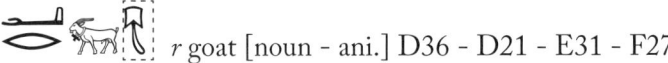 r goat [noun - ani.] D36 - D21 - E31 - F27

Hieroglyphs Z2 - W24 / rotated / modified (dashes as dots inside circle) / Linear A symbol L91
As we have seen previously (and as set out in Appendix 6), this symbol, representing Hieroglyphs Z2 - W24, represents the ordinal:

ḫmt nw third [ordinal number] Z2 - W24

These two symbols therefore mean "goats [for the] third [month]".

Example 9: Superscript reference to third month (believed to be 3 Šmw, the penultimate month of the year) next to last item on list
Tablet HT 33 gives us our best indication that the meaning we have inferred for subscript ordinals (or superscript ordinals, as here) next to items on a list (here, the last item on a list) is correct. Here we see the following:

506   The Decipherment of Linear A

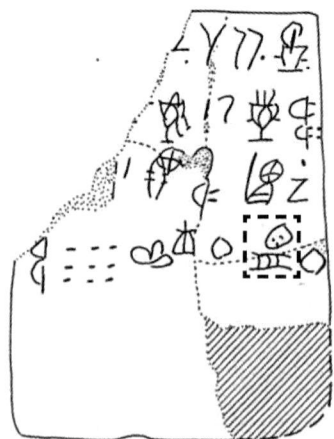

Hieroglyph O43 𓎺 (not rotated) / simplified / Linear A symbol L1 (here, rotated) 𐙁
As we have seen previously, this symbol represents the first hieroglyph in the word

𓎺 𓂡 *šsp* to receive [verb] O43 - U30 - D40 - M33

Here, the scribe decided not to rotate Hieroglyph O43 to become Linear A symbol L1, leaving it with the same orientation as the hieroglyph that it represents. With Linear A symbol L91 on top of it, it takes up the same amount of space, horizontally, as Linear A symbol L1 would written normally (rotated by 90 degrees) with Linear A symbol L91 next to it, so the scribe presumably felt there was no need to rotate it to save space.

Superscript Hieroglyphs Z2 - W24 ꜥ / rotated ꜥ / modified (dashes as dots inside circle) / Linear A symbol L91 ☺
As we have seen previously (and as set out in Appendix 6), this symbol, representing Hieroglyphs Z2 - W24, represents the ordinal:

𓏤𓏤𓏤 *ḥmt nw* third [ordinal number] Z2 - W24

These two symbols therefore mean "receive[d for the] third [month]". The scribe, writing in the second month, did not repeat the description of the item (which related to the part of the consignment received in, and for use in, the second month), but simply notes that a portion received in the second month was to be carried forward for use in the third month. Recording something as received in one period but noting it was for use in the next is not too far removed from modern accrual accounting (and, again, evidences that the temple created and relied upon forecasts in conducting its operations). With the hints of use of concepts not far removed from double entry bookkeeping that we noted in Chapter Five, while the temple ledgers themselves have not survived, the standard of accounting employed appears unlikely to have been surpassed in sophistication until the Middle Ages.

Type Four: Next to the grand total

In order to indicate the date of summation of a grand total on a tablet (in particular, when a date was not given in the tablet heading and the relevant date nonetheless needed to be made clear), the symbol(s) for the specific date could be incised next to that for grand total.

Example 10: Grand total of tablet with a date of summation of New Year's Day (*wpt rnpt*)

Tablet HT 102 perhaps sets this out the clearest:

Hieroglyph F14 / rotated / simplified / Linear A symbol L98

As we have seen previously, this symbol represents the first hieroglyph in the word:

wpt rnpt New Year's Day (and its festivals) [noun] F14 - W3

wpt rnpt New Year's Day (and its festivals) [noun] F15 - W3 - N5

Hieroglyph N14 / modified / Linear A symbol L22 +

As we have seen previously, this symbol represents the first hieroglyph in the word:

dmḏ smꜣ grand total [noun] N14 - F36

These two symbols therefore mean "[on] New Year's Day, grand total", and this is followed by the grand total of the items recorded on the tablet as at that specific date.

Select Bibliography

It might take two lifetimes to read everything that has ever been written on Linear A and the history of Egypto-Cretan relations in the Middle and Late Bronze Ages. This work has, therefore, necessarily had to be selective in its approach.

As regards Linear A, however, this is not problematic for this book is the result of a focus on the primary evidence rather than secondary sources that discuss the primary evidence (indeed, in trying to bring a fresh perspective to decipherment, this was deliberate). As with the decipherment of Linear B, decipherment of Linear A has, in any event, made prior works on the subject largely if not wholly redundant.

As regards the history of Egypto-Cretan relations in the Middle and Late Bronze Ages, it is perhaps unsurprising, with significant explicit evidence omitted from current histories, that a major revision of the historical narrative would take place once a comprehensive reassessment of all the evidence was undertaken (such evidence now also including, but the resulting reassessment not being reliant upon, a deciphered Linear A). Again, prior works on the subject have been made at least partially redundant.

Only a select bibliography is provided here, therefore, covering those works that I found the most useful in the course of writing this book and which I think the reader will find of most use consulting after having read this book. As to how this select bibliography is organised, I have categorised works by the subject areas in which I found them of most use (which is not necessarily the areas that they covered in their entirety).

Part 1: Languages and Scripts

Linear A

Articles

Emmett L. Bennett Jr, "The Mycenae Tablets", *Proceedings of the American Philosophical Society* 97(4)(1953), pp422–470

Gerald Cadogan, "Pyrgos, Crete, 1970–1977", *Archaeological Reports* 24(1977–1978), pp70–84

Ilse Schoep, "Tablets and Territories? Reconstructing Late Minoan IB Political Geography through Undeciphered Documents", *American Journal of Archaeology* 103(2)(April 1999), pp201–221

Jacques Raison, "Du nouveau sur la chronologie du linéaire A", *Bulletin de l'Association Guillaume Budé* 3(October 1960), pp315–324

Books

W. C. Brice, *Inscriptions in the Minoan Linear Script of Class A* (Oxford: Oxford University Press, 1961)

Louis Godart and Jean-Pierre Olivier, *Recueil des Inscriptions en Linéaire A, Volume 1: Tablettes éditées avant 1970* (Athens: École Française D'Athènes, 1976)

Louis Godart and Jean-Pierre Olivier, *Recueil des Inscriptions en Linéaire A, Volume 3: Tablettes, Nodules et Rondelles éditées en 1975 et 1976* (Athens: École Française D'Athènes, 1976)

Chapters in edited books

Maurizio Del Freo, "Rapport 2001–2005 sur les textes en Écriture Hiéroglyphique Crétoise, en Linéaire A et en Linéaire B" in A. Sacconi, M. del Freo, L. Godart & M. Negri (Eds.), *Colloquium Romanum: Atti del XII Colloquio Internazionale de Micenologia. Roma, 20–25 febbraio, 2006* (Pisa and Rome: Pasiphae, 2007), pp3–30

Ilse Schoep, "The Inscribed Document" in C. F. Macdonald & C. Knappett (Eds.), *Knossos: Protopalatial deposits in early magazine A and south-west houses* (British School of Athens Supplementary Volume 41)(London: British School of Archaeology at Athens, 2007), pp131–134

Ruth Palmer, "Linear A commodities: a comparison of resources", in Robert Laffineur and Wolf-Dietrich Niemeier, *Politea: Society and State in the Aegean Bronze Age: proceedings of the 5th International Aegean Conference/5e Rencontre égéenne internationale, University of Heidelberg, Archäologisches Institut, 10–13 April, 1994* (Bruxelles & Austin: Université de Liège & University of Texas at Austin, 1994), pp133–154

Giovanni Pugliese Carratelli, "Nuove epigrafi minoiche di Festo", in *Annuario della Scuola Archeologica di Atene e delle Missioni Italiane in Oriente* (Vol. XXXV-XXXVI) (Nuova Serie XIX-XX) (1957–1958) (Roma: Instituto Poligrafico Dello Stato, 1958)

Massimo Perna, "The Birth of Administration and Writing in Minoan Crete", in Dimitri Nakassis, Joann Gulizio, Sarah A. James (Eds.), *KE-RA-ME-JA: Studies Presented to Cynthia W. Shelmerdine* (Philadelphia: INSTAP Academic Press, 2014), pp251–259

Videos

Helena Tomas – It's All Linear B to Me
https://www.youtube.com/watch?v=OBUIMjXkHZU (accessed 11 October 2020)

Linear B

Ancient texts

Sir Arthur Evans, *Scripta Minoa: The Written Documents of Minoan Crete, with special reference to the archives of Knossos, Volume II* (Oxford: Clarendon Press, 1952)

Articles

Lydia Baumbach, "The Dilemma of the Horns – An Analysis of the Knossos Mc Tablets", *Acta Classica* 14(1971), pp1–16

José L. Melena, "On the Knossos Mc Tablets", *Minos* 13(1972), pp29–54

Books

John Chadwick, *The Decipherment of Linear B* (2nd Ed.)(Cambridge: Cambridge University Press, 1967)

Michael Ventris & John Chadwick, *Documents in Mycenaean Greek* (2nd Ed.)(Cambridge: Cambridge University Press, 1973)

Websites

Database of Mycenaean at Oslo: https://damos.hf.uio.no/

Chapters in edited books

José L. Melena, "Mycenaean Writing" in Yves Duhoux & Anna Morpurgo Davies (Eds.), *A Companion to Linear B Mycenaean Greek Texts and their World* (Louvain-La-Neuve & Walpole, MA: Peeters, 2014)

Helena Tomas, "Saving on Clay: The Linear B Practice of Cutting Tablets", in Kathryn E. Piquette & Ruth D. Whitehouse, *Writing as Material Practice: Substance, Surface and Medium* (London: Ubiquity Press, 2013), pp175–192

Videos

The Minoans: Ancient Worlds (Bettany Hughes)
https://www.youtube.com/watch?v=7VJqnTlbCS0 (accessed 11 October 2020)

Greek and Greek shorthand method

Ancient texts

Cicero, *Letters to Atticus*

Diogenes Laertius, *Lives of Eminent Philosophers*

Plutarch, *Parallel Lives: The Life of Cato the Younger*

Articles

F. W. G. Foat, "On Old Greek Tachygraphy", *The Journal of Hellenic Studies* 21 (1901), pp238–267

T. W. Allen, "Miscellanea", *The Classical Quarterly* 24(1)(1930), pp40–41

Books

L. H. Jeffery, *The local scripts of archaic Greece: a study of the origin of the Greek alphabet and its development from the eighth to the fifth centuries B.C.* (Oxford: Clarendon Press, 1961)

H. J. M. Milne, *Greek Shorthand Manuals: Syllabary and Commentary* (London: Egypt Exploration Society, 1934)

Middle Egyptian language and hieroglyphic script

Articles

Alan H. Gardiner, "The Transcription of New Kingdom Hieratic", *The Journal of Egyptian Archaeology* 15(1929), pp48–55

Books

A.H. Gardiner, *Egyptian Grammar: Being an Introduction to the Study of Hieroglyphs* (3rd Ed.)(Oxford: Griffith Institute, 1957)

Alan H. Gardiner, *Late-Egyptian Stories* (Bruxelles: Édition de la Fondation Egyptologique Reine Elisabeth, 1932)

Alan H. Gardener, *Late Egyptian Miscellanies* (Bruxelles: Édition de la Fondation Egyptologique Reine Elisabeth, 1937)

John F. Healey, *The Early Alphabet* (Berkeley & Los Angeles: University of California Press, 1990)

Jac J. Janssen, *Commodity Prices from the Ramessid Period: an economic study of the village of necropolis workmen at Thebes* (Leiden: E. J. Brill, 1975)

Boris Jerorović, *A Concise Dictionary of Middle Egyptian* (Oxford: Griffith Institute, Ashmolean Museum, 2002)

Leonard H. Lesko (Ed.), *A Dictionary of Late Egyptian: Volume I* (2nd Ed.)(Providence RI: BC Scribe Publications, 2002)

Leonard H. Lesko (Ed.), *A Dictionary of Late Egyptian: Volume II* (2nd Ed.)(Providence RI: BC Scribe Publications, 2004)

Boyo G. Ockinga, *A Concise Grammar of Middle Egyptian* (Darmstadt/Mainz: Verlag Philipp von Zabern, 2012)

Websites

Thesaurus Linguae Aegyptiae: https://aaew.bbaw.d

Mark Vygus' online Middle Egyptian dictionary: https://www.egyptologyarchive.com/2018/10/book-no2-middle-egyptian-dictionary.html

Egyptian mathematics

Articles

Helena Lopez Palma, "Egyptian Fractional Numerals: The grammar of Egyptian NPs and statements with fractional number expressions", *LingAeg* 23(2015), pp197–228

Books

Annette Imhausen, *Mathematics in Ancient Egypt: A Contextual History* (Princeton & Woodstock: Princeton University Press, 2016)

Paul Benoit, Karine Chemla, and Jim Ritter, *Histoire de fractions, fractions d'histoire* (Basel, Boston, & Berlin: Birkhäuser Verlag, 1992)

Latin

Articles

J. N. Adams, "The Latin of the New Vindolanda Tablets", *Britannia* 50(2019), pp253–263

J. N. Adams, "The Latin of the New Vindolanda Tablets", *The Classical Quarterly* 53(2)(2003), pp530–575

Books

Oxford Latin Dictionary (Oxford: Clarendon Press, 1968)

Proto-Sinaitic

Articles

Alan H. Gardiner, "The Egyptian Origin of the Semitic Alphabet", *The Journal of Egyptian Archaeology* 3(1)(1916), pp1–16

F. Simons, "Proto-Sinaitic – Progenitor of the Alphabet", *Rosetta* 9(2011), pp16–40

Part 2: Archaeology and History

Archaeology and history of Crete (and the Aegean)

Ancient texts, translations thereof, and commentaries thereon

Diodorus Siculus, *Bibliotheca Historica*

Herodotus, *The Histories*

George Rawlinson, *History of Herodotus* (D. Appleton and Company: New York, 1882)

Homer, *The Iliad*

Plutarch, *Life of Theseus*

Thucydides, *History of the Peloponnesian War*

Strabo, *Geography*

Malcolm M. Willcock, *A Companion to the Iliad, based on the translation by Richard Lattimore* (Chicago: The University of Chicago Press, 1976)

Articles

Paul Halstead, "Missing Sheep: On the Meaning and Wider Significance of O in Knossos Sheep Records", *The Annual of the British School at Athens* 94(1999), pp145–166

Julie M. Hansen, "Agriculture in the Prehistoric Aegean: Data versus Speculation", *American Journal of Archaeology* 92(1)(1988), pp39–52

J. T. Killen, "The Wool Industry of Crete in the Late Bronze Age", *Journal of the British School at Athens* 59(1964), pp1–15

Thomas F. Strasser, "Location and Perspective in the Theran Flotilla Fresco", *Journal of Mediterranean Archaeology* 23(1)(2010), pp3–26

L. Vance Watrous, "The Harbor Complex of the Minoan Town at Gournia", *American Journal of Archaeology* 116(3)(2012), pp521–541

Books

James Henry Breasted, *Ancient Times: A History of the Early World* (Ginn and Company, Boston, 1944)

Gerald Cadogan, *Palaces of Minoan Crete* (London: Barrie & Jenkins Ltd, 1976)

Jan Driessen & Colin F. MacDonald, *The Troubled Island: Minoan Crete Before and After the Santorini Eruption* (Liège: Université de Liège, 1997)

Sir Arthur Evans, *The Palace of Minos: A comparative account of the successive stages of the early Cretan civilization as illustrated by the discoveries at Knossos. Volume 1* (London: Macmillan and Co, Ltd, 1921)

Hara Georgiou, *The Late Minoan Destruction of Crete: Metal Groups and Stratigraphic Considerations. Monograph IX* (Los Angeles: Institute of Archaeology, University of California, 1979)

J. Alexander MacGillivray, *Minotaur: Sir Arthur Evans and the archaeology of the Minoan Myth* (London: Jonathan Cape, 2000)

J. D. S. Pendlebury, *A Handbook to the Place of Minos: Knossos* (2nd Ed.)(London: Macdonald and Jane's, 1974)

Peter Warren, *The Making of the Past: The Aegean Civilizations* (London: Elsevier-Phaidon, 1975)

Chapters in edited books

Maria Andreadaki-Vlazaki, "LM 1B pottery in Khania", in Thomas M. Brogan and Erik Hallager (Eds.), *LM IB Pottery: Relative Chronology and Regional Differences. Acts of a Workshop Held at the Danish Institute at Athens in Collaboration with the INSTAP Study Center for East Crete, 27–29 June 2007 - Monographs of the Danish Institute at Athens, Volume 11,1* (Athens: The Danish Institute at Athens, 2011), pp55–74

Philip P. Betancourt and Ioannis Frangakis, "The Slingstones", in Cheryl R. Floyd, Philip P, Betancourt, Costis Davaras, *Pseira III: The Plateia Building* (Philadelphia: University of Pennsylvania Museum, 1998), pp117–124

Eric H. Cline, "The Nature of the Economic Relations of Crete with Egypt and the Near East during the Late Bronze Age", in Angelos Chaniotis (Ed.), *From Minoan Farmers to Roman Traders: Sidelights of the Economy of Ancient Crete* (Stuttgart: Franz Steiner Verlag, 1999), pp115–144

Tim Cunningham, "Havoc: The destruction of power and the power of destruction in Minoan Crete", in J. Bretschneider, J. Driessen, and K Van. Lerberghe (Eds.), *Power and Architecture: Monumental Public Architecture in the Bronze Age Near East and Aegean* (Leuven, Paris & Dudley: Uitgeverij Peeters, 2007), pp23–44

Sinclair Hood, "Warlike Destruction in Crete c.1450 BC", in Theocharēs Eustratiou Detorakēs (Ed.) *Pepragmena tou 5. Diethnous Krētologikou Synedriou (Hagios Nikolaos, 25 Septemvriou-1 Oktōvriou 1981)* (Héraklion, 1985), pp170–178

Dimitri Nakassis, "The Extractive Systems of the Mycenaean World", in Jonathan Valk and Irene Soto Marín (Eds.), *Ancient Taxation: The Mechanics of Extraction in Comparative Perspective* (New York: New York University Press, 2021), pp93–127

Ruth Palmer, "Bridging the Gap: The Continuity of Greek Agriculture from the Mycenaean to the Historical Period", in David W. Tandy, *Prehistory and History: Ethnicity, Class and Political Economy* (London: Black Rose Books, 2001), pp41–84

Lefteris Platon, "Zakros: one or two destructions around the end of the LM IB period", in Thomas M. Brogan and Erik Hallager (Eds.), *LM IB Pottery: Relative Chronology and Regional Differences. Acts of a Workshop Held at the Danish Institute at Athens in Collaboration with the INSTAP Study Center for East Crete, 27–29 June 2007 - Monographs of the Danish Institute at Athens, Volume 11,2* (Athens: The Danish Institute at Athens, 2011), pp595–612

Malcolm H. Weiner, "The Mycenaean Conquest of Minoan Crete", in Colin F. McDonald, Eleni Hatzaki, and Stelios Andreou (Eds.), *The Great Islands: Studies of Crete and Cyprus presented to Gerald Cadogan* (Kapon Editions: Athens, 2015), pp131–142

Helène Whittaker, "Symbolic Aspects of Warfare in Ancient Crete", in Geoff Lee, Helène Whittaker, Graham Wrightson, *Ancient Warfare: Introducing Current Research: Volume 1* (Newcastle upon Tyne: Cambridge Scholars Publishing, 2015), pp1–13

Websites – archaeology
The Assembly on the Hill and Shipwreck Fresco:
https://web.archive.org/web/20120306172922/
http://www.therafoundation.org/wallpaintingexhibition/assembly-on-the-hill-and-shipwreck/wallpainting

The Flotilla Fresco:
https://web.archive.org/web/20120308114124/
http://www.therafoundation.org/wallpaintingexhibition/flotilla/wallpainting

Websites – animal biology
Feeding Lambs: http://www.sheep101.info/201/feedinglambs.html
Mitata in Crete: http://www.wondergreece.gr/v1/en/Articles/Architecture/8721-Mitata_in_Crete
Shearing sheeps in Crete!: https://www.arolithos.com/blog/shearing-sheeps-in-crete/
The ruminant digestive system: https://extension.umn.edu/dairy-nutrition/ruminant-digestive-system
What Do Goats Eat? A Guide to Goat Feed: https://www.tractorsupply.com/tsc/cms/life-out-here/the-barn/animal-medication-for-goats/nutritional-requirements-for-goats
What is the gestation period for sheep?: https://www.provicorural.com.au/what-is-the-gestation-period-for-sheep-what-to-know-when-raising-sheep/

History of Greece and the Greek world (excluding Crete specific items)

Ancient texts
Doukas, *Historia Turco-Byzantina*
Apprenticeship to a shorthand writer: http://papyri.info/ddbdp/p.oxy;4;724

Books
Jonathan Harris, *Byzantium and the Crusades* (2nd Ed.)(London: Bloomsbury Publishing Plc, 2014)
R. Janin, *Constantinople Byzantine. Developpement Urbain et Repertoire Topographique* (2nd Ed.)(Paris: Institut Français d'études Byzantines, 1964)

Chapters in edited books
Marja Vierros, "Scribes and other writers in the Petra Papyri", in Rodney Ast, Malcolm Choat, Jennifer Cromwell, Julia Lougovaya, and Rachel Yuen-Collingridge (Eds.), *Observing the Scribe at Work: Scribal Practice in the Ancient World* (Leuven, Paris, Bristol, CT: Peeters, 2021), pp101–115

Archaeology and history of Egypt, its foreign interests, and its empire (excluding Crete)

Ancient texts and translations thereof
William L. Moran, *The Amarna Letters* (Baltimore & London: The John Hopkins University Press, 1992)
James Henry Breasted, "The Report of Wenamon", *The American Journal of Semitic Languages and Literatures* 21(2)(1905), pp100–109
James Henry Breasted, *Ancient Records of Egypt: Volume 2* (Champaign: University of Illinois Press, 2001)
James Henry Breasted, *Ancient Records of Egypt, Volume 4: The Twentieth to the Twenty-Sixth Dynasties* (Chicago: University of Chicago Press, 1906)
Miriam Lichtheim, *Ancient Egyptian Literature: Volume II* (Berkeley: University of California Press, 1976)
David Lorton, *The Juridical Terminology of International Relations in Egyptian Texts through Dynasty XVIII* (The John Hopkins University Press: Baltimore, 1974)
William J. Murnane, *Texts from the Amarna period in Egypt* (Atlanta: Scholars Press, 1995)
Kurt Sethe, *Urkunden der 18. Dynastie, Abteilung IV, Band III* (Leipzig: JC Hinrichs'sche Buchandlung, 1907)

Academic Theses
Eleanor Beth Simmance, *Communication with the Divine in Ancient Egypt: Hearing Deities, Intermediary Statues, and Sistrophores* (PhD: University of Birmingham, 2017)
William Cooney, "Egypt's encounter with the West: Race, Culture and Identity", *Durham theses* (Durham University, 2011) (http://etheses.dur.ac.uk/910)

Barbara Ann Richter, *The Theology of Hathor of Dendera: Aural and Visual Scribal Techniques in the Per-Wer Sanctuary* (PhD: University of California, Berkeley, 2012)

Hana Vymazalová, *The accounting documents from the papyrus archive of Neferre and their specific terminology* (PhD: Charles University in Prague, 2005)

Articles

John Baines, "Literacy and Ancient Egyptian Society", *Man* 18(3)(September 1983), pp572–599

Stefan Bergdoll, *The Temple of Deir El Bahari* (Berlin: epubli, 2013)

Manfred Bietak, "The Tuthmoside stronghold of Perunefer", *Egyptian Archaeology: The Bulletin of the Egyptian Exploration Society* 26(2005), pp13–17

Manfred Bietak, "Perunefer: the principal New Kingdom naval base", *Egyptian Archaeology: The Bulletin of the Egyptian Exploration Society* 34(2009), pp15–17

Manfred Bietak, "Minoan presence in the pharaonic naval base of "Peru-nefer"", *British School at Athens* 18(2010), pp11–24

Eric H. Cline and Steven M. Stannish, "Sailing the Great Green Sea? Amenhotep III's "Aegean List: from Kom el-Hetan, Once More", *Journal of Ancient Egyptian Interconnections* 3(2)(2011), pp6–16

A. R. David, *The Pyramid Builders of Ancient Egypt: A Modern Investigation of Pharoah's Workforce* (Boston: Routledge and Kegan Paul, 1986)

Aiden Dodson, "The Coregency Conundrum", *Kmt: A Modern Journal of Ancient Egypt* 25(2)(2014), pp28–35

Paul Faure, "Toponymes Créto-Mycéniens Dans Une Liste D'Aménophis III (environ 1380 avant J. C.)", *Kadmos* 7(1968), pp138–149

Alan B. Lloyd, "The Egyptian Labyrinth", *The Journal of Egyptian Archaeology* 56 (1970), pp81–100

Susan Tower Hollis, "Hathor and Isis in Byblos in the Second and First Millennia BCE", *Journal of Ancient Egyptian Interconnection* 1(2)(2009), pp1–8

Christine Lilyquist, "The Gold Bowl Naming General Djehuty: A Study of Objects and Early Egyptology", *Metropolitan Museum Journal* 23(1988), pp5–69

Anthony Spalinger, "A Critical Analysis of the "Annals" of Thutmose III (Stücke V-VI)", *Journal of the American Research Centre in Egypt* 14(1977), pp41–54

Antony Spalinger, "Further Remarks on the Old Kingdom Phyle System", *Orientalia* 83(3)(2013), pp 157–206

B. Switalski Lesko, "The Senmut Problem", *Journal of the American Research Centre in Egypt* 6(1967), pp113–118

R. S. Merrillees, "Aegean Bronze Age Relations with Egypt", *American Journal of Archaeology* 76(3)(1972), pp 281–294

J. J. Shirley, "Viceroys, Viziers & The Amun Precinct: The Power of Heredity and Strategic Marriage in the early 18th Dynasty", *Journal of Egyptian History* 3(1)(2010), pp73–113

Books

C. J. Bleeker, *Hathor and Thoth: Two Key Figures of the Ancient Egyptian Religion* (Leiden: E. J. Brill, 1973)

Anna Lucille Boozer, *Amheida II: A Late Romano-Egyptian House in the Dakhla Oasis / Amheida House B2* (New York: New York University Press, 2016)

Eric Cline, *1177 B.C. The Year Civilization Collapsed* (Princeton: Princeton University Press, 2014)

Marianne Eaton-Krauss, *The Unknown Tutankhamun* (London and New York: Bloomsbury Academic, 2016)

Nina de Garis Davies, *Ancient Egyptian Paintings I* (Chicago: Oriental Institute of Press, 1936)

Norman de Garis Davies, *The Tomb of Rekh-mi-re' at Thebes: Volume 1* (New York: The Metropolitan Museum of Art Egyptian Expedition, 1943)

Eberhard Dziobek, Erik Hornung & Yvonne Marzoni Fecia di Cossato, *Die Gräber des Vezirs User-Amun Theben Nr. 61 und 131* (Mainz am Rhein: Verlag Philipp von Zabern, 1994)

Richard A. Gabriel, *Thutmose III: The Military Biography of Egypt's Greatest Warrior King* (Washington, D.C.: Potomac Books, Inc., 2009)

Sigrid Hodel-Hoenes, *Life and Death in Ancient Egypt: Scenes from Private Tombs in New Kingdom Thebes* (Ithaca and London: Cornell University Press, 2000)

Colleen Manassa, *Imagining the Past: Historical Fiction in New Kingdom Egypt* (Oxford & New York: Oxford University Press, 2013)

William L. Moran, *The Amarna Letters* (Baltimore: The John Hopkins University Press, 1992)

Brian P. Muhs, *The Ancient Egyptian Economy: 3000–30 BCE* (Cambridge: Cambridge University Press, 2016)

A. Leo Oppenheim, *Letters from Mesopotamia: Official, Business, and Personal Letters on Clay Tablets from Two Millennia* (Chicago & London: The University of Chicago Press, 1967)

Richard Anthony Parker, *The Calendars of Ancient Egypt* (Chicago: The University of Chicago Press, 1950)

Donald B. Redford, *History and Chronology of the 18th dynasty of Egypt: Seven studies* (Toronto: University of Toronto Press, 1967)

Susan Redford, *The Harem Conspiracy: The Murder of Ramesses III* (DeKalb: North Illinois University Press, 2002)

Nicholas Reeves, *Akhenaten: Egypt's False Prophet* (London: Thames & Hudson, 2001)

Torgny Säve-Söderbergh, *The Navy of the Eighteenth Dynasty* (Uppsala, Sweden: Uppsala University Press, 1946)

Ann Macy Roth, *Egyptian Phyles in the Old Kingdom: The Evolution of a System of Social Organisation – Studies in Ancient Oriental Civilization No. 48* (The Oriental Institute of the University of Chicago: Chicago, 1991)

Ian Shaw, *The Oxford History of Ancient Egypt* (Oxford & New York: Oxford University Press, 2003)

John Strange, *Caphtor / Keftiu: A new investigation* (Acta theologica Danica Vol. 14, Leiden: Brill, 1980)

The Epigraphic Survey in cooperation with the Department of Antiquities of Egypt, *The Tomb of Kheruef: Theban Tomb 192* (Chicago: The Oriental Institute of the University of Chicago, 1980)

Chapters in edited books

Manfred Bietak, "Harbours and Coastal Military Bases in Egypt in the Second Millennium B.C.: Avaris, Peru-nefer, Pi-Ramesse", in Harco Willems and Jan-Michael Dahms (Eds.), *The Nile: Natural and Cultural Landscape in Egypt* (Germany: transcript Verlag, 2017), pp53–70

Olaf E. Kaper, "The Western Oases", in Christina Riggs (Ed.) *The Oxford Handbook of Roman Egypt* (Oxford: Oxford University Press, 2012), pp717–735

Diamantis Panagiotopoulos, "Foreigners in Egypt in the Time of Hatshepsut and Thutmose III", in E. Cline & D. O'Connor (Eds.), *Thutmose III: A New Biography* (Ann Arbor: University of Michigan Press, 2006), pp370–412

Laure Pantalacci, "Balat, A Frontier Town and its Archive", in Juan Carlos Moreno García (Ed.), *Ancient Egyptian Administration* (Leiden & Boston: Brill, 2013), pp197–214

Laure Pantalacci, "Between Old and Middle Kingdom: paleography of the clay documents from Balat", in S. A. Gülden, K. van der Moczel, and U. Verhoeven (Eds.), *Ägyptologische "Binsen" – Weisheiten III Formen und Funktionen von Zeichenliste und Paläographie. Akten der internationalen und interdisziplinären Tagung in der Akademie der Wissenschaften und der Literatur Mainz im April 2016* (Stuttgart: Franz Steiner Verlag, 2018), pp217–231

Juan-Pablo Vita & José-Ángel Zamora, "The Byblos Script", in Silvia Ferrara and Miguel Valério (Eds.), *Paths into Script Formation in the Ancient Mediterranean* (Rome: Edizioni Quasar, 2018), pp75–102

Klaas A. Worp & Colin A. Hope, "A Greek Account on a Clay Tablet from the Dakhleh Oasis", in Rudolf De Smet, H. M. Melaerts, & Cecilia Saerens (Eds.), *Papyri in Honorem: Johannis Bingen Octogenarii* (Leuven: Uitgeverij Peeters, 2000), pp471–485

James M. Weinstein, "The World Abroad: Egypt and the Levant in the Reign of Amenhotep III", in David O'Connor and Eric H. Cline (Eds.), *Amenhotep III: Perspectives on His Reign* (Ann Arbor: The University of Michigan Press, 2001), pp223–270

Websites

Statue assise de Nḫt-wsr(?) tenant un emblème d'Hathor. Caire JE 36719: http://www.ifao.egnet.net/bases/cachette/?id=81

The Golden Bowl of General Djehuty: https://www.louvre.fr/en/oeuvre-notices/bowl-general-djehuty

The Tell e' Daba Late Minoan Wall Paintings https://www.orea.oeaw.ac.at/en/research/tell-el-daba-publications/tell-el-daba-late-minoan-wall-paintings

Part 3: Other

Ancient texts
Sun-Tzu, *The Art of War* (Melbourne: Penguin Group (Australia), 2009)

Academic theses
Patrick Melby, *Insatiable Shipyards: The Impact of the Royal Navy on the World's Forests, 1200–1850* (Dissertation: Western Oregon University, 2012)

Articles
C. J. Gadd and R. Campbell Thompson, "A Middle-Babylonian Chemical Text", *Iraq* 3(1)(1936), pp87–96
Peter Hanrahan, *Agriculture Notes: Ram Percentage* (February 2003): https://www.vgls.vic.gov.au/client/en_AU/search/asset/1280773/0
David Williamson, "Was Hitler a weak dictator?", *History Review* 42(2002), pp9–14

Books
Robert G. Albion, *Forests and Sea Power: The Problem of the Royal Navy 1652–1862* (Cambridge: Harvard University Press, 1926)
E. H. Carr, *What is History?* (2nd Ed.)(Camberwell, Vic: Penguin, 2008)
Winston S. Churchill, *The World Crisis, Volume 3* (New York: Charles Scriber's Sons, 1927)
Norman F. Dixon, *On the Psychology of Military Incompetence* (London: Jonathan Cape, 1976)
Financial Accounting Standards Board, *Statement of Financial Accounting Concepts Statement No. 1: Objectives of Financial Reporting by Business Enterprises* (Norwalk (Conn.): Financial Accounting Standards Board, November 1978)
David Kahn, *The Codebreakers: A Comprehensive History of Secret Communication from Ancient Times to the Internet* (New York: Scribner, 1996)
Frank Wood & Sheila Robinson, *Book-Keeping & Accounts* (5th Ed.)(Harlow: Financial Times Prentice Hall, 2001)

Chapters in edited books
Patricia R. McDonald, "By Who and for Whom? British Reactions to the Landscape of New South Wales, 1788–1830", in *The World Upside Down: Australia 1788–1830* (Canberra: National Library of Australia, 2000), pp27–34

Radio Programmes
In Our Time: The Alphabet (18 December 2003)
https://www.bbc.co.uk/sounds/play/p0054950

Films
All the President's Men (1976)
Minority Report (2002)
Starsky & Hutch (2004)

Websites
Was the 'New Coke' Fiasco Just a Clever Marketing Ploy?
https://www.snopes.com/fact-check/new-coke-fiasco/

Index

A Canterbury Tale (1944 British film), 97
Abusir papyrus archive of the funerary temple of King Neferirkare / King Neferefre / Queen Khentkaus (5th Dynasty), 201, 250, 253, 372, 493
Accounting
  Procedures at Hagia Triada, 149, 157, 228–229, 401
  Accrual accounting, 506
Acrophony, 218–219, 461
Akhenaten (Egyptian 18th Dynasty King), 78, 91, 118–121, 459, 460
Amarna Correspondence, 77–78, 91, 460
Amenhotep II (Egyptian 18th Dynasty King), 64, 67, 108, 109, 110, 114, 459
Amenhotep III (Egyptian 18th Dynasty King), 78, 91, 111, 112, 114, 116–120, 244, 257, 364, 459, 460, 476, 478
Andreadaki-Vlazaki, Maria (historian), 106
Annals, The, 51, 58, 66, 71, 76, 77, 81, 82, 83, 84, 85, 86, 87, 89, 90, 91, 101, 102, 103, 104, 108, 109, 110, 459
  Botanical Gardens of Thutmose III, 83, 84, 85, 101, 103
  Third Campaign of Thutmose III, 83, 84, 86
  Fourth Campaign of Thutmose III, 84, 86, 87, 90
  Removal of references to Crete by Amenhotep II, 85, 86, 109–110, 459
Antoninus Pius (Roman Emperor), 26

Battle of Jutland (1916), 73
Battle of Megiddo (1457 BC), 51, 66, 67, 71, 76, 86, 101
Bechuanaland Protectorate, 76
Bennett Jr, Emmett L. (historian), 2, 3
Bietak, Manfred (historian), 88
Botanical Gardens of Thutmose III, *see* Annals
Breasted, James Henry (historian), 80, 81, 90, 91, 104
Breath of life, The (Egyptian juridical expression), 70, 71, 76, 78, 79, 84, 86, 101, 111, 114, 118, 119, 120

Brighton Pavilion, 89
British India, 62, 89
Byblos Script, 45, 461
Byzantine Empire, 25, 53, 69

Cadogan, Gerald (historian), 103, 160, 485
Callimachus (Hellenistic Greek poet), 461
Chadwick, John (historian), 2, 6, 11, 25, 140, 156, 164, 169, 171, 196, 228–229, 230, 234, 240–241, 457–458, 469, 475–476
Churchill, Winston (British statesman), 73
Cicero (Roman statesman), 26
Cline, Eric (historian), 61, 64, 66, 70, 108, 113, 114
Clinton, Bill (44th US President), 111
Constantine IX Monomachos (Byzantine Emperor), 53
Constantinople, fall of (AD 1453), 170, 241
Cyprus, Egyptian subjugation of, 89–91

Diodorus Siculus (Romano-Greek historian), 54, 72
Djehuty (Egyptian General of Thutmose III), 58, 79, 80, 82, 85, 158, 458
Documents in Mycenaean Greek (book), 2, 6, 140, 164, 240, 469, 475
Double entry bookkeeping, 190–191, 499, 506
Doukas (Byzantine historian), 77
Dunbabin, T. J. (historian), 6, 19

Egyptian temple chapels on Crete, 54–55, 56
Egyptian Late Bronze Age commercial wares found on Crete, 58, 59–63
Egyptian shorthand method, *see* Linear A
Egyptian navy, 56, 84, 87–91
Egyptian scorched earth policy on withdrawal from Crete, 106–108
Evans, Sir Arthur (archaeologist), 54, 64, 75, 99, 457

Faure, Paul (philologist), 102
Flotilla Fresco, 58, 72, 84, 92–102
Foat, F. W. G. (historian), 26, 27
Fourth Crusade (AD 1202–1204), 53

Gabriel, Richard A. (military historian), 88
Gardiner, Sir Alan H. (philologist), 18, 128, 136, 253, 362, 405, 474
Gebelein papyrus records of provincial administration (late 4th / early 5th Dynasty), 154
Golden Bowl of General Djehuty, 79–80, 458
Greek Orthodox Church, 170, 241
Greek shorthand method
   Characteristics, 28–29
   Known history, 25–26
   Likely levels of use, 26–27
   Rotation and reversal of symbols, 21
   Surviving examples, 269

Hansen, Julie M. (historian), 493
Hathor (Egyptian Goddess), 54, 55, 64, 461
   References to, in the Linear A corpus, 124, 240, 272, 320, 321, 325–326, 328, 332, 375, 377, 386, 390, 433, 441–442
   Priests of Hathor, references to in the Linear A corpus, 268, 311, 315, 383, 385, 436, 442, 443, 444, 455, 456
Hatshepsut (Egyptian Queen, wife of Thutmose II), 63, 67, 85–86
Healey, John F. (historian), 219
Herodotus (Classical Greek historian), 52, 72, 73, 87, 104, 105, 109–111
   Bias of, 109–111
Hieratic (Egyptian script), 56–57, 59, 126, 142, 154, 253, 278, 361, 372, 459, 470–471
Hodel-Hoenes, Sigrid (historian), 109
Homer (Archaic Greek author), 103
Horemheb (Egyptian 18th Dynasty King), 82, 158
Huya (Chief Steward of Queen Tiye etc.), tomb of, 119–120

India, 62–63
Inw (tribute or diplomatic gifts), 70, 71, 91, 108
Isaac II Angelus (Byzantine Emperor), 53
Ismay, Hastings (first Secretary General of NATO), 76

Janssen, Jac J. (historian), 472–473
Jellicoe, Admiral Sir John (Royal Navy), 73
Judson, Anna (historian), 196

Kahun papyrus accounting records of a pyramid town (12th Dynasty), 253
Khama III (King of Bechuanaland), 76

Kheruef (Steward to Queen Tiye etc.), tomb of, 116–118
Killen, J. T. (historian), 158–159
Kober, Alice (major contributor to the decipherment of Linear B), 1, 2, 3, 5
Kom el-Hetan (mortuary temple of Amenhotep III), 111–115, 118–121, 244, 257, 364, 476

Labyrinth, The (Cretan myth), 54, 73
Lance, Bert (23rd Director of the Office of Management and Budget, USA), 59
Lepsius, Karl Richard (historian), 54
Lesko, Barbara Switalski (historian), 65
Lesko, Leonard H. (historian), 473
Linear A
   Pictorially comparative school of attempted decipherment, 3–6
   Place names mentioned in tablets
      Amnisos, 160, 243–244, 253, 256, 475, 476–477
      Knossos, 160, 257–258, 265, 266, 278, 279, 475, 476, 477–479
      Phaistos, 160, 333, 362, 364, 369, 475, 476, 479–480
   Summary of methodology, 39–42, 151–152, 188
   Syllabic comparative school of attempted decipherment, 2–3, 218
   Tablets, attributed dates, 48, 49
Linear B
   Dk series of Linear B tablets, 11–13, 17, 123, 131, 140, 151, 152, 156, 163–170, 234, 241, 242
   E series of Linear B tablets, 130, 132
   Mc series of Linear B tablets, 124, 190, 191, 208, 229–234, 234–235, 235–240, 240–242, 469
Linear B relationship to Linear A, 12, 108, 123, 216, 217–221, 460–461
Lorton, David (historian), 70, 79, 114, 120
Loukas Notaras (last Byzantine *megas doux* and *mesazon*), 77

Mehmet II (Ottoman Sultan), 170, 241
Menkheperraseneb (High Priest of Amun), tomb of, 104
Merrillees, R. S. (historian), 66
Merneptah (Egyptian 19th Dynasty King), 473
Meryre II (Royal scribe etc.), tomb of, 119–120
Michael VIII Palaiologos (Byzantine Emperor), 53

Milne, H. J. M. (historian), 26, 28, 29, 37, 46, 151, 152, 203
Minoan Empire, 51–52, 73, 74, 75, 83, 85, 89, 91, 92, 98, 99, 101, 109
  End of, 72–77, 83, 85, 91, 101, 109, 457
Minoan units of measure of weight, 156, 163, 234–235
Minos (Minoan King), 51, 54, 72–74, 75
Minotaur (Cretan myth), 64, 73–74, 105
Muhs, Brian (historian), 279
Mycenaeans
  Arrival on Crete, 103–105, 109–110
  Rebellion of, 105–107, 108–109

NATO (North Atlantic Treaty Organization), 76
Nefertiti (Egyptian Queen, wife of Akhenaten), 119–120
New South Wales, British colony of, 96–97
North German Confederation, 51, 52

Palmer, Ruth (historian), 3–4, 17–18, 135, 494
Panagiotopoulos, Diamantis (historian), 70, 77, 78, 79, 83, 86
Pendlebury, J. D. S. (historian), 75
Peru-nefer (naval base), 88, 91–98
Peru-nefer (palace of Thutmose III), 89
Petrie, Flinders (historian), 54
Phoenician alphabet, 21, 219
Plutarch (Romano-Greek philosopher and historian), 74
Poetical Stela of Thutmose III, 90
Proto-Sinaitic script, 57, 219
Prussia, Kingdom of, 51, 52
Ptolemaic Egypt, 26, 27, 194

Ramesses III (Egyptian 20th Dynasty King), 102
  Golden river barque, 102
Reeves, Nicholas (historian), 113, 120
Rekhmire (Vizier of Thutmose III and Amenhotep II), 63, 64, 109
  Tomb of, 51, 52, 67–71, 76, 77, 78, 79, 85, 86, 103, 104, 105, 106, 108–109, 114
  Fall from power, 100
Report of Wenamum, 78
Restoration Stela of Tutankhamun, 90, 354
Rice-Davies, Mandy (model and showgirl), 457

Rosetta Stone, 6, 19
Royal Navy, 75
  Timber problem, 75

Schoep, Ilse (historian), 494
Senenmut (Egyptian royal architect of Hatshepsut and Thutmose III), 63–65
  Tomb of, 63, 64–66, 68, 71, 85, 86, 109
Seti II (Egyptian 19th Dynasty King), 472
Socrates (Greek philosopher), 26
Spalinger, Anthony (historian), 84, 90
Stannish, Steven M. (historian), 70
Strabo (Romano-Greek geographer and historian), 51
Sun-Tzu (Chinese military strategist), 106

Thera (modern Santorini), eruption of, 52, 57
Thutmose II (Egyptian 18th Dynasty King), 85
Thutmose III (Egyptian 18th Dynasty King), 50, 51, 56, 58, 59, 62, 63, 64, 65, 66, 67, 71, 72, 76, 77, 79, 80, 81, 82–83, 84, 85, 86, 87–90, 91, 101, 102–103, 104–105, 108, 109, 278, 459
Thutmose IV (Egyptian 18th Dynasty King), 116
Tiye (Egyptian Queen, wife of Amenhotep III), 116, 117, 119
Tomas, Helena (historian), 3
Tutankhamun (Egyptian 18th Dynasty King), 82, 354

Useramun (Vizier of Thutmose III), 63–64
  Tomb of, 63, 65, 66, 67, 68, 71, 79, 85, 86, 87, 101, 104

Ventris, Michael (decipherer of Linear B), 1, 2, 6, 11, 24, 140, 156, 164, 169, 171, 179, 196, 218, 228, 229, 230, 234, 240, 241, 458, 469, 475, 476
Vercoutter, Jean (historian), 66, 108
Vindolanda Tablets, 472
Vymazalová, Hana (historian), 201, 250, 372

Weiner, Malcolm H. (historian), 103
Window Tax (tax in England, 1696–1851), 159

Xenophon (Greek general and historian), 26

Dear Reader,

We hope you have enjoyed this book, but why not share your views on social media? You can also follow our pages to see more about our other products: facebook.com/penandswordbooks or follow us on X @penswordbooks

You can also view our products at www.pen-and-sword.co.uk (UK and ROW) or www.penandswordbooks.com (North America).

To keep up to date with our latest releases and online catalogues, please sign up to our newsletter at: www.pen-and-sword.co.uk/newsletter

If you would like a printed catalogue with our latest books, then please email: enquiries@pen-and-sword.co.uk or telephone: 01226 734555 (UK and ROW) or email: uspen-and-sword@casematepublishers.com or telephone: (610) 853-9131 (North America).

We respect your privacy and we will only use personal information to send you information about our products.

Thank you!